Dedication

To Tessa, la migliore fabbra, and to Dan and Beth—R.G.G.

To Louise, and her own personal inheritance hierarchy: Moira, Elizabeth, Louis, Vera, and Thomas—J.A.M.

Java™
First Contact

Second Edition

Roger Garside
John Mariani

Lancaster University

THOMSON

BROOKS/COLE   Australia • Canada • Mexico • Singapore • Spain
United Kingdom • United States

THOMSON

BROOKS/COLE

Editor: *Kallie Swanson*
Senior Editorial Assistant: *Carla Vera*
Technology Project Manager: *Burke Taft*
Executive Marketing Manager: *Tom Ziolkowski*
Marketing Assistant: *Darcie Pool*
Advertising Project Manager: *Laura Hubrich*
Project Manager, Editorial Production: *Kelsey McGee*
Print/Media Buyer: *Vena M. Dyer*

Permissions Editor: *Connie Dowcett*
Production Service: *The Book Company*
Copy Editor: *Frank Hubert*
Cover Designer: *Denise Davidson*
Cover Image: *Imtek Imagineering/Masterfile*
Cover Printing, Printing, and Binding: *Webcom, Limited*
Compositor: *Pre-Press Company, Inc.*

Printed in Canada
1 2 3 4 5 6 7 06 05 04 03 02

For more information about our products, contact us at:
Thomson Learning Academic Resource Center
1-800-423-0563

For permission to use material from this text, contact us by: **Phone:** 1-800-730-2214
Fax: 1-800-730-2215
Web: http://www.thomsonrights.com

Library of Congress Control Number: 2002105968

ISBN 0-534-37816-1

Brooks/Cole–Thomson Learning
511 Forest Lodge Road
Pacific Grove, CA 93950
USA

Asia
Thomson Learning
5 Shenton Way #01-01
UIC Building
Singapore 068808

Australia
Nelson Thomson Learning
102 Dodds Street
South Melbourne, Victoria 3205
Australia

Canada
Nelson Thomson Learning
1120 Birchmount Road
Toronto, Ontario M1K 5G4
Canada

Europe/Middle East/Africa
Thomson Learning
High Holborn House
50/51 Bedford Row
London WC1R 4LR
United Kingdom

Latin America
Thomson Learning
Seneca, 53
Colonia Polanco
11560 Mexico D.F.
Mexico

Spain
Paraninfo Thomson Learning
Calle/Magallanes, 25
28015 Madrid, Spain

Contents

Part 1   Using Objects

Programming and the Java Language   2

1.1   Programs and Programming   2
1.2   Algorithms   3
1.3   High-Level Languages and Programs   5
1.4   A Simple Computer   8
1.5   Machine Code   9
1.6   Files and the Filing System   14
1.7   The World Wide Web   15
1.8   The Java Programming Language   17
1.9   Getting Started with Java   20
1.10   A First Java Program   21
1.11   The print and println Methods   24
1.12   How This Book Is Arranged   25
1.13   Key Points in Chapter 1   26
1.14   Exercises   27

2   Object Orientation   29

2.1   Objects and Classes   29
2.2   Software Objects   32
2.3   More about Single Objects   36
2.4   An Object-Oriented Program   39
2.5   Types   40
2.6   Classes and Instances Revisited   43

2.7   Key Points in Chapter 2   46

2.8   Exercises   47

3   Declaring Objects and Calling Methods   48

3.1   Program Structure   48

3.2   The class Person   49

3.3   A Program to Manipulate a Person   51

3.4   The import Statement   52

3.5   Declaring Objects   53

3.6   Using Methods to Set the Attributes of Objects   57

3.7   Using Methods to Extract Object Attributes   60

3.8   Using Constants in Java   63

3.9   Using Objects and Methods   65

3.10   A Variety of Methods   66

3.11   Constructors Revisited   68

3.12   Input to a Program (Optional)   72

3.13   Key Points in Chapter 3   73

3.14   Exercises   74

4   Selecting Among Alternatives   77

4.1   Reading Values from the Keyboard   77

4.2   More on Integer Variables   80

4.3   Type Checking   84

4.4   Making Decisions   85

4.5   Selection Statements in Java   89

       4.5.1   Statements   90

       4.5.2   Relational Operators and Boolean Expressions   92

4.6   The Boolean Type   96

4.7   The switch Statement   101

4.8   Testing a New Class   107

4.9   Key Points in Chapter 4   110

4.10   Exercises   111

5   Repetition   113

5.1   Repetition as a Basic Control Structure   113

5.2   Looping a Predetermined Number of Times: The for Statement   115

5.3   Looping an Indeterminate Number of Times: The `while` Statement   121
5.4   Stopping in the Middle of an Iteration   124
5.5   `for` Loops and `while` Loops   126
5.6   Nested Loops   127
5.7   Boolean Expressions for Loops   126
5.8   Testing at the End of the Loop   134
5.9   Other Java Loop Features   136
5.10   Key Points in Chapter 5   138
5.11   Exercises   139

6   Basic Java Data Types   142
6.1   Objects and Basic Data Types   142
       6.1.1   Declaration   142
       6.1.2   Setting a Value   144
       6.1.3   Obtaining a Value   146
       6.1.4   Arguments to Methods   147
6.2   The `int` Data Type   147
6.3   Other Whole Number Data Types in Java (Optional)   151
6.4   Floating-Point Data Types   153
6.5   The `boolean` Data Type   155
6.6   The `char` Data Type   156
6.7   The `String` Class   157
6.8   Methods for the `String` Class   161
6.9   Wrapper Classes (Optional)   162
6.10   Key Points in Chapter 6   165
6.11   Exercises   166

Part 2   Writing Objects

7   A Simple Class   169
7.1   What We Are Trying to Achieve   169
7.2   Providing the `Person` Class   172
7.3   Methods for the `Person` Class   175
7.4   Actual and Formal Arguments   178
7.5   Modes of Argument Passing   182
7.6   Return Values   185

7.7   Lexical Conventions within a Class   185

7.8   Key Points in Chapter 7   186

7.9   Exercises   187

8   More on the Simple Class   189

8.1   Constructor Methods   189

8.2   Overloading   193

8.3   Class Constants   195

8.4   Class Variables   196

8.5   Private Methods   198

8.6   Class or Static Methods   201

8.7   Revisiting the Main Class   202

8.8   Packages and Directories   206

    8.8.1   The import Statement   209

8.9   Scope and Visibility   210

    8.9.1   Intraclass Visibility   210

    8.9.2   Use of this   214

    8.9.3   Interclass Visibility   214

8.10   Key Points in Chapter 8   215

8.11   Exercises   216

9   Arrays   218

9.1   Collections of Elements   218

9.2   Arrays of Objects   221

9.3   Searching an Array   223

9.4   Binary Search   226

9.5   Sorting an Array   227

9.6   Arrays as Arguments   234

9.7   Multidimensional Arrays   237

9.8   Nonrectangular Arrays (Optional)   241

9.9   Key Points in Chapter 9   242

9.10   Exercises   244

10   Objects within Objects   249

10.1   What We Are Trying to Achieve   249

10.2   Writing the OurDate Class   250

10.3   Using the OurDate Class   251
10.4   Objects as Arguments   253
10.5   Multiple References to the Same Object   255
10.6   Objects as Arguments and Return Values: Call by Reference   260
       10.6.1   Changing the Contents of the Formal and Actual Arguments   263
10.7   Hiding References to Other Objects   266
10.8   Key Points in Chapter 10   267
10.9   Exercises   268

11   Putting Objects to Work   270
11.1   A Task Organizer Program   270
11.2   A Priority Queue Class   271
11.3   Implementing a Priority Queue with an Array   275
11.4   Alternative Implementations of PriorityQueue (Optional)   281
11.5   Testing the PriorityQueue Class   282
11.6   Using the PriorityQueue Class   287
11.7   Outstanding Issues   289
11.8   Key Points in Chapter 11   291
11.9   Exercises   291

Part 3   Advanced Objects

12   Introduction to Inheritance   293
12.1   Motivation   293
       12.1.1   Data Modeling   293
       12.1.2   Programming   298
12.2   What's the Difference?   299
12.3   Overriding Inherited Methods   300
12.4   Access Rights and Subclasses   304
12.5   Airplane Reservations: An Example   305
12.6   Key Points in Chapter 12   310
12.7   Exercises   311

13   Class and Method Polymorphism   313
13.1   Person and Student: An Example   313

13.2   Constructor Methods and Inheritance   314
        13.2.1   Constructor Chaining   315
13.3   Multiple Levels of Inheritance: The Inheritance Hierarchy   316
13.4   The Class `Object`   317
13.5   Polymorphism   319
13.6   Polymorphism and Heterogeneous Collections   322
        13.6.1   Dynamic Method Binding (Late Binding)   325
13.7   Calling Overridden Methods   325
13.8   Methods in Derived Classes   327
13.9   Key Points in Chapter 13   329
13.10   Exercises   330

14   Abstract Classes and Interfaces   333
14.1   Abstract Classes   333
14.2   Polymorphism   338
14.3   Interfaces   340
14.4   Key Points in Chapter 14   346
14.5   Exercises   347

15   Throwing and Catching Exceptions   351
15.1   Motivation: Robust Programs   351
15.2   Defining a New Exception   353
15.3   Throwing an Exception   354
15.4   Catching an Exception   355
        15.4.1   The `finally` Clause (Optional)   361
15.5   Key Points in Chapter 15   363
15.6   Exercises   365

16   Graphics and the Abstract Windowing Toolkit   366
16.1   Graphical User Interfaces   366
16.2   A Simple Program with a Graphical Interface   368
16.3   Writing the `Chapter16n0` Class   372
        16.3.1   The Constructor for the `Chapter16n0` Class   372
        16.3.2   Other Layout Managers   375
        16.3.3   The `main` Method for the `Chapter16n0` Class   376
        16.3.4   The `actionPerformed` Method of the `Chapter16n0` Class   376
        16.3.5   The `windowClosing` Method of the `Chapter16n0` Class   377

16.4   Writing the `Canvas0` Class   378

16.5   Writing Text on the Canvas   382

16.6   Animating the Simple Graphics Program   383

16.7   Input of Character Strings in a Graphical Interface   386
    16.7.1   Setting Up the Picture   387
    16.7.2   Getting a String from a `TextField`   389
    16.7.3   Drawing the Thermometer   391

16.8   Menus, Files, and Images (Optional)   392
    16.8.1   Setting Up Menus   393
    16.8.2   Selecting a File   397
    16.8.3   Displaying an Image   398
    16.8.4   Tracking the Mouse   399

16.9   Key Points in Chapter 16   400

16.10   Exercises   401

Part 4   Advanced Java

17   Linked Data Structures   406

17.1   Linear and Linked Data Structures   406

17.2   Implementing a Priority Queue Using a Linked Data Structure   409

17.3   Methods for the `PriorityQueue` Class   413
    17.3.1   The `length` Method   413
    17.3.2   The `first` Method   415
    17.3.3   The `remove` Method   416

17.4   The `insert` Method   417

17.5   Deletion from a Linked Data Structure (Optional)   423

17.6   Doubly Linked Lists (Optional)   425

17.7   Using Linked Data Structures   428

17.8   Key Points in Chapter 17   429

17.9   Exercises   430

18   Recursion and Binary Trees   434

18.1   Recursion   434

18.2   Solving the Towers of Hanoi Problem   437
    18.2.1   A Recursive Solution to the Towers of Hanoi Problem   439
    18.2.2   An Iterative Solution to the Towers of Hanoi Problem   441

18.3   Binary Trees   442
    18.3.1   Searching and Updating a Binary Tree   445
    18.3.2   Writing the Code for the Binary Tree   447
    18.3.3   Adding a Word Occurrence to the Lexicon   448
    18.3.4   Outputting the Lexicon Information   451
18.4   Key Points in Chapter 18   452
18.5   Exercises   452

19   Input and Output in Java   457
19.1   Input and Output Systems   457
19.2   The Java Classes for Input and Output   460
19.3   The PrintStream Class and System.out   462
    19.3.1   Output Redirection   465
19.4   The BufferedReader Class and System.in   466
    19.4.1   Tokenizing an Input Line   467
    19.4.2   Converting Strings to Numeric Values   468
    19.4.3   Redirecting Input   470
19.5   Files and File Handling   471
19.6   Reading and Writing Files   472
    19.6.1   Writing to a File   473
    19.6.2   Reading from a File   474
19.7   Binary Files (Optional)   476
19.8   Random Access Files (Optional)   477
19.9   Accessing Other Computers (Optional)   478
19.10   Key Points in Chapter 19   479
19.11   Exercises   481

20   Creating and Using Applets   484
20.1   Creating Applets   484
20.2   Using Applets   486
20.3   More about Applets   489
20.4   A Useful Applet   490
    20.4.1   The readIndex Method   493
    20.4.2   The actionPerformed Method   494
20.5   Security Aspects of the Use of Applets   495
20.6   Key Points in Chapter 20   496
20.7   Exercises   496

21   Other Features of Java   499

21.1   Vectors and Other Java Data Structures   499
    21.1.1   The Vector Class   499
    21.1.2   The Hashtable Class   503

21.2   Strings and StringBuffers   505

21.3   Run-Time Type Information (Optional)   506

21.4   Threads (Optional)   507
    21.4.1   Synchronizing Threads   513

21.5   Key Points in Chapter 21   514

21.6   Exercises   515

Part 5   Object-Oriented Design

22   Object-Oriented Design   518

22.1   Software Engineering   518

22.2   The Software Life Cycle   519
    22.2.1   Requirements   520
    22.2.2   Design   520
    22.2.3   Coding   520
    22.2.4   Testing   520
    22.2.5   Maintenance   520

22.3   Design   521
    22.3.1   The Design Process   521
    22.3.2   Functional Design   522

22.4   Object-Oriented Design (OOD)   522
    22.4.1   Capturing Our Design: A Design Notation   522
    22.4.2   Object Identification   524

22.5   Key Points in Chapter 22   527

22.6   Exercises   528

22.7   References   529

23   Case Study: Implementing the Personal Organizer 1   530

23.1   First Steps in the Design   530

23.2   File Organization   530
    23.2.1   Index Sequential Access   530
    23.2.2   The Main File   532

23.2.3 The `RandomAccessFile` Class   535

23.2.4 The Index   536

23.2.5 Suitability of the `Vector` Class for Internal Representation of the Index   536

23.2.6 Suitability of the `Hashtable` Class for Internal Representation of the Index   537

23.2.7 Using the `Vector` Class Indirectly   538

23.3   The Classes in Detail   538

23.3.1 Filing System Considerations   540

23.3.2 Clientship   542

23.4   Moving toward Implementation   544

23.4.1 The `DirBase` Class   544

23.4.2 The `DirEntry` Class   544

23.4.3 The `IndexElem` Class   546

23.4.4 The Index Class   546

23.5   Key Points in Chapter 23   547

23.6   Exercise   548

23.7   Reference   548

24 Case Study: Implementing the Personal Organizer 2   549

24.1   Completing the Implementation   549

24.2   Implementation of `DirBase`, `Index`, `IndexElem`, and `DirEntry`   549

24.2.1 `DirEntry` Class Source and Commentary   549

24.2.2 `IndexElem` Class Source and Commentary   552

24.2.3 Index Class Source and Commentary   554

24.2.4 `DirBase` Class Source and Commentary   560

24.3   Testing What We Have Done So Far   564

24.3.1 Using a `StreamTokenizer`   564

24.3.2 Test-Based Interface: Intermediate Application and Testing   568

24.3.3 What Are We Testing?   570

24.4   Graphical User Interface: The Final Prototype Application   571

24.4.1 Testing the Graphical Interface   574

24.5   Using Inheritance   575

24.6   Key Points in Chapter 24   576

24.7   Exercises   577

25 Criteria for a Good Object-Oriented Design   579

25.1   Introduction   579

25.2   Cohesion   579

25.3   Coupling   582
    25.3.1   The Law of Demeter   583

25.4   Clarity   584

25.5   Extensibility of Our Design   585
    25.5.1   Adding an Email Attribute to a Directory Entry   585
    25.5.2   Adding a Diary Feature to the Personal Organizer   586

25.6   Key Points in Chapter 25   586

25.7   Exercises   587

25.8   References   587

Part 6   Appendixes

A Getting Started with Java   588

B Keywords in Java   589

C ASCII and Unicode Characters   590

D Program Listings   593

D.1   Person.Java   593

D.2   Chapter2On2.java   599

D.3   The GUI Source Code for the Java Personal Organizer   604
    D.3.1   The Gui Class   604
    D.3.2   The DirGui Class   606
    D.3.3   The BrowseRecGui Class   608
    D.3.4   The NewRecGui Class   610
    D.3.5   The AlertDialog Class   612

Index   614

Preface

This is a book about programming in the Java™ programming language. It is intended for people who have no previous programming experience, so it is unlike many other Java programming books, which appear to have been written by experts for experts. It was written from scratch and not based on previous C or C++ textbooks by the same authors, which also makes it different from many other books. This book was developed for a specific purpose and is not an evolution from an earlier book. The book is thus well suited for a first-year undergraduate programming course. This edition has been thoroughly revised and updated for the latest versions of Java.

The authors have between them taught the first-year programming course at Lancaster University for more than 14 years, first in Pascal, then in Ada, and since 1996–1997 in Java, one of the first British universities to use the Java language for first-year programming. This book is based on our experience of teaching the language to classes of some 150 students. One author has experience in object-oriented software development and database management systems from Objective-C to C++ and ONTOS to POET. The other has written a number of textbooks on natural language processing and computer architecture.

Java is an interesting development in the field of programming languages. We briefly explore some of the history of Java in our first chapter, but for now, suffice it to say that it is very much a language for the new millennium. Part of the "buzz" around Java is because it is the language of the World Wide Web (itself a major aspect of computing now and in the future), but a significant feature of the language is that it is *object-oriented*. This means that we can think of systems as composed of a number of *objects* that provide and request services from each other to accomplish an overall task. The object model can be applied from the earliest stages of system requirements and design and carried through to coding, testing, and maintenance.

Rather than avoid or delay object orientation, we have decided to make objects our departure point. We present our study of Java in terms of objects from the very start rather than begin as a conventional programming text and graft on objects at a later point.

We believe that Java is an elegant language with an extensive class library that supports the programming of graphical interfaces and the use of computer networks. We therefore believe it is a good language with which to introduce the concepts of computing, and it is rewarding because the programmer is able to write significant pieces of code quickly.

The book consists of five parts:

- In Part 1, we concentrate on using objects. Here objects are supplied either from the standard Java library of classes or from example classes of our own creation. The programmer writes applications that call upon the services of these preexisting objects and interprets the results.

- In Part 2, we change emphasis and look at what is required to write (and use) objects of our own.

- In Part 3, we explore a major concept in object models, that of *inheritance*, and how we can apply it in Java. This part also covers two areas of Java that rely heavily on inheritance: the use of exceptions for dealing with error conditions in programs and the Abstract Windowing Toolkit (AWT), which supports the creation of graphical user interfaces.

- In Part 4, we examine more advanced features of Java, such as the input/output facilities, and how applets—applications that can be executed over the World Wide Web—can be written. We also examine how common data structures can be realized in Java, introducing ideas about the use of pointers and linked data structures.

- In Part 5, we look at object-oriented design and show how we can identify objects from the requirements of a system and move forward through design and into coding. This section is supported by examining the development of a system from start to finish.

We cover all the major parts of the basic language except multithreading, which we introduce only briefly in Chapter 21. In a book of this size, it is possible to cover only a small part of the extensive facilities provided by Java. Thus, we introduce only a few of the main classes of the AWT, and we consider access to networks only in terms of the communication between an applet and its originating computer. Some of the sections are marked as optional on a first reading. We see Java as having a future as a good general-purpose programming language rather than as only a vehicle for Web programming. We therefore spend most of the book discussing normal application programs and discuss how applets can be written to be executed over the Web only in Chapter 20.

The book contains many examples and exercises to illustrate the principles discussed. All example programs are also available through a Web site (see Appendix A).

A number of environments are available for developing Java programs. This book describes Version 1.3 of Java, and the development environment it describes is the basic Software Development Kit (SDK) from Sun Microsystems. The examples have all been tested under the Windows NT and UNIX operating systems. Appendix A describes how to obtain a copy of the SDK, as well as the special classes used in this book.

We believe that Java is an exciting development in programming language design. We hope you will enjoy this introduction to the world of Java programming.

R.G.G. & J.A.M.
Lancaster

Acknowledgments

We would like to thank Professors Doug Shepherd and Ian Sommerville of the Computing Department at Lancaster University for supporting our efforts with this book. We introduced Java as our first-year teaching language in October 1996, one of the first UK universities to do so. We would also like to thank Richard Cardoe for his assistance in developing course material and Ian Warren for his help with the material in Part 5. We would especially like to thank our first-year students for serving as guinea pigs for various versions of the material and exercises in this book. Finally, we would like to thank our long-suffering wives for putting up with us during the long process of producing this book.

R.G.G.
J.A.M.
Lancaster

PART 1

Using Objects

1 **Programming and the Java™ Language**

2 **Object Orientation**

3 **Declaring Objects and Calling Methods**

4 **Selecting Among Alternatives**

5 **Repetition**

6 **Basic Java Data Types**

CHAPTER 1

Programming and the Java Language

1.1 Programs and Programming

Most of us use computers and computer programs nearly every day of our lives. When we want to write something, we start up a word-processing program such as Microsoft® Word or Word-Perfect® . When we have to do some calculations, we use a spreadsheet such as Microsoft® Excel. When we want to find some up-to-date information, we turn to a browser such as Netscape® Navigator or Microsoft® Internet Explorer to search the World Wide Web. These are all examples of computer *programs* written by a programmer (or more likely, a team of programmers) for our use.

A computer itself has no intelligence. As you will see, all it can do is follow a rather detailed set of instructions. A program is simply a detailed set of instructions in a suitable format that tells the computer how to carry out a task. For example, a programmer writing a word-processing program has to specify how the computer is to deal with text typed in by the user, how to format the text as a series of lines of characters, how to change the format according to instructions from the user, how to check the spelling of each word against a dictionary of valid words, how to pass the text to a printer to produce a printed version, and so on.

Nowadays, there are computer programs in places you might not expect. A modern washing machine contains one or more small computers or *processors*, which control the sequence of operations carried out by the machine according to the instructions of the user and the state of the wash (Is the machine full of water? Is it at the right temperature? Has the user specified a long spin cycle? and so on). Similarly, a car has several processors to control the ignition system according to the state of the engine, to check that the seat belts are used correctly, and so on. Each of the processors in these *embedded systems* follows a program, or set of instructions, specifying in detail how the system should react to any particular combination of input information sensed by the processor.

The programs we have discussed so far are called *application* programs; that is, there is some particular task that we want carried out, and the program is designed to deal with it, perhaps (as in the word-processing and spreadsheet examples) in collaboration with the user. However, there are other programs that do not directly carry out an application task but make it easier for an application program to do so. One very important such program is the *operating system* in the computer (e.g., Microsoft® Windows 2000 or UNIX). This program organizes and manages the resources of the computer system as instructed by the user. For example, we can request, by typing in a sequence of characters as a command to the operating system or by clicking on an icon representing a particular program, that a word-processing program be run. We can request that the resultant file (a letter or a report) be passed to a suitable printer, and the operating system will organize the queue of files waiting to be printed. Or we can store the resultant file in a *filing system* so that we can retrieve it by name for use at a later time, and we can arrange our various different files in a way that enables us to find them easily the next time we need them.

This book is about learning to write programs. That is, we must learn to specify how to carry out a task in a clear step-by-step procedure, in sufficient detail, and in an appropriate format so that the computer can understand and carry out the task. We want to organize this programming task in such a way that the task will be correctly carried out, and the program will make a suitable response if the information supplied to it is invalid in some way (even if the response is simply to display an error message for the user). And we want to design the program so that modifying it is as straightforward as possible if we want to extend or revise how the task is to be carried out.

To write a program, or set of instructions, for a computer to carry out, we have to write in a language the computer can understand, a *programming language*. Over the years, a vast number of programming languages have been designed for different types of programming tasks. They have incorporated different ideas of how a programming language should be designed to make it as easy as possible to write (and later rewrite) a program with as few errors (or "bugs") as possible.

In this book, we use *Java*® as the programming language. Java was released by Sun Microsystems in 1995. There has been a lot of interest in Java, partly because of its ability to deliver programs across the World Wide Web. But we use Java in this book because we think it is also a clear and elegant programming language, suitable as a first language for teaching programming.

1.2 Algorithms

If we are going to carry out any step-by-step procedure, we must have a clear and unambiguous specification of the steps needed. This clear specification, called an *algorithm*, doesn't have to be written in a programming language; it could be in some form of English or in some other more formal language. The problem with using English (or any other natural language) is its ambiguity, so we may turn to more formal languages to be more precise.

Here is an example of part of an algorithm for calculating the date Easter falls on in a given year. The algorithm is in the 17th-century language of the Church of England *Book of Common Prayer*. Actually, this part works out the position of the sun in a 19-year period called the "saros cycle" because this information is needed by the Easter Day calculation:

```
To find the Golden Number, or Prime, add One to the Year of our Lord, and then
divide by 19; the Remainder, if any, is the Golden Number; but if nothing
remaineth, then 19 is the Golden Number.
```

Here is the beginning of another algorithm, written in the formal language of knitting patterns:

```
SLEEVES

Size 4 mm (8) needles.
Working in St. St.
Pick up 70 (76, 82, 88, 102, 108, 114, 118) Sts. around armhole edge.
Work 10 (10, 10, 10, 12, 2, 0, 0) rows in St. St.
Next Row K.2. K.2. Tog. T.B.L. K. to last 4 Sts. K.2 Tog. K.2
```

And Figure 1.1 is part of a third algorithm, expressed in an even more formal language.

Figure 1.1: An algorithm expressed in the formal language of music

What are our requirements of an algorithm to specify how a programming task is to be carried out?

- The steps of the algorithm must be *precise* and *unambiguous*. We must know, at least in principle, how we would specify each step in the programming language we are using.

- We also need to be precise about what type of *input data* is required by our algorithm. In the Easter Day algorithm, a single piece of data is required—the year for which we want to find the date of Easter—but the algorithm states that it is valid only for years "from the present time till the year 2199 inclusive."

- The algorithm must be *correct*. We must know that if we set the algorithm going with suitable data, it will eventually finish its calculation and deliver a result that is appropriate for the given input data.

- The algorithm should be *efficient*. For programs that are run rarely or that do not require much calculation, efficiency is not very important. But many programs become useful only if they can deliver a result in a time short enough to be useful (tomorrow's weather forecast is useful only if we can calculate it before tomorrow) and in a space (amount of memory) small enough to fit into the computer that is to perform the task. So for most algorithms, we will be interested in how much time and space are needed (for a particular amount of input data).

When we code the algorithm in a programming language, the preceding factors remain important, and some further factors become relevant:

- A new issue becomes important when we consider *correctness*. We need to have the program check that the input data are valid for the task to be performed. If they are not valid, we need to ensure that the program displays clear and unambiguous error messages explaining what is wrong with the input data and exactly what the program has done about it. For example, it could abandon the task for this set of data, or it could try and adjust the values in some way to obtain a valid set of input data.

■ We need to consider the *maintainability* of the program. Inevitably, errors ("bugs") will be found in the program and will need to be corrected; changes will occur in the outside world that require corresponding changes to the program; and there may be a desire to extend the tasks carried out by the program. It is difficult enough making changes to a program that we last worked on several months or years ago, but the changes to a program may have to be made by a different programmer (the original programmer may have moved to another job or at least to a different programming task). All this requires us to arrange the structure of our program as clearly as possible. It needs to be obvious what parts of the program need to be modified for any particular change in the task. And we need to be assured that, as far as possible, changes to one part of a program do not affect other parts. A major issue of programming language design has been how to split up a program into its constituent parts so that a modification to one part has a minimal effect on all the other parts.

1.3   High-Level Languages and Programs

High-level programming languages have been in use since the early 1950s. Most computer languages, from early examples like FORTRAN and ALGOL to more recent languages like C and Ada, have been imperative or procedural. A computer program in a language of this type consists of:

■ A collection of *variables* (named places, or "pigeonholes," in the computer), each of which at any stage contains a certain value (a number, a character, a string of characters, etc.).

■ A collection of *statements* that change the values of these variables. The new value (which replaces the previous value of a variable) could be a fixed value specified in the program. Or it could be a value computed from values held in other variables. These statements will be interspersed with tests on values held in variables to decide in what order the statements of the program are to be executed (and consequently, what the final result of the program will be).

A programming language of this style is called an *imperative* language because the basic operation is a command to change the value in a variable to a suitable new value. This style of programming is based on the style of the underlying hardware of the computer, or machine code (see Section 1.5), but with a clearer syntax for specifying how new values are to be calculated and how tests are to affect the ordering of statements.

Early experience in the difficulties of writing programs revealed that it was important to divide a program into a number of more-or-less independent pieces so that the programmer could concentrate on writing one piece at a time. A typical piece would be a program in miniature, consisting of a sequence of statements to assign values to variables, with tests applied to the values of variables already read in or calculated. Such a subdivision of a program is usually called a *procedure*. Since imperative languages generally rely on some form of procedure as the basic building block of a program, they are often called *procedural* languages.

Consider the following problem. Someone has given us a list of all the salaries at the place we work, and we want to know the largest salary (actually, we probably would also like to know who receives it, but let's keep the problem simple). There are several hundred employees, so we need some sort of systematic way of going about it (i.e., we need an algorithm). Written in an imperative style, we could have a procedure, called (let's say) maxList, which, given a list of numbers stored in a variable called list, proceeds as follows:

```
1 We assume that the number of salaries in list is stored in a variable called
count
2 Copy the first salary in list to a variable called max
3 Set a variable i to the number 2
4 Copy the ith salary in list to a variable called current
5 if the number in current is greater than that in max
6    copy the number in current into max
7 add 1 to the number in i
8 if the number in i is not greater than the number in count, repeat from step 4
9 print the number in max
```

In this imperative programming example, we have several variables—pigeonholes—that each have a name and hold a value. Some, such as count and current, can hold only a single value (here it is a whole number or integer, but in another program it might be a number with a decimal part or a character). The value in count does not change (i.e., it is a *constant*) in this piece of code, whereas the value in current probably changes several times. The variable list holds a whole collection of items, all of the same type (they are all whole numbers). Sometimes all the items in a collection in a program can be expected to be of the same type, but not always. In some of the statements, we specify an actual value—2 in statement 3 and 1 in statement 7—these are called *literals*.

Each of the statements 1 to 9 either calculates a new value to be stored in a variable from other values already available or (as with statement 8) specifies a test to decide which of two actions is to occur (repeat from statement 4 or implicitly proceed to statement 9).

We assume in the preceding program that, if we have a variable i containing a number, we can easily extract (or change) the ith element of the list. This is a common operation in imperative languages, and it uses a mechanism called an *array*, which we discuss in Chapter 9. Figure 1.2 shows the situation just after the computer has checked the fourth salary in the list and is about to return to step 4 with the variable i set to 5.

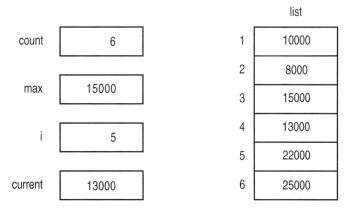

Figure 1.2: Variables in the maxList procedure

Note that we must be careful with this program. It assumes that there are at least two salaries in the list. We could easily revise the algorithm so that it still works correctly with a list consisting of a single salary (how would you do it?). But if there are no salaries in the list, the correct action for the program to take is not clear. Perhaps the program should check for this situation and stop after printing an error message.

We have here a program written in a *high-level* language. A computer cannot directly understand a program written in this form. As you will see, a computer executes a much more basic type of language called *machine code*. But the computer can come to the rescue and translate the program written in the high-level language into an equivalent program in machine code. Such a translation program is called a *compiler*, and we would need one for the particular high-level language in which our program is written and for the particular computer and machine code on which we want our program to run (Figure 1.3).

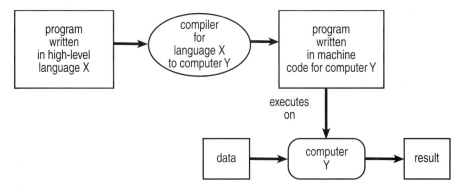

Figure 1.3: Compiling and executing a program

A more recent style of programming language is *object-oriented programming*, which is based on this imperative or procedural style. Because Java is an object-oriented language, the features of this style of programming language are discussed in detail in the next chapter.

1.4 A Simple Computer

To motivate some of the discussion later in this book, you need to have a basic idea of what a computer is. The most important distinction is between software and hardware.

The *software* is the set of programs that tells the computer how to carry out any particular task. One important piece of software is the operating system; this program automatically starts to run when the computer is switched on. It responds to user commands—for example, to run some piece of application software, such as a word-processing program, a Computer-Aided Design program, a game, or a Java program. When the application program finishes, control is returned to the operating system, which awaits the user's next command.

The *hardware* is the basic electronics of the computer itself and its associated peripheral or input/output equipment. The latter usually includes a keyboard and display, disk storage (perhaps of various types), a printer, and some form of connection to a local or wide area network (Figure 1.4).

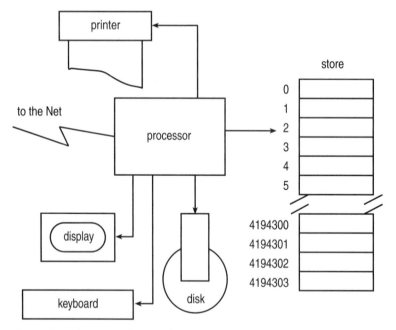

Figure 1.4: The parts of a simple computer

The computer itself is divided into a *processor* and a *store*. Ultimately, everything is controlled by the processor, which has a repertoire of operations it can carry out. It can, for example:

- Add two numbers.

- Test to see if one number is the same as another.

- Request the next character to be read in from a particular input device (e.g., from the keyboard or from a particular location on the disk).

- Request that a character be written to a particular output device (causing it to be displayed on the screen or printed by the printer).

The store consists of a number of store *locations* that hold the data (the numbers or characters) upon which the operations take place. The store locations are all the same size, usually a *byte* of 8 binary *bits*. Such a store location is capable of holding 256 different values, each representing a character in the ASCII character set, or a number in the range -128 to $+127$. To access an individual location in the store, we must have some unique way of referring to it. Because the store is a long sequence of locations, we simply use the position in this sequence as the *address* of this location in a range from 0 to, say, 4,194,303 (for a 4 megabyte store).

Since a byte is rather small, we use a group of adjacent bytes to hold a larger item of data. Thus, the designer of the computer might decide that a group of 4 adjacent bytes could be treated as a *word*, capable of holding an integer in the range $-2,147,483,648$ to $+2,147,483,647$. We specify a particular word by the address of its first byte (i.e., the byte with the lowest address). For example, Figure 1.5 illustrates a word at address 1024 holding the number 1,512,345.

1024	1025	1026	1027
00000000	00010111	00010011	10011001

Figure 1.5: Four adjacent bytes holding the value 1,512,345

A *program* consists of a set of instructions to be carried out by a computer to complete some task. An *instruction* is a specification of an operation to be carried out together with the address of the data to be used for the operation. A basic insight from the early days of computing is that such an instruction can be considered as just a set of numeric values and can therefore also be stored in a sequence of bytes in the store.

1.5 Machine Code

Let us consider a concrete example. We assume a very simple computer with a store of only 65,536 bytes (numbered with addresses from 0 to 65,535). An instruction consists of 3 bytes:

- The first byte specifies the operation to be carried out. One byte gives 256 different possibilities, but we are going to use only a small number of different operations in this simple computer, as listed in Table 1.1.

Value	Function
0	load
1	add
2	subtract
3	multiply
4	divide
5	store
6	. . .

Table 1.1: Operations for a Simple Computer

- The second and third bytes, taken together, represent a value in the range 0 to 65,535. So these 2 bytes give the address of a store location whose contents are to be used in the specified operation.

Most arithmetic operations, such as add and subtract, require two pieces of data. One is found in the store location specified in the instruction. The other is in a special location in the processor called the *accumulator*. To get a calculation started, we have a *load* operation to bring a value into this accumulator. When the calculation is finished, we can use the *store* operation to put the result in a specified store location.

Let us assume that we never need to perform arithmetic on values outside the range −32,768 to +32,767. Then the accumulator needs to be 16 bits long (equivalent to 2 bytes). We also assume that, in this computer, an instruction specifies the store address of a location containing a number by giving the address of the lower of the 2 bytes making it up.

Suppose in an electricity billing program that we want to perform the calculation

(unitsConsumed * costPerUnit) + standingCharge

with the values unitsConsumed, costPerUnit, and standingCharge in locations

```
unitsConsumed    123–124
costPerUnit      125–126
standingCharge   127–128
```

The result (totalCharge) is to go in location 129–130. To keep things simple, we assume all values are held as whole numbers of pence. This calculation would be accomplished by the fragment of a program in Figure 1.6. The code fragment starts at location 1005.

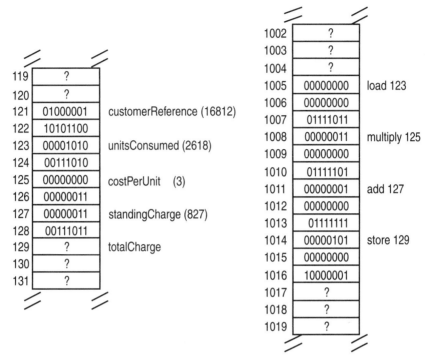

Figure 1.6: Part of an electricity billing program

This program of instructions is carried out as follows. The processor contains another register, the *program counter*, which always holds the address in store of the next instruction to be executed. The basic *instruction cycle* of the processor repeatedly carries out the following sequence of steps:

1. Copy to the processor the instruction in the store starting at the address given by the program counter (in this computer, occupying the addressed byte and the next 2 bytes).

2. Update the program counter so that it refers to the next instruction (in this computer, the program counter is updated by adding 3).

3. Execute the instruction that has been copied from the store. This may involve reading from or writing to a store location at the address specified in the instruction.

4. And repeat.

If the program counter starts by containing the value 1005, then by the time it contains the value 1017 (and is ready to execute the next instruction after our code fragment), the instructions will have evaluated the value 2618 × 3 + 827 and stored the result (8681) in the 2 bytes at locations 129–130. We can imagine that the instructions before location 1005 calculated the unitsConsumed from the two most recent meter readings. The instructions from location 1017 onward print a bill containing the total charge (in location 129–130) together with the customer reference number, which we assume is the number 16812 stored in locations 121–122. In a real billing program, of course, there will be a lot more information associated with the customer such as the name and address, the current and previous meter readings, and so on.

There are major difficulties in trying to write such a program in what is called machine code, which is broken down into a detailed set of steps corresponding to the requirements of this particular computer. But we can enlist the help of the computer itself. As discussed in Section 1.3, we can design a high-level programming language that is easier to use than machine code and have a program called a compiler to translate it into machine code to be executed. In a high-level language, the preceding calculation could be written in a much clearer form, such as:

```
totalCharge = unitsConsumed * costPerUnit + standingCharge ;
```

We can design the language so that the programmer's intentions are more explicitly declared in a program, and the compiler can cross-check that the program and the programmer's intentions match. For instance, if we declare that a certain store location in a program holds a character, then some operations that our program tries to perform on it are likely to be valid (e.g., displaying it on the screen or comparing it to another character) but others are not (e.g., adding 3.7 to it). The ability to do as much checking as possible of the validity of a particular operation on a particular piece of data is called *type checking*. If our programming language specifies what type of data each variable can hold, the type checking can be done during the compilation process (i.e., at *compile time*) rather than when the program is running with test data or, even worse, when the program is in use (i.e., at *run time*). This is a powerful factor in reducing the cost of developing and maintaining a program written in a high-level language.

Let us return to the electricity billing program. We had a set of store locations (starting at address 121) that held the data corresponding to some particular customer (customer 16812), and we had a piece of code to perform the billing calculation—the fragment we looked at started at location 1005, and the code to print the bill presumably started at location 1017. If we wished to calculate the electricity bill for a number of different customers, we might have the details of each customer in a separate area of store together with a table containing the addresses of these areas (Figure 1.7).

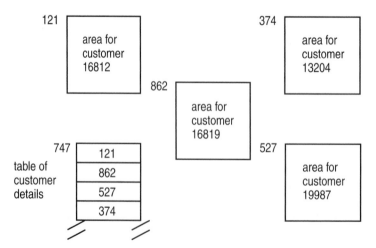

Figure 1.7: Sets of data for different customers

The billing program would have to be modified slightly so that, each time we execute it, the instructions refer to the appropriate set of locations for the customer currently being dealt with. The machine code of a modern computer has facilities that enable the programmer to establish the address of a particular piece of data if it is given the address of the store area containing it (and if all the areas of store have the same layout). For example, the units consumed by customer 19987 will be 2 bytes on from the beginning of the area allocated to this customer—that is, 529–530.

The point of this illustration is to make clear that a store location can contain any one of several different types of information:

■ It may contain a *value*, such as the number of units consumed by customer 16812 (i.e., 2618) in bytes 123–124.

■ It may contain an *instruction*, such as the multiply instruction in bytes 1008–1010.

■ It may contain an *address*, such as the address 121 of the store area containing details for customer 16812, in bytes 747–748. We call this address a *reference*. Because we are usually not concerned with the exact address of a store area, our diagrams generally show such a reference as a pointer from the location containing the reference to the area of store referred to (Figure 1.8).

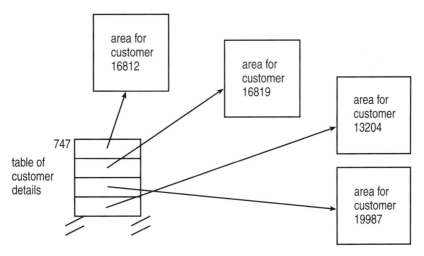

Figure 1.8: Sets of data for different customers: version 2

It is important when studying Java programs to be clear when a store location contains a value (e.g., 2618) and when it contains a reference (e.g., the address of the area associated with customer 16812). The store areas we have considered in this example contained only values (customer reference number, units consumed, etc.). But they could also (or instead) have contained instructions. We could have had a table specifying that the instructions for calculating the units consumed start at, say, location 996; the instructions for calculating the total charge start at location 1005; the instructions for printing the bill start at 1017; and so on. Or the area could have contained a further reference—perhaps the address of the customer, a string of characters located somewhere else in the store.

1.6   Files and the Filing System

Useful information (the text of a letter, the text of a high-level language program, the machine code version of this program, data to be read in by a program, data produced by a program, etc.) is held in *files* in the *filing system* of a computer. We briefly review the terminology of filing systems in this section. If you are familiar with the terminology, you can skip to the next section.

Files may be grouped together into *directories* or *folders*. Since a directory is like a file, we can further group directories (and other files if we wish) into other directories. Thus, the complete filing system looks like a tree (growing downward, as is usual in computer science) starting at a particular directory called the *root* of the filing system. Figure 1.9 shows an example.

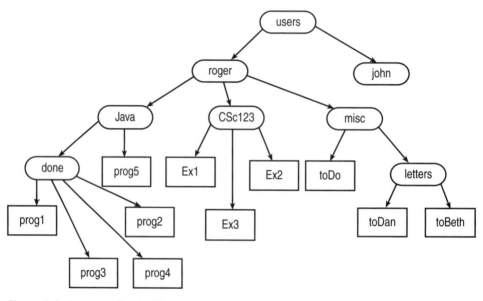

Figure 1.9: An example of a filing system

When we start to use a computer (when we switch on, or log on), we are placed at some position within this tree, the *current directory*, and there are facilities for making some other directory the current directory.

If we want to refer to a file in the current directory, we simply specify its name. Thus, if the current directory is `roger`, we specify the file `misc` (which happens to be a directory) by simply quoting its name. If we want to access a file in some other directory, we have to specify a *pathname*, which gives the sequence of directories from the current directory or from the root directory to the file in question. On a UNIX system, we could specify the file `toBeth` (assuming the current directory is still `roger`) as

```
misc/letters/toBeth
```

or we could specify it as a path from the root directory as

`/users/roger/misc/letters/toBeth`

Here, the initial / character indicates that we are starting from the root directory (an *absolute* pathname) rather than from the current directory (a *relative* pathname). On other systems, we would do something similar. On a Windows system, we would specify the same file (assuming our current directory is `roger`) as

`misc\letters\toBeth`

where the separator between one file name and the next is the character \ instead of /.

1.7   The World Wide Web

There has been phenomenal growth in the World Wide Web as a source of information and entertainment since the first sites and browsers became available in 1991. There is, of course, a lot of hype over what can be achieved with the Web, but it clearly has great potential for making available, at a locally accessible computer, up-to-date information or interesting entertainment from all over the world.

The Web (Figure 1.10) is based on a set of standard formats for data of various types together with computer software that can access data if they are in one of these standard formats on a computer connected to the *Internet*. The Internet is a network of computers (originally in Europe and North America, but now in almost every country in the world). It probably makes no sense to ask how many computers are connected to the Internet because it would be out of date immediately, but it must be hundreds of millions. The Internet is based on a set of communication protocols—that is, a set of standard formats for forwarding data from one computer to another and getting a reply.

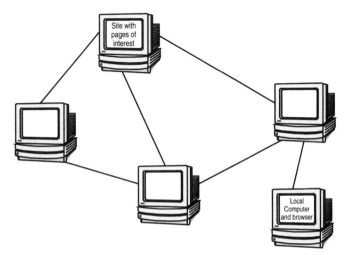

Figure 1.10: Part of the World Wide Web

We access information on the Web with a program called a *browser*, such as Netscape Navigator or Microsoft Internet Explorer. The information making up the World Wide Web is held as a number of *pages*, which contain the information itself together with formatting information written in *Hypertext Markup Language (HTML)*. The browser displays the page, laid out according to the HTML instructions (specifying which pieces of text are headings, where to display images, etc.), as shown in Figure 1.11.

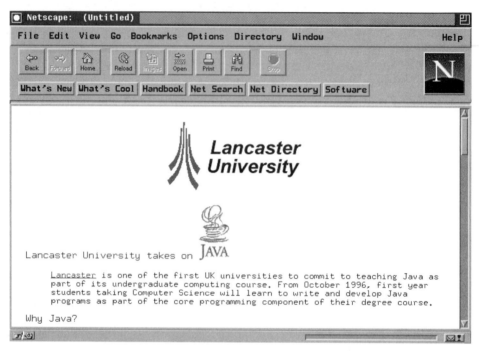

Figure 1.11: A Web page displayed in a browser

The HTML instructions can indicate a *link* to another page (e.g., the underlined word Lancaster in Figure 1.11). If we click on text marked in this way, the browser fetches a page specified by the HTML instructions and displays it. In this case, it would bring up a page describing general features about Lancaster university. This page is usually called the university's *home page*.

Originally, pages in HTML were essentially passive objects. We could read the text and look at the images; we could click on a reference and display a new page; we could fill in a form and pass it back to the originator of a page; we could send an email message to a specified address.

With the advent of Java, things changed. Now a page can contain a reference to a Java program or *applet*. If the browser is *Java aware*, it brings a copy of the program from the originating Web site to the local computer, where the browser is running, and executes the program as part of the page being displayed. The Java program can create moving images within the page; it can collect information from the user, perform some sort of calculation, and display the results; it can extract information from the Web, filter it in some way according to the instructions of the user, and display it locally. The applet could play a game with the user; it could animate some subject of educational interest (e.g., show how planetary orbits are affected by a change in the force of gravity); it could extract stock information selected by the user and display it in various useful ways. And so on.

There are two issues that need to be dealt with before applets can be routinely downloaded from the Web and run on your local computer. One issue is *security*. Downloading a program from a remote Web site and running it on our machine seems like an invitation for computer viruses to destroy our hard disk or to copy all our private data files back to the originating Web site. The Java language and system have been designed to cope with this threat. Severe restrictions can be placed on an applet that is downloaded from a remote site by a Web browser. For example, the applet can be refused access to the files on our disks, and its access to the Web could be only to its originating site (but it could interact with a program at the originating site to access information at other locations).

A second issue is *platform independence*. Our local computer might be a PC, a Macintosh, or a UNIX system, and each of these has a different machine code and operating system. Does the writer of the applet have to supply a version of the applet for each such machine code, and how does the browser make sure it picks the right version? In the next section, we look at the Java solution to this question.

1.8   The Java Programming Language

Java is based on the C and C++ programming languages. C was an imperative language designed in the early 1970s; it became well known as the language in which the UNIX operating system was written and, by the early 1980s, was perhaps the most popular language among software developers and researchers. It is characterized by what its supporters would call its flexibility in allowing the programmer to mix variables of different types (numbers, addresses, characters, etc.). Its detractors would call this a dangerous lack of rigor because it does not carry out as much type checking as possible at compile time (and consequently, leaves bugs to be discovered at run time, when they are much more dangerous in their effects and more expensive to correct).

By the early 1980s, it had become clear that C was an extremely popular language among programmers and that *object-oriented* programming was an influential way of organizing the task of writing software. The result was the C++ programming language, which is essentially the C language (with a few changes) with the features of object-oriented programming added onto it. This language has in its turn become very popular. But C++ is a large language to learn, containing nearly all the features of C together with a full set of features for object-oriented programming. Some people felt that a new and more radical departure was called for.

In 1990–1991, the Java language was designed by a team from Sun Microsystems lead by James Gosling (the language was at the time called Oak). The designers started with the basic syntax of C and C++, but they did not feel constrained to include all the features of these languages. Their aim was to create a small language, which was parsimonious in features. But they decided that it should be object-oriented. The language was first intended for use in "information appliances" such as cellular phones. By 1993, it had become clear to Sun that the language (now called Java) could be used to provide animation and interaction on the World Wide Web, which was rapidly becoming popular at that time. Java caught the popular imagination in 1995 with the announcement that the next version of the Netscape Navigator browser would be able to download and run Java applets. And the rest is history.

Let us now return to the problem of platform independence of Java applets downloaded across the Web. We want to download a Java applet to our local machine and execute it there, and we want to do this whatever our local machine is (a PC, a Macintosh, a UNIX system, each with their own machine code and operating system). As shown in Figure 1.12, we could compile the program for each of the main platforms and try to ensure that the most appropriate copy is downloaded, but this requires a potentially large number of different copies every time we recompile.

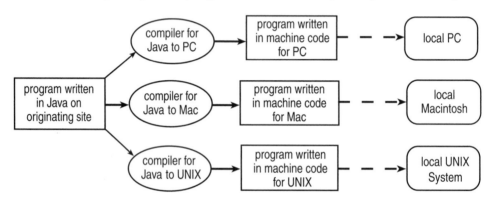

Figure 1.12: Compiling for different platforms: the problem

Alternatively, we could download the Java source text, compile it locally into the appropriate machine code for our local platform, and then execute it (Figure 1.13). But this requires an extra step for the user and the availability of a suitable Java compiler and associated software. It also requires the developers of the program to be prepared to make available the source text (which may be commercially valuable) to anyone who wants to use it.

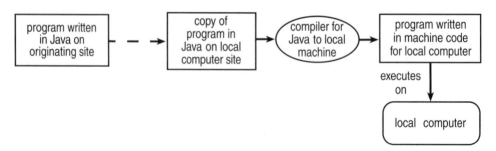

Figure 1.13: Compiling for different platforms: downloading the source program

The solution arrived at by the Java developers, illustrated in Figure 1.14, was to compile the Java source code, not into some particular machine code, but into a machine code (*byte-codes*) for a hypothetical machine, and this is what is downloaded to the local machine. But the bytecodes are not the native machine code of the local computer, so how do they get executed? We need a program in the local machine (called an *interpreter*) that reads the bytecodes, interprets what operations have to be carried out on what data, and then carries them out. It turns out that it is easier to write an interpreter for the Java bytecodes than it is to write a compiler for the Java source code. As long as we have a bytecode interpreter on our local machine, we can download a Java program and execute it.

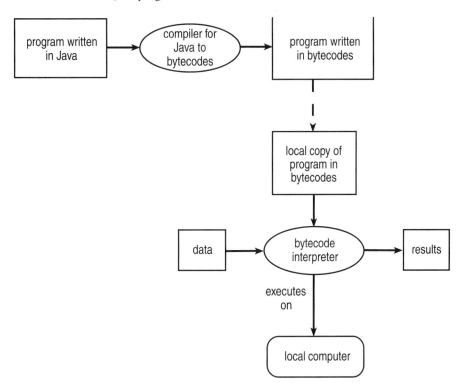

Figure 1.14: Compiling for different platforms: the Java solution

How do we obtain a bytecode interpreter? Most Web browsers nowadays are *Java aware*. That is, they contain an interpreter, so when they read an HTML page containing a reference to a Java applet, they can download the bytecodes and execute the applet while they are displaying the page.

The Java programs we have discussed in this section are all *applets*; that is, they are designed to be downloaded and run from within a Net browser. With other programming languages, we write programs that are not run from within a browser. They are usually run as isolated programs, invoked by specifying the name of the program at the command-line interface or by clicking on a program icon in a graphical user interface (GUI). It is possible to write programs of this type in Java, and the Java term for a program not run from within a browser is an *application*.[1] We concentrate on writing Java applications for most of this book, starting with a simple application in Section 1.10. By Chapter 20, we will have introduced sufficient concepts of the Java language to be able to return to the writing of applets.

1.9 Getting Started with Java

To learn to use the Java language, you need access to a Java compiler, which converts a file containing the text of a Java program into a file of bytecodes, and the bytecode interpreter, which enables you to run the Java program you have written. Sun Microsystems provides a version of these two programs, together with some other useful programs, in something called the *Software Development Kit (SDK)* or *Java Development Kit (JDK)*. This is available for various computers such as PCs (running Windows operating systems), Macintoshes, and UNIX systems. The SDK can be obtained from various sources, including over the Internet. Details of how to obtain it are in Appendix A.

In this book, we assume that you are using the SDK on a PC or a UNIX system. This is the environment we describe, for example, when we explain how to compile and run a Java program in the next section. This book describes Version 1.3 of Java.

The user interface to the SDK is fairly primitive because we have to type a command string to carry out each step while developing a Java program. There are a number of other Java development environments that provide a more sophisticated, integrated environment in which to do the development. If you are using one of these environments, you should substitute the appropriate procedure for compiling and running a Java program.

One very important resource provided by the SDK is the *Application Program Interface (API)* which gives details of all the classes provided by Sun Microsystems for the Java language. It is important to have access to the API when writing a program because it allows you to check all the details of the classes you are using. You need to use a browser to access this documentation. Details of the API are also in Appendix A.

In this book, we make use of a number of classes to illustrate features of Java or to provide simple access to some of Java's more sophisticated features (e.g., input and output). Versions of these classes and the accompanying documentation or API are available on this book's Web site. See Appendix A for more information.

We illustrate programming concepts with examples of code fragments or complete programs. The relevant portion of the code, and sometimes the complete program, is printed in the appropriate part of the book. Complete versions of all programs discussed in this book are available on this book's Web site. See Appendix A for more information.

---

[1]Java applications and applets are both application programs in the sense mentioned in Section 1.1 because they execute a particular task we want carried out.

1.10   A First Java Program

In this section, we demonstrate a very simple Java program to illustrate the basic format of a program and to introduce the procedure to compile and run it. It is common in books on programming in the C tradition to start with a program to display the message "Hello, World" on the terminal screen. This is a slightly unusual program, as it requires no input from the user (or from anywhere else) when it runs. Every time, it boringly does the same thing.

This first Java example is an application rather than an applet. It is executed by quoting its name at the command prompt rather than from an HTML page being accessed by a Web browser.

Java source code must be in a file whose name ends in the characters .java; this first program is in a file called Hello.java. It is important for you to be aware that the case of individual letters (capital or lowercase) is significant in the Java language. Java makes a distinction between the characters Hello and the characters hello. You will unfortunately find that peculiar things happen if you use the wrong case in writing a Java program. It is worth getting into the habit early of checking the case of everything you write in Java, and it will soon become second nature. You have been warned!

Here are the contents of the file Hello.java:

```
/*
 *
 * demonstration of the simplest Java application program
 *
 * Written by: Roger Garside
 *
 * First Written: June 12, 2002
 * Last Rewritten: July 14, 2002
 *
 */

public class Hello
    {

    /*
     *
     * main
     *
     */

    public static void main(String[] args)
        {
        System.out.println("Hello, World") ;
        } // end of method main
    } // end of class Hello
```

The program commences with some text between the characters /* and */. This is one way of marking the beginning and end of a *comment* in Java. Comments are ignored by the Java system and so can be used to insert "signposts" in the code to enable a human reader to follow the structure of the program. Each separate file of Java code should have a header comment giving details of the status of the code along the lines illustrated here.

Everything in a Java program has to be part of a *class*. In the next chapter, we will explain exactly what a class is, but in this program the line

```
public class Hello
```

introduces or *defines* a class called `Hello` (not `hello`). The word `public` is what is called an *access modifier* and specifies the circumstances in which the class can be accessed; this class is publicly accessible. It is a rule in Java that if there is a public class in a file (and there cannot be more than one public class per file), the name of the public class (`Hello` in this case) must be the same as the first part of the name of the file (i.e., up to the period).

The contents of the class `Hello` start at the { character immediately after the `class` statement and finish with the } character at the end of the program. To make it easy to match braces (also called curly brackets), we have put a comment after the } character. This uses the other way of introducing comments in Java with the characters // (the comment finishes at the end of the line).

The class `Hello` contains only one thing, a *method* (i.e., a named piece of code to carry out some task) called `main`. This method is introduced by the *method header* line:

```
public static void main(String[] args)
```

Again, we will explain later what the words `public static void` and `(String[] args)` tell us about the method `main`. For the moment, simply assume that this is required to get things off the ground. The *body* of the `main` method (i.e., the specification of its detailed steps) starts at the { character immediately after the method header line and finishes with the } character on the second to the last line of the program. Again, we have used a comment to make this clear.

The braces { and } are used to delimit the beginnings and ends of classes and methods and of various other features in the Java language. It is easy to insert one too many or one too few of these braces. To help a human reader understand how the braces match up, it is usual to indent each pair of braces a fixed number of character positions further to the right than the braces that enclose them. In this book's programs, we indent successive pairs of braces by four characters.

When you look at Java programs written by other people, you will find that there are a number of alternative conventions for laying out the pairs of braces. In this book, we use a simple one of lining up vertically the beginning and ending braces and all the enclosed lines of text. It needs also to be pointed out that these indentation conventions are used solely to guide the human reader of a program; the Java system itself makes no use of the convention. But it is important, as the programs you write become larger, to get into the habit of laying out your programs according to a convention that makes clear the program's structure. You will be amazed how unfamiliar a program looks if you come back to it several months after first writing it!

The contents, or *body*, of a method consists of one or more *statements*. Each statement in Java must end with a semicolon (;). This allows a long statement to spread over several lines. In this program, there is only one statement:

```
System.out.println("Hello, World") ;
```

The Java system provides a number of mechanisms for the output of results from a program, and output to the user's terminal is associated with an *object* called `System.out`. Like the terms *class* and *method*, we will explain the term *object* in the next chapter. This statement invokes, or *calls*, a method called `println` (print and go to next line) belonging to the `System.out` object, and this `println` method outputs a value to the screen.

The value to be output is supplied as an *argument*, or *parameter*, to the method and is specified in parentheses (...) after the method name. In this example, the argument we supply is a fixed character string, a character string *literal*. We write a character string literal by putting the characters between double quote marks:

```
"Hello, World"
```

Later, we will see arguments that are not literals; the string we want to print will have been constructed from other strings or read in from the user or from a file.

The procedure for compiling and running a Java program (using the SDK environment on a UNIX system or in the Command Prompt window under Windows on a PC) is as follows:

1. Create the Java source code as a file (here called `Hello.java`) using a suitable editor.

2. Compile the source code with the command `javac` followed by the name of the file to be compiled:

   ```
   javac Hello.java
   ```

   If there are no compilation errors, a new file `Hello.class` is created.

3. Run the resulting program with the command:

   ```
   java Hello
   ```

This causes the Java bytecode interpreter `java` to be executed. It first looks for a file called `Hello.class`. If it finds the file, it looks in it for a method called `main` and executes it. It starts at the first statement, executes it, and goes onto the next. In our simple program, there is only one statement, a call of the `println` method of the `System.out` object, with the argument `"Hello, World"`. This results in the text being displayed on the screen, so you should see

```
Hello, World
```

displayed at your terminal. After the message has been displayed, the program terminates.

If there is a grammatical error in your program, the compiler will display an error message together with an indication of where it thought the error occurred. Try deleting the semicolon from the end of the statement:

```
System.out.println("Hello, World")
```

Then rerun the compiler with this file. You will get an error message indicating that it expects the semicolon.

Now delete the / character at the end of the first comment in the original file and recompile the program. Can you explain what has happened?

1.11   The `print` and `println` Methods

The `println` method does two things:

1. First it prints the string we have specified (here `"Hello, World"`).

2. Then it prepares to output the next piece of information by positioning itself at the beginning of the next line.

You can see how this works if we replace the single statement with:

```
System.out.println("Hello,") ;
System.out.println("World") ;
```

Now the first `println` writes the string `"Hello,"` and positions itself at the beginning of the next line. Then the second `println` writes `"World"` on this new line (and moves to the beginning of the next line).

There is another slightly different output method called `print`. This displays a string, but it does not move to the next line. If we replace the first `println` with `print`

```
System.out.print("Hello,") ;
System.out.println("World") ;
```

we get `"Hello,World"` all on one line. Notice that no space has been left between `"Hello,"` and `"World"`. The `print` and `println` methods output exactly what we specify. If we want a gap between the words, we must insert it explicitly:

```
System.out.print("Hello, ") ;
System.out.println("World") ;
```

What happens if you replace the second `println` with `print`? If you do this, you will find that (at least on some systems) nothing gets output to the screen. What has happened is that the Java system always displays a complete line at a time. If you write a series of `print` calls, the system saves up (or *buffers*) the characters to be output, waiting for more characters to be added to the line for display or until a call of `println` tells it that the end of the line has been reached and the line can be displayed. If the `println` method is never called, the line is never displayed.

There is in fact another way of making Java output the characters in the buffer to the screen without waiting for a call of `println` to move onto the next line. This is with the method `flush`:

```
System.out.print("Hello, World") ;
System.out.flush() ;
System.out.println("Look, we are still on the same line!") ;
```

Unlike the print and println methods, the flush method does not need any argument. But notice that we still have to put in the parentheses.

1.12   How This Book Is Arranged

It is important when using an object-oriented language such as Java that you are completely familiar with the way objects are used in the language. We have therefore designed this book so that it starts off by introducing the basic concepts of setting up and manipulating objects in the language. The other concepts you require for programming in Java can then be introduced using these basic object-oriented ideas.

The book is divided into five parts:

- The first part (Chapters 1 to 6) introduces the basic concepts of setting up and using classes and objects. We then build on these basic concepts to introduce the procedures for adjusting the flow of control from one statement to another by using the selection and repetition mechanisms provided by Java. Not everything in Java is in fact an object, so we conclude this first part with a discussion of the basic data types provided by Java, such as characters and numbers.

- The classes and objects manipulated in the first part have already been written for you; they are either part of the basic language provided by Sun, or they have been provided by the authors of this book. In the second part of the book (Chapters 7 to 11), we take a look at how these classes were originally set up and allow you to create classes of your own. These first classes are quite simple, but the later chapters of this part introduce more complex features we might wish to use in our classes.

- There is a very important concept in object-oriented programming called *inheritance*, which allows us to create classes by reusing classes written by someone else rather than always having to start again from scratch. The concept of inheritance is introduced in the third part of the book (Chapters 12 to 16). This part concludes with a discussion of the means provided in Java to enable you to design and create graphical user interfaces for your programs.

- In the fourth part (Chapters 17 to 21), we introduce further features of the Java programming language, leading to a discussion (in Chapter 20) of how to create Java applets that can be downloaded from the Net and run by a browser.

- The final part (Chapters 22 to 25) introduces the ideas of object-oriented *design*, discussing the question of how to take a specification of a task and to design and implement a set of classes to carry it out.

Each chapter ends with a list of key points, summarizing the main concepts introduced in the chapter, and a selection of exercises. Programming is a practical craft, and the only way to learn it is to do it. We encourage you to try the exercises in each chapter.

1.13   Key Points in Chapter 1

- An *algorithm* embodies a set of steps or instructions to be followed to reach a goal. An algorithm should be clear and unambiguous. It can be specified in a natural language (e.g., English) or in some other more formal (and usually specialized) language or notation.

- A *program* is a version of an algorithm that can be executed on a computer. A program in an *imperative* style consists of a number of *variables* with values and a sequence of *statements* to compute new values for some of the variables. Computer *software* includes *application* programs to carry out particular tasks and an *operating system* to manage the resources of the computer. A program in a high-level language has to be translated by a *compiler* into machine code before it can be executed on a computer.

- Computer *hardware* is the electronics of the computer and consists of a *processor* and *store* together with associated peripheral or input/output equipment. The store consists of a collection of *locations*, each usually 1 *byte* (8 binary bits) in size and with a unique *address*. A group of adjacent bytes can be used to represent a larger unit, or *word*. The store contains data *values*, *instructions* specifying an operation to be carried out by the processor, or addresses of (*references* to) other areas of the store.

- A computer's filing system consists of a set of *files* grouped into *directories* or *folders*. A file can be specified by a *pathname*, starting from the *current directory* (a *relative* pathname) or from the *root* directory (an *absolute* pathname).

- The *World Wide Web* is a global information resource made up of *pages* of data held at different sites across the world. A page contains some information, some formatting instructions, and *links* to other pages, all specified in a language called *HTML*. These pages can be viewed with a *browser*, which can follow links from one page to another.

- *Java* is a programming language. Programs in Java are compiled into an intermediate form called *bytecodes*, which are executed by a program called an *interpreter*. A browser can contain such an interpreter, which enables a Java *applet* to be downloaded from a site on the World Wide Web and executed on our local computer, whatever type of machine it is. Alternatively, we can write and run a program on our local computer without using a browser; such a Java program is called an *application*.

- A Java program consists of a *class* containing one or more *methods* made up of a *header* and a series of *statements*, each terminated with a semicolon. *Comments*, which are ignored by the Java compiler but are useful to the human reader, start with the characters /* and finish with the characters */ or start with the characters // and finish at the end of the line. Extra blank lines and indentation should be used to make clear the program structure. The print and println methods of the System.out object can be used to output messages to the computer screen.

- A Java program resides in a file with the name `Something.java`. It can be compiled using the SDK command `javac`, which produces a file `Something.class`. This can then be run with the SDK command `java`.

1.14 Exercises

1. Have a look at some examples of algorithms in everyday life. Some places to look are:

   - The recipes in a cookbook.
   - The instructions for some piece of equipment (e.g., the instructions for programming your video recorder to record a TV program).
   - The constructions in a geometry book.

   To what extent do these algorithms meet the criteria set out in Section 1.2? What sort of notation do they use to specify the algorithm? If they use English, how precise and unambiguous is it?

2. Try to specify a precise algorithm for checking the spelling of all the words in a piece of text, such as the text of this question. A dictionary probably contains the word *word* but not *words* because it assumes you know how to form plurals. Does your algorithm know how to deal with this? Will it work with *boxes* and *tries*?

3. In a spreadsheet, each cell can contain a number or a formula to calculate a value for this cell from the values in other cells. The formulas can include any of the usual arithmetic operations. Sketch out an algorithm that a spreadsheet program could use to recalculate all the values after the user has changed a few of the numbers or formulas. You need to consider in what order the formulas are to be evaluated. What would happen if the formulas in two cells each referred to the value in the other cell? Is this question a clear statement of what is required from your algorithm, or have you had to make assumptions about what the question means?

4. Carry out the program given in Section 1.3 to find the largest in a list of salaries for each of the following lists of salaries:

   - 10,000 8,000 15,000 13,000 22,000 25,000
   - 10,000 8,000 15,000 13,000 15,000
   - 10,000

5. Consider an office worker sitting at a desk with an in-box, an out-box, and a filing cabinet containing information that needs to be referred to from time to time. Compare this worker with the hardware of the computer system described in Section 1.4 and map the components of the office (including the worker) onto the components of the computer system. What corresponds to the software of the computer system? What corresponds to the Net connection?

6. Use a browser to visit some sites on the World Wide Web that contain applets and try running some applets that look interesting:

   - The Web site for this book contains an applet HelloApplet. This is a very simple applet corresponding to the "Hello, World" program in Section 1.10. Have a look at the HTML page (HelloApplet.html) to see how it refers to the applet and have a look at the code (in HelloApplet.java) to see how it differs from Hello.java. More details are in Chapter 20.

   - There are a number of places on the Web that are sources for interesting applets (URLs are in Appendix A). Explore the resources there.

7. Compile and run the "Hello, World" program in Section 1.10.

   - Make some changes to the code and try recompiling it, trying to understand what sort of error the compiler is indicating. For example, delete the semicolon at the end of the print statement. Delete the / character at the end of the first comment. Change the name of the class from Hello to Hello1 (without changing the file name).

   - Try making the changes to the print statement given in Section 1.11 and observe the changes.

   - Change the print statement to

     ```
     System.out.println("Hello, " + args[0]) ;
     ```

     Recompile the program and run the program with:

     ```
     java Hello Mary
     ```

     Try it again with Mary changed to Bill and then changed to your first name. Then try running it again with:

     ```
     java Hello
     ```

     See Section 3.12 for a discussion of this.

CHAPTER 2

Object Orientation

2.1 Objects and Classes

Object orientation (or OO) is a technique that has pervaded all aspects of computer science over the past decade or so. Object-oriented ways of thinking have been applied to software system design, operating systems, programming languages, and database systems, to name but a few areas on which this technology has had an impact. In this chapter, we introduce some of the basic concepts of object orientation.

One of the main claims made for object orientation is that it is a natural way of thinking about things. In the world we live in, we are surrounded by *objects*. Once a problem has been clearly stated, it should be possible to identify an object involved in the problem and the actions we can perform on that object, as well as the actions it may ask of us and other objects. Moreover, an object has some kind of *state* that dictates its actions in response to requests. Consider a radio receiver, which has as part of its state a wave band (e.g., AM/FM) and the frequency to which it is currently tuned. Actions that we can perform on the radio are to change the wave band and to tune in to another broadcasting station.

Let's elaborate on this with another example. If we consider a CD player as an object, we can list the actions we can ask the CD player to undertake. This is very straightforward, as we need only look at the control panel of the CD player to find out what it can do. The control panel (Figure 2.1) forms the "user interface" to the CD player object.

We can:

- Play
- Pause
- Seek a particular track
- Fast forward
- Fast reverse
- Eject the CD

Notice also that the CD player has some state. For example, does it currently contain a CD? The answer to that question has an impact on how the player responds to user requests; if we ask it to play while it does not contain a disk, it will simply do nothing or it may flash an indicator light.

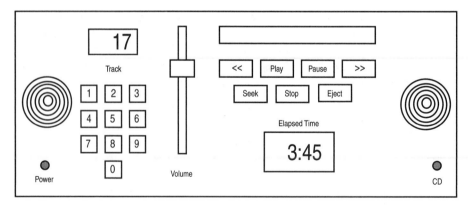

Figure 2.1: CD player control and display panel

The control panel of a CD player has more than just ways for users to express their desires; it also has some *readouts*, which give users information about its state such as which track is currently playing and how many minutes we are into the track.

Notice that the control panel reveals only the information that the user is directly interested in. In no sense do we need to know how the CD player actually works, that it contains a laser, what the current intensity of the laser is, and so on. The CD player is an example of a "black box" mechanism; most of the details of how it works are hidden from the user.

The CD player object illustrates some valuable features of object orientation:

- The idea that an object provides a set of operations that the user may invoke. These operations are known as *methods*.

- An object has an internal *state*. Some of that state may be available to the user, either directly or through the use of methods.

- An object is a *black box*. Some of its internal state is hidden from the user. Moreover, how the methods actually work is also hidden, as is how they manipulate the internal state.

So far, we have discussed a single CD player. However, as you know, there are millions of such players throughout the world. CD players of the same make and model have exactly the same functionality. But even players of different makes and models all provide the same basic core functionality of allowing the user to insert a CD and play it!

In object-orientation terminology, we can therefore identify a *class* of CD players. In this class, we can specify the operations (or actions or methods) we expect each CD player to provide and list the state it will maintain. At this point, when we discuss the state of a CD player, we are talking in a general sense about the kind of state all CD players will maintain—for example, the number of the current track being played. Obviously, here we are not considering a single instance of a CD player, so we do not need to think of a single value for the state; rather, we need to consider the kind or type of value that would be sensible. For example, a character value would not be sensible because CD tracks are numbered. Floating-point values (decimal fractions) are also unsuitable. Clearly, integers (whole numbers) are best. We can even go so far as to say that positive nonzero integers are exactly what we want. To summarize, we are talking about state in a general sense and how it will apply to all CD players rather than the actual state (or particular value) of an individual CD player.

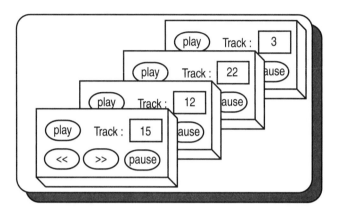

Figure 2.2: Instances of the class of CD players

Specific, individual CD players are *instances* of the *class* of CD players (Figure 2.2). They all share the same operations, but they will usually have states that differ from each other. For two distinct players, asking them to play the first track may result in different tunes being played because each CD player contains a different disk. Moreover, even if they contain the same CD, asking to play the next track may result in different music because they may currently be at different positions within the CD. In general, an object is in fact an instance of a class. In this case, an individual CD player object is a single instance of the CD player class.

We have, till now, concentrated on a single type of object: a CD player. We can use the concept of objects to model quite complicated real-world systems that consist of many different kinds of objects and many instances thereof. Consider, for example, a university. A university (among other things) typically consists of a number of academic departments. These departments in turn consist of a number of staff members. A department offers a number of courses. Each course is taken by a number of students.

From this very simple textual description, we can already identify a number of classes of objects:

- University
- Academic department
- Staff member
- Course
- Student

We can move forward and identify the state of each class and a set of operations (or methods). From these class definitions, we can generate as many instances as we require—for example, a student "object" for each student we have in a course. Indeed, we can use these classes to represent as many universities as we like.

2.2 Software Objects

Let's move on to a software object. We wish to represent information about a person. The kind of information we wish to model will, of course, depend on the application (what we want to use the information for), but for now we will consider some basic data about people. A person has a name, a gender, and an age. Figure 2.3 shows this represented as a class specification.

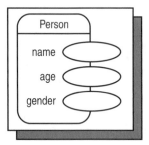

Figure 2.3: Class specification of Person

We have introduced three simple *attributes*. These attributes make up the state of a Person object. If we wish a person object to represent fred, we can declare this as shown in Figure 2.4. We can set the values of these attributes directly by placing values within them (Figure 2.5).

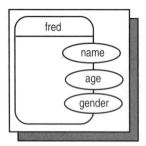

Figure 2.4: A Person instance called fred

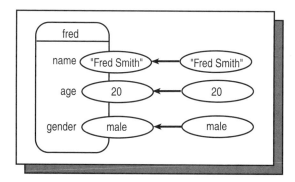

Figure 2.5: Setting the attributes of fred

However, in this case, the attributes of a Person object are all visible to the user and are not hidden at all. It is often desirable to hide attributes and to provide methods that allow access. This means that direct access is no longer possible, and the methods can contain code that allows checks to be made on the access. For example, when setting someone's age, it is not sensible to allow negative numbers or numbers greater than, say, 150. By forcing access to an attribute through a method, we can control the setting of the attribute's value.

Moreover, some of the state of the object may never be accessible by the user, although the methods make use of them. Let's make all the attributes of the person object hidden from the user (Figure 2.6). We can now provide a group of get and set methods (Figure 2.7).

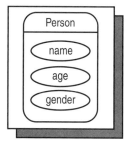

Figure 2.6: Revised class specification of Person

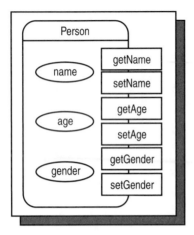

Figure 2.7: Providing methods to access the hidden attributes of Person

In Figure 2.8, we see a newly declared instance of the Person class, fred. The values of the attributes are unknown. We can set the values of the attributes using the set methods (Figure 2.9). Similarly, we can extract the values using the get methods (Figure 2.10).

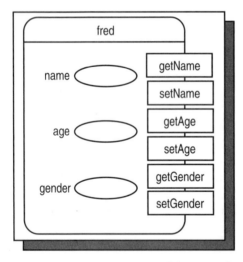

Figure 2.8: An instance fred of the revised Person class

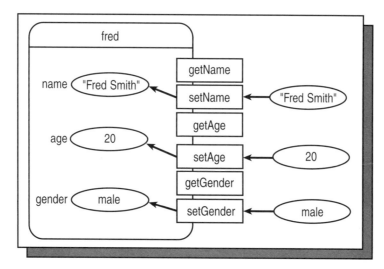

Figure 2.9: Using the access methods to set fred's attributes

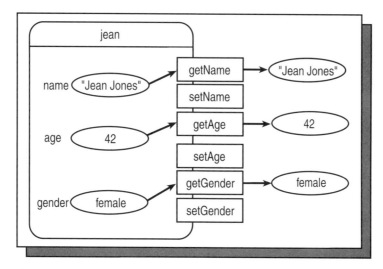

Figure 2.10: Using the access methods to get jean's attributes

An object-oriented program consists of a set of object definitions (e.g., Person) and instances of actual objects (e.g., fred and jean). A Java program (an "application"—see the end of Section 1.8) contains a main method that initiates the program. The methods of an object are invoked by requests from other objects. For the moment, however, we return to our study of a single object.

2.3   More about Single Objects

As we have said, a single object consists of two main parts: its state, which can be defined as a set of *attributes*, some or all of which may be hidden from the user, and its *methods*, which access and manipulate the state of the object. Broadly speaking, the state is the data of the object, and the methods are the code or processing part of the object.

Even at this rudimentary level, the object meets some important criteria for *software engineering*. Software engineering was the response to the "software crisis" identified in the late 1960s. Basically, software engineering acknowledges the fact that if we are building a bridge across a river, we cannot use the same techniques as we would to place a plank over a stream. Software systems are now among the most complicated artifacts made by humans; we cannot expect the same approach we might use to write a 20-line program to scale up to those millions of lines of code used to implement a complex system.

Early efforts concentrated on the design and coding of software. One of the oldest problem-solving approaches is to "divide and conquer"; if the problem we face is just too large, then we should split it up into a set of subproblems. We can repeat this process as often as required; if a subproblem is still too big, split it into a set of subsubproblems and so on.

We should end up with a set of subproblems that are "directly" solvable. It was realized that the software systems intended to solve our original problem should mirror this structure. A program can be subdivided into a set of subprograms. For the moment, we can think of subprograms as analogous to methods.

It was also realized that sets of useful subprograms could be grouped together in a construct that is neither a program nor a subprogram. This construct is known as a *module*. For decades, the concept of a module has been a major part of software engineering. A module is a software black box. It provides a set of subprograms that can be invoked by users of the box. The state of the box is encapsulated within it and is accessible only through its *interface* to the outside world. Does this sound familiar? It should!

One of the most important concepts supported by the module is that of *information hiding*. When a module provides a service, the user is interested only in the results of that service, not in how it is provided or realized. The actual implementation of how the service is realized—both its code and its internal hidden state—is completely invisible to the user. Like the CD player, we don't need to know how it works to use it. We don't have to understand the complex electronics and mechanics behind the control panel if we want to hear some music. The impact for the *service provider* is equally great. If we discover a better way to implement the same service, we can freely change the insides of the black box. As long as the user interface does not change, this has no impact on the user (other than ideally to improve the service).

The simple object we have introduced in this chapter is very similar to a module. The methods are the subprograms that manipulate the state of an object. An object then encapsulates both data (internal state) and operations (methods). How do we ask an object to carry out an operation? We simply issue a request to an object.

The code that realizes a method will make use of data from two sources:

- The actual state of the object. No part of the internal state of the object is hidden from the object itself, so a method can freely access all of the state information.
- Data provided along with the request. These are referred to as *arguments* or *parameters*.

For example, when we want to set someone's age, we issue the request shown in Figure 2.11. In this diagram, we see bill as the name of the object; it is the destination of our request. Our request in this case consists of two parts. It has the name of the method we wish the object to carry out, together with some data that the object will need to carry out our request. In this case, it is the actual age that we want bill to have. The effect of this request is seen in Figure 2.12.

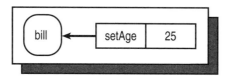

Figure 2.11: Sending a request to an object

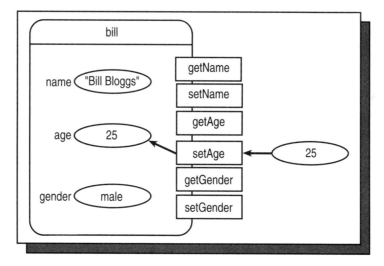

Figure 2.12: Setting bill's age attribute

Note that we are not reading any of the state of the person; we are only setting the value of the age attribute to that of the value supplied when we call the setAge method. In this extremely simple example, we are writing to one attribute of the state. The setAge method does not make use of any of the current state of the person.

Figure 2.13 shows us making a request to extract information from an object. Here, our request has no associated arguments. We are simply reading the value of one of the object's attributes. We are accessing the state, but only for the sake of returning it.

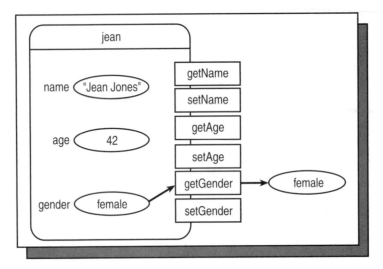

Figure 2.13: Getting jean's gender attribute

Let's take an example where we do make use of the state of the object. Consider a video cassette recorder (VCR) as an object like our CD player. One function that a VCR possesses that a CD player does not is that of recording; it is also possible to program the VCR to record at a given time for a given period. We do this by specifying a start and stop time and a TV channel.

The VCR object stores, as part of its state, the current date and time. When we issue the request to start "programming the timer," the object accesses this state and presents it to the user; it may even use this to give an initial value to the proposed start time.

Back to software. Consider a software object representing a personal telephone book, with lists of our friends' and colleagues' names and their telephone numbers. We can sketch this as shown in Figure 2.14. The state of the object includes the actual telephone index. To access a number, we issue a request that includes the person's name (Figure 2.15). The object returns the data we require.

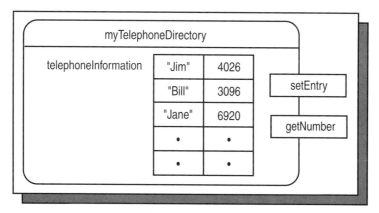

Figure 2.14: A telephone directory object

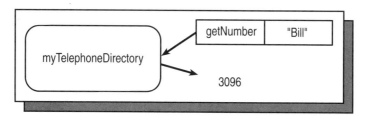

Figure 2.15: Making a request of the object

Notice that we, as users of `myTelephoneDirectory`, do not need to know or care how the internal state of the object is structured and stored; all that matters is that we know how to get a telephone number back out of the object.

2.4   An Object-Oriented Program

An object-oriented program, then, is made up of sets of class definitions (e.g., the `Person` class) and object declarations (e.g., `fred`). Java applications have a `main` method that starts the ball rolling. Thereafter, objects may *call methods* of other objects, and they in turn can *request services* from further objects. Notice that these are two ways of describing the same thing.

One way of thinking about this is to visualize each object individually within an object space. If an object is inactive, it is simply waiting to receive a request from another object in the space. We can say that the objects communicate by passing messages from one to the other. A message consists of three parts:

- Its destination. Which object is it addressed to?

- The service it requires. If the destination is `fred`, what method do we want to invoke?

- The message arguments. Is there any additional information that the receiving object needs to know to carry out the service properly? For example, the telephone directory `getNumber` method needs a subscriber name.

The reply to a message usually consists of the result of the request. If we ask the `fred` object to execute `getAge`, then we will get back a number that represents `fred`'s age in years.

In many object-oriented languages, there is exactly one active object. The currently active object is the one that is executing a method body. If in the course of this execution we call a method of another object, control switches to that other object, and thereafter it is the currently active object. When a method finishes execution, control returns to the calling object.

In a world where the use of computers linked by communications networks is ever increasing, it is useful to have a model where there can be many active objects at the same time. Indeed, even on single processor machines, it is possible to have multiple active objects. Java supports this approach, but it is largely beyond the scope of this book. Nevertheless, we introduce the concept in Chapter 21.

2.5   Types

When we declare a class in Java, it consists of a set of attributes and a set of methods. If we think of attributes as entities in a data space, we can visualize the contents of an object (Figure 2.16).

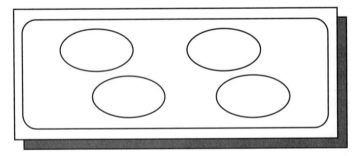

Figure 2.16: Four attributes contained within an object

Let's say we are modeling a person. This graphical definition shows us only that a person has four attributes. We cannot uniquely select and use one because there is no way to specify which one we want. One technique for differentiating among a set of entities is to give each entity a unique name. As we are modeling a person, the four attributes could have the names in Figure 2.17.

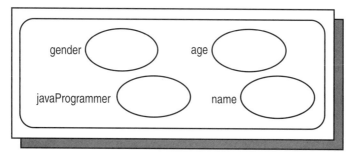

Figure 2.17: Four named attributes contained within an object

Naming can be an issue of great importance, particularly where the maintenance of software is concerned. For example, if we used names such as x1, x2, x3, and x4 instead of the names in Figure 2.17, it means that someone reading our class definition really has no idea what each attribute is intended to represent. In a sense, we have almost returned to the first situation (in Figure 2.16) where there are no names. Yes, we can specify each individual attribute, but they all seem to be exactly the same; we have no indication of the underlying semantics or meaning of each attribute. What does it represent? How is it to be used?

It is very important to give attributes (and classes and objects, for that matter) meaningful names. This increases the readability and understandability of our software both for ourselves and for others. When we are producing classes that others will use, this is particularly crucial.

Looking at our set of named attributes, are there still any problems? Well, for one thing, all the attributes look exactly the same. Is this sensible? Surely an attribute that will store the value of a person's age should look different from one that will store a person's name.

The issue we are raising here is one of *type*. Different attributes will store different kinds (or types) of data. For example, a person's age will be an integer value. Normally, when we discuss someone's age, we give it in terms of whole years. We do not normally talk about someone being 24.523 years old, so we would not expect to use floating-point numbers to represent someone's age. Also, we would not write that someone was *twenty-four*, so we would not use characters to store information about someone's age. Similarly, a person's name cannot be represented as an integer or a floating-point number, but rather, it is a sequence (or string) of characters.

The Java programming language provides a set of basic types. These can be used to specify the type of some attributes. The basic types include:

```
boolean
char
byte
short
int
long
float
double
```

We will explore these types in more detail later in the book. For the moment, we concentrate on the `boolean` and `int` types. Boolean attributes can store only one of two possible values: true or false. You will see later how Boolean variables can be used to control the flow of a program; for now, however, we examine their suitability for modeling one attribute of a person.

There are aspects of a person that can be considered true or false. For example, `wears-Glasses` can be true or false. Similarly, `hasDegree` or `javaProgrammer` can be true or false. Either you have a degree or you have not; either you have programmed in Java or you have not.

We have already discussed how we can use integers (Java's `int`) to represent a person's age. We can also use integers to encode information; for example, we can represent a person's gender by deciding to represent male by the value 1 and female by the value 2. You will see later how you can declare constant values to associate meaningful names (`MALE` and `FEMALE`) with your choice of encoded values (1 and 2).

In our graphical representation of a class declaration, we choose to represent Booleans, integers, doubles (numbers containing a decimal point), and characters (Java's `char`) as follows:

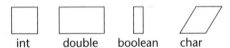

int   double   boolean   char

A person's name cannot be represented as one of these basic types. A name is made up of a *sequence*, or a *string*, of characters. For now, we represent a string graphically as follows:

string

We are now in a position to return to our definition of a `Person` class and use the graphical type specifications (Figure 2.18).

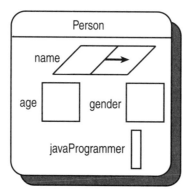

Figure 2.18: `Person` class definition showing named and typed attributes

2.6 Classes and Instances Revisited

We have discussed classes and instances. Let's revise these concepts here. We can think of a class as an abstraction over a group of entities. Rather than discuss individuals, we can talk about a class. We can say that, by and large, people have two eyes. This is a lot simpler than having to name every individual person in the world and state that they each have two eyes. Once we have this kind of abstraction, we can think, reason, and talk about the group as a whole, and this can make life much easier.

This allows us to identify a number of attributes that members of a group will possess. People normally have a name, an age, and a gender. We can think of the class as a blueprint for the individual instances we will create.

Once we have reasoned in this manner, we can create a class definition for people in general. We have done so in this chapter and called it `Person`. We can also think of the class definition as a template for individual objects in that class. Once we create instances of the class, we know they will have a name, age, and gender by looking at the template, and we know what methods they possess.

Consider another example: We might want to model the concept of a house as a class. Again, by and large, houses have a fixed location, details of which are captured as the address of the house. Such an address usually consists of a number, street, and town. Further attributes could be the type of house (bungalow, detached, semidetached, etc.) and the date of its construction. Without considering the type of each attribute, we can model our class definition graphically (Figure 2.19).

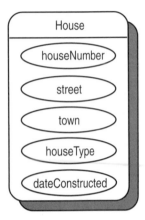

Figure 2.19: House class definition

Later, it becomes necessary to model the concept of a (family) home. A home has among its attributes the name of the family that lives there and the date they moved in. It also has all the attributes of a house as a physical location. It seems silly to have to define a Home class from scratch, ignoring the existence of the House class. It would be nice to have a mechanism that allows us to define a Home class in terms of the House class, basically saying that a Home is the same as a House except for these additional details (Figure 2.20).

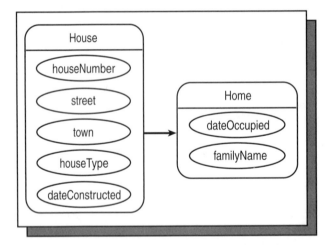

Figure 2.20: Defining the Home class with the help of the House class

Object orientation has a mechanism, called *inheritance*, to define one class in terms of modifications to another class; we will begin to look at inheritance in Chapter 12. This means we can introduce a new class, such as Home, that we do not need to define from scratch; instead, we base our new class on an existing one, such as House. We need only specify the differences between Home and House.

We can think of a factory that processes our requests to create new instances of a class. The factory receives our request, which includes the name of the class. The factory generates new instances of the class. Such a factory for the Person class is shown in Figure 2.21.

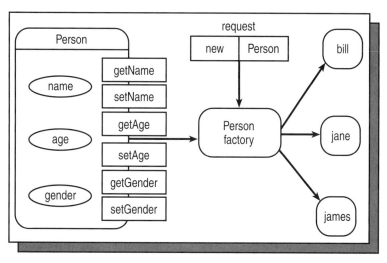

Figure 2.21: The Person factory

Here, we have a class "template" that we use to create individual instances of people. However, it is also possible to describe a class as a set of individual objects that possess the same attributes and methods. Theoretically, this means we have examined a group of objects, extracted a set of common features, and used this to form a new abstraction. It would be as if we knew nothing about people in general but had a number of specimens to examine. After this examination, we might know that bill, jane, and james all had two eyes, a name, an age, and a gender. From this, we might formulate a new class definition and call it Person.

In Java programs, we will always proceed from the class definition to create a set of instances. Because all the Person instances are manufactured using the same Person definition, they will all automatically have a set of common features. Thus, we can see that all Person objects form part of the group that makes up the Person class. In this book (and elsewhere), the term *class* has at least two meanings. It is the class definition itself and the group of instances that belong to that class (Figure 2.22).

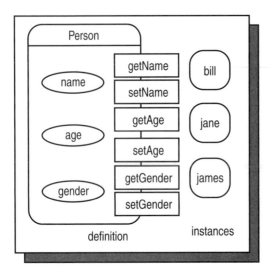

Figure 2.22: Class as a definition and a collection of instances

However, once we have a group of people and we need to manipulate the state of these people, we can't generally treat them as a group. We have to move from the abstract to the concrete individual. For example, reasoning about people as a group does not help us update Fred's age. We have to identify the single object that represents Fred and send it a request that will update his age.

2.7 Key Points in Chapter 2

- We can think of the real world as consisting of *objects*.
- Objects provide a set of operations or *methods* for the user. They maintain internal *state*, which is either:
  - Directly accessible to the user.
  - Accessible indirectly through the methods.
  - Completely hidden.
- An object's state is defined by a set of *attributes*. Attributes have both a distinguishing name and a *type*.
- Objects support the concept of *information hiding*.
- Objects can *call* or *invoke* methods (or request services) from other objects. We can think of this in terms of *message passing*.

- A *class* can be thought of in two ways
  - As a template that describes objects in the class in a general way. It lists the names and types of attributes/methods that objects in the class possess. The actual values of attributes are held in individual objects.
  - As a collection of all the objects, or *instances*, belonging to the class.

2.8 Exercises

1. Think of an everyday real-world object that you use such as a household appliance, a tool, a vehicle, and so on. Model it as a software object by
   - Identifying operations (methods) that you can invoke.
   - Identifying state information that it maintains and list these as attributes.

2. Imagine that you have a collection of Person objects. Outline an algorithm that would allow you to calculate the average age of the people in your collection. How would you access the age of an individual?

CHAPTER 3

Declaring Objects and Calling Methods

3.1 Program Structure

In Chapter 2, you were introduced to the idea of object-oriented programming. A program consists of a number of *objects*, each an instance of a certain *class*, and the action carried out by the program is a series of calls or invocations of the *methods* of one object by the methods of another. The remainder of the book shows you how this is actually done in the Java language. To begin, in Chapters 3 through 6, we assume that someone has already written all of the classes we need, and we are simply going to declare objects from these classes and call methods associated with them. Some of the classes are part of the standard Java environment (you have already met an object System.out of this type in Chapter 1), and some have been specially written for this book. Starting in Chapter 7, we will begin to show you how to "open the box" and create simple classes of your own.

All the programs we write until we reach Chapter 20 are going to be *applications* rather than *applets*. Applications are executed directly by the Java bytecode interpreter java. In Chapter 20, you will see how a Web browser executes an applet when it finds a reference to the applet in a page it is displaying. An application contains a main method, which is started by the bytecode interpreter to set the action of the program in motion. The structure of the program is going to look like this:

```
/*
 *
 * brief description of the program
 *
 * Written by: author
 *
 * First Written: date
 * Last Rewritten: date
 *
 */
```

```
public class ClassName
   {
   /*
    *
    * main
    *
    */

   public static void main(String[] args)
      {

      body of the main method

      } // end of main method

   } // end of class ClassName
```

The program starts with a comment giving a short description of what it does, who wrote it, and when it was written (in particular, when it was last modified). This could be expanded to give further information about the program—for instance, how to use the program, what input and output it requires, a history of the changes made to the program, and so on. When we show you a program in this book, we often omit these comments to save space, but you will see that we include them in all the programs on this book's Web site (see Appendix A). Similarly, all your programs should start with a comment giving all this information.

The rest of the program consists of a class definition (here the class ClassName). This contains a method called main, and the body of this method contains statements that set up suitable objects and manipulate them.

It is a convention in Java that class names start with a capital letter, and a capital letter marks each new word in the class name. The classes of our demonstration programs all have names of the form Chapter3n1 (the first program discussed in Chapter 3) or Chapter15n5, and they are always in a file with a corresponding name ending in the characters .java (e.g., Chapter3n1.java). The Java compiler insists on this correspondence, as you will see if you change the class or file name. When we compile the program, we will get a new file with a name such as Chapter3n1.class.

3.2   The class Person

The first class of objects we are going to introduce is called Person. It represents a few simple facts about a person: a surname, a (single) forename, an age, and a gender (Figure 3.1).

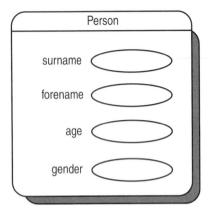

Figure 3.1: The class `Person`

This class has a number of methods to allow us to set up instances of this class, to extract the various facts held about a particular person, and to specify the facts about a person in the first place. This class is not built into the standard Java environment; we have supplied it as part of this book. We have also supplied documentation to tell you everything you need to know about objects of this class, and this is available on this book's Web site (see Appendix A).

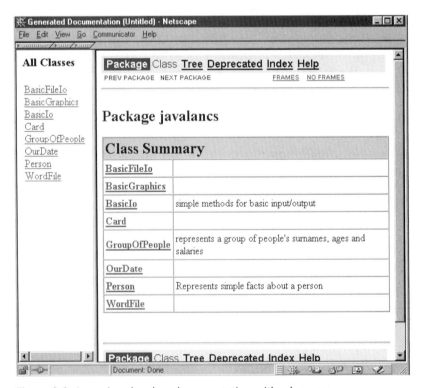

Figure 3.2: Accessing the class documentation with a browser

If we look at this documentation with a browser (Figure 3.2), it lists all the classes provided to accompany the book. At the moment, we are interested only in the `Person` class, so we can click on the reference to this class in the list to look at its documentation. The documentation tells us mainly about the methods available for the `Person` class: what they are called, what they do, what their arguments are, what value (if any) they return, and so on. But it does not tell us what the internals of the objects are, which should be of no concern when we are using an object from the class. Of course, in this case, we will in fact start to show you the internals of the `Person` class in Chapter 7.

The documentation for the `Person` class is similar to the documentation for the standard Java classes and methods, called the Java Application Programming Interface (API), which we discuss later.

3.3   A Program to Manipulate a `Person`

In this first simple program, we are going to

- Set up two objects of type `Person`.

- Set the attributes of the objects to suitable values.

- Display the attributes of the objects to prove that they have the values we have set.

Here is the Java program, which is a `main` method in a class called `Chapter3n1` in a file called `Chapter3n1.java`:

```
import javalancs.* ;

public class Chapter3n1
    {

    public static void main(String[] args)
        {
        // step 1 - declare two "Person" variables
        Person person1 = new Person() ;
        Person person2 = new Person() ;

        // step 2 - set the attributes of "person1"
        person1.setForename("John") ;
        person1.setSurname("Smith") ;
        person1.setAge(24) ;

        // step 3 - set the attributes of "person2"
        person2.setForename("Peter") ;
        person2.setSurname("Wright") ;
        person2.setAge(19) ;
```

```
// step 4 - display the attributes of "person2"
System.out.print("the second person is ") ;
System.out.print(person2.getForename()) ;
System.out.print(" ") ;
System.out.print(person2.getSurname()) ;
System.out.print(" (") ;
System.out.print(person2.getAge()) ;
System.out.println(")") ;

// step 5 - leave a blank line
System.out.println() ;

// step 6 - display the attributes of "person1"
System.out.print("the first person is ") ;
System.out.print(person1.getForename()) ;
System.out.print(" ") ;
System.out.print(person1.getSurname()) ;
System.out.print(" (") ;
System.out.print(person1.getAge()) ;
System.out.println(")") ;
} // end of method main

} // end of class Chapter3n1
```

In the next sections, we look at the parts of this program one by one.

3.4   The `import` Statement

We are going to set up a number of objects of the class `Person`, which has been written specially for this book. How does the compiler know where to find information about this class? In Java, a group of related classes can be collected together into a larger unit called a *package*. All the classes supplied for this book, including the `Person` class, are collected into a package called `javalancs`. The Java compiler is given some information called the *classpath* that tells it a sequence of places in the computer's filing system in which to look for the class information it requires; more details of classpath are given in Section 8.8. As long as the compiler can find the classes it requires in one of the places specified, it will be able to compile our program.

The full name of the `Person` class is `javalancs.Person` (i.e., package name–dot–class name), and we could use this full name every time we want to refer to the class. But there is a shortcut, which is the `import` statement that begins our program:

```
import javalancs.* ;
```

This tells the compiler to expect the following program to contain references to any of the classes found in the package `javalancs`. Furthermore, we do not have to specify the full class name; `Person` is sufficient.

If we wanted to refer (as in this program) only to the `Person` class in the `javalancs` package, we could write

```
import javalancs.Person ;
```

but there is no penalty overhead for importing all the `javalancs` classes (later, we are going to use other classes from this package). Incidentally, if you make a mistake in typing this line (which must be the first line in your program, except for comments) the Java compiler is likely to signal a cascade of further errors on every line containing a reference to an object of one of the imported classes. Simply correct the `import` statement and recompile the program.

You will have noticed that this program (and indeed the "Hello, World" program in Chapter 1) refers to an object `System.out` but does not have a corresponding `import` line. The `System.out` object is in a standard package called `java.lang`. But since the things provided in this package would be needed in almost any program, the Java compiler acts as if each Java file starts with

```
import java.lang.* ;
```

Thus, we can refer to `System.out` rather than `java.lang.System.out`, even though we have not written an `import` statement for the package.

3.5   Declaring Objects

We first need to set up an instance of the `Person` class, and we do this by declaring a *variable* of type `Person`. This is done with the statement:

```
Person person1 = new Person() ;
```

Let us look at this statement in detail. The first part (up to the = sign) declares a *local* variable of type `Person`—that is, a pigeonhole of a certain shape. Furthermore, it specifies that we have decided to call this variable `person1`. We say that the *scope* of the variable `person1` is *local*, which means that the variable is part of the `main` method and is not visible to other parts of the program outside this method. We will discuss the scope of variables in more detail later.

The statement declares that this variable is of type `Person`, so the compiler can check that it is used only in ways that match the specification of objects of this class. Note that this checking is done at *compile time*. Thus, errors are found as soon as possible, and we don't have to wait until the program is run with test data to catch the errors. The danger of leaving it until *run time* to catch errors is that we may not catch them during the testing phase if our test data are not comprehensive enough. Hence, it would be possible for some parts of the program to be visited for the first time only when the program is in use, with all the problems that could cause.

We have decided that this variable should be named person1. The Java rules for an *identifier* allow any sequence of upper- and lowercase letters and digits together with the character _. An identifier must start with a letter, and it must not be the same as any of the Java *reserved* words such as class, public, and so on (a full list of Java reserved words is in Appendix B). Thus, all the following are valid identifiers:

```
person1
ClassOne
THIS_IS_A_RATHER_LONG_IDENTIFIER
thisIsAnotherRatherLongIdentifier
```

and the following are not:

```
this-is-an-identifier      (contains the character '-')
1st_person                 (starts with a digit)
```

It is important to give your identifiers meaningful names to help the reader understand the usage of variables in your programs. It would not be helpful to the reader (although perfectly acceptable to the Java compiler) for your variables to be called x1, x2, x3, and so on. The Java convention for variables like this is that an identifier should be made up of a sequence of words, with the first letter of each word (except the first) capitalized:

```
testResult
```

Remember that case is important in Java—thisResult and thisresult (and ThisResult) are all names of different variables, although it would be rather trying to the person reading the program to use more than one of them in a single program!

So far, we have set aside an area of the store of the computer, named it person1, and specified that it can be used only to refer to objects of type Person. But what does the area that we have set aside actually hold? The part of the statement to the right of the = sign tells us:

```
Person person1 = new Person() ;
```

The characters Person( ) in fact refer to a *method*, and this is signified by the parentheses ( ). A call of a method consists of its name followed by its arguments in parentheses. You have to insert a pair of parentheses even if (as here) there are no arguments. Since this method call appears after the Java reserved word new, it is a special type of method called a *constructor* method. The fact that it is a constructor method is also revealed by the fact that the method name is the same as the name of the class with which it is associated, namely, Person.

An object is likely to be large and complex, with a number of attributes and methods. It will possibly take up an area of quite a large number of bytes or words. What the constructor method does is create a new *instance* of the specified object; that is, it works like the instance factory at the end of Chapter 2. When we get to write the definition of a class of objects for ourselves in Chapters 7 and 8, we will be writing constructor methods for this class; as you will see then, we can specify an initial value for each of the attributes of the object when we set it up. For the moment, we simply check the documentation for this constructor method for the Person class (Figure 3.3), and this reveals that the forename and surname are each initialized to the string of characters "NONE", the age is initialized to the number zero, and the gender is initialized to a special value UNKNOWN (more about this later).

```
● Person
    public Person()

        Creates an instance of the Person class with default values (forename =
        "NONE", surname = "NONE", age = 0, gender = UNKNOWN)
```

Figure 3.3: Documentation for the Person constructor method

Thus, the expression new Person() constructs a new instance of the Person class and initializes the attributes of this instance as specified by the constructor method. But the aim of the statement is that we shall be able to refer to this instance of the Person class by the name person1. What happens is that the constructor method passes back a *reference* to the store area (actually the address of the beginning of the area) holding this new instance. This reference is stored in the location named person1. Figure 3.4 shows what has happened.

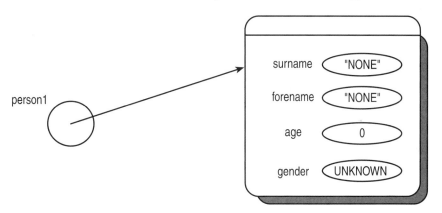

Figure 3.4: The result of declaring the object person1

Notice the form of this first statement:

```
Person person1 = new Person() ;
```

The part to the left of the = sign sets up a location in the computer's memory that is capable of holding a reference to (the address of) an instance of the Person class. The part to the right of the = sign sets up a Person instance with suitable initial values and passes back a reference to the instance. We can interpret new Person() as an expression that (among other things) returns a value that is a reference to a Person instance, just the right sort of thing to be stored in the location person1.

The = is the *assignment* or "becomes" symbol indicating that the value generated by the expression to the right of the symbol should be stored in the location specified to its left (replacing whatever value might have been there before). Thus, the = operator in Java (and in other languages derived from C) does not test for equality of the things on either side of it. Rather, it is an indication that the assignment of a value to a variable is to be carried out.[1]

The second statement

```
Person person2 = new Person( ) ;
```

similarly uses the constructor method Person( ) to generate a new, different instance of the Person class, initializes its attributes, and stores the reference in a new local Person variable called person2. Figure 3.5 shows the situation now.

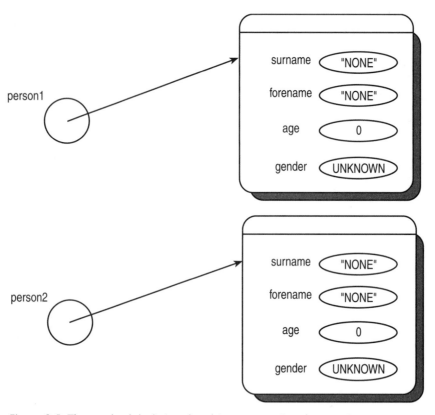

Figure 3.5: The result of declaring the objects person1 and person2

Finally, note the line preceding the declaration statements, which begins with the characters //. This is the second way to write a comment in Java, mentioned in Chapter 1; the comment extends from the // characters to the end of the line. If we are writing a comment that consists of a single line—here we are indicating the aim of each set of following program statements—then this form of the comment is appropriate. If we are writing a more extended comment, it is more appropriate to use the /* ... */ form.

3.6 Using Methods to Set the Attributes of Objects

We have set up some `Person` objects, and their attributes have the default values provided by the constructor method. We now want to be able to set the attributes to more interesting values. For this, we are going to call some methods associated with the `Person` class. When we examine the documentation for `Person`, we see that there are a number of methods with which we can change the attributes of an object. It is a convention in Java (although not always adhered to) for what are called *mutator* methods, which we can use to change the values of one or more of an object's attributes, to have names starting with the characters `set`.

To call a method, we need to know four things:

- The name of the object to which the method is to be applied.

- The name of the method.

- Any argument values required by the method to carry out its task.

- What to do with any information passed back by the method.

We can look at the documentation for the method (Figure 3.6) to find out what it requires in the way of arguments and return values.

```
⦿ setForename

  public void setForename(String f)

      set the forename attribute of the person
      Parameters:
          f - the forename of the person
```

Figure 3.6: Documentation for the `setForename` method

If we wish to set the forename attribute of the object `person1` to the string `"John"`, then the four pieces of information are as follows:

- The name of the object to which the method is to be applied is `person1`.

- The name of the method (taken from the documentation) is `setForename`.

- The `setForename` method needs to know what value the forename should be given, so there is a single argument to the method. Java insists (quite rightly) on knowing what type of thing the argument is—the document specifies that the single argument is of type `String` (note the capital S); that is, a string of zero or more characters.

- It is possible (as you will see shortly) for a method to pass back a "return" value. This is not required for the `setForename` method; the documentation indicates this with the reserved word `void` immediately before the name of the method. You have already met this reserved word in Chapter 1, where it indicates that the `main` method (like the `setForename` method) does not pass back any value when its execution terminates.

A method call has the format:

- Name of object
- Dot
- Name of method
- Left parenthesis
- Zero or more arguments, separated by commas if there are more than one
- Right parenthesis

Thus, to set the forename attribute of the `person1` object to `"John"`, we write the statement:

```
person1.setForename("John") ;
```

There is no value passed back by this method, so the call is a statement in its own right (terminated with a semicolon). The method requires a single `String` argument, and we have supplied an appropriate value for this string (enclosed in double quote marks). The specification of an actual string value, enclosed in double quote marks, is called a character string literal.

We set the surname of `person1` in a similar way, with the `setSurname` method (which similarly requires a character string argument):

```
person1.setSurname("Smith") ;
```

Now we want to set the age attribute of the `person1` object to, say, 24. This is a number rather than a string of characters. We consult the documentation for the `setAge` method (Figure 3.7). We see that the `setAge` method requires a single argument of type `int` (note the lack of an initial capital). This means the age is going to be an integer or whole number such as 14 or 52. The designers of this class decided that ages are stored as whole numbers (of years) and not as numbers with a decimal part such as 14.6 or 52.95. We supply the argument to `setAge` as a numeric *literal*; note that there are no quote marks:

```
person1.setAge(24) ;
```

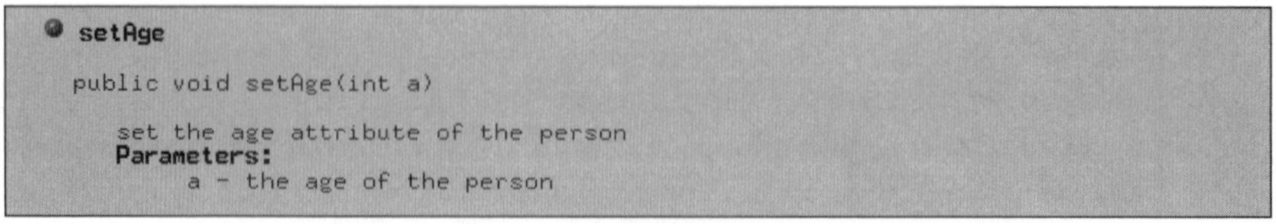

```
● setAge

    public void setAge(int a)

        set the age attribute of the person
        Parameters:
            a - the age of the person
```

Figure 3.7: Documentation for the setAge method

Figure 3.8 shows the situation now.

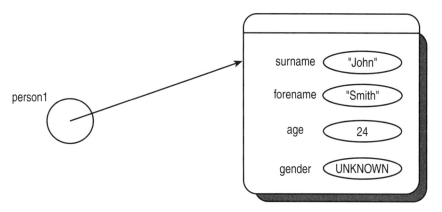

Figure 3.8: The person1 object after initialization

We have laid out the statements that make up the body of the main method one after the other in a sequence, each on a separate line. When we have a number of statements in a program, there is an implicit question:

- When we have finished executing one statement, what shall we do next?

This program illustrates the simplest way of answering this question: When we have finished one statement, we go on to the next in sequence. We can imagine one of those bouncing balls that guides the audience in singing the choruses in a pantomime by bouncing from one statement to the next in sequence. The way the ball bounces from one statement to the next is called the *flow of control,* and the different ways control can flow from one statement to the next are called *control structures.* The simplest control structure is thus *sequencing* from one statement to the one that follows it next in the program text:

- First we set up the person1 object.
- Then we set up the person2 object.
- Then we set the forename attribute of person1.
- Then we set the surname attribute of person1.
- Then we set the age attribute of person1.
- And so on.

Notice that the order of some of these statements is forced on us by the logic of the situation—we have to set up the person1 object before we can set its surname or age. But we could have set up the surname, forename, and age of the person1 object in any order.

There are a number of other control structures, and we introduce the two other main ones in Chapter 4 (*selection*) and Chapter 5 (*repetition*) and another one in Chapter 15 (*throwing and catching exceptions*). There are other possible control structures, but they lead to programs that are exceptionally difficult to design and correct, and we do not discuss them in this book.

Note that there is only one flow of control in a program here; there is only one bouncing ball. It is possible to write Java programs with more than one flow of control (more than one bouncing ball, a red one for the left half of the audience and a blue one for the right half of the audience). In Java, these multiple flows of control are called *threads*; we briefly discuss threads in Chapter 21, but a full treatment is beyond the scope of this book.

3.7   Using Methods to Extract Object Attributes

Having set the attributes of the objects person1 and person2, we now want to extract the attributes and output them to the screen. For this, we have a collection of *selector* methods, and the Java convention is that their names generally start with the characters get. For example, the method getForename extracts the value of the forename attribute for the specified object.

The getForename method is going to pass back the forename, a string of characters, and we are then going to display this string on the screen. But we know how to display strings; we use the statement

```
System.out.print( ... ) ;
```

and we put the string we want printed in place of the dots. Note that we want to write the forename and surname on the same line (with a space in between), so we want print rather than println.

```
 getForename

    public String getForename()

        returns the forename attribute of the person
        Returns:
            the forename attribute of the person
```

Figure 3.9: Documentation for the getForename method

If we now look at the documentation for the getForename method (Figure 3.9), we see that it has the word String just before the method name (where setForename had the word void). This means that the method passes back a string of characters as its *return value*. Anywhere in a program we expect to see a String, we could insert a method that returns a String. We know that the print method requires a String as its argument, so we can insert as its argument any method that returns a String. Thus, we write:

```
System.out.print( person2.getForename() ) ;
```

If we check the documentation for getForename, we see that it requires no arguments. But we still have to include the parentheses that would enclose the argument if there had been one.

How does this work? When the Java system reaches this statement, it decides that it must call the print method of the System.out object, and this method requires a single argument of type String. But the argument provided is a method call that returns a value of type String. The method getForename associated with the object person2 is therefore called, and it returns a String, in this case, "Peter". We can imagine this returned value as replacing the call of the getForename method, so the effect is as if the statement had been:

```
System.out.print( "Peter" ) ;
```

Thus, the string "Peter" is displayed at the terminal (or it will be after any further print calls followed by a println call).

We now want to output the surname associated with the person2 object, so we write:

```
System.out.print(person2.getSurname()) ;
```

We want a gap of one blank character between the forename and surname, so we want to write a character string literal consisting of a single character:

```
System.out.print(" ") ;
```

This statement goes in between the printing of the forename and the printing of the surname because we want the correct sequence:

- First we print the forename.

- Then we print the space.

- Then we print the surname.

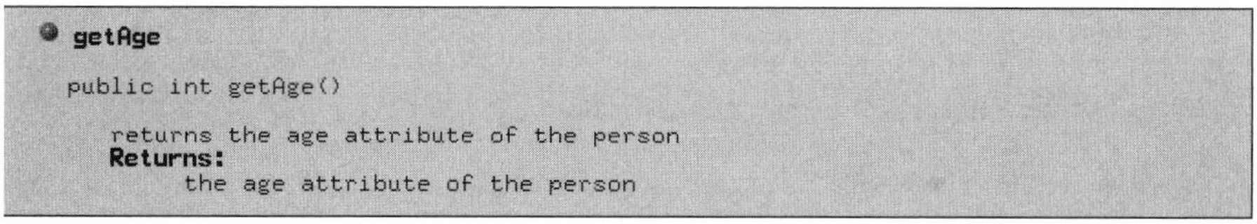

```
● getAge

  public int getAge()

     returns the age attribute of the person
  Returns:
        the age attribute of the person
```

Figure 3.10: Documentation for the getAge method

Now we want to print the age attribute of the person2 object. We extract this with the getAge method, which we see from the documentation (Figure 3.10) has a return value of type int; that is, it will return a whole number. We have print and println methods for displaying strings. What can we do with an integer? The Java system also supplies methods to display integers. They are called print and println depending whether we want to remain positioned on the same line afterward or move on to the beginning of the next line. Hence, we can display the age with:

```
System.out.print(person2.getAge()) ;
```

The Java system knows the type of any argument passed to the print method, so it can work out the appropriate version of the method to call.

Have a look at how the number is displayed. It takes up as much space as is required by the size of the value (including a leading minus sign, if necessary). If we want to leave a gap, we must do this explicitly.

To complete the display of information, we have added further calls of `print` and `println` to output an introductory string `"the second person is "` (notice the additional space after `is`—try leaving it out), to put parentheses around the age, and to leave a space between the surname and the age.

We could have used another version of the `print` method to output the gap between the forename and surname. The method call

```
System.out.print(" ") ;
```

outputs a string literal, a string one character long consisting of a space character. Alternatively, we could have written:

```
System.out.print(' ') ;
```

Note that the double quote marks have been replaced by single quote marks. Now we are passing a single character literal, a space character, rather than a string of characters that happens to be one character long. And the appropriate version of `print`, the one for dealing with individual characters, will be invoked. Of course, in this case, it makes little difference which we use. But later, we will have to be clear whether we are talking of *characters* or of *strings of characters* (which might happen to be only one character long). If we want to specify a single character literal, it goes between single quote marks; if we want to specify a `String` literal, it goes between double quote marks.

After we have displayed the details of the `person2` object, we display the details of the `person1` object with a similar sequence of calls of the `print` and `println` methods. The statement

```
System.out.println() ;
```

is used to output nothing and go to the beginning of the next line. This inserts a blank line between the details of the two `Person` objects. It is another version of `println`.

So far, each separate element (string, character, number) that we want to output requires a separate call of `print` or `println`. But things are not as bad as that. We can join two strings, or a string and a character, with the *concatenate* operator + and pass this longer string as an argument. Thus,

```
System.out.println(person1.getForename() + ' ' +
                person2.getSurname()) ;
```

passes as argument to the `println` method a string consisting of the forename attribute of `person1`, then a space, and then the surname attribute of `person2`.

You can even mix strings and integers, and the concatenate operator is clever enough to cope. For example, we could write:

```
System.out.println("the first person is " +
                person1.getForename() + ' ' +
                person1.getSurname() + " (" +
                person1.getAge() + ')') ;
```

We have spread out the statement over several lines to make it easy to follow. Here the concatenate operator understands that the `getAge` method returns a number rather than a string, so it converts it to a string for concatenating with other parts of the expression.[2]

When we have extracted the value of an attribute from an instance, the only use we have yet made of it is to output it to the screen. But we could use it anywhere in a program that requires a value of that type. Suppose we wanted to set up `Person` instances for two sisters. We could write:

```
Person person1 = new Person() ;
person1.setForename("Mary") ;
person1.setSurname("Smith") ;
person1.setAge(23) ;

Person person2 = new Person() ;
person2.setForename("Susan") ;
person2.setSurname(person1.getSurname()) ;
```

The `setSurname` method requires a `String` as argument, and the `getSurname` method returns a `String`, so this statement extracts the surname attribute from `person1` and sets the surname attribute of `person2` to this value. Similarly, if these sisters are twins, we could set the age attribute of `person2` from the age attribute of `person1`:

```
person2.setAge(person1.getAge()) ;
```

If Susan were 2 years older than Mary, we could set the ages accordingly:

```
person2.setAge(person1.getAge() + 2) ;
```

This extracts the age attribute from `person1`, adds 2 to it, and then sets the age attribute for `person2` with the resulting value.

3.8   Using Constants in Java

We have discussed setting and extracting the forename and surname attributes, which are `Strings`, and the age attribute, which is an `int` or integer. What about the gender attribute? This can be any one of three things; female, male, or unknown.

How should we model this attribute? In some programming languages, there are facilities for specifying what are called *enumerated types*, whereby we can specify that a particular at-

---

[2]However, the concatenate operator does not always give you the result you expect—for example, with a character and an integer. If you write

```
System.out.println('X' + 3) ;
```

(expecting it to convert the integer to a character string and output "X3"), it in fact converts the character to its Unicode value (see Chapter 6) and then adds the integer 3, and the resulting integer is output. Here the **+** symbol represents the plus operator between integers rather than the concatenate operator between strings. Try it.

tribute can take on any one of a set of values that we can list or enumerate. Thus, here we would specify that the gender attribute can take on any one of the values female, male, and unknown. We would not need to worry exactly what sort of thing such an attribute was because the programming language would automatically police its use and ensure that only these three values are available for it.

The Java language does not provide enumerated types. Instead, we have to use an attribute of type int to model the gender type. We would allocate different integers to the three possible values (perhaps 1 for male, 2 for female, and 99 for unknown) and then use these values to keep track of the gender.

But this is not a very good idea because it is easy to forget which integer we have decided to allocate to which value. It would perhaps not be too difficult in this case, where we have only three possible values to worry about, but we might have to remember values for four card suits, a dozen or more colors, or a hundred places. What Java allows us to do is to specify names for the different values, so we can use the names and not try to remember the values they correspond to.

In the Person class, we have defined the names FEMALE, MALE, and UNKNOWN for the three values the gender attribute can take (see the documentation in Figure 3.11). These are *constants*, and it is a convention in Java (though it is not always adhered to) to give them names all in capitals.

Variable Index

- **FEMALE**
    Constant – female gender
- **MALE**
    Constant – male gender
- **UNKNOWN**
    Constant – unknown gender

Figure 3.11: Documentation for the Person constants

Thus, if we want to set the gender of the person1 object to female, we would write the statement:

```
person1.setGender(Person.FEMALE) ;
```

Notice that Java requires us to include the name of the class that the constant belongs to; that is, class name–dot–constant name, or here Person.FEMALE. If we consult the documentation for the setGender method, we will see that its argument is an int, but the method checks the value passed to it and will not accept any but the values allocated to FEMALE, MALE, and UNKNOWN.

If we extract the value of the gender attribute, it will of course be an int. Hence, if we write

```
System.out.println("the gender of the first person is " +
                person1.getGender()) ;
```

the program outputs:

```
the gender of the first person is 2
```

In the next chapter, you will see techniques that enable us to create more meaningful messages from attributes with a limited range of values. In the meantime, the `Person` class has an extra method, `getGenderString`, which passes back a `String` version of the gender attribute:

```
System.out.println("the gender of the first person is " +
                    person1.getGenderString()) ;
```

Its output is:

```
the gender of the first person is female
```

It is good programming practice not to make use of the knowledge of what number is associated with a particular conceptual value in these types of attributes. If you want to refer to a particular value, you should use the constant provided. This will make your program much easier for others to follow.

3.9   Using Objects and Methods

We have introduced a class `Person` of objects with attributes forename, surname, age, and gender. Why do we bother? A primary reason is that all the information relating to one instance of this class is held together in one place and can be referred to as a single entity. If we have two instances of the class, the information for one is completely separate from the other. In the earlier example program, the changes to the attributes of `person1` have no effect on `person2`.

A further reason is that we can arrange to validate any changes we attempt to make to the attributes of an object before accepting them. For instance, the `setAge` method has been designed to accept only ages in a certain range. What this range should be is, of course, a design issue. Should the upper limit be 100 years, 120 years, or even 150 years? Suppose we write the statement:

```
person1.setAge(155) ;
```

The `setAge` method checks the argument and discovers it is outside the valid range. What does it do about this? The method is designed to bring the program to a halt with a suitable error message. Similarly, the methods that set the forename and surname bring the program to a halt if we give them an argument string that is zero characters long. Try:

```
person1.setForename("") ;
```

At the moment, these methods have no option but to halt the program. Later, we will see a more refined way of dealing with situations like this with what are called *exceptions*.

If we are writing a program and wish to ensure that it supplies only valid arguments to any method calls, we might wish to check that the argument lies in a suitable range before we call the setAge method. But to do this, we need access to information about what this range actually is, so the Person class provides a method called getUpperAgeLimit, which returns the upper limit of the age range (an int).

There is a peculiarity about this method. Up to now, all the calls of methods belonging to the Person class are associated with some particular instance of this class. It makes no sense to try to extract the age attribute without having a Person instance of which it is an attribute. It makes no sense to set a surname attribute without a Person instance whose attribute is to be set. All these methods are therefore called *instance* methods because they must be associated with some particular instance of the class, and they are invoked with the syntax "instance variable–dot–method name (arguments)."

But it makes perfectly good sense to find out the upper age limit of the Person class without there being any instances of the Person class about. This method is therefore called a *class* method because it is properly associated with the class rather than any instance of the class. A class method is sometimes called a static method in Java because all such methods have the word static in their headers, as you can see from the documentation (Figure 3.12).

```
 getUpperAgeLimit

   public static int getUpperAgeLimit()

      returns the upper limit for a valid age
      Returns:
         the upper limit for a valid age
```

Figure 3.12: Documentation for the getUpperAgeLimit method

A class or static method is invoked with the syntax "class name–dot–method name (arguments)." Thus,

```
System.out.println("the upper age limit is " +
                   Person.getUpperAgeLimit()) ;
```

would output:

```
the upper age limit is 150
```

In the next chapter, you will learn how to make use of the value returned by the getUpperAgeLimit method to check a number to see if it is a valid age.

3.10   A Variety of Methods

We have a number of methods in the Person class with which we can set individual attributes of an object. But it makes sense to be able to set the forename and surname at the same time. The method setFullName (note the capitalization) allows us to do this. If you examine the documentation for this method (Figure 3.13), you see it has two arguments, both of type String, the first being the forename and the second the surname.

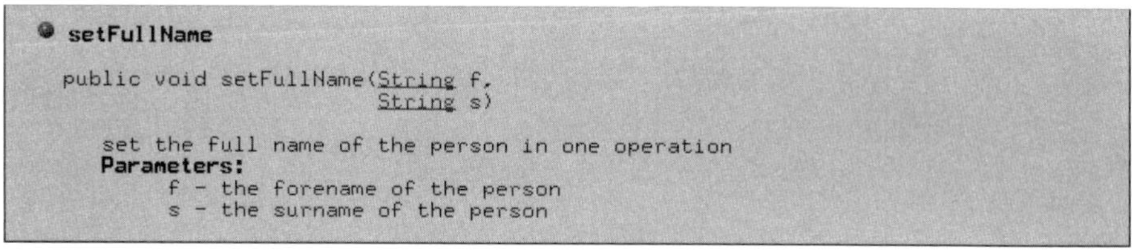

```
● setFullName

  public void setFullName(String f,
                          String s)

     set the full name of the person in one operation
  Parameters:
          f - the forename of the person
          s - the surname of the person
```

Figure 3.13: Documentation for the setFullName method

We can invoke this method with a statement such as:

```
person1.setFullName("Bill", "Watson") ;
```

The method does not return any value (it is a void method), so it is invoked, like the other set methods, as a statement. The two arguments are written in between the argument parentheses, separated by a comma. We must ensure the arguments are in the right order—first the forename and then the surname—because the method uses the position in the list to work out which argument is which.

In some methods, the arguments might be of different types (e.g., if we set the surname and the age in a single method, one argument would be a String and the other an int). In such a case, the Java compiler would complain if the types of the expected (or *formal*) arguments did not match the types of the argument values we supplied (the *actual* arguments). But here both arguments are of type String, and it would be rather difficult to make the method check that the forename passed to it (for instance) was or was not a legitimate one. (How could you construct a list of all and only the names that could be valid forenames? What about names that can be used as either a surname or a forename?)

So far, the methods you have seen have either been constructor methods or they have set or extracted one or more of an instance's attributes. But a method could do a more substantial task than this. It is difficult to give good examples for the Person class—you will see examples with other classes later—but it does have two methods that are slightly different from the patterns seen thus far:

- The method increaseAge adds the number of years specified as the integer argument to the age attribute of the object associated with the method.

  ```
  System.out.println("The age is " + person1.getAge()) ;
  person1.increaseAge(4) ;
  System.out.println("The age is " + person1.getAge()) ;
  ```

  This outputs:

  ```
  The age is 24
  The age is 28
  ```

■ The method `formalTitle` returns a string that is a formal title for the person and is constructed from one of the strings `"Mr"` and `"Ms"` (according to the gender attribute), the first initial of the forename, and the surname.

```
person1.setForename("Bill") ;
person1.setSurname("Sowerbuts") ;
person1.setGender(Person.MALE) ;
System.out.println("Dear " + person1.formalTitle() +
                        ',') ;
System.out.println("I am writing to you ... ") ;
```

It outputs:

```
Dear Mr B. Sowerbuts,
I am writing to you ...
```

3.11   Constructors Revisited

We created a `Person` object with a statement like this:

```
Person person1 = new Person() ;
```

This called the constructor method `Person()` to create and initialize a new object. The documentation for the constructor method tells us that the attributes are set to suitable values (`"NONE"` for the names, zero for the age, `UNKNOWN` for the gender). But it is possible to have several different constructors for the `Person` object initializing the object in various different ways. If you again consult the documentation (Figure 3.14), you will see that there is a second constructor.

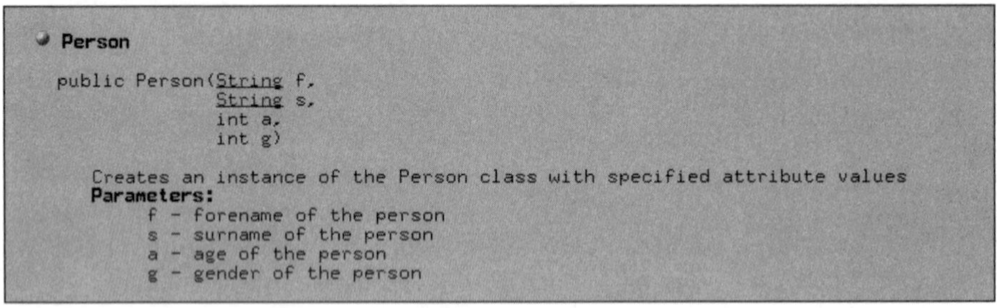

```
● Person

    public Person(String f,
                  String s,
                  int a,
                  int g)

        Creates an instance of the Person class with specified attribute values
        Parameters:
            f - forename of the person
            s - surname of the person
            a - age of the person
            g - gender of the person
```

Figure 3.14: Documentation for a `Person` constructor with several arguments

This allows us to initialize the object to specific values for the forename, surname, age, and gender. Thus, we could write:

```
Person person3 = new Person("Bill", "Watson", 45,
                            Person.MALE) ;
```

This would have the result shown in Figure 3.15.

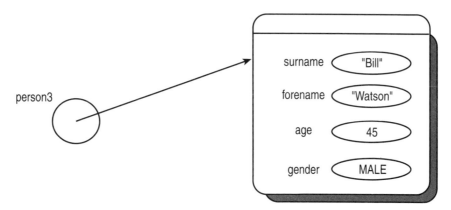

Figure 3.15: The result of declaring the person3 object

We now have two versions of the constructor for Person: one with no arguments and one with four (and both with the name Person). This is an example of *overloading*, where we have several methods with the same name that are differentiated by the number and types of the arguments. All constructors for Person instances have the name Person, and the Java system selects the right version by checking the number and type of the actual arguments supplied (here two Strings and two ints) against the formal arguments provided for each constructor method.

In Java, you can declare an object variable without initializing an object for it to refer to:

```
Person person4 ;
```

What is happening here? As shown in Figure 3.16, the variable person4 contains some unknown value.

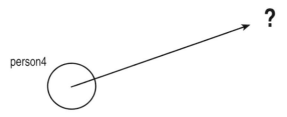

Figure 3.16: The result of declaring person4 without calling a constructor

If we do not want to create an object for the variable person4 to refer to when we declare it, it is safer to set person4 to the special value null. This makes it clear that it is deliberate and that the variable person4 does not refer to a Person instance at present:

```
Person person4 = null ;
```

This has the result shown in Figure 3.17.

person4

Figure 3.17: The result of declaring person4 and setting it to null

Later, we could make person4 refer to an instance of the Person class, with the keyword new and a constructor method:

```
person4 = new Person("Henrietta", "Lime", 21,
                     Person.FEMALE) ;
```

Notice that there is no Person at the beginning of this statement. The variable person4 has already been declared as a local variable in the main method; it already exists as an identifiable named location in the store and does not need to be redeclared. It simply needs to be assigned a value (to replace the value null) by storing in it a reference to a new instance of the Person class, using the assignment ("becomes") symbol to store in it a reference to a new instance of the Person class. The result is shown in Figure 3.18.

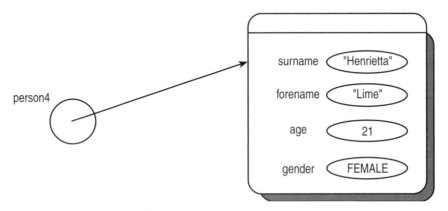

Figure 3.18: The result of assigning a new Person instance to person4

Suppose we had declared an object variable and initialized it to null and then neglected to create a Person object for it to refer to. If we then invoke a method associated with this variable, the program will halt with an exception (i.e., an erroneous condition) NullPointer-Exception at run time; we are trying to invoke a method attached to a nonexistent object. Of course, if we tried to write this statement and we had not declared the person4 variable earlier, the compiler would complain because all Java variables must be declared before they are used.

Finally, suppose we write the following:

```
Person person4 = new Person("Henrietta", "Lime", 21,
                              Person.FEMALE) ;
Person person5 = person4 ;
```

We know that the first statement declares a Person variable called person4 and makes it refer to a new instance of the Person class with the specified attributes. The second statement also declares a Person variable, this time called person5. We assign to it the value contained in the variable person4, and this is the reference to the Person instance just created, so person4 and person5 refer to the same object (Figure 3.19).

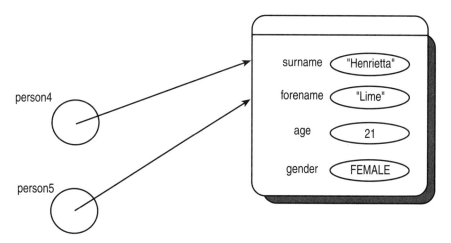

Figure 3.19: Two variables referring to the same object

We can set an attribute via one variable and retrieve it via the other:

```
person4.setSurname("Williams") ;
System.out.println(person5.getSurname()) ;
```

Hence, we can see that the two variables refer to the same instance.

3.12   Input to a Program (Optional)

In the programs we have written so far, there is no scope for the program to seek information from outside. If we want to change the effect of a program, we have to revise the Java source text with an editor, recompile it, and then run it again. This is, of course, inappropriate in most cases (and impossible if the user of the program knows nothing about Java). In the next chapter, we will start to introduce mechanisms for the program to seek information from the outside world—initially from the user at the keyboard and later from files on disk.

For the present, we reveal a simple way to pass small amounts of information to a program without recompiling it. This is by means of *command-line parameters*. When we call for a Java program to be executed with the Java bytecode interpreter `java`, we can write a number of strings on the same line after the name of the file we want executed:

```
java Chapter3n2 Fred Smith
```

In the header line for the `main` method, we have seen the characters (`String[] args`) after the method name. This specifies that `args` is where to find these command-line parameters (actually, it is an array of `String`s, as you will see in Chapter 9). The first parameter (`"Fred"` in this example) is referred to as `args[0]` because counting in Java (as in the C and C++ programming languages) usually starts at 0 rather than 1. The second parameter (`"Smith"` in this example) is referred to as `args[1]` and so on.

Suppose we want to set the forename and surname of object `person1` to the first and second command-line parameters. This can be done with the statement:

```
person1.setFullName(args[0], args[1]) ;
```

We have to be careful that there are two command-line parameters. If there are not, we will get an `ArrayIndexOutOfBoundsException` error condition or exception. Try it. The value `args.length` tells you how many command-line parameters there are. In this example, the statement

```
System.out.println("No of parameters is " +
                   args.length) ;
```

displays:

```
No of parameters is 2
```

After the next chapter, you will be able to use a selection statement to check that there are enough command-line parameters before making use of them.

3.13   Key Points in Chapter 3

- To declare and create a new object, we write:

  `<object class> <object identifier> = new <object class> () ;`

  For example:

  `Car fiatUno = new Car() ;`

  We can now refer to the object by its identifier (here `fiatUno`).

- The expression to the right of the assignment symbol—here `new Car()`—is an example of a special type of method call, a *constructor* method. A constructor method creates a new object of the required class (in this case, `Car`) and returns a reference to the object (which, in this case, is stored in the variable called `fiatUno`).

- Identifiers must obey the following rules:

  - Must start with a letter.
  - Can be any sequence of upper- and lowercase letters, digits, and the underscore character _.
  - Must not be the same as any of the Java reserved words.

- It is important to be using meaningful identifiers.

- To invoke a method, we must know the following four things:

  - The name of the object to which the method is to be applied.
  - The name of the method.
  - Any arguments required by the method.
  - What to do with any information passed back by the method.

- We can identify two common types of method:

  - *Mutators*, which allow us to change the values of attributes; by convention, the names of mutator methods start with `set`.
  - *Selectors*, which allow us to obtain the values of attributes; by convention, the names of selector methods start with `get`.

- To call a method, we write:

  `<object identifier> . <method name> ( <argument values> )`

  Even if there are no argument values, the parentheses are still required. If there is more than one argument value, they are separated by commas.

  If a method returns no value, the method invocation would be written as a statement:

  `<object identifier> . <method name> ( <argument values> ) ;`

  If a method returns a value, then the method invocation would be written in a place inside a statement where you would expect a value of this type (e.g., as an argument to a `print` method):

```
System.out.print( <object identifier> . <method name>
                    (<argument values>) ) ;
```

- It is possible to *overload* method names—that is, to have two or more methods with the same name. However, they must be differentiated by the number and types of their arguments. One common use of overloading is to have several different constructor methods for the same class.

- If we have an attribute that can take only a certain range of values, we may have a set of constants that name these values. We refer to such a constant with the notation

  ```
  <class name> . <CONSTANT name>
  ```

- Most methods are *instance* methods because they are associated with a particular instance of the class. But *class* or *static* methods are possible; they are not associated with a particular instance, but with the whole class. To call a class method, we write:

  ```
  <class name> . <method name> ( <argument values> )
  ```

- Two or more strings can be joined together with the concatenation operator +. If we concatenate a number to a string, it is converted to a string first.

3.14   Exercises

1. Write a Java program called `FirstExercise` that:

   a. Sets up an instance of the `Person` class.

   b. Sets the name, age, and gender attributes of this instance to your name, age, and gender (using the appropriate `set` mutator methods).

   c. Outputs the attributes of this instance (using the appropriate `get` selector methods and the `print` and `println` methods) in the form:

   ```
   this person is John Smith (21, male)
   ```

2. Modify your program for Exercise 1 as follows:

   a. Output the information in the form:

   ```
   Smith, John is 21 years old
   ```

   b. Use the `formalTitle` method (and other methods, as required) to output the information in the form:

   ```
   Mr J. Smith is 21 years old
   ```

   c. Use the `increaseAge` method with an argument of 10 and then output the information again using the `formalTitle` and other methods.

3. Write a Java program to:

   a. Set up a `Person` instance for Peter Booth, a male aged 30, and output a line giving the values of all the attributes.

b. Set up a second `Person` instance for Gail Turner, a female aged 28, and output a line giving the values of all the attributes.

c. Since Peter and Gail are getting married, write a statement that makes Gail's surname the same as Peter's and output the new values of the attributes for both instances.

4. There is a `Card` class in the `javalancs` package, modeling the basic facts about a playing card, its suit, and value. Have a look at the documentation supplied. Note that the `Card` constructor method (with no arguments) chooses a random card and sets its suit and value and that there are `get` methods for returning suit and value as strings and as integers.

   Write a program that sets up two `Card` instances and prints out their values. For example:

```
The first card is the four of Hearts
The second card is the Queen of Clubs
```

5. The `Date` and `GregorianCalendar` classes are part of the standard Java API in the `java.util` package. They provide a way of holding and manipulating date and time information. The documentation of these two classes in the Sun API (see Appendix A) is quite difficult to follow because you must also consult the documentation for the class `Calendar` (in the same package) for some of the methods and constants required. (The class `Calendar` is in fact an abstract class from which `GregorianCalendar` is derived; you will find out what these terms mean in Chapter 14.) A synopsis of what you need to know for the simple use of dates and times is:

   a. The constructor method `Date()` sets up a `Date` instance initialized to the current date and time:

```
Date myDate = new Date() ;
```

   b. There are several calendars in use around the world. In most of the Western world, the Gregorian calendar is used, and has (usually) been since some time in the 18th century. You next have to specify that you are using the Gregorian calendar and that you are going to interpret your `Date` instance according to this calendar:

```
GregorianCalendar myCalendar = new GregorianCalendar() ;
myCalendar.setTime(myDate) ;
```

   c. You can then extract the attributes you are interested in with the `get` method. This requires an argument that is a constant from the `Calendar` class to specify which attribute you are interested in. For example, to get the day of the month (an integer in the range 1 to 31), you could write:

```
int myDayOfMonth = myCalendar.get(Calendar.DAY_OF_MONTH) ;
```

   Other useful constants in the `Calendar` class are `HOUR_OF_DAY` (in the 24-hour clock—i.e., in the range 0 to 23), `MINUTE` (in the range 0 to 59), `MONTH` (which gives an integer in the range 0 to 11 instead of 1 to 12—be careful with this), and `YEAR`.

   Write a program to obtain the current date and time and then display them in the format:

```
The time (sponsored by Java) is 11:47 on 2/2/2002
```

Note ■

You will need the line

```
import java.util.* ;
```

near the top of your program, so you can access the classes you need in the java.util package.

6. BasicGraphics is another class provided as part of the javalancs package to enable you to display a window on the computer screen containing simple shapes of different kinds, sizes, positions, and colors. In Chapter 16, you will learn details of how to write your own programs to draw shapes like these (and others), directly using the facilities provided as part of the Java language.

The BasicGraphics class draws an area 600 units (or *pixels*) wide by 400 units high, with the origin (0, 0) at the top left corner of the area. We have supplied documentation for this class. You need to look up information on the BasicGraphics constructor method, the methods setShape, setDimensions, and setColor to specify what you want drawn, and the method draw to display the window on your computer screen.

a. Write a program to set up a BasicGraphics instance, specify a single red square centered at (200, 200) with side 60, and display it.

b. Write a program to set up a BasicGraphics instance, specify a red square centered at (200, 200) with side 60 and a blue circle centered at (400, 200) with diameter 80, and display them.

c. Write a program to declare two BasicGraphics instances, specify a red square centered at (200, 200) with side 60 in the first and a blue circle centered at (400, 200) with diameter 80 in the second, and display them both.

d. Experiment with rearranging the order of the statements of the programs you have written.

e. Write a program to declare a BasicGraphics instance, specify two red equilateral triangles centered at (200, 200) with sides 100 and 150, and display them.

f. Experiment with the other facilities provided by the BasicGraphics class.

Note ■

1. The argument for the setShape method is one of a set of constants provided by the BasicGraphics class—BasicGraphics.RECTANGLE for rectangles (including squares), BasicGraphics.OVAL for ovals (including circles), BasicGraphics.TRIANGLE for triangles, and so on.
2. There are four arguments to the setDimensions method. If you imagine a rectangle drawn around the shape you are displaying, the first two arguments give the x- and y-coordinates of its top left corner and the next two are its width and height.
3. The argument for the setColor method is one of the colors provided by the standard class Color in the package java.awt—Color.red, Color.blue, Color.green, Color.yellow, and so on (see the list on page 394). You will need to import the java.awt package into your programs.

CHAPTER 4

Selecting Among Alternatives

4.1   Reading Values from the Keyboard

In this chapter, we begin by considering how to read in values for attributes. This involves thinking further about different sorts of *variables*, a concept introduced in the previous chapter. We then embark on a study of Java's selection statements: the `if` statement and the `switch` statement.

In the previous chapter, we wrote a program that:

- Set up some local variables for `Person` instances.
- Set the attributes of these instances to suitable values.
- Output the values of the instance attributes so that we could check them.

The values we used as attributes were all "built into" the program. If we wanted to set an attribute to a different value, we would revise the program with an editor, then recompile it, and finally run it again—a rather laborious process. What we would prefer to do is have the program request a suitable attribute value from the user and then use the value that the user types in.

Java provides a number of powerful facilities for reading values from the keyboard or from a file in the filing system. The problem is that these facilities (in a package called `java.io`) are rather difficult to use when you are starting to write programs. We have provided a set of simplified ways to allow the user to type a value at the keyboard and have it read and used by the program. These facilities are collected together as a class called `BasicIo`, and this class is held in the same `javalancs` package that holds the `Person` class used in the previous chapter. If we want to use any of the `BasicIo` facilities, we must have the appropriate import statement at the beginning of our program:

```
import javalancs.* ;
```

If our program wants the user to type in a value, it must output a message saying so. For this task, the `BasicIo` class provides a method called `prompt`, which takes a single argument, the message to be output. This is a *class* or *static* method, so we have to precede it with the name of the class:

```
BasicIo.prompt("type surname of first person ") ;
```

Now the user types a string of characters and presses the Return key. For the program to read in this string, the `BasicIo` class has a method `readString`. This method has no arguments but returns the string typed by the user at the keyboard.

Where shall we put the string returned by this method? What we want to do is set up a named location to hold the string until we are ready to make use of it in the same way as we have locations (or local *variables*) to hold the `Person` instances. In Java, we can set up a variable called `string1` to hold a string of characters `"This is a string of characters"`:

```
String string1 = "This is a string of characters" ;
```

The first word in this statement, `String`, specifies the sort of thing we can store in this variable. The type `String` is provided by the Java language to hold strings of zero or more characters. Notice that it is spelled with a capital S because it is in fact a class provided by the Java language (see Section 6.7). Next comes the name of the variable, then the "becomes" symbol, and finally the value (the string of characters) that we want stored (Figure 4.1).

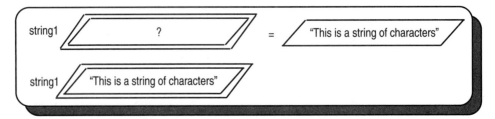

Figure 4.1: Assigning a `String` value to a `String` variable

Similarly, we can set up a variable called `surname` that can hold a string typed in by the user:

```
String surname = BasicIo.readString() ;
```

The part after the = symbol reads the character string typed by the user at the keyboard (using the class method `readString` in the `BasicIo` class) and returns this string to be stored in the variable `surname`.

Whenever we want to refer to the string typed in, we give the name of the variable `surname` holding it. For example, we could set the surname attribute of the `person1` instance with:

```
person1.setSurname(surname) ;
```

We can now read a string from the user for the surname and forename attributes. What about the age attribute? This is not a string of characters but a number; actually it is an integer—that is, a whole number with no fractional part. There is a method `readInteger` in the `BasicIo` class to read such a value typed in at the keyboard. But we must store it in a different type of variable:

```
int age = BasicIo.readInteger() ;
```

Here we have declared a local variable called age that is the right shape to hold an integer or whole number. Notice that in Java it is spelled int with a lowercase i, and it is one of the basic data types provided by Java as a building block for all the rest (more details are in Section 6.2). We can use the value held in this variable to set the age attribute of the person2 instance:

```
person2.setAge(age) ;
```

Here is a complete program

1. to prompt the user for a string, to read it in, and then to output it again for confirmation.

2. to prompt the user for an integer, to read it in, and then to output it again for confirmation.

The comments have been left out.

```
import javalancs.* ;

public class Chapter4n1
   {
   public static void main(String[] args)
                           throws Exception
      {
      // read in and output a String
      BasicIo.prompt("please type in a string ") ;
      String string1 = BasicIo.readString() ;
      System.out.println("the string you typed was **" + string1 + "**") ;

      System.out.println() ;

      // read in and output an integer
      BasicIo.prompt("please type in an integer ") ;
      int intValue = BasicIo.readInteger() ;
      System.out.println("the integer you typed was "
                        + intValue) ;
      } // end of method main
   } // end of class Chapter4n1
```

If we compile and run this program, we will have a dialog like the following (where the user input is in bold):

```
please type in a string Hello Everyone
the string you typed was **Hello Everyone**

please type in an integer 6
the integer you typed was 6
```

Suppose that, in response to the second message, we typed something that Java couldn't interpret as an integer. In this case, the readInteger method "throws up its hands in horror and abandons its task"; in Java language, it "throws an exception":

```
please type in an integer abc
Exception in thread "main" java.io.IOException: invalid integer
        at javalancs.BasicIo.readInteger(BasicIo.java:72)
        at Chapter4n1.main(Chapter4n1.java:25)
```

Here the Java system is telling us that it has abandoned our program because of an exception called `IOException`, and it occurred at line 25 of the file `Chapter4n1.java`. At the moment, there is nothing we can do about this exception; in Chapter 15, you will learn how to have your program *catch* the exception so that it can do something about it.

The Java system always wants to know when an exception might be thrown. All the `read` methods in the `BasicIo` class can throw exceptions, so we have to tell the Java system that our `main` method is not going to catch any of these exceptions but will simply allow them to stop our program. That is why we have written:

```
... throws Exception
```

at the end of the header line for our `main` method. We need to do this whenever the `main` method contains any calls of these `BasicIo` methods.

4.2   More on Integer Variables

As you have seen, variables can refer to instances of objects, or they can refer to more basic types. You have met only the one basic type, `int`, so far, but there will be others shortly. For now, we will concentrate on basic types, using `int` as an example. We can declare a local variable called `total` that can store an integer value:

```
int total ;
```

The result is shown in Figure 4.2. We have set aside an area, a pigeonhole, in the computer that is the right size and shape for an integer value and called it `total`. We have not set it to any particular value.

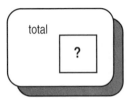

Figure 4.2: An integer variable called `total`

It is possible to initialize a variable by giving it a value when we declare it. For example, we could have declared the variable `total` as follows:

```
int total = 4 ;
```

The result is shown in Figure 4.3.

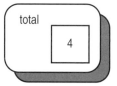

Figure 4.3: Initializing `total` to the value 4

We can change the value of `total` anywhere within the method in which it is declared (we have called it a *local* variable because it is local to the body of the `main` method and cannot be accessed from outside the method). We can write:

```
total = 6 ;
```

This is an example of the assignment statement, which you first met in Chapter 3. We have assigned the value 6 to the variable `total`. It is because of the fact that we can change or vary the value of a variable that they are so called. In algebraic or arithmetic terms, we are using an equal sign here as the assignment operator. It looks like an equal sign, but it can be read as "becomes." In other words, "the value of `total` becomes 6."

Thus, we have integer variables that can be visualized as "integer-shaped" boxes. Into these boxes, we can place integer-shaped values (Figure 4.4).

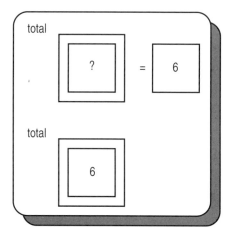

Figure 4.4: Assigning the value 6 to `total`

We can assign the value of an integer variable to another integer variable; we do this by taking the value contained in one box and placing a copy of it in another box (leaving the original unchanged). So, for example:

```
int final ;
final = total ;
```

The result is shown in Figure 4.5.

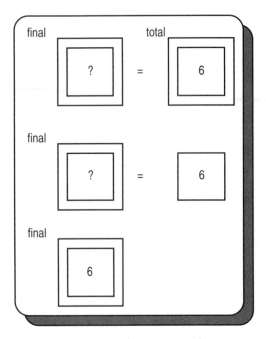

Figure 4.5: Assigning the contents of `total` to `final`

It is possible to form integer *expressions*; these are expressions that can involve integer variables and values combined using arithmetic operators. An integer expression is one that, once evaluated, results in a single integer value. This value can then, of course, be assigned to an integer variable. For example:

```
int x ;
int y = 6 ;
x = y + 4 ;
```

The result is shown in Figure 4.6.

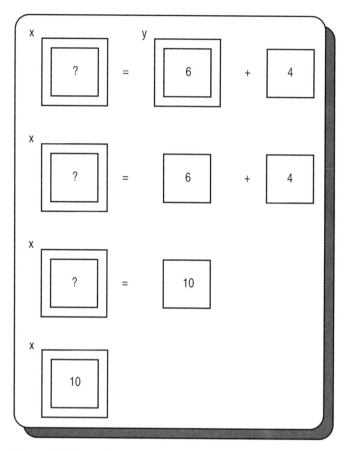

Figure 4.6: Evaluating an expression involving y and assigning the result to x

Finally, it is possible to have an assignment statement such as:

```
total = total + 2;
```

If we look at this algebraically, it makes no sense at all. Remember, however, we read the = sign as "becomes," so this statement should be read "the value of total becomes the (previous) value of total plus 2." This is explored in Figure 4.7.

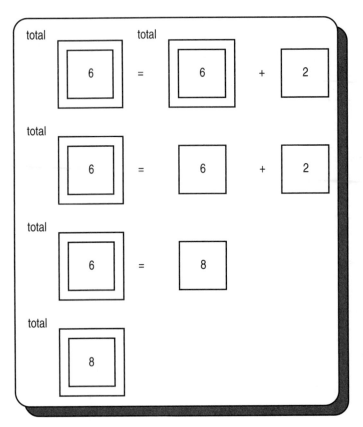

Figure 4.7: Assigning to total the value of an expression involving total

Hence, the statement makes perfect sense: Make the value of total 2 more than its previous value.

4.3 Type Checking

Java is what is called a *strongly typed* language. This means that whenever we try to assign a value of type X, we can do so only to a variable of type X. So, for example, a successful assignment would be:

```
int final = 4 ;
```

Consider the following statement:

```
int final = someValue ;
```

This may or may not be valid. We can tell only by finding out how someValue was declared. If it was declared to be of type int, this assignment will be all right. If it was declared as some other type, we will have problems. The Java compiler will generate an error, and we will have to fix it before we can continue.

If we consider our graphical version, it should be obvious why any attempt to place a value of one type into a variable of another will fail; they are simply the wrong shape.

```
int total = 6.2 ;
```

We are trying to store a value that is a number with a decimal point (sometimes called a *real* or *floating-point* number) in a variable that is the right shape only for an integer (Figure 4.8).

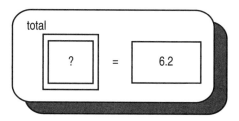

Figure 4.8: Trying to assign a floating-point-number-shaped value to an integer-shaped box

As you have seen, this kind of checking also occurs when inputting information. If we are using the readInteger method and the user types letters instead of digits, we will get a runtime error (an exception) unless we, the programmers, take steps to handle such an error.

4.4 Making Decisions

In the course of an average day, we make thousands of commonplace decisions.

This evening, shall I:

  a. Stay in and study programming?
  b. Go out?

These two decisions can lead to others:

  a-1. Write solutions to the exercises at the end of this chapter, which I can type in and
         try out when I next have access to a computer?
  a-2. Read over the last chapter?
  b-1. Go to the pub?
  b-2. Go to the movies?
  b-3. Go to the sports center?

As humans, we base our decisions on feelings and information. We might go to the movies if the film showing is one we want to see. To make that decision, we need to know what movie is playing this evening. Computers make decisions based only on information:

- If it is 10:30 A.M. and a weekday, it is coffee time.
- If it is coffee time and I am not busy, I will take a break.

Computers use binary arithmetic and manipulation. We can base our programs' decisions on a binary value of true or false. There are certain kinds of statements that we can make in English that are either true or false; there is no other interpretation of them. For example, if someone asks if it is raining then we can only say (factually) "yes" or "no." Thus, the statement "It is raining" will be true if it is raining and false otherwise. We can venture an opinion, "No, it isn't raining now but it looks like it is clouding over." Nevertheless, although we think it might rain later, the statement "It is raining" is still false until such time as it starts raining.

This kind of factual statement (based on available information) allows us to write programs that have a more complex flow of control. In the programs we have written so far, statements are executed one after the other in the order in which we have placed them. It is often useful to be able to decide to do one set of statements rather than another set. Also, as you will see in the next chapter, we may wish to repeat a set of statements. The "flow of control" through the programs we have written so far can be visualized as a straight line, linking each statement to the next (Figure 4.9).

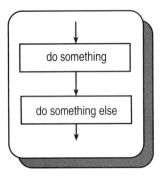

Figure 4.9: Sequential action

Using selection statements in a program leads to a more complicated diagram. We shall use a rather old-fashioned technique, flowcharting, to illustrate the flow of control when using selection.

In most programming languages, the selection statement begins with the keyword if. This is followed by an expression that can only ever be either true or false. Such expressions are known as *Boolean* expressions. Boolean expressions, when evaluated, have a value of true or false, just as arithmetic expressions have an arithmetic value. We look at Boolean expressions in more detail later in this chapter. Depending on the result of the Boolean expression, we can choose to do one of two sets of actions:

- If the Boolean expression is true, then do this.
- Otherwise, do that.

Associated with some Boolean value, then, we can have two actions: "do this" and "do that." We choose which action to carry out depending on whether the value is true or false. If it is true, we carry out the "do this" action; if it if false, we carry out the "do that" action. This is illustrated by the flowchart in Figure 4.10.

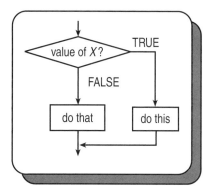

Figure 4.10: Choosing to do this or do that

Let us examine the syntax of the diagram in Figure 4.10. In the diamond box, we place the Boolean expression. Now, instead of a single line, we have two alternative lines emanating from the diamond "decision" box. The two lines are labeled true and false to indicate which path we should follow depending on the value of the Boolean expression within the decision box.

One line leads to a box containing one or more statements ("do this"), and the other line leads to a different box containing a different set of statements ("do that"). Finally, note that once the selection statement is completed, the two different lines join up, and we are back to our simple, sequential flow of control.

Notice that the "do that" action might be to do nothing.

- If (I feel like drinking a cup of coffee), then get one; otherwise, do nothing.
- If (X is true), then do this; otherwise, do nothing.

We can simply omit the "otherwise, do nothing" part of the statement, as illustrated by the flowchart in Figure 4.11.

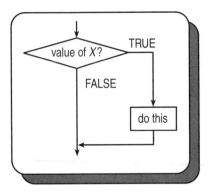

Figure 4.11: Choosing to do this or do nothing

Being limited to two choices may seem restrictive, but any multiway decision can be broken down into a sequence of binary decisions:

If the animal is an elephant, put it in the elephant enclosure; or else if it is a tiger, put it in the tiger cage; or else if it is a shark, put it in the shark tank.

This is illustrated by the flowchart in Figure 4.12. Notice that we may make one, two, or three choices, but we carry out only one of the actions. (We certainly wouldn't want to put an elephant in the elephant enclosure and then put it in the shark tank!)

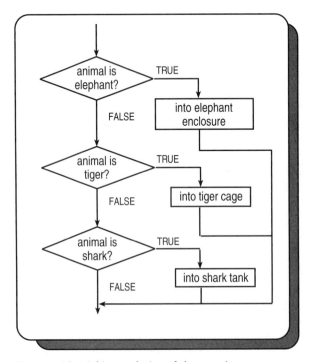

Figure 4.12: Making a choice of three actions

We can try to clarify the textual representation of our conditional statement by using indentation:

```
if (animal is elephant), then
        put in elephant enclosure
else if (animal is tiger), then
        put in tiger cage
else if (animal is shark), then
        put in shark tank
```

4.5   Selection Statements in Java

We now return to our use of the Person class. Let us suppose that we wish to classify the current person according to his or her age. A simple program might examine the value of a person's age and, depending on that value, tell us if the person is an adult:

```
if (person1.getAge() > 18)
    {
    System.out.print(person1.getForename() + ' ' +
                    person1.getSurname()) ;
    System.out.print(" is an adult") ;
    System.out.println() ;
    }
```

Notice that the if keyword is followed by a Boolean expression in parentheses. Either a person is older than 18 or he or she is not. The only possible outcome of this question is true or false. If the expression evaluates to true, then we execute the set of statements contained in the curly braces.

This might be suitable in some situations, but notice that if the person is younger than 18, this program prints nothing. It might be useful to make some other statement about a person's age classification if it is not adult:

```
System.out.print(person1.getForename() + ' ' +
                person1.getSurname()) ;
System.out.print(" is ") ;
if (person1.getAge() > 18)
    System.out.print("an adult") ;
else
    System.out.print("a minor") ;
System.out.println() ;
```

Notice that here we have a simple statement following the Boolean expression. It becomes even more important that we use indentation sensibly so that we can see the flow of control through this sequence of statements. Moreover, we introduce another keyword, else. This allows us to specify the second path emanating from the decision box. We show this sequence in Figure 4.13. If the person is older than 18, we will execute the statement which prints out that the person is an adult. Otherwise, we will execute the statement that prints out that the person is a minor.

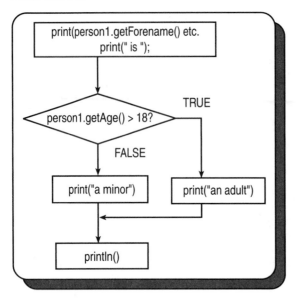

Figure 4.13: Deciding if a person is an adult or a minor

4.5.1 Statements

In this section, we consider the grammar and construction of a statement. We can identify two kinds of statements: *single* (or simple) and *compound*. An example of a single statement could be an assignment statement:

```
x = 4 ;
```

A compound statement is a sequence of statements enclosed in curly braces:

```
{
x = 4 ;
System.out.println("about to do something with x") ;
y = x * 2 ;
}
```

A statement can be either a single statement or a compound statement; both are grammatically correct. This means that wherever we expect a statement to appear, we can have a single statement or a compound statement.

If we then say that the general structure of an if statement is

```
if (Boolean expression) statement else statement
```

then where we have statement, we could have a single or a compound statement. Consider the following example:

```
if (age >= 60)
    System.out.print(person1.getSurname()) ;
    System.out.println(" is an old age pensioner") ;
```

What we intend to happen is that if age is greater than or equal to 60, we output the person's surname and a suitable message. However, despite our indentation, the statement following our Boolean expression is a single one. This means that regardless of the result of the test, we will always output the message " is an old age pensioner". If we flowchart this if statement (Figure 4.14), it should be clear what is happening.

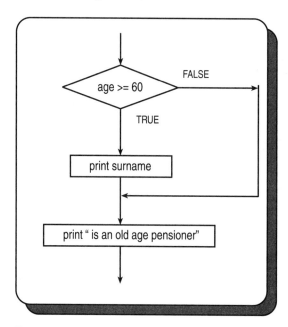

Figure 4.14: Printing " is an old age pensioner" every time

We must use the curly braces to create a compound statement:

```
if (age >= 60)
    {
    System.out.print(person1.getSurname()) ;
    System.out.println(" is an old age pensioner") ;
    }
```

Now if we flowchart this statement (Figure 4.15), we can see that it behaves as expected.

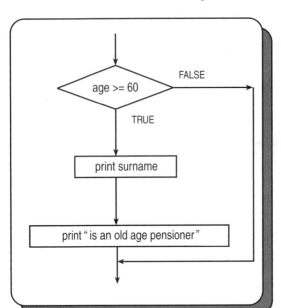

Figure 4.15: Printing the surname of old age pensioners with suitable message

4.5.2 Relational Operators and Boolean Expressions

Boolean expressions can be formed using the *relational operators* (Table 4.1). These allow us to compare one value with another value of the same type.

==	equals
!=	not equals
<	less than
<=	less than or equal to
>	greater than
>=	greater than or equal to

Table 4.1: Relational Operators

We have already been using a couple of these operators—greater than and greater than or equal to—when we've been comparing the value of a person's age with the integer constants 18 and 60. This was okay because both values are integers. We can also compare other values of the same types—for example, two characters. However, we cannot compare two values of different types because this does not make sense.

An important point to note is the use of == (two equal signs in a row) to denote equality. The equal sign (=) is already used in Java to denote the assignment operator, so we cannot use it again here as the relational equality operator. It is very important not to get these operators mixed up. It can cause some problems at compile time.

As you saw earlier in our example concerning animals and the dilemma facing the zookeepers as to which enclosure the animals belong in, sometimes we need to make a multi-way decision. Concerning a person's age, we can classify it with a finer granularity than just adult and minor. For example, we can have four categories: child, teenager, adult, and pensioner. We can lay this out as in Table 4.2.

Condition Based on Age	Classification
less than 13	child
greater than or equal to 13 and less than 18	teenager
greater than or equal to 18 and less than 60	adult
greater than or equal to 60	pensioner

Table 4.2: Conditions and Classifications

We can implement this as a sequence of if-else statements as follows:

```
System.out.print(person1.getForename() +' ' +
                 person1.getSurname()) ;
System.out.print(" is ") ;
if (person1.getAge() < 13)
    System.out.print("a child") ;
else if (person1.getAge() < 18)
    System.out.print("a teenager") ;
else if (person1.getAge() < 60)
    System.out.print("an adult") ;
else
    System.out.print("a pensioner") ;
System.out.println() ;
```

This is illustrated by the flowchart in Figure 4.16.

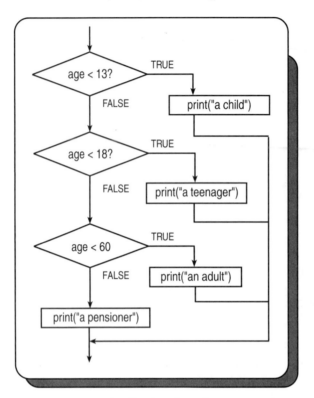

Figure 4.16: Four classifications based on a person's age

Consider now the following. At present and for a few more years, deciding whether some-one is a pensioner in the United Kingdom involves more information than just the person's age. This is because at present women retire at 60 and men at 65.

As we saw in Chapter 3, the Person class provides a gender attribute and a set of integer constants—MALE, FEMALE, and UNKNOWN. As users of the Person class, we do not need to know what integer values these constants have; we simply use the semantics that they represent—the possible information we may have regarding a person's gender.

```
System.out.print(person1.getForename() + ' ' +
                 person1.getSurname()) ;
System.out.print(" is ") ;
if (person1.getAge() < 13)
    System.out.print("a child") ;
else if (person1.getAge() < 18)
    System.out.print("a teenager") ;
```

```
else if (person1.getGender() == Person.FEMALE)
    {
    if (person1.getAge() < 60)
        System.out.print("an adult") ;
    else
        System.out.print("a pensioner") ;
    }
else
    {
    if (person1.getAge() < 65)
        System.out.print("an adult") ;
    else
        System.out.print("a pensioner") ;
    }
System.out.println() ;
```

The last two parts of this multiway decision are shown in Figure 4.17.

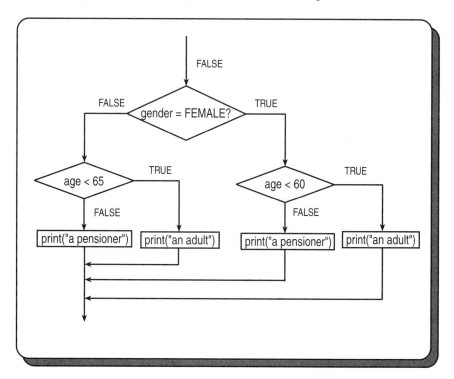

Figure 4.17: Multiway decision based on age and gender

4.6   The Boolean Type

As well as having Boolean expressions as the result of statements containing relational operations, we can have variables of type `boolean` in Java. For example, we can have the following:

```
boolean myBool = true ;
```

This is similar to having an integer variable and giving it an integer value. As you know, integer variables can also be given the value of an integer expression:

```
int x = 4 +(9 * 20) / y ;
```

Similarly, a variable of type `boolean` can be assigned the result of a Boolean expression:

```
myBool = (person1.getAge() > 18) ;
```

Depending on the value of a person's age, `myBool` will be given the value true or false. We can construct more complicated Boolean expressions by using the set of *logical operators*. In Java, the logical operators in Table 4.3 may be used with Boolean expressions. Tables 4.4 through 4.7 define the operators AND, OR, NOT, and EQUALS (here b and d are Boolean values).

AND	&	logical conjunction (both)
OR	|	logical disjunction (one or the other or both)
NOT	!	logical negation
EQUALS	==	equivalence

Table 4.3: Logical Operators That May Be Used with Boolean Expressions

b	d	b AND d
false	false	false
false	true	false
true	false	false
true	true	true

Table 4.4: The AND Operator

b	d	b OR d
false	false	false
false	true	true
true	false	true
true	true	true

Table 4.5: The OR Operator

b	NOT b
false	true
true	false

Table 4.6: The NOT Operator

b	d	b EQUALS d
false	false	true
false	true	false
true	false	false
true	true	true

Table 4.7: The EQUALS Operator

The tables are known as *truth tables*. Because there are only two possible values for a Boolean, it is possible to write down all possible combinations of two Booleans and the result of the operation. (Imagine doing this for integers and the plus operation!) For the results of an AND to be true, both operands must be true. For the result of an OR to be true, any of the operands must be true. There is a formal algebra (Boolean algebra) built up around these operators and the values of the operands.

Now that we have introduced the logical operators, we can take a second look at the problem of male and female pensioners. If we wish to examine a person and decide if they are a pensioner, we can have the following selection statement:

```
boolean isPensioner = false ;
if (person1.getGender() == Person.FEMALE)
    {
    if (person1.getAge() >= 60)
        isPensioner = true ;
    }
else
    {
    if (person1.getAge() >= 65)
        isPensioner = true ;
    }
```

Here you see the nested if statements, executed depending on whether a person is male or female. Notice how we make the initial assumption that the person is not a pensioner and subsequently check for "pensioner-hood."

In this particular example, we can use the logical operators to combine the Boolean expression from the outer `if` statement with the inner `if` statement and thus remove the need for a nested `if` statement:

```
boolean isPensioner = false ;
if (
      (
        (person1.getGender() == Person.FEMALE)
        &
        (person1.getAge() >= 60)
      )
      |
      (person1.getAge() >= 65)
    )
        isPensioner = true ;
```

We have indented the parentheses in this example to highlight the structure of the Boolean expression; we can, of course, write it more compactly as follows:

```
boolean isPensioner = false ;
if (((person1.getGender() == Person.FEMALE) &
      (person1.getAge() >= 60)) |
     (person1.getAge() >= 65))
    isPensioner = true ;
```

In this Boolean expression, we have placed parentheses around each individual part. It is possible to leave out some of the parentheses, but we have to be careful that the priority, or *precedence*, of the Boolean operators does not affect the final result of the expression. The three Boolean operators we have introduced have the precedences shown in Table 4.8 (in Chapter 6, you will see a fuller version of this table that includes other operators).

Precedence	Operator	Description
high	!	NOT
medium	&	AND
low			OR

Table 4.8: Precedence for Logical Operators

Those operators with a higher priority are executed first so that, for instance, AND operators are evaluated before OR operators.

In our expression that tests for pensioners, we want to make sure that we test for females over 60 before we test for anybody over 65. The expression that tests for females over 60 links two simpler expressions with an AND operation. We can see from Table 4.8 that AND is executed before OR; therefore, we will indeed test for females over 60 before we OR that result with the test for anyone over 65.

In this particular case, then, we do not need to parenthesize the "females over 60" expression and can write the overall expression as follows:

```
boolean isPensioner = false ;
if ((person1.getGender() == Person.FEMALE) &
    (person1.getAge() >= 60) |
    (person1.getAge() >= 65))
    isPensioner = true ;
```

Although the additional parentheses we had earlier are not actually necessary—the operator precedences ensure that the expressions are evaluated in the order we require—they do add to the readability of the expression and reflect the programmer's intention explicitly. In a moment, we will look at an example of an expression where the parentheses do affect the outcome.

Let's take our pensioner expression as a worked example of how Boolean expressions are evaluated. Table 4.9 considers Joan, aged 18, and Bill, aged 72.

	Joan	Bill
gender = FEMALE	true	false
age >= 60	false	true
(gender = FEMALE) AND (age >=60)	false	false
age >= 65	false	true
((gender = FEMALE) AND (age >= 60)) OR (age >= 65)	false	true

Table 4.9: Joan, Bill, and the Value of the Boolean Expressions

In the first and second rows, we evaluate the two simple Boolean expressions contained within the larger AND expression. In the third row, we evaluate the AND. We can do this by looking at the AND truth table presented earlier (Table 4.4), or we can remember the rule that AND results in true only if both the operands are true. In both cases, one of the operands is false, so we know immediately that the result of the AND is false. In the fourth row, we evaluate the last simple Boolean expression that we must OR with the result of the AND. Finally, in the fifth row, we OR the results shown in rows three and four. Again, we can do this by referring to the OR truth table (Table 4.5), or we can remember the rule that the result of an OR is true if either of the operands is true.

Returning to operator priority and parentheses, consider the following expression:

```
switch4 = ( ! ( switch1 | switch2 ) ) & switch3 ;
```

Table 4.10 gives the evaluation of this Boolean expression for a particular set of values for the Boolean variables.

switch1	true
switch2	true
switch3	true
switch1 OR switch2	true
NOT (switch1 OR switch2)	false
NOT (switch1 OR switch2) AND switch3	false

Table 4.10: Evaluating the switch Boolean Expression

Now let us take the parentheses out completely:

```
switch4 = ! switch1 | switch2 & switch3 ;
```

Table 4.11 gives the new evaluation of this expression.

switch1	true
switch2	true
switch3	true
NOT switch1	false
switch2 AND switch3	true
NOT switch1 OR switch2 AND switch3	true

Table 4.11: Evaluating the switch Boolean Expression without Parentheses

From the tables, you can see how the operations are being executed in a different order because of operator precedence and, in this case, arrive at a different result.

Consider the pensioner example again. We are checking the value of a Boolean expression. If it is true, we set the value of a boolean variable to true. If it is false, we set it to false. In this particular case, there is no need for the if statement at all. We can do all the work with the boolean expression itself and an assignment statement as follows:

```
Boolean isPensioner = (((person1.getGender() ==
                     Person.FEMALE) &
              (person1.getAge() >= 60)) |
              (person1.getAge() >= 65)) ;
```

As well as the & and | forms of the AND and OR operators, there are the && and || operators. These are known as *short-circuit* versions of the AND and OR operators, and they function as follows:

- If we inspect the AND truth table (Table 4.4), we find that for "b AND d" to be true, both *b* and *d* must be true. As soon as either *b* or *d* is false, we know the overall result of "b AND d" must also be false. If *b* or *d* are Boolean expressions, once we have evaluated *b* to false, there is clearly no need to go on and evaluate *d*; regardless of whether *d* is true or false, the result of "b AND d" must be false.

- Similarly, the OR truth table (Table 4.5) shows us that for "b OR d" to be false, both *b* and *d* must be false. As soon as either *b* or *d* is true, the result of "b OR d" must also be true.

In Java, we can use the short-circuit AND (&&) and OR (||) operators to avoid the needless evaluation of the second Boolean expression:

```
switch4 = ! switch1 || switch2 && switch3 ;
```

4.7 The switch Statement

Clearly, it is possible to split a multiway decision into a series of binary decisions. However, it is sometimes possible to replace a sequence of if statements with a switch statement. The switch statement more directly models the multiway decision, making life easier for both the programmer and the maintainer: It is easier to read and understand something that more accurately captures the semantics of what is being done.

Let's begin with a simple example. Grades denoted by letters of the alphabet (A, B, C, D and F) have been assigned to students. However, for the purposes of deciding whether a student should progress to the next year of study, these grades need to be converted into points that are then added together. If the result is greater than some nominal threshold, the student is allowed to proceed. We can achieve the transformation from grade to points using the following switch statement:

```
char grade = ...
...
int points = 0 ;
switch (grade)
    {
    case 'A' :
        points = 4 ;
        break ;
    case 'B' :
        points = 3 ;
        break ;
    case 'C' :
        points = 2 ;
        break ;
```

```
    case 'D' :
        points = 1 ;
        break ;
    case 'F' :
        points = 0 ;
        break ;
    }
```

The switch keyword is followed by an expression or variable name in parentheses. The value of the expression or variable must belong to an *ordinal* type. An ordinal type is one whose values form an ordered list and which differ in complete steps. For example, int is an example of an ordinal type because its values range from the smallest integer to the largest in steps of one. The char type is also an ordinal type, but the double and String types are not.

Following the *controlling expression* (in this example, grade), we have a list of case statements. The value of the controlling expression is compared with each case label in turn. When we find a match, the statements associated with the matching label are executed. If grade was equal to 'B', then the statements points = 3 and break would be executed.

The break statement transfers control to the statement following the switch statement. If we omit the break statement, it would mean we execute all the case statements following the one we matched grade with. You will see examples of this later.

Compare this with the if statement that would achieve the same effect:

```
char grade = ...
...
int points = 0 ;
if (grade == 'A')
    points = 4 ;
else if (grade == 'B')
    points = 3 ;
else if (grade == 'C')
    points = 2 ;
else if (grade == 'D')
    points = 1 ;
else if (grade == 'F')
    points = 0 ;
```

Actually, this doesn't look too bad. However, consider a statement with 20-odd decision points.

Consider now an application where we represent the months of the year as 12 integer constants JAN to DEC. We need to be able to obtain the number of days in the current month. We could use the following switch statement as an almost direct realization of the rhyme:

30 days hath September,
April, June, and November,
All the rest have 31,
Except February, which has 28 days clear,
And 29 in each leap year.

```
int month = ...
...
int days = 0 ;
switch (month)
    {
    case SEP : case APR : case JUN : case NOV :
        days = 30 ;
        break ;
    case FEB : // assume not a leap year, at present
        days = 28 ;
        break ;
    default :
        days = 31 ;
        break ;
    }
```

In this example, we have introduced the default case statement. Clearly, a controlling expression can potentially return any value from the ordinal type. For example, month here is an int and could in principle contain any integer value in the range (for our example to work correctly, they should really be in the range JAN to DEC, but that's another story). Rather than provide a case statement for every possible value of month (a rather tedious and boring task), we can use the "catchall" default statement instead. In our example, if month does not contain SEP, APR, JUN, NOV, or FEB, we assume it contains either one of the other valid months or some other integer and set the value of days to 31.

The default statement matches any value of the controlling expression that is not listed as part of any of the other case labels.

Consider writing the 30-days option as an if statement:

```
if ((month == SEP) | (month == APR) |
    (month == JUN) | (month == SEP))
    ...
```

This example illustrates a number of important points about the switch statement. It may appear as if we have only listed the four options for 30 days, but this is purely a matter of layout. If we view the overall switch statement as follows

```
switch (month)
    {
    case SEP :
        // empty statement
    case APR :
        // empty statement
    case JUN :
        // empty statement
```

```
        case NOV :
            days = 30 ;
            break;
        case FEB : // assume not a leap year, at present
            days = 28 ;
            break;
        default :
            days = 31 ;
            break ;
    }
```

we can see that we have five identified cases plus the sixth default case (more about this in a moment). Once we have entered a case, we execute all subsequent statements until we encounter the end of the overall switch statement or a break statement. If the month was APR, then we would "execute" the empty statement associated with the APR case, continue onto the empty statement associated with JUN, execute the days = 30 assignment statement associated with NOV, reach the break statement, and exit from the switch statement.

If the month is SEP, APR, or JUN, we will enter at the appropriate case statement but end up executing the code associated with NOV. This is as it should be. Notice that if the month is NOV, we execute only the single assignment statement and leave. We do not continue onto the FEB case.

If there were no break statements in this example, the value of the days variable would always end up being that of the last case statement. In this example, that is the default statement, and therefore, days would always have the value 31.

Consider now a pay raise being granted to employees and managers. Employees are to receive a 10 percent raise, as are managers. However, before this raise is applied, managers are also to receive a $50 increase. One way of achieving this would be:

```
if (status == MANAGER)
    {
    salary = salary + 50 ;
    }
if ((status == EMPLOYEE) | (status == MANAGER))
    {
    salary = salary + ((salary / 100) * 10) ;
    }
```

Taking advantage of our ability to execute consecutive case statements, we can handle this as a switch statement:

```
switch (status)
    {
    case MANAGER :
        salary = salary + 50 ;
```

```
    case EMPLOYEE :
        salary = salary + ((salary / 100) * 10) ;
        break ;
    default :
        // do something appropriate
    }
```

Now, if status is MANAGER, not only do we get our $50 raise, but we "fall through" to the EMPLOYEE case and get our 10 percent increase on top of that.

What would happen if we placed a break statement at the end of the MANAGER case? Would our manager be very pleased about this mistake? The use and nonuse of break statements has to be handled very carefully; it can be a source of errors that are quite difficult to spot.

Let us return to our days of the month example. The original rhyme has a nice "get out clause"; it covers the 4 months that have 30 days, handles the oddball February, and then simply says "all the rest have 31." If we wanted to be pedantic about things, we could have:

```
switch (month)
    {
    case SEP : case APR : case JUN : case NOV :
        days = 30 ;
        break ;
    case FEB :
        // assume not a leap year, at present
        days = 28 ;
        break ;
    case JAN : case MAR : case MAY : case JUL :
    case AUG : case OCT : case DEC :
        days = 31 ;
        break ;
    }
```

If we cannot know for sure that only valid month values will be given to this switch statement, then we need to be pedantic (or careful) in order to catch and handle any invalid attempt to use the switch.

```
switch (month)
    {
    case SEP : case APR : case JUN : case NOV :
        days = 30 ;
        break ;
    case FEB :
        // assume not a leap year, at present
        days = 28 ;
        break ;
```

```
    case JAN : case MAR : case MAY : case JUL :
    case AUG : case OCT : case DEC :
        days = 31 ;
        break ;
    default :
        System.out.print("month not valid!") ;
    }
```

Imagine now a very rudimentary integer calculator implemented as a Java program. The user types in an operand, followed by an operator (one of the characters +, −, *, /), followed by a final operand. The operands are read with the readInteger method, and the operator, which is a single character, is read with the readCharacter method. The operator is applied to the operands, and the result is output. We can use the switch statement to help realize this program:

```
BasicIo.prompt("type the first operand: ") ;
int operand1 = BasicIo.readInteger() ;
BasicIo.prompt("type an operator (+, −, * or /): ") ;
int operator = BasicIo.readCharacter() ;
BasicIo.prompt("type the second operand: ") ;
int operand2 = BasicIo.readInteger() ;
int result = 0 ;
switch (operator)
    {
    case '+' :
        result = operand1 + operand2 ;
        break ;
    case '−' :
        result = operand1 − operand2 ;
        break ;
    case '*' :
        result = operand1 * operand2 ;
        break ;
    case '/' :
        result = operand1 / operand2 ;
        break ;
    default :
        System.out.print("operator not valid") ;
    }
System.out.println("the result is " + result) ;
```

The statement or statements that follow a case specifier can be complex. This means we can use if statements in conjunction with switch statements, and vice versa. To complete our implementation of the days of the month example, we need to tackle the problem of February. This is not just a simple value, but it depends on whether the year involved is a leap year or not. We need to know the year, and we need a Boolean expression that tells us whether it is a leap year:

```
case FEB :
   days = 28 ;
   if (year % 4 == 0)
      days = days + 1 ;
   break ;
```

The expression `year % 4` means "calculate the remainder from dividing `year` by 4." This is not a full leap-year calculation because a century year is a leap year only if it is divisible by 400; thus, 2000 was a leap year, but 1900 was not. Can you rewrite this expression to do the full calculation?

4.8   Testing a New Class

When developing a new class or using an existing one, it is important to test the class as thoroughly as possible before issuing it or using it in a real application. One technique is to develop a *test harness* or *driver program*. As you have seen, the object orientation of Java allows us to build software with a strict, enforced interface. Users of a class have access to a list of available methods. We can use this as the basis of our interactive test harness.

Programmers using the test harness can select which method they want to test; the harness then prompts for the arguments for the method, calls the method under test, and outputs any return value. The following is a test harness for the `Person` class, which tests the getting and setting of forename, surname, age, and gender using a `switch` statement to select which method is to be called. We obviously want to try out a *sequence* of method calls, so we have used a loop or repetition statement—the `while (continueLoop)` statement (this will be explained in the next chapter).

```
import javalancs.* ;

public class Chapter4n2
   {
   public static void main(String[] args)
                             throws Exception
      {
      Person myPerson = new Person() ;
      boolean continueLoop = true ;

      while (continueLoop)
         {
         // get the command (a character)
         BasicIo.prompt("type command character: ") ;
         char command = BasicIo.readCharacter() ;
         int age = 0 ;
         String response = null ;
```

```
// call the appropriate method
switch (command)
    {
    case 'a' : // set forename
        BasicIo.prompt("type a forename: ") ;
        response = BasicIo.readString() ;
        myPerson.setForename(response) ;
        break ;

    case 'b' : // set surname
        BasicIo.prompt("type a surname: ") ;
        response = BasicIo.readString() ;
        myPerson.setSurname(response) ;
        break ;

    case 'c' : // set age
        BasicIo.prompt("type an age: ") ;
        age = BasicIo.readInteger() ;
        myPerson.setAge(age) ;
        break ;

    case 'd' : // set gender
        BasicIo.prompt("type a gender: ") ;
        response = BasicIo.readString() ;
        if (response.equals("male"))
            myPerson.setGender(Person.MALE) ;
        else if (response.equals("female"))

            myPerson.setGender(Person.FEMALE) ;
        else
            myPerson.setGender(Person.UNKNOWN) ;
        break ;

    case 'e' : // get forename
        System.out.print("forename is ") ;

        System.out.println(myPerson.getForename()) ;
        break ;

    case 'f' : // get surname
        System.out.print("surname is ") ;

        System.out.println(myPerson.getSurname()) ;
        break ;

    case 'g' : // get age
        System.out.print("age is ") ;
        System.out.println(myPerson.getAge()) ;
        break ;
```

```
          case 'h' : // get gender
              System.out.print("gender is ") ;
              switch (myPerson.getGender())
                    {
                  case Person.MALE :

                      System.out.println("male") ;
                      break ;
                  case Person.FEMALE :

                      System.out.println("female") ;
                      break ;
                  default :

                      System.out.println("unknown") ;
                    }

              break ;
          case '?' : // print 'help' information
              System.out.println("a : set forename") ;
              System.out.println("b : set surname") ;
              System.out.println("c : set age") ;
              System.out.println("d : set gender") ;
              System.out.println("e : get forename") ;
              System.out.println("f : get surname") ;
              System.out.println("g : get age") ;
              System.out.println("h : get gender") ;
              System.out.println("? : output this message") ;
              System.out.println("s : stop the program") ;
              break ;

          case 's' : // stop the program
              continueLoop = false ;
              break ;

          default :
              System.out.println("illegal command") ;
          }
      }
    } // end of method main
  } // end of class Chapter4n2
```

Notice how the gender attribute was handled. The argument to the setGender method is an integer, and the Person class provides the constants MALE, FEMALE, and UNKNOWN. We don't want the user to have to remember the values of these constants, so we allow the user to type in one of the strings "male" and "female" (any other string is treated as an UNKNOWN value). Hence, we need to test the input string (response) to see if it is the string "male"—if so, we set the gender attribute to the MALE constant:

```
if (response.equals("male"))
   myPerson.setGender(Person.MALE) ;
...
```

We cannot compare strings with the == relational operator. Instead, Java provides an equals method that returns the value true if the argument string is the same as the string to which the method is applied and the value false otherwise. If the string was not "male", we need to test for the string "female":

```
else if (response.equals("female"))
   myPerson.setGender(Person.FEMALE) ;
...
```

If this also fails, we set the value accordingly:

```
else
   myPerson.setGender(Person.UNKNOWN) ;
```

It would be nice if the user could type "Male" or "MALE" as well as "male", so we could write:

```
if ((response.equals("male")) ||
   (response.equals("Male")) ||
   (response.equals("MALE")))
   myPerson.setGender(Person.MALE) ;
...
```

Alternatively, we could convert the response string all to lowercase before doing any tests. You will see how to do this in Chapter 6.

When printing the gender, we want to output a string rather than an integer. We use a switch statement to convert from one to the other (instead of the getGenderString method provided).

4.9 Key Points in Chapter 4

- A program that allows only a linear progression through a sequence of statements would have very limited functionality. A program needs to decide which of two or more sets of actions should be carried out based on the current circumstances.

- An if statement has the form

  ```
  if (BOOLEAN EXPRESSION)
     FIRST SET OF STATEMENTS
  else
     SECOND SET OF STATEMENTS
  ```

  If the BOOLEAN EXPRESSION evaluates to true, the FIRST SET OF STATEMENTS is executed; otherwise, the SECOND SET OF STATEMENTS is executed. If there are more than one statement in FIRST/SECOND SET OF STATEMENTS, they must be enclosed in curly braces.

The else and the SECOND SET OF STATEMENTS can be omitted.

- if statements can be written in sequence, or nested, to allow more complex tests.
- We can compare two values with a set of relational operators ==, !=, <, <=, > and >=. The relational operator == means test for equality; != means test for nonequality.
- Boolean variables and expressions can take on only the values true and false. We can combine Boolean values with the Boolean operators AND (&), OR (|), and NOT (!).
- The operators && and || are *short-circuit* versions of & and |, respectively. They do not evaluate the second operand if the value of the result can be deduced from the value of the first operand.
- Java also provides a switch statement that has the form:

```
switch (EXPRESSION)
    {
    case FIRST_VALUE :
        FIRST SET OF STATEMENTS ;
        break ;
    case SECOND_VALUE :
        SECOND SET OF STATEMENTS ;
        break ;
...
    default :
        FINAL SET OF STATEMENTS ;
    }
```

The value of EXPRESSION must be an ordinal type. Typically, it is an int or a char (see Section 6.6); it cannot be a double (see Section 6.4) or a String.

If the break is omitted, execution "falls through" to the next set of statements. If the EXPRESSION does not match FIRST_VALUE, or SECOND_VALUE, and so on, the FINAL SET OF STATEMENTS for the default case is executed.

4.10 Exercises

1. Write a program that sets up a Person instance with suitable attributes and then prints the person's name (forename followed by surname) followed by "is a man" or "is a woman" as appropriate.

   Modify the program so that it prints the name followed by:

   is a girl
   is a boy
   is a woman
   is a man

   as appropriate (a boy or girl is defined as age 17 or younger).

2. Write a program that sets up two `Person` instances with suitable attributes, finds the elder, and prints the name of the elder, followed by `"is older than"`, followed by the name of the younger.

   Modify your program to check for the two age attributes being the same and print a suitable message in this case.

3. Modify your answer to Exercise 3.1 to prompt the user to type in a forename, surname, age, and gender. Then set the attributes of a `Person` instance to these values and print them.

   Make use of the class method `getUpperAgeLimit` to test that the age typed in by the user is valid. If it is not valid, output an error message and stop the program with a call of the `System.exit` method:

   ```
   System.exit(1) ;
   ```

   This is a method (in the `java.lang` package) that causes your program to stop immediately. The argument is a status code; it should be zero if everything worked satisfactorily or nonzero if (as here) the program terminated with some sort of error condition.

4. In Exercise 3.4, two cards are selected at random and displayed. Assuming that the first card selected is for the computer and the second is for the user, print who wins according to the value of the cards.

   Modify your program so that ace counts as higher than king.

5. In a card game, the user selects a card value and suit, and then the computer does the same. If the computer selected a red card (hearts or diamonds), the highest value wins, but if the computer selected a black card (spades or clubs), the lowest value wins. Aces always count as high.

   Write a program to prompt the user for his or her card selection and store the result as a `Card` instance. The computer then selects a card at random, decides who is the winner, and outputs what the cards were and the result of the game.

6. Modify your answer to Exercise 3.5 to print today's date and time in the form:

   ```
   The time (sponsored by Java) is 11:47 on 2 2nd 2002
   ```

   Use the `switch` statement to put the correct suffix on the end of the number of the day within the month; for example, 1st, 2nd, 3rd, 4th, and so on.

   Further modify the program to print the name of the month instead of the number:

   ```
   The time (sponsored by Java) is 11:47 on February 2nd 2002
   ```

7. Modify your answer to Exercise 3.6 to prompt the user to type in the name of a shape (one of the strings `"square"`, `"circle"`, or `"triangle"`), the dimensions and color of the shape, and then draw the specified shape on the screen using the `BasicGraphics` class. You should check the input from the user for validity, stopping the program with a suitable error message if the data are not valid.

CHAPTER 5

Repetition

5.1   Repetition as a Basic Control Structure

So far, you have met two *control structures*—two ways in which we can answer the question: After we have finished this statement, what shall we do next? You met basic *sequencing* in Chapter 3 and *selection* in Chapter 4. In this chapter, we discuss the remaining major control structure: After we have finished this statement, perhaps we should *repeat* it.

Let's look at an example from cooking. The instructions for a recipe for Christmas pudding say: Add three tablespoons of brandy to the mixture, mixing well after each spoonful. We can write this more formally as follows:

```
do the preceding step
do the following three times
    add a tablespoonful of brandy to the mixture
    mix well
do the next step
```

This is an example of a *repetition statement*, or *loop*. The *body* of the loop, that is, the statements

```
    add a tablespoonful of brandy to the mixture
    mix well
```

are to be repeated a certain number of times (in this case, three times). Notice that we have indented the body of the loop to make clear to the reader which statements form part of the body and which do not. Notice also that in this loop, we know how many times we are going to go around the loop (three times) *before* we start it.

In this example, we do the same thing on each iteration of the loop. Another recipe contains the instructions: Add the next three ingredients, stirring well after each one (where the next three ingredients are orange juice, olive oil, and cider vinegar). The loop written out formally looks something like:

```
do the preceding step
do the following three times
    add the ith ingredient to the mixture
    mix well
do the next step
```

Here we assume that we are counting the iterations 1, 2, 3, and i indicates the number of the iteration we are currently performing.

Another recipe contains the instruction: Whisk the egg whites until they stand in soft peaks. We write this formally as:

```
do the preceding step
repeat
    whisk the egg whites for a bit
    look at the result
until the result forms soft peaks
do the next step
```

Again, we have a body

```
    whisk the egg whites for a bit
    look at the result
```

that we indent for clarity. We are going to repeat this a number of times, but we do not know before we start how many times we are going to repeat it. We perform the iteration and then conduct a test to decide whether to do it again or whether we can terminate the loop and proceed with the next step.

There is a problem with the preceding loop. Occasionally, when we attempt to follow this recipe, we cannot seem to reach the soft-peaks stage. Instead, the egg whites eventually separate, and we know the only option is to throw this mixture away and start again. There are two ways of taking account of this possibility in the instructions.

We could have a more elaborate test—until the result forms soft peaks or the result has separated. The next step after the loop would have to check what happened and take two different actions depending on which of the two possibilities caused us to terminate the loop.

Alternatively, we could decide that the mixture separating is an error condition (it certainly is) and that it occurs rarely (yes, that too). We could test for the separation of the mixture inside the loop and, if so, *throw an error exception*. If we do nothing about the exception, it would cause the whole recipe to be abandoned with an error message. A more sophisticated cookery program would *catch* the exception somewhere and take appropriate action, perhaps restarting the recipe at a suitable point after clearing up the mess.

Let us now turn to programming. We want to carry out a set of statements a number of times. Sometimes we know before we start how many times we are going to perform the iteration, and sometimes we have to conduct a test during each iteration to decide whether or not we require another. Most computer languages provide two different mechanisms for efficiently carrying out these two different types of repetition.

Java, following the example of the C and C++ programming languages, has two different repetition statements: for and while. As with most other computer languages, the Java while statement provides a repetition structure that performs a test on each iteration. But the for statement in Java provides a rather more powerful repetition structure than the basic "do this a fixed number of times" mechanism of the first example. It is also more powerful than the version of for provided by many other programming languages. In this chapter, we introduce only a simple version of Java's for statement.

Consider again the egg white whisking example. We whisked for a bit and then tested to see if we had done enough; if not, we had a second iteration—whisk, test, and so on. Thus, the test is done at the end of the iteration. We always do at least one iteration before the first test.

But suppose the egg whites miraculously started out forming soft peaks (maybe my wife has already done the whisking for us). Then to ensure we do not waste any effort, we would need to do the test at the beginning of each iteration. If we are lucky, we may perform no iterations of the loop.

In writing loops that involve a test on each iteration, we must decide whether the test goes at the beginning of the loop (this is by far the most common form), at the end, or perhaps somewhere in the middle of the loop. In this final case, we carry out part of the iteration, and that puts us in a position to decide whether we require no further iterations (in which case, we leave the loop and go to the step after the loop), or we complete this iteration and then at least commence the next iteration.

Finally, consider the following loop found on a shampoo bottle:

```
wet the hair
apply a generous amount of the shampoo and work in
rinse with clean water
repeat
```

This is an *infinite* loop; we will never get out of the loop (unless the empty bottle generates an exception)! Furthermore, how can we "wet the hair" on the second and subsequent iterations? The loop would be more carefully written as follows:

```
wet the hair
do the following twice
    apply a generous amount of the shampoo and work in
    rinse with clean water
```

Luckily, we (unlike a computer program) are able to do what it means rather than what it says.

5.2   Looping a Predetermined Number of Times: The for Statement

We begin with the case where we know before we begin the looping how many iterations there are going to be. The basic idea is that we have a counter, or *control variable,* that keeps track of how many times we have been around the loop and stops the repetition when the counter has recorded that we have iterated the appropriate number of times. The control variable is going to take on a *range* of values; hence, if we want to repeat a loop 10 times:

- We could start the control variable at the value 1.

- At the end of each iteration, we could add 1 to the value of the control variable

- We could keep testing the control variable, stopping when it reaches the value 10.

Or perhaps we stop when we have reached the value 11. It is very easy in writing loops to make an "out-by-one" error; in a loop where we want to go around 10 times, we go round 9 or 11 times by mistake. We have to be careful where we add 1 to the control variable in relation to where we test the value of the control variable.

To perform this type of loop, when we know before entering the loop how many iterations there are going to be and when we are going to count a control variable through a range of values, Java provides the for statement. This takes the form:

```
for ( INITIALIZATION ; TESTING ; MODIFICATION )
    LOOP BODY
```

This specifies a loop with the structure shown in Figure 5.1.

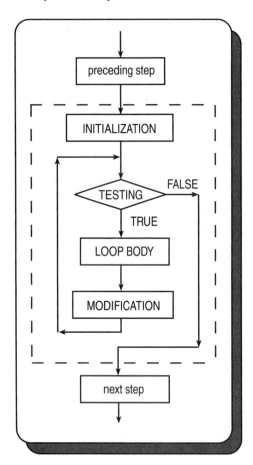

Figure 5.1: The structure of the for loop

Before we start the loop, we carry out the INITIALIZATION. Then we have the statements executed on each iteration of the loop. We carry out the TESTING at the beginning of each iteration to decide whether to proceed with this iteration. If we proceed, we next carry out the LOOP BODY, and finally, we carry out the MODIFICATION at the end of each iteration.

For a simple version of the for statement, we are going to use a *control variable* to ensure we execute the LOOP BODY 10 times. In the INITIALIZATION section, we need to declare a suitable control variable and set it to its initial value. For example,

```
int i = 0
```

declares an int variable called i and assigns it the initial value 0. It is usual in Java, for reasons that will become clear later, to start counting at 0 rather than 1. Because we have declared the variable i as part of the for statement, it is available only inside the body of the for loop.

In the MODIFICATION section, we specify what has to be done to the control variable at the end of each iteration. We write:

```
i++
```

This is an incrementation statement. It takes the value in the variable i, adds 1 to it, and restores the new value in the variable.

Finally, we have the TESTING section. This is a Boolean expression that is evaluated at the beginning of each iteration. As long as the expression evaluates to true, we proceed with the iteration; when it evaluates to false, the loop is terminated and we proceed to the next statement after the loop. We want to execute the loop 10 times, so our TESTING section is:

```
i < 10
```

What shall we do on each iteration? For this first example, we are simply going to display the current value of the control variable in the body of the loop so that we can see that it is taking on the correct sequence of values. Here is the code:

```
System.out.println("Before the beginning of the loop") ;
for (int i = 0 ; i < 10 ; i++)
    System.out.println(i) ;
System.out.println("After the end of the loop") ;
```

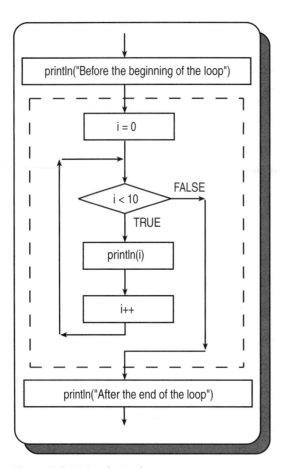

Figure 5.2: A simple for loop

Figure 5.2 is a diagram of the loop, and this is what happens:

- The text "Before the beginning of the loop" is displayed.
- The variable i is declared and initialized to the value 0.
- We start the first iteration.
  - The Boolean expression i < 10 is evaluated (i has the value 0); this gives the value true, so we proceed with this iteration.
  - We execute the body of the loop—display the current value of i, which is 0.
  - We increment the control variable i, so its value is now 1.

- We start the next iteration.
  - The Boolean expression i < 10 is evaluated (i has the value 1); this gives the value true, so we proceed with this iteration.
  - We execute the body of the loop—display the current value of i, which is 1.
  - We increment the control variable i, so its value is now 2.
- We start the next iteration.
  - The Boolean expression i < 10 is evaluated (i has the value 2); this gives the value true, so we proceed with this iteration.
  - We execute the body of the loop—display the current value of i, which is 2.
  - We increment the control variable i, so its value is now 3.

And so on.

- We start the next iteration.
  - The Boolean expression i < 10 is evaluated (i has the value 8); this gives the value true, so we proceed with this iteration.
  - We execute the body of the loop—display the current value of i, which is 8.
  - We increment the control variable i, so its value is now 9.
- We start the next iteration.
  - The Boolean expression i < 10 is evaluated (i has the value 9); this gives the value true, so we proceed with this iteration.
  - We execute the body of the loop—display the current value of i, which is 9.
  - We increment the control variable i, so its value is now 10.
- We start the next iteration.
  - The Boolean expression i < 10 is evaluated (i has the value 10); this gives the value false, so we terminate the loop.
- The text "After the end of the loop" is displayed.

The loop has been executed with the control variable i having the successive values 0, 1, 2, 3, 4, 5, 6, 7, 8, and 9. Thus, the loop was executed 10 times.

We are now going to rewrite our loop slightly because we want to display a table of numbers together with their squares. Here is the code:

```
System.out.println("Table of Squares") ;
for (int i = 0 ; i < 10 ; i++)
    {
    System.out.print("the square of " + i) ;
    System.out.println(" is " + (i * i)) ;
    }
System.out.println("**end of table**") ;
```

The body of the loop now consists of two statements, although we could have written it as one if we had made more use of the concatenate operator +. But the body of a for loop (like each of the branches of an if statement) must be a *single* statement. The solution is the same as for the if statement; if we want the loop body to consist of more than a single statement, we must make it a *compound* statement by enclosing the sequence of statements in curly braces { ... }.

Notice that we have indented the body of the loop in both of the preceding examples to make it clear to the reader which statements are part of the loop and which are not. The Java compiler makes no use of the indentation. If we forgot to insert the braces around the two statements in the last example, the compiler would ignore the indentation and assume that only the first statement was part of the loop and the second statement follows the loop.

Some programmers advocate always inserting the curly braces, even for loops with bodies that are only one statement long. The argument is that inserting the braces around the loop body is a good practice to follow, and it makes things easier (and less likely to cause an error) if we have to insert more statements into the loop body later.

The INITIALIZATION, TESTING, and MODIFICATION sections of the for statement can, in Java, be more complex than the example we have given. However, it is good programming practice to limit them to initializing, testing, and incrementing a single simple control variable.

Another simple example would allow us to start the control value at a value typed in by the user and count it down toward zero. We are going to prompt the user for a string and then output the characters of the string one per line in reverse order. If we have a String, we can use the length method to find out how many characters there are, and we can extract the individual characters of the string with the charAt method (the characters are numbered from 0 to 1 less than the length of the string). Here is the code:

```
BasicIo.prompt("type a string") ;
String response = BasicIo.readString() ;

for (int i = response.length() - 1 ; i >= 0 ; i--)
    System.out.println(response.charAt(i)) ;
```

First we prompt the user and store in the variable response the string typed in. In the for loop, we initialize the control variable to a value 1 less than the length of the string; that is, response.length() - 1. We test for i being greater than or equal to 0. The MODIFICATION section i-- means "take the value of the variable i, reduce its value by 1, and restore it as the new value of i." Before you run the program, check how many iterations there will be with a string of length 7 (e.g., "welcome"). The loop will be executed for control variable values of 6, 5, 4, 3, 2, 1, and 0, so the loop is actually executed seven times, and this is what we want the program to do.

What would happen if the string had no characters? That is, what happens if the user immediately presses Return at the prompt? The variable i gets initialized to −1, so on the first iteration, the test i >= 0 fails immediately, and no iterations are performed. The program simply skips the loop and moves to the next statement.

5.3   Looping an Indeterminate Number of Times: The while Statement

We use the Java for statement when we want to repeat a loop a predetermined number of times. We use the Java while statement when we do not know before entering the loop how many iterations we are going to perform; on each iteration, we perform a test to decide whether or not to perform another iteration. The while statement takes the form:

```
while ( BOOLEAN EXPRESSION )
    LOOP BODY
```

The structure of the while statement is shown in Figure 5.3.

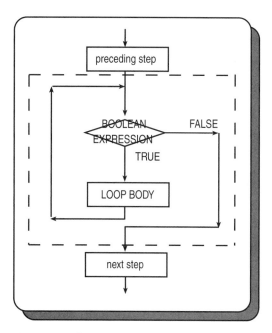

Figure 5.3: The structure of the while loop

We start by evaluating the BOOLEAN EXPRESSION. If it is true, we execute LOOP BODY for a first iteration and then reevaluate the BOOLEAN EXPRESSION for a second time. If it is still true, we execute LOOP BODY for a second iteration and then reevaluate BOOLEAN EXPRESSION for a third time. And so on. When the BOOLEAN EXPRESSION evaluates to false, no more iterations are performed, and control proceeds to the statement following the loop. Notice that there is no INITIALIZATION or MODIFICATION section as there was with the for statement. Any INITIALIZATION must be done before entering the while statement. Any MODIFICATION must be done as part of the LOOP BODY (presumably at the end).

A class `GroupOfPeople` (in the `javalancs` package) holds information about a group of individuals. For the present, our `GroupOfPeople` instance is going to hold a collection of people's surnames. When we set up an instance of this class, it contains no surnames, and we can always find out how many surnames are held with a `getCount` method (which returns an integer). We can add a surname with an `addSurname` method; this requires a single `String` argument, the new surname we wish to add to the collection.

We are going to write a program that allows the user to type a sequence of surnames, and we are going to store them in a `GroupOfPeople` instance that we have declared. How will the program know when there are no more surnames to be stored? We are going to instruct the user to press Return when there are no more surnames, so the program will recognize a zero-length surname as the end of the list. Since the program starts executing the loop without knowing how many iterations there are going to be, we use a `while` statement. Here is the code:

```
GroupOfPeople computing = new GroupOfPeople() ;

System.out.println("Type a surname, then press 'return'") ;
System.out.println("(press 'return' if no more surnames)") ;
String nextString = BasicIo.readString() ;
while (nextString.length() != 0)
    {
    computing.addSurname(nextString) ;
    System.out.println("inserted surname " + nextString) ;

    System.out.println("Type a surname, then press 'return'") ;
    System.out.println("(press 'return' if no more surnames)") ;
    nextString = BasicIo.readString() ;
    }
System.out.print("There are " + computing.getCount()) ;
System.out.println("people in the group") ;
```

We declare an object of type `GroupOfPeople` called `computing`. We prompt the user for the first surname and read it into a variable `nextString` with the method `readString`.

In the loop, we test for a string of length zero. If the string `nextString` that we have read in is of length zero, we terminate the loop immediately. If the string is not of zero length, it is a valid surname, so we insert it in the `computing` object with the method `addSurname` and we tell the user that we have done so. Now we need to prompt for the next surname, which is the remainder of this iteration. The body of a `while` must be a single statement; because we want a sequence of statements to be executed on each iteration, we put curly braces { ... } around the sequence in the usual way.

Suppose the user types in the surnames "Smith", "Jones", and "Williams". What happens is as follows:

- The computer prompts for the first surname, and the user types "Smith" into nextString.
- On the first iteration,
  - The string nextString is not of length zero, so we proceed with the body of the iteration.
  - The string "Smith" is inserted in computing, and the user is informed.
  - The computer prompts for the next surname, and the user types "Jones" into nextString.
- On the next iteration,
  - The string nextString is not of length zero, so we proceed with the body of the iteration.
  - The string "Jones" is inserted in computing, and the user is informed.
  - The computer prompts for the next surname, and the user types "Williams" into nextString.
- On the next iteration,
  - The string nextString is not of length zero, so we proceed with the body of the iteration.
  - The string "Williams" is inserted in computing, and the user is informed.
  - The computer prompts for the next surname, and the user presses Return (i.e., nextString is set to an empty string).
- On the next iteration,
  - The string nextString is of length zero, so the loop terminates.

As usual, if the first string we typed in was of length zero, then no iterations of the loop are performed.

We can now print the surnames we have stored. The getSurname method takes an integer argument, say i, and returns surname number i. The numbering system is the order in which the surnames were added starting at zero. Since we now know how many surnames there are (the getCount method tells us), we can use a for loop:

```
for (int i = 0 ; i < computing.getCount() ; i++)
   {
   System.out.print("The " + (i + 1) + "th surname is ") ;
   System.out.println(computing.getSurname(i));
   }
```

One flaw in this code is that the computer displays "1th" instead of "1st", "2th" instead of "2nd", and so on. Can you fix this?

5.4 Stopping in the Middle of an Iteration

If we return to the code we used to read in the surnames, you will have noticed that we read the next surname in at the end of this iteration. Furthermore, we had to write twice the statements to prompt the user and read in the surname—before the loop for the first surname and at the end of the loop body for all the rest. Many programmers try to avoid writing the same code more than once; in part, this may be laziness, but it is partly because, if we decide to change a piece of code, it is more difficult to get it right if there are several different places where it has to be changed.

How can we arrange to have the prompting and reading done at one place in the program? The problem is that the looping test has to come at the beginning of the loop. If we could put the test somewhere in the middle of the loop, we could write everything only once. We can do this with a version of the break statement; in Chapter 4, we used it to break out at the end of the individual cases of the switch statement, and here we use it to break out of the middle of a loop. Here's how:

```
GroupOfPeople computing = new GroupOfPeople() ;

while (true)
    {
    System.out.println("Type a surname, then press 'return'") ;
    System.out.println("(press 'return' when no more surnames)") ;
    String nextString = BasicIo.readString() ;

    if (nextString.length() == 0)
        break ;

    computing.addSurname(nextString) ;
    System.out.print("inserted surname " + nextString) ;
    }

System.out.print("There are " + computing.getCount()) ;
System.out.println(" people in the department") ;
```

The BOOLEAN EXPRESSION in this loop is true, which of course always evaluates to true; thus, in principle, we will go around the loop forever. Inside the loop, we prompt the user and read in the string nextString. Then we test the length of the string; if it is of length zero, we execute the break statement. This takes us out of the loop immediately, and the next statement executed is the first one after the loop. If the length of the string is not zero, we proceed to the statement following the if statement, insert the string nextString in the computing object, and inform the user. Then we start the next iteration.

Notice that we had to invert the test. The BOOLEAN EXPRESSION in the while in the original program tested for nonzero length; with the break statement here, we are testing for zero length.

The layout of this new looping structure is shown in Figure 5.4.

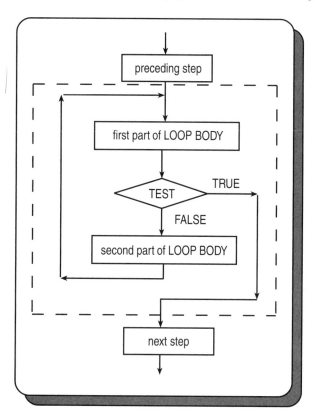

Figure 5.4: Breaking out of the middle of a loop

Suppose, as before, the user types in the surnames `"Smith"`, `"Jones"`, and `"Williams"`. What happens is as follows:

- On the first iteration,

    - The computer prompts for a surname, and the user types `"Smith"` into `nextString`.
    - The string `nextString` is not of length zero, so we proceed with the rest of this iteration.
    - The string `"Smith"` is inserted in `computing`, and the user is informed.

- On the next iteration,
  - The computer prompts for the next surname, and the user types `"Jones"` into `nextString`.
  - The string `nextString` is not of length zero, so we proceed with the rest of this iteration.
  - The string `"Jones"` is inserted in `computing`, and the user is informed.
- On the next iteration,
  - The computer prompts for the next surname, and the user types `"Williams"` into `nextString`.
  - The string `nextString` is not of length zero, so we proceed with the rest of this iteration.
  - The string `"Williams"` is inserted in `computing`, and the user is informed.
- On the next iteration,
  - The computer prompts for the next surname, and the user presses `Return` (i.e., `nextString` is set to an empty string).
  - The string `nextString` is of length zero, so the break is executed and the loop terminates.

As usual, if the first string we typed in was of length zero, then only the first half of the first iteration is performed.

5.5 for **Loops and** while **Loops**

It has probably not escaped your attention that we don't really need both the `for` and the `while` mechanisms. Suppose we have a `for` loop like this:

```
for (i = 0 ; i < n ; i++)
    LOOP BODY ;
```

Then we could have written this as a `while` loop:

```
i = 0 ;
while (i < n)
    {
    LOOP BODY ;
    i++ ;
    }
```

One advantage of the `for` loop is that it collects together all the parts of the loop. If the LOOP BODY in this `while` is lengthy, then the `i++` statement is a long way from the `i < n` test, and it may not be easy to see the structure of what is going on.

Similarly, if we have a `while` loop

```
while (s.length() != 0)
    LOOP BODY ;
```

then we could write this as a `for` loop

```
for ( ; s.length() != 0 ; )
    LOOP BODY ;
```

where the INITIALIZATION and MODIFICATION sections are empty (or we could insert something unrelated to the test, although this would be very poor programming style).

However, it makes your programs easier to follow if you use `for` and `while` in different programming situations. We recommend the following rules:

- If the number of times the loop is to be executed is known before entering the loop, then use a `for` loop. More generally, if the situation is such that you are processing your way through a complete set of data, set up before entering the loop, and expect to reach the end, then a `for` is appropriate. You will see examples of this more general situation in Chapter 17.

- If we do not know when we start the loop how many times we will execute it, use a `while` loop. More generally, if we are processing through a set of data but expect that we might stop before reaching the end of the data, then it is appropriate to use a `while`. For example, if we are searching a set of data for a particular value and find it, we will not look at the remainder of the data; thus, a `while` is appropriate.

5.6 Nested Loops

The body of a loop can contain any statement. Thus, it is possible for a loop to contain another loop (Figure 5.5). This is called a *nested* loop. For each iteration of the outer loop, there will be zero or more iterations of the inner loop.

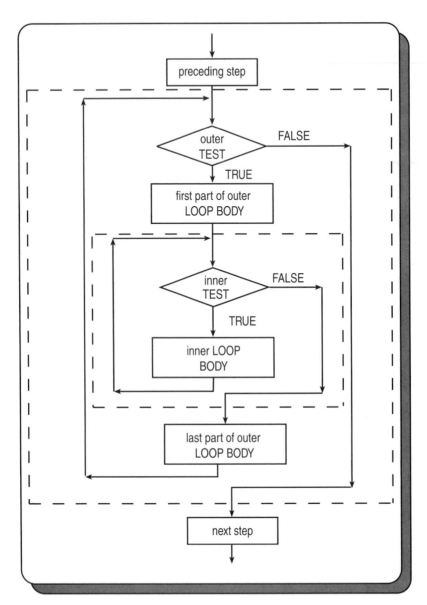

Figure 5.5: A nested loop

Suppose we are reading in surnames as before and want to store a surname only if we have not already stored it. We need to test each new surname against all the surnames that have already been read and stored, and this requires a nested loop. The program will have this structure:

```
set up the GroupOfPeople instance
    prompt the user
    get the next surname
    if the string length is zero, then leave outer loop
    start at beginning of list of surnames stored so far
        look for a match with each stored surname in turn
    if we found no match
        add the surname
    otherwise
        print an error message
output the number of surnames stored
```

Notice in this sketch of the solution, and in the Java code that follows, that we have indented the body of the inner loop within the indented body of the outer loop to clarify the structure of the program. Here is the code:

```java
GroupOfPeople computing = new GroupOfPeople() ;

while (true)
    {
    System.out.println("Type a surname followed by 'return'") ;
    System.out.println("(type 'return' when no more surnames)") ;
    String nextString = BasicIo.readString() ;

    if (nextString.length() == 0)
        break ;

    // explanation starts HERE
    int i = 0 ;
    while (i < computing.getCount())
        {
        if (nextString.equals(computing.getSurname(i)))
            break ;
        i++ ;
        }
    if (i == computing.getCount())
        {
        // search did not find a match
        computing.addSurname(nextString) ;
        System.out.print("inserted surname " +
                        nextString) ;
        }
    else
        {
        // search did find a match
```

```
        System.out.println("WARNING: surname " +
                            nextString + " duplicated") ;
        System.out.println("not added to the list") ;
        }
    // explanation finishes HERE
    }

System.out.print("There are " + computing.getCount()) ;
System.out.println(" people in the department") ;
```

Here's how the inner loop works. Remember that we are checking whether the surname the user has just typed is already stored in the computing object. We start at the comment explanation starts HERE:

- We declare an integer variable i and initialize it to zero. This is a control variable for the while statement that follows it. We have decided that it should be a while statement, because stopping before we looked at all the stored surnames is a distinct possibility.

- On each iteration of the inner loop, we test i against the number of surnames stored in computing. If it is the first iteration of the outer loop, there will be no surnames in the computing object, so the getCount method returns zero, and no iterations of the inner loop will be performed.

- If there is at least one surname in the computing object, this BOOLEAN EXPRESSION will succeed, and we will check the string nextString against the first surname held in the computing object, returned by computing.getSurname(i) with i set to zero. The String method equals tests its String argument against the String with which the method is associated (here nextString) and returns true if they are equal (i.e., the same length, with the same characters) and false otherwise.

- If the strings match, we execute the break statement. This always breaks out of the innermost loop that contains it. So we break out of the surname-matching loop, but not the outer loop that reads in a surname on each iteration. The break in fact sends us to the if statement immediately after the inner loop.

- If the strings did not match, the variable i is incremented, and we prepare to start the next iteration of the inner loop.

- If there are at least two surnames stored, we will enter the second iteration of the inner loop and test the string nextString against the next surname stored (the one associated with the value 1 for the argument to the getSurname method). And so on.

- Eventually, we will leave the inner loop either because we have run out of surnames to look at (so we didn't find a match) or because we have broken out of the loop early (because we did find a match). We need to distinguish between these two cases, and this is what the if statement does.

If we broke out of the inner loop early, the control variable i will be set to the value at which nextString matched a surname in computing. We know that there are computing.getCount() surnames in this object, and they are therefore numbered from 0 up to computing.getCount() − 1. So in this case, i will have a value in the range 0 to computing.getCount() − 1.

If we did not break out of the inner loop, we must have looked at the final surname, and this would have had the number computing.getCount() − 1. Since the equals method returned true, we did not break out of the loop. Instead, we incremented the control variable i and prepared to start the next iteration of the loop with i set to computing.getCount(). The BOOLEAN EXPRESSION of the inner loop would have evaluated to false, so we would not have started a further iteration. Hence, we would have stopped with i holding the value computing.getCount().

Thus, if there were seven stored surnames, i would have had a value of 7 if no match had been found and a value in the range 0 to 6 if a match had been found.

The if statement checks the final value of the control variable i against the value returned by computing.getCount(). If they are equal, the search failed to find a match, and we can add the surname to the computing object and inform the user. Notice that we inserted comments to remind us which was which of the two branches of the if statement; it is easy to mix up the two branches.

If the BOOLEAN EXPRESSION in the if statement evaluates to false, we must have broken out of the loop early because we found a duplicate. We want to inform the user and not add the surname to the list. Note that the error message tells the user there was a duplicate, what the duplicated surname was, and what the program has done about it (i.e., the surname was ignored and not added to the list). It might be important in certain circumstances also to display the position at which we found the duplicate (i.e., the value of i), but we have not done so here.

To see exactly what is happening, we can add statements to output some information as we traverse the inner loop:

```
// explanation starts HERE
int i = 0 ;
System.out.println("TEST: starting inner loop: count="
                   + computing.getCount()) ;
while (i < computing.getCount())
    {
    System.out.print("TEST: start inner iteration: i="
                     + i) ;
    if (nextString.equals(computing.getSurname(i)))
        break ;
    i++ ;
    System.out.print("TEST: finish inner iteration: i="
                     + i) ;
    }
```

```
System.out.print("TEST: leaving inner loop: i=" + i) ;
if (i == computing.getCount())
    {
    // search did not find a match
    computing.addSurname(nextString) ;
    System.out.print("inserted surname " +
                    nextString) ;
    }
else
    {
    // search did find a match
    System.out.println("WARNING: surname " +
                    nextString + " duplicated") ;
    System.out.println("not added to the list") ;
    }
// explanation finishes HERE
```

Now try running the program with different sets of surnames, some with duplicates and some without. Make sure you are confident you can explain all the values that get printed by these test statements. In particular, convince yourself that the program works properly (a) on the first iteration, when there are no surnames to match against and (b) when a pair of duplicates occurs together so that we find the match on the last iteration of the inner loop.

5.7 Boolean Expressions for Loops

In the last example, we wrote the inner loop like this:

```
int i = 0 ;
while (i < computing.getCount())
    {
    if (nextString.equals(computing.getSurname(i)))
        break ;
    i++ ;
    }
if (i == computing.getCount())
    . . .
```

There are several different ways to write this loop. An alternative is:

```
int i = 0 ;
while ((i < computing.getCount()) &&
        (!nextString.equals(computing.getSurname(i))))
    i++ ;
if (i == computing.getCount())
    . . .
```

Look carefully at the BOOLEAN EXPRESSION here. It says continue with another iteration if both of the following are true:

- The control variable i has not yet reached the end of the list of surnames (i.e., it is a valid argument for the getSurname method).

- The new surname nextString is not equal to the surname in the list at position i.

If both are true, we can go around the loop another time and increment the variable i with the statement i++. If either of the tests fails, we must terminate the loop. As before, the value of i tells us whether we found a match or not.

To see how this works, we insert some output statements as before and try some test data.

```
int i = 0 ;
System.out.println("TEST: starting inner loop: count=" +
                    computing.getCount()) ;
while ((i < computing.getCount()) &&
       (!nextString.equals(computing.getSurname(i))))
    {
    System.out.print("TEST: start inner iteration: i=" + i) ;
    i++ ;
    System.out.print("TEST: finish inner iteration: i=" + i) ;
    }
System.out.print("TEST: leaving inner loop: i=" + i) ;
if (i == computing.getCount())
    ...
```

Note that when we inserted the output statements in the loop, we had to insert curly braces { ... } around the loop body. We did not need these when the loop body was a single statement.

Notice that we have written the operator && instead of the normal AND operator &. There is a subtlety about this BOOLEAN EXPRESSION of which you need to be aware. In the purely logical meaning of the AND operation, we can evaluate both operands of the AND and then work out the value of the AND. Suppose we try that here, when we have reached the final iteration and i has reached the value computer.getCount(). The left operand of the AND operation has the value false. But what about the right operand, which contains the expression computing.getSurname(i)? This is not valid because there is no surname with this number. Perhaps the programmer who wrote the GroupOfPeople class has been kind enough to ensure that an invalid argument still causes a valid response. But in general, this cannot be relied on.

So we have replaced the & operator, with the && operator, which is sometimes called a *short-circuit* operator. If its first operand evaluates to false, then it knows that the result of the &&

operation must be false and does not evaluate the second operand. Thus, in fact, this expression is always valid; if the first expression decides that there is no surname, the second expression is not evaluated, and the correct result of false is returned.[1]

A third way of writing this loop avoids the break statement and has a clearer test after the loop. Here is the code:

```
int i = 0 ;
boolean duplicateFound = false ;
while ((i < computing.getCount()) && (!duplicateFound))
    {
    if (nextString.equals(computing.getSurname(i)))
        duplicateFound = true ;
    i++ ;
    }
if (!duplicateFound)
    . . .
```

We have declared a boolean variable to record whether we have found a duplicate, and before entering the loop, we have initialized it to false. The body of the loop sets the Boolean variable to true when it finds a match. The loop terminates because either (a) we have tried all the elements in the list or (b) the Boolean variable has been set to true on the previous iteration (because we found a match). The if statement following the loop can then test the Boolean variable to decide whether or not a duplicate was found. What value does i have if a duplicate is found?

5.8   Testing at the End of the Loop

We have looked at loops that test at the beginning of the iteration (the for statement and the while statement without a break) and loops that test in the middle of the iteration (the while statement with the break). Java provides another form of the repetition statement with the test at the end (so the loop is always executed at least once). It looks like this:

```
do
    LOOP BODY
while ( BOOLEAN EXPRESSION ) ;
```

and has the structure shown in Figure 5.6.

---

[1]Unlike Java, some programming languages (e.g., Pascal) do not have a short-circuit version of the AND operation, and this form of the loop would not be possible.

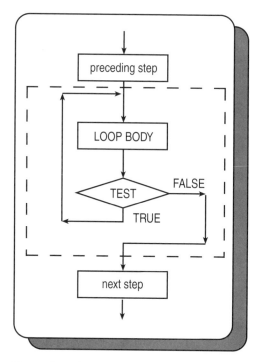

Figure 5.6: The structure of the do loop

The LOOP BODY is executed once, and the BOOLEAN EXPRESSION is then evaluated. If it is true, the iteration and test are repeated. If it evaluates to false, the loop terminates and the statement following the loop is executed. Of course, if the LOOP BODY is more than one statement long, we need to insert curly braces { . . . } as usual.

Suppose we have a program to work out the square of a number specified by the user. If we run the program, we presumably have at least one number for which we want the program to calculate a square, so we know we want to do the calculation at least once. But we might want to do it more than once. Thus, after calculating a square, we can ask the user if he or she wants another calculation.

In our loop, we will accept a number from the user and calculate its square. Then we will ask the user if he or she wants any further calculations; if so, we repeat the loop. We will always execute the loop at least once, and we test the user's response at the end of the loop to see if another iteration is in order. So the do . . . while statement is the one to use:

```
String response ;

do
    {
    BasicIo.prompt("type a number ") ;
    int n = BasicIo.readInteger() ;
    System.out.print("the value of " + n) ;
    System.out.println(" squared is " + (n * n)) ;

    BasicIo.prompt("calculate more numbers (y or n)? ") ;
    response = BasicIo.readString() ;
    }
while (response.charAt(0) == 'y') ;
```

The loop is repeated as long as the user types in a string whose first letter is `'y'`. A slightly better version would allow the user to type in a string starting `'y'` or `'Y'`, making use of the `String` method `toLowerCase` to convert the user response to lowercase before doing the test. There would still be problems if the user typed in a line containing no characters, but we can fix that as well:

```
String response ;

do
    {
    BasicIo.prompt("type a number ") ;
    int n = BasicIo.readInteger() ;
    System.out.print("the value of " + n) ;
    System.out.println(" squared is " (n * n)) ;
    BasicIo.prompt("calculate more numbers (y or n)? ") ;
    response = BasicIo.readString().toLowerCase() ;
    }
while ((response.length() > 0) && (response.charAt(0) == 'y')) ;
```

This form of loop, with the test at the end, is less common than the `for` and the `while` with a test at the beginning.

5.9   Other Java Loop Features

The break statement always terminates the current iteration immediately and then terminates the loop. There is also a `continue` statement, which also terminates the current iteration immediately but then proceeds to start the next iteration. A typical use for this might have a loop that resembles the following:

```
while (BOOLEAN EXPRESSION1)
    {
    STATEMENTS1 ;
    if (BOOLEAN EXPRESSION2)
        continue ;
    STATEMENTS2 ;
    }
```

This could have been written without the `continue` as follows:

```
While (BOOLEAN EXPRESSION1)
    {
    STATEMENTS1 ;
    if (!BOOLEAN EXPRESSION2)
        {
        STATEMENTS2 ;
        }
    }
```

The advantage of the version with `continue` is that it allows the STATEMENTS2 to be written with less indentation than the version without.

Finally, Java has an additional form of the `break` statement called the *labeled break*. The normal (unlabeled) form of `break` leaves the innermost loop—that is, the first looping statement that you encounter if you work back from the `break` statement. Sometimes you may want to break out of a number of nested loops. An example would look something like this:

```
loopLabel : while ...
    {
    ...
    while ...
        {
        ...
        if ( BOOLEAN EXPRESSION )
            break loopLabel ;
        ...
        }
    ...
    }
NEXT STATEMENT ;
```

If BOOLEAN EXPRESSION evaluates to true, the labeled `break` statement takes us out of both loops to the statement NEXT STATEMENT. That is, it goes to the first statement after the end of the loop labeled loopLabel.

5.10 Key Points in Chapter 5

- We often need to repeat a group of statements several times, and Java provides a number of *looping* statements to allow this. The main ones are the `for` statement and the `while` statement.

- We use the `for` statement when we know before we start how many times we are going to repeat the loop. It has the form:

```
for (INITIALIZATION ; TESTING ; MODIFICATION)
    LOOP BODY
```

A typical loop, to be executed n times with a control variable i set to 0, 1, 2, 3 . . . up to n − 1, would be:

```
for (int i = 0 ; i < n ; i++)
    LOOP BODY
```

- We use the `while` loop when we do not know beforehand how many iterations are going to be required. It has the form:

```
while (BOOLEAN EXPRESSION)
    LOOP BODY
```

Each iteration starts with a test of the BOOLEAN EXPRESSION. If it is true, it does one more iteration. If it is false, it does no more iterations but proceeds to the statement after the loop.

If the BOOLEAN EXPRESSION evaluates to false when the loop is entered for the first time, no iterations are performed.

- The `break` statement allows us to break out from inside a loop and proceed immediately to the statement after the loop. This allows us to have the loop test in the middle of the body of the loop.

- It is possible to "nest" one loop inside another.

- In a BOOLEAN EXPRESSION for a loop, it is often important to use the short-circuit operator && so that only the valid operands are evaluated.

- There is a version of the `while` loop with the test at the end. This has the form:

```
do
    LOOP BODY
while (BOOLEAN EXPRESSION) ;
```

5.11 Exercises

1. Rewrite this program from Section 5.2 earlier in this chapter

```
System.out.println("Table of Squares") ;
for (int i = 0 ; i < 10 ; i++)
    {
    System.out.print("the square of " + i) ;
    System.out.println(" is " + (i * i)) ;
    }
System.out.println("**end of table**") ;
```

so that it outputs the cube of each number from 0 to 9 as well as the square, making sure that it outputs suitable accompanying text.

Modify the program so that it deals with the numbers from 1 to 25 instead of 0 to 9.

2. Rewrite this part of the program from Section 5.3 earlier in this chapter

```
for (int i = 0 ; i < computing.getCount() ; i++)
    {
    System.out.print("The " + (i + 1) + "th surname is ") ;
    System.out.println(computing.getSurname(i))
    }
```

so that it outputs the correct letters after each number (1st, 2nd, 3rd, 4th, etc.)

3. Use the Card class to implement a simple card game between the computer and the user. The computer chooses five cards for the user. If their total value comes to 21 or less, the user has won; if their total value comes to more than 21, the computer has won. The value of a Jack is 11, of a Queen 12, and of a King 13.

The program should choose each card in turn, reveal to the user what it is, and inform the user of the total value of the cards chosen so far.

Modify the program so that, after each card has been chosen, the user can specify whether to draw the next card or whether to "stick" with the cards chosen.

Note ▪

The Card constructor with no arguments, which chooses a card at random, is arranged so that it never chooses the same card twice. When we want the random drawing of cards from the deck to start again (i.e., we are allowed to pick a card that we have picked before), we call the restart method.

4. Write programs that use a for statement and the BasicGraphics class to draw:

a. A sequence of 10 red squares, each 20 units wider and higher than the previous one, but all with the same top left corner.

    b. A sequence of 10 green squares, all the same size and with successive top left corners 20 units further along the *x*- and *y*-axes.

    c. A sequence of 10 blue circles, all with their centers at the same place but with the diameter decreasing successively by 20 units.

5. Modify your answer to Exercise 4.7 so that the user can specify a number of different shapes to be drawn. When the user has finished specifying a shape, the program should ask if the user wants to specify another shape. If so, it should prompt the user for details of the next shape. Finally, the program should display all the shapes specified.

6. Modify your answer to Exercise 5.5 so that the information is read in from a file in the filing system. The file should be created using an editor and might look like this:

```
square
200
200
60
red
circle
300
350
40
yellow
EndOfFile
```

The program should terminate when it reads a shape EndOfFile from the file.

Note ■

For this, you need the BasicFileIo class (in the javalancs package). To read from a file called shapes.data, you call the constructor BasicFileIo with two arguments: (a) the constant BasicFileIo.INPUT and (b) the name of the file. For example:

```
BasicFileIo fileIn = new BasicFileIo(BasicFileIo.INPUT,
                                     "shapes.data") ;
```

Then you can read a complete line from the file as a string

```
String s = fileIn.readString() ;
```

or you can read a complete line from the file as an integer

```
int n = fileIn.readInteger() ;
```

A set of methods for reading from a file is provided similar to the read methods in the BasicIo class. When you have finished reading from the file, you should close it with:

```
fileIn.closeFile() ;
```

7. Use the facilities of the BasicGraphics class to draw two octaves of a piano keyboard (Figure 5.7).

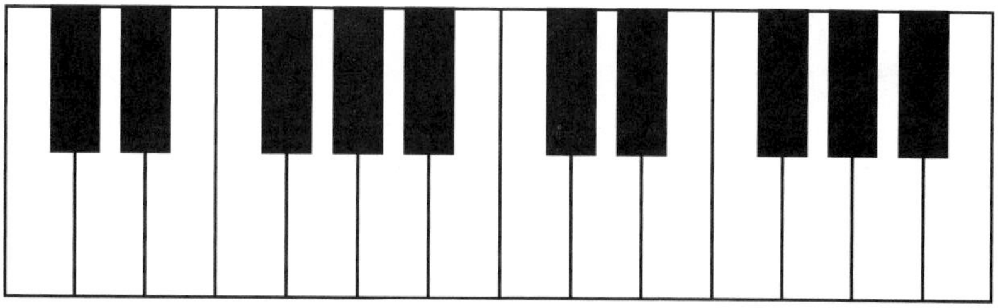

Figure 5.7: A piano keyboard

Try to use looping and selection statements as much as possible in this program.

CHAPTER 6

Basic Java Data Types

6.1 Objects and Basic Data Types

In some object-oriented languages, all the data elements of a program are objects; that is, all the variables in a program refer to objects of one type or another. In Java, many elements are objects, but for efficiency, there are a few types of elements that are not, and these form the basic blocks out of which we can build objects. You have already met the int and boolean types in Chapters 4 and 5. In this chapter, we review these and Java's other six basic data types, and we recap the differences between variables of these types and variables that refer to objects. In this chapter, we also discuss the String type, which in fact is a class of object.

There are a number of differences between the way we handle objects in Java and the way we handle these basic data types.

6.1.1 Declaration

We declare a variable that refers to an object with a statement such as:

```
Person person1 = new Person("John", "Smith", 55,
                            Person.MALE) ;
```

This creates a variable—a location or pigeonhole in the computer—called person1 that is capable of holding a *reference* to an instance of the class Person. In this case, it actually refers to an instance of a Person object whose attributes have been initialized to suitable values by the constructor method Person(...). The result is shown in Figure 6.1.

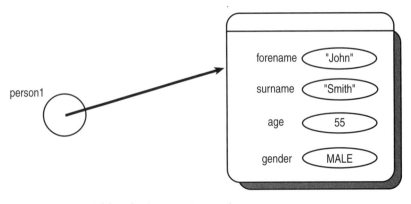

Figure 6.1: A variable referring to a Person instance

If we do not invoke a constructor method, we should set the value of the variable `person1` to the special value `null`

```
Person person2 = null ;
```

to indicate that the variable does not at present refer to a specific instance (Figure 6.2).

person 2

Figure 6.2: A `Person` variable initialized to `null`

Later, we could set up an instance and have the variable `person2` refer to it:

```
person2 = new Person("Jane", "Black", 35, Person.FEMALE) ;
```

Notice that there is no `Person` at the beginning of this line. We are not declaring a variable `person2` because it already exists; we are simply making it point to a new object (Figure 6.3).

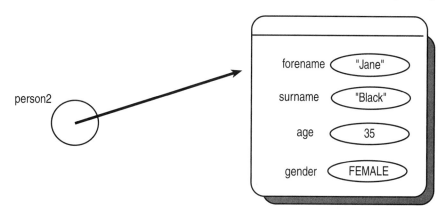

Figure 6.3: The `person2` variable now referring to a `Person` instance

We declare a variable of one of the basic types with a statement such as:

```
int countOfMembers = 4 ;
```

This creates a variable—a location or pigeonhole in the computer—called `countOfMembers`, which is capable of holding an integer *value*. In this case, we have initialized the variable to hold the value 4 (Figure 6.4).

countOfMembers

4

Figure 6.4: An initialized `int` variable

We could have left the variable uninitialized, in which case the variable would contain an unknown value. It is usually best to initialize each variable to a suitable value when declaring it.

6.1.2   Setting a Value

We set a value for one of the attributes of an object by invoking a suitable method associated with the object. This will be a *mutator* method, often with a name starting with `set`. For example:

```
person1.setSurname("Jones") ;
```

This method changes the value of the surname attribute of the `person1` object to the string `"Jones"`. Whatever previous value this attribute had (whether initialized by a constructor method or changed by an earlier call of a mutator method) will be overwritten and lost. The result is shown in Figure 6.5.

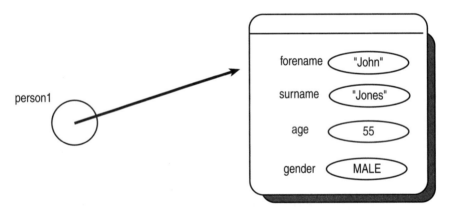

Figure 6.5: A new value for the surname attribute

In this case, no other attributes of the `person1` object have been changed. But in principle, a method could be written that changes some other attribute or attributes as a side effect of its task. For example, if there was another attribute recording the number of characters in the surname (perhaps so that it can be displayed neatly), this attribute would also be changed by the `setSurname` method. We have also seen the `setFullName` method, which explicitly sets two attribute values.

The value of a basic data type is changed by the *assignment* statement. This has the form:

```
nameOfBasicVariable = EXPRESSION ;
```

The EXPRESSION is evaluated, and the result becomes the value of the variable named to the left of the = sign. The previous value of the variable is lost. Thus, suppose we had declared `firstValue` and `secondValue` as integer variables and set them to initial values specified by the user:

```
BasicIo.prompt("type the first value ") ;
int firstValue = BasicIo.readInteger() ;
BasicIo.prompt("type the second value ") ;
int secondValue = BasicIo.readInteger() ;
```

The result of the execution of these statements might be as shown in Figure 6.6.

Figure 6.6: Two `int` variables initialized

We could set the value of `secondValue` to be twice the value of `firstValue` with:

```
secondValue = 2 * firstValue ;
```

The symbol * is the multiplication operator. The multiplication operator cannot be omitted as it can in many mathematical formulas (e.g., where $2\pi r$ means "2 times π times r"); it must always be written explicitly in Java.

After execution of this assignment statement, the value of `secondValue` will be set to twice the value of `firstValue` and lose its original value (Figure 6.7). The value of `firstValue` is unchanged.

Figure 6.7: The result of an assignment to `secondValue`

Note that the assignment symbol is the character =, which we distinguish from the equality relational operator, which is the symbol == in Java. Some people are confused by statements such as:

```
x = x + 1 ;
```

This does not assert that the value of x is equal to a value 1 larger than itself. It is an assignment statement that specifies that 1 should be added to the value in x. As you have already seen, we could instead write this:

```
x++ ;
```

Note that we wrote the assignment statement:

```
secondValue = 2 * firstValue ;
```

There is no int at the beginning of the statement. In this case, we are not declaring a new variable because the variable secondValue already exists; we are simply assigning it a new value.

6.1.3 Obtaining a Value

We extract the value of one of the attributes of an object by calling a suitable method associated with the object. This will be a *selector* method, often with a name starting with get. For example,

```
person1.getAge()
```

extracts the age attribute of the object instance person1, an integer. Since this method call returns a value, the call is not a statement but an expression and must appear in a position where an expression is appropriate. It could appear as the argument of a suitable method call (e.g., System.out.println) because this is a position where an expression is valid:

```
System.out.println(person1.getAge()) ;
```

Another place an expression is valid is the right side of an assignment statement. Thus, if the variable thisAge has not yet been declared, we could write:

```
int thisAge = person1.getAge() ;
```

The variable thisAge now contains the value of the age attribute of the person1 object ready for further manipulation. Or we could write

```
thisAge = person1.getAge() - 4 ;
```

which sets the (preexisting) variable thisAge to a value 4 less than the age attribute of person1.

We access the value of a variable of a basic type by simply quoting the variable name. Thus, in the statement,

```
secondValue = 2 * firstValue ;
```

we extracted the value of the integer variable firstValue by quoting the variable name (and then multiplied the value by 2 before storing it as the value of the variable secondValue).

6.1.4 *Arguments to Methods*

Each of the arguments of a method can be an expression. Thus, it can be:

- A constant value or *literal* such as 44 or "Smith":

```
person1.setSurname("Smith") ;
person1.setAge(44) ;
person1.setGender(Person.FEMALE) ;
```

- The name of a variable of a suitable basic type or String, in which case the value of the variable is passed to the method:

```
BasicIo.prompt("type in a string ")
String surname = BasicIo.readString() ;
int ageValue = 27 ;
int female = Person.FEMALE ;

person1.setSurname(surname) ;
person1.setAge(ageValue) ;
person1.setGender(female) ;
```

Notice that, because we are passing the *value* of the variable to the method, there is no way that the method can get at the variable and change its value.

- A method that returns a value of a suitable type:

```
person1.setSurname(person2.getSurname()) ;
person1.setAge(person2.getAge()) ;
person1.setGender(person2.getGender)) ;
```

- Any suitable combination of the foregoing:

```
person1.setSurname(person2.getSurname() + "son") ;
person1.setAge((person2.getAge() + person3.getAge())/2) ;
```

Here the first line sets the surname of person1 to that of person2 with "son" added on the end. The second line sets the age of person1 to the average of the ages of person2 and person3.

6.2 The int Data Type

A variable of the int data type can hold an integer, a whole number without fractions or decimal places, in the range $-2,147,483,648$ to $+2,147,483,647$.

In many programming languages, different versions of the language on different computers (or even on the same computer) have different definitions of the range of the basic integer type, although the better languages have mechanisms that allow the program to find out what the range is and take action accordingly. But a result of Java's insistence on platform independence is that each of the various numerical types has a fixed range on all platforms. Thus, we can assume that an int can hold the aforementioned range of values whatever machine our program runs on.

The usual arithmetic operations of addition (+), subtraction (–), multiplication (*), and division (/) are available between integers. As we have mentioned, the multiplication operator * must not be omitted, as is sometimes done in mathematics, but must be written explicitly. Some examples are:

```
int x1 = 4, x2 = 6, x3 = 7, x4 = 9 ;
int result = x1 + x2 ;          // result has the value 10
result = x2 - x3 ;              // result now has the value -1
result = x3 * x4 ;              // result now has the value 63
```

The division operation between integers is called *integer division*; any fractional part is thrown away. There is an *integer remainder* or *modulus* operation (%), which returns the fractional part that the integer divide throws away. This is illustrated by the code:

```
int x5 = 21, x6 = 4 ;
result = x5 / x6 ;              // result now has the value 5
result = x5 % x6 ;              // result now has the value 1
x5 = -21 ;
x6 = 4 ;
result = x5 / x6 ;              // result now has the value -5
result = x5 % x6 ;              // result now has the value -1
```

Investigate what happens if x6 is negative or both x5 and x6 are negative.

A very common operation is to add 1 to, or subtract 1 from, a variable. Instead of writing

```
counter = counter + 1 ;
```

you can use a special Java notation: the incrementation operator ++. If the integer variable counter contains the value 5, after the statement

```
counter++ ;
```

it will contain the value 6.

Similarly, there is a decrementation operator ––, which reduces the value of the variable by 1:

```
counter-- ;
```

Another fairly common operation for which Java provides special notation is to add a constant (other than 1) to the value of a variable. For example, instead of writing

```
taxablePay = taxablePay + 125 ;
```

in Java, we can write the more concise form:

```
taxablePay += 125 ;
```

Similarly, instead of

```
x1 = x1 - 3 ;
x2 = x2 * 4 ;
x3 = x3 / 5 ;
x4 = x4 % 6 ;
```

we can write, respectively:

```
x1 -= 3 ;
x2 *= 4 ;
x3 /= 5 ;
x4 %= 6 ;
```

The += operator is probably the most useful of these four.

Our GroupOfPeople class allows us to store the age for each member as well as a surname. We could work out the average age with the following code:

```
int num = computing.getCount() ;
int sum = 0 ;
for (int i = 0 ; i < num ; i++)
    sum += computing.getAge(i) ;
System.out.println("The average age is " + (sum / num)) ;
```

We declare and initialize two integer variables, num for the total number of individuals in this group and sum to total up all the ages. Note that it is very important to initialize sum to zero; we cannot assume that the programming language will do it for us. We then add successive ages to sum using a for loop and the += operator. Finally, we calculate the average by dividing sum by num. Since the argument to a method can be an expression, we give the expression sum / num as the argument to println. Because the operands are integers, this is *integer* division; we will have a result truncated to the next lower integer.

Consider now a piece of code to calculate the area of a field whose dimensions are supplied by the user:

```
BasicIo.prompt("type the field length in feet: ") ;
int length = BasicIo.readInteger() ;
BasicIo("type the field breadth in feet: ") ;
int breadth = BasicIo.readInteger() ;
System.out.print("the area of field " + length +
                " feet by ") ;
System.out.print(breadth + " feet is ") ;
System.out.print(2 * length + breadth) ;
System.out.println(" feet") ;
```

Before you run this program, what should the results be for a length of 4 feet and a breadth of 5 feet? What do you get when you run the program with these values? Why are they different?

The reason for the error is *precedence*, which decides the order in which the operations in an expression are carried out. The basic rule in Java is the same as that in most other programming languages and in mathematics. First, all multiplications and divisions are carried out from left to right, and then all additions and subtractions are carried out, again from left to right. So in this case, the multiplication 2 * length is carried out first and then breadth is added to this result. If we want to change the order in which operations are carried out, we must insert parentheses. Thus, the erroneous line should be rewritten:

```
System.out.print(2 * (length + breadth)) ;
```

The relational operators (==, !=, <=, <, etc.) and Boolean operators (!, &, |, &&, and ||) were introduced in Chapter 4. In this section, we have mentioned a number of arithmetic operators (+, −, *, /, %, ++, −−, +=, −=, *=, /=, and %=). The precedence for all these operators is given in Table 6.1 (Java has a number of other operators that we have omitted from this table).

Precedence	Operators
Level 1	++ --
Level 2	unary + unary − !
Level 3	* / %
Level 4	+ −
Level 5	< <= > >=
Level 6	== !=
Level 7	&
Level 8	|
Level 9	&&
Level 10	||
Level 11	= += −= *= /= %=

Table 6.1: A (Partial) List of Java Operators
and Their Precedence Level

In an expression containing no parentheses, operators at a lower numbered level are performed before operators at a high-numbered level. Operators at the same level are performed from left to right through the expression, except for operators at levels 2 and 11, which are performed from right to left through the expression. If an expression contains parentheses, these rules are applied to the contents of each pair of parentheses in turn, starting with the innermost set of parentheses.

Unary + and unary − are the operators appearing in +4 and −x, to be contrasted with the binary versions of these operators in x + 4 and 5 − x. Thus, the expression − 4 − − 5 means (− 4) − (− 5).

Here are some of the consequences of these rules:

- `2 * length + breadth` means `( 2 * length ) + breadth`

- `a * b / c * d` means `(((a * b) / c ) * d)` rather than `(a * b) / (c * d)`, which is what one might expect from the mathematical convention

- `a + 2 > b` means `( a + 2 ) > b`

- `a > b && a < c` means `( a > b ) && ( a < c )`

- `a < b < c` means `( a < b ) < c`; the expression in parentheses evaluates to a Boolean, so this is an invalid expression—we would have to write `(a < b) && (b < c)`

It is difficult to remember the full precedence ordering of a language's operators (and in fact the full precedence table in Java contains more than 40 operators), especially as another language's ordering will not be exactly the same. It is always possible to insert parentheses even if the precedence ordering does not strictly require them. You should always insert sufficient parentheses to make it clear to yourself and the average reader what the order of the operations will be.

6.3 Other Whole Number Data Types in Java (Optional)

The Java `int` data type occupies four 8-bit bytes of storage to hold a value. Java provides three other basic data types which, like `int`, hold whole numbers but occupy different amounts of storage and therefore have different ranges of values. They are listed in Table 6.2.

Data Type	Storage	Range of Values
int	4 bytes	−2,147,483,648 to +2,147,483,647
byte	1 byte	−128 to +127
short	2 bytes	−32,768 to +32,767
long	8 bytes	−9,223,372,036,854,775,808 to +9,223,372,036,854,775,807

Table 6.2: Whole Number Data Types in Java

The `long` data type is provided for situations where the range of the `int` data type is too small. The `byte` and `short` data types are provided for situations where we need to save space in storing large numbers of integer values, each with a smaller range than `int`. In this book, we use only the `int` data type for values that are whole numbers.

As we noted in Chapter 4, Java is generally what is called a *strongly typed* language; that is, it is very careful not to allow the programmer inadvertently to mix values of one type with values of another type. For example, Java will not allow you to store a `boolean` value in an `int` variable. It would be possible for Java to apply these strong typing rules to the various whole number data types. For example, it could refuse to add together a short and a long value. In some other programming languages, a programmer has to specify explicitly that some sort of conversion of the short value to a long value is to take place before such an addition is allowed. But this would make it rather difficult to work with the different whole number data types, so Java relaxes the rules in this area. Java always allows a value with a smaller potential range to be stored in a variable with a larger range. Thus, the following assignments are valid:

```
byte byteValue = 12 ;
short shortValue = byteValue ;
int intValue = shortValue ;
long longValue = intValue ;
```

In each case, we are taking a value from a variable with a smaller potential range and storing it in a variable with a larger potential range, and this is guaranteed not to cause a problem. For example, in the second line, we are taking a value that must be in the range −128 to +127 and storing it in a variable capable of holding a value in the range −32,768 to +32,767.

Similarly, in an expression that involves variables of different whole number types, values of a type with a limited range are, where necessary, "promoted" to have the larger range. So, for example, in adding a short and a long value, the short value is automatically converted to a long value before the addition:

```
longValue = shortValue + longValue ;
```

But suppose we want to store a value with a larger potential range in a variable with a smaller range—for example, a value of type short in a variable of type byte:

```
byteValue = shortValue ;
```

There could be a problem with this statement if the actual value to be stored is outside the range of the variable in which it is to be stored. Hence, the compiler would reject this statement as it stands and require the programmer to indicate that a statement of this type is not an error but an intended part of the program. We do this by specifying explicitly that a type conversion is required to convert a value with a larger potential range to one with a smaller range. This is done with a *cast*; we specify the required type in parentheses before the value or expression:

```
byteValue = (byte) shortValue ;
```

The cast here says "the expression on the right potentially gives a value in the short range (−32,768 to +32,767), and we want to store the value in a variable which is of type byte and can therefore accept only a value in the range −128 to +127; but this is all right because we are expecting the actual value of the expression to lie within the smaller range." The compiler will arrange for the value to be suitably converted from one type to the other.

Using casts (because we are storing values with a wider range in variables with a narrower range), all the following statements are possible:

```
long longValue = 12L ;
int intValue = (int) longValue ;
short shortValue = (short) intValue ;
byte byteValue = (byte) shortValue ;
```

Note that we can specify a `long` integer literal value with the letter L as a suffix.

6.4 Floating-Point Data Types

The `int` data type always holds whole numbers. If we want to hold numbers with a fractional part, such as 3.7 and −123.45, there is a separate basic data type called `float`. The name comes from the term floating-point, which refers to the format in which such numbers are held. A floating-point number is stored in such a way as to preserve as much precision (i.e., as many significant decimal places) as possible.[1]

A value in the Java `float` data type occupies 4 bytes and holds about seven significant decimal digits. Because seven significant decimal places are often insufficient for a typical calculation, Java provides another floating-point type called `double`. A value in this format occupies 8 bytes and holds about fifteen significant decimal digits. We will use `double` for all floating-point calculations in this book. The type `float` is available if we need to save space in storing large numbers of floating-point values and are prepared to lose some precision.

We can specify a floating point value in either of two ways:

- For small values, in the normal way—for example, 3.7, −123.45.

- In *scientific notation,* where a power of 10 can be specified. In Java, the power of 10 is written after the letter e. Thus, the value 123.456e3 represents 123.456 times "10 to the power 3," or 123456.0, and 123.456e−3 represents 123.456 times "10 to the power −3," or 0.123456.

A literal value in either of these two formats is assumed to be a `double` value, with the appropriate amount of precision, unless it has the letter f or F following it, which specifies that it is a `float` value and is therefore stored to lower precision. Thus, 1.2 is a `double` value, and 1.2f or 1.2F is a `float` value. So we can write:

```
double doubleValue = 1.2 ;
doubleValue = 2.4f ;              // promoted to larger precision
float floatValue = 3.6f ;
floatValue = (float) 4.8 ;        // cast to smaller precision
```

In the first line, we are storing a `double` value in a `double` variable, and in the third line, we are storing a `float` value in a `float` variable, so these statements present no problems. In the second line, we are storing a `float` value with a low precision (a smaller number of signif-

---

[1]For more details about the floating-point representation, see, for example, Arthur B. MacCabe, *Computer Systems: Architecture, Organization, and Programming* (Chicago: Irwin, 1993), Chapter 8.

icant digits) in a `double` variable with higher precision (a larger number of significant digits), so Java allows us to do this.

In the final line, we are storing a value with a larger number of significant digits (since we do not specify the type after the value, it is a `double` value) in a variable capable of holding only a smaller number of significant digits. Java requires programmers to indicate with a cast that they intend the possible loss of precision.

For the floating-point data types, all the arithmetic operators are provided: addition (+), subtraction (-), multiplication (*), and division (/). Division between floating-point values is the normal one. Thus, the expression `21.0 / 4.0` applies the division operator to two floating-point (actually `double`) values, and the result is 5.25. Here is a simple example of a floating-point calculation:

```
BasicIo.prompt("type the radius: ") ;
double radius = BasicIo.readDouble() ;
double circumference = 2 * Math.PI * radius ;
System.out.print("a circle of radius " + radius) ;
System.out.println(" has circumference " + circumference) ;
```

There is a double constant `PI` (representing 3.14159 . . .) provided in the `Math` class in the `java.lang` package (there is also the constant `E` for 2.71828 . . .). Hence, we can refer to it with `Math.PI`; we do not need an import statement for this package.

There is no exponentiation operator in Java, but there is a method `pow` in the `Math` class. The expression `Math.pow(5.0, 3.0)` represents the first argument (5.0) raised to the power of the second argument (3.0), giving 125.0. The `Math` class contains methods for a number of other useful functions, such as logarithms and the trigonometric functions.

The integer and floating-point data types are different types, but the strong typing rules of Java are again relaxed here. We can store an integer value in a floating-point variable

```
int intValue = 3 ;
double doubleValue = intValue ;  // stores 3.0
```

and we can mix integer and floating-point values and variables in an expression:

```
BasicIo.prompt("type the radius ") ;
int radius = BasicIo.readInteger() ;
double circumference = 2 * Math.PI * radius ;
System.out.print("a circle of radius " + radius) ;
System.out.println(" has circumference " + circumference) ;
```

Storing a floating-point value in an integer variable is potentially dangerous because some precision may be lost. Java therefore requires the programmer's intentions to be marked explicitly with a cast:

```
doubleValue = 1.9 ;
intValue = (int) doubleValue ;   // stores 1
```

The fractional part of the floating-point number (if any) will be ignored; that is, the floating-point value will be *truncated* to an integer (1) before storing it in the integer variable. Of course, the value stored in the variable doubleValue is not changed.

There is a method round (in the Math class) to convert a double value to an integer value by rounding:

```
intValue = (int) Math.round(doubleValue) ; // stores 2
```

The version of round that takes a double argument actually returns a long value, so we have to cast it to an int.

6.5   The boolean Data Type

You first met the boolean data type in Chapter 4. A variable of this type can hold only one of two values: true and false. In some languages (including C and C++), numerical values can be treated as Boolean values—for example, zero representing false and any nonzero value representing true. This is not possible in Java.

We can assign a value to a boolean variable with an assignment statement, but the expression on the right side of the = sign must be a Boolean expression:

```
boolean found = true ;
boolean variableInRange = (intValue > 20) && (intValue < 40) ;
```

Notice the second assignment. If the value of the (integer) variable intValue lies in the range 21 to 39, the Boolean expression evaluates to true, and this value is assigned to variableInRange. If the value of intValue is 20 or less or 40 or more, the value false is assigned to variableInRange. It is not necessary to use an if statement to set the variable to true or false in cases such as this.

Variables of type boolean can be used as the BOOLEAN EXPRESSION in an if or while statement. For example, we could write:

```
if (variableInRange)
    . . .
```

Notice how the test works. If the value of variableInRange is true, the first (or only) branch of the if statement will be executed. If the value is false, the else branch (if any) is executed. It is unnecessary to write

```
if (variableInRange == true)
    . . .
```

Similarly, to carry out a sequence of statements if a boolean variable is false (e.g., if, in this case, the variable is out of the range), we can use the NOT operator (!) and write:

```
if (!variableInRange)
    . . .
```

6.6   The `char` Data Type

A variable of type `char` holds a single character. There is not much we can do with a single character other than set it to a value or test its value. We are usually more concerned with strings of one or more characters, discussed in the next section.

There are a large number of different character sets in use on different computers. Probably the best known is the ASCII (American Standard Code for Information Interchange) character set, and you may already be familiar with this because it is used on many PCs. Java uses an international standard called the *Unicode* character set. A Unicode character occupies 2 bytes of storage, so there is room for up to 65,536 different characters, sufficient to cover a large number of different scripts from around the world.

Although Java uses Unicode internally, a Java program is able to manipulate ASCII characters because the input and output methods can translate between ASCII and Unicode where necessary. Thus, an input method such as `readString` can read ASCII characters from the keyboard or a file and turn them immediately into Unicode for internal processing. An output method such as `print` can take the internal Unicode characters and output them as ASCII characters to the screen or to a file.

Unicode character literal values in a Java program are written between single quotation marks:

```
char charValue = 'b' ;

if ((thisCharacter == 'a') || (thisCharacter == 'A'))
   . . .

while (nextCharacter != '.')
   . . .
```

There are some special characters that cannot be represented in this way. Instead, they are represented by an *escape sequence*—that is, the *escape character* \ followed by a letter to denote the particular special character. The most useful are listed in Table 6.3.

Special Character	Meaning
\t	tab
\n	newline character
\'	single quote character
\"	double quote character
\\	backslash (i.e., the character \ itself)

Table 6.3: Special Escape Sequences in Java

Thus, we could check to see if a character is a space or a tab character with:

```
if ((thisCharacter == ' ') || (thisCharacter == '\t'))
   . . .
```

It is also possible to specify a character by quoting its number within the Unicode character set. The numbering system runs from 0 to 65535, but it must be specified in hexadecimal following the prefix \u, so it runs from \u0000 to \uFFFF. The printable ASCII characters occupy the beginning of this numbering sequence from \u0020 to \u007E and are listed in Appendix C. For example, because the Unicode character E is allocated the (decimal) number 69, we could specify this character in either of two ways:

```
char thisCharacter = 'E' ;
```

or

```
char thisCharacter = '\u0045' ; \\ decimal 69 or 'E'
```

In this book, we do not really need to consider the differences between Unicode and ASCII, and the printable ASCII subset of Unicode is all we will use. We will specify character literals by writing the character itself in single quotes or by using one of the escape sequences listed in Table 6.3.

6.7 The String Class

The String data type is not a basic data type. It is in fact a *class* like Person. However, the String class is fundamental to the Java language, and it has a number of features that we do not find in other classes, so we discuss it in this chapter. Remember the spelling is String, not string.

A String is a sequence of zero or more characters from the Unicode character set. We can declare a string variable s1:

```
String s1 = "Tweedle" ;
```

You can see from this example that, although a String is an object, it is initialized by specifying a literal constant rather than by calling a constructor method with new. A String literal is written between double quote marks. Figure 6.8 shows the result of this declaration.

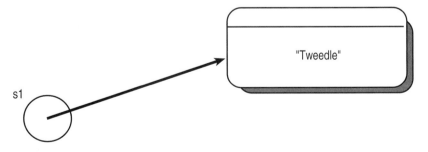

Figure 6.8: Declaration of a String variable

We can declare some more `String` variables:

```
String s2 = "dum" ;
String s3 = s1 + s2 ; // i.e. "Tweedledum"
String s4 = s1 + ' ' + s2 ; // i.e. "Tweedle dum"
String s5 = "He said \"Go Home\"." ;
String s6 = "First Line\nSecond Line" ;
```

The declarations of variables s3 and s4 shows the use of the concatenation operator + to join strings or strings and characters together. If you want a space to separate the two strings you are joining, you must explicitly insert one.

The double quote mark indicates the end of a string. To have a double quote mark in the string, you must write it as an escape sequence, as illustrated by the declaration of variable s5. To set up a string that will print on two lines, you can write a newline character as an escape sequence, as illustrated by the declaration of s6.

```
String s7 = "   " ;              // three spaces
String s8 = "" ;                 // the empty String
String s9 ;                      // no String at all
```

Finally, notice the difference between the strings referred to by the variables s7, s8, and s9; the results are shown in Figure 6.9. Variable s7 refers to a string of a certain number of spaces (in this case, three). Variable s8 refers to an empty string, a string that is zero characters long. But variable s9 does not refer to a string at all at present; we should really have written:

```
String s9 = null ;               // no String at all
```

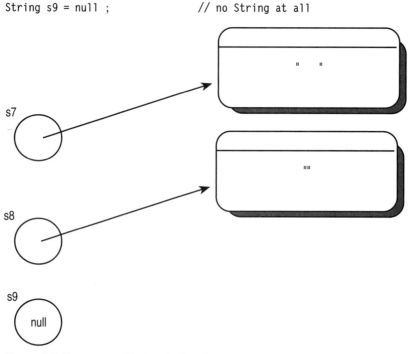

Figure 6.9: Some more `String` declarations

We can find out how long a string is by using the method length( ). Do not forget the parentheses (you will see in Chapter 9 that arrays use a reserved word length without parentheses, but here we are referring to a method, so we do need the parentheses). Thus, s1.length( ) is 7, s2.length( ) is 3, and s3.length( ) is 10. Similarly, s7.length( ) is 3 and s8.length( ) is zero. But s9.length( ) is invalid because s9 does not at present refer to an object; a call of this method would cause a NullPointerException.

We could use an assignment statement to change the String that one of these variables refers to:

```
s2 = "dedee" ;
s3 = s1 + s2 ;                          // that is, "Tweedlededee"
```

Figure 6.10 shows what the three String variables looked like before executing these assignment statements, and Figure 6.11 shows what the String variables look like after the assignments. We still have the three variables, but s2 and s3 now point to different (in this case, longer) strings. What happened to the old strings? When each of the assignments takes place, the Java system does the following:

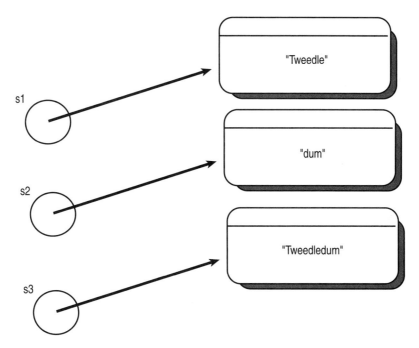

Figure 6.10: Variables s1, s2, and s3 before the assignments

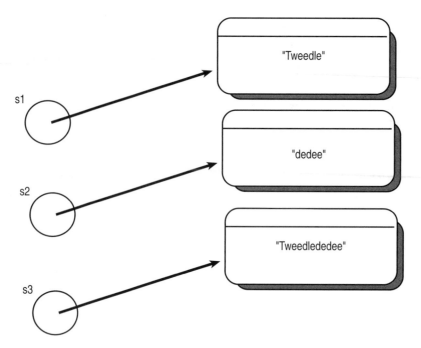

Figure 6.11: Variables s1, s2, and s3 after the assignments

- Allocates a new area of a sufficient size from the store area for strings.
- Writes the new string into this new area—for the first assignment, this is "dedee".
- Puts a reference to this area into the variable—for the first example, this is s2.
- No variable now refers to the area containing the string "dum". Eventually, the Java system will recognize that this string area is unused and return it to the pool for later use. This process, called *garbage collection*, is completely automatic in Java.

In Java, Strings are said to be *immutable*; that is, once a String has been set up, it is never changed. Every time we modify a String, even if we want to change only one character, the Java system in fact makes a new one and throws the old one away. If we are making a lot of changes to a string (perhaps we are constructing it one character at a time), this may be a bit inefficient. In Chapter 21, we discuss another way of holding a string of characters, called a StringBuffer, which is more efficient if we are making a lot of modifications. But for now, the String class provides the facilities we need.

6.8 Methods for the String Class

We have already introduced the length method for the String class, which gave us the number of characters in a string. Some other useful methods in this class are:

- charAt(...) returns the character at a specified position in a string (the first character is at position zero). Thus, s1.charAt(4) returns the 'd' of "Tweedle":

```
s1 = "Tweedle" ;
char aCharacter = s1.charAt(4) ; // stores 'd'
```

- substring(...) returns a new String containing the substring starting and finishing at specified positions in the original string. The first argument is the position of the first character of the substring. The second argument specifies a position just after the last character of the substring. Thus, s1.substring(1, 4) returns the substring from position 1 to position 3 of s1 (i.e., "wee").

   There is a second version of the substring method with a single argument, the starting position of the substring. The substring extends to the end of the string. Thus, s1.substring(4) returns "dle".

```
s1 = "Tweedle" ;
System.out.println(s1.substring(1, 4)) ; // outputs "wee"
System.out.println(s1.substring(4)) ;    // outputs "dle"
```

- Since a String is an object and not a basic type, you cannot compare Strings with the relational operator ==. Instead, you must use the String method equals(...). This method compares the String with which the method is associated with the String provided as the argument to the method. Each character at each position in the two Strings must match. Characters in different cases do not match with this method. For example, 'a' and 'A' are different characters. Thus, s1.equals("Tweedle") returns true, s1.equals("tweedle") returns false, and s3.equals(s4) also returns false.

```
if (s1.equals("tweedle"))
    . . .
if (s1.equals(s4))
    . . .
```

Other useful String methods for comparison include:

- equalsIgnoreCase(...). This works like the equals method but ignores the case of the individual characters. With this method, 'a' and 'A' are treated as the same character. Thus, s1.equalsIgnoreCase("tweedle") returns true.

- startsWith(...) and endsWith(...) match the argument String against the beginning or the end of the String with which the method is associated. Hence, s1.startsWith("Twee") returns true, and s1.endsWith("dlE") returns false.

- indexOf(...) returns the position of the first (i.e., the leftmost) occurrence of the argument `String` in the `String` with which the method is associated. Thus, `s1.indexOf("ee")` returns 2 (remember the character positions are numbered from 0 upward). If there is no occurrence of the argument `String`, the method returns −1. It is the leftmost occurrence that is returned:

```
String s3 = "Tweedledee" ;
System.out.println(s3.indexOf("ee")) ;        // outputs 2
```

There is also a method `lastIndexOf( ... )` to return the position of the last (i.e., the rightmost) occurrence of the argument `String` in the `String` with which the method is associated:

```
String s3 = "Tweedledee" ;
System.out.println(s3.lastIndexOf("ee")) ;    // outputs 8
```

- The method `trim()` returns the `String` with all leading and trailing spaces and tab characters removed, `toLowerCase()` returns the `String` with all uppercase characters converted to lowercase, and `toUpperCase()` returns the `String` with all lowercase characters converted to uppercase. Consider the statements:

```
BasicIo.prompt("type in a string ") ;
String response =
            BasicIo.readString().trim().toLowerCase() ;
```

If the user types in a string, this converts it to a standard form in the variable `response`, with all leading and trailing tabs and spaces removed and all alphabetic characters converted to lowercase.

- replace(...) replaces all occurrences of the first character argument with the second character argument. Thus, `s1.replace('e', 'o')` returns "Twoodlo". The statement

```
BasicIo.prompt("type in a string ") ;
String response =
            BasicIo.readString().trim().toLowerCase().replace(
                            '\t', ' ') ;
```

ensures that any tab characters are converted to space characters.

Full details of all these (and other) methods can be found in the documentation for the `String` class in the `java.lang` package.

6.9   Wrapper Classes (Optional)

In some object-oriented languages (e.g., Smalltalk), everything is an object. For efficiency, Java makes a distinction between objects and the basic data types discussed in this chapter. But occasionally, we need to treat a basic data type as an object. Java has one special class of objects associated with each basic data type. These are called *wrapper* classes (they "wrap up" the basic data types as objects), and they are listed in Table 6.4.

Basic Type	Wrapper Class
boolean	Boolean
char	Character
byte	Byte
short	Short
int	Integer
long	Long
float	Float
double	Double

Table 6.4: Wrapper Classes

We use the basic types most of the time because operations are more efficient on such types. We can create an instance of a wrapper object by calling a constructor method with a value of the basic type as argument. So

```
int iBasic = 42 ;
Integer iWrapper = new Integer(iBasic) ;
```

declares an instance of the Integer wrapper class with the value 42.

Each wrapper class has an appropriately named method for extracting a basic value from the wrapper class. So

```
int iNewValue = iWrapper.intValue() ;
```

extracts the value 42 from the iWrapper object and stores it in the (basic) int variable iNewValue.

We have seen a number of useful methods associated with the String class—for example, to force a string to all upper- or all lowercase or to trim off leading and trailing spaces. But there are a number of similar tasks we might like to carry out for the basic data types—for example, to force an individual character to upper- or lowercase. But these basic types are by definition not objects, so they cannot have associated methods to carry out these useful tasks. The wrapper classes are a suitable place to put methods like this.

Most of these methods are *class* or *static* methods; that is, they are associated with the class rather than an object of that class. To call them, you specify the name of the *class*, followed by a dot, followed by the method name and arguments.

Useful methods from the Character class include:

- toUpperCase(...) and toLowerCase(...) to change, respectively, a lowercase letter (passed as the argument) to uppercase (the returned value) and an uppercase letter to lowercase. Other characters are left unchanged. So

```
char firstChar = 'A' ;
char secondChar = Character.toLowerCase(firstChar) ;
```

puts the value 'a' in the character variable secondChar (the value of firstChar is, of course, unchanged).

- isLetter(...), isDigit(...), isLowerCase(...), isUpperCase(...), isWhitespace(...). These are all class methods that take a char argument and return a boolean value indicating whether or not the character argument is in the set of characters specified in the name of the method. For example,

```
Character.isDigit(response)
```

returns true if response is a digit character in the range 0 to 9 and false otherwise.

```
Character.isLowerCase(response)
```

returns true if response is a lowercase letter in the range 'a' to 'z' and false otherwise.

```
Character.isWhitespace(response)
```

returns true if response is one of the *whitespace* characters (i.e., the space, tab, and newline characters and two less common ones, form feed and carriage return) and false otherwise.

The Integer class contains the useful (class or static) method parseInt. This method takes a String argument and returns the corresponding int value. So

```
String stringValue = "123" ;
int intValue = Integer.parseInt(stringValue) ;
```

puts the value 123 in intValue. If the String argument is not a valid integer, we get a NumberFormatException exception.

We can convert an int value to a String with the (class or static) method toString. So

```
int intValue = 456 ;
String newStringValue = Integer.toString(intValue) ;
```

puts the value "456" in newStringValue.

Both parseInt and toString have versions that allow the programmer to specify a radix other than 10 for the string of digits.

Similarly, the Double class contains the useful parseDouble and toString methods for converting between Strings and doubles.

6.10   Key Points in Chapter 6

■ Java provides a number of *basic data types*. The main ones are `int`, `double`, `boolean`, and `char`.

Variables of these types are declared as follows:

```
<name of basic type> <name of variable> = <initial value> ;
```

A variable of one of these types can be assigned a new value with an assignment statement:

```
<name of variable> = <expression> ;
```

■ The `int` type can store a whole number value in the range −2,147,483,648 to +2,147,483,647.

Operations that can be performed on integer values include addition (+), subtraction (−), multiplication (*), integer division (/), and remainder (%).

The order in which operations are carried out in an expression depends on the *precedence* of the operators (see Table 6.1).

■ The `double` type can store a number with a fractional part with about 15 decimal places of accuracy. Operations that can be performed on these values include addition (+), subtraction (−), multiplication (*), and division (/).

■ In an expression with both `int` and `double` values, an `int` value is automatically converted to a `double` value where necessary.

If a `double` needs to be converted to an `int` value, the programmer must indicate this with a *cast*; the `double` value will be *truncated* to an `int` value.

```
<int variable> = (int) <double expression>
```

■ Strings of characters are held as instances of the `String` class. We can set up a `String` variable with a particular value:

```
String stringName = "This is a String" ;
```

We can set this `String` variable to a different value:

```
stringName = "This is a different String" ;
```

The `String` class provides the `length` method to return the length of the string, `charAt` to return a particular character (numbered from zero), `toUpperCase` and `toLowerCase`, and so on. Comparisons between `Strings` must be done with the `equals` method, not with the `==` operator.

■ There is a wrapper class corresponding to each basic data type. The `Character`, `Integer`, and `Double` classes contain some useful (static or class) methods.

6.11   Exercises

1. Write a program to prompt the user to input an amount in ounces and return the amount in grams (1 ounce = 28 grams).

   Modify the program so that the user can type in a number of ounces to be converted to grams or a number of pints to be converted to liters (1 pint = 0.568 liters).

   Modify the program so that the user can do a sequence of metric conversions.

2. Write a program to prompt the user to type in an amount in pence. Your program should then work out the least number of the following coins needed for this amount of money:

   £1 (i.e., 100 pence), 50p, 10p, 1p

   For example, the least number of coins for 195 pence is:

   1 × 1 pound, 1 × 50 pence, 4 × 10 pence, 5 × 1 pence

Note ∎

There will be a significant amount of repetition in parts of your solution because you have not yet learned how to use an array to store the different coin values. This is why you have not been asked to handle all possible denominations of British notes and coins.

3. Write a program to read in a string of characters from the user and output the characters one per line on the screen (see the example at the end of Section 5.2).

   Modify the program so that all vowels are output in uppercase and all consonants in lowercase so the string "Hello" would appear as:

   h
   E
   l
   l
   O

4. Write a program to read in a string of characters typed by the user and test if it is palindromic. That is, test whether the string reads the same in both directions. The matching of the characters should ignore case, so the word "Madam" is considered palindromic.

   Modify the program so that the user can type in a sequence of strings and have the program indicate for each one whether it is palindromic or not.

5. Write a program that takes two strings and tests whether or not the first string is contained within the second. For example, the string "pen" is contained within the string "independent".

   Modify the program so that it reports the starting position of the first string within the second if it is so contained.

   Modify the program so that it always looks for the shorter string within the larger, whatever order they are typed in.

6. You have been invited to participate in a game show where you could win a free star prize. When you play, you are asked to choose one box from three. Only one of the boxes contains a prize; the other two boxes contain lemons. When you have chosen your box, but before you open it, the game show host will open one of the two remaining boxes and show you a lemon. At this point, you have three possible strategies:

   a. Keep the box you chose initially and open it.

   b. Take the remaining box, which the game show host did not open.

   c. Flip a coin to decide whether to open the box you originally chose or the remaining box, which the game show host did not open.

   When you play the game, which of the three strategies should you adopt? Write a Java program to help you decide. The program should simulate playing the game a large number of times (to be specified by the user) with each of the three strategies to see which one offers you the best chance of winning. You may be surprised at the result.

Note ◾

Java provides the Random class (in the `java.util` package) to generate random numbers. You can declare

```
static Random rand = new Random() ;
```

and then the following method returns a random integer in the (inclusive) range 1 to the value of the argument supplied:

```
public static int random(int n)
    {
    return (int) (1 + (Math.abs(rand.nextInt()) % n)) ;
    } // end of method random
```

PART 2

Writing Objects

7 A Simple Class

8 More on the Simple Class

9 Arrays

10 Objects Within Objects

11 Putting Objects to Work

CHAPTER 7

A Simple Class

7.1 What We Are Trying to Achieve

Object-oriented programming provides us with a mechanism—the object itself—that supports a number of important concepts in software engineering. As the software artifacts we build become ever more complex, we need much more control over the structure and use of their components. One of the crucial features of objects is that they can be gathered together under the general concept of *encapsulation*, long heralded as a vital feature for modern software components.

Encapsulation has an impact on a number of areas. It gives us a structuring mechanism whereby we can gather together, in one place, logically related program elements. It also, for example, makes it possible to

- Gather together a number of related functions in one module.
- Group both the code and the data it manipulates.

Over and above this useful grouping mechanism that allows us to structure our components (and the systems we build from them) in a logical and sensible fashion, we can also use the module concept to support *information hiding*. Essentially, the users of the modules have information about them on a "need-to-know" basis. If we have a geometry module that supports shapes and functions that operate on those shapes (e.g., circles, radii, and perimeters), we do not need to know how the function that calculates radii works; we need to know only how to call it.

The module should also be self-contained. It should contain everything it needs to function appropriately. Module users should not need to declare additional data or provide additional code in their program to support the module.

The classic example of a module that contains a data structure and related state information is the stack. A stack is a data structure that supports an LIFO (last-in, first-out) list. You will find out more about stacks later in the book. For the moment, all you need to know is that we can add data to a stack, and get data back from it. However, the stack is organized in such a way that the last item added will be the first one back. Two essential operations for stack users are *push*, to add a data item to the stack, and *pop*, to get a data item back from the stack.

The point is that users of the stack need to understand only the general LIFO concept and what the push and pop operators do. They do not have to know how the operators work or the nitty-gritty details of how the stack is implemented. This kind of information hiding makes the module easier to use. In addition, the fact that the module is self-contained means that there is generally no need to provide additional code or data structures to make the module work.

Encapsulation is also beneficial for the module provider. If the module provider decides that there is a more efficient way to implement the stack—either through a new data structure or a new algorithm for the operators—these changes can be made with impunity, as long as they do not have an impact on the appearance and behavior of the module as far as the users are concerned.

Most, if not all, of the data within a module is hidden from the user. The only way we can access hidden data is through the methods the module provides. For example, if we model a person's age as a visible integer, we can do anything to that age that we could do to an integer. This includes assigning it a negative value. As far as people's ages are concerned, this action is semantically incorrect. If we hide the person's age within a module, however, and provide a method setAge, then the module provider can check to make sure that the value provided by the user is semantically valid—that is, greater than 0 and less than, say, 150. You will see later in this chapter how this can be done. This is a simple example of how module providers can ensure objects can be manipulated only in valid, sensible ways.

In this chapter, we consider three types of people involved in writing and using elements of a Java program:

- The *class provider* is the person (or team) responsible for the definition and implementation of the class. This person identifies and defines the attributes and the methods of the class and decides whether they should be hidden (private) or available to the class user (public).

- The *class user* is the person who takes the classes provided and uses them to write a Java program. This is the role we have adopted thus far in the book. You will see how to use classes to write other classes later in this book.

- The *end user* is the person who takes the Java program we have written and executes it either as an application or as an applet accessed over the Web. The end user interacts with our program as it executes and may be prompted to provide data via the keyboard and/or some graphical input artifact (e.g., a menu).

As you have already seen, from the perspective of class users, classes support the encapsulation mechanism. In this chapter, we switch hats and start to look at objects from the viewpoint of the class provider. We progress by continuing to use the Person class as our example.

Each class should provide some documentation aimed at the class user. This documentation should detail the publicly available aspects of the class; this may include constants, attributes, and methods. The information provided should be enough to allow class users to employ the class successfully as part of their application(s).

Here is a list of the methods available for the user of the `Person` class:

```
public Person()
public Person(String f, String s, int a, int g)
public String getForename()
public String getSurname()
public int getAge()
public int getGender()
public String getGenderString()
public void setForename(String f)
public void setSurname(String s)
public void setAge(int a)
public void setGender(int g)
public void increaseAge(int n)
public void setFullName(String f, String s)
public static int getUpperAgeLimit()
public String formalTitle()
public String toString()
public Person copy()
```

Notice the group of `get` and `set` methods. These allow us to get and set the values of the person's forename, surname, age, and gender. We can extract or change these values, but only indirectly, through the provided methods. We can thus assume that this information—the state of a person—is encapsulated within the object.

Note the provision of the `toString` method. Many classes, such as those contained in the Java libraries, provide this method. Its intention is to provide a representation of the object as a `String`, which can then be printed. For example, if we have an instance of the `Person` class called `bill`, we can obtain the `String` representation as follows:

```
bill.toString()
```

We could use this in conjunction with the `System.out.println` method:

```
System.out.println("the person is " + bill.toString()) ;
```

However, for reasons presented in Chapter 14, we can omit the call to `toString` in these particular circumstances because `System.out.println` is clever enough to apply the method on our behalf to a variable that is not of type `String`.

Notice also that the `getUpperAgeLimit` method is declared as `static`. We will examine what this means in Section 8.6.

How do we declare and use an object of this class? The class provider gives us at least one constructor method. We can tell which methods are constructors because they have the same name as the class; here it is `Person`. We can also tell that it is a constructor because it does not have a return type specified. You can see that we have two constructor methods in the `Person` class. One has no arguments, and the other has four. The way to use the constructors is in conjunction with the keyword `new`:

```
Person aPerson = new Person() ;
aPerson.setForename("James") ;
aPerson.setSurname("Kirk") ;
aPerson.setAge(34) ;
aPerson.setGender(Person.MALE) ;
```

Once we have created the new person, we can use any of the methods provided. Here we are using the four `set` methods to give aPerson some state. We are setting the four values or attributes encapsulated within the object. Alternatively, we could use the second constructor:

```
Person aPerson = new Person("James", "Kirk", 34,
                            Person.MALE) ;
```

This second constructor takes four arguments, which map onto the four attributes (forename, surname, age, and gender). For the fourth argument, we use one of the gender constants provided by the `Person` class.

On the birthday of aPerson, we need to increment their age by 1. We can do this using the `getAge` and `setAge` methods.

```
int temp = aPerson.getAge() ;
temp = temp + 1 ;
aPerson.setAge(temp) ;
```

However, looking back at the list of methods provided, we can see there is an `increaseAge` method. We can use this as follows:

```
aPerson.increaseAge(1) ;
```

7.2 Providing the Person Class

It is finally time to swap hats and examine the `Person` class as a class provider. We begin by looking at a skeleton declaration of this class (the complete class is listed in Appendix D.1):

```
public class Person
    {

    // Person class constants

    public static final int UNKNOWN = 99 ;
    public static final int MALE = 1 ;
    public static final int FEMALE = 2 ;

    private static final int UPPER_AGE = 150 ;

    // Person instance variables
```

```
private String forename ;
private String surname ;
private int age ;
private int gender ;

// Person Constructor methods

public Person() { ... body removed ... }
public Person(String f, String s, int a, int g) { ... }

// selector methods for Person instance fields

public String getForename() { ... }
public String getSurname() { ... }
public int getAge() { ... }
public int getGender() { ... }
public String getGenderString() { ... }

// methods for setting Person instance fields

public void setForename(String f) { ... }
public void setSurname(String s) { ... }
public void setAge(int a) { ... }
public void setGender(int g) { ... }

// other Person methods

public void increaseAge(int n) { ... }
public void setFullName(String f, String s) { ... }
public static int getUpperAgeLimit() { ... }
public String formalTitle() { ... }
public String toString() { ... }
} // end of Person class
```

Let us look first at the head of the class.

It starts with the keywords `public` and `class` followed by `Person`, the name of the class. It is followed by the body of the class, enclosed in curly braces. Next we have a group of three public and one private class constants. These will be discussed in more detail in Section 8.2. Suffice it to say the first three constants are intended to model the possible values of a person's gender: Either it is male or female, or else we simply do not have access to that information yet.

Next we have a set of variables that stores the state of a `Person` object, one for each attribute: A person, as we are modeling one, has a forename, a surname, an age, and a gender. As you can see, these are of type `int` or `String`. In the class body, they are declared much as local variables have been declared in the `main` method: the type to which they belong followed by the name of the variable. The major difference here is that they are encapsulated within the class body. We make them hidden by prefacing their declaration with the keyword private. The user of the class cannot directly reference them. These variables are known as *instance variables* or *attributes*.

Notice, however, that all attributes, regardless of whether they have been declared as public or private, are accessible to all methods contained within the same class. Let's explore this further. If we had the following class definition

```
public class Car
    {
    private String carName ;
    public int mileage ;

    // methods ...
    } // end of class Car
```

then a class user can try to write

```
Car aCar = new Car() ;
aCar.mileage = 10000 ;            // valid
System.out.print(aCar.carName) ; // not valid
```

When an instance variable is declared as public, we can access it directly as part of the object with the notation "instance name–dot–attribute name." Thus, we can directly assign an integer value to aCar's mileage. There is no need for a get or set method. However, when we try directly to access a private attribute (e.g., carName), this will not work. Attributes should usually be private.

The Car class specification does not actually contain two instance variables called carName and mileage; it contains only their specification. We cannot say, for example,

```
Car.mileage = 100 ;
```

Object instances of the Car class have their own distinct copies of the two instance variables (Figure 7.1). They have the same name and form, but we can access them only through the object that contains them:

```
Car bCar = new Car() ;
bCar.mileage = 105 ;
```

We use the name of the object to select which set of instance variables we wish to use.

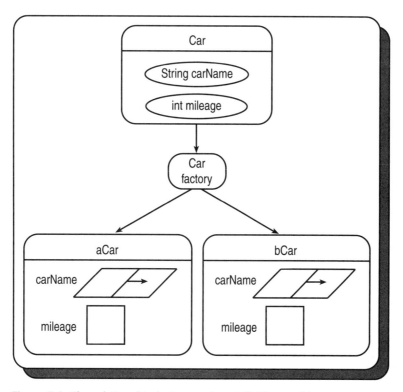

Figure 7.1: The relationship between class definition and instances

7.3   Methods for the Person Class

Returning to the Person class, next we have two constructor methods; these will be discussed in more detail in Section 8.1. Finally, we have a set of methods used to extract or insert information or, generally, to manipulate the values contained in the instance variables. We now examine these methods in more detail.

The general form of a method header is

```
public-or-private return-value-type name arguments-in-parentheses
```

This is followed by the code, contained in curly braces, that implements the method. This is known as the *body* of the method.

Just as for the instance variables we have seen so far, the keyword public indicates that the method is available to the class user. That is, the class user can call the method. It is also possible to have private methods. These can be called by the other methods in the class, but no method outside the body of the class can call a private method. They are hidden from the user but will be of great importance in implementing the public methods the user can call. In other words, they can be called only indirectly by the user. We shall discuss this further later.

The `return-value-type` specifies

- Whether the method returns a value or not.
- What type the value will have.

The keyword `void` specifies that no value will be returned. In the current implementation of the `Person` class, none of the `set` methods return a value and thus all feature the `void` keyword. You will look at an example of a `set` method shortly.

On the other hand, we can see methods that do return a value, such as `getAge`. Because the instance variable `age` has type `int`, when we return this as the result of a method, we are returning a value of type `int`. Hence, the `getAge` header looks like:

```
public int getAge()
```

When the user calls `getAge`, it can be as follows:

```
int oneAge = aPerson.getAge() ;
```

As always, we need an integer variable to hold an integer value.

Now we examine the actual bodies of our methods. They contain code just like the code you have seen so far in this book. Let's begin with the simplest kind of method, one that returns the otherwise hidden value of an instance variable:

```
public int getAge()
    {
    return age ;
    }// end of method getAge
```

Here the body of the method consists of a single statement. It uses the keyword `return` to prefix the value it is going to return as the result of the user calling this method. Because the instance variable `age` has the type `int`, the "`return-value-type`" specifier in the method header must also be `int`.

Now consider the following:

```
public String getSurname()
    {
    return surname ;
    } // end of method getSurname
```

Here the instance variable `surname` has type `String`, so the "`return-value-type`" specifier is `String`.

So far, we have considered methods that return a value, one of those belonging to the hidden instance variables; these are the so-called `get` methods. Let us now examine methods that allow us to change the value of the hidden instance variables—the `set` methods:

```
public void setAge(int a)
   {
   age = a ;
   } // end of method setAge
```

Here we see a *formal argument* a, of type int. When class users call this method, they will provide a corresponding *actual argument*, a value of type int.

```
aPerson.setAge(uAge) ;
```

The formal argument a takes the value of the actual argument (in this case, uAge). In the body of the method, we have an assignment statement that assigns the value of a to the attribute age. We have taken the value provided by the class user as an actual argument, copied it into the formal argument, and assigned it to the attribute. This has the desired effect. We describe this whole process in more detail in the next section.

Notice that the types of the formal arguments of the set methods must match the types of the instance variables. Thus, setAge has an argument of type int to match that of the age instance variable, and setForename has an argument of type String to match that of the forename instance variable.

However, as we discussed earlier, we can do a bit more in the set methods to try to ensure that only sensible (semantically valid) values can be passed into the instance variables. In this case, we might say that ages must be in the range 0 to 150. We can enhance the setAge method using a selection statement as follows:

```
public void setAge(int a)
   {
   if ((a < 0) || (a > UPPER_AGE))
      {
      System.out.println("invalid age in 'setAge'") ;
      System.exit(1) ;
      }
   else
      age = a ;
   } // end of method setAge
```

Here we are making the entire application program shut down in response to an invalid age value.

We can of course do something similar with most of the set methods; consider setForename:

```
public void setForename(String f)
   {
   if (f.length() < 1)
      {
      System.out.println("invalid forename in 'setForename'") ;
      System.exit(1) ;
      }
```

```
        else
            forename = f ;
    } // end of method setForename
```

Here we are saying that the smallest acceptable forename has at least one letter.

7.4   Actual and Formal Arguments

To understand what is actually happening when we call a method, we need to explain the terminology of actual and formal arguments. To make matters worse, we have to swap hats quite quickly between class user and class provider.

We take the setAge method as our first example. Let's say that the class user has written some code that allows the end user to type in someone's age. This is stored in an integer variable before it is used as the actual argument to the setAge method:

```
Person aPerson = new Person() ;
BasicIo.prompt("Type in the person's age ") ;
int uAge = BasicIo.readInteger() ;
aPerson.setAge(uAge) ;
```

The actual argument, then, is whatever variable or value we provide when we call the method. In this case, it is the integer variable uAge. It could have just as easily been a single integer value (e.g., 5) or an integer expression that results in a single integer value.

For that matter, it could even have been a call to a method that returns a single integer value. Let's say we have brother and sister who are twins. Once we have set the age of one, we can use that information to set that of the other:

```
boy.setAge(girl.getAge()) ;
```

On the other hand, if they are not twins, and we know the boy is 1 year older than the girl, we could have

```
int uAge = girl.getAge() ;
boy.setAge(uAge + 1) ;
```

or

```
boy.setAge(girl.getAge() + 1) ;
```

Now let's put on our class-provider hat and look again at the declaration of setAge:

```
public void setAge(int a)
    {
    ...
    } // end of method setAge
```

Here again we see that it is a method called setAge, which doesn't return a value and is available to the class user. Inside the parentheses is the formal argument. We see that it is named a and is of type int. It is the type of the formal argument that dictates the type of actual argument. This is why a call of setAge can have only a single integer variable or value as its actual argument.

Note also that we can see there is only one formal argument. Of course, it is possible to have as many as necessary for the method to carry out its work. Because there is only one in this case, calls of setAge can have only one actual argument; any more or less would be illegal.

```
aPerson.setAge(5) ;                // valid
aPerson.setAge() ;                 // not valid - no arguments
aPerson.setAge(uAge, 6, 9) ;       // not valid - three arguments
                                   // instead of one
aPerson.setAge("fred") ;           // not valid - one argument,
                                   // but wrong type
```

Thus, by examining the formal arguments of a method, we can learn a lot about how we can call the method: specifically, what types of arguments we can have and how many.

Where we have many formal arguments, we have to be careful that the types of the actual and formal arguments match up. For example, we could extend our Car class with engine capacity modeled as an integer, registration number as a string, and roadworthiness as a Boolean. We could have a method that allows the class user to set up these instance variables as follows:

```
public void setup(String regNo, int engCap, boolean
                  onRoad)
    {
    ...
```

When we call this method, we must ensure that the first argument is a String, the second an int, and the third a boolean. Any other ordering is an illegal situation:

```
aCar.setup("D54VBV", 999, true) ;  // valid
aCar.setup(999, true, "D54VBV") ;  // not valid
```

Thus, the ordering of formal and actual arguments is important.

Let's return to setAge. We are calling it with an actual argument of uAge:

```
aPerson.setAge(uAge) ;
```

Whatever the contents of that integer variable is (for the sake of this example, let's say it is 21), we want to set the value of the instance variable age to the value contained in the actual argument. If we look at the body of setAge, there is no reference at all to uAge, only to the formal argument a. How does the value of uAge end up in the formal argument a? This occurs through the *calling process*.

Before a method is called, its formal arguments do not exist. If the body of the method contains any declarations of variables, those variables also do not exist. When a method is called, the formal arguments and the variables come into existence so that they can be used by the instructions contained in the method body as they are executed. When a method is finished, the formal arguments and the variables again cease to exist.

The variables contained within the body of a method are said to be *local* variables. This is because they can be referenced (and accessed) only by the instructions contained in the method body.

When the formal arguments come into existence, the values of the actual arguments are copied into the formal arguments. It is as if an assignment statement had taken place. In our example, this would be:

```
a = uAge ;
```

Before the method is called, and no one is using the aPerson object, it appears as shown in Figure 7.2. We can see the four instance variables, forename, surname, gender, and age. Because age is the one that most interests us, we have shown it here as a labeled box. It contains an integer value, denoted by ??, because we neither know nor care what value it currently has. We want to replace it with the value stored in uAge.

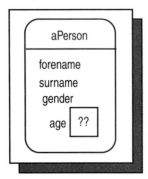

Figure 7.2: The aPerson object

When we call setAge with the actual argument uAge, the temporary existence of the formal argument a begins. We show the temporary data in the lower half of the aPerson object in Figure 7.3. The formal argument a is given the same value as the actual argument uAge. In this way, we can say that the value 21 is being passed into the object.

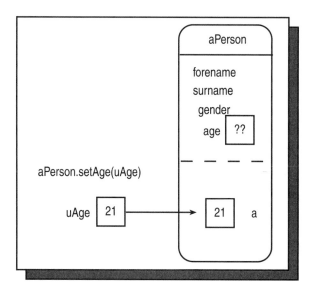

Figure 7.3: Calling `setAge`

To complete the process, the method body is now executed, and the value 21 is passed from **a** into the instance variable **age** (Figure 7.4).

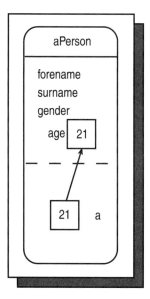

Figure 7.4: Executing `setAge`

Finally, when `setAge` terminates, any temporary variables (formal arguments and local variables) cease to exist. This leaves us with `aPerson` after the method has been executed (Figure 7.5).

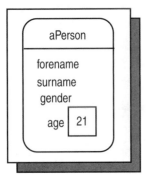

Figure 7.5: After `setAge`

7.5 Modes of Argument Passing

In this section, we return to the mechanism of passing a argument, where the type of the argument is one of the basic types (`boolean`, `int`, etc.) or a `String`. By this, we mean the process of taking a value from the actual argument and "passing it into" the formal argument.

We can pass values only in one direction: from the actual argument to the formal argument. Any changes we make to the formal argument have no effect on the actual argument. Suppose we have a class `Dog` with a method `setAge`:

```
class Dog
    {
    private int age, dogAge ;

    public void setAge(int a)
        {
1.      age = a ;
2.      a = a * 7 ;     // map onto dog years
3.      dogAge = a ;
        } // end of method setAge
    } // end of class Dog
```

We call this `setAge` method as follows:

```
int mda = 2 ;
myDog.setAge(mda) ;
```

Before we call the method, we have the situation shown in Figure 7.6. When we call the method, the value of the actual argument is copied into the formal argument (Figure 7.7).

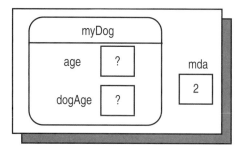

Figure 7.6: Before the call of setAge

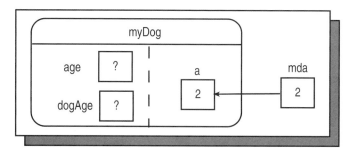

Figure 7.7: Creating the formal argument and copying the actual argument into it

From this point on, the actual argument is no longer relevant to the execution of the method. Line 1 of the method sets the age attribute to the value of the formal argument (Figure 7.8). Line 2 multiplies the formal argument by 7 (Figure 7.9). This has no effect on the actual argument.

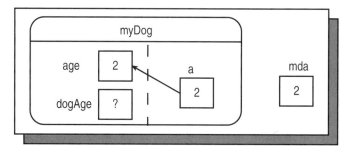

Figure 7.8: Assigning the formal argument to the attribute

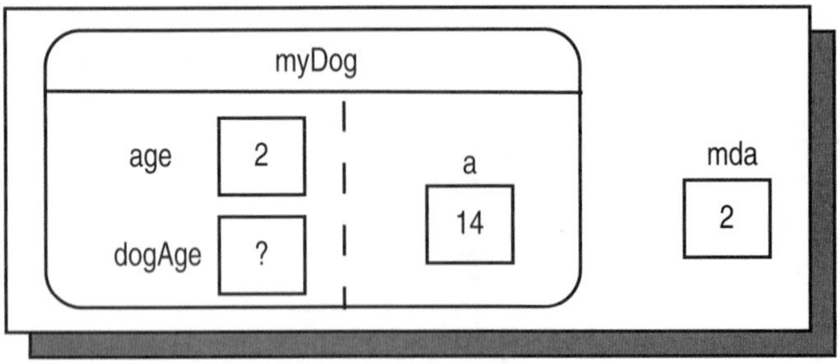

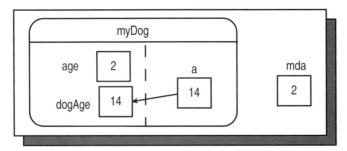

Figure 7.9: After multiplying the formal argument

Line 3 sets the value of the `dogAge` attribute to the new value of the formal argument (Figure 7.10). The method concludes, the formal argument disappears, and as you can see in Figure 7.11, the attribute values have been set as we would expect, and the actual argument remains unaltered.

Figure 7.10: Assigning the formal argument to the second attribute

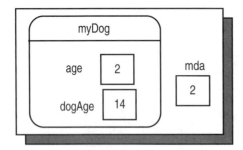

Figure 7.11: After the call of `setAge`

Traditionally, this is known as *call by value*; values are passed into the formal argument. Some languages support *call by value returned*, whereby values are passed out of the formal argument back into the actual argument. If this were the case in Java, Figure 7.10 would have an arrow leading from a to mda, and mda would contain the value 14.

It is not possible in Java to use actual arguments of the basic types to pass values back out of the method. The only way methods can pass values back to the calling program is if the method has a return value. In Chapter 10, we will examine the use of objects as arguments.

7.6   Return Values

As you have seen, some methods return a value. For example, any `get` method will normally return a value of the same type as the attribute it is associated with. We usually do this by returning the value of the attribute itself.

However, as we have seen in connection with variables, we can assign an integer value on the right side of an assignment statement to an integer variable on the left side. The integer value may be a literal integer value, it may be taken from another integer variable, or it may be the result of evaluating an integer expression. Similarly, the value returned from a method may be a literal, the contents of a variable, or the result of evaluating an expression.

In our `Dog` class, we chose to store the value that represented a dog's age in dog years. However, as we store the age in normal years, we could always calculate the dog years version of the age whenever it was requested. We could provide the following method:

```
public int getAgeInDogYears()
   {
   return age * 7 ;
   } // end of method getAgeInDogYears
```

Here you can see that following the `return` keyword, we have an expression involving an integer literal (the number 7) and an integer attribute. This integer expression evaluates to produce a single integer value, which we return as the result of the method call.

7.7   Lexical Conventions within a Class

It is often useful to have conventions for the textual representation of elements within a class. By this, we mean ways of varying the appearance of text to impart information to readers, so they can tell at a glance whether the word they are looking at is a class name or an attribute name.

The main techniques we explore here involve the use of capitalization and "visible" spaces. When we want to give something a name that involves two (or more) words, we cannot use actual space characters because the name of something in Java has to be a continuous string of characters (with no spaces). There are two main techniques for handling this problem: (a) using capitals to represent the start of the next word in the sequence or (b) using the underscore character _ to represent the space. So the name *dog age* can be represented as `dogAge` or `dog_age`. We will adopt the former convention for the names of attributes, variables, instances, and methods.

To differentiate the name of a class, we use a capital first letter. Thus, the name of the class modeling a person is `Person`. Other class names you have already met are `GroupOfPeople` and `BasicIo`.

Finally, we wish to distinguish constant names from all others; we have chosen to represent these as all capital letters. Of course, our visible space solution will not work under these circumstances, so we resort to the use of the underscore character. Hence, *VAT rate* is represented as `VAT_RATE`.

These are the conventions we have tried to apply throughout this book. We make no particular claim for them; the important point is that you should decide on the conventions you will use and stick with them.

7.8 Key Points in Chapter 7

- *Encapsulation* is an important aspect of modern software engineering. It allows us to collect together data, and instructions that manipulate those data, in one place, to protect the data and instructions if required, and to present a strict interface to the end user. Java classes allow us to use encapsulation.

- We can identify three types of people by their relationship to Java software:
  - A class provider, who writes the class definition.
  - A class user, who uses the class and its instances to implement an application.
  - An end user, who uses a Java application.

- It is possible to provide different constructors for the same class (see Chapter 8). We use constructors to create new instances of a class.

- A class definition contains:
  - Class constants (e.g., MALE, FEMALE, etc.).
  - Instance variables or attributes (e.g., forename, gender, etc.).
  - Methods.

  We shall generally refer to these contents as *elements* of the class.

- The contents of a class definition can be specified as `public` or `private`. This relates to the visibility (or availability) of the element. A `private` element is available only within the class (to the class provider), and a `public` element is generally accessible (to the class provider and class user).

- Methods consist of sets of instructions that manipulate the data contained within the instance. A method has two parts: a *header* and a *body*.

- The general form of a method header is:

  `public-or-private return-value-type name arguments-in-parentheses`

- Like any element of a class, we can make a method `public` or `private`.

- A method may return a value as part of its function. We specify in the header the type of value it returns. If it does not return a value, we specify this as `void`.

- The body of a method consists of a set of Java statements. If the method returns a value, it must contain at least one `return` statement.

- The *formal arguments* of a method appear in the method header and will be referred to in the method body. Formal arguments form a run-time link to the *actual arguments*, which are the values or variables used when the method was called. We use arguments to pass data into the method.

7.9 Exercises

1. Complete the definition of the `Dog` class. Provide a suitable driver application to test your class.

2. Extend the `Person` class as follows:

   a. Introduce a new instance variable `maritalStatus`.

   b. A person can be single, married, divorced, or widowed. Since class constants are not introduced until Section 8.3, for the present you'll have to use the integers, say, 1, 2, 3, and 4, for the four possible values of this attribute (or look ahead at the next chapter).

   c. Add new `get` and `set` methods to deal with the marital status. Make sure the `set` method semantically validates the value being passed into the object.

   d. A person is eligible to marry if they are above or on the age of consent (say, 18) and are not married. Write a method, `eligibleToMarry`, which returns true if the person can be married and false otherwise.

   e. Write a driver program that uses your extended `Person` class and allows you to test your new code fully.

3. We saw earlier that the `Person.setAge` method simply abandons the execution of the application if an age that is out of range is provided as an argument. This might seem a bit excessive, and there are a number of approaches we can take to make this a friendlier method. One thing we can do is to change the method so that it returns a Boolean value that indicates whether the class user's attempt to set the person's age was successful or not. Let's say we return true if the attempt succeeded and false otherwise.

   Rewrite the `setAge` method to reflect this and provide a driver application that checks the return status of the operation. For example, you could provide a loop that repeatedly asks the end user to provide an age until a valid age is supplied.

   Exercises 4 onward require you to implement a class and to provide an appropriate driver application. These drivers should be interactive and should prompt the end user to select a command and provide the necessary arguments. They should consist of a main loop that continuously prompts the user for a command, interprets the command, and calls the appropriate methods. You should include commands that

   a. Allow the end user to find out what commands are available.

   b. Terminate the application gracefully.

4. Write a class called Distance that maintains two attributes to represent a distance in miles and in kilometers (1 mile = 1.609 km). Provide suitable get, set, and toString methods. Write an appropriate driver application to test this class.

5. Write a class called Rectangle that maintains two attributes to represent the length and breadth of a rectangle. Provide suitable get, set, and toString methods plus two methods that return the perimeter and area of the rectangle. Write an appropriate driver application to test this class.

6. Write a class called Journey that maintains statistics about a journey undertaken by a car. At the beginning of a journey, a car's odometer reads S miles and the fuel tank is full. After the journey, the reading is F miles and it takes G gallons to fill the tank. The Journey class should maintain these data and provide a method that returns the fuel consumption in gallons per 100 miles. Declare the class with appropriate methods using more meaningful attribute names than S, F, and G. Write an appropriate driver application to test this class.

7. In the last three exercises, we assume the values provided by the end user will all be non-negative. Alter the class set methods to ensure valid values have been provided; they should return a boolean result: true if valid and false otherwise. Update your driver applications to check this result and take appropriate action.

CHAPTER 8

More on the Simple Class

8.1 Constructor Methods

You will recall from earlier chapters how we can declare and initialize objects in our programs. Continuing our use of the `Person` class, we begin by declaring a variable of type `Person`.

```
Person aPerson ;
```

We can then use a class *constructor method* to set up the actual `Person` instance. In essence, the `aPerson` just declared is a reference to an instance we have yet to create. When we provide a class, if we do not provide a constructor method, Java provides a default one. However, we can provide as many constructor methods as we like (with different lists of arguments). The simplest kind of constructor method is one that takes no arguments (the default constructor provided by Java has this form). For example, in our class definition, we can have:

```
public Person()
    {
    // do nothing
    } // end of constructor method
```

This is pretty much what Java's default constructor would look like, but you will see in a moment how we can usefully extend the functionality of our own constructor. To use the constructor, we write the following statement:

```
Person aPerson = new Person() ;
```

Notice that the name of the constructor method is always the name of the class. We do not need to specify the type of return value. All this does is to set up the space for the actual object's attributes or instance variables. So, in this case, we have a new instance (Figure 8.1).

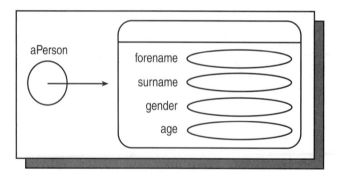

Figure 8.1: A new instance

There is something important to note about declaring any kind of variable in this way, be it a simple basic type (e.g., `int`) or an object type (e.g., `Person`). We have simply allocated the space for the object; we have said nothing about what value might currently occupy that space. This is an example of an *uninitialized* variable.

Why might this cause problems? Well, for example, an integer variable might be intended to contain the current heading (in degrees) of a rocket. Let's declare it as follows:

```
int heading ;
```

Let's assume, as in Figure 8.2, that 0 degrees is to the left, 90 is up, 180 is to the right, and 270 is down. Now we need to update that heading due to new information. Let's say we assume the rocket is heading straight up (90 degrees) and we want it to shift 10 degrees to the right. The variable `change` contains the value 10.

```
heading = heading + change ;
```

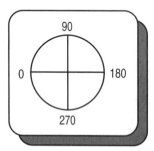

Figure 8.2: Points of the compass

What can we say about the new value of `heading`? Before the assignment, `heading` will contain some integer value, but it may not be 90. It could be, say, 260. Adding 10 to this and then interpreting it as the direction we should be heading in gives us 270 degrees, straight down.

It is important to note that the Java language system initializes attributes (but not local variables) on our behalf if we forget to do so. The default values are listed in Table 8.1.

boolean	char	byte	short	int	long	float	double
false	\u0000	0	0	0	0	0.0	0.0

Table 8.1: Default Values

However, it may be that we have more sensible initial values. For example, our enumerated integer attribute gender would be initialized by the Java system to 0. However, this value has no meaning. We should always initialize an integer attribute that is modeling gender to UNKNOWN.

Equally important, when you move to other programming languages, you have no guarantee that they will behave like Java. They may or may not initialize variables for you, so we believe it is important that you get in the habit of initializing your own variables sensibly and not be lazy and leave it to the system.

Constructor methods give us a powerful mechanism for avoiding the uninitialized attribute problem. We, the class providers, can ensure that sensible initial values are given to the attribute when the class user chooses not to allocate the values themselves. Thus, we can extend our declaration of the constructor method as follows:

```
public Person( )
    {
    forename = "NONE" ;
    surname = "NONE" ;
    age = 0 ;
    gender = UNKNOWN ;
    } // end of constructor method
```

Now, when a user calls this particular method, we create the instance shown in Figure 8.3. In our method, we have tried to ensure that sensible, interpretable values have been given to the attributes of the object rather than unknown and unpredictable values.

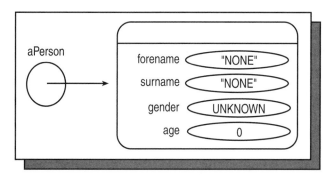

Figure 8.3: An instance with default values

Now that the class user has created the object, he or she can use the other methods provided to manipulate the contents of the object. Thus, if the class user now wants to represent a person called James Kirk, we can issue the following instructions:

```
aPerson.setForename("James") ;
aPerson.setSurname("Kirk") ;
aPerson.setAge(34) ;
aPerson.setGender(Person.MALE) ;
```

This would give us the object shown in Figure 8.4.

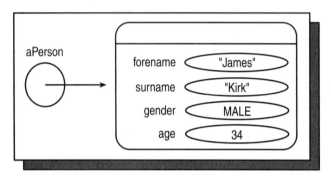

Figure 8.4: An initialized instance

However, perhaps the class user knows these details when the object is created and would like to set these values at the same time. We can allow for this by having a constructor method with arguments. For example:

```
public Person(String f, String s, int a, int g)
    {
    forename = f ;
    surname = s ;
    age = a ;
    gender = g ;
    } // end of constructor method
```

Here the class provider has included a method, also called Person, but this time with four arguments. The formal arguments f, s, a, and g are intended to represent the forename, surname, age, and gender of the person. Now the class user can write:

```
Person aPerson = new Person("James", "Kirk", 34,
                            Person.MALE) ;
```

The result is identical to Figure 8.4.

8.2 Overloading

It is important to note that we haven't replaced the original, argumentless constructor; instead, we have added a new one with four arguments. Both these methods have exactly the same name (Person). How is this possible? Won't the compiler and language system complain that we have used the same name twice? Try declaring two attributes or two local variables with the same name and see what happens.

The situation with methods is somewhat different. A method can be said to have a *signature*. The signature of a method is the number, order, and type of its formal arguments. Table 8.2 gives some examples. And Table 8.3 lists the constructor methods we have written.

Method Name	Formal Arguments
getForename	none
setForename	String
getAge	none
setAge	int

Table 8.2: Examples of Signatures

Method Name	Formal Arguments
Person	none
Person	String, String, int, int

Table 8.3: Signatures for Constructors Methods

For us to have a true "name clash," the signatures of two methods must match in every respect. Here, we can see the two methods have the same name; however, they differ in their list of formal arguments. This means there is enough distinction between the two methods that the compiler and the language system can treat them as being, indeed, two different methods.

As far as the compiler is concerned, when it processes our Person class definition, these two constructor definitions offer no problem whatsoever.

```
// first constructor
public Person( )
    {
    forename = "NONE" ;
    surname = "NONE" ;
    age = 0 ;
    gender = UNKNOWN ;
    } // end of constructor method
```

```
// second constructor
public Person(String f, String s, int a, int g)
    {
    forename = f ;
    surname = s ;
    age = a ;
    gender = g ;
    } // end of constructor method
```

What happens for the class user, however?

```
Person aPerson, bPerson ;
aPerson = new Person() ;
bPerson = new Person("James" , "Kirk", 34, Person.MALE) ;
```

How does the compiler know which version of the constructor to call for aPerson and bPerson? Again, it turns to the signature information. When we call a constructor for aPerson, it can see that it has no actual arguments. This matches the signature for the first constructor, and that is the one we shall call.

For bPerson, we can see the constructor call has four actual arguments, and the types are in the order (String, String, int, int). This matches the signature for the second constructor.

This concept of having methods with the same name but different signatures is generally available for all types of methods. For example, we could have two methods called increaseAge. Their signatures and behavior are given in Table 8.4.

Method Name	Formal Arguments	Behavior
increaseAge	int	adds the value of the argument to the age attribute
increaseAge	none	adds 1 to the age attribute

Table 8.4: Signatures and Behaviors for increaseAge

The new variant of increaseAge is:

```
public void increaseAge()
    {
    age = age + 1 ;
    } // end of method increaseAge
```

We can call the two versions as follows:

```
aPerson.increaseAge(10) ;   // adds 10 to the age of aPerson
aPerson.increaseAge() ;     // adds 1 to the age of aPerson
```

The general term for this mechanism is *overloading* because we are using the same name but in different circumstances; thus, we are overloading the name with multiple uses.

8.3 Class Constants

As you have already seen, it is often desirable to have some named *constant* values that we can use (either as a class provider or a class user) when dealing with an object. In our `Person` example, we want to model a person's gender in a more meaningful, semantic way. Although in Java we have to use an integer to store a person's gender, we don't want to use simple integer values (1, 2, 99) to represent the gender. Such values are completely meaningless in this context. The use of constants gives us a simple mechanism for naming these values sensibly in a way that someone reading our code can understand. Thus, in our `Person` class, we declare the following constants.

```
// Person class constants
public static final int UNKNOWN = 99 ;
public static final int MALE = 1 ;
public static final int FEMALE = 2 ;
```

Thereafter, whenever we wish to refer to someone's gender, we can use the terms `MALE`, `FEMALE`, and `UNKNOWN` rather than 1, 2, and 99.

We can, of course, use other kinds of constants. For example, a class that calculates the price of consumer goods needs to include information on VAT (value-added tax). VAT is a rate that is subject to change only at budget times, so here again it is useful to model this as a constant between budgets. For this example, we will assume VAT is set at 10 percent:

```
public static final double VAT_RATE = 10.0 ;
```

In this way, throughout the class and the program that uses it, we can refer to VAT_RATE rather than its actual value. Why is this useful?

Imagine the situation where you have used the VAT rate extensively throughout your program. The budget is announced and the rate has changed. Now you must search through your program and change the rate wherever it occurs. Moreover, you have to be sure that only the occurrences of 10.0 that represent the VAT rate are changed; if it represents something else, it should not be changed.

If you have used a class constant, however, no such difficulties arise. You have only to change the constant definition and recompile your program. We have already encountered a class constant in the `Person` class, namely, UPPER_AGE, which was declared as `private`.

To declare a class constant, the general form is:

```
public-or-private static final <type> <constant name> = <value> ;
```

The keyword `static` indicates that this belongs to the class rather than every individual instance. For example, Figure 8.5 shows the result of the code:

```
public class Car
    {
    private String carName ;
    public int mileage ;
```

```
public static final int TOP_SPEED = 150 ;
// methods ...
} // end of class Car
```

As we noted in the previous chapter, we represent constants by using all capital letters, with the underscore character as a visible space between words.

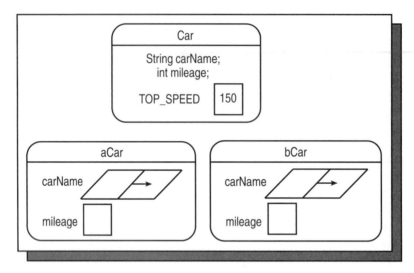

Figure 8.5: The Car class, a constant, and two instances

This also means that we can access the value of TOP_SPEED without declaring any instances of the class:

```
System.out.println("The top speed is " + Car.TOP_SPEED) ;
```

We access the value via the class name, not an instance name.

The keyword final means this is the final value this "variable" can have. It happens to be its first as well.

One benefit of Java's approach is that a constant is strongly typed; in our example, TOP_SPEED is an integer-shaped box and can be used anywhere that an ordinary integer can (except, of course, on the left side of an assignment statement).

Constants must be declared at the class level; you cannot have constant declarations within a method body.

8.4 Class Variables

Just as we can have class constants, it is possible to declare class variables. For example, we may wish to keep a count of how many Car objects have been made. It seems natural to keep this count with the Car class. This would be declared and initialized in the following code, and the result is shown in Figure 8.6.

```
public class Car
    {
    private String carName ;
    public int mileage ;

    public static final int TOP_SPEED = 150 ;
    public static int carCount = 0 ;

    // methods ...
    } // end of class Car
```

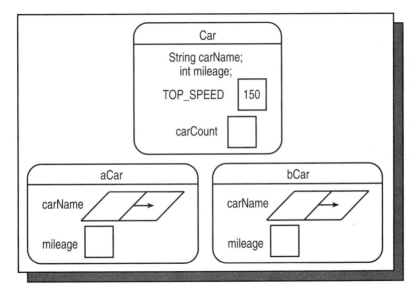

Figure 8.6: The Car class, a constant, a class variable, and two instances

Now, our constructor method(s) must remember to increment this count every time they are called:

```
public Car()
    {
    // initialize instance variables
    // to appropriate values
    carCount++ ;
    } // end of constructor method
```

To find out how many Car instances have been created at any time, we can write the following:

```
System.out.println("number of cars is " + Car.carCount) ;
```

8.5 Private Methods

The methods you have seen so far have all been declared as public. This means they can be accessed and used by any class user. However, it is also possible to declare methods as private. This means they are hidden from the class user and are accessible only to the class provider. What possible use can private methods have?

A private method is unavailable (directly) to the class user; however, the class provider may use it to support the public methods. What does this mean? Well, for example, whenever we set the age attribute of a person, it is possible (as you have seen) and useful to ensure that we set that attribute only to a sensible value. Because of this, we have written the setAge method as follows:

```
public void setAge(int a)
    {
    if ((a < 0) || (a > UPPER_AGE))
        {
        System.out.println("invalid age in 'setAge'") ;
        System.exit(1) ;
        }
    else
        age = a ;
    } // end of method setAge
```

However, we can set the age of a person in more than one method—for example, in one or more of our constructor methods. If we want to check the age is valid, we would have to repeat the foregoing if statement everywhere we set the age. One possibility is to encapsulate the testing code in a private method:

```
private boolean isValidAge(int a)
    {
    return ((a >= 0) && (a <= UPPER_AGE)) ;
    } // end of method isValidAge
```

Now we can rewrite the setAge method as follows:

```
public void setAge(int a)
    {
    if (!isValidAge(a))
        {
        System.out.println("invalid age in 'setAge'") ;
        System.exit(1) ;
        }
    else
        age = a ;
    } // end of method setAge
```

And we can revise the second constructor method:

```
public Person(String f, String s, int a, int g)
    {
    forename = f ;
    surname = s ;
    if (isValidAge(a))
        age = a ;
    else
        age = AGE_UNKNOWN ;
    gender = g ;
    } // end of constructor method
```

Here we are simply setting a default value (which we would need to declare) to the incorrectly valued age.

In our next example, we model temperature as a class. This class has two `private` instance variables, `celsius` and `fahr`, to hold the temperature in Celsius and Fahrenheit, respectively. We have the normal `get` and `set` methods associated with these variables. However, we have decided that these two variables should be kept in step. That is to say, whatever is the temperature in `celsius`, the `fahr` variable contains the matching value in Fahrenheit, and vice versa.

To achieve this, we have provided two `private` methods to take care of the conversion: `celsiusToFahr` and `fahrToCelsius`:

```
public class Temperature
    {
    private double celsius, fahr ;

    public Temperature()
        {
        setCelsius(0.0) ;
        celsiusToFahr() ;
        } // end of constructor method

    public double getCelsius()
        {
        return celsius ;
        } // end of method getCelsius

    public double getFahr()
        {
        return fahr ;
        } // end of method getFahr

    private void celsiusToFahr()
        {
        fahr = ( 1.8 * celsius ) + 32 ;
        } // end of method celsiusToFahr
```

```
public void setCelsius(double c)
   {
   celsius = c ;
   celsiusToFahr() ;
   } // end of method setCelsius

private void fahrToCelsius()
   {
   celsius = (5.0 / 9.0) * ( fahr - 32 ) ;
   } // end of method fahrToCelsius

public void setFahr(float f)
   {
   fahr = f ;
   fahrToCelsius() ;
   } // end of method setFahr
} // end of class Temperature
```

Notice that when we call setCelsius, we not only set the value of celsius but we use the celsiusToFahr method to convert this into Fahrenheit and to set the value of fahr. We do the same within setFahr.

If you are familiar with spreadsheets, you can think of celsius and fahr as two cells in the sheet. They are linked with each other through the formulas contained in the two private conversion methods. Whenever a user directly updates one of these cells, the other is also updated according to the formula. The same thing is happening here.

Both the conversion formulas and the methods that use them are hidden from the class user. In our main program, if we want to convert from one temperature scale to the other, all we have to do is set one and then get the other:

```
public static void main(String[] args)
   {
   Temperature aTemp = new Temperature() ;

   aTemp.setFahr(104.3) ;
   System.out.print("Celsius = " + aTemp.getCelsius() +
                    " Fahr = " + aTemp.getFahr()) ;
   System.out.println() ;
   } // end of main method
```

Thus, private methods support the functionality of the public ones. In some cases, it may be arguable whether a method should be private rather than public. But this is essentially a design decision that may change once the class is in general use.

Often, when we write the main class that drives an application, we find that within the class, as well as the main method, we need a number of "helper" methods. These methods are acting as private methods that assist the main method. You will see examples of this situation later in the book.

8.6 Class or Static Methods

It is possible to declare methods as static; just as with constants, this means they belong to the class rather than an instance. For example, if the static constant TOP_SPEED in the Car class had been declared as private, the class user would be unable to access it directly. We would need a get method to do the job. However, as TOP_SPEED belongs to the class, the getTopSpeed method should also belong to the class rather than instances of that class.

```
public class Car
    {
    private String carName ;
    public int mileage ;

    private static final int TOP_SPEED = 150 ;

    public static int getTopSpeed()
        {
        return TOP_SPEED ;
        } // end of method getTopSpeed
    // other methods ...
    } // end of class Car
```

Thus, we can write:

```
System.out.println("top speed is " + Car.getTopSpeed()) ;
```

The Person class provides similar functionality with the static method, getUpperAgeLimit.

If we examine some of the Java system-supplied classes, we can find some static (or class) methods. For example, the class Math (in the java.lang package) is never intended to have any instances. Instead, it gathers together some constants and methods that can be used in general, in association with ints and doubles as arguments and/or return values. For example, a method that takes two ints as arguments and returns the smaller of the two can be called as follows:

```
int smaller = Math.min(x, y) ;
```

The Integer wrapper class (see Section 6.9) provides a toString method. This method takes an int value and converts it into a String. We can call this as follows:

```
int x = ... ;
...
String xStr = Integer.toString(x) ;
```

In this example of a method, it is not clear where else this could be placed. There is no int class, as int is a primitive type. It has been put in the Integer class, although it does not operate on instances of Integers, but on ints.

It is often difficult to decide whether a method should be implemented as an ordinary instance method or as a class method. You will see an example later in this chapter.

8.7 Revisiting the Main Class

It is time to consider again the main class of any Java application. Although we can envisage our object instances as floating within an object space and exchanging messages as requests to other objects to execute methods on our behalf, there is clearly the need for some initial event to set the ball rolling. In Java, that event is the main class. Here initial objects can be created and requests made of them.

The main class is the class that is specified when we run the Java interpreter java. To execute a class (say, User.class), we type:

```
java User
```

For our application to execute, the named class must contain a class (static) method called main. The header for this should be:

```
public static void main(String[] args)
```

The args argument allows us to provide *command-line parameters* when we execute the Java interpreter. (By the way, the actual name of the String array is arbitrary; we do not need to use the name args, but it is often used by convention.) As a simple example, consider a Java application that prints the command-line parameters, each on its own line.

```
public class CommandLine
    {

    public static void main(String[] args)
        {
        for (int i = 0 ; i < args.length ; i++)
            System.out.println(args[i]) ;
        } // end of main method

    } // end of class CommandLine
```

The argument to the main method in our example is String[] args. This is an array of String objects. You will study arrays in more detail in Chapter 9. For the moment, suffice it to say that we can access each individual String in this array by using an index. In the for loop in the body of the main method, the variable i will index each individual element and allow us to treat each like a single String (e.g., we can print it).

Further, the attribute length of the array lets us find out how many elements are present in args. This will, of course, be the number of command-line parameters we provide when we execute the application. To execute the application, we type

```
java CommandLine one two three
```

and the results are:

```
one
two
three
```

Returning to our Temperature class, we can write an application that takes temperatures in Celsius from the command-line parameter and prints the equivalent temperature in Fahrenheit:

```
public class Temperature
    {
    private double celsius, fahr ;

    // as before plus a new method ...

    public String toString()
        {
        return celsius + " degrees Celsius " +
                fahr + " degrees Fahrenheit" ;
        } // end of method toString

    } // end of class Temperature
```

We have added a new toString method. This produces a String that contains the temperature in Celsius and Fahrenheit with some explanatory text.

```
public class Chapter8n1
    {
    public static void main(String[] args)
        {
        Temperature temperature = new Temperature() ;

        for (int i = 0 ; i < args.length ; i++)
            {
            boolean valid = true ;
            String strCel = args[i] ;
            double cel = 0.0 ;

            try    {
                cel = Double.parseDouble(strCel) ;
                }
            catch (NumberFormatException e)
                {
                System.out.println("parameter provided ["
                                + strCel +
                                "] not in double format") ;
                valid = false;
                }

            if (valid)
                {
                temperature.setCelsius(cel) ;
```

```
                    System.out.println(temperature) ;
                    }
                }
            } // end of main method
        } // end of class Chapter8n1
```

If we type

```
java Chapter8n1 12.1 gur 34.1
```

the results are:

```
12.1 degrees Celsius 53.78 degrees Fahrenheit
parameter provided [gur] not in double format
34.1 degrees Celsius 93.38 degrees Fahrenheit
```

Notice that when we call System.out.println(temperature) it in turn calls toString to obtain a printable text version of the temperature object. We provided a toString method so that we could use println in this way.

The command line could also include *flags*. We could have a flag –c to specify that the input temperature is in Celsius and a flag –f for Fahrenheit.

```
public class Chapter8n2
    {
    public static void main(String[] args)
        {
        Temperature temperature = new Temperature() ;

        // have we got two parameters?
        if (args.length != 2)
            {
            System.out.println("incorrect number of parameters") ;
            System.exit(1) ;
            }

        // does the first parameter look like a flag?
        String flag = args[0] ;
        if (flag.charAt(0) != '-')
            {
            System.out.println("first parameter not a flag") ;
            System.exit(1) ;
            }

        // ok it's a flag but is it valid?
        char flagChar = flag.charAt(1);
```

```
            switch (flagChar)
                {
                case 'f' :
                case 'c' :
                    break ;
                default :
                    System.out.println("unknown flag [" +
                                        flagChar + "] used") ;
                    System.exit(1) ;
                }

        String strCel = args[1] ;
        boolean valid = true ;
        double temp = 0.0 ;
        try     {
            temp = Double.parseDouble(strCel) ;
            }
        catch (NumberFormatException e)
            {
            System.out.println("parameter provided ["
                            + strCel +
                            "] not in double format") ;

            valid = false ;
            }

        if (valid)
            {
            switch (flagChar)
                {
                case 'f' :
                    temperature.setFahr(temp) ;
                    break ;
                case 'c' :
                    temperature.setCelsius(temp) ;
                }
            System.out.println(temperature) ;
            }
        }// end of main method

    } // end of class Chapter8n2
```

If we type

```
java Chapter8n2 -f 93.38
```

the result is:

`34.1 degrees Celsius 93.38 degrees Fahrenheit`

If we type

`java Chapter8n2 -c 12.1`

the result is:

`12.1 degrees Celsius 53.78 degrees Fahrenheit`

The class that contains the `main` method is not intended to have any instances. It is the "main program" of our application. Hence, the `main` method is declared as `static`, as a class method. Clearly, the Java interpreter sets out by executing the `main` method of the named class—in our example, `Chapter8n2.main`. The `main` method is thus no different from other class methods; they are methods that can be executed whether or not instances of the class exist.

Just as with normal classes, the main class can contain class variables and declarations of methods. These methods can be called only in the `main` method of the main class and can manipulate the class variables of the main class. The relationship between the `main` method and `private` methods within the same class is very close to the relationship between the main program and the first-level subprograms in the traditional world.

In our approach to the `main` method and the main class, we have tried not to deviate too far from the traditional world. However, we stress that this has been only an approach (and attempt to simplify the treatment) and not a requirement in Java. Any concrete class can provide a `main` method; this means that we can run such an individual class without the need for a driver application. This can be a very useful debugging technique.

8.8 Packages and Directories

In this section, we review the use of *packages* in the Java programming environment. Classes can be grouped together into packages. They are related very closely to the underlying file and directory structure of the operating system supporting the Java programming environment, which we reviewed in Section 1.6.

The source text for a Java class is contained in a file. It is possible to have more than one Java class source in a single file, but if so, only one of the classes can be declared `public`. It is perhaps more usual to have a single class source in a single file. Whatever the situation, the single public class must have the same name as the file. The file, however, additionally has the extension `.java`.

We have treated each class as a stand-alone entity, which contains a selection of variables, constants, and methods. In fact, it is possible to have a class defined inside another class. This is called an *inner* class. Inner classes are beyond the scope of this book.

The `Temperature` class of Section 8.5 should be contained in a file called `Temperature.java`. When the source text is compiled successfully, the Java bytecodes are contained in a single `.class` file. The results of compiling a valid `Temperature` class will be contained in `Tempera-`

ture.class. Where a source file contains more than one class definition, there will be multiple .class files, one for each class defined.

Suppose now that John wishes to collect together the classes he has developed into a package called johnsClasses. He can do this by creating a directory called johnsClasses in his john directory and placing there the compiled Java bytecodes for the classes in question. For the sake of example, assume that John has written the Temperature class and wishes it to be part of the johnsClasses package. The file Temperature.class must be stored in the directory johnsClasses. One way to do this is to put the file Temperature.java in the johnsClasses directory, go to this directory, and then compile the file with the javac command.

As well as doing this, John would have to edit the source file so that the first line of text in the file reads:

```
package johnsClasses ;
```

This tells the compiler the name of the package that the class belongs to. Note also that the declaration of the class Temperature has to be public:

```
public class Temperature

    {
    ...
```

Now suppose that John has, in the directory john, a file Tdrive.java containing Java source code that uses the class Temperature. So that the compiler can find the Temperature class, we add the following import directive at the beginning of Tdrive.java:

```
import johnsClasses.* ;
```

This tells the compiler that this code will need to access one or more classes to be found in the johnsClasses directory (Figure 8.7).

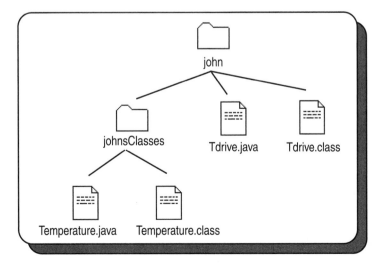

Figure 8.7: John's directories and files

The Java system knows that the bytecodes for the Temperature class are in a file called Temperature.class and (because this class is in the package johnsClasses) that this file will be in a directory called johnsClasses. How does it know where this directory is?

The operating systems under which Java can be used have a number of environment variables, which can be set by the user or contained in files that are executed when the user logs on. By setting the environment variable CLASSPATH to the pathname of the directory containing our package, we can allow the Java interpreter to find our user classes.

For example, in UNIX, we would execute the command:

```
setenv CLASSPATH .:/usr/local/classes
```

This tells the Java system to look for any classes it needs in the current directory (called .) or in the directory /usr/local/classes. Thus, the Java system looks in the current directory john, where it finds the directory johnsClasses which it is looking for.

What if we wish to share the classes written by our colleagues? For example, John wishes to use Roger's Car class, which is in a package called rogersClasses, to write a simple program Tcuser.java that uses both cars and temperatures. A possible situation is shown in Figure 8.8.

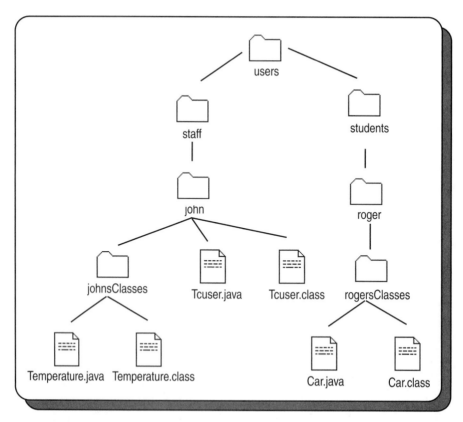

Figure 8.8: Directories and files belonging to John and Roger

Since the class he wants is in the `rogersClasses` package, John adds the following import line to his `Tcuser.java` source file:

```
import rogersClasses.* ;
```

Now the Java system will be expecting to find a directory called `rogersClasses` containing a file `Car.class`, and the CLASSPATH environment variable tells it that the `rogersClasses` directory should be either in the current directory `john` or in the directory `/usr/local/classes`. Because the file is in neither directory, we need to modify the CLASSPATH variable. How we do this depends on what operating system we are using; for example, in UNIX, we would use the `setenv` (set environment variable) command:

```
setenv CLASSPATH .:/usr/local/classes:/users/students/roger
```

This tells the Java system that another place to look for the `rogersClasses` directory is in `/users/students/roger`, and this time the search will be successful.

If a class does not contain a `package` statement, then it is part of an unnamed default package, which is usually the directory that the class was compiled in. This is useful for small test programs or development and is probably the situation you are in at present.

The Java API (Application Programming Interface) provides a set of standard classes, grouped together in more than 40 packages. The ones we discuss in this book are listed in Table 8.5. Your Java environment is usually set up to ensure that these packages are visible to the Java system when needed by having their (known) location included in your CLASS-PATH environment variable.

Package Name	Contents
`java.applet`	classes for implementing applets (see Chapter 20)
`java.awt`	classes for graphics, text, windows, and GUIs (see Chapter 16)
`java.awt.event`	classes for GUI button, mouse actions, etc. (see Chapter 16)
`java.io`	classes for input and output (see Chapter 19)
`java.lang`	classes for the core language
`java.net`	classes for networking (see Chapter 19)
`java.util`	classes for useful data types (see Chapter 21)

Table 8.5: Part of the Java API

8.8.1   *The* import *Statement*

It is worth noting the `import` statement does not actually import code from other places. It simply tells the compiler where the other code can be found (in conjunction with the CLASS-PATH environment variable and the underlying file system). You can have as many `import` statements as you like; they must appear before any class definitions and after the optional `package` statement at the start of the file.

We examine two forms of the statement:

(a) `import package.class ;`
(b) `import package.* ;`

Form (a) allows the class in the package to be referred to by its class name only. For example:

`import java.util.Hashtable ;`

Let us use the name `Hashtable` instead of `java.util.Hashtable`.

Form (b) means that all classes within a package are accessible by class name only. For example, if `johnsClasses` contained `Car.class` and `Temperature.class`, then to refer to these classes by name only, we need:

`import johnsClasses.* ;`

It should be noted that where a dot . separator appears in a package name it denotes a subdirectory (like the slash / separator in a UNIX file name). Any classes in a subdirectory to an imported directory will not be imported. Thus, an `import` statement

`import java.awt.* ;`

imports any classes in the package `java.awt` but not classes in the package `java.awt.event`. To import the latter classes, we need an extra import statement:

`import java.awt.event.* ;`

8.9   Scope and Visibility

In this section, we consider the visibility and accessibility of attributes, variables, and methods. We have already discussed issues of hidden attributes and methods; here we give a general treatment to the various circumstances and properties of "hiding" things.

We begin by considering a class that contains some attributes and methods. We first consider only availability of attributes and methods within the class (*intraclass*). We turn to *interclass* availability (i.e., availability between classes) later in this section. Within the class, all attributes and methods are visible to everything else, even if they have been specified as `private`. The `private` specification holds only for interclass visibility.

8.9.1   *Intraclass Visibility*

The range over which something is visible is called its *scope*. So, for example, in the `Temperature` class, the attributes `celsius` and `fahr` have the entire class as their scope. Any method within the class can access and use these attributes. The same holds for the methods; any method within `Temperature` can call any of the others.

Moreover, in Java, the textual organization of attributes and methods does not affect their visibility. In some programming languages, things have to be declared before (i.e., earlier in the file than) they are used; in essence, their scope ranges from their point of declaration to the end of the programming unit. This is not so in Java; items declared at the end of a class still have the entire class as their scope.

On a software engineering note, this is not necessarily a good thing. An important aid to understandability and readability (and thus, to reuse and maintenance) is that items within a programming unit are organized in a sensible manner. It would probably help us understand a class more easily if the attributes are at the start of the class rather than at the end of it, even though Java does not require this. Just because we can get away with something does not mean we should do it! This is a situation where good programming practice is not enforced by the language syntax.

So far, we have dealt with attributes (instance variables) and methods. However, methods themselves contain declarations of formal arguments and of local variables. Local variables are so called because they are local to the body of the method. Unlike attributes within a class, which can be accessed anywhere within the class, local variables exist only within the method body. Their scope is limited to the method in which they are declared. For example, consider the following piece of code:

```
public class Chapter8n3a
    {
    public void method1()
        {
        int year = 4 ;
        // code ...
        } // end of method method1

    public void method2()
        {
        int y = year + 1 ;
        // code ...
        } // end of method method2
    } // end of class Chapter8n3a
```

Here we assume there are no attributes called year in the class Chapter8n3a.

When we try in method2 to access year, a local variable belonging to method1, we get a compile-time error. This is because year does not exist as far as method2 is concerned. The scope of year is only within method1.

What happens if we use the same name for a local variable as we do for an attribute? Consider the following code:

```
public class Chapter8n3b
    {

    private int year = 1 ;      // attribute

    public void method1()
        {
        int year = 4 ;
        System.out.println("method1 year = " + year) ;
        } // end of method method1
```

```
public void method2()
    {
    method1() ;
    System.out.println("method2 year = " + year) ;
    } // end of method method2
} // end of class Chapter8n3b
```

This would print the following:

```
method1 year = 4
method2 year = 1
```

This is because the year referred to within method1 is the local variable declared within the method. When control returns to method2, the year referred to is the instance variable. The local variable has its value set to 4; the instance variable is unaffected.

What is happening here is that there is a *hole* in the scope of the year instance variable. This hole is exactly the same size as the scope of the year local variable. This is obviously something that we must be wary of. In Table 8.6, you see the scope of the instance variable year and how a hole can be made in the scope by a local variable of the same name.

Scope of year Instance Variable	Value	Scope of year Local Variable	Value	Code
•	1			`int year = 1 ;`
•	1			
		•		`public void method1()`
		•		`{`
		•	0	`int year = 4 ;`
		•	4	`System.out.println(`
				`"method1 year = " + year) ;`
		•		`} // end of method method1`
•	1			
•	1			`public void method2()`
•	1			`{`
•	1			`method1() ;`
•	1			`System.out.println(`
				`"method2 year = " + year) ;`
•	1			`} // end of method method2`

Table 8.6: The Scope of the year Instance Variable and year Local Variable

In `for` loops, we can declare the control variable inside the initialization part of the loop. For example:

```
for (int i = 0 ; i < MAX ; i++)
    ...
```

The scope of this integer `i` is the body of the loop. If we use the same name as a local variable, this creates a hole in the scope of the local variable.

Another way to punch a hole in the scope of an instance variable is to have a formal argument with the same name.

```
public class OurDate
    {
    int day, month, year ;

    public void incrementYear(int year)
        {
        year = year + 1 ;
        } // end of method increment
    } // end of class OurDate
```

The `year` that is incremented will be the formal argument `year`, not the instance variable `year`. Notice that the actual argument will remain unaltered. Sometimes, however, you might have a valid reason for using the same names:

```
public void setYear(int year)
    {
    year = year ;
    } // end of method setYear
```

Whatever this strange looking method does, it does not do what we expect or want. We want this method to take the values of the formal argument and pass it into the corresponding instance variable. One option is to change the name of the formal argument:

```
public void setYear(int y)
    {
    year = y ;
    } // end of method setYear
```

A further option is to distinguish between the names—to specify that on the left side of the assignment we mean the attributes belonging to the instance of the class rather than the formal arguments appearing on the right side of the assignment. We can use the dot . notation for this. You have already seen how we can specify a (public) constant within a class:

```
System.out.println("top speed is " + Car.TOP_SPEED) ;
```

We can do the same to access a public instance variable:

```
System.out.println("current mileage is " + aCar.mileage) ;
```

We could place the name of the instance on the left side, followed by a dot, followed by the attribute name. The problem here is that, as class providers, we cannot possibly know the name of the instance! Only the class users will know this at some point in the future.

8.9.2 Use of this

Java provides the keyword this, which stands for the current instance of the class that is calling this method. Hence, class providers can write the following:

```
public void setYear(int year)
    {
    this.year = year ;
    } // end of method setYear
```

Thus, when as class users we have the following code:

```
christmas.setYear(2002) ;
```

everywhere we have this appearing in setYear, it is as if we had christmas. We can think of this as a kind of implicit argument to the methods.

8.9.3 Interclass Visibility

There are four levels of access permission; here we list them from least to most restrictive: public, protected, default (package visibility), and private. The protected permission relates to subclasses, so we delay discussion of this access level until Chapter 12.

A class either has the access modifier public or none (which specifies the default level). When we apply the public modifier to a class, this means it is visible everywhere. The default level means the class is visible only to other classes in the same package.

A method or constant or attribute can be public, default, or private. When they are public, they are visible everywhere. If they are default, they are visible to other classes in the same package. If they are private, they can be accessed only within their own class.

Normally, classes and constants are public, attributes are private, and methods are either public or private. This is because classes are usually intended as "building blocks" for an application and wouldn't be of much use if they were private. Constants are usually public as they are intended for use by the class users; for example, a class that contains useful mathematical constants would normally make them publicly available. Attributes, as they represent the state of an object, are normally subject to information hiding and are thus private. Finally, methods that are public are provided to allow the class user to manipulate instances of the class, with private methods being used to support the implementation of the public methods.

8.10   Key Points in Chapter 8

- *Constructor* methods allocate sufficient space for an object instance. It is often useful to make the constructor sensibly initialize the attributes of the instance.

- It is possible to have multiple versions of any method (including constructors), as long as their signatures differ. This is called *overloading*.

- Elements in a class definition can belong to the class rather than to instances of the class. This is denoted by the key word `static`. We can use static elements even if no instances of the class exist. The `static` keyword is useful for the following:

  - Defining constants applicable to all instances (e.g., `MALE`, `FEMALE`, etc.).
  - Maintaining data about the collection of instances rather than individual instances (e.g., `carCount`).
  - Collecting together methods where there is no associated object (e.g., a math library).

- A `private` method is accessible only to the class provider. It would be used to support the functionality of other (`private` or `public`) methods within the class.

- The `main` method is a `static` (class) method that is the first one (in an application) executed by the Java interpreter.

- *Packages* are constructs that allow us to group classes together. Classes are kept in individual files; files are kept in directories, and we can treat a directory as a package. To tell the system which package (if any) a class belongs to, we use the `package` statement. To use the classes contained in a package, we use the `import` statement.

- The concept of *scope* relates to the visibility of attributes, variables, and methods. Within a class, scope is closely related to the idea of *global* and *local* variables. For example, a variable declared anywhere in a class definition, except within a method, is said to be *global* to that class. It can be referred to in any statement, anywhere in the class. If a variable is declared within a method (as a variable or a formal argument), it is `local` to that method; we can refer to it only within the method body.

- However, *holes* in scope can arise due to

  - Local variables in method bodies.
  - Formal arguments to methods.

- For class users, scope is defined by the four levels of access permission. At this point in our study of Java, these collapse onto the three levels shown in Table 8.7.

Permission Level	Meaning
`private`	visible only within own class
(default)	visible within own class and other classes in the same package
`public`	visible everywhere

Table 8.7: Access Permissions Levels

8.11   Exercises

1. Write a class `MonthManager` that provides the following facilities:

   a. Static constants JAN, FEB, ... DEC starting from 1.

   b. Static conversion methods that take the following styles of month names

      `"JAN"`, `"Jan"`, `"January"`

      and return the appropriate constant.

   c. A static conversion method that takes a constant and returns a string containing the full name of the month.

   Write a driver application to test your class.

2. Develop your `Rectangle` class from Exercise 7.5 to include:

   a. An argumentless constructor that initializes the length and breadth attributes to zero.

   b. A constructor that takes two arguments to initialize the length and breadth of the rectangle.

3. You need to represent the manufacturer of a car as a constant. The manufacturers you are concerned with include CHEVROLET, FORD, MERCURY, and DODGE.

   Develop the `Car` class so that it includes:

   a. Constants to represent the four manufacturers.

   b. An attribute that stores the manufacturer of the car.

   c. You also wish to represent the particular model of a car; the models you are concerned with are shown in Table 8.8.

Manufacturer	Model	Engine Capacity
Chevrolet	Malibu	999
Chevrolet	Impala	1,100
Ford	Taurus	1,200
Ford	Thunderbird	1,250
Mercury	Sable	999
Mercury	Cougar	1,000
Dodge	Stratus	1,150
Dodge	Intrepid	1,300

Table 8.8: Car Data

You need a method that will convert a car manufacturer constant and the car model attribute into a string. For example, if the manufacturer is Ford and the model is Taurus, then this method should return `"Ford Taurus"`. This method should be defined as `private` and called `toName`.

d. A toString method that returns the manufacturer, the model, and the engine capacity of the car. It should of course make use of the private method toName given earlier.

   You also need method(s) that allows the end user to type in data about a particular car as text and to convert this information into the appropriate internal representation using the foregoing constants.

e. A method encodeManufacturer to take the String version of the data and return the appropriate constant (if it is known).

f. Suitable constructors to initialize the contents of a Car instance.

g. A suitable driver application to test your development of the Car class.

4. Continuing our work on the Car class, provide a method that allows us to compare two Car instances. It should return

   ■ −1 if the first Car is less powerful than the second.
   ■ 0 if they have the same engine capacity.
   ■ 1 if the first Car is more powerful than the second.

5. In this exercise, you need to create two classes as follows:

   a. A Cooker class, which defines an oven for cooking food.

   b. A Dish class, which defines some food you wish to cook.

   Each instance of these classes maintains the current temperature of itself.

   When you place a Dish in the Cooker, you specify how long (in seconds) you want the Dish to be cooked. Assume that for every second the Dish remains in the oven, its temperature increases by (cooker temperature − dish temperature) / 10. Obviously, the dish cannot become hotter than the cooker.

   Specify and implement the necessary methods and attributes to support an application that allows the end user to:

   ■ Input the current temperature of a dish.
   ■ Input the current temperature of the oven.
   ■ Input how long the dish is to remain in the oven.

   The application responds by displaying the temperature of the dish when the time expires.

   Notice that the Dish's current temperature should be updated appropriately during (and after) its time in the Cooker.

6. Write a class Videotape to model the details of an individual recording of a TV program on a videotape. The attributes should be:

   ■ classification—at least film, comedy, education, other
   ■ title
   ■ playing time (a whole number of minutes)

   Write a driver program to allow the user to test your Videotape class.

CHAPTER 9

Arrays

9.1 Collections of Elements

So far, we have usually been dealing with variables that refer to individual elements such as a single integer, a single string of characters, a single instance of the Person class. If we need more than one element of the same type, then we have simply declared several elements all of the same type, each with its own name.

But we often want to refer to large numbers of elements all of the same type such as a collection of integers to hold a number of salaries, let's say, or a collection of strings to hold a number of lines making up a page. We could of course declare a number of individual elements

```
int firstSalary ;
int secondSalary ;
int thirdSalary ;
```

and so on.

However, this takes a lot of writing, and we have to decide at the time we write the program how many of these salary elements we are going to need. Furthermore, we would have difficulty processing these elements because we have to write a separate statement to process each one. What we need is some systematic way of naming the elements so that we can process them inside a loop, referring to successive elements in successive iterations of the loop.

Java provides a mechanism called an *array* to hold a collection of elements all of the same type. For example, if we want to hold a collection of 10 integers, we declare:

```
int[] salaries = new int[10] ;
```

This creates a programming element called salaries. It is of type int[], which is pronounced "array of int"; the characters [] appended to a type indicate an array of that type. The reserved word new introduces a constructor for the array, and we need to specify how many elements are going to be in the array; here there will be 10.

This array declaration is rather like the declaration of an object variable. What in fact happens is that the variable salaries contains a reference to an area of store containing a set of elements of the type specified (Figure 9.1).

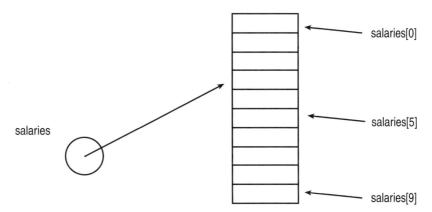

salaries[0]

salaries

salaries[5]

salaries[9]

Figure 9.1: An array of 10 ints

We refer to an individual element of this array by writing the name of the array (here salaries) followed by the number of the element, the *index*, in square brackets. In Java, following the convention of the C and C++ programming languages, the numbering of the elements of an array starts at zero. Thus, the first element of this array is salaries[0] and the last is salaries[9]; they are of type int, of course. It is important to remember that the index of the last element is 1 less than the number of elements we have declared.

If we have an int variable i, we can refer to the ith element of the array with salaries[i]. As long as i takes one of the values in the range 0 to 9, the appropriate element of the array is accessed. If i has a value outside this range, then an attempt to access the array will cause the exception ArrayIndexOutOfBoundsException to be thrown.

So far, we have set up this array salaries capable of holding 10 integers, but we have not yet set them to any particular value. We could set them in a for loop:

```
for (int i = 0 ; i < salaries.length ; i++)
    salaries[i] = i * 10000 ;
```

We can find out the number of elements in the array salaries by writing salaries.length. Of course, in this case, we could have written i < 10. But if we later decided that the length of the array should be, say, 20, we would then have to go through the program changing all the 10s that referred to the length of this array and remember not to change all the 10s that refer to something else. Thus, it is better to use the length attribute of the array where we can. Notice that we do not put parentheses after length; it is not a method like the length() method of the String class.

This is a typical loop for processing an array. We start with the index set to zero, and the last iteration is with the index set to 1 less than the length of the array.

There is an alternative way to initialize an array in Java using a *literal array expression*. The language allows us to write the initial values for an array as a sequence of expressions separated by commas and surrounded by curly braces. So we could have declared and initialized the salaries array as follows:

```
int[] salaries = {0, 10000, 20000, 30000, 40000, 50000,
                    60000, 70000, 80000, 90000} ;
```

The declaration is able to calculate how many array elements there should be (here 10, numbered from 0 up as before).

When we used the for loop to initialize the array, it was perhaps unusual to be able to calculate the value in the array from the index. Why would we need to store all the values? A more typical array initialization would be one where there is no systematic way of going from the index value to the contents of an element, such as for an array of the number of days in each month:

```
int[] daysInMonth = {31, 28, 31, 30, 31, 30, 31, 31, 30,
                      31, 30, 31} ;
```

An alternative way of assigning values to the salaries array might be to read them in from the user:

```
int noOfSalaries = 0 ;
int[] salaries = new int[10] ;
while (true)
    {
    System.out.println("Type the " + noOfSalaries
                        + "th salary") ;
    System.out.println("\ttype zero after final salary") ;
    int response = BasicIO.readInteger() ;
    if (response == 0)
        break ;
    if (noOfSalaries == salaries.length)
        {
        System.out.println("ERROR: too many salaries")
        System.out.println("salary " + response +
                            " ignored") ;
        break ;
        }
    salaries[noOfSalaries] = response ;
    noOfSalaries++ ;
    }
```

We prompt the user for a salary value and read it into the integer variable response. If the value is zero, we can leave the loop with a break statement. We keep track of how many salaries we have read in with the variable noOfSalaries. We check that we have not read in too many salaries with the test:

```
if (noOfSalaries == salaries.length)
    ...
```

Is this the correct form of the test? If we failed to perform this test, we would be storing an element into the array with index value salaries.length. But we know that the index values must lie in the range zero to 1 less than the length of the array. So the test is in the correct form.

If the number of salaries is not too large, we can store the new value in the next array element and then increment the count of salary values we have seen. After we leave the loop, we have to remember that for the rest of the program the valid salaries have index values in the range zero to noOfSalaries − 1. To print them, we could write a for loop:

```
for (int i = 0 ; i < noOfSalaries ; i++)
    System.out.println(salaries[i]) ;
```

9.2 Arrays of Objects

So far, we have declared arrays of a basic data type int. But we can also declare arrays of objects. For example, we could declare an array of 100 Person instances as follows:

```
Person[] personGroup = new Person[100] ;
```

What does this do? It sets up a variable personGroup (of type "array of Person", written Person[]) and this refers to a block of 100 elements of type Person (numbered from zero to 1 less than personGroup.length). This is shown in Figure 9.2.

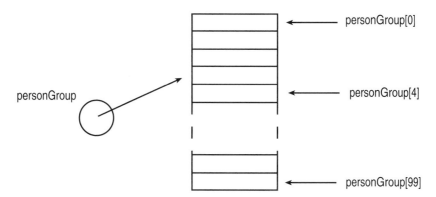

Figure 9.2: An array of 100 Person instances

But just like the integer array, the Person elements in this array have not yet been initialized; they do not refer to instances of the Person class. If we try to set one of the attributes of, say, personGroup[0], we get a NullPointerException. We could again initialize the array elements in a for loop, using a constructor method:

```
for (int i = 0 ; i < personGroup.length ; i++)
    personGroup[i] = new Person() ;
```

This sets each element of the array to refer to an instance of the Person class (Figure 9.3). Each of these objects has been set up with whatever initial values are provided by the Person constructor method with no arguments (strings "NONE" for the names, zero age, and UNKNOWN for the gender; see the documentation for the Person class).

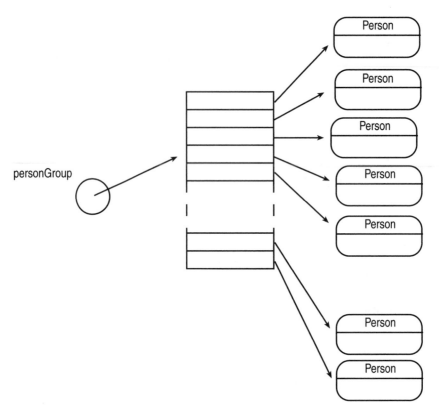

Figure 9.3: An initialized array of Person instances

Alternatively, we could read the values in. This time we will read them in from a file:

```
Person[] personGroup = new Person[100] ;
BasicFileIo file = new BasicFileIo(BasicFileIo.INPUT,
                                    "person.data") ;
int noOfPersons = 0 ;
while (true)
    {
    String fore = file.readString() ;
    if (fore == null)
        break ;
    String sur = file.readString() ;
    int age = file.readInteger() ;
    String x = file.readString() ;
    int gender ;
    if (x.equalsIgnoreCase("MALE"))
        gender = Person.MALE ;
    else if (x.equalsIgnoreCase("FEMALE"))
        gender = Person.FEMALE ;
```

```
        else
            gender = Person.UNKNOWN ;
        if (noOfPersons == personGroup.length)
            {
            System.out.println("ERROR: too many people")
            System.out.println(fore + " " + sur +
                                " ignored") ;
            break ;
            }
        personGroup[noOfPersons] = new Person(fore, sur,
                                     age, gender) ;
        noOfPersons++ ;
        }
file.closeFile() ;
```

This program reads a succession of values of forename, surname, age, and gender. When it has a set of values, it creates a new instance of the Person class initialized with the values just read in. In the case of gender, a string of characters read in has to be converted to an integer constant. When the program reaches the end of the file, the readString method returns a null reference rather than a String, and the program tests for this null reference to terminate the loop.

We can extract an attribute of one of the array elements by writing something like personGroup[i].getSurname():

- First we specify the array name so that we have something of type "array of Person".

- Then we specify the index value in square brackets; this gives us something of type Person.

- Then we apply the method name and any arguments.

We could display all the surnames we have read into the array with:

```
for (int i = 0 ; i < noOfPersons ; i++)
    System.out.println(personGroup[i].getSurname()) ;
```

Java provides another way to hold a collection of elements all of the same type, a *Vector*. We will discuss this other mechanism further in Chapter 21.

9.3 Searching an Array

Suppose we have read a set of personal details into the array personGroup. We now read a surname into a String variable surname and wish to find all the personal details relating to this surname. Here is some code to carry out this task:

```
int i = 0 ;
while ((i < noOfPersons) &&
       (!personGroup[i].getSurname().equals(surname)))
    i++ ;
```

We use a `while` loop because there are two possible outcomes: (a) we search right through the array and do not find what we are looking for or (b) part of the way through the array we find a matching surname. Because we may stop early, we do not use a `for` loop.

We have a control variable `i` initialized to zero, which we increment as long as (a) this value is a legitimate index into the `personGroup` array, and (b) the surname of the `Person` instance at this index value does not match the surname we are looking for. This latter test is done by extracting the surname from the `i`th array element (with `personGroup[i].getSurname()`) and then using the `equals` method from the `String` class to compare it to the variable `surname`; hence:

```
personGroup[i].getSurname().equals(surname)
```

Finally, the Boolean value required is the opposite of this, so we add the NOT operator !.

When we leave the loop, the control variable `i` will be set either to the value `noOfPersons`, indicating that the surname we sought was not among those held, or it will be a value in the range zero to `noOfPersons − 1`, indicating that we have found a match at that index position in the array.

Perhaps there are several `Person` instances with this surname. What would happen in this case? It is obvious that the preceding loop would find the first such `Person` instance. If we wanted, for some reason, to find the last such `Person` instance, we could search backward through the loop, starting the index variable at `noOfPersons - 1` and stopping when `i` reaches the value −1; we need to check the `Person` at offset 0, as this could be a match.

If we want to know whether there are multiple matches, we could write:

```
int matchIndex = -1 ;
int noOfMatches = 0 ;
for (int i = 0 ; i < noOfPersons ; i++)
    if (personGroup[i].getSurname().equals(surname))
        {
        matchIndex = i ;
        noOfMatches++ ;
        }
```

We have to traverse the entire array now to make sure we have counted all the matches; hence, we use a `for` loop. When we find a matching surname, we remember where it occurred in `matchIndex`. This is the index of the last match because that was the easiest to write. How would you modify the code so that it remembered the first match? The number of matches will be in `noOfMatches` (a value of zero meaning there were no matches, of course).

If we wanted to have a list of all the matches, we could store each index value in a new array of matches when we find it. Try writing this version.

Let us return to the original code for searching the array, where we stop as soon as we find the first match. How efficient is this algorithm? The amount of time required to run the program will be proportional to the number of times around the loop, so the number of iterations is a good measure of how much time the program will take. If there is a matching surname at index position `i` in the array, then we must go around the loop `i + 1` times. If the surname is not in the array, we will look at each surname in the array, which means `personGroup.length` iterations. Thus, in the worst case (when there is no match), for an array of n elements, we require n iterations, or an amount of time proportional to n. We say that this linear search is an O(n) algorithm, pronounced "order n algorithm." If we double the size of the array, we double the amount of work to be done (in the worst case).

Suppose now that we *sorted* the array on the surnames; that is, we rearranged the elements in the array so that the Person instance at index position 0 had the earliest surname alphabetically, and the Person instance at index position noOfPersons − 1 had the latest surname alphabetically. You will see later how to make this rearrangement; for the moment, let us just assume that it has been done. We can rewrite the searching algorithm to stop the search as soon as we find ourselves starting to look at surnames alphabetically later than the one we want because we then know that later ones are higher still in the alphabet and therefore could not match:

```
int i = 0 ;
boolean matchSurname = false ;
while (i < noOfPersons)
    {
    int result =
            personGroup[i].getSurname().compareTo(surname) ;
    if (result == 0)
        {
        matchSurname = true ;
        break ;
        }
    else if (result > 0)
        break ;
    }
```

The method compareTo compares the String to which it is applied with the String argument (like the equals method), but the return value is an integer representing three possibilities:

- The value zero if the two Strings match.

- A value less than zero if the instance's String is alphabetically earlier than the argument String.

- A value greater than zero if the instance's String is alphabetically later than the argument String.

If we are in an iteration where we find that the surname at this position in the array is later than the one we are looking for, we know that there is no point in looking further, and we can break out of the loop. Similarly, if we find a match, we can also break out, but we need to set the boolean variable matchSurname to true.

How good is this algorithm? If we find a match at index value i, we need i + 1 iterations, as before. If we don't find a match, then we generally no longer need to search all the way through the array. Sometimes we will be lucky and decide at the first array position that the surname we are looking for is not in the array; other times we will be unlucky and decide only at the last array position. On average, we are likely to have to search about halfway through the array. So we have improved the searching. In fact, we still call this an O(n) algorithm because it requires time proportional to the size of the array n. If we double the size of the array, the amount of time required is approximately doubled. However, the proportionality constant is smaller.

One way to improve the average performance (though not the worst case performance) might be to find out which are the values most commonly sought, put them at the beginning of the array, and then use the original linear search. If some surnames are much more commonly searched for than others, this would improve the average searching time. For example, if this is a list of all my email aliases, it is certainly true that there is a small number of aliases I use several times a day and others I use once a month or less. This is a case where ordering by frequency of access might pay off.

9.4 Binary Search

A more general alternative is to make better use of the fact that we have put the array into alphabetical surname order. We can use a technique called *binary search*, which works as follows:

- First we look at the array element at (or near) the middle of the array. If this is the element we want, then we have finished. If it is not the element we want, we at least now know (because the array is ordered) whether the element is in the first half of the array or in the second half (if it is there at all).

- We now look at the middle element of the appropriate half. Again, we may find what we want. But if not, we now know which quarter (if any) the element is in.

- We look at the middle element of the appropriate quarter and so on, looking at the middle element of smaller and smaller sections of the array.

- We stop when we have either found what we want or the section of the array we are looking in has dwindled to nothing.

Here is the code for binary search of an ordered array:

```
int i = -1 ;
int j = noOfPersons ;
int k = 0 ;
boolean matchSurname = false ;
while ((i + 1 < j) && (!matchSurname))
    {
    k = (i + j) / 2 ;
    int result =
            personGroup[k].getSurname().compareTo(surname) ;
    if (result == 0)
        matchSurname = true ;
    else if (result < 0)
        i = k ;
    else // that is, result > 0
        j = k ;
    }
```

On each iteration, the section to be searched is from just after the value i to just before the value j. We initialize these values before the first iteration to include all the elements in the array, and we test on each iteration to find out if the section we are searching has shrunk to contain no elements. We set the variable k to point to the middle element of the section, using integer divide to get a valid index value. We compare the surname at this position with the surname we are searching for, using the `compareTo` method and putting the result of the comparison in the variable `result`.

If `result` is zero, we have a match and can terminate the search; k now holds the index value for the matching surname in the array. If `result` is less than zero, the element we want must be in the second half of the section we have just searched. In this case, we change the value of the variable i, which indicates the bottom of the section to be searched. If `result` is greater than zero, the element we want must be in the first half of the section we have just searched. In this case, we change the value of the variable j, which indicates the top of the section to be searched.

How well does this work? It can easily be shown that binary search of an array of n elements takes approximately "logarithm of n to base 2" iterations. Thus, binary search of an array of 1,024 elements would take no more than 10 iterations (where with linear search we would expect to need something like 500 iterations on average). So we say binary search is an O(log n) algorithm.

Two further points need to be made about searching:

- If there are several elements in the array with the same surname, we cannot be sure which one a binary search will find. It will not necessarily be the first, the last, or any predictable position. It will depend on the positioning of the surnames with respect to the binary subdivision of the array.

- When we are searching for a surname, our search will be efficient because we have rearranged the array to make it so. But if we now want to search for a particular forename or a particular age, we are back with the O(n) linear search because the array cannot be ordered on these attributes and on the surname as well.

9.5   Sorting an Array

We now need to consider how to *sort* the array—that is, to rearrange it in alphabetical order by surname so that it can be searched efficiently. There are a large number of algorithms for sorting arrays.[1] We are going to demonstrate only one of these algorithms and set another as an exercise.

The first sorting algorithm is called *insertion sort.* Suppose we have already put some of the array in order; elements 0 to i − 1 are in order, and elements i to noOfPersons − 1 are still to be sorted. We can take the element at position i, find out where it should go within the elements 0 to i − 1, and then insert it. Then we repeat this with element i + 1. Here is the code:

---

[1]There are in fact complete books on the subject. A definitive but rather dated one is Donald Knuth, *Art of Computer Programming, Volume 3: Sorting and Searching* (Reading, MA: Addison-Wesley, 1999); see also Sara Baase, *Computer Algorithms* (Reading, MA: Addison-Wesley, 2000), Chapter 2.

```
for (int i = 1 ; i < noOfPersons ; i++)
    {
    int j = i ;
    String s = personGroup[i].getSurname() ;
    Person p = personGroup[i] ;
    while ((j > 0) &&
           (personGroup[j - 1].getSurname().compareTo(s) > 0))
        {
        personGroup[j] = personGroup[j - 1] ;
        j-- ;
        }
    personGroup[j] = p ;
    }
```

On each iteration of the outer loop, we put the ith array element in its correct location within the sorted array of elements 0 to i (inclusive). An array consisting of a single element can be considered already sorted. Thus, we do not need to perform an iteration for i set to 0, to position the 0th element in the sorted array consisting only of the 0th element. Thus, we start with i set to 1 and finish with i set to noOfPersons - 1.

We are going to move the element at position i to position j, so the inner loop needs to find the correct value of j. We start with j set to the value of i because the ith element might already be in the right place. We then scan down through the elements that are already sorted, making a gap at the appropriate place for the ith element. If the element at position j - 1 has a surname alphabetically later than that at position i, we move the element at position j - 1 up one and then decrement j by one so that there is a gap at position j. We continue doing this until we find an element that should appear before the element at position i or until we have scanned right to the beginning of the array (i.e., the ith element should be at position 0).

Since we are shuffling the elements up through the array, we need first to clear out the element at position i to a temporary Person variable p. We also make a copy (in the String variable s) of the surname of the original ith element to make the comparison statement a bit shorter.

Let us now watch how the sort works. Suppose there are four elements in the array, and initially, they have surnames in the order Smith, Jones, Thomas, Matthews (Figure 9.4). We assume that the section of the array consisting only of element 0 (i.e., the Person instance with the surname Smith) is in the correct order, as indicated by the thick line drawn across the array below this element.

We start the first iteration of the outer loop, with i set to 1 and, consequently, with j set to 1 and s set to Jones. Finally, we copy the value in the array element at position 1 to the variable p so that p refers to the instance containing the surname Jones. Figure 9.5 shows the current state.

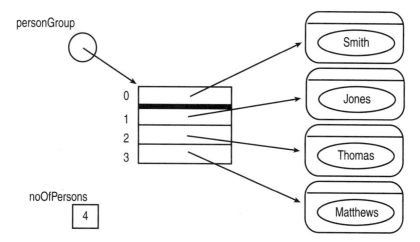

Figure 9.4: The original unsorted array

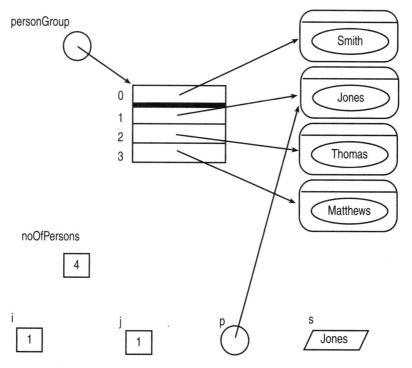

Figure 9.5: Beginning the first iteration of the inner loop

We start executing the inner loop. We test that j is greater than 0 (which is true) and that `personGroup[j - 1].getSurname()` (which is `Smith`) is alphabetically later than s (which is `Jones`), and this is also true. So we perform an iteration of the inner loop, making the element at position j refer to the same object instance as that at position j - 1 (with the statement `personGroup[j] = personGroup[j - 1]`) and decreasing the value of j by 1. Figure 9.6 shows the result.

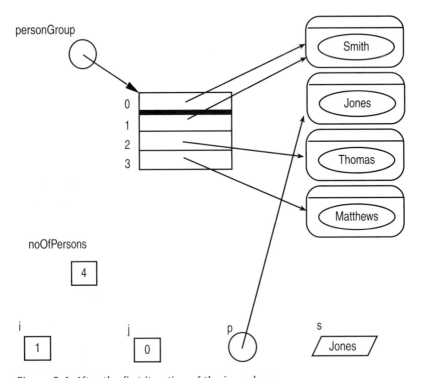

Figure 9.6: After the first iteration of the inner loop

The variable j now has the value 0, so we do not perform any more iterations of the inner loop. We execute the statement:

`personGroup[j] = p ;`

This makes the jth element of the array (i.e., the one at position 0) refer to the object instance with surname `Jones`. We have what is shown in Figure 9.7. The section of the array `personGroup[0 . . . 1]` is now in order as indicated by the thick line.

We commence the next iteration of the outer loop, with i set to 2, j to 2, s to `Thomas`, and p referring to the object instance with surname `Thomas`. Figure 9.8 shows the result.

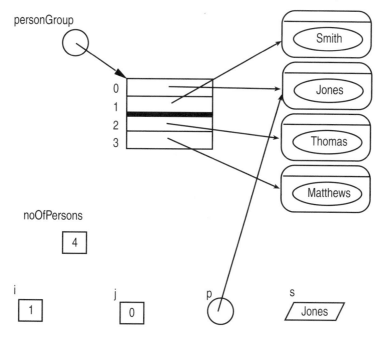

Figure 9.7: After the first iteration of the outer loop

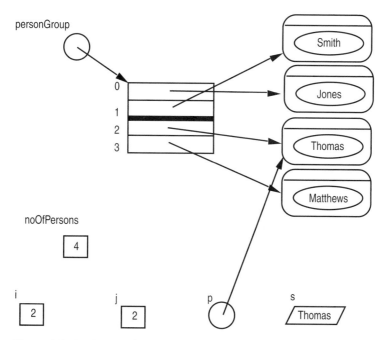

Figure 9.8: Beginning the second iteration of the outer loop

We prepare to reenter the inner loop. The value of j is greater than 0, but the method com-pareTo as applied to the value of personGroup[j - 1].getSurname() which is (Smith), and the value of which is s (Thomas) returns a negative value. Hence, the iteration test fails, and we perform no iterations of the inner loop.

Thus, we copy back the reference to the Thomas instance into the jth element (i.e., the one at position 2), leaving what is shown in Figure 9.9. In other words nothing has changed, but we now know that the sorted section of the array is personGroup[0 . . . 2]. We could have arranged not to do the copying of the references in this case because it is unnecessary. But it probably makes the code more difficult to follow, with little improvement in efficiency (re-member, we are copying references to objects, not the objects themselves), so we leave the code as it is.

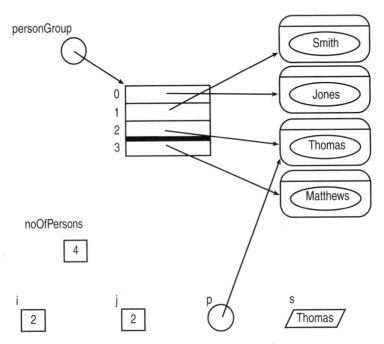

Figure 9.9: After the second iteration of the outer loop

We are now ready for the next (and last) iteration of the outer loop, with i set to 3. If you follow the code step by step, you will find that the two surnames Thomas and Smith will be shifted up one position and Matthews shifted into position 1, leaving what you see in Figure 9.10. The algorithm terminates, and the array section personGroup[0 . . . 3], which is the entire relevant portion of the array, is now sorted.

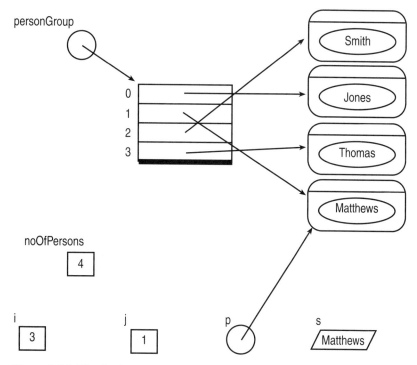

Figure 9.10: The final sorted array

How much effort does this insertion sorting algorithm take? We go around the outer loop noOfPersons - 1 times. How many times do we go around the inner loop? In the worst case (when the array to be sorted is exactly in the wrong order—in decreasing alphabetical order in this case), we have to go through the whole sorted array each time. Thus, we have one inner loop iteration for i set to 2, two for i set to 3, and so on. In the worst case, this is 1 + 2 + 3 . . . + noOfPersons - 2. If there are n elements in the array, this comes to $n(n - 1)/2$. Thus, insertion sort is an $O(n^2)$ algorithm, pronounced "order n squared."

This is not the best we can do. There are sorting algorithms that are $O(n \log n)$; that is, of order "n times log n to base 2," which is considerably better. If n is 1,000, n^2 is 1,000,000, and $n \log n$ is about 10,000, it is a factor of 100 better for this value of n.

What happens if we have two elements with the same surname? We have carefully written our sorting algorithm so that it is *stable*; that is, if two arrays elements have the same sorting field, they are left in the same order as in the original array. Check that you understand how this algorithm ensures this stability. With some other sorting algorithms, it is not as easy to ensure stability.

9.6 Arrays as Arguments

So far, our program consists of a single main method to read in the values for the array, to sort it into alphabetical order by surname, and then to search it for a succession of surnames typed in by the user. It would be better to organize our program into a simpler main method, which calls separate private methods (readArray, sortArray, and searchArray) to carry out these three steps.

Here is the sortArray method:

```
private static void sortArray(Person[] array,
                            int arrayLength)
   {
   for (int i = 1 ; i < arrayLength ; i++)
      {
      int j = i ;
      String s = array[i].getSurname() ;
      Person p = array[i] ;
      while ((j > 0) &&
             (array[j - 1].getSurname().compareTo(s) > 0))
         {
         array[j] = array[j - 1] ;
         j-- ;
         }
      array[j] = p ;
      }
   } // end of method sortArray
```

There are two arguments to this method. The first is the array to be sorted (of type Person[]—that is, an array of Person instances), and the second is the number of elements to be sorted (of type int).

In the main method, we declare the array and a count of how many people we have read into the array:

```
int maxNoOfPersons = 100 ;
Person[] personGroup = new personGroup[maxNoOfPersons] ;
int noOfPersons ;
```

We read the data into the array, setting noOfPersons while we do it, and then we sort the array:

```
sortArray(personGroup, noOfPersons) ;
```

Figure 9.11 shows the situation while this method is being executed.

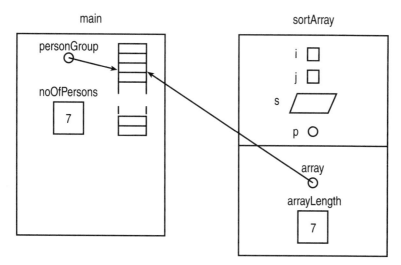

Figure 9.11: Calling the sortArray method

In the main method, there is an array variable personGroup and an int variable noOfPersons, which are passed as actual arguments to the sortArray method, corresponding to its formal arguments array and arrayLength, respectively. We know how int arguments are passed. The value of the actual argument noOfPersons, let's say 7, is copied into the formal argument arrayLength for use inside the method. With an array argument, a *reference* is passed across, and we can refer to individual elements of the array from inside the sortArray method—for example, array[0] or array[arrayLength – 1].

Because only the value of an int argument is passed to the method, a change to the formal argument arrayLength will not affect the actual argument noOfPersons. But because a reference to the array has been passed across, any modifications to the array from inside the sortArray method using the formal argument array will affect the actual array personGroup in the main method. In particular, the elements of the array will be rearranged into sorted order.

We have a problem with the readArray method because we need to pass back two pieces of information: the array with the values copied into it and the number of elements inserted. We can pass the array as an argument, as before, but we have to pass the count of elements as a return value:

```
private static int readArray(String name, Person[] array)
                             throws IOException
    {
    BasicFileIo file = new BasicFileIo(BasicFileIo.INPUT,
                                       name) ;
    int arrayLength = 0 ;

    while (true)
        {
        String fore = file.readString() ;
```

```
        if (fore == null)
            break ;
        String sur = file.readString() ;
        int age = file.readInteger() ;
        String x = file.readString() ;
        int gender ;
        if (x.equalsIgnoreCase("MALE"))
            gender = Person.MALE ;
        else if (x.equalsIgnoreCase("FEMALE"))
            gender = Person.FEMALE ;
        else
            gender = Person.UNKNOWN ;
        if (arrayLength == array.length)
            {
            System.out.println("ERROR: too many people") ;
            System.out.println(fore + " " + sur +
                                    "ignored") ;
            break ;
            }

        array[arrayLength] = new Person(fore, sur, age,
                                    gender) ;
        arrayLength++ ;
        }

    file.close() ;
    return arrayLength ;
    } // end of method readArray
```

We call this method as follows:

```
BasicIo.prompt("type file name ") ;
String fileName = BasicIo.readString() ;
noOfPersons = readArray(fileName, personGroup) ;
System.out.println("read " + noOfPersons +
                " elements from file " + fileName) ;
```

You will recall that the main method usually has a single formal argument args:

```
public static void main(String[] args)
```

It is now clear that this is an array of Strings, the *command-line parameters* passed to the program when it begins to run. Thus, if we run a Java application program with

```
java JavaProgram now is the hour
```

in the `main` method `args.length` is 4, `args[0]` is "now", and `args[3]` is"hour".

9.7 Multidimensional Arrays

So far, we have discussed *one-dimensional* arrays, which are a single sequence of elements all of the same type. We can introduce *two-dimensional* arrays to represent matrices from mathematics, boards from games like chess, computer display screens, and so on. In all these cases, there are two dimensions or index values, usually called the *row* and the *column*, and a particular element is specified by its row and column number. As before, all elements of the array must be of the same type.

We are going to illustrate two-dimensional arrays by starting to create a class to represent a game of tick-tack-toe (noughts-and-crosses). A typical board, with three rows and three columns, is shown in Figure 9.12.

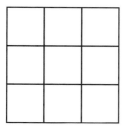

Figure 9.12: A board for a game of tick-tack-toe (noughts-and-crosses)

The squares of the board need to contain only a blank, a tick (X), or a tack (O); thus, we declare some constants:

```
public static final int BLANK = 0 ;
public static final int O = 1 ;
public static final int X = 2 ;
```

and then we declare a two-dimensional array `board`:

```
private int[][] board = new int[3][3] ;
```

The variable array `board` is of type `int[][]`, pronounced "array of array of `int`." Unlike some programming languages, in Java, we cannot directly create a two-dimensional array; instead, we create a one-dimensional array of one-dimensional arrays (Figure 9.13).

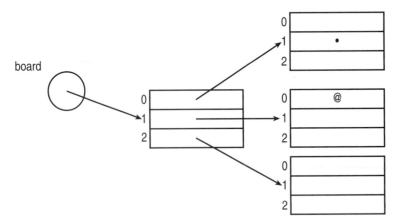

Figure 9.13: A two-dimensional array in Java

We refer to an individual element with an extension to the notation for one-dimensional arrays. The element at row 0 column 1 (indicated with a blob • in Figure 9.13) is `board[0][1]`. Notice that the first declared dimension is also the one specified first when referring to an individual element. The element `board[1][0]` (i.e., row 1 column 0) is the one with the @ symbol in the figure.

We can initialize an empty board, before starting to play a game, using a nested loop:

```
for (int i = 0 ; i < 3 ; i++)
    for (int j = 0 ; j < 3 ; j++)
        board[i][j] = BLANK ;
```

Alternatively, Java allows us to initialize a multidimensional array by listing the values in an extension of the literal array expression notation provided for a one-dimensioned array:

```
private int[][] board = {{BLANK, BLANK, BLANK},
                         {BLANK, BLANK, BLANK},
                         {BLANK, BLANK, BLANK}} ;
```

The outermost pair of curly braces encloses the whole initialization expression, and each inner pair of curly braces encloses a row; the row expressions, like the expressions for the individual elements of the row, are separated by commas. The compiler can deduce from this expression that there are three rows in the array (numbered 0 to 2), and each has three elements (numbered 0 to 2). In this situation, we want to set all the elements to the same value, but we could set some of the elements to different values:

```
private int[][] board = {{X, BLANK, BLANK},
                         {BLANK, X, BLANK},
                         {BLANK, BLANK, X}} ;
```

Figure 9.14 shows the result.

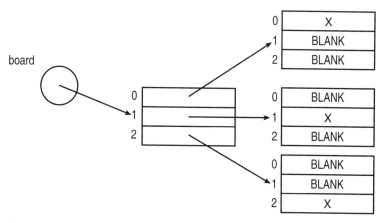

Figure 9.14: An initialized two-dimensional array

We could test for a win on the diagonal from top left to bottom right with the test:

```
if ((board[0][0] == board[1][1]) &&
    (board[1][1] == board[2][2]))
    . . .
```

Actually, there is something wrong with this code as a test for a winning move. Our first attempt to write a program to play this game had the preceding code, and we were surprised to find it was claiming a victory before any moves had been made. The code has to be rewritten to ensure that the contents of the three positions is either a 0 or a X (i.e., not a BLANK). For example:

```
if ((board[0][0] == board[1][1]) &&
    (board[1][1] == board[2][2]) &&
    (board[0][0] != BLANK))
    . . .
```

This was a square array with the same number of rows and columns. We can of course declare rectangular arrays. For example, to declare an array rainfall to hold a double value for the rainfall for each month of a period of 10 years, we could write:

```
double[][] rainfall = new double[10][12] ;
```

The result of this declaration is shown in Figure 9.15.

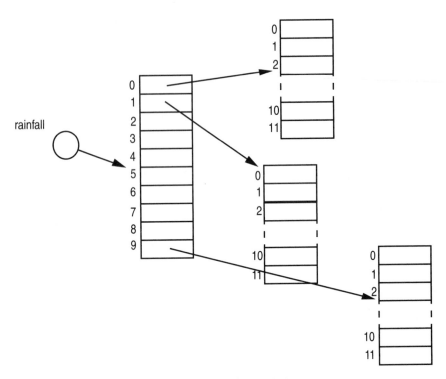

Figure 9.15: A rectangular two-dimensional array in Java

The first index is for the 10 years, say, 2000 to 2009, represented by index values 0 to 9, and the second for the months; notice that the latter takes the range 0 to 11 rather than 1 to 12. The value for, say, June 2006, would be `rainfall[6][5]`.

We can declare arrays with more than two dimensions, although three dimensions are probably the most we are likely to find useful. An array for rainfall figures for each month of a 10-year period for each of 20 locations could be declared as:

```
double[][][] rainfall = new double[10][12][20] ;
```

The value for, say, June 2006 for location 15 (numbered 0 to 19), would be `rainfall[6][5][15]`.

We are going to have difficulty remembering which location is which, so we could declare a set of constants to give a location name to each of the 20 index values for the third index.

If we take the length of the `rainfall` array (with `rainfall.length`), we get the length, of the array of row references, which here is 10. Applying it to one of the row arrays (with, say, `rainfall[0].length`) gives 12. The expression `rainfall[0][0].length` gives 20.

9.8 Nonrectangular Arrays (Optional)

In Java, it is possible to have arrays that are not rectangular. Suppose we wanted an array to hold Pascal's triangle, which looks like this:

```
        1  1
      1   2   1
    1   3   3 1
  1 4   6   4 1
1 5 10 10 5 1
```

Each row starts and finishes with the value 1, and the remaining values are the sum of the two values above it. The first 3 in the third row is 1 + 2 from the row above, for example. We could hold this in a normal rectangular array (and waste some space), but in Java, we could also use a triangular array. We first declare a two-dimensional array with the second dimension unspecified:

```
int[][] pascal = new int[10][] ;
```

Figure 9.16 shows what is created by this declaration.

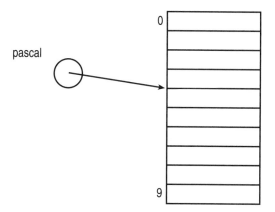

Figure 9.16: Declaring a nonrectangular array in Java: Step 1

The elements of this array are of type int[]; they can each refer to an array of integers but do not yet do so. We now set up an array of the correct size and put its reference into the appropriate place in the array we have just declared:

```
for (int i = 0 ; i < pascal.length ; i++)
    {
    pascal[i] = new int[i + 2] ;
    pascal[i][0] = 1 ;
    pascal[i][i + 1] = 1 ;
    for (int j = 0 ; j < i ; j++)
```

```
        pascal[i][j + 1] = pascal[i - 1][j] +
                           pascal[i - 1][j + 1] ;
    }
```

The first line in the body of the loop generates an array of i + 2 integers and stores a reference to it, as the ith row, in pascal[i]. The second and third lines fill in the first and last values, and the for loop in the final line fills in the rest of the values in the row. Figure 9.17 shows the result.

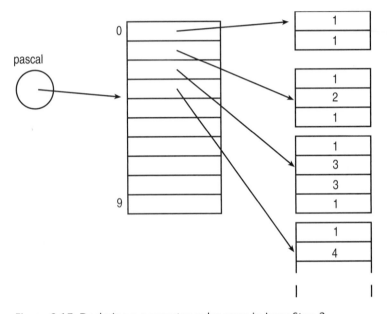

Figure 9.17: Declaring a nonrectangular array in Java: Step 2

The elements of the array can be accessed in the usual way. Thus, pascal[3][2] has the value 6. Accessing the element pascal[0][2] would cause an exception to be thrown.

9.9   Key Points in Chapter 9

- It is often necessary to maintain, manipulate, and process collections of data. We use the Java *array* mechanism to support this.

- A typical declaration of an array would be:

  ```
  int[] years = new years[5] ;
  ```

  This declares an array of ints called years with five elements.

- To access an individual element of an array, we use an *index*. An index is an integer value that uniquely identifies a position within an array.

- The `years` array has five elements indexed by the values 0 to 4. An individual element (say, `years[3]`) can be treated exactly the same as a single integer variable.

- We can initialize the contents of an array when we declare it:

```
int[] years = {1957, 1962, 1969, 1974, 1978} ;
```

- Just as we can have arrays of the basic data types (e.g., `int`s), we can also have arrays of objects.

- Arrays and loops are made for each other. We use loops to process each element of an array in sequence.

- We can sort and search the contents of an array. The algorithms we can apply for searching are affected by the ordering of the array elements. For example, if an array of objects including a search attribute (e.g., the surname) is in random order, then to search for all occurrences of a surname means we must sequentially examine all the surnames.

  If the array is sorted in alphabetical order by surname, however, we can use the binary search algorithm and significantly reduce the number of elements we must examine.

- It is possible to declare, initialize, and use multidimensional arrays:

```
int[][] matrix = new int[2][2] ;
```

The logical view of this (directly supported in some languages) would be:

```
     0   1                         matrix [0][0] = 1
  0 | 1 | 2 |                      matrix [0][1] = 2
  1 | 3 | 4 |                      matrix [1][0] = 3
                                   matrix [1][1] = 4
```

The actual implementation in Java, however, is that of an array whose elements are further arrays (Figure 9.18).

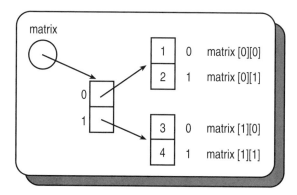

Figure 9.18: A two-dimensional array in Java

9.10 Exercises

1. Rewrite the code in Section 9.3 to find all the `Person` instances with a matching surname, not just the first or last. You should set up an array for the matching index values, together with an integer variable `noOfMatches`.

2. Write a method `evaluateHand` with one argument, an array of five `Card` instances that models a hand in the game of poker. Your program should return an indication of the value of the hand, which could be four of a kind, full house (three of a kind plus a pair), three of a kind, two pairs, a pair, or nothing.

   Write a program to test your method.

   Expand your method to test for all the possible winning combinations of a poker hand.

3. Here is a second way of sorting an array (called a *bubble sort*—can you see why?):

   Go through the array looking at each adjacent pair of elements in turn. If they are in the wrong order, interchange them, and then go on to look at the next pair. If any changes were made, repeat the process. Figures 9.19 and 9.20 show the first and second passes through a particular unsorted array.

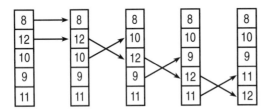

Figure 9.19: The first pass of a bubble sort

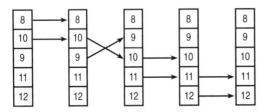

Figure 9.20: The second pass of a bubble sort

As Figure 9.21 shows, on the third pass, we would make no changes (and so realize that we don't need any more passes).

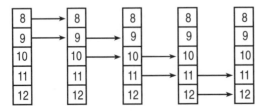

Figure 9.21: The third (and final) pass of a bubble sort

Write a method that uses this sorting algorithm to replace the version of `sortArray` given in Section 9.5.

4. In Section 9.7, we declared an array `board` to represent a position in the game of tick-tack-toe (noughts-and-crosses). Write a method:

`boolean winForSomeone(int[][] board)`

that, given a position `board` in the game, returns true if it is win for one of the two players (i.e., there is a row, horizontal, vertical, or diagonal, of either all Xs or all Os). Otherwise, it should return false.

5. Write a class `Sentence` that provides the following functionality:

   a. Reads in and stores a sentence from the keyboard (using the `readString` method in the `BasicIo` class). The sentence becomes part of the hidden state of the class.

   b. On request, returns the next word from the sentence with an indication as to whether there are still words to be returned from the sentence or not.

   You should supply the following methods:

   `public void getSentence()`

   This reads in a sentence from the keyboard and stores it within the body of the instance in a suitable data structure (e.g., a `String`).

   `public String nextWord()`

   This extracts the next word in sequence from the sentence and returns it.

   `public boolean hasMoreWords()`

   This returns true if there are still words left in the sentence and false otherwise.

   Write a suitable driver application; for example, one that allows the end user to type in a sentence and print it one word per line.

   Be careful to define the appropriate elements of the `Sentence` class as `private` (i.e., all the state of the instance and any methods you may write to support the functionality of the three public methods listed earlier).

6. Write an application to store and update changes to a set of monthly unemployment figures for a particular year for a small urban area. Your application should allow the user to enter numbers of jobs gained or lost (a negative number indicates jobs lost) during any month.

   With each iteration through a loop, the user selects one of three choices:

   a. To enter the number of jobs gained or lost for a particular event (e.g., a factory opening or closing) and the month in which the event occurred. For example, to indicate that 27 jobs have been created in August by the opening of a new factory, the user types:

   `August 27`

   b. To calculate statistics for the data entered so far. Note that you are interested only in the overall trend in employment for each month:
      i. The net change in unemployment over the year; that is, the sum of each month's figures.
      ii. The month(s) during which most jobs were lost; that is, the month(s) with the lowest value.
      iii. The month(s) during which fewest jobs were lost; that is, the month(s) with the largest value.

c. To quit.

You don't know the number of unemployed at the start of the year, so you need to store the change in unemployment for each month.

Your objective is to implement this application by providing a class `EmploymentStatistics` that maintains the monthly unemployment figures and provides methods that support the needs of the application (adding new information and producing the three statistics; the latter methods might be called `netChange`, worstMonth, and bestMonth).

If the user types in the following information:

> August 27; February –6; March 120; April 62; May –90; June 21; May 30; July 82; October 100; August –4; September 22; December 43; October – 20; September 15; October 40

this should result in the net figures for the year shown in Table 9.1.

Month	Net Jobs
January	0
February	–6
March	120
April	62
May	–90 + 30 = –60
June	21
July	82
August	27 – 4 = 23
September	22 + 15 = 37
October	100 – 20 + 40 = 120
November	0
December	43

Table 9.1: Net Figures for the Months

Thus, in response to requests of type:

b. i. the total number of jobs for the year: 442

b. ii. the month(s) with the smallest value: May

b. iii. the month(s) with the largest value: March and October

Remember to provide a suitable initializing constructor for the class.

7. A millionaire has a car collection. An application is to be written to calculate the average power of the collection. Using the `Car` class, write an application that allows the end user to input data about a set of cars and produces the average power of the collection. You may assume there will be no more than 50 cars in a collection.

8. a. Define a class to hold the information for a university timetable slot (course number, course title, lecturer, and location).

b. Write a file `timetable.data` containing timetable information for a computer science course in the format:

```
day
time
course number
course title
lecturer
location
```

For example:

```
Fri

9

CSc112

Programming in Java

Roger Garside

GF1
```

c. Write a program that reads in the timetable data from the file `timetable.data` and stores it in an array of timetable slot instances of the class you have declared. You can assume that there is no more than one teaching event at a time and each event is 1 hour.
Display the details of a timetable slot given a user request from the terminal specifying a day and time. A suitable response should be given if there is no teaching at the time specified.

d. Write a method to display a list of all the timetable slots for a lecturer, specified as the single `String` argument to the method. The slots should be displayed in chronological order, and a suitable message should be displayed if there are no slots for the specified lecturer. Use this to allow a user of your program to list the timetable slots for a lecturer specified by the user at the terminal.
How would you modify your program if there could be more than one teaching event at a time?

9. Magic squares are squares that contain numbers arranged in such a way that all the rows and columns add up to the same number. Examples of magic squares of size $n = 3$ and $n = 5$ are shown in Figure 9.22.

15	8	1	24	17
16	14	7	5	23
22	20	13	6	4
3	21	19	12	10
9	2	25	18	11

6	1	8
7	5	3
2	9	4

Figure 9.22: Magic squares

An algorithm exists to determine where numbers should be placed so that rows and columns will add up to the same number. The algorithm works for odd n only and is as follows (for a square of size n):

1. Start with k set to 1 and insert this value in the top center square.

2. Repeat the following steps until (a multiple of) n numbers are in place:

   ▪ Add 1 to k.

   ▪ Move left one square and up one square (see note 1) and insert the number k.

3. Add 1 to k.

4. Move down one square from the last number you placed and insert the number k.

5. Go back to step 2 until all squares are filled.

   Write a program to implement this magic square algorithm. Your program should prompt the user for the required size (n) and then, assuming n is valid, it should print a magic square of that size. To check that your square is in fact magic, have the program calculate and print out the sum of each row, column, and diagonal and confirm that they are all identical.

Note 1 ▪

This algorithm assumes that rows and columns *wrap around*. If a move is off the top of the square, start again at the bottom; similarly, if a move is off the left of the square, start again at the right (see the examples in Figure 9.22).

Note 2 ▪

For practical reasons when running your program, n should not be too big!

CHAPTER 10

Objects within Objects

10.1   What We Are Trying to Achieve

So far, the classes we have written have contained a set of instance variables that were all examples of the basic types (`boolean`, `char`, `int`, and `double`). We have also used the type `String`; as you know, `String` is not a basic type or even an array. `String` is an example of a system-provided class, so we can say it is an *object* type.

This means that an instance variable belonging to one object can in fact be a reference to a further object. In our `Person` class, the forename and surname instance variables are references to two `String` objects. Just as `String` is a class, we can use any classes—system provided or written by ourselves—in the same way. Part of the state of an object, then, can be modeled by a further object.

This phenomenon is familiar to those working with databases and is known as the *parts-explosion* situation. If we model a car as an object, there may be certain attributes of that car that we can handle with basic types. For example, the number of wheels a car has can be stored as an integer value. In Java, the name of the car must be stored in a `String` object, so here we have already left the basic types behind. However, there are other parts of the car such as the engine, which in turn are made up of other complex parts such as the fuel injectors, and so on.

Thus, you can see how we can begin with a single conceptual object such as a car, but when we start to explore the components that make up that object, we find that they too must be modeled as objects rather than basic types. This is what we mean by a parts explosion.

As our main Java example, we are going again to consider the `Person` class. So far, we have modeled a person's name (as `String`s) and their age and gender (as `int`s). Our application now requires that we know the person's date of birth. A date can be thought of as a triple of integers: one for the day of the month, one for the month, and one for the year. We could model this directly within the `Person` class as three separate instance variables, all of type `int`. However, this is not very satisfying for a number of reasons.

First, as we have said, classes are a way of collecting data that logically belong together and the methods that operate on those data. Second, classes are a way of modeling real-world entities more directly. The concept of a date is a real-world entity. It feels more natural to declare a class `Date` that has these three integers as its state, and thereafter, we can provide a number of methods that operate on dates. This also makes the `Date` class available to any other applications that require them—for example, an electronic diary or calendar. Other classes may have dates analogous to a person's birth date—for example, the date a car rolled off the assembly line. If we went ahead with our initial plan of including the three integers within `Person` itself, we would be greatly reducing the possibilities of reusing the `Date` concept and methods elsewhere.

In fact, the Date class is so useful, it is a system-provided class in the package `java.util`. However, that class does not provide quite the facilities we are going to require for manipulating dates. We are therefore going to write our own class, OurDate, to represent people's birth dates.

10.2   Writing the OurDate Class

We have decided to model the actual date as a set of three integers, one for day of the month, one for the month, and one for the year. These will be the instance variables of the class. We have also provided a constructor that expects all three values to be specified when an instance of OurDate is created. Finally, we have a group of set and get methods that allow us to inspect the state of a OurDate instance:

```java
public class OurDate
    {
    private int dayOfMonth, month, year ;

    public OurDate(int y, int m, int d)
        {
        dayOfMonth = d ;
        month = m ;
        year = y ;
        } // end of constructor method

    public int getDayOfMonth()
        {
        return dayOfMonth ;
        } // end of method getDayOfMonth

    public int getMonth()
        {
        return month ;
        } // end of method getMonth

    public int getYear()
        {
        return year ;
        } // end of method getYear

    public void setDayOfMonth(int d)
        {
        dayOfMonth = d ;
        } // end of method setDayOfMonth

    public void setMonth(int m)
        {
        month = m ;
        } // end of method setMonth
```

```
public void setYear(int y)
    {
    year = y ;
    } // end of method setYear

} // end of class OurDate
```

The set methods that operate on the day and month should contain checks to ensure that only valid integers are being used; for example, the month should lie between 1 and 12.

10.3 Using the OurDate Class

We update the Person class with the following instance variable and methods:

```
// new instance variable
private OurDate dateOfBirth ;

public void setDateOfBirth(OurDate d)
    {
    dateOfBirth = d ;
    } // end of method setDateOfBirth

public OurDate getDateOfBirth()
    {
    return dateOfBirth ;
    } // end of method getDateOfBirth
```

The treatment is the same as for the age or gender attributes. However, notice that we are here using an object rather than a basic type.

In our main class, we add a method called displayPerson as follows:

```
private static void displayPerson(Person person)
    {
    System.out.print(person.getForename()) ;
    System.out.print(' ') ;
    System.out.print(person.getSurname()) ;
    System.out.print(' ') ;
    System.out.print(person.getAge() + " ") ;
    OurDate tDate = person.getDateOfBirth() ;
    System.out.print(tDate.getMonth() + "/"
                    + tDate.getDayOfMonth() + "/"  + tDate.getYear()) ;
    } // end of method displayPerson
```

Here we are using an instance as the formal argument to a method. We will discuss this further in the next section.

To gain access to the information about the person's date of birth, we have a local variable tDate, which is of type OurDate. We use the getDateOfBirth method associated with the Person class to return a reference to the OurDate object contained within the Person instance.

Once we have that reference, we can call the OurDate methods directly on the referenced OurDate instance. Thus, in the statement

```
System.out.print(tDate.getMonth() + "/" + tDate.getDayOfMonth() + "/" +
        tDate.getYear()) ;
```

we can quite happily apply the methods getMonth, getDayOfMonth, and getYear to the instance tDate.

Here is an example from our main class:

```
public static void main (String [] args)
    {
    Person aPerson = new Person("James", "Kirk", 32,
                            Person.MALE) ;

    // set up a Person's date of birth
    OurDate birthday = new OurDate(1957, 3, 8) ;
    aPerson.setDateOfBirth(birthday) ;

    displayPerson(aPerson) ;
    System.out.println() ;
    } // end of main method
```

Notice that here again we have a "temporary" object, in this case, birthday. We first use the OurDate constructor to set up a suitable instance of the class. Then we use the setDateOf-Birth method to set the dateOfBirth attribute of the Person instance to refer to the birthday instance. This resembles what you see in Figure 10.1.

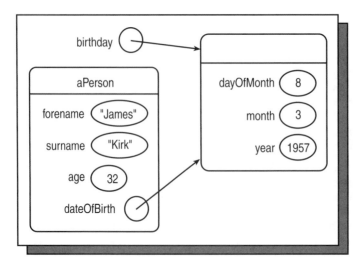

Figure 10.1: A single OurDate object with two references

The result of running this code is:

```
James Kirk 32 3/8/1957
```

10.4 Objects as Arguments

We have an application in mind. We wish to provide a program that allows the end user to enter his or her date of birth; the application then calculates and displays the following:

- The actual day of the week the end user was born.

- The appropriate line of the following nursery rhyme:
  Monday's child is fair of face,
  Tuesday's child is full of grace,
  Wednesday's child is full of woe,
  Thursday's child has far to go,
  Friday's child is loving and giving,
  Saturday's child works hard for a living,
  Sunday's child is fair and wise and good and gay.

- The astrological sign the end user was born under.

- The length of life of the end user so far.

To calculate the length of life, we have to define a kind of "subtraction" operator that takes two OurDate instances as operands and returns the elapsed time as an integer number of days. In an object-oriented fashion, we can look at the idea of sending an OurDate object a subtract request with another OurDate as argument. The destination object subtracts the argument object from itself and returns an integer result:

```
public class OurDate
    {
    // declarations ...

    public int subtract(OurDate operand)
        {
        // body
        } // end of method subtract

    } // end of class OurDate
```

This could be used as follows:

```
OurDate aDate, bDate ;
// code ...
int lifeLength = aDate.subtract(bDate) ;
```

It is purely a matter of taste, but it seems more natural to model "subtraction" as a dyadic operator between two operands rather than as a monadic operation where the second operator is an argument. If this is the preferred option, we can model this as a class method:

```
public class OurDate
    {
    // declarations ...

    public static int subtract(OurDate oper1, OurDate oper2)
        {
        // body
        } // end of method subtract

    } // end of class OurDate
```

This version could be applied as follows:

```
OurDate aDate, bDate ;
// code ...
int lifeLength = OurDate.subtract(aDate, bDate) ;
```

A possible implementation of this subtract method is:

```
/* contained as private methods in the OurDate class are the following:

    dayOfTheYear: this operates on the attributes of OurDate to
        calculate which day of the year the current OurDate falls
        on, in the range 1 to 366

    leapyear: this operates on the "year" attribute and returns
        true if the current OurDate lies within a leap year,
        false otherwise.
*/

public static int subtract(OurDate low, OurDate high)
/*
    given two "OurDates" (where 'low' < 'high') this
    subtracts (high - low) and returns the result
    as an integer (of days)
*/
    {
    int lowdoty = low.dayOfTheYear() ;
    int highdoty = high.dayOfTheYear() ;
    int days = 0 ;
    if (low.year == high.year)
        {
        days = highdoty - lowdoty ;
        return days ;
        }
```

```
        int lowyear = low.year + 1 ;
        int highyear = high.year - 1 ;
        for (int i <= lowyear ; i = highyear ; i++)
            {
            days = days + 365 ;
            if (leapyear(i))
                days++ ;
            }
        int daysleft = 365 - lowdoty ;
        if (leapyear(low.year))
            daysleft++ ;
        days = days + highdoty + daysleft ;
        return days ;
        } // end of method subtract
```

Note that we can directly access the private attributes of aDate and bDate. This is because the body of subtract is declared within the OurDate class itself; all things are visible within the body of the class.

Let's say we cannot change the OurDate class, but we are users of the class. We decide that we need a method that will print the date in a standard format; for some reason, the class providers have not supplied this method. We can write a method in our main program of the form:

```
private static void displayOurDate(OurDate d)
    {
    // body of method
    } // end of method displayOurDate
```

Here we have a method, outside the class of object it takes as argument, which has an object instance as argument. We can, as usual, use the get and set methods to access the attributes of an instance. Hence the body of the method might be:

```
{
System.out.print(d.getMonth() + "/" + d.getDayOfMonth()
                + "/" + d.getYear()) ;
} // end of method displayOurDate
```

10.5 Multiple References to the Same Object

We need to address a possible danger. If, in our main class, we continue to use birthday as follows

```
birthday.setMonth(6) ;
displayPerson(aPerson) ;
System.out.println() ;
```

what do you think the results of this second displayPerson call are?

`James Kirk 32 6/8/1957`

   This is because we can think of this OurDate instance as having two distinct references to it. It doesn't matter whether we use either birthday or aPerson.dateOfBirth to update it. We may not be able to access aPerson.dateOfBirth directly, as it is a private instance variable, but we can get yet another reference to it through the getDateOfBirth method. When we say:

`birthday.setMonth(6) ;`

the situation becomes what is shown in Figure 10.2: The value of the month attribute of birthday is set to 6, as we would expect. But we mustn't forget the true picture (Figure 10.3) where the month of James Kirk's birthday is now 6.

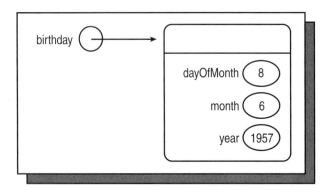

Figure 10.2: The result of birthday.setMonth(6)

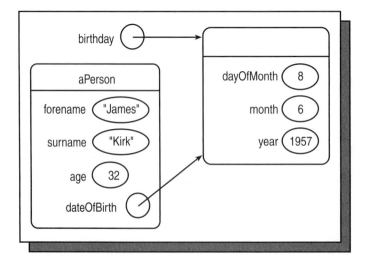

Figure 10.3: Remember, this single object has two references

There are a number of problems with this scenario; one is that one of the references may go "out of scope" and disappear. For example, if birthday happened to be a local variable or a formal argument, once the method that contains it terminates, the local variable or formal argument vanishes. This means that the associated object cannot be reached through that reference anymore, but as long as there are others, the object continues to exist. This isn't a problem, really, as long as there are other references.

The other point to note is that sometimes updating an object via different references may be a desirable behavior, but at other times it may not. If we want the dateOfBirth attribute of aPerson to be a totally independent object with no other references to it, we have to make what is called a *deep copy* of the birthday object.

What we have done so far in the setDateOfBirth method is to make a *shallow copy* of birthday. This simply means we have taken a copy of the object reference. What we need to do now is a deep copy where we actually create a brand new object but make sure all its instance variables are the same as the original.

To achieve this, we have added a copy method to the OurDate class as follows:

```
public OurDate copy()
    {
    OurDate t ;
    t = new OurDate() ;
    t.dayOfMonth = dayOfMonth ;
    t.month = month ;
    t.year = year ;
    return t ;
    } // end of method copy
```

This is used in a revised version of the setDateOfBirth method of Person as follows:

```
public void setDateOfBirth(OurDate d)
    {
    dateOfBirth = d.copy() ;
    } // end of method setDateOfBirth
```

Figure 10.4 shows what happens when setDateOfBirth is called with the actual argument birthday.

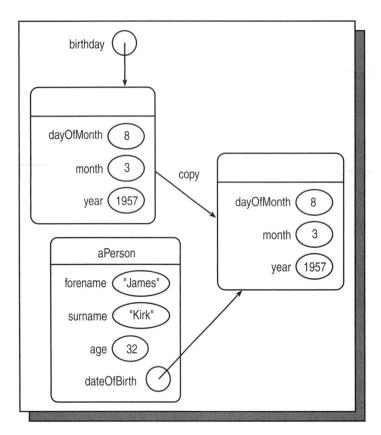

Figure 10.4: The actual argument is copied, and we store the reference to the copy in
`aPerson.dateOfBirth`

Now if we change the month of the `OurDate` object referenced by `birthday`, we have the
situation shown in Figure 10.5. The `aPerson.dateOfBirth` object no longer references the
same object as `birthday`. Thus, the `aPerson.dateOfBirth` object's month attribute remains
as it was before.

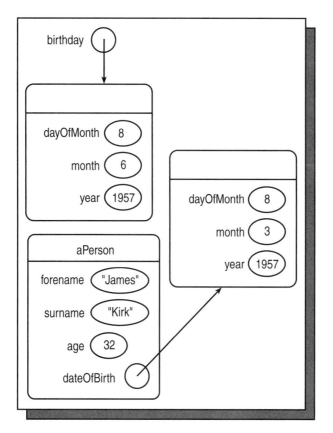

Figure 10.5: Changing `birthday.month` has no effect on the copy `aPerson.dateOfBirth`

Another way to try to avoid the problem of a "floating reference" is not to have an intermediate object reference. In essence, the only reason `birthday` exists is to allow us to set up an `OurDate` instance that we then pass into the `Person` instance `aPerson`. We can create the `OurDate` instance we need without `birthday` as follows:

`aPerson.setDateOfBirth(new OurDate(1957, 3, 8))` ;

As before, the call of `new OurDate` creates an `OurDate` instance, but instead of placing its reference in an intermediate variable, we pass it directly as an argument to the `Person` method `setDateOfBirth`. In a sense, we have an "anonymous" reference because we never name it. Because it is anonymous, we cannot now in our main method directly access the `OurDate` instance.

10.6 Objects as Arguments and Return Values: Call by Reference

Let's continue our study of object references with particular regard to how they are used with methods: as arguments and as the returned result. First, let's consider them as arguments. We have already seen a method that takes an object as an argument: setDateOfBirth in class Person. Let's begin with our original version, which used a shallow copy. This sets the value of the OurDate object reference to that of the object in the argument. Let's examine what happens step by step:

- Figure 10.6 shows the temporary creation of the formal argument d, which is given the same object reference as birthday.

- In Figure 10.7, the body of setDateOfBirth has executed, and dateOfBirth has been assigned the same reference as the formal argument d.

- Figure 10.8 shows the situation after setDateOfBirth has completed execution and the temporary formal argument d has vanished.

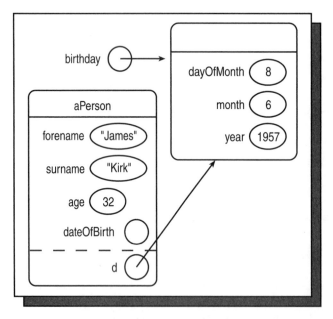

Figure 10.6: Formal and actual argument to setDateOfBirth

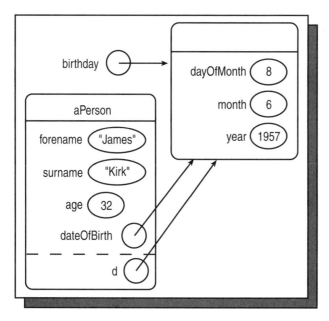

Figure 10.7: Setting the value of the dateOfBirth attribute

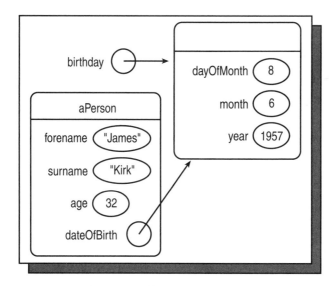

Figure 10.8: After the method has finished

We now consider objects as return values; more correctly, these are return references. Take the getDateOfBirth method of class Person. This returns the reference that it stores in the dateOfBirth attribute:

```
OurDate someBirthday = null ;
someBirthday = aPerson.getDateOfBirth() ;
```

Figure 10.9 shows the situation before the method is called.

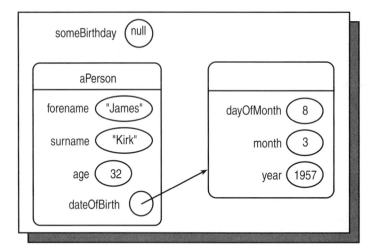

Figure 10.9: Before aPerson.getDateOfBirth is called

After the method has been called, the reference that was in the dateOfBirth attribute of aPerson is also in the someBirthday object reference (Figure 10.10).

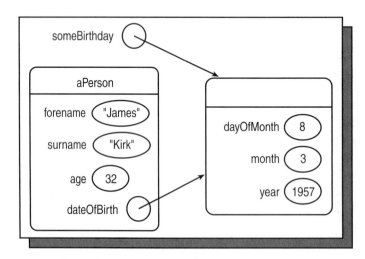

Figure 10.10: After aPerson.getDateOfBirth has been called

Again, we have the situation where there is a single physical object but two references; that is, there are two ways of accessing the methods associated with that object.

10.6.1   *Changing the Contents of the Formal and Actual Arguments*

When we change the contents of an object acting as a formal argument, we also change the contents as far as the actual argument is concerned. This should be obvious because, as you have already seen in connection with a `Person`'s `dateOfBirth` object, there is only one object but more than one reference to it. This is in marked contrast to the situation with the basic types and `String`s discussed in Section 7.5.

We can access and update the attributes of an object argument if the suitable `get` and `set` methods are available. Consider the following method belonging to a main class acting as a client of the `OurDate` class.

```
public static void incrementMonth(OurDate d)
    {
    int month = d.getMonth() ;
    month = month + 1 ;
    if (month > OurDate.DEC)
        {
        System.out.println("oops!") ;
        System.exit(1) ;
        }
    d.setMonth(month) ;
    } // end of method incrementMonth
```

In this code, we assume the class provider has declared 12 static integer constants (`JAN` . . . `DEC`) to represent the months of the year.

How does this work? When we call `incrementMonth`, the formal argument(s) and local variable(s) come into existence.

```
incrementMonth(today) ;
```

The formal argument d is given the same value as the actual argument `today`. Because `today` is an object reference, `today` and d both refer to exactly the same object (Figure 10.11).

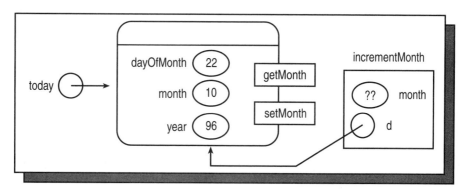

Figure 10.11: After calling `incrementMonth`, the formal argument and local variable are created

When we execute getMonth on the OurDate object d, the value 10 is returned and placed in the local variable month (Figure 10.12).

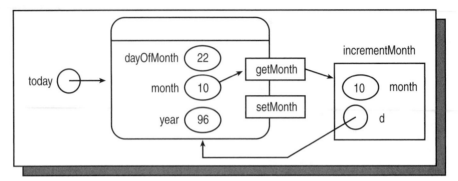

Figure 10.12: Setting the value of the local variable month

The incrementMonth method now adds 1 to the value of the month variable. Next, this value is passed into the OurDate object referenced by d using the setMonth method (Figure 10.13).

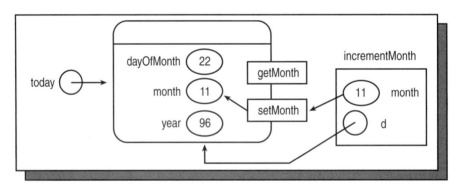

Figure 10.13: Putting back the incremented month value

Finally, when incrementMonth terminates, we are left with the situation shown in Figure 10.14.

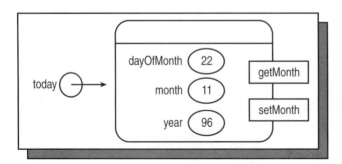

Figure 10.14: After the call of incrementMonth

As a further example, consider a `Marriage` class that models the fact that two people are married. As attributes, it contains two `Person` objects, husband and wife. Traditionally in Western countries, a wife takes on her husband's surname. When we create a `Marriage` object, we change the wife's surname to that of her husband. In the following code, we show the `Marriage` class:

```
public class Marriage
    {

    private Person husband, wife ;

    public Marriage(Person h, Person w)
        {
        w.setSurname(h.getSurname()) ;

        husband = h ;
        wife = w ;
        } // end of constructor method


    public String toString()
        {
        return (husband + " and " + wife) ;
        } // end of method toString

    } // end of class Marriage
```

Here is the main class that uses the `Marriage` class:

```
public class Chapter10n1
    {
    public static void main(String[] args)
        {
        Person hus, wife ;
        Marriage wedding ;
        hus = new Person("Bill", "Jones", 35,
                        Person.MALE) ;
        wife = new Person("Jenny", "Smith", 32,
                        Person.FEMALE) ;

        System.out.println("husband is " + hus +
                        " and wife is " + wife) ;
        wedding = new Marriage(hus, wife) ;
        System.out.println("wedding : " + wedding) ;
        System.out.println("husband is " + hus +
                        " and wife is " + wife) ;
        } // end of main method

    } // end of class Chapter10n1
```

The result of executing this program is:

```
husband is Bill Jones and wife is Jenny Smith
wedding : Bill Jones and Jenny Jones
husband is Bill Jones and wife is Jenny Jones
```

You can see that although the formal argument w was used in the body of the Marriage constructor, the surname of the actual argument wife was also changed. This is because the object references named w and wife are both referring to exactly the same object.

10.7   Hiding References to Other Objects

Just as in earlier examples, you have seen objects provide services to the main class; here you can see that a server class (Person) can act as a client to another server (OurDate). However, this is not the whole story. The main class has also had to declare and use objects of class Our-Date to set up the birthday object before it could be passed into a Person object.

It would, of course, be possible to organize matters so that the OurDate class was not known by the main class at all. This could be done by adding a method to the Person class as follows:

```
void setDateOfBirth(int y, int m, int d)
    {
    dateOfBirth = new OurDate(y, m, d) ;
    } // end of method setDateOfBirth
```

Getting back someone's date of birth without using the OurDate class is slightly trickier. Our current getDateOfBirth returns an object of type OurDate. Now, however, we are proposing that this is not allowed. We are left with the position that we return the individual components of OurDate—that is, the three integers that represent the day, month, and year. It is not possible to write a method that returns three values; we can only ever return a single value of a basic type or an object reference.

Here, we have ruled out the possibility of returning an object reference of type OurDate. The alternatives are:

- Have three get methods that return the day, month, and year, respectively.

- Introduce a new class expressly for the purpose of allowing these three values to be returned in an object reference.

The latter seems a bit strange because we would be duplicating the OurDate effort. Let's take the first approach:

```
public int getDayDateOfBirth()
    {
    return dateOfBirth.getDayOfMonth() ;
    } // end of method getDayDateOfBirth
```

```
public int getMonthDateOfBirth()
    {
    return dateOfBirth.getMonth() ;
    } // end of method getMonthDateOfBirth

public int getYearDateOfBirth()
    {
    return dateOfBirth.getYear() ;
    } // end of method getYearDateOfBirth
```

Now we have a `Person` class that completely hides the fact that it is using the `OurDate` class from its clients.

It feels as if there is more effort involved in ensuring this level of information hiding; however, as always, there are certain advantages to information hiding. If the `OurDate` class changes, this will have an impact on all classes that use it. By insulating clients of `Person`, we limit the amount of potential damage due to the `OurDate` changes. We will have to update only the `Person` class to take account of these changes, but all clients of `Person` should not see any effects (unless, of course, the changes to `OurDate` are so extreme that they change the `Person` class itself).

In effect, what we have done is to "pass calls on." Instead of the user of `Person` obtaining an object reference to `Person.dateOfBirth` and then directly executing methods on that reference, we are making a request to `Person`, which then passes the calls on (internally) to `Person.dateOfBirth`. We will discuss these issues again in Chapter 25.

10.8   Key Points in Chapter 10

- Objects may contain references to further objects. For example, a `Person`'s date of birth could be modeled as an `OurDate` object.

- We can pass object references into and out of objects using `get` and `set` methods.

- If we provide a `get` method for an object that is part of another object's state, we must take care! If we simply hand back a reference to someone's date of birth, we have made a *shallow copy* of the date of birth object. If we change the contents of the date of birth object via either reference, we may not get the results we were hoping for. This is generally true for any situation where we have more than one reference to the same object.

  If this is not the desired effect, we must make a *deep copy*—that is, create a new object of the same type and copy each individual attribute of the old object to the new object. This means we have two different references to two different objects.

  The problem is, if we have a shallow copy but believe we have a deep copy and then change our copy and find the original has also changed, this is not the effect we were after.

- When we pass an object reference into a method, effectively what we have done is to set up the formal argument as a shallow copy of the actual argument. This means if we change the attributes of the object via the formal argument (the "copy"), then we are of course changing the attributes of the actual argument (the "original"). In general, this would be the desired effect.

- It may not be desirable to provide set and get methods that use object references directly because this affects information hiding. Remember that a client of Person must now also be a client of OurDate if they wish to use the date of birth attribute of Person. If OurDate changes, not only will this affect Person (which is a direct client of OurDate) but also clients of Person (who are now necessarily also direct clients of OurDate). If Person's use of OurDate is completely hidden from the client of Person, then any "knock-on" effects of OurDate's alteration rest solely with Person and not the client of Person.

10.9   Exercises

1. In this chapter, we updated the Person class to store a person's date of birth as an instance of the OurDate class. This means it is a bit redundant to store the person's age because you can always calculate it given today's date and subtracting the person's date of birth from it.

   Update the Person class so that:

   a. It no longer holds a person's age as an attribute.

   b. It no longer provides a setAge method.

   c. The getAge method calculates the person's age and returns the result.

2. You need to model the concept of a family. For your needs, a family will consist of:

   - A father and a mother.
   - A number of children (no more than 10).

     You can model these individual elements as instances of the Person class. Implement the Family class and provide appropriate methods for setting the elements of the class. Don't forget to provide suitable initializing constructors and a toString method.

     We would suggest that you add children to the family one at a time.

     Provide a suitable driver application to test your Family class.

3. You now need to calculate the average age of the children in a family. Provide an averageAge method for your Family class and update your application to allow for testing of this method.

4. Families can consist of a single parent. You want to model this in your Family class. Extend the class as required and, of course, the application to test your work.

5. In this exercise, you want to model two different classes. The first is a compact disk that has the following attributes:

   - Name of recording artist(s)
   - Name of album
   - A track listing

The second is a CD player. You can load the CD player with any of your CDs, and select a track to be played. Among the methods are:

- Load with a CD
- Select track
- Eject CD

When you select a track, the CD player should display the name of the artist(s), the name of the album, and the number of the track. If the track number you provide is nonexistent (negative or zero or greater than the last track number), you should get an appropriate warning. If you try to select a track and the CD player is currently empty, again you should be warned. You can eject disks and load others as required.

Write an application to test both these classes.

6. You want to model the state of the board during a game of checkers (draughts). For this problem, you need to model the board (as a two-dimensional array of squares); squares can be empty or can contain a Piece. A Piece in turn has a color and, for the sake of redundancy, also contains its current location on the board.

Implement the three classes. Write a test application that:

a. Sets up the starting state of the board.

b. Allows the players to specify a move.

c. Checks if the move is valid.

d. If the move is valid, makes the move, updates the piece(s) involved, updates the board, and displays the board to the player(s).

CHAPTER 11

Putting Objects to Work

11.1 A Task Organizer Program

In this chapter, we are going to put to work the concepts and techniques we have learned so far in programming in Java. We are going to design and implement a program to carry out a simple task; as a by-product, we will be led to implement a useful sort of object that we will use in later chapters in this book.

The program we are going to write is a very simple system to keep track of all the different tasks we need to remember to carry out. A list might resemble the following:

- Mow the lawn.
- Complete the programming assignment.
- Look at recipes for Saturday's party.
- Read the next chapter of the book on Java.
- And so on.

If you are anything like us, this list will be extremely long, containing tasks that we must do today and tasks that we might do if there was any free time available. So we would like to assign each task a priority. This is going to be an integer in the range 1 to 4, with lower numbers being higher priorities: 1 means URGENT, 2 means HIGH, 3 means MEDIUM, and 4 means LOW. Our list might now look like this:

- 2 Mow the lawn.
- 1 Complete the programming assignment.
- 4 Look at recipes for Saturday's party.
- 4 Read the next chapter of the book on Java.
- And so on.

We are going to have an application program constantly running on our computer that allows us access to this list. We will want to add new tasks to the list when we are committed to doing them, and we remove items from the list when they are complete. When we start the program at the beginning of the day, we will read the current version of the list from a file on the disk. At the end of the day, before we turn the computer off, we will make an up-to-date copy of the list in a file that we can reload tomorrow.

We are going to keep this extremely simple. One important restriction will be that we only remove from the list the item with the highest priority.

11.2 A Priority Queue Class

This list of tasks is a *queue*, like a line waiting at a bank or a tollbooth. We add new tasks to the queue, and we remove the task at the front of the queue. But this is not the normal sort of queue, where items are always added to the back and removed from the front of the queue in the same order as they were added to the back (what is called a *first in, first-out,* or *FIFO,* queue). Instead, an item is added to the queue at a position corresponding to how its priority matches the priority of the items already in the queue. This is a *priority queue* (Figure 11.1).

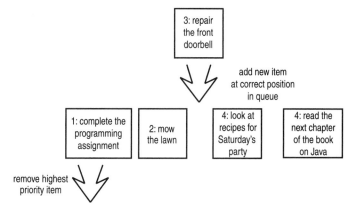

Figure 11.1: A priority queue

A priority queue might be a useful feature in other programs we have to write. We are therefore going to consider writing a new class `PriorityQueue` to provide this useful type of data structure. For our task organizer, which has only four levels of priority, we could have kept four separate queues, one for each priority level. But since we have decided to write a more generally useful class, we will allow any positive integer as the priority number, with low values being higher priorities, and we are going to have a single queue, with the priority stored with the other information.

We start by deciding what methods such a class should have. We have already mentioned two of them:

- We need to add a task to the queue in the correct position, bearing in mind its priority.

- We need to remove the item at the front of the queue (the highest priority item) because we have completed this task.

Thinking about the task further, we see the need for the following additional methods:

- We suggested that we remove an item from the queue only when we have completed it. Thus, we need to be able to look at the first item in the queue without removing it. In fact, we might like to look at any or all the items in the queue, but we are going to simplify things by allowing only the first item, the item with the highest priority, to be viewed.

- Since we are not going to be allowed to look at any but the first item, it might be useful to know how many items are in the queue. We might also like to have a method to tell us whether or not there is anything at all in the queue before we take a look. Depending on how we implement the queue, there might be circumstances in which the queue could be completely full, so it would be useful to have a way to find this out if we are trying to add another item.

- We are going to need a constructor method to set up a new empty queue. We may also need a method to take a preexisting queue and set it back to empty.

If we think about the methods to remove an item from the queue or to look at the item at the front of the queue, we will see that two items of information must be passed back: a specification of the task to be carried out (a String) and the priority (an int) because we probably need to know how important the task is. Hence, we are going to create a subsidiary class, QueueElement, which contains these two items of information. An instance of this class will be what the "remove" and "look at first item" methods return. It also makes sense for the "insertion" method to have such an object as its single argument, although we could have provided two arguments: the task (a String) and the priority (an int).

The QueueElement class will need a constructor method to set up an object with a specified task, and there will need to be methods to get (and possibly to set) the two attributes:

```java
public class QueueElement
    {
    private int priority ;
    private String data ;

    public QueueElement()
        {
        priority = 0 ;
        data = "" ;
        } // end of constructor method

    public QueueElement(int p, String d)
        {
        priority = p ;
        data = d ;
        } // end of constructor method

    public void setPriority(int p)
        {
        priority = p ;
        } // end of method setPriority
```

```
public void setData(String d)
    {
    data = d ;
    } // end of method setData

public int getPriority()
    {
    return priority ;
    } // end of method getPriority

public String getData()
    {
    return data ;
    } // end of method getData

} // end of class QueueElement
```

This class needs to be `public` because an application using the `PriorityQueue` class also needs access to this class. We put it in a separate file `QueueElement.java`.

A suitable set of methods for our `PriorityQueue` class is the following:

- A constructor method for this class:

```
public PriorityQueue()
```

- An initializer method, which resets the instance to empty:

```
public void initialize()
```

- A method for inserting an item in the queue at the correct point. This needs one argument of type `QueueElement`, containing the information (task and priority) to add to the queue:

```
public void insert(QueueElement d)
```

- A method to remove the item with highest priority from the queue. This method has no arguments but returns a `QueueElement`:

```
public QueueElement remove()
```

- A method to provide information about the highest priority item without removing it from the queue. Like the `remove` method, this has no arguments but returns a `QueueElement`:

```
public QueueElement first()
```

- A method to return how many items are in the queue, an integer:

```
public int length()
```

- Two Boolean methods to tell us if the queue is empty and if it is full. We will discuss later whether the latter method is the best way to deal with the possibility of queue overflow:

```
public boolean isEmpty()
public boolean isFull()
```

The overall structure of our code is:

```
public class PriorityQueue
    {
    ... constants and instance variables ...

    public PriorityQueue()
        {
        ...
        } // end of constructor method

    public void initialize()
        {
        ...
        } // end of method initialize

    public void insert(QueueElement d)
        {
        ...
        } // end of method insert

    public QueueElement first()
        {
        ...
        } // end of method first

    public QueueElement remove()
        {
        ...
        } // end of method remove

    public int length()
        {
        ...
        } // end of method length

    public boolean isFull()
        {
        ...
        } // end of method isFull
```

```
public boolean isEmpty()
    {
    ...
    } // end of method isEmpty

} // end of class PriorityQueue
```

This code is in a file PriorityQueue.java. A complete version of the code for this example is on this book's Web site (see Appendix A).

11.3   Implementing a Priority Queue with an Array

How shall we implement a priority queue? We are going to need to store a collection of items, each of which looks much the same: a priority (int) and the data (a String) making up a QueueElement. It is natural to think of using arrays for this (you will see an alternative way of storing this queue, as a *linked list*, in Chapter 17).

We need to have an array of QueueElements for the items in the queue and an integer variable to remember how many items are in the queue. Thus, we declare:

```
private QueueElement[] buffer = new
                        QueueElement[MAX_BUFFER_SIZE] ;

int queueLength ;
```

It is not clear how big the array should be for this queue, so we are going to declare a constant:

```
private static final int MAX_BUFFER_SIZE = 100 ;
```

It will be easy to change the value of this constant if we need to rather than go through the program looking for all the places we need to change the value. An alternative implementation might be to allow the user to specify the maximum size of the queue as an argument for the constructor method.

The constructor method is obvious:

```
public PriorityQueue()
    {
    queueLength = 0 ;
    } // end of constructor method
```

The initialize method is similar:

```
public void initialize()
    {
    queueLength = 0 ;
    } // end of method initialize
```

The length and Boolean functions are also easy:

```
public int length()
    {
    return queueLength ;
    } // end of method length

public boolean isEmpty()
    {
    return (queueLength == 0) ;
    } // end of method isEmpty

public boolean isFull()
    {
    return (queueLength == MAX_BUFFER_SIZE) ;
    } // end of method isFull
```

Notice that we return the Boolean value that is the result of evaluating a Boolean expression (e.g., queueLength == 0); we do not need to write:

```
if (queueLength == 0)
    return true ;
else
    return false ;
```

There are several ways of using the array to hold the queue items. We will always insert a new item at its correct place in the array according to its priority. And we are going to have the items stored in descending order of priority with the first item (the item with the highest priority) in array position zero. When we remove this first item, we are going to shuffle all the other items, with the item in position one going into position zero, that in position two going into position one, and so on. There are a number of alternative ways to store the information in the array, which we discuss in the next section. Figure 11.2 shows a typical example of the priority queue we have described.

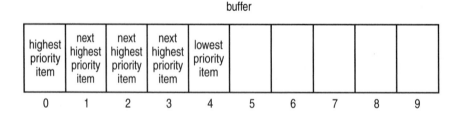

Figure 11.2: Holding items in descending order of priority

With this design, the first method is easy:

```
public QueueElement first()
    {
    if (isEmpty())
        {
        System.out.println("queue underflow") ;
        System.exit(1) ;
        }
    return buffer[0] ;
    } // end of method first
```

We first use our isEmpty method to check that the queue is not empty. We should always do this and not rely on the programmer who uses our package (it might be ourselves!) to remember to check before calling this method. If the queue is empty, we abandon the program with an error message (which is probably too terse) and a call of the System.exit method. A better solution would probably be to throw an exception (you will learn how to do this in Chapter 15).

The remove method is similar but needs to do the shuffle down:

```
public QueueElement remove()
    {
    // check for empty queue
    if (isEmpty())
        {
        System.out.println("queue underflow") ;
        System.exit(1) ;
        }

    // remember the first item
    QueueElement temp = buffer[0] ;

    // shuffle everything else up
    for (int i = 0 ; i < queueLength - 1 ; i++)
        buffer[i] = buffer[i + 1] ;

    // adjust the length
    queueLength-- ;

    // return the first item
    return temp ;
    } // end of method remove
```

There are several ways to write the shuffling loop. Another is:

```
    for (int i = 1 ; i < queueLength ; i++)
        buffer[i - 1] = buffer[i] ;
```

We chose the first way because it is clearer what the range of the index variable i should be. The elements of the queue after the removal are in locations 0 to queueLength - 1.

Finally, we have to write the most complicated method, insert, which we have been putting off for as long as possible. Here it is:

```
public void insert(QueueElement d)
    {
    // check that the queue is not full
    if (isFull())
        {
        System.out.println("queue overflow") ;
        System.exit(1) ;
        }

    // search for the correct insertion position "i"
    int i = 0 ;
    while ((i< queueLength) &&
           (buffer[i].getPriority() <= d.getPriority()))
        i++ ;

    // shuffle the data up (if necessary)
    for (int j = queueLength ; j > i ; j--)
        buffer[j] = buffer[j - 1] ;

    // insert the item
    buffer[i] = d ;

    // adjust queue length
    queueLength++ ;
    } // end of method insert
```

We first check that the queue is not full. We then scan through the array leaving the variable i pointing to the place the new item should go according to its priority. We continue to scan until either (a) we reach the end of the queue or (b) we meet a queue element with a priority value larger (i.e., with a lower priority) than the one we are adding. The test on the priorities is "less than or equal" (<=) rather than "less than" (<) so that, if we have several items with the same priority, they will be inserted in the order they were added to the queue (i.e., the queue is FIFO within priority).

If the queue is empty or the new item has a lower priority value than all the items already in the queue, we will be adding the item in the first free item after any items already in the queue. But otherwise, we have to shuffle up the items from position i (inclusive) to the end of the array. The next loop does this. Finally, we insert the data and priority in the appropriate place in the array and update the queue length.

Actually, there is a problem with this implementation, and it relates to the issue of *shallow* and *deep* copying raised in the previous chapter. We have inserted the new item in the queue with an assignment statement:

```
buffer[i] = d ;
```

This causes the ith element of the array buffer to refer to the formal argument, the object d; that is, it refers to the actual argument of the insert method. Suppose we do the following:

```
PriorityQueue q = new PriorityQueue() ;
QueueElement temp = new QueueElement(1, "first item") ;
q.insert(temp) ;
```

Then, because we copied a *reference* to temp into buffer[0], the situation is as shown in Figure 11.3.

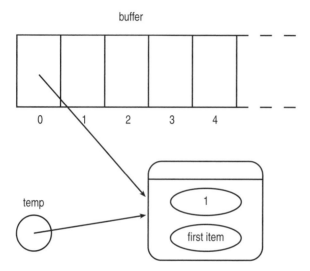

Figure 11.3: A first object inserted into the priority queue

If we now attempt to insert a new element in the queue with the following code, it will not work:

```
temp.setPriority(2) ;
temp.setData("second item") ;
q.insert(temp) ;
```

What happens is that the insert method copies only a reference into the array; that is, we are doing a shallow copy, and we will change the element occupying the first location in the queue (Figure 11.4). This is presumably not what we want.

buffer

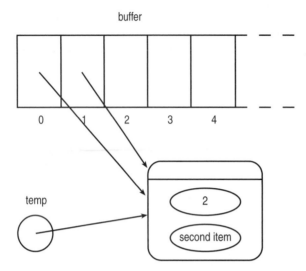

Figure 11.4: A second object inserted into the priority queue

We need to make a deep copy of the element we are inserting in the queue, so the correct form of the assignment statement in the insert method is:

```
buffer[i] = new QueueElement(d.getPriority(),
                            d.getData()) ;
```

We generate a new QueueElement instance for buffer[i] to refer to and use the constructor method to set its attributes from those of the instance d.

There is a similar problem with the first method. We have written:

```
return buffer[0] ;
```

Suppose we call this method as follows:

```
QueueElement x = q.first() ;
x.setPriority(5) ;
```

We would now find that the first element in the queue has had its priority changed to 5. We should have taken a copy of the element in the first method:

```
return new QueueElement(buffer[0].getPriority(),
                        buffer[0].getData()) ;
```

The remove method does not have this problem because the object is actually removed from the queue. Thus, once we have returned from the method, the only reference to the object is in the actual argument.

11.4   Alternative Implementations of `PriorityQueue` (Optional)

The array implementation in the last section involves inserting a new element at the correct position in the queue (which may involve shuffling element references about) and doing more shuffling when the highest priority element is removed. An alternative implementation would store the elements in reverse order, with the lowest priority element in position zero in the buffer and with increasing priority as we move through the array (Figure 11.5).

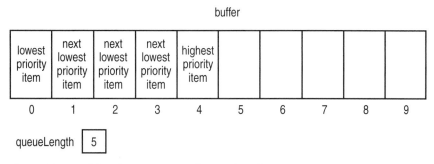

Figure 11.5: Holding items in ascending order of priority

The highest priority item (the "first" or "front" item) is at location `queueLength` − 1. This means that we can remove this item without any shuffling; the shuffling is always done on input.

Suppose we want to revert to the original scenario of having priority decreasing as we move up through the array. We are forced to do any shuffling required by the `insert` method because we are committed to keeping the elements in priority order. But we can avoid the shuffling in the `remove` method by using what is called a *circular buffer*, where an item stays in the same array location while it is in the queue. In a simple first-in, first-out queue, we could use a similar circular buffer to eliminate all shuffling.

The idea is that when we remove the first queue item from array location zero, we remember that the new first element in the queue is now at array location one and so on. We would declare instance variables for this implementation (Figure 11.6) as follows:

```
private QueueElement[] buffer = new
                            QueueElement[MAX_BUFFER_SIZE] ;
int firstPointer, lastPointer ;
```

What happens now is that, as items are added to and removed from the queue, the queue data migrate up through the array. We simply have to assume that the last element of the array is followed by the first element (Figure 11.7), and this is where the term *circular* buffer comes from.

buffer

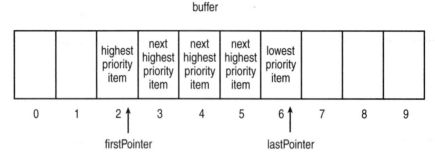

Figure 11.6: Using a circular buffer

buffer

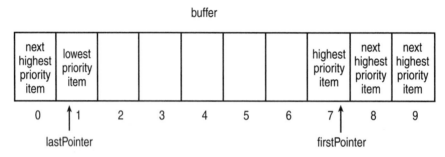

Figure 11.7: A circular buffer when `lastPointer` is behind `firstPointer`

This is easy to program; you have to ensure that the `lastPointer` never catches up with the `firstPointer`. It is best to retain the variable `queueLength` to make it easy to test for this condition.

A more radical alternative would be not to store the elements in priority order but to insert each one in the next free location in the array. Then we would extract the highest priority item by scanning through the array looking for it when required.

11.5   Testing the `PriorityQueue` Class

We have written our `PriorityQueue` class, and we now need to make sure that it works. We may have already written the program that is going to make use of this class, in which case we might hope that running the program with the new class will iron out any bugs. But this is not a good way to proceed:

■ It may be very difficult to make the program systematically try out all the different ways of calling the methods of the new class because it depends on the particular ways the program uses the `PriorityQueue` methods for particular sets of data.

- If the results are not what we expect, the problem could be in the `PriorityQueue` class code, or it could be in the code of the program using it.

- Finally, in this case, we have not in fact yet written the program code for the overall task.

So we are going to write a simple driver program or test harness, which we can use to exercise our `PriorityQueue` class. Here it is:

```
public static void main(String[] args) throws IOException
    {
    boolean continueLoop = true ;
    PriorityQueue q = new priorityQueue() ;
    QueueElement temp = new QueueElement() ;

    while (continueLoop)
        {
        displayMenu() ;
        int priority ;
        String data ;

        String response =
            BasicIo.readString().toLowerCase() ;
        if (response.length() == 0)
            response = "x" ;
        switch (response.charAt(0))
            {
            case '1' :
                q.initialize() ;
                System.out.println("queue initialized") ;
                break ;

            case '2' :
                BasicIo.prompt("priority? ") ;
                priority = BasicIo.readInteger() ;
                BasicIo.prompt("string to insert? ") ;
                data = BasicIo.readString() ;
                temp.setPriority(priority) ;
                temp.setData(data) ;
                q.insert(temp) ;
                System.out.print("'" + data) ;
                System.out.print("' inserted in queue with priority ") ;
                System.out.println(priority) ;
                break ;
```

```
case '3' :
    temp = q.first() ;
    System.out.print("'" + temp.getData()) ;
    System.out.print("' at head of queue with priority ") ;
    System.out.println(temp.getPriority()) ;
    break ;

case '4' :
    temp = q.remove() ;
    System.out.print("'" +
                    temp.getData()) ;
    System.out.print("' removed from queue with priority ") ;
    System.out.println(temp.getPriority()) ;
    break ;

case '5' :
    System.out.print("there are " +
                    q.length()) ;
    System.out.println(" items in the queue") ;
    break ;

case '6' :
    System.out.print("the queue is ") ;
    if (!q.isFull())
        System.out.print("not") ;
    System.out.println(" full") ;
    break ;

case '7' :
    System.out.print("the queue is ") ;
    if (!q.isEmpty())
        System.out.print("not") ;
    System.out.println(" empty") ;
    break ;

case '8' :
    while (true)
        {
        BasicIo.prompt("priority (0 to terminate)? ") ;
        priority = BasicIo.readInteger()
        if (priority == 0)
            break ;
        BasicIo.prompt("string to insert? ") ;
        data = BasicIo.readString() ;
        temp.setPriority(priority) ;
```

```
                    temp.setData(data) ;
                    q.insert(temp) ;
                    }
                break ;

            case '9' :
                while (!q.isEmpty())
                    {
                    temp = q.remove() ;
                    System.out.print("'" + temp.getData()) ;
                    System.out.print("' with priority ") ;
                    System.out.println(temp.getPriority()) ;
                    }
                System.out.println("**end of queue**") ;
                break ;

            case 'a' :
                q.print() ;
                break ;

            case 'q' :
                continueLoop = false ;
                break ;

            default :
                System.out.println("invalid response") ;
                break ;
            }
        if (continueLoop)
            {
            BasicIo.prompt("press RETURN to continue ") ;
            response = BasicIo.readString() ;
            }
        }
    System.out.println("program terminating") ;
    } // end of method main

private static void displayMenu()
    {
    System.out.println() ;
    System.out.println("Options to Exercise the Priority Queue") ;
    System.out.println() ;
    System.out.println("1 : initialize") ;
    System.out.println("2 : insert") ;
    System.out.println("3 : first") ;
    System.out.println("4 : remove") ;
```

```
        System.out.println("5 : length") ;
        System.out.println("6 : is full") ;
        System.out.println("7 : is empty") ;
        System.out.println() ;
        System.out.println("8 : multiple item insert") ;
        System.out.println("9 : scan and empty queue") ;
        System.out.println("a : print queue contents") ;
        System.out.println() ;
        System.out.println("q : quit") ;
        } // end of method displayMenu

private void print()
    {
    System.out.println("the queue is (highest priority first)") ;
    for (int i = 0 ; i < queueLength ; i++)
        {
        System.out.print(i) ;
        System.out.print(": priority = " +
                        buffer[i].getPriority()) ;
        System.out.print(": data = '" +
                        buffer[i].getData()) ;
        System.out.println("'") ;
        }
    } // end of method print
```

Notice that we have written this driver program as the `main` method in the `PriorityQueue` class. The idea is that it is part of the class, allowing us to test it whenever necessary—for example, if we add new methods or make a change to a method. If we call this class with

```
java PriorityQueue
```

the `main` method is called in the usual way. It sets up an instance of the `PriorityQueue` class, and then the user can exercise this with the commands provided, which invoke the various methods with suitable data provided by the user, afterward indicating the result of the call.

A test of the `PriorityQueue` class should include at least the following:

- Some straightforward tests that a sequence of inserts followed by a sequence of removes returns the correct values in the correct order.

- A test of inserting a sequence of values, removing some of them, then inserting some more, and finally removing all of them, at all times returning the correct values in the correct order.

- Tests to determine that insertions into an empty queue, at the beginning of a queue, at the end of a queue, and in the middle all give the correct results.

- Tests to determine that insertion of multiple items with the same priority all give the correct results.

- Tests to determine that while the preceding sequences are being performed, the methods `first`, `isEmpty`, and `length` return the correct results and that `remove` and `first` work correctly on an empty queue.

- A test of reinitializing a `PriorityQueue` and then seeing that insertion, removal, and the other method calls still work.

- A test of the `isFull` method and of what happens if you try to insert an item into a full queue. Notice that a special command has been provided in the driver program to allow these capacity tests to be done with reasonable ease.

11.6 Using the `PriorityQueue` Class

We can now return to our original task organizer program. The basic structure of the program is:

- When the program starts up, set up a `PriorityQueue` instance, open the file of tasks, and read them into the queue using the `insert` method.

- Manipulate the queue using `insert` to add new tasks, `first` to look at the highest priority task (the next one to be carried out), and `remove` to remove it when completed.

- When the program closes down, reopen the file of tasks on disk and copy the current set of tasks from the queue (with `remove`) to the file.

The code for a simple version of this program is as follows:

```
import java.io.* ;
import javalancs.* ;

public class TaskOrganizer
    {
    public static void main(String[] args)
                              throws IOException
        {
        PriorityQueue p = new PriorityQueue() ;
        QueueElement temp = new QueueElement() ;

        BasicIo.prompt("type name of file containing tasks ") ;
        String fileName = BasicIo.readString() ;
        BasicFileIo fileIn = new
            BasicFileIo(BasicFileIo.INPUT, fileName) ;
        while (true)
            {
            int priority = fileIn.readInteger() ;
            if (priority == 0)
                break ;
            String task = fileIn.readString() ;
            temp.setPriority(priority) ;
```

```
                temp.setData(task) ;
                p.insert(temp) ;
                }
        fileIn.close() ;
        System.out.println("there are " + p.length() +
                            " tasks") ;

        int priority ;
        String data ;
        boolean continueLoop = true ;

        while (continueLoop)
            {
            displayMenu() ;

            String response = BasicIo.readString().toLowerCase() ;
            if (response.length() == 0)
                response = "x" ;

            switch (response.charAt(0))
                {
                case 'a' :
                    BasicIo.prompt("task to add ") ;
                    data = BasicIo.readString() ;
                    BasicIo.prompt("priority? ") ;
                    priority = BasicIo.readInteger() ;
                    temp.setPriority(priority) ;
                    temp.setData(data) ;
                    p.insert(temp) ;
                    break ;

                case 'f' :
                    temp = p.first() ;
                    System.out.print("'" + temp.getData()) ;
                    System.out.print("' at head of list with priority ") ;
                    System.out.println(temp.getPriority()) ;
                    break ;

                case 'r' :
                    temp = p.remove() ;
                    System.out.print("'" +
                                    temp.getData()) ;
                    System.out.print("' removed from list with priority ") ;
                    System.out.println(temp.getPriority()) ;
                    break ;

                case 'q' :
                    continueLoop = false ;
                    break ;
```

```
                            default :
                                System.out.println("invalid response") ;
                                break ;
                        }

                    if (continueLoop)
                        {
                        BasicIo.prompt("press RETURN to continue ") ;
                        response = BasicIo.readString() ;
                        }
                    }

            BasicFileIo fileOut = new
                BasicFileIo(BasicFileIo.OUTPUT, fileName) ;
            while (!p.isEmpty())
                {
                temp = p.remove() ;
                fileOut.println(temp.getPriority()) ;
                fileOut.println(temp.getData()) ;
                }
            fileOut.println(0) ;
            fileOut.close() ;
            } // end of main method
        private static void displayMenu()
            {
            System.out.println() ;
            System.out.println("Options to Manipulate Task List") ;
            System.out.println() ;
            System.out.println("a : add new task") ;
            System.out.println("f : look at first task") ;
            System.out.println("r : remove first task") ;
            System.out.println() ;
            System.out.println("q : quit") ;
            } // end of method displayMenu

    } // end of class TaskOrganizer
```

11.7   Outstanding Issues

In writing our TaskOrganizer program and its PriorityQueue class, a number of issues arise, which we will revisit later in the book.

We created our PriorityQueue class in two stages. First, we decided what operations we would like to carry out on objects of this type. Second, we decided how we would implement objects of this type. We decided to use arrays for the moment, despite the fact that it forced us to consider issues like the maximum size of a queue and how best to shuffle items (which might cost quite a bit of time if the queue was very long).

In Chapter 17, you will see that there is an alternative way of implementing a priority queue. We can build a priority queue class that provides the same set of methods as the one described in this chapter, but we use a linked list structure instead of an array. We will no longer have to consider the maximum queue size, and we will no longer have to shuffle items around. But the cost is that the concepts and coding involved are slightly more complicated, and we have to take extra care with the implementation.

As far as we are concerned, a priority queue is defined in terms of what operations are allowed (i.e., what method calls we can make). We are free to choose whatever implementation we like; we can start off with a simple but inefficient implementation and later return to the task of making a more complex but more efficient version of the queue. We have used the object-oriented nature of Java to ensure that a programmer who uses the class cannot make use of any knowledge about how the class is actually implemented because it is all encapsulated inside the class. This is the basic idea of *information hiding*, which you have met in several places in this book.

When we define a type of programming element and specify what type of operations can be performed on it, we call this a *data type*. For example, Java's basic data type int is defined in terms of what values it can take and what operations can be performed on values of this type—all the arithmetic operations, for example, but not Boolean AND or string concatenate. Similarly, our priority queue is defined in terms of what values it can take (a collection of strings of characters with associated priority values) and what operations can be performed on it (insert, remove, etc.). We call this an *abstract data type*. It is abstract because we define the operations but not how they are to be implemented.

This priority queue is actually a priority queue of strings of characters. We might wish to store along with our task definition some additional information, such as an estimate of how long it will take or what other resources are needed to complete it. We could collect all this information together as a new class (perhaps called TaskDetails). We would now like our priority queue to be a priority queue of TaskDetails instances.

Some programming languages allow us to define a priority queue of some incompletely specified object. We could later use this partially specified abstract data type to generate a completely specified priority queue by indicating what the basic queue item is to be. This concept is sometimes called *genericity*. We specify what a priority queue means in terms of a "generic" ELEMENT, and then we have a mechanism to say "take the generic priority queue and make it into a specific type of priority queue where the ELEMENT is actually a String, a TaskDetails instance, or whatever."

Java handles this genericity requirement in a different way. We first have to introduce the concept of inheritance and the inheritance hierarchy of objects in the next three chapters before we can explore this.

If we attempt to extract an item from an empty queue or insert an item in a full queue, we have written the methods to display an error message and stop the program (using the System.exit method). This is fairly drastic, and it would be better to throw an exception to allow the program using the PriorityQueue class to attempt to recover if possible. To tell the full story of how to manipulate exceptions again requires an understanding of inheritance, so we will return to the topic of exceptions and exception handling in Chapter 15.

11.8 Key Points in Chapter 11

- You should consider the behavior of a new class (what methods it provides) before considering how to implement this behavior.
- Arrays can be used to build data structures with a variety of behaviors.
- Care must be taken to use deep copying when appropriate to create independent instances within the data structure.
- If we write a class to model some concept, we can put a `main` method inside the class to provide a test harness.
- Whenever we modify the class, we should use the test harness to do a full check on the facilities provided by the class.
- An *abstract data type* is a class of objects with a range of facilities provided by a set of methods, where the behavior of the class is defined in terms of the behavior of the methods and not in terms of how they are implemented.

11.9 Exercises

1. Add the following methods to the `PriorityQueue` class:

   a. A second `insert` method, where the information to be inserted into the queue is passed as two arguments, the task (a `String`) and the priority (an `int`):

      `public void insert(String task, int priority)`

   b. Methods `getTopData` and `getTopPriority` to return, respectively, the data and the priority of the element in the queue with the highest priority:

      `public String getTopData()`

      `public int getTopPriority()`

   Modify the test harness and fully test your new methods.
2. Reimplement the `PriorityQueue` using the alternative array implementations discussed in Section 11.4. Fully test your new versions. Is one implementation particularly simpler to program than the others and (if so) why?
3. Define a class `BookDetails` to hold information about books: the title, the author's name, and the year of publication.

   Implement a simple first-in, first-out (FIFO) queue of `BookDetails` instances where the element removed is the element added to the queue longest ago.

   You should provide a similar set of methods to the `PriorityQueue` class, and you can use any of the array implementations discussed in this chapter.

   Write a program to allow you to test your implementation.

PART 3

Advanced Objects

12 Introduction to Inheritance

13 Class and Method Polymorphism

14 Abstract Classes and Interfaces

15 Throwing and Catching Exceptions

16 Graphics and the Abstract Windowing Toolkit

CHAPTER 12

Introduction to Inheritance

12.1 Motivation

Inheritance is a very important part of the object model. Unfortunately, it is also one of the model's more complex aspects. It is crucial that you gain a thorough understanding of the concept to make full use of the mechanism. We begin by examining the concept in connection with data modeling; for the moment, we ignore programming features such as methods.

12.1.1 Data Modeling

As you have seen, a class can be viewed as a set of objects that share common features. This means we can have the universal set of all objects in our universe, and by examining all of them, we can identify subsets. Membership of a subset will be dictated by the features (or attributes) of each object. For example, we could have subsets males and females; membership would be based on the value of an object's "gender" attribute.

As a side issue, we hope you can envision how set membership could be automated using selection statements and Boolean conditions. It is worth noting, however, that it is possible to form sets that cannot be automatically formed because they are based on subjective assessment of an object's features. For example, if we have a set of books and wish to form a subset of good books, membership of this latter set must be based on a personal assessment.

In a programming language such as Java, set membership is automatic. When we declare an object of type Person, we know it will have a group of features in common with all other instances of type Person; hence, it is a member of that set (or class).

However, just as we start with the universal set of all objects and can form various subsets of that set, it should be obvious that we can repeat this procedure as often as we like. For example, we can examine a subset and decide that it, too, can form the basis for subsequent subsets. Indeed, there may be so many possible subsets that it becomes difficult to decide which sets to use. Obviously, in programming terms, we can use the application requirements to help us choose.

Regardless, let's continue with our general model with the initial set "object" (Figure 12.1). Now, we may choose to have subsets for people and animals. We can look at the people and say we want to split them up into young people and old people. We can look at the young people and say we want to split them up into toddlers, school pupils, undergraduates, and so on.

What exactly are we doing as we move away from the root of the tree and out toward the leaves? We are moving from the most general concept—the object—to a set of much more specialized ones—toddlers, school pupils, undergraduates. In data modeling terms, we are using the concepts of *generalization* and *specialization*.

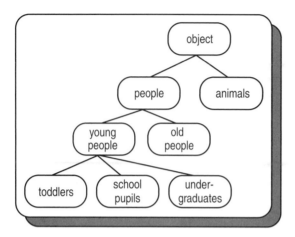

Figure 12.1: A generalization/specialization tree

Specialization means that we examine the features of a set and identify a group of objects that share one or more additional features that others within the set do not possess. For example, in the set of young people, we find that some have a feature that they are registered for a degree at a university. Clearly, this is a feature that not all young people have (the toddlers, school pupils, etc.). Thus, we form a new subset, undergraduates, and make all relevant objects members of this subset.

Generalization means we are examining the features of a number of sets and identifying a group of features common to members of all those sets. We should use this conclusion to generate a new "superset," and then all the involved sets become subsets of it. For example, consider an academic set of publications shown in Figure 12.2. These may be the sets books, journal papers, and conference papers.

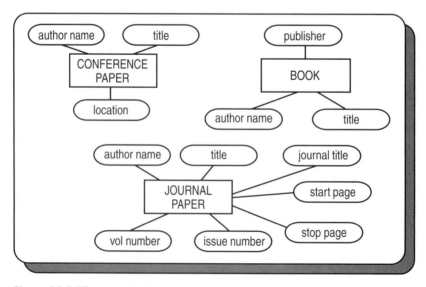

Figure 12.2: Three separate sets

We can see that all three groups share a set of features; that is, author name and title. We can thus form a new set, publications, and make the three existing sets subsets of this new set (Figure 12.3).

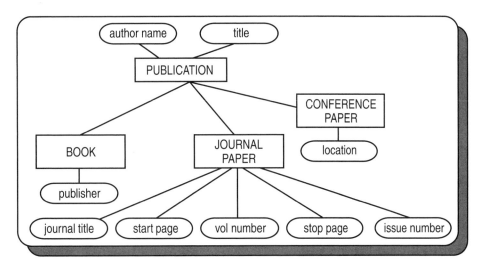

Figure 12.3: A superset and three subsets

Let's pause for a moment and see what it means for an object to be a member of a subset. Let's declare some objects in a Java-style syntax:

```
Publication p1 ;
Book b1, b2, b3 ;
JournalPaper j1, j2 ;
ConfPaper c1, c2 ;
```

Object b1 has been directly declared to be of type Book; this means it is a member of the set of Books. However, because Book is a subset of Publication, it is also a member of the set of Publications. If we write this in set notation, we have:

```
Books = {b1, b2, b3}
JournalPapers = {j1, j2}
ConfPapers = {c1, c2}
Publications = {p1, b1, b2, b3, j1, j2, c1, c2}
```

Although object c1 was not declared as type Publication, because it is of type ConfPaper, it shares a set of features with all Publication objects—that is, author name and title. It is therefore a member of the set of Publications. We can draw a diagram (Figure 12.4) to represent the relation between sets and subsets as a tree.

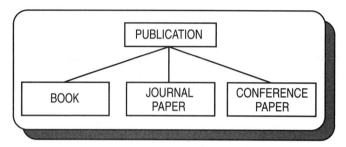

Figure 12.4: Sets and subsets as a tree

We can also use standard Venn diagrams (Figure 12.5) to represent the relationship between elements, sets, and subsets.

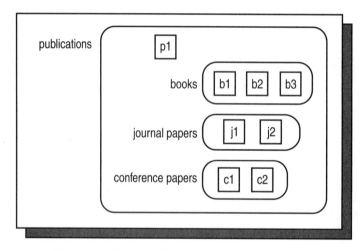

Figure 12.5: Venn diagram of sets and subsets

In a Javalike syntax, how might we represent the declarations of these four sets? We may proceed as we have up until now:

```
public class Publication
    {
    String authorName, title ;
    } // end of class Publication

public class JournalPaper
    {
    String authorName, title ;
```

```
     String journalTitle ;
     int startPage, stopPage, volNumber, issueNumber ;
     } // end of class JournalPaper

public class ConferencePaper
     {
     String authorName, title ;

     String location ;
     } // end of class ConferencePaper

public class Book
     {
     String authorName, title ;

     String publisher ;
     } // end of class Book
```

This may reproduce some of the effects we desire, but it is seriously lacking in a number of areas:

- We haven't captured the information that Book is a subset of Publication. By inspecting the attributes or features, we can deduce this, but we shouldn't have to. It should be clearly indicated. This is a matter of unclear semantics.

- On a pragmatic level, what happens if we realized Publication should have an additional attribute (e.g., date of publication)? Now we must remember to add it to all the subsets as well, and as noted earlier, we have no easy or quick way of finding all those subsets.

- On a language level, when we declare an instance of Book, it will be a member only of the set of Books. There is no way of knowing that it is also a member of the set of Publications.

Java provides us with a keyword extends, which allows us to overcome the three problems just listed. Now we can write our declarations as follows:

```
public class Publication
     {
     String authorName, title ;
     } // end of class Publication

public class JournalPaper extends Publication
     {
     String journalTitle ;
     int startPage, stopPage, volNumber, issueNumber ;
     } // end of class JournalPaper

public class ConferencePaper extends Publication
     {
     String location ;
     } // end of class ConferencePaper
```

```
public class Book extends Publication
    {
    String publisher ;
    } // end of class Book
```

Notice that something interesting has happened: Now, when we declare Book, we do not need to repeat the declarations of the attributes contained in Publication. An instance of Book has the attributes directly associated with the declaration of Book (publisher), but it also automatically has those associated with the class it extends (those of Publication—authorName and title). Book is said to *inherit* the features of Publication.

There is quite a bit of loose terminology in the area of inheritance. As you have seen, a new class may extend an existing class. In our example, Book extends Publication. Book is a specialization of Publication. We can describe the participants in an "extending" relationship in various ways (Table 12.1).

existing class	new class
superclass	subclass
base	derived
parent	child

Table 12.1: Participants in an Extending Relationship

It can get confusing, so we will usually refer to *superclasses* and *subclasses* in the remainder of this book.

12.1.2 Programming

We have considered the impact of inheritance on data modeling. In this section, we turn our attention to software. Inheritance gives us a mechanism for extending an existing class. This is a powerful way of adapting an existing class that provides most, but not all, of the functionality we need without having to rewrite the existing class.

For example, consider the work we did earlier using the OurDate class (Chapter 10). As we have said, there is already a system-provided class called Date. However, we used OurDate as an example, and it contains three methods that Date does not. The most important is subtract, which allows us to subtract one date from another, returning an integer result that is the number of days elapsed between the two dates.

If we started again without OurDate and wanted to use the system Date, it would provide most of the functionality we require, but not the subtract method. In a non-object-oriented system, how would we adapt the Date module to provide this new functionality? It could prove to be rather awkward.

In Java, we can use the inheritance mechanism. We declare a new class, say, Date2, which extends the existing class Date. As we have seen earlier, when we declare a subclass, we do not need to repeat the declarations of the attributes and methods of the superclass. All we have to specify is the difference between the subclass and the superclass. In this case, the difference is the subtract method and the two methods that directly support it, dayOfTheYear and leapyear.

Moving from a base class to a derived class is the *specialization* process. We are adding more detail and more functionality as we move from the superclass to the subclass. In this example, we have added more functionality.

It should be seen that inheritance is a powerful mechanism for supporting software reuse. Developing `Date2` by extending `Date` means that:

- We can use all the existing public methods and attributes of `Date` in implementing `Date2`.

- The information hiding principle, so important in software engineering and modular construction, is upheld. We may never need to know how the `Date` methods are implemented to provide the extended functionality of `Date2`.

We are, in the truest sense, building on existing work rather than tearing it all down and starting again.

We can also apply the generalization approach. There may already exist a number of classes that provide similar functionality. We can identify a new superclass that we can use to factor out the common code from the existing classes.

For example, if we were developing classes for Java's AWT (Abstract Windowing Toolkit; see Chapter 16), we could imagine independently developing (test) classes for `Panels`, `Frames`, and `Dialogs`. We would quickly find that we were carrying out the same kinds of operations on these basic graphical constructs—for example, adding other graphical components (e.g., buttons, labels, and text fields) and managing these components.

As a result, we might identify that our three graphical classes are in fact all types of containers for other components. We could then introduce a new class, `Container`, which would bring together the necessary shared methods and act as a superclass to `Panels`, `Frames`, and `Dialogs`.

The bonuses here include:

- There is a single place where the common code resides. Previously, the same (or similar) code would be in a number of different classes. If a modification is made in one class, how can we ensure it is updated everywhere?

- Chances are that the common code will represent a useful "abstract" concept that can now be reused in other specializations. If we hadn't factored it out, it might have stayed hidden, "buried" within the other classes.

12.2 What's the Difference?

As we indicated earlier, one way of figuring out what we need in the derived class is thinking about the difference between the existing base class and the proposed derived class. In terms of data modeling, if we have a `Person` class and now need to represent an `Employee` class, we need to think about the difference between people in general and someone who has a job. If we look at the `Person` class, we find out that people have a name, an age, and a gender. So do employees, as we would expect. What does an employee have that a person doesn't? Employees have a salary and a tax code. Thus, we can define an `Employee` class as follows:

```
public class Employee extends Person
    {
    double salary ;
    String taxCode ;
    } // end of class Employee
```

All we have to declare are the differences between a `Person` and an `Employee`. The similarities are taken care of by inheritance.

```
Employee - Person = {salary, taxCode }
```

This holds for methods as well as attributes. What we define in our derived class are the additional attributes and methods that make up the difference. The difference between `Date` and `Date2` is the methods `subtract`, `dayOfTheYear`, and `leapyear`.

```
Date2 - Date = {subtract, dayOfTheYear, leapyear}
```

So you have seen how we can supply additional methods.

12.3 Overriding Inherited Methods

It is also possible to replace existing methods (which we inherit from the superclass) by ones that are more suited to the derived class. For example, we can define a class to represent a square with a subclass rectangle. With geometric shapes such as these, it is often useful to provide methods such as `area` and `perimeter`.

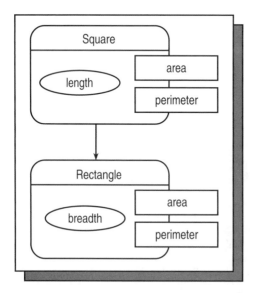

Figure 12.6: The `Square` and `Rectangle` classes

From Figure 12.6, we can see that Square has one attribute, length. Rectangle provides one attribute, breadth, and inherits length from Square. Square has two methods: area and perimeter. The algorithms for calculating the area and perimeter of a square use the length of the square as in Table 12.2.

area	length * length
perimeter	4 * length

Table 12.2: Algorithms for Area and Perimeter of a Square

The definition of the Square class is as follows:

```
public class Square
    {
    protected int length ;

    public Square()
        {
        length = 0 ;
        } // end of constructor method

    public Square(int 1)
        {
        length = 1 ;
        } // end of constructor method

    public int getLength()
        {
        return length ;
        } // end of method getLength

    public int area()
        {
        return length * length ;
        } // end of method area

    public int perimeter()
        {
        return 4 * length ;
        } // end of method perimeter

    } // end of class Square
```

Note that the length attribute has been declared as protected; we shall discuss what this means later.

Rectangle also has two methods with the same names. However, the algorithms use more than the length attribute; they have to use both the length and the breadth (Table 12.3).

area	length * breadth
perimeter	2 * (length + breadth)

Table 12.3: Algorithms for Area and Perimeter of a Rectangle

It would be quite inappropriate for instances of Rectangle to use the area and perimeter methods provided by the superclass. We wish to override or replace the Square methods with new, more suitable ones for the Rectangle. We simply do this by redefining them in the Rectangle class:

```
public class Rectangle extends Square
    {
    private int breadth ;

    public Rectangle()
        {
        length = 0 ;
        breadth = 0 ;
        } // end of constructor method

    public Rectangle(int 1, int b)
        {
        length = 1 ;
        breadth = b ;
        } // end of constructor method

    public int getBreadth()
        {
        return breadth ;
        } // end of method getBreadth

    public int area()
        {
        return length * breadth ;
        } // end of method area

    public int perimeter()
        {
        return 2 * (length + breadth) ;
        } // end of method perimeter

    } // end of class Rectangle
```

Table 12.4 summarizes what is provided by Square and what is inherited, added, or overridden by Rectangle.

Square	length		getLength		area, perimeter
Rectangle	inherited	breadth	inherited	getBreadth	overridden

Table 12.4: Methods and Attributes of Square and Rectangle

Those of you who know about geometric figures will realize that it is usual to consider Square as a specialization of Rectangle rather than vice versa. In our defense, we have done it this way because it is a good example (!), and we revisit the situation later.

To end this section, we present a small test program of the Square and Rectangle classes:

```
public class Chapter12n1
    {
    public static void main(String[] args)
        {
        Square s1 = new Square(5) ;
        Rectangle r1 = new Rectangle (4, 2) ;
        System.out.println("square of side " +
                        s1.getLength() +
                        " has area "+s1.area()+
                        " and perimeter "+ s1.perimeter()) ;
        System.out.println("rectangle of length " +
                        r1.getLength() +
                        " and breadth " + r1.getBreadth() +
                        " has area "+ r1.area() +
                        " and perimeter "+ r1.perimeter()) ;
        } // end of main method
    } // end of class Chapter12n1
```

The appropriate method is called in each case. For example, when the compiler processes the method call

```
r1.area()
```

it knows the type of r1 from the declarations at the start of the main method; it knows that r1 is a Rectangle. When it encounters the call of area, therefore, it knows that it should call the area method that belongs to the Rectangle class.

On the other hand, when we call

```
r1.getLength()
```

we know that the Rectangle class does not directly possess a method called getLength. However, through inheritance, we know that a Rectangle is also a Square, and the Square class does have a getLength method. We will therefore call the getLength method belonging to the Square class.

12.4 Access Rights and Subclasses

Now that we have introduced the concept of subclasses, we need to revisit the access rights introduced in Section 8.9.3. We discussed the four levels of access permission: `public`, `protected`, default, and `private`. The two ends of the spectrum, `public` and `private`, remain as before. The issue of subclasses does not affect them. When a method or variable is `public`, it can be accessed from anywhere. When a method or variable is `private`, it can be accessed only from within the class in which it is declared.

In `Rectangle`, we wish to represent both the length and the breadth of a rectangle. `Square` already contains an instance variable, `length`, which we wish to use by inheritance. However, if in `Square` we had defined the variable `length` as `private`, there is no way we could inherit and use it directly in `Rectangle`. We could, of course, still access it with the `getLength` method.

One solution might be to make the `length` `public`; however, this means it is generally accessible and not hidden in any way. For example, we could interfere directly with the value of this instance variable by writing a value into it (using an assignment statement from any part of the program that contains a reference to the object). This completely circumvents the read-only access we intended by making `length` `private` and providing a `getLength` method.

What we desire to do is to keep `length` hidden from general use but available to any subclasses of `Square`. We do this by using the `protected` level. A `protected` attribute or method is visible within its own class and subclasses and also to any classes within the same package. This is why in `Rectangle` we can quite happily use the inherited instance variable `length` in conjunction with our own new attribute, `breadth`.

Now that we have introduced both packages and subclasses, we can summarize the access levels in Table 12.5.[1]

situation	public	protected	**default**	private
Accessible to subclass in same package?	yes	yes	yes	no
Accessible to nonsubclass in same package?	yes	yes	yes	no
Accessible to subclass in different package?	yes	yes	no	no
Accessible to nonsubclass in different package?	yes	no	no	no
Inherited by subclass in same package?	yes	yes	yes	no
Inherited by subclass in different package?	yes	yes	no	no

Table 12.5: Access Levels

[1]Based on David Flanagan, *Java in a Nutshell* (3rd ed.). Sebastapol, CA: O'Reilly & Associates, 1999.

Consider the situation where B is a subclass of A, and B contains a reference to an instance of A. The protected attributes are inherited by subclasses and can be accessed in instances of those subclasses. However, subclass B cannot access these attributes in instances of A.

To illustrate a possible use of the `private` access level between superclass and subclass, we revisit our `Square` and `Rectangle` example. Originally, we had `Square` as the superclass and `Rectangle` as the subclass. However, in set theory, we can think of `Rectangle` as the superclass of `Square`. A square is a special example of a rectangle. The set of all squares is a subset of all rectangles.

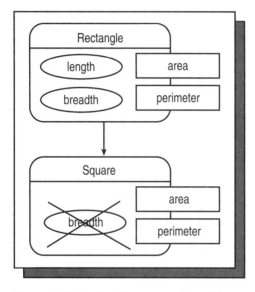

Figure 12.7: `Rectangle` as superclass of `Square`

If we model this in Java, Figure 12.7 shows that (as before) the subclass overrides the superclass methods. The `Square` subclass does not want to add any new attributes but only inherit from `Rectangle`. Further, it does not want all the attributes from `Rectangle`, only `length`.

We have already seen how to block direct access to attributes; in `Rectangle`, we declare `breadth` as `private`. This means that no other class, including any subclasses, may directly access this attribute.

12.5   Airplane Reservations: An Example

In the following example,[2] we consider different kinds of airline reservations. The basic type of reservation maintains a date of travel, a flight number, and a seat number. There is a more

---

[2]See John Barnes, *Programming in Ada 95*. Reading, MA: Addison-Wesley, 1999.

expensive style of reservation, a "nice" reservation, that allows us to specify the kind of seat we want (aisle or window) and the kind of meal we want (green for vegetarians, white for fish or fowl, and red for meat). Finally, if we can afford it, we can make a "posh" reservation so that a limousine meets us at the airport and takes us to our final destination.

The *inheritance hierarchy* (Figure 12.8) shows the superclass/subclass relationship as a hierarchy. A hierarchy is an example of a very common data structure in computing: an inverted tree. It is inverted because the root of the tree is normally at the top of the diagram (in this example, Reservation) and the leaves of the tree appear at the bottom (here BasicReservation and PoshReservation). We can recognize the leaves because they are nodes (e.g., Reservation, BasicReservation, NiceReservation, and PoshReservation) that are not linked to any further nodes.

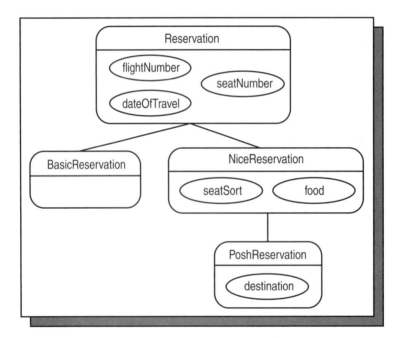

Figure 12.8: The reservation inheritance hierarchy

In Figure 12.8, we have additional information in the form of the attributes defined by different classes (and subclasses). As before, we can define the subclasses in terms of what they offer that is different from their superclass. We can see that a reservation offers a flight number, a date of travel, and a seat number. There is no difference between a basic reservation and a reservation, so the new subclass has no additional attributes. The difference between a posh reservation and a nice reservation is the limousine, so the additional attribute specifies a destination:

```
BasicReservation - Reservation = { }
NiceReservation - Reservation = {seatSort, food}
PoshReservation - NiceReservation = {destination}
```

Let's look at the Java declarations necessary to capture our data model:

```
public class Reservation
    {
    private int flightNumber ;
    private Date dateOfTravel ;
    private int seatNumber ;
    } // end of class Reservation

public class BasicReservation extends Reservation
    {
    } // end of class BasicReservation

public class NiceReservation extends Reservation
    {
    public static final int AISLE = 1, WINDOW = 2 ;
    public static final int GREEN = 1, WHITE = 2, RED = 3 ;
    private int seatSort ;
    private int food ;
    } // end of class NiceReservation

public class PoshReservation extends NiceReservation
    {
    private String destination ;
    } // end of class PoshReservation
```

In our example application, we want to provide an interactive system that a travel agent can use to enter the details (excluding the date of travel to simplify the example) of a customer's reservation. To do this, each class provides a read method. Without regard for the inheritance of methods, one way of doing this would be to provide a method that reads all the attributes of each class. For example:

```
public class PoshReservation extends NiceReservation
    {

    public void readPosh() throws IOException
        {
        BasicIo.prompt("flight number? ") ;
        flightNumber = BasicIo.readInteger() ;
        BasicIo.prompt("seat number? ") ;
        seatNumber = BasicIo.readInteger() ;
        BasicIo.prompt("kind of food? 1 (green), 2 (white), 3 (red): ") ;
        food = BasicIo.readInteger() ;
        BasicIo.prompt("kind of seat? 1 (aisle), 2 (window): ") ;
        seatSort = BasicIo.readInteger() ;
        BasicIo.prompt("Destination address? ") ;
        destination = BasicIo.readString() ;
        } // end of method readPosh
```

```
   other methods ...
   } // end of class PoshReservation
```

Let's look at the read method for `NiceReservation`:

```
public class NiceReservation extends Reservation
   {

   public void readNice() throws IOException
      {
      BasicIo.prompt("Flight number? ") ;
      flightNumber = BasicIo.readInteger() ;
      BasicIo.prompt("Seat number? ") ;
      seatNumber = BasicIo.readInteger() ;
      BasicIo.prompt("kind of food? 1 (green), 2 (white), 3 (red): ") ;
      food = BasicIo.readInteger() ;
      BasicIo.prompt("kind of seat? 1 (aisle), 2 (window): ") ;
      seatSort = BasicIo.readInteger() ;
      } // end of method readNice

   other methods...
   } // end of class NiceReservation
```

Finally, here is the read method for `Reservation`:

```
public class Reservation
   {

   public void readRes() throws IOException
      {
      BasicIo.prompt("Flight number? ") ;
      flightNumber = BasicIo.readInteger() ;
      BasicIo.prompt("Seat number? ") ;
      seatNumber = BasicIo.readInteger() ;
      } // end of method readRes

   other methods
   } // end of class Reservation
```

The problem we have here is that although we are using inheritance of attributes, we are not using inheritance of methods! Look at the code duplication between the read methods of `NiceReservation` and `PoshReservation`; there are only two lines of difference. `Posh Reservation` needs the extra lines to prompt for, and read in, the value of the `destination` attribute. This is logical because `destination` is the difference between `PoshReservation` and `NiceReservation`.

What we should be doing here is allowing each class to take responsibility for reading its own set of attributes. If `readPosh` can assume that `readNice` is reading the attributes it supplies, then `readPosh` can call `readNice` before reading its own attributes. Similarly, `readNice` depends on `readRes` to read the attributes provided by `Reservation`.

Table 12.6 summarizes the attributes and the method responsible for reading those attributes.

Reservation	NiceReservation	PoshReservation	Responsibility
flightNumber			readRes
seatNumber			readRes
	seatSort		readNice
	food		readNice
		destination	readPosh

Table 12.6: Responsibilities for Reading Attributes

Unsurprisingly, the responsibility lies with the class that provided the attribute(s) in the first place.

Let's look at the revised set of read methods for each class:

```
public class Reservation
    {

    public void readRes() throws IOException
        {
        BasicIo.prompt("Flight number? ") ;
        flightNumber = BasicIo.readInteger() ;
        BasicIo.prompt("Seat number? ") ;
        seatNumber = BasicIo.readInteger() ;
        } // end of method readRes

    other methods ...
    } // end of class Reservation

public class NiceReservation extends Reservation
    {

    public void readNice() throws IOException
        {
        readRes() ;
        BasicIo.prompt("kind of food? 1 (green), 2 (white), 3 (red): ") ;
        food = BasicIo.readInteger() ;
        BasicIo.prompt("kind of seat? 1 (aisle), 2 (window): ") ;
        seatSort = BasicIo.readInteger() ;
        } // end of method readNice
```

```
    other methods ...
    } // end of class NiceReservation

public class PoshReservation extends NiceReservation
    {

    public void readPosh() throws IOException
        {
        readNice() ;
        BasicIo.prompt("Destination address? ") ;
        destination = BasicIo.readString() ;
        } // end of method readPosh

    other methods ...
    } // end of class PoshReservation
```

So we now have the situation where each class has its own read method, each with a unique name. We shall see in the next chapter that it is possible, and useful, for each read method to have the same name!

12.6   Key Points in Chapter 12

- A class can be viewed as a set of objects that share common features.

- From the set of all objects, we can identify subsets.

- In Java, set membership is automatic. When we declare an instance of type Person, we know it has a group of features in common with all other instances of type Person, hence, it is a member of that set (or class).

- As we examine a set (e.g., of people), we can identify subsets (e.g., young people and old people). In turn, we can identify subsets of young people (toddlers, school pupils, undergraduates).

- As we move from sets to increasingly more detailed subsets, we are moving from general concepts to more specialized ones. This is known as *specialization*.

- If we examine several sets and identify common features that we can represent as a subset, we are moving from specialized concepts to a more general one. This is known as *generalization*.

- We can represent the relationship between sets and subsets as an inverted tree.

- In Java, when we introduce a new subclass of an existing class, we use the keyword extends.

- When declaring a new subclass, we need to specify only the elements (attributes, method) that are different. For example, if Employee is to be a subclass of Person, we need to ask ourselves what is the difference between a Person and an Employee. What does an employee have that a person doesn't?

We do not need to specify again the elements of the Person class; the Employee class is said to *inherit* the elements of its superclass.

- It is possible to replace existing (inherited) methods by more appropriate ones in the inheriting class; this is known as *overriding*.

- Now that we have introduced the subclass concept, the four access levels supported by Java for element visibility are now distinct and are summarized in Table 12.7.

Permission Level	Meaning
public	visible to everyone
protected	visible to all classes in the same package and to all subclasses
default	visible to all classes and subclasses in the same package
private	visible only within the same class

Table 12.7: Access Permission Levels

12.7   Exercises

1. Figure 12.9 shows an inheritance hierarchy linking together classes that describe vehicles that operate on land.

   a. Set up the LandVehicles hierarchy as a set of Java classes.

   b. Provide appropriate get and set methods.

   c. Create instances of a car, a truck, and a bicycle.

   d. Write a simple driver application to illustrate your classes.

2. In Exercise 10.2, we chose to model parents as part of a family. We now intend to model Parent as a subclass of Person. A Parent is different from a Person in that he or she has one or more children. A Parent may also have a spouse or a partner.

   Declare a class Parent according to the description in the previous paragraph. As always, remember that appropriate initialization constructor(s) should be provided. Provide a driver application.

   As you did for Exercise 10.3, provide an averageAge method that operates on the children.

3. a. Write a class, Circle, that has one attribute, radius, and a method, space, that returns the area of the circle. The formula for calculating the area of a circle is πr^2, where r is the radius. Provide additional methods as required, and a driver application.

   b. Write a class, Sphere, as a subclass of Circle. It also has one attribute, radius, and a method, space, that returns the volume of the sphere. The formula for calculating the volume of a sphere is $4/3\pi r^3$, where r is the radius. Provide additional methods as required and a driver application.

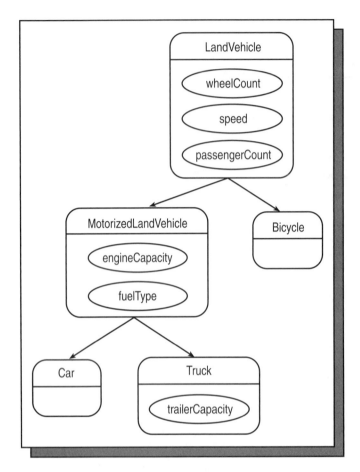

Figure 12.9: A LandVehicles hierarchy

    c. Vary the access permissions to the inherited radius attribute and note the effects on the Sphere subclass.

4. a. Write a class, Time, that holds the time in hours and minutes. Provide suitable get and set methods, along with a toString method. Write a driver application. Make the attributes protected.

    b. You now discover you need a method earlier to compare two Time instances to find out if one is earlier in the day than the other. Pretend that the Time class is a library class and that you do not have access to the source. You must extend the functionality by inheritance. Do so, creating a new class, Time2, and update your driver application.

    c. Change the attribute access levels of Time from protected to private. How does this affect your Time2 class? Update it accordingly.

CHAPTER 13

Class and Method Polymorphism

13.1 Person **and** Student: **An Example**

In this chapter, we revisit our Person example and show how it can be used as the base class for a new class, Student, to represent college students. In this simple example, the difference between a Person and a Student is that a Student is enrolled in some major subject. The Student class inherits all the attributes of the Person class and adds a new attribute, major.

```
public class Student extends Person
    {
    private String major ;

    public Student()
        {
        super() ; // call constructor of Person
        major = "UNKNOWN" ;
        } // end of constructor method

    public Student(String f, String s, int a, int g, String m)
        {
        super(f, s, a, g) ; // call constructor of Person
        major = m ;
        } // end of constructor method

    public String getMajor()
        {
        return major ;
        } // end of method getMajor

    public void setMajor(String m)
        {
        major = m ;
        } // end of method setMajor
```

```
public String toString()
   {
   return super.toString() + " " + major ;
   } // end of method toString

} // end of class Student
```

13.2 Constructor Methods and Inheritance

You have seen how classes provide one or more constructor methods. We can use these to ensure that the attributes of a new instance of a class have meaningful "default" values. What impact does inheritance have on constructor methods? Consider our example of Person and Student. Person provides a constructor; so, too, does Student. How can we ensure that when we initialize a Student we also initialize those attributes it inherits from Person?

Here we introduce the keyword super and show how it can be used in conjunction with constructor methods. When we declare an instance of Student

```
Student fred = new Student() ;
```

we are calling one of the constructors provided by the Student class. We expect this to set aside space for the attributes and perhaps to initialize them to meaningful default values. Student has only one directly defined attribute: major. But what about the inherited attributes (the ones from the Person class)? How are they to be initialized? If we look at the Student class, we find:

```
public Student()
   {
   super() ;
   major = "UNKNOWN" ;
   } // end of constructor method
```

We see that, as usual, the attribute of Student is given a suitable initial value. But the first line of the method body is the one of interest. Here it appears as if we are calling a method called super. What we are actually doing is calling the constructor of the base class, Person.

The terminology is derived from the idea of a superclass and a subclass. Here Student is the subclass and Person is the superclass. We are calling the constructor belonging to the superclass; hence, super.

There are two rules about this use of super:

- It can be used in this way only in a constructor method.
- If it appears in the constructor method at all, it must be the first statement within the constructor method, even before variable declarations.

Notice again the use of super in our version of a constructor that allows the user to specify the initial values for the inherited attributes:

```
public Student(String f, String s, int a, int g, String m)
    {
    super(f, s, a, g) ;
    major = m ;
    } // end of constructor method
```

Again, the call to super appears as the first statement in the body of the constructor.

13.2.1   Constructor Chaining

The Java language system guarantees that whenever an instance of a class is created, the class's constructor method is called. However, it also guarantees that the constructor is called whenever an instance of any subclass is created. Thus, when we create an instance of class Student, not only is the Student constructor called but so, too, is the Person constructor.

To meet this guarantee, Java must ensure that every constructor method of a subclass calls one of the constructors of its superclass. In our Student example, we have provided a super call in both our constructors; Java can check that we have done so and know that the guarantee is being upheld. Our Student constructors call different versions of the overloaded Person constructor methods, as indicated by the arguments.

If we are lazy and do not include the super call, Java will implicitly insert a call to super(). For example:

```
public Student()
    {
    // super() ;
    // we've omitted the call but it is implicitly put in by Java
    major = "UNKNOWN" ;
    } // end of constructor method
```

Being lazy usually has a price:

```
public Student(String f, String s, int a, int g, String m)
    {
    // super() ;
    // we've omitted the call so Java calls "super()" for us
    major = m ;
    } // end of constructor method
```

In this case, Java calls the argumentless version of the constructor. We might as well have not bothered supplying the formal arguments f, s, a, and g for all the use they are going to be. Try it out for yourselves!

13.3 Multiple Levels of Inheritance: The Inheritance Hierarchy

It is possible to have multiple levels of inheritance. The hierarchies you have seen so far in the book typically have two or, at most, three levels. Theoretically at least, we can have as many as we like. In this section, we present two examples of multilevel hierarchies. If you examine some of the Java libraries, you will find many more.

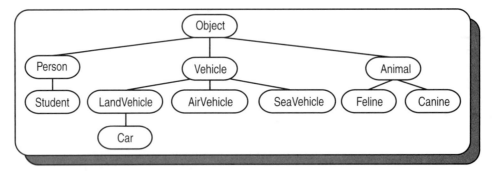

Figure 13.1: An inheritance hierarchy

In our first example (Figure 13.1), we introduce the Object class as the root of the tree. We shall examine the Object class in more detail in the next section. In the example, it acts as superclass to Person, Vehicle, and Animal. You can see we further subclass Person to Student, Vehicle to LandVehicle, AirVehicle, and SeaVehicle, and Animal to Feline and Canine. Finally, at our lowest level (two nodes removed from the root), we have LandVehicle as super-class to Car. In this example, we have concentrated on classes and ignored methods and attributes.

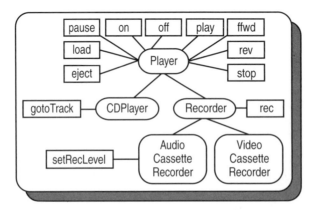

Figure 13.2: Inheritance hierarchy showing methods

In our second example (Figure 13.2), we return to the CD player introduced in Chapter 2. This time, however, we position it in a possible hierarchy that relates various home entertainment systems that play prerecorded CDs or audio/video cassettes and also offer the possibility of recording. Here we include methods, and it should be noted that it is possible to capture quite a large amount of commonality between CD players, audiocassette recorders, and videocassette recorders (VCRs).

This hierarchy has only three levels, but it is a graphic example of how inheritance allows us to capture commonality and to apply generalization to existing (physical) objects to produce a specialization hierarchy.

It is possible to prevent any further inheritance. As class providers, we may decide that it is not sensible to have any subclasses of Car; there are no vehicles that are specializations of Car. We require a mechanism to prevent further extends. We reuse the keyword final.

When we declare a class that is to have no subclass extensions, we include final in the declaration:

```
public final class Car ....
```

13.4   The Class Object

As you have seen, the superclass/subclass relationship forms an inheritance hierarchy. For instance, in the airplane reservations example, we formed an inheritance hierarchy with Reservation as the root and its subclasses as nodes further down the tree.

This seems logical when we examine the declarations of the Reservation subclasses; they each include an extends statement that names their superclass. The Reservation class declaration itself does not include such a statement. We have seen several examples similar to this one—for instance, the Person and Student superclass and subclass.

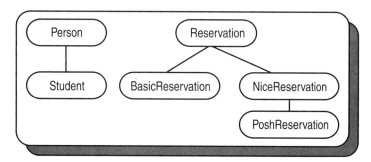

Figure 13.3: Two inheritance hierarchies

However, in Java, there is an implicit root to the overall inheritance hierarchy. We can use this to bring together the two separate subtrees in Figure 13.3. Where a class is defined without an extends statement, it is as if one is inserted on that class's behalf. As shown in Figure 13.4, every such class is a subclass of the system `Object` class (in the `java.lang` package). For illustration purposes, it is possible to insert the `extends Object` statement explicitly. For example, `public class Person extends Object` and `public class Reservation extends Object` are the same as `public class Person` and `public class Reservation`.

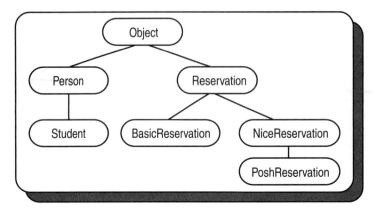

Figure 13.4: A single inheritance hierarchy

The `Object` class is the only Java class that does not have a superclass. Also notice that any class may call (or override) the methods provided by the `Object` class. This is due to the inheritance mechanism. All classes we declare can be considered subclasses of the `Object` class.

One method that the `Object` class provides is `toString`. You may have noticed in some of our class definitions that we have been overriding `toString` to provide our own version. The basic `toString` provided by `Object` when applied to an instance returns a `String` in the format:

```
<class which instance belongs to>@<numerical value>
```

The numerical value need not concern us here; it relates to the low-level representation of the instance. For example, if we have an instance of `Student` and we have not overridden the `toString` method in the `Student` class definition (or in any of its superclasses), we would have a result similar to the following:

```
Student@123456
```

Overriding `toString` allows us to specialize the method to suit the needs of the specific class and ourselves; we can provide a more meaningful representation of the instance and its contents.

The `toString` method is of further interest because the method `System.out.print` makes use of it. Because `toString` is declared as part of the `Object` class, `System.out.print` can safely make the assumption that every object in a Java program has access to that method. It can safely invoke the method without raising an exception or causing an error.

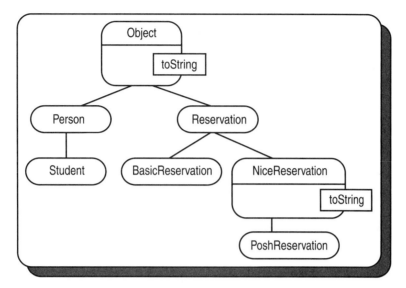

Figure 13.5: Overriding toString

When we override it to provide a more meaningful mapping from the instance to a String, it is our overriding toString method that System.out.print will call. Thus, in some of our example test programs, we are able to include statements like:

```
NiceReservation nr1 ....
System.out.print("Nice Reservation is " + nr1) ;
```

The System.out.print method knows that nr1 is a reference to an object and calls toString on it. If this was not the case, we would have to call it explicitly:

```
System.out.print("Nice Reservation is " + nr1.toString()) ;
```

13.5 Polymorphism

Polymorphism is a powerful mechanism that is exploited fully in object-oriented systems. Essentially, it means there are a number of different classes of objects that will respond to the same request. We return to our example of Person and Student.

We can describe instances of a class as members of the set of instances of that class. For example, consider the statement:

```
Person p1, p2 ;
```

Instances p1 and p2 are members of the set (of instances) of Person (Figure 13.6).

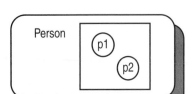

Figure 13.6: A Venn diagram showing two instances of Person

Now consider the statement:

```
Student s1, s2 ;
```

Instances s1 and s2 are members of the set (of instances) of Student (Figure 13.7).

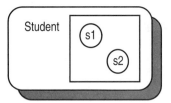

Figure 13.7: A Venn diagram showing two instances of Student

Because Student is a subclass of Person, however, we can say that the set of instances of Student is a subset of the Person set (Figure 13.8). In other words, s1 is a member of the set of students but is also a member of the set of (simple) persons. Thus, s1 is a Person as well as a Student.

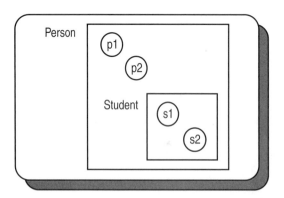

Figure 13.8: A Venn diagram showing Person with the Student subset

In addition to having those methods and attributes directly associated with Student, an instance of Student also possesses (via inheritance) those associated with Person (Figure 13.9).

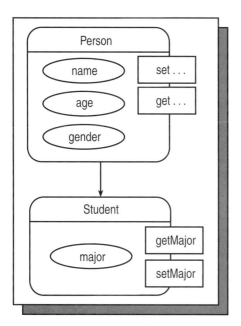

Figure 13.9: Person and its subclass Student

Thus, just as we expect a Person to have the four attributes forename, surname, age, and gender, and the associated get and set methods, we can also expect a Student to have them as well.

We can apply setAge to an instance of Student just as we can to an instance of Person. Everything a Person possesses and the methods it can respond to are shared by a Student:

```
Person p1 ;
Student s1 ;
...
p1.setAge(40) ; // applying a Person method to a Person
s1.setAge(18) ; // applying a Person method to a Student
```

Everywhere we expect a Person instance, we can use a Student instance:

```
p1 = s1 ;
p1.setGender(Person.MALE) ;
```

This is because an object that is a member of the class Student is, by inheritance, also a member of the class Person. Consider the following procedure:

```
public void printPersonName(Person ppn)
   {
   System.out.println("A person's name is " + ppn.getSurname()) ;
   } // end of method printPersonName
```

We can call this with an actual argument of type `Person` or `Student`:

```
printPersonName(p1) ;
printPersonName(s1) ;
```

The general rule is that everywhere an instance of a class is expected, we can use an instance of any of its subclasses (or subsubclasses etc.). This is a precise example of polymorphic behavior. Notice, however, we cannot go in the opposite direction:

```
s1 = (Student) p1 ; // invalid
```

First, to avoid a compile-time error, we must explicitly cast the type of the object on the right side (`Person`) into that of the type of the object on the left side (`Student`). Second, although this statement compiles, at run time it generates a `ClassCastException` exception. Consider the following:

```
public void printStudentMajor (Student psm)
    {
    System.out.println("A student's major is " + psm.getMajor()) ;
    } // end of method printStudentMajor
```

```
printStudentMajor(s1) ;     // OK
printStudentMajor(p1) ;     // invalid
```

The second attempt to call the method with a `Person` actual argument generates a compile-time error because the compiler cannot find a method called `printStudentMajor` that expects a `Person` actual argument.

These attempts generate different types of errors, but the fundamental problem they alert us to is the same. Although `Person` and `Student` share some behavior (that of `Person`), they do not share all of each other's behavior (that of `Student`). A `Student` can behave the same as a `Person`, but the opposite is not true. `Student` has an additional attribute and two extra methods; a `Person` instance cannot handle a `getMajor` method call.

In brief, an object that is a member of a subclass shares all the behavior of the superclass. An object that is a member of a superclass does not share all the behavior of the subclass.

13.6 Polymorphism and Heterogeneous Collections

The situation we wish to explore is that of a *heterogeneous* collection of objects. To start our examination, we return to our reservation example. It is possible to imagine a collection of reservations to be processed at a travel agent. For example, if we wish to print the different reservations, we need to traverse the collection in some way, examine each reservation in turn, and print each one.

As you will see, we can model collections in a number of ways: as an array or as a linked list (see Chapters 11 and 17). We use the array here. In our simple test program, we set up an array of four reservations: a basic one, two nice ones, and a posh one:

```
Reservation[] collection = new Reservation[4] ;

BasicReservation br = new BasicReservation() ;
br.set(12, 23) ;
collection[0] = br ;

NiceReservation nr1 = new NiceReservation() ;
nr1.set(34, 45, NiceReservation.AISLE, NiceReservation.GREEN) ;
collection[1] = nr1 ;

NiceReservation nr2 = new NiceReservation() ;
nr2.set(45, 56, NiceReservation.WINDOW, NiceReservation.RED) ;
collection[2] = nr2 ;

PoshReservation pr = new PoshReservation() ;
pr.set(67, 78, NiceReservation.AISLE, NiceReservation.WHITE, "Birmingham") ;
collection[3] = pr ;
```

We begin by declaring an array called collection; each element is of type Reservation. Then we declare four variables: one of type BasicReservation, two of type NiceReservation, and one of type PoshReservation. Since we last examined these classes, we have added a new method to each. It is called set, and we use it to set all the attributes of the class to which it belongs. After setting up these instances appropriately, we assign them to the collection array.

Here are some points to notice. Polymorphism has already come into play in our example. Just as you saw earlier, it is possible to use an instance of a subclass where the superclass is expected. As each element of the collection array is of type Reservation, we can assign objects of class Reservation or any of its subclasses. This is why we can successfully assign objects of class BasicReservation, NiceReservation, or even PoshReservation (a subsubclass of Reservation) to the elements of the collection array.

We have created a heterogeneous collection of objects (Figure 13.10) in which not all the objects in the collection have the same type, but they are interrelated (Figure 13.11).

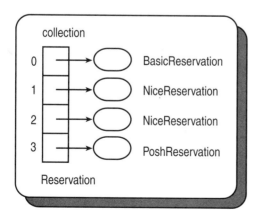

Figure 13.10: A heterogeneous collection of Reservations

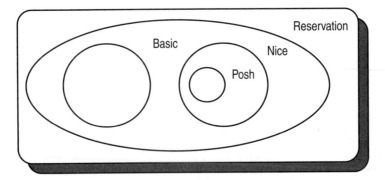

Figure 13.11: A Venn diagram showing subsets of `Reservations`

When we declare a heterogeneous collection of objects, we need to find at least one common superclass. As you saw earlier in this chapter, we are guaranteed to find such a superclass—namely, `Object`. It is a question of finding the lowest class in the inheritance hierarchy that is an ancestor of all the classes we want to put in the collection.

If we wish to make a collection that will contain references to instances of `BasicReservation`, `NiceReservation`, and `PoshReservation`, we can make the collection of type `Reservation`. There is no need to go "all the way back" to the `Object` root. On the other hand, if we want references to instances of `PoshReservation` and `Students`, we must make the collection of type `Object` because this is the only superclass that the instances have in common.

Our next problem is to process the contents of `collection` and to print each element of the array. Here is a skeleton of the code we need to write:

```
for (int i = 0 ; i < collection.length ; i++)
    {
    /* print out the contents of the ith element of the collection array */
    System.out.println() ;    // print a new line to
                              // separate the elements
    }
```

The problem now is how to implement the actions detailed in the first comment. Clearly, we wish to delegate responsibility for how an object is to print itself to the object itself. This means that for each class, from `Reservation` down, we need to implement a method to do this.

If we chose not to take advantage of polymorphism, we may have implemented the methods correctly but given them different names in each class (Table 13.1).

Class	Method Name
Reservation	printRes
NiceReservation	printNice
PoshReservation	printPosh

Table 13.1: print Method Names for the Reservation Classes

If we do this, we are introducing another problem. When we wish to print `collection[i]`, which method should we call? Should it be `collection[i].printRes()`, `collection[i].printNice()`, or `collection[i].printPosh()`?

The method we call depends on the type of the object indicated by `collection[i]`. To pursue this approach further, we would need some way of finding out the type of the object at run time and attempt to use this to direct a `switch` statement to call the appropriate method. This is actually possible, as you will see in Chapter 21. However, as you have seen in the `Person` and `Student` example, calling a method on an inappropriate object can lead to a compile- or run-time error.

The fact is that we can arrange things so that the problem of which method to call is left to the language system. We do this by exploiting polymorphism. In this case, we rename all the print methods to `print`. This leads to the final solution, which is as follows:

```
for (int i = 0 ; i < collection.length ; i++)
    {
    collection[i].print() ;
    System.out.println() ;
    }
```

13.6.1 Dynamic Method Binding (Late Binding)

When we are processing a collection of reservations and we invoke the `print` method (as in our example in the previous section), how do we know which version of the `print` method to call? After all, there are three such methods, one for each `Reservation` class.

When we use a superclass reference (an element of `collection`, the `Reservation` array) to refer to a subclass object and invoke the `print` method, the program selects the correct subclass print method dynamically (at run time). This is known as *dynamic method binding*.

Although the compiler doesn't know which subclass a superclass reference is referring to, the Java interpreter does. In our example, it knows which `Reservation` collection array elements are basic, nice, and posh and can thus ensure that the correct `print` method is called.

Instead of the programmer doing the work, we leave it to the system to work out the class of the reference and which method to call. Imagine that we introduce yet another kind of reservation to our hierarchy (say, `SuperReservation`). An instance of `SuperReservation` could be an element of our collection. As long as we give `SuperReservation` a method called `print`, the solution shown earlier should not need altering and will work as is. If we were doing the work with an `if` statement, we would have to add a new arm to the statement to handle `SuperReservations`.

Although dynamic method binding is fast, it is not as fast as invoking a method directly. Wherever there is no possibility of overriding, we can use direct method invocation. Methods declared as `static`, `private`, and/or `final` cannot be overridden, and thus, we do not need to use dynamic method binding.

13.7 Calling Overridden Methods

We now continue with our airline reservations example; in the previous chapter, each class provided its own `read` method as shown in Table 13.2.

Class	read **Method**
Reservation	readRes()
NiceReservation	readNice()
PoshReservation	readPosh()

Table 13.2: read Method Names for the
Reservation Classes

However, using different names like this raises the same problems for a heterogeneous collection of different types of reservations, as did the different print method names earlier in this chapter.

Imagine that we want to process a collection of reservations and read in the values for each one. The skeleton code is remarkably similar to that for our printing of the collection:

```
for (int i = 0 ; i < collection.length ; i++)
    {
    // read in the contents of the ith element
    // of the collection array
    System.out.println() ; // print a new line to separate the reads
    }
```

To tackle this, we wish to give every read method the same name, read.

```
for (int i = 0 ; i < collection.length ; i++)
    {
    collection[i].read() ;
    System.out.println() ;
    }
```

We have decided to call the method responsible for reading the attributes of an instance read. We have done this in each class so that we have overloaded the name. We have overridden the superclass method, just as we did in our Square and Rectangle example in Chapter 12. Whenever we have an instance of a reservation (be it basic, nice, or posh), we always know how to invoke the appropriate read method; it is called read in every case.

However, this leaves us with a problem: How do we call the read method of the superclass? In the PoshReservation.read method, if we said

```
public void read()
    {
    read() ; // used to be "readNice()"
    BasicIo.prompt("Destination address? ") ;
    destination = BasicIo.readString() ;
    } // end of method read
```

this would be an unintentional (and completely useless) use of a technique called *recursion* (see Chapter 18). Essentially, PoshReservation.read would call itself; this call would then call itself again; this third call would call PoshReservation.read again; and so on into infinity.

Fortunately, the keyword super comes to the rescue. We can use this keyword to indicate the superclass. For the PoshReservation.read method to call NiceReservation.read, we prefix the name of the method in the superclass that we want to call (here read) with the keyword super. The final version of the PoshReservation.read method looks like the following:

```
public void read()
   {
   super.read() ;  // call read method belonging to superclass
                   // in this case NiceReservation.read
   BasicIo.prompt("Destination address? ") ;
   destination = BasicIo.readString() ;
   } // end of method read
```

Notice that super is being used in two different ways—as super and super():

- In the former case, it is acting like a class reference. We use it to access a method belonging to our superclass and apply it to the current instance. It is a bit like using this, which acts directly as an instance reference to the current instance. When we use super, we use it to reference the superclass of the class of this instance. We can then supply the name of a method belonging to that superclass, usually one that we have overridden. This means that we can override a method but still have access to that method should we require it.

- In the latter case, it is a method call to a constructor belonging again to our superclass.

13.8   Methods in Derived Classes

We have discussed in earlier chapters the importance of information hiding in modern software engineering. Information hiding allows us to think of modules or classes as black boxes; we know how they behave, what messages or requests they can process, and what kinds of results they return. We use the black boxes on a "need-to-know" basis. This means we do not need to know exactly how they work but only what they do. This reduces the level of complexity in using the black box. In addition, as long as the interface and behavior remain unchanged, the box providers can make any changes they wish as to how the box provides its services.

The issue we wish to raise at this point is the impact information hiding has on inheritance. If we program by extending (or refining) existing classes (by adding attributes and methods), is there any way we can extend the functionality and behavior of an existing method without knowing how the original method works?

Until now, we have used methods in derived classes in one of two ways. First, we have used them as additional methods intended to extend the functionality of the base class. Second, we have used them as refinements of existing classes—for example, the read method in PoshReservation. In general, this new read method has the same basic functionality as the read method in the NiceReservation class, the base class. We can still access this functionality using the super.read notation to call the read method in the NiceReservation class. However, we are free to provide additional code that refines the existing code and make the new read method more suitable for the PoshReservation class.

The airline reservations classes contain a number of examples of refinement. The methods read, print, and set are all defined in terms of their corresponding superclass method. You have already seen the read methods. Let us now look at the set methods and how they refine their superclass method by adding more functionality without changing the inherited behavior:

```
public class Reservation
    {
    public void set (int fn, int sn)
        {
        flightNumber = fn ;
        seatNumber = sn ;
        } // end of method set
    ...

public class NiceReservation
    {
    public void set (int fn, int sn, int st, int f)
        {
        super.set(fn,sn) ;
        seatType = st ;
        food = f ;
        } // end of method set
    ...

public class PoshReservation
    {
    public void set(int fn, int sn, int st, int f, String d)
        {
        super.set(fn, sn, st, f)    ;
        destination = d ;
        } // end of method set
    ...
```

Another example is as follows. We have the class Manager as subclass of Employee. There is a method (increment) used to calculate an Employee's annual increment. Managers are entitled to the same increment with a bonus based on their department's productivity. As before, we can define the class Manager by the difference between it and the class Employee. From the details given so far, the difference is:

- An attribute to denote their department's productivity (deptProd).
- An overriding version of increment.

We can thus define the new version of increment as follows:

```
public double increment()
    {
    double res = super.increment() ;
    res = res + deptProd * 0.1 ;
    return res ;
    } // end of method increment
```

You can see that we do not need to know how an employee's increment is calculated or what attributes are used. All we need to know is how a manager's additional bonus is calculated. If, at some future point, a new way is introduced for how an employee's increment is calculated, this will have no impact on the manager's increment method; we will automatically inherit (and use) the revised version. The principle of information hiding is being maintained through the inheritance mechanism.

As a final example, consider the Student class, which inherits from the Person class. If we want to produce a toString method for Student, which will simply provide details from the Person class plus the major attribute from Student, why should we have to write a completely new toString method from scratch? Instead, we want to use Person.toString and append the major details. We can do this using the keyword super as follows:

```
public String toString()
    {
    return super.toString() + " " + major ;
    } // end of method toString
```

13.9   Key Points in Chapter 13

- Whenever an instance of a class is created, the class's constructor method is called. It is also called whenever an instance of any subclass is created.

- We can explicitly ensure the superclass constructor is called by including a call to super( ). We can use super in this way only in a constructor method, and it must be the first statement.

- If we do not include a call to super( ), Java automatically inserts one. Notice that it always calls the argumentless version (this may or may not be the one that we want).

- It is possible to have multiple levels of inheritance and create an inheritance hierarchy.

- There is an implicit root to Java's inheritance hierarchy. Any class declared without an extends statement is automatically a subclass of the system Object class.

- Class providers may wish to block inheritance. We can prevent access to inherited elements by specifying private access to those elements. If we don't want to have any subclasses at all, we can declare our class as final. Note also that if you don't want to have a method overridden, you can declare it as final as well.

- *Polymorphism* means instances of different classes can respond to the same request. For example, if Student is a subclass of Person, every place we expect a Person instance, we can use a Student instance. This is because a Student instance has inherited all the elements of a Person instance and can thus handle any Person method call. Notice that we cannot expect polymorphism from subclass to superclass.

■ Because of polymorphism, we can set up and process heterogeneous collections of objects. We can have an array of Reservations that contains BasicReservations, NiceReservations, and PoshReservations. If each class provides a method (of the same name and signature), we can execute the appropriate method on each element of the array.

■ It is useful to be able to call an overridden method (often within the method that overrides it). We can again use the keyword super to refer to our superclass. This means we can extend the functionality of an inherited method without understanding how it is implemented.

■ Inheritance allows us to extend the functionality of inherited methods without compromising information hiding. We can override the inherited method (but still call it within the overriding method using super) and add the code that refines the functionality.

13.10   Exercises

1. Zeller's congruence is a formula for determining the day of the week on which a calendar date falls. It works for any U.K. and U.S. date since 1752, when the Gregorian calendar was introduced in Britain and its colonies.

   The formula is as follows:

   $$W = (k + [(2.6 * m) - 0.2] - (2 * C) + Y + [Y / 4] + [C / 4]) \bmod 7$$

   where:

   ■ Expressions in [] give rounded-down integer results.

   ■ k is the day of the month (1 to 31).

   ■ m is the month. This is slightly peculiar in that 1 = March, 2 = April, . . . 10 = December, 11 = January, 12 = February, with January and February being treated as months of the preceding year. See Y.

   ■ C is the century. Thus, 2002 has $C = 20$.

   ■ Y is the year. Thus, March 2002 to February 2003 have $Y = 02$, while January and February 2002 have $Y = 01$. See m.

   ■ W is the day of the week, where 0 = Sunday and 6 = Saturday.

   Write a program that repeatedly prompts the user for dates and returns the corresponding day of the week for each. If the user types:

   October 16, 2002

   The answer returned is:

   Wednesday

   We propose that you tackle this problem by:

   a. Extending the OurDate class to include a method that calculates the day of the week.

b. The new subclass should include a `String` attribute `weekday`, which stores the result of the method.

c. Whenever a method is called to set the date, you should call the Zeller method to update the `weekday` attribute.

Remember to make elements of the class `private` if they should be.

2. a. Write a class called `House` to hold details of the location (street number, street name, town) and (if known) the year of construction and the property tax band.

b. Write a derived class `Home` with additional instance variables for the name of the occupying family and the date they moved in. You should use the `OurDate` class from the `javalancs` package.

Note the following:

■ There should be two constructor methods:

```
public Home(int house, String street, String town,
            String family, Date movedIn)
```

and

```
public Home(int house, String street, String town,
            int yearConstructed, char taxBand, String family,
            Date movedIn)
```

These should make use of the keyword `super` where appropriate.

■ There should be the usual methods to set and extract the values of the new instance fields:

```
setFamily
getFamily
setDateMovedIn
getDateMovedIn
```

■ There should be a `printDetails` method that calls the `printDetails` method provided by the `House` class to display the address of the house and then displays the text `"has been occupied by SOMEONE since DATE"` with suitable values inserted.

3. Write a program that contains an array of `Houses`:

```
House[] collection = new House[100] ;
```

The user inserts elements in this array as follows. The program prompts the user for the number, street, town, and (if the user wishes) a family name and date of moving in. The program should then create an instance of the appropriate class (`House` or `Home`) and store it as the next element of the array `collection`.

Finally, the program should scan through the array `collection` calling the `printDetails` method for each element. Check that Java correctly calls the appropriate version of this method in each case.

4. Continuing your development of the `Time` class from Chapter 12, it is now found that you need to maintain the time to an accuracy of seconds. Assume now that `Time` and `Time2` are both library classes. Create a `Time3` class that allows you to keep hours, minutes, and seconds and provides new versions of the `toString` and `earlier` methods. As usual, provide a suitable driver application to test your methods.

5. Consider again the problems of modeling people within a university. There are undergraduate students, postgraduate students, and staff members. You should decide what attributes and methods should be possessed by an instance of each of these classes and develop an inheritance hierarchy (with the Person class as its base). Declare a heterogeneous collection for university member objects and write an application that prints each element of the collection.

6. Write a program to read two text files with names specified by the user at the terminal. The program should match each line of one file with the corresponding line of the other and display a list of the lines that do not match, together with a count of the total number of mismatching lines.

   Two lines match if they differ only (a) in the number of leading or trailing spaces or tab characters, (b) in the case (upper or lower) of the letters, or (c) when one line contains multiple spaces or tab marks at a position where the other has a different number of spaces or tabs (but not zero).

   Thus,

   ```
   The   Cat   Sat   ON   The   Mat
   ```

   matches

   ```
   the cat sat on the mat
   ```

   Implement this program by deriving a class from BasicFileIo and adding a method

   ```
   public String getCanonicalLine()
   ```

   to read a text line from a file and return it in canonical form.

   Initially, this method could be the readString method from the BasicFileIo class, while you write the matching program to use it. Then rewrite the method to (a) strip out leading and trailing spaces from the line read before returning it, (b) force all letters to lowercase, (c) replace a sequence of two or more spaces by one space, and finally (d) deal with the tab character in the same way you deal with a space.

   Test the program by trying it out on a file containing a suitable program text (perhaps the very same program you have just written).

Note 1 ■

Canonical means "in a standard form." The getCanonicalLine method returns a line transcribed into a form standardized with respect to case of letters and the presence of whitespace (e.g., spaces and tab characters).

Note 2 ■

The match is line by line. You do not have to deal with lines inserted into or deleted from one of the files, which is a much more difficult problem.

CHAPTER 14

Abstract Classes and Interfaces

14.1 Abstract Classes

In this chapter, we introduce the concept of an *abstract* class. The classes you have seen so far are all examples of *concrete* classes. A concrete class is one that has direct instances. For example, the Person class provides the template for a number of Person instances. Similarly, we can have instances of Employees or Students. An abstract class does not have such direct instances. It is provided only to have other classes derived from it (some of which eventually will have instances). In this chapter, our main example of an abstract class is the Solid class. We would therefore never write in a Java program:

```
Solid aSolid = new Solid() ;
```

In one sense, we are returning to the issues of data modeling and sets of objects. In a generalization exercise, we can identify a whole host of geometric solids, such as cuboids, spheres and cylinders. These three entities have some features in common; for example, they all have an enclosed volume and a surface area. We should thus identify a common superclass that possesses these features, and the three subclasses should inherit from the superclass, which we will call Solid (Figure 14.1).

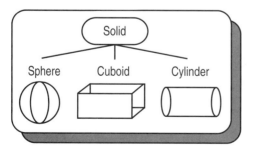

Figure 14.1: The Solid class and its subclasses

Next, we need to decide whether these features (volume and surface area) should be modeled as attributes or methods. Clearly, we would want the object to calculate its own volume and surface area rather than the user, who would then provide these values through a set method. Thus, we want them to be methods.

How are we to implement these methods? At this point, we run into difficulties. The formula for calculating the surface area of a cuboid is quite different from that for the surface area of a sphere. These formulas are in Table 14.1.

	Attributes	**Surface Area**	**Volume**
cuboid	length, breadth, height	2 * ((length * breadth) + (length * height) + (breadth * height))	length * breadth * height
cylinder	radius, height	2 * ((π * radius * radius) + (π * radius * height))	π * radius * radius * height
sphere	radius	4 * π * radius * radius	4/3 * π * radius * radius * radius

Table 14.1: Formulas for Cuboids, Cylinders, and Spheres

Notice that the formulas make reference to features that the solids do not all have in common. For example, a sphere and a cylinder have a radius. A sphere has no height of side, whereas a cuboid and cylinder do. These features belong only to the specific class; they do not belong to the shared superclass Solid.

How then can we specify these algorithms as methods within the Solid class? They need access to instance variables that do not belong in Solid. We can say that Solid is an *abstract* class. It specifies two abstract methods, called volume and surfaceArea, both of which have no arguments and return a double. We can specify this as follows:

```
public abstract class Solid
    {
    public abstract double surfaceArea() ;
    public abstract double volume() ;
    } // end of class Solid
```

Note that we do not provide the method bodies because we are quite unable to do so. You should be able to understand now why we cannot have direct instances of Solid. How would you interpret the following?

```
Solid aSolid = new Solid() ;
double res = aSolid.surfaceArea() ;     // meaningless
```

We can now begin to define the subclasses, Sphere, Cuboid, and Cylinder, as follows:

```
public class Sphere extends Solid
    {
    private double radius ;
```

```java
   public Sphere()
      {
      radius = 0.0 ;
      } // end of constructor method

   public Sphere(double r)
      {
      radius = r ;
      } // end of constructor method

   public double volume()
      {
      return 4.0 / 3.0 * Math.PI * radius * radius * radius ;
      } // end of method volume

   public double surfaceArea()
      {
      return 4.0 * Math.PI * radius * radius ;
      } // end of method surfaceArea

   public String toString()
      {
      return "Sphere radius " + radius + " volume " +
             volume() + " surface area " + surfaceArea() ;
      } // end of method toString

   other methods ...
   } // end of class Sphere

public class Cuboid extends Solid
   {
   private double height, breadth, length ;

   public Cuboid()
      {
      length = 0.0 ;
      breadth = 0.0 ;
      height = 0.0 ;
      } // end of constructor method

   public Cuboid(double l, double b, double h)
      {
      length = l ;
      breadth = b ;
      height = h ;
      } // end of constructor method
```

```
public double volume()
    {
    return length * breadth * height ;
    } // end of method volume

public double surfaceArea()
    {
    return 2 * ((length * breadth) + (length *
            height) + (breadth * height)) ;
    } // end of method surfaceArea

public String toString()
    {
    return "Cuboid length " + length + " breadth " +
            breadth + " height " + height + " surface area " +
            surfaceArea() + " volume " + volume() ;
    } // end of method toString

    other methods ...
    } // end of class Cuboid

public class Cylinder extends Solid
    {
    private double height, radius ;

public Cylinder()
    {
    radius = 0.0 ;
    height = 0.0 ;
    } // end of constructor method

public Cylinder(double r, double h)
    {
    radius = r ;
    height = h ;
    } // end of constructor method

public double volume()
    {
    return Math.PI * radius * radius * height ;
    } // end of method volume

public double surfaceArea()
    {
    return 2 * ((Math.PI * radius * radius) +
            (Math.PI * radius * height)) ;
    } // end of method surfaceArea
```

```
public String toString()
   {
   return "Cylinder height " + height + " radius " + radius +
          " surface area " + surfaceArea() + " volume " + volume() ;
   } // end of method toString

other methods ...
} // end of class Cylinder
```

Note that these subclasses now contain the instance variables they need to implement the formulas as methods.

At this point, you may be wondering why we should bother with the Solid class at all. It hasn't saved us any work because we still had to define the methods for each subclass. We didn't inherit any concrete methods or attributes from it at all.

Well, as you have seen, it is useful to have generalization and specialization in data modeling. The Solid class allows us to state that there is a general thing called Solid, of which Sphere, Cuboid, and Cylinder are three specializations. It allows us to state that every shape has common features, namely, a surface area and a volume. The compiler will check that the eventual concrete class has the named methods and appropriate arguments and return value types. You will see in a moment how polymorphism allows us to have some practical advantages from abstract classes as well.

It is the responsibility of the concrete derived class to provide a physical implementation of each abstract method. As you have seen, the inheritance hierarchy can be several levels deep. It may be several levels before we can make every aspect of an abstract class concrete. In this case, as long as a derived class contains an abstract method, then that class is itself abstract. It is only when all methods have been given a body that the class becomes concrete and we can set up instances of the class.

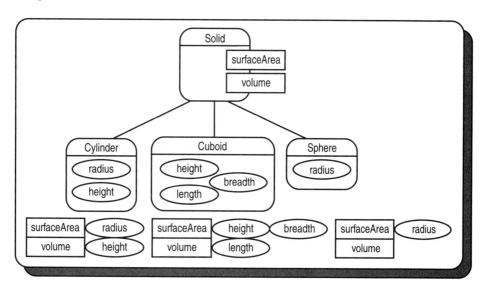

Figure 14.2: The inheritance hierarchy for solids, showing the features added at each level and the final set of features for the concrete classes

Figure 14.2 presents the inheritance hierarchy for the Solid class and its immediate subclasses. We show the attributes and methods defined at each level and finally summarize the set of methods and attributes available to instances of the subclasses.

14.2 Polymorphism

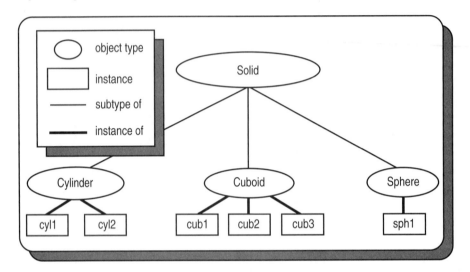

Figure 14.3: The inheritance hierarchy showing instances of the concrete classes

Figure 14.3 shows the hierarchy, but this time we show some object instances of the subclasses. These instances will expect the methods and attributes at the bottom of Figure 14.2.

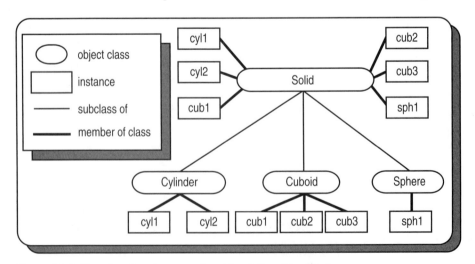

Figure 14.4: Showing the class membership of the object instances

In Figure 14.4, we consider the classes as collections or sets of object instances. For example, the sph1 instance of Sphere is directly a member of the set of spheres but also a member of the set of solids. Finally, Figure 14.5 shows set membership in a traditional Venn diagram.

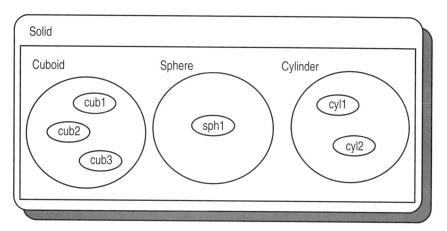

Figure 14.5: Showing the class memberships as a Venn diagram

In the Venn diagram, you can see how objects that have been directly declared as instances of the concrete classes are also members of the superclass. Through polymorphism, anywhere we expect a Solid, we can also use a Cuboid, Cylinder, or Sphere. For example:

```
Solid aSolid ;    // valid declaration. Note we haven't
                  // used a constructor.
Sphere aSphere = new Sphere(4.0) ;
aSolid = aSphere ;
System.out.println(aSolid.volume()) ;
```

We can use the aSolid variable more directly:

```
Solid aSolid = new Sphere(4.0) ;
System.out.println(aSolid.volume()) ;
```

Just as you saw in the previous chapter, we can set up a collection of different classes that share a common superclass. We used an array of type Reservation to store elements of the different subclasses of Reservation (BasicReservation, NiceReservation, and PoshReservation). In that example, Reservation was not an abstract class; it contained two attributes (flightNumber and seatNumber) and matching get and set methods.

Even though Solid is an abstract class, we can set up a collection of instances of its subclasses. In this example (Figure 14.6), we build an array of class Solid with different elements (Sphere, Cuboid, and Cylinder) and calculate their total volume.

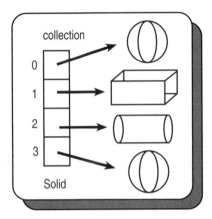

Figure 14.6: A heterogeneous collection of solids

```
Solid[] collection = new Solid[4] ;

Sphere s1 = new Sphere(4.0) ;
collection[0] = s1 ;

Cuboid c1 = new Cuboid(2.0, 3.0, 4.0) ;
collection[1] = c1 ;

Cylinder cyl = new Cylinder(4.0, 2.0) ;
collection[2] = cyl ;

Sphere s2 = new Sphere(3.0) ;
collection[3] = s2 ;

double totalVolume = 0.0 ;
for (int i = 0; i < 4; i++)
    {
    totalVolume += collection[i].volume() ;
    }
System.out.println("total volume = " + totalVolume) ;
```

As described in Section 13.6.1, the system uses dynamic method binding at run time to select the version of the volume method associated with the appropriate class.

14.3 Interfaces

You may have noticed in all our examples that a subclass can have only a single immediate superclass. The Student class has Person, BasicReservation has Reservation, and so on. This restriction means that the graph that represents the superclass-subclass relationship is a hierarchy—that is, a tree with a single root—hence, inheritance *hierarchy*.

Some systems allow multiple superclasses; for example, the class ToyTruck may inherit from Toy and Truck. The class NuclearSubmarine may inherit from NuclearPoweredVehicle and Submarine. In such systems, the superclass-subclass relationship is a network or lattice—hence, inheritance *lattice*.

Java allows only *single* inheritance as opposed to *multiple* inheritance. This restriction means we can inherit functionality and data only from a single superclass. In an attempt to alleviate this limitation, Java supports the concept of *interfaces*.

Polymorphism maintains that a set of objects has a common set of methods or behaviors; for example, we can find out the volume of a set of objects that were declared as members of different classes (albeit sharing a common "root" class). A consequence is that it might be useful if we can expect instances of different classes to provide common methods. If we do not provide these specifications through inheritance, how then are we to implement polymorphism?

Interfaces resemble abstract classes in that they define a set of methods (or behaviors) that a class can be expected to provide. They can also provide a set of constants. They do not define attributes, however.

If we return to our player example in Section 13.3, we can identify videocassette recorders (VCRs) in the hierarchy. One very common use of VCRs is to record programs at a given day and time. We need to include a set of methods (and attributes) that allow us to program the VCR. However, elsewhere in our home entertainment hierarchy, we may find a satellite receiver (Figure 14.7). This is also programmable. Is there any way we can capture the fact that these two pieces of equipment share the same behavior?

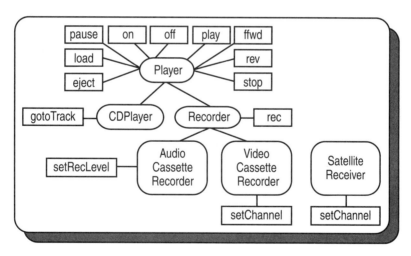

Figure 14.7: A hierarchy of home entertainment

If Java supported multiple inheritance, we could introduce a new class, Programmable-Timer, and have VideoCassetteRecorder and SatelliteReceiver inherit from it (Figure 14.8).

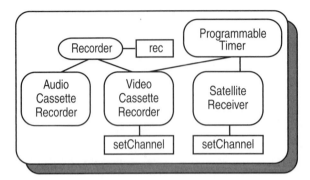

Figure 14.8: A lattice of home entertainment

However, this is not possible in Java. Instead, we define an interface, `Programmable`, which specifies the (abstract) methods that a programmable VCR or satellite receiver would need (Figure 14.9).

```
public interface Programmable
    {
    public void setCurrentTime(int day, int month, int hour, int minute) ;
    public void setChannel(int channel) ;
    public void setStart(int day, int hour, int minute) ;
    public void setStop(int day, int hour, int minute) ;
    } // end of interface Programmable
```

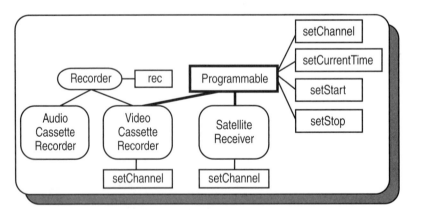

Figure 14.9: Interfaces as well as classes

The interface provides a set of specifications of methods; it does not provide any code that we can reuse or extend. It is the responsibility of the class to implement the methods (just as it is with abstract methods). An interface is a guarantee, enforced by the compiler, that certain methods will appear with certain names, arguments, and return values. Let us illustrate the concept with the help of the example shown in Figure 14.10.

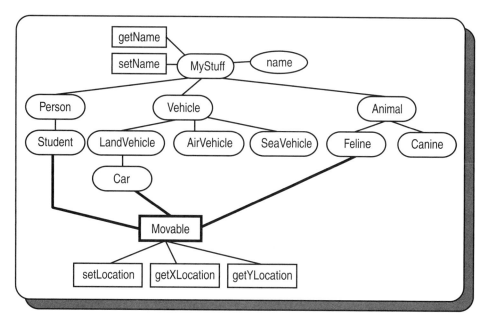

Figure 14.10: Inheritance plus interfaces

Here we have an inheritance hierarchy linking a number of disparate kinds of real-world objects. We decided quite early that all the objects of interest to us should have a name. We captured this by placing a name attribute and associated get and set methods in the MyStuff class. Later, we decided that some classes should be movable; that is, they can be moved from one position to another on a two-dimensional plane. We need to represent this by a pair of Cartesian coordinates and associated get and set methods.

As you have seen, we cannot do this by means of multiple inheritance. We must use the Java interface mechanism. We provide the following interface definition:

```
public interface Movable
    {
    public void setLocation(int x, int y) ;
    public int getXLocation() ;
    public int getYLocation() ;
    } // end of interface Movable
```

Note that we store this in a file called Movable.java and compile it as usual. This produces a file called Movable.class.

We now identify the classes that we wish to make movable; these are Student, Car, and Feline. We change their class definition to include the fact that they are going to implement the Movable interface as follows:

```
public class Student extends Person implements Movable
    {
    ...
```

```
public class Car extends LandVehicle implements Movable
    {
    ...

public class Feline extends Animal implements Movable
    {
    ...
```

At this point, the class providers of Student, Car, and Feline must implement the three methods listed in the Movable interface specification. We cannot inherit any attributes or code from the interface; this may mean that we have to introduce completely new attributes and the associated code. In this example, each class may use exactly the same code as follows:

```
// implementing the Movable interface methods
    private int x, y ;
    public void setLocation(int x1, int y1)
        {
        x = x1 ;
        y = y1 ;
        } // end of method setLocation

    public int getXLocation()
        {
        return x ;
        } // end of method getXLocation

    public int getYLocation()
        {
        return y ;
        } // end of method getYLocation
```

This is very similar to inheriting from an abstract class. Polymorphism is supported now because all Movable classes can respond to requests for the setLocation, getXLocation, and getYLocation methods. Let us now examine an example that uses our Movable classes.

```
public class Chapter14n1
    {
    public static void main(String[] args)
        {
        MyStuff[] collection = new MyStuff[3] ;
        Movable[] moveCol = new Movable[3] ;

        Student stud = new Student() ;
        stud.setName("James T. Kirk") ;
        stud.setLocation(0, 0) ;
        collection[0] = stud ;
        moveCol[0] = stud ;
```

```
Car aCar = new Car() ;
aCar.setName("Fiat Uno") ;
aCar.setLocation(1, 1) ;
collection[1] = aCar ;
moveCol[1] = aCar ;

Feline aCheetah = new Feline() ;
aCheetah.setName("The Flash") ;
aCheetah.setLocation(2, 2) ;
collection[2] = aCheetah ;
moveCol[2] = aCheetah ;

// access object directly
System.out.println("Name of aCar is " +
    aCar.getName() + " Current location is " +
    aCar.getXLocation() + ", " + aCar.getYLocation()) ;
System.out.println() ;

// access objects indirectly
for (int i = 0 ; i < 3 ; i++)
    {
    System.out.println("Name of "+ i +
        "th element is " + collection[i].getName()) ;
    System.out.println("Current location is "
        + moveCol[i].getXLocation() + ", " +
        moveCol[i].getYLocation()) ;
    System.out.println() ;
    }
} // end of main method

} // end of class Chapter14n1
```

As before, we set up a collection of objects. Here we set up two exact duplicates; one is of class MyStuff and the other is of interface Movable.

Notice, however, when we use a single object directly (aCar), we do not need to refer to it via two different references, MyStuff or Movable. We know what class aCar belongs to, and we know it can respond to its own methods, the methods it inherited, and the methods it implemented to conform to the Movable interface. We can thus apply these methods directly.

When we come to processing the elements of the heterogeneous collections, however, we must take care to apply the methods to the appropriate collection. The MyStuff array elements expect only method invocations that the MyStuff class can handle—for example, get-Name. If we try to write

```
collection[i].getYLocation()
```

this will result in a compile-time error. We must have a Movable collection so that the compiler understands we are calling a Movable interface method.

Unlike classes, where we can extend only a single class, it is possible to implement multiple interfaces. We may want to make our `Movable` objects have a graphical representation and for those representations to be placed at *x, y* screen locations. We could define our classes as follows:

```
public class Car extends Land implements Movable, Drawable
    {
    ...
```

Finally, just as classes can have subclasses, interfaces can have subinterfaces. A subinterface inherits all the abstract methods and constants of its superinterface and may add new ones of its own. Again, we have the ability to handle multiple interfaces because an interface can extend more than one interface.

```
public interface Transformable extends Scalable,
                               Rotatable, Reflectable
    {
    ...

public interface DrawingObject extends Drawable,
                               Transformable
    {
    ...

public class Solid implements DrawingObject
    {
    ...
```

14.4   Key Points in Chapter 14

- A *concrete* class is one that we expect to have direct instances. An *abstract* class will not; it exists only to have other (abstract or concrete) classes derived from it.

- Abstract classes can contain abstract methods; these are methods that do not (and often cannot) exist within the abstract class but that we expect subclasses to override by providing implementations of the method.

- Abstract classes support polymorphism. For example, an abstract class `Shape` could have a number of concrete subclasses such as `Triangle`, `Rectangle`, and `Circle`. We can now set up a heterogeneous collection of `Triangles`, `Rectangles`, and `Circles` as an array of `Shapes`. If `Shape` has an abstract method `area`, then we expect the subclasses to provide implementations of that method suitable for their own geometry. Thereafter, the `Shape` subclasses will respond to the same method request(s).

- Any class with at least one abstract method must be declared abstract.

- Some systems support multiple inheritance—for example, ToyTruck inheriting from Toy and Truck. Java supports inheritance only from a single superclass; hence, we have an inheritance *hierarchy* rather than *lattice* or network.

- What if we identify two sets of behavior such as finding out the volume of objects from different classes? How do we support polymorphism under these circumstances if multiple inheritance is not allowed? Java's answer to this is the *interface*.

- An interface resembles an abstract class because it defines a set of methods it expects a class to provide. Unlike an abstract class, an interface can contain no concrete code. The interface can also provide a set of constants but not attributes.

- We can thus use inheritance and interfaces to model the following situation. We have a home entertainment system hierarchy, and this includes a VCR and a satellite receiver, both of which are programmable. We can't make these subclasses of a ProgrammableDevice superclass because the VCR is already a subclass of Recorder. Instead, we define a Programmable interface and specify that the VCR and satellite receiver both implement that interface. The onus is on the class provider to implement the methods specified in the interface.

- We can have collections of objects that are polymorphic because they all implement a common interface and can thus respond to requests for the interface methods.

14.5   Exercises

1. You have a number of classes to represent institutions (Figure 14.11). The Institution class is abstract and has two concrete subclasses, Educational and Commercial.

   An Institution has a value associated with it. For the Educational class, this is calculated as follows:

   ```
   assets = number of students * fees - running costs
   ```

   For the Commercial class, you have:

   ```
   profits = gains - losses
   ```

   a. Model the hierarchy as a collection of Java classes with appropriate method and attribute definitions as required.

   b. Create a heterogeneous collection of Educational and Commercial instances.

   c. Provide a driver application that allows you to find
      - The total value of your collection.
      - The names of the institutions with the highest and lowest values.

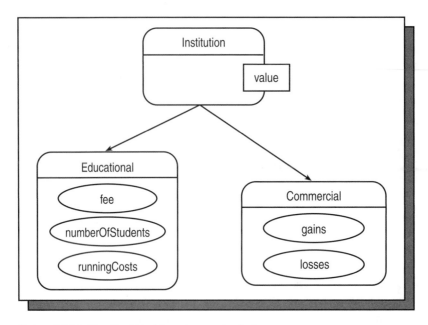

Figure 14.11: The Institution class and subclasses

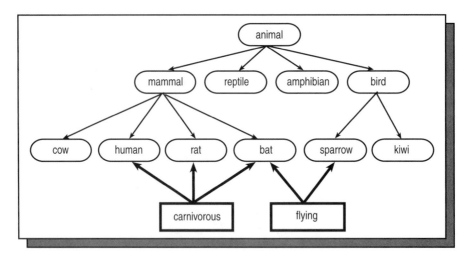

Figure 14.12: Animal inheritance and interfaces

2. Figure 14.12 is a portion of a classification hierarchy for the natural world.

   a. Show how you can use interfaces to specify the following:

   - Bats and sparrows can fly (a possible method might be maximumTimeInFlight).
   - Humans, rats, and bats are carnivorous (a possible method might be huntingRadius).

   b. Realize the relevant portions of the hierarchy and interfaces in Java.

   c. Provide a driver application to test your classes and interfaces.

3. You have three different classes: `Person`, `Car`, and (household) `Appliance`.

   You wish to provide a method `getSummary` that allows you to get a `String` containing a summary of the instance (rather than a perhaps too detailed `toString`). For a `Person`, you wish to get the title and surname; for a `Car`, the make and model; for an `Appliance`, the manufacturer and model.

   There are two different approaches. You can have `Person`, `Car`, and `Appliance` all inherit from a shared abstract class (called `MyObject`), which has the method specifier `getSummary`. You then implement it in the three subclasses (Figure 14.13).

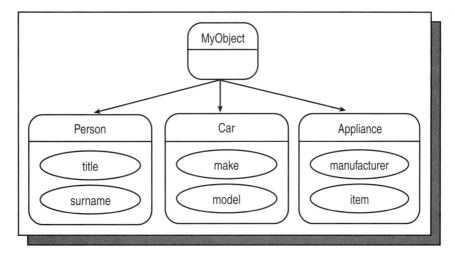

Figure 14.13: Inheritance and four classes for Exercise 14.3

   If you are unable to reorganize the inheritance hierarchy, you can provide an interface `Summarizable`, again with the method specifier `getSummary` (Figure 14.14).

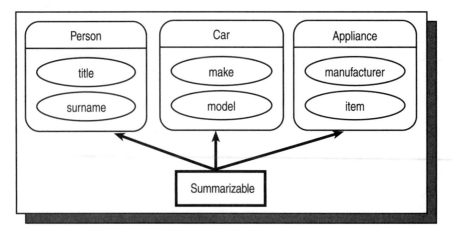

Figure 14.14: Three classes and an interface for Exercise 14.3

    a. Implement both solutions just presented.

    b. For both cases, create a heterogeneous collection of instances of the three classes.

    c. For both cases, provide a driver application to test your classes and interfaces.

4. You wish to model a game of chess. As in Exercise 10.6, you again wish to model the board, the squares, and the pieces. However, you now want to make use of abstract classes. You have an abstract class `ChessPiece`, which provides a concrete method and attributes to represent a piece's location but also the abstract method `isMoveLegal`. You have a number of concrete classes inheriting from `ChessPiece` (e.g., `Pawn`, `Rook`, `Knight`, etc.), and their responsibility is to provide a concrete implementation of `isMoveLegal` for their own characteristics.

    As in Exercise 10.6, set up the board for the start of the game and allow player(s) to specify moves that are checked for legality before the move is made.

CHAPTER 15

Throwing and Catching Exceptions

15.1 Motivation: Robust Programs

One of the problems with writing a program is to make sure it is *robust*. That is, when something unexpected occurs (e.g., an invalid piece of data has been typed in by the user or an access to the Internet has failed), we have to ensure that the program can detect what has happened and do something about it. The program could modify the processing as appropriate in the light of what has happened, it could perhaps retry the operation (e.g., reaccess the Internet), or it could at least close down the program in a "safe" way with a suitable error message.

If we are going to test for and then cope with a large number of special situations, our program may end up as a spaghetti of code, most of which is there to handle one of a large number of possible special situations, none of which occur very frequently. A common system would be for each method to pass back a special indication of any failure and for the calling method to detect this and pass it back in its turn. Such a system may make it difficult to write the code that handles the standard, common situations in a well-structured way. What we need is a mechanism that allows each special condition to be checked for at the point where it could occur. But when the condition does occur, we want control to be passed automatically to a section of code at a suitable location (which may be at some distance from where the condition was detected) for the appropriate action to be taken.

The mechanism supplied for this in the Java language is the *exception* (Figure 15.1). An exception is an indication that some special condition has occurred; as you will see, it is in fact an instance of a class derived from the Exception class (in the java.lang package). The piece of code that detects that the condition has occurred creates an exception of the appropriate type; it is said to *throw* the exception. Somewhere else in the program, there may be a piece of code that is able to deal with the condition (i.e., some form of error handler). We can arrange for the code to *catch* the exception and then deal with it. Because there may be several error handlers in the program, there needs to be a technique by which an exception is caught only by a handler that can deal with it. If the handler cannot, the exception will be passed on for another handler to deal with it. If no handler is found, the program will be brought to a halt with a suitable error message.

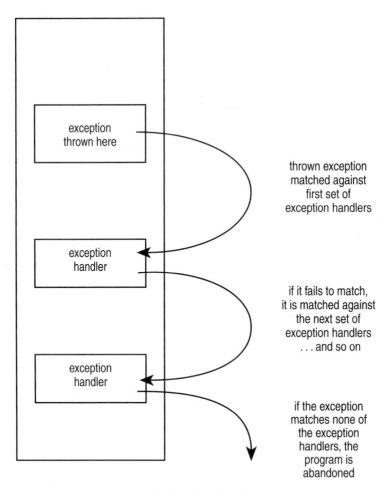

exception
thrown here

thrown exception
matched against
first set of
exception handlers

exception
handler

if it fails to match,
it is matched against
the next set of
exception handlers
. . . and so on

exception
handler

if the exception
matches none of
the exception
handlers, the
program is
abandoned

Figure 15.1: An exception looking for a handler

You have in fact already met the concept of an exception. When we are using the BasicIo or BasicFileIo classes, various things can go wrong. For example, when the program is trying to read an integer with the readInteger method, the user could type the string"two", or we could attempt to write to a file that was read-only. In situations such as these, the methods of these classes throw an exception from a class called IOException (in the java.io package and derived from the Exception class). In the code we have written so far, we have made no attempt to catch and do anything about these exceptions; we have simply allowed the program to be abandoned. But we have already found that Java insists on strict accounting for exceptions. If we have a method that calls other methods that may throw exceptions, and our method is not going to do anything about them, then as far as Java is concerned our method is responsible for possibly throwing an exception. We have to report this in our method header with a throws clause.

Thus, whenever we write a method that calls any of the `BasicIo` or `BasicFileIo` methods, we have to indicate that our method may throw an `IOException`:

```
public static void main(String[] args) throws IOException
    {
    . . .
```

In Chapter 11, we implemented a `PriorityQueue` class. We are going to discuss exceptions in terms of this class. You will recall that if we attempt to extract an item from an empty queue or insert an item in a full queue, we have set up the methods to stop the program (using the `System.exit` method). This is fairly drastic, and it would be better to throw an exception to allow the program using the class to attempt to recover if possible. We need to do the following:

- Define the exceptions that we might need to throw.

- Throw an exception at an appropriate point.

- Set up handler code at appropriate places and make it catch the appropriate exception or exceptions.

15.2   Defining a New Exception

First we have to decide what exceptions we want to throw. Sometimes we want to throw an exception that has already been defined in the standard Java language. For example, as was mentioned earlier, we have written all the methods of the `BasicIo` and `BasicFileIo` classes so that they throw the standard exception `IOException`.

At other times, we will want to define our own class of exceptions. This is a new class that inherits from one of the standard Java exceptions. In the case of the `PriorityQueue` class, we want to define a new class of exception called `QueueEmptyException` to be thrown when either of the methods `first` or `remove` is called on to access the "first" element in an empty queue.

We define this exception by extending one of the standard Java exception classes (or one of the exception classes that we have defined earlier):

```
public class QueueEmptyException extends Exception
    {
    . . .
    } end of class QueueEmptyException
```

This is going to be a `public` class (because we will want to refer to it in other programs where we are coding exception handlers), so it will be in a separate file `QueueEmptyException.java`.

What do we need to put in our new class? We need to provide only a pair of constructor methods: a default method and a method with a single `String` argument. The `String` argument can give more information about the exception than is available from its name. For example, if we were throwing an exception because an argument to a method was invalid, we might want the string to include information about the particular argument value that caused the problem.

The body of these constructors simply calls the appropriate constructor of the base class either implicitly or explicitly:

```
public QueueEmptyException()
    {
    } // end of constructor method

public QueueEmptyException(String message)
    {
    super(message) ;
    } // end of constructor method
```

15.3 Throwing an Exception

When a program detects a condition that requires an exception to be reported, it creates an instance of that exception (using the appropriate constructor method) and throws it. Thus, in the `remove` method, we test for there being nothing to remove. If so, we create and throw an instance of the `QueueEmptyException` exception:

```
if (isEmpty())
    throw new QueueEmptyException() ;
```

or

```
if (isEmpty())
    throw new QueueEmptyException("'remove' from empty queue") ;
```

The Java system requires the programmer to inform it of what exceptions could be thrown by each method. Thus, the header line of the remove method becomes:

```
public QueueElement remove() throws QueueEmptyException
```

Actually, not all exceptions need to be reported in the `throws` part of a method header. Some exceptions (e.g., `NullPointerException`) could be thrown by almost any piece of Java code, so it would be necessary to list this exception in almost every method header. The rule is that the `throws` list must include all exceptions derived from the `Exception` class but not those derived from its subclass `RuntimeException`.

If the `throw` statement is reached in the `remove` code, the flow of control does not proceed any further through the code of the method nor does it return to the method that called it. Instead, the Java system searches for an exception handler that is able to handle this type of exception. If it does not find one, it terminates the program with a suitable error message.

Similarly, we insert a `throw` statement in the `first` method (and a `throws` clause in its header):

```
public QueueElement first() throws QueueEmptyException
    {
    if (isEmpty())
    throw new QueueEmptyException("'first' on empty queue") ;
    . . .
```

In the `insert` method, we need to throw a `QueueFullException` (with a `throws` clause in its header):

```
public void insert(QueueElement d) throws QueueFullException
    {
    if (isFull())
    throw new QueueFullException("'insert' in full queue") ;
    ...
```

Of course, we need to define this `QueueFullException` class first, as we did with the `QueueEmptyException` class.

If we compile the `PriorityQueue.java` file now, we will find another problem. We left in the class a `main` method for testing purposes. This calls all three of our modified methods, which means that exceptions may be thrown that `main` does nothing about. Hence, we have to modify the header:

```
public static void main(String[] args) throws IOException,
                QueueFullException, QueueEmptyException
```

Because we call `BasicIo` methods, we are already warning that instances of `IOException` may be thrown.

15.4   Catching an Exception

If we now try our new version of the `PriorityQueue` with the `main` method that we left for testing purposes, we find that attempting to remove from an empty queue causes the program to be abandoned with a suitable error message

```
Exception in thread "main" QueueEmptyException: 'remove' from empty queue
        at PriorityQueue.remove(PriorityQueue.java:94)
        at PriorityQueue.main(PriorityQueue.java:192)
```

if we used the `QueueEmptyException` constructor with an argument, or

```
Exception in thread "main" QueueEmptyException:
        at PriorityQueue.remove(PriorityQueue.java:94)
        at PriorityQueue.main(PriorityQueue.java:192)
```

if we used the `QueueEmptyException` constructor without an argument.

But now we want to catch these exceptions in the `main` method so that we can continue with the testing. If we wish to deal with some or all of the exceptions in a certain sequence of code, we have to make it into a `try` block:

```
try {
    SEQUENCE OF STATEMENTS WHERE WE WISH TO CATCH EXCEPTIONS
    }
```

```
catch (EXCEPTION-CLASS-1 variable-name)
    {
    CODE TO DEAL WITH EXCEPTIONS OF THE SPECIFIED CLASS
    }
catch (EXCEPTION-CLASS-2 variable-name)
    {
    CODE TO DEAL WITH EXCEPTIONS OF THE SPECIFIED CLASS
    }
catch (EXCEPTION-CLASS-3 variable-name)
    {
    CODE TO DEAL WITH EXCEPTIONS OF THE SPECIFIED CLASS
    }
```

The basic idea (Figure 15.2) is that if an exception is thrown in the try block, it is tested against each of the catch clauses in turn, starting at the first one. The first matching catch clause is executed, and then control passes to the code immediately after the last catch clause. That is, only one of the catch clauses is executed, the first one that matches, and then the program continues from after the try-catch code.

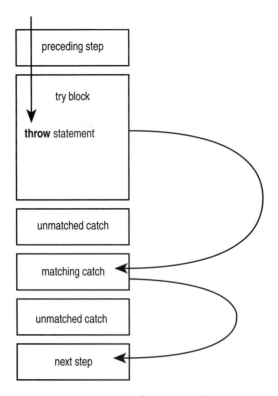

Figure 15.2: Sequence of execution for a caught exception

If none of the catch clauses matches the exception that has been thrown, the Java system has still not caught the exception, and it will look for an enclosing try clause so that it can try to match the exception against each of its catch statements in turn (Figure 15.3).

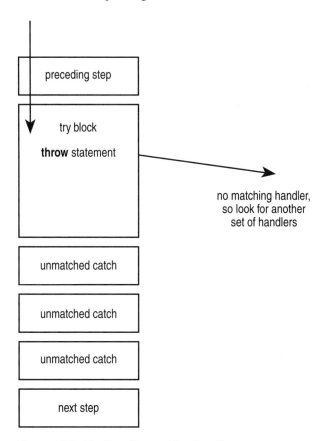

Figure 15.3: No "local" matching handler

If no exception is thrown, control proceeds to the end of the try block, ignores all the catch clauses, and proceeds with the code after the last catch clause (Figure 15.4).

We now take the loop in the main method of the PriorityQueue class:

```
while (continueLoop)
    {
    displayMenu() ;
    ...
    switch (response.charAt(0))
        {
        case '1' :
            ...
            code that includes calls of insert (which may throw
```

```
                    QueueFullException) and first and remove (which may throw
                    QueueEmptyException)

                    ...
            default :
                    System.out.println("invalid response") ;
                    break ;
            } // end of switch

      if (continueLoop)
            {
            BasicIo.prompt("press RETURN to continue") ;
            response = Basicio.readString() ;
            } // end of if
      } // end of loop
```

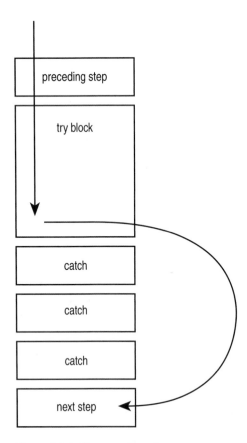

Figure 15.4: No exception thrown

We insert a try block in it to catch the exceptions for the "queue full" and "queue empty" conditions:

```
while (continueLoop)
    {
    displayMenu() ;
    ...
    try {
        switch (response.charAt(0))
            {
            case '1' :
            ...
            code that includes calls of insert (which may
                throw QueueFullException) and first and remove (which may
                throw QueueEmptyException)
                ...
            default :
                System.out.println("invalid response") ;
                break ;
            } // end of switch
        } // end of try block
    catch (QueueFullException ex)
        {
        System.out.println("no more room in the queue") ;
        }
    catch (QueueEmptyException ex)
        {
        System.out.println("no elements in the queue") ;
        }

    if (continueLoop)
        {
        BasicIo.prompt("press RETURN to continue") ;
        response = BasicIo.readString() ;
        }
    } // end of loop
```

We are now catching the two new exceptions rather than allowing them to be thrown out of our main method, so we no longer need to tell the Java system that we are throwing them (we could still throw an IOException):

```
public static void main(String[] args) throws IOException
```

In the normal course of events, when no exceptions are thrown, the program executes the statements of the try block, ignores the catch clauses, and proceeds to the if test at the end of the loop before proceeding in the normal way to the next iteration of the loop.

Suppose we now try to remove an element from an empty queue. The remove method will be abandoned when it reaches the throw statement. Since the exception was thrown inside the try block, the flow of control immediately proceeds to the appropriate exception handler, which will deal with it by printing an error message. It will ignore the other catch clause and proceed to the if statement and then to the next iteration of the loop.

If any other exception is thrown (e.g., an instance of the IOException class), no matching exception handler has been provided. The system looks for an enclosing try block, does not find it, and the program terminates with an error message.

A catch clause looks a bit like a method with a single formal argument of some class derived from Exception (and in this example, given the name ex):

```
catch (QueueEmptyException ex)
    {
    . . .
    }
```

We can refer to the exception inside the catch clause if we want. There is a toString method in the Exception class, and this is inherited by the derived classes; it prints the exception name and any message associated with it. Thus, we could write:

```
catch (QueueEmptyException ex)
    {
    System.out.println("ERROR: " + ex) ;
    }
```

This causes the toString method associated with the instance ex to be called automatically (see Section 13.4) to print a suitable error message.

We stated that a thrown exception was tested against each of the catch clauses in turn to find the first one that matched. If we have thrown an instance of the QueueEmptyException class, the first catch clause it matches is:

```
catch (QueueEmptyException ex)
    . . .
```

An alternative way of writing the preceding code is:

```
while (continueLoop)
    {
    displayMenu() ;
    . . .
    try {
        switch (response.charAt(0))
            {
```

```
                case '1' :
                    ...
                    code that includes calls of insert (which may
                    throw QueueFullException) and first and remove (which may
                    throw QueueEmptyException)
                    ...
                default :
                    System.out.println("invalid response") ;
                    break ;
                } // end of switch
            } // end of try block
        catch (Exception ex)
            {
            System.out.println("ERROR: " + ex) ;
            }

        if (continueLoop)
            {
            BasicIo.prompt("press RETURN to continue") ;
            response = Basicio.readString() ;
            }
        } // end of loop
```

Here we have provided only one `catch` clause:

```
catch (Exception ex)
    ...
```

But the `QueueEmptyException` class is derived from the `Exception` class, so (by polymorphism) a `QueueEmptyException` instance is also an `Exception` instance. Thus, all the exceptions will be caught by this `catch` clause (including `IOException`).

15.4.1   *The* `finally` *Clause (Optional)*

There is a slight problem if we have a lot of `catch` clauses:

```
try {
    SEQUENCE OF STATEMENTS WHERE WE WISH TO CATCH EXCEPTIONS
    }
catch (EXCEPTION-CLASS-1 variable-name)
    {
    CODE TO DEAL WITH EXCEPTIONS OF THE SPECIFIED CLASS
    }
catch (EXCEPTION-CLASS-2 variable-name)
    {
    CODE TO DEAL WITH EXCEPTIONS OF THE SPECIFIED CLASS
    }
```

```
catch (EXCEPTION-CLASS-3 variable-name)
    {
    CODE TO DEAL WITH EXCEPTIONS OF THE SPECIFIED CLASS
    }
catch (EXCEPTION-CLASS-4 variable-name)
    {
    CODE TO DEAL WITH EXCEPTIONS OF THE SPECIFIED CLASS
    }
```

If we have some tidying up to do after dealing with an individual exception, we would have to put it at the end of each of the catch clauses. To avoid this problem, Java provides a finally clause, which is always executed after any of the catch clauses have been executed:

```
try {
    SEQUENCE OF STATEMENTS WHERE WE WISH TO CATCH EXCEPTIONS
    }
catch (EXCEPTION-CLASS-1 variable-name)
    {
    CODE TO DEAL WITH EXCEPTIONS OF THE SPECIFIED CLASS
    }
catch (EXCEPTION-CLASS-2 variable-name)
    {
    CODE TO DEAL WITH EXCEPTIONS OF THE SPECIFIED CLASS
    }
catch (EXCEPTION-CLASS-3 variable-name)
    {
    CODE TO DEAL WITH EXCEPTIONS OF THE SPECIFIED CLASS
    }
catch (EXCEPTION-CLASS-4 variable-name)
    {
    CODE TO DEAL WITH EXCEPTIONS OF THE SPECIFIED CLASS
    }
finally
    {
    CODE TO DO ANY TIDYING UP
    }
```

The effect of the keyword finally is shown in Figure 15.5.

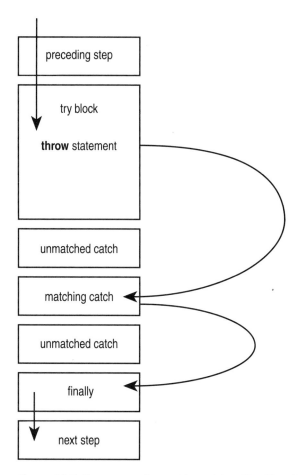

Figure 15.5: Sequence of execution with a `finally` clause

In fact, the `finally` clause is executed however the `try` block is left, whether it leaves normally without throwing an exception, or it throws an exception that is not caught by any of these `catch` clauses. Thus, we can put in the `finally` clause any tidying-up code that we must guarantee to execute.

15.5   Key Points in Chapter 15

- If we have an unusual condition, we can *throw* an *exception* at the point where the condition is detected and *catch* it at a distant point in the program, where we can handle the condition.

- We define new exceptions by deriving them from the `Exception` class (or a class derived from it). We need to define a default constructor and a constructor with one `String` argument:

```
public class NewException extends Exception
    {
    public NewException()
        {
        } // end of constructor method

    public NewException(String message)
        {
        super(message) ;
        } // end of constructor method
    } // end of class NewException
```

- We throw an exception by setting up a new instance of the class and then using the keyword `throw`:

```
if (CONDITION)
    throw new NewException(" ... ") ;
...
```

- We can catch exceptions that are thrown in a sequence of statements (including those thrown by methods called from the sequence) with a `try` block:

```
try {
    SEQUENCE OF STATEMENTS WHICH MAY THROW EXCEPTIONS
    }
catch (EXCEPTION-CLASS-1 ex)
    {
    HANDLER FOR EXCEPTION-CLASS-1
    }
catch (EXCEPTION-CLASS-2 ex)
    {
    HANDLER FOR EXCEPTION-CLASS-2
    }
```

If no exceptions are thrown, the `catch` clauses are ignored. If an exception is thrown, the rest of the SEQUENCE OF STATEMENTS is abandoned, and only the matching `catch` clause is executed. If none of the `catch` clauses match, the system searches for an enclosing `try` block. If no match occurs anywhere in the program, it will be abandoned with an error message.

■ If an exception is thrown by a method (or by a method that it calls) and the method does not handle the exception, it has to be mentioned in a throws clause in the method header:

```
public ... methodName( ... arguments ... ) throws NewException
```

15.6   Exercises

1. Rewrite the Person class so that an exception NonvalidPersonAttribute is thrown if any of the set methods is passed an argument that is not valid (e.g., a surname of length zero or a negative age).

    Rewrite the test harness program for the Person class (see Section 4.8) so that it catches the NonvalidPersonAttribute but not any IOExceptions.

    Rewrite the test harness further so that it also catches any IOExceptions.

2. Implement a stack of characters as an abstract data type in the class CharacterStack. The stack should be implemented as an array of characters, together with a count of how many elements are currently stored in the stack. It should have the following methods:

    ■ public void initialize( ) to initialize an empty stack.

    ■ public void push(char ch) to push a character ch on the top of the stack, throwing StackOverflowException if there is no room.

    ■ public char pop( ) to pop the top character off the stack and return it, throwing StackUnderflowException if the stack is empty.

    ■ public boolean isEmpty( ) to return whether or not the stack is empty.

    ■ public int size( ) to return the number of elements in the stack.

    Write a driver program to allow the stack to be tested by a user from the terminal. The user should be able to specify the next method to call from a menu and then specify any arguments, and the program should print any return values for checking.

3. Use the CharacterStack class to implement a program to check an expression for matching enclosure symbols.

    The types of enclosure symbols it should recognize are parentheses (and), square brackets [and], and curly braces { and }. Thus, {([])} and {(())[()()]} are valid expressions, whereas {(} and ( ) are not. The expression should be entered by the user as a string.

    The algorithm for this program is as follows:

    Starting with an empty stack and a string of characters, take each successive character in the string. If the character is an opening symbol of some sort, push it on the stack. If it is a closing symbol of some sort and either the stack is empty or the character popped from the top of the stack is not an opening symbol of the same type, then the string is unbalanced. A balanced string will leave an empty stack when the string has been processed.

CHAPTER 16

Graphics and the Abstract Windowing Toolkit

16.1 Graphical User Interfaces

So far in this book, our programs have communicated with the user by reading and writing strings of characters. Typically, the program starts and then requires some input information. It prompts the user for a piece of data using the BasicIo.prompt method or some of the System.out.print methods. Then it reads in a value from the user using an appropriate method from the BasicIo class. It repeats this for each required piece of input data. Finally, it carries out some form of calculation and then outputs the results for the user, again using some of the System.out.print methods.

Today, many programs provide a different format for interacting with the user: a *graphical user interface,* or *GUI* (pronounced *gooey*). The user is presented with one or more "windows" containing text, drawings, diagrams of various types, or perhaps pictures or "images." The user communicates with the program by typing into designated areas of the display or by moving the mouse to a particular position and clicking the mouse button. This action is used to press buttons of various kinds on the screen, to scroll a window across a larger diagram or area of text, to indicate a particular location within a drawing at which some action or redrawing must take place, and so on. You saw a good example of this in the network browser introduced in Chapter 1. The browser displays a page, and we can press various buttons to carry out actions (e.g., to add the URL of the current page to our bookmark file), to scroll through the page if it is larger than the display area, and to click on a link in the page, which the browser interprets as a call to read the designated page from the Web and display it.

One of the problems in creating a graphical user interface in the past has been *platform independence.* Even if we write our program in a standard language such as C, different operating systems (e.g., UNIX, Microsoft Windows, and the Macintosh operating system) have a different set of facilities for providing a GUI, with a different set of behaviors.

In this chapter, we describe how to build a graphical user interface for a program written in Java. Java provides a set of facilities called the *Abstract Windowing Toolkit,* or *AWT,* and this provides a standard set of facilities for building GUIs that is the same across all platforms. It does this by mapping the facilities provided by the AWT onto the facilities provided by the particular operating system on which the program is running.

In fact, Java provides two sets of facilities for writing GUI programs: the AWT and a more advanced set called *Swing*. In this chapter, we concentrate on the AWT, but Swing versions of all programs described in this chapter are available on this book's Web site (see Appendix A). You can usually obtain the Swing name for a GUI component from the AWT name by adding a J at the beginning; thus, the Swing components `JFrame`, `JButton`, `JLabel`, `JPanel`, and `JTextField` correspond to the AWT components `Frame`, `Button`, `Label`, `Panel`, and `TextField` described in this chapter.

There are more than 70 classes in the current version of the AWT. Therefore, we do not attempt to describe in detail all the facilities available. To illustrate the general features of the facilities provided by the AWT, we instead introduce a number of short programs that use the AWT to provide simple graphical interfaces. To find more information, you can study the Java API documentation or read any of a number of books that describe the AWT in much more detail.

We write graphical interface programs in Java by deriving new classes from the classes provided in the Abstract Windowing Toolkit, so this is also a good introduction to the use of the inheritance features described in Chapters 12 to 14.

There is a significant difference between a program with a text interface, the type we have used up to now, and one with a graphical interface, the type to be discussed in this chapter. This difference relates to the range of events that the program has to be able to handle. When a program with a text interface is awaiting input from the user, the only event that will happen is that the user eventually types in some sequence of characters. The program has to interpret these characters, decide whether or not they are valid, and then take the appropriate action. In a graphical interface, there could be several different text areas, drawing areas, and buttons. The user could type into any one of the text areas, click on any part of a drawing, or press any one of the buttons.

Furthermore, the user could have several other windows on the screen that are connected to other programs. The user could move one of these windows over the top of the window connected to our Java program, partially or fully obscuring this window. Later, the user could bring the Java window back to the front, and the system has to know how to redraw the parts of the window that have become visible again. The user could "resize" the Java window (i.e., make it larger or smaller), and again the system has to know how to redraw the graphical interface at this new size.

A central feature of a graphical program is therefore an *event loop*. The program waits for some event to occur and, when it occurs, causes the appropriate action to be taken. If the window has become exposed after being hidden behind another window or if the window has had its size changed by the user, it will call a method to redraw the window. If a button has been pressed, it will call a suitable method to deal with this event; presumably, some calculation will be carried out, after which some part of the window may need to be redrawn. After the action appropriate to the event has been carried out, the program returns to waiting in the event loop. We say that such a program is *event driven*.

This event loop is inside the code that implements the AWT, and it does not appear explicitly as part of the code of our program. Our program normally does some initialization and setting up of the graphical components to be displayed and then goes into the event loop inside the AWT. The rest of our program will be a number of short fragments (typically methods), each of which is called by the AWT event loop to deal with a certain type of event (e.g., a button depression or a mouse click at a particular location on a diagram).

There is another feature of graphical programming that needs to be mentioned, and that will be illustrated in the example programs later in this chapter. As you will see, we are going to write a method to redraw a portion of a window based on the current state of various program variables. In Java, this method is usually called paint. When an event occurs, such as to press a button or move the mouse, the corresponding action should normally record details of the event and then request that the AWT carry out a redraw of the appropriate part of the screen at a suitable time. This request in Java is a call of the repaint method. For example, the method called as a result of clicking the mouse at a certain position should record the position and call repaint. This allows the action corresponding to an event to occur quickly so that the program can keep up with events as they happen. The redrawing of the parts of the window by the paint method, which is likely to be rather slower, will be carried out at a time scheduled by the AWT.

16.2   A Simple Program with a Graphical Interface

Our first simple graphical program displays a window such as the one in Figure 16.1.

Figure 16.1: A first Java program with a graphical interface

A happy face is displayed. If we click the Change button, it becomes a sad face, and if we click Change again, it becomes happy again. We can leave the program by clicking the Quit button. If you try running the program, you will see that if you cover this window with that from another program and then reveal it again, the face is redrawn. If you resize the window, you will see that the happy face is redrawn in the new center of the area.

In fact, we are going to start with the slightly simpler program shown in Figure 16.2.

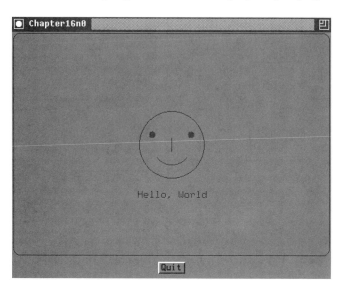

Figure 16.2: A simplified first graphical program

This version does not have a Change button; rather boringly, the face is always happy. However, we have retained the Quit button so that we can abandon the program when we wish. Here is the code for this program, which we explain in the next few sections; the program is in the file Chapter16n0.java.

```java
import java.awt.* ;
import java.awt.event.* ;

public class Chapter16n0 extends Frame
                              implements WindowListener, ActionListener
    {
    public Chapter16n0()
        {
        super() ;

        // set up basic window
        setTitle("Chapter16n0") ;
        setBackground(Color.green) ;
        setSize(500, 400) ;
        addWindowListener(this) ;

        // set up area for face
        Canvas0 canvas = new Canvas0() ;
        add("Center", canvas) ;
```

```
// set up area with buttons
Panel p = new Panel() ;
p.setLayout(new FlowLayout()) ;
Button quit = new Button("Quit") ;
p.add(quit) ;
quit.addActionListener(this) ;
add("South", p) ;
} // end of constructor method

public static void main(String[] args)
{
Chapter16n0 f = new Chapter16n0() ;
f.setVisible(true) ;
} // end of main method

public void actionPerformed(ActionEvent event)
{
// deal with "Quit" button
dispose();
System.exit(0);
} // end of method actionPerformed

public void windowClosing(WindowEvent event)
{
dispose() ;
System.exit(0) ;
} // end of method windowClosing

public void windowOpened(WindowEvent event) {}
public void windowIconified(WindowEvent event) {}
public void windowDeiconified(WindowEvent event) {}
public void windowClosed(WindowEvent event) {}
public void windowActivated(WindowEvent event) {}
public void windowDeactivated(WindowEvent event) {}
} // end of class Chapter16n0

class Canvas0 extends Canvas
{
public Canvas0()
{
super() ;
} // end of constructor method

public void paint(Graphics g)
{
// set up some dimensions for the drawing
Dimension d = getSize() ;
```

```
    int cx = d.width / 2,
        cy = d.height /2,
        faceRadius = 50,
        noseLength = 20,
        mouthRadius = 30,
        mouthAngle = 50,
        eyeRadius = 5 ;

// draw the frame
g.setColor(Color.black) ;
g.drawRoundRect(2, 2, d.width - 5, d.height - 5, 20, 20) ;

// draw the face
g.setColor(Color.red) ;
g.drawOval(cx - faceRadius,
           cy - faceRadius,
           faceRadius * 2,
           faceRadius * 2) ;
g.setColor(Color.blue) ;
g.fillOval(cx - 30 - eyeRadius,
           cy - 20,
           eyeRadius * 2,
           eyeRadius * 2) ;
g.fillOval(cx + 30 - eyeRadius,
           cy - 20,
           eyeRadius * 2,
           eyeRadius * 2) ;
g.setColor(Color.red) ;
g.drawLine(cx, cy - (noseLength / 2),
           cx, cy + (noseLength / 2)) ;
g.drawArc(cx - mouthRadius,
          cy - mouthRadius,
          mouthRadius * 2,
          mouthRadius * 2,
          270 - mouthAngle,
          mouthAngle * 2) ;

// write the text
Font f1 = new Font("TimesRoman", Font.PLAIN, 14) ;
Font f2 = new Font("TimesRoman", Font.ITALIC, 14) ;
FontMetrics fm1 = g.getFontMetrics(f1) ;
FontMetrics fm2 = g.getFontMetrics(f2) ;
String s1 = "Hello, " ;
String s2 = "World" ;
int w1 = fm1.stringWidth(s1) ;
int w2 = fm2.stringWidth(s2) ;
g.setColor(Color.black) ;
```

```
        g.setFont(f1) ;
        int ctx = cx - ((w1 + w2) / 2) ;
        int cty = cy + faceRadius + 30 ;
        g.drawString(s1, ctx, cty) ;
        ctx += w1 ;
        g.setFont(f2) ;
        g.drawString(s2, ctx, cty) ;
        } // end of method paint
    } // end of class Canvas0
```

The Java class that implements an independent window on the screen is called `Frame`. Our version of `Frame` is going to contain an area upon which we will draw the happy face; this is a version of another Java class that provides a drawing area or canvas, called `Canvas`. We have an area below the canvas that contains the Quit button (and later the Change button). Thus, our program consists of two classes:

- A public class called `Chapter16n0`, derived from `Frame`. This provides the basic layout of the window, sets the program running in the first place, and specifies the action that should result if the Quit button (and later the Change button) is pressed.

- A class called `Canvas0`, derived from `Canvas`. This contains details of how to draw the happy face and accompanying text.

The classes and methods for programming with the AWT are in two packages, `java.awt` and `java.awt.event`, so we import both.

16.3   Writing the `Chapter16n0` Class

The class `Chapter16n0` contains no instance variables but has four methods:

- A constructor method to specify the layout of the window.
- A `main` method to set the program going.
- An `actionPerformed` method to deal with pressing the Quit button.
- A `windowClosing` method, which is a necessary part of any Java graphics program, to ensure that we are able to kill off the program if it is not working properly. As you will see, it is also necessary to have several more dummy methods to deal with other possible things that can happen to a window.

We deal with each of these methods in turn.

16.3.1   *The Constructor for the* `Chapter16n0` *Class*

The constructor method `Chapter16n0` provides the basic layout of our window. First we specify a title to go in the title area at the top of our window using the `setTitle` method:

```
setTitle("Chapter16n0") ;
```

We have provided as title the string Chapter16n0, but we could have used something less boring. If we omit this step, a default title is displayed, such as all spaces.

Then we set the background color for our window using the setBackground method:

```
setBackground(Color.green) ;
```

The argument to this method is an instance of the Color class. This class provides a number of color names as constants; we have used green (Color.green), but the full list is

- black
- blue
- cyan
- darkGray
- gray
- green
- lightGray
- magenta
- orange
- pink
- red
- white
- yellow

It is in fact possible to construct other shades of color with the Color class, but it is beyond the scope of this book. On our system, if we omit to call the setBackground method, the default color is lightGray.

Next we specify the initial size of the window with the setSize method:

```
setSize(500, 400) ;
```

This takes two integer arguments: the horizontal width followed by the vertical height of the window. The units of these arguments are *pixels*. A pixel, or picture element, is the basic unit of resolution on the screen; it is the smallest addressable area on the screen, and it is the unit in which coordinates within the window are specified (from an origin in the top left corner). You should not omit this step because the AWT needs to have some initial idea about the size of your window.

We discuss the call of the addWindowListener method in Section 16.3.5.

Now we can start to put the basic elements of the layout in our window. The main part of our window is going to be an area containing the happy face. This will be derived from the class Canvas, and our derived class is going to be called Canvas0. We declare a local variable canvas of this type, referring to an object created with the constructor method Canvas0 (there is more about the Canvas0 class and constructor method later).

```
Canvas0 canvas = new Canvas0() ;
```

We want the canvas to appear as the main item in our picture with the button (or buttons) below it. If we wished, we could calculate the exact position of each item and tell the AWT to position the item at that point. But usually, we want to arrange the items in specified relative positions and have the AWT work out the exact positioning (particularly as we cannot anticipate exactly how each platform may display the components of the picture, and the end user may later wish to resize the window). To simplify the problem of layout, the AWT provides a number of *layout managers* to do most of the work of positioning picture components within a larger "container" component. The default layout manager for classes derived from `Frame` is the *border* layout manager.

We add a picture component to a container component with a version of the `add` method, one of whose arguments is the picture component to be added:

```
add("Center", canvas) ;
```

If we are using the border layout manager, the `add` method needs another argument to specify the positioning. This, the first argument, is one of the strings`"Center"`, `"North"`, `"South"`, `"East"`, or`"West"` to specify the relative position of the picture elements according to the diagram in Figure 16.3.

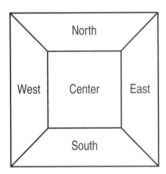

Figure 16.3: Positions in the border layout

Thus, the `Canvas0` instance `canvas` goes at the `Center`, and the group of buttons will go at `South` (i.e., at the bottom of the window). As you can see from this example, not all positions in a border layout need to be filled.

Now we set up the Quit button. We are going to put the buttons on a panel, which is a general window component that can contain other components, so we declare a `Panel` instance p:

```
Panel p = new Panel() ;
```

We specify (with the `setLayout` method) that the panel should have another layout manager, the *flow* layout manager, which lays out components in a generally helpful way, filling up rows from left to right and then top to bottom.

```
p.setLayout(new FlowLayout()) ;
```

We then create a button labeled `Quit`. We create an instance of the `Button` class with the label as the argument to its constructor, and we add it to the panel `p` with the `add` method. Since the button is being added to the panel under the control of the flow layout manager, the only argument to the `add` method is the component being added.

```
Button quit = new Button("Quit") ;
p.add(quit) ;
```

We discuss the call of the `addActionListener` method in Section 16.3.4.

Finally, we add the panel `p` to the class derived from `Frame`, requiring it to be positioned at the bottom of the window (i.e.,`"South"`), as we have already mentioned:

```
add("South", p) ;
```

16.3.2 Other Layout Managers

We have used the `FlowLayout` and `BorderLayout` managers in this example. There are a number of other layout managers, perhaps the most useful of which is the `GridLayout` manager. This allows a set of components to be laid out in a specified number of rows and columns. When we set up this manager, we specify the number of rows and columns:

```
p.setLayout(new GridLayout(2, 3)) ; // 2 rows, 3 columns
```

Then we add the components with the `add` method (with no additional arguments)—first the components of the first row, from left to right, then the components of the second row, from left to right, and so on:

```
p.add(row0column0) ;
p.add(row0column1) ;
p.add(row0column2) ;
p.add(row1column0) ;
p.add(row1column1) ;
p.add(row1column2) ;
```

This gives the layout shown in Figure 16.4.

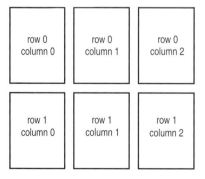

Figure 16.4: Using the `GridLayout` Manager

It is possible to be much more specific about how components are laid out (e.g., with a layout manager called `GridBagLayout`), but this is beyond the scope of this book. The fore-going three layout managers will be sufficient for the tasks we want to carry out here. We can build up more complex layouts by using combinations of these three. For example, we could have a component with a `GridLayout` manager with two rows and a single column, and adding to it two components each with a `GridLayout` manager with a single row and several columns, leading to a layout resembling the one in Figure 16.5.

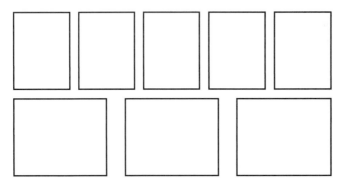

Figure 16.5: More complex use of the `GridLayout` manager

16.3.3 *The* main *Method for the* Chapter16n0 *Class*

We move on now to the `main` method of our `Chapter16n0` class. We first declare a local variable of type `Chapter16n0` and initialize it with the constructor method we have just described:

```
Chapter16n0 f = new Chapter16n0() ;
```

Then we call the method `setVisible`:

```
f.setVisible(true) ;
```

This displays the object on the screen and enters the AWT event loop, waiting for and then responding to events as they occur.

16.3.4 *The* actionPerformed *Method of the* Chapter16n0 *Class*

Next we have to specify what is to happen when we click Quit. If we click a button, the AWT system calls a method `actionPerformed`, which belongs to the `ActionListener` interface (in fact, it is the only method in this interface). We therefore first have to tell Java that our class `Chapter16n0` implements this interface:

```
public class Chapter16n0 extends Frame implements ActionListener
```

For each button, we need to tell the AWT which class contains the `actionPerformed` method for this button. In the examples in this book, it will always be the class that contains the constructor that set up the button in the first place. Thus, we can use the keyword `this` as an argument to the `addActionListener` method applied to the button when we have set it up in the constructor method:

```
quit.addActionListener(this) ;
```

We now have to write the `actionPerformed` method. This has a single argument, an `ActionEvent`, and this gives details of what has happened:

```
public void actionPerformed(ActionEvent event)
    {
    ...
```

For the moment, we have only a single button. So, if this method has been called, we can assume that the Quit button must have been pressed. If so, we abandon the program by calling the `System.exit` method. Since this is a normal exit from the program, we give an argument value of zero. Before we do this, we make sure we have returned all the system resources used by this object using the method `dispose`:

```
    // deal with "Quit" button
    dispose();
    System.exit(0);
    } // end of method actionPerformed
```

16.3.5   *The* `windowClosing` *Method of the* `Chapter16n0` *Class*

Finally, we need a `windowClosing` method to make sure the user can always abandon the program if things go wrong and the Quit button is inaccessible. We have to tell Java that we are implementing the `WindowListener` interface:

```
public class Chapter16n0 extends Frame implements WindowListener, ActionListener
```

We then have to specify that the `windowClosing` method is to be found in this class (`Chapter16n0`), so we insert in the constructor the statement:

```
addWindowListener(this) ;
```

The `windowClosing` method then abandons the program:

```
public void windowClosing(WindowEvent event)
    {
    dispose() ;
    System.exit(0) ;
    } // end of method windowClosing
```

Unfortunately, having promised to implement the interface `WindowListener`, we have to provide six other methods to deal with various things that can happen to a window. We provide dummy methods that do nothing:

```
public void windowOpened(WindowEvent event) {}
public void windowIconified(WindowEvent event) {}
public void windowDeiconified(WindowEvent event) {}
public void windowClosed(WindowEvent event) {}
public void windowActivated(WindowEvent event) {}
public void windowDeActivated(WindowEvent event) {}
```

You can simply copy the code we have provided here into the class derived from `Frame` (i.e., effectively the main class) in each program you write.

This completes the discussion of the code for the class `Chapter16n0`. We now turn to the class `Canvas0`.

16.4 Writing the `Canvas0` Class

The class `Canvas0` contains no instance variables, only a constructor, and one other method, `paint`. We use a default constructor method for this class:

```
public Canvas0()
    {
    super() ;
    } // end of constructor method
```

The `paint` method is called when the window is first displayed and whenever the AWT needs to redraw the canvas such as after part or all the window has been hidden and then revealed again or when the window has been resized. Later, when we implement the Change button, we will tell the AWT that the canvas needs redrawing each time the button is pressed, and this will eventually result in this `paint` method being called.

To draw the canvas correctly, we need to know the current size of the area. This is provided by the `getSize` method, which returns an instance of the class `Dimension`. We extract the values of the instance variables `width` and `depth` from this object, and these are the current width and height of the canvas in pixels. From this, we can calculate the center point of the canvas (`cx`, `cy`) and draw a line around the edge of the canvas.

The `paint` method has one argument, which is of type `Graphics`:

```
public void paint(Graphics g)
    {
    ...
```

When we draw lines, fill areas with color, write text characters, and so on, we do so by calling methods associated with this object. We have called this formal argument of the `paint` method g, so we call the method to draw a rectangle with rounded corners (`drawRoundRect`) with:

```
g.drawRoundRect( ... arguments ... ) ;
```

There is a large collection of methods to draw in various ways on the canvas. We list the most useful ones here, and we illustrate some of them in the code for drawing the face in our class Canvas0. Each one draws using the current color, and we set this when required with the setColor method.

- drawLine draws a line in the current color (e.g., the nose in the example program). The four arguments are, in order, the *x*- and *y*-coordinates of the two ends of the line. These arguments are integers, and the units are pixels, with the origin of the coordinates (0, 0) at the top left corner. So

  ```
  g.drawLine(10, 20, 30, 10);
  ```

  draws the line shown in Figure 16.6.

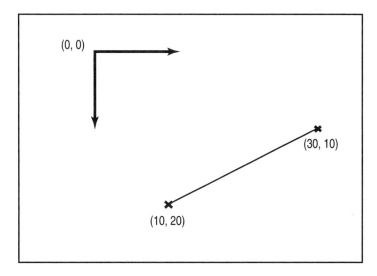

Figure 16.6: Using the drawLine method

- drawRect draws a rectangle in the current color. The first two arguments are the *x*- and *y*-coordinates of the top left corner of the rectangle. The third and fourth arguments are the width and height (respectively) of the rectangle in pixels. If the third and fourth arguments are equal, the rectangle would be a square. So

  ```
  g.drawRect(10, 5, 20, 15) ;
  ```

  draws the rectangle shown in Figure 16.7.

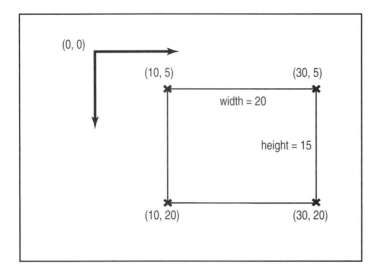

Figure 16.7: Using the `drawRect` method

- `drawRoundRect` draws a rectangle in the current color with rounded corners; this is used in the example program to draw a line just inside the edge of the canvas. The first four arguments are the coordinates of the top left corner, the width, and the height, as for the `drawRect` method. The fifth and sixth arguments are the horizontal and vertical diameters of the arcs at the corners (in pixels).

- `drawOval` draws an oval in the current color. You need to imagine a rectangle enclosing the oval that you want to draw, and you then specify the x- and y-coordinates of the top left corner and the width and the height of the bounding rectangle, just as with the `drawRect` method. So

```
g.drawOval(10, 5, 30, 20) ;
```

draws the oval shown in Figure 16.8. If the third and fourth arguments are equal, the oval would be a circle.

In some ways, defining the position by the top left corner is not the most convenient procedure, but this is what most of these AWT methods use. In the code of the example program, you will see that in most cases the calculation works out the position of the top left corner from the position of the center of the figure, and this is probably a more logical way of specifying a position. Notice generally that this code has been written to make clear how the positions, sizes, angles, and so on are specified in terms of the various basic dimensions that define the face.

- `drawArc` draws part of a circle or oval. We have to specify the circle or oval by the top left corner and the width and height of the bounding rectangle, just as with the `drawOval` method. The last two arguments (the fifth and sixth) specify which part of the arc to draw. The fifth argument specifies the angle at which to start, in degrees, with zero degrees being due east (as in the normal mathematical convention). The arc is

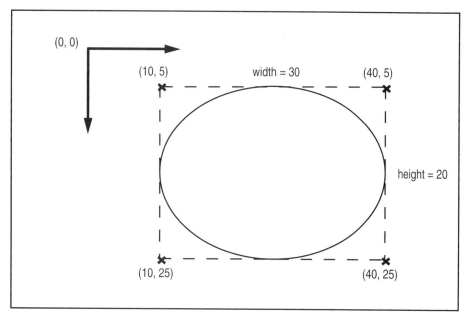

Figure 16.8: Using the drawOval method

drawn from this angle counterclockwise for the number of degrees specified by the sixth argument. Note that the sixth argument is not the final angle (an easy mistake to make)—the final angle would in fact be the sum of the fifth and sixth arguments.

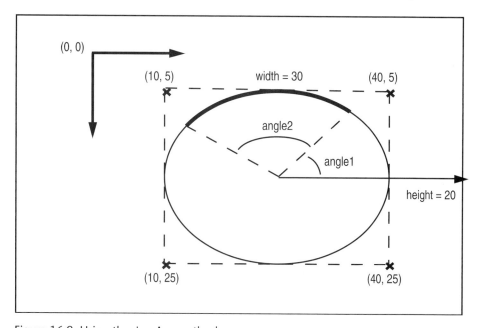

Figure 16.9: Using the drawArc method

So we draw the smile on the happy face in terms of the center of the canvas (cx, cy), the radius of the circle (mouthRadius) of which the smile is an arc, and a mouthAngle (50 degrees) for half the mouth with:

```
g.drawArc(cx - mouthRadius,
          cy - mouthRadius,
          mouthRadius * 2,
          mouthRadius * 2,
          270 - mouthAngle,
          mouthAngle * 2) ;
```

- There are methods fillRect, fillRoundRect, and fillOval that are variations on drawRect, drawRoundRect, and drawOval, respectively (with the same set of arguments). They fill the space enclosed by the drawing with the current color. The eyes in the example program are blue circles drawn with fillOval.

- There are methods drawPolygon and fillPolygon to draw an irregular figure between a number of points. The three arguments are an array of the *x*-coordinates of the points, an array of the *y*-coordinates of the points, and a count of the number of points.

16.5   Writing Text on the Canvas

Having drawn the face, we want to write a piece of text just below it. To illustrate the features provided by the AWT for writing character strings, we are going to write "Hello" in a normal typeface and "World" in italics. The basic method is drawString, which writes the specified text (the first argument) at the specified position (the *x*- and *y*-coordinates are the second and third arguments); for example, we would write "Happy Birthday" with:

```
g.drawString("Happy Birthday", 100, 150) ;
```

The *x*-coordinate is the position of the left edge of the first character, as you would expect. The *y*-coordinate is the position of the *baseline* upon which most characters lie; some characters (e.g., *g* and *y*) may descend below the baseline (Figure 16.10).

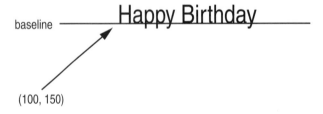

Figure 16.10: Using the drawString method

The string is drawn in the current color and font. You are familiar with the concept of the current color, but we need to set the font with the setFont method, and this requires an argument of type Font. We create instances of the Font class by calling a suitable constructor. For example:

```
Font f1 = new Font("TimesRoman", Font.PLAIN, 14) ;
```

The first argument is the name of the font. Other commonly available font names are "Helvetica", "Courier", "Dialog", and "Symbol". There may be other fonts available on particular platforms, but this cannot be relied on.

The second argument is the font style. This should be one of the constants Font.PLAIN, Font.BOLD, or Font.ITALIC. It is possible also to use the expression Font.BOLD + Font.ITALIC for this argument, giving a bold italic style of lettering if it is available for this font.

The third argument is the point size required for the font. Typical sizes would be 8 for a small size, 12 for a typical size, and 36 or more for large sizes.

If we want to write a sequence of character strings, perhaps in varying fonts, Java expects us to specify exactly where to position them. For this, we need to know how much room a particular sequence of characters takes up in a particular font. The class FontMetrics provides this information. We set up an instance of this class for a particular Graphics object and Font:

```
FontMetrics fm1 = g.getFontMetrics(f1) ;
```

We can then find out the width of a particular character string in the specified font:

```
int w1 = fm1.stringWidth("We want the space used by this String") ;
```

In the example program, we use string widths obtained in this way to calculate the *x*-coordinate ctx for the beginning of the string so that it is centrally positioned in the window, and then we update this value to get the position of the next portion of the string.

16.6   Animating the Simple Graphics Program

We are now going to add the Change button to this program so that we can switch backward and forward between drawing a happy and a sad face. We will also make another small change by allowing the user to type in a name as a command-line parameter (see Section 3.12); if a name is typed in, it is used instead of the word World in the greetings message.

We find now that we have to be able to pass more information between the class derived from Frame (in this version of the program called Chapter16n1) and the class derived from Canvas (here called Canvas1). The Chapter16n1 code needs to have a reference to the instance of the Canvas1 class so that it can call for the face to be redrawn when the Change button has been pressed. We do this by making the variable referring to the canvas an instance variable of the Chapter16n1 class rather than a local variable of its constructor. Since our actionPerformed method now needs to distinguish between a click on Change and a click on Quit, we similarly make the variables referring to the buttons into instance variables of the Chapter16n1 class. The Canvas1 code needs to have a reference to the instance of the Chapter16n1 class so that it can access its instance variables as required (e.g., so it can find out whether to draw a happy or a sad face). We do this by passing a suitable reference when we call the `Canvas1` constructor, and this is stored as an instance variable of the `Canvas1` class for later use.

The `Chapter16n1` class now has five instance variables:

- A variable `canvas`, of type `Canvas1`, which refers to the instance we have created of this class so that we can require it to be repainted.

- Two variables `change` and `quit`, of type `Button`, for the two buttons.

- A `String` variable `name`, which will contain the word `World` or the name from the command-line parameter. The `main` method checks the command-line parameter (if any) and passes the appropriate `String` as the argument to the `Chapter16n1` constructor method, which stores it in the variable `name`.

- A Boolean variable `isSmiling` to record whether the face should currently be smiling or not. We initialize this in the `Chapter16n1` constructor method to true (we want to start off happy).

```
public class Chapter16n1 extends Frame
                           implements WindowListener, ActionListener
    {
    Canvas1 canvas ;
    Button change, quit ;
    String name ;
    boolean isSmiling ;
    . . .
```

The `Canvas1` class now has a single instance variable `parent`, of type `Chapter16n1`, which refers to the instance we have created of that class:

```
class Canvas1 extends Canvas
    {
    Chapter16n1 parent ;
    . . .
```

The constructor method for the `Canvas1` class now needs an argument, so we can pass a reference to the `Chapter16n1` instance to be stored in the `parent` instance variable:

```
public Canvas1(Chapter16n1 f)
    {
    super() ;
    parent = f ;
    } // end of constructor method
```

We call this constructor from inside the `Chapter16n1` constructor as follows:

```
canvas = new Canvas1(this) ;
```

The keyword `this` is a reference to the current instance of the `Chapter16n1` class (see Section 8.9.2). That is, we are passing to the constructor for the `Canvas1` class a reference to the `Chapter16n1` instance that is creating it so that it can be stored in `parent`.

In the Chapter16n1 constructor method, we have added the new Change button and registered that actionPerformed is to be called if it is clicked. We rely on the flow layout manager of the Panel it is in to position it correctly:

```
change = new Button("Change") ;
p.add(change) ;
change.addActionListener(this) ;
```

In the actionPerformed method, we need to test for which of the two buttons has been pressed. The ActionEvent instance passed as the method's argument contains a reference to the button pressed, and we can extract this with the getSource method:

```
if (event.getSource() == quit)
    ...
```

If the Change button has been pressed, we invert the value of the isSmiling variable. We then need to ensure that the canvas is redrawn by calling the repaint method associated with the canvas instance:

```
public void actionPerformed(ActionEvent event)
    {
    if (event.getSource() == quit)
        {
        dispose() ;
        System.exit(0) ;
        }
    else if (event.getSource() == change)
        {
        isSmiling = !isSmiling ;
        canvas.repaint() ;
        }
    } // end of method actionPerformed
```

The result is that the paint method of the Canvas1 class is eventually called, and the entire canvas is redrawn.

The paint method of the Canvas1 class is very similar to the original version. The method refers to the isSmiling variable in the Chapter16n1 class (using the notation **parent.** isSmiling). This establishes whether the mouth should be happy or sad, and paint redraws it accordingly using the drawArc method:

```
if (parent.isSmiling)
    g.drawArc(cx - mouthRadius,
              cy - mouthRadius,
              mouthRadius * 2,
              mouthRadius * 2,
              270 - mouthAngle,
              mouthAngle * 2) ;
```

```
else
    g.drawArc(cx - mouthRadius,
                cy - mouthRadius + 50,
                mouthRadius * 2,
                mouthRadius * 2,
                90 - mouthAngle,
                mouthAngle * 2) ;
```

Similarly, the second part of the text to be displayed is at parent.name:

```
String s2 = parent.name ;
.  .  .
g.drawString(s2, ctx, cty) ;
```

16.7   Input of Character Strings in a Graphical Interface

In the previous program, the only way the user could communicate with the program was to press one of the two buttons. Another desirable type of communication is for the user to type a sequence of characters into a text field for the program to interpret. We illustrate this type of interaction with another sample program, Chapter16n2.java (Figure 16.11). This makes use of the Temperature class introduced in Chapter 8.

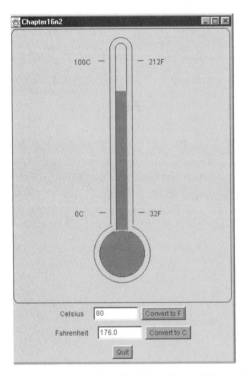

Figure 16.11: A graphical interface with text input

We can type a temperature in degrees Celsius in the text field labeled `"Celsius"`. If we now press the `"Convert to F"` button, the program uses the `Temperature` class (see Section 8.5) to calculate the equivalent temperature in Fahrenheit and displays it in the text field labeled `"Fahrenheit"`. Similarly, we can type a temperature in degrees Fahrenheit in the field labeled `"Fahrenheit"` and have it converted to degrees Celsius in the other text area. We have to take care to check the validity of any string typed in. To make the program slightly more interesting, we draw a thermometer and display a mercury column showing the temperature.

16.7.1   Setting Up the Picture

As before, we have a class `Chapter16n2` derived from `Frame` and a class `Canvas2` derived from `Canvas`. In the `Chapter16n2` class, we have seven instance variables:

- A variable `temp1` of the `Temperature` class to provide the Celsius-to-Fahrenheit conversion.

- A variable `canvas` of the `Canvas2` class upon which we are going to draw the thermometer. This needs to be an instance variable rather than a local variable because we need to request that it be redrawn when the temperature changes.

- Two variables of the `TextField` class called `celsiusField` and `fahrField`. The `TextField` class implements a small area into which the user can type a sequence of characters that the program can then extract and process in some way. We need to declare these two variables here so that we can call methods associated with them in the `actionPerformed` method.

- Three variables of the `Button` class (`toF`, `toC`, and `quit`) to allow the `actionPerformed` method to check which button has been pressed.

```
public class Chapter16n2 extends Frame
                             implements WindowListener, ActionListener
    {
    Temperature temp1 ;
    TextField celsiusField,
            fahrField ;
    Canvas2 canvas ;
    Button toF, toC, quit ;
```

The constructor method `Chapter16n2` looks very similar to that of the earlier programs:

```
public Chapter16n2()
    {
    super() ;

    temp1 = new Temperature() ;

    setTitle("Chapter16n2") ;
    setBackground(Color.green) ;
    setSize(400, 600) ;
    addWindowListener(this) ;
```

```
canvas = new Canvas2(this) ;
add("Center", canvas) ;
...
```

- We create an instance of the `Temperature` class for the variable `temp1` to refer to.

- We set up the window title and the background color and size, as before.

- We create an instance of the new class `Canvas2` upon which the thermometer will be drawn, and we position this in the center of the window (using the default border layout manager).

We now want a collection of graphical components at the bottom of the window laid out as three lines of components. The first and second lines are rather similar. Each requires:

- A text field in the middle where we can type a temperature; this is an instance of the `TextField` class of graphical components. The constructor for this class takes two arguments: the initial string to appear in the text field (we set it to blank) and an integer specifying how wide the field should be in "columns"—it is best to make this one or two longer than the maximum number of characters you are expecting in this field (we have chosen 8).

- On the left, a character string to specify what type of temperature this is. We use an instance of the `Label` class of graphical components whose only task is to display a character string. When we construct a `Label` instance, we pass the labeling string as the argument (in the first line, it is `"Celsius"`).

- A button to invoke the temperature conversion; this is an instance of the `Button` class, which you have met before. On the first line, it has the label `"Convert to F"`.

We want to keep the three components of the first line together, so we put them in a panel p1 with a flow layout manager:

```
Panel p1 = new Panel() ;
p1.setLayout(new FlowLayout()) ;

p1.add(new Label("Celsius")) ;

celsiusField = new TextField("", 8) ;
p1.add(celsiusField) ;

toF = new Button("Convert to F") ;
p1.add(toF) ;
toF.addActionListener(this) ;
```

We do the same for the second line in a panel p2:

```
Panel p2 = new Panel() ;
p2.setLayout(new FlowLayout()) ;

p2.add(new Label("Fahrenheit")) ;
```

```
fahrField = new TextField("", 8) ;
p2.add(fahrField) ;

toC = new Button("Convert to C") ;
p2.add(toC) ;
toC.addActionListener(this) ;
```

Finally, we set up a panel p3 containing only the Quit button:

```
Panel p3 = new Panel() ;
p3.setLayout(new FlowLayout()) ;
quit = new Button("Quit") ;
p3.add(quit) ;
quit.addActionListener(this) ;
```

We want these three panels to appear one above the other, so we declare a new panel p, specify that it should use the grid layout manager with three rows and one column, and then add the three panels p1, p2, and p3 in that order. We specify that the panel p shall appear "South" in the main window, as we did in the previous programs:

```
Panel p = new Panel() ;
p.setLayout(new GridLayout(3, 1)) ;
p.add(p1) ;
p.add(p2) ;
p.add(p3) ;
add("South", p) ;
```

Figure 16.12 shows the overall situation of the display.

The main method simply creates an instance of the Chapter16n2 class and calls the setVisible method to get things started:

```
public static void main(String[] args)
    {
    Chapter16n2 f = new Chapter16n2() ;
    f.setVisible(true) ;
    } // end of method main
```

The windowClosing method is exactly the same as before.

16.7.2   Getting a String from a TextField

The general structure of the actionPerformed method is similar to what you have met before. We test in sequence for the label of each button that could have been pressed and take action accordingly. We look in detail at the action to be taken if the "Convert to F" button is pressed; the action for "Convert to C" is similar. Here is the piece of code:

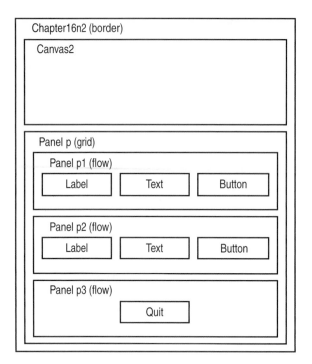

Figure 16.12: Layout of the graphical components of the `Chapter16n2` program

```
. . .
else if (event.getSource() == toF)
    {
    String c1 = celsiusField.getText() ;
    double c2 = 0.0 ;
    boolean isValid ;
    try {
        c2 = Double.parseDouble(c1) ;
        isValid = true ;
        }
    catch (NumberFormatException ex)
        {
        isValid = false ;
        }
    if (isValid)
        {
        temp1.setCelsius(c2) ;
        double f2 = temp1.getFahr() ;
        f2 = ((double) Math.round(f2 * 100)) / 100 ;
        String f1 = Double.toString(f2) ;
        fahrField.setText(f1) ;
```

```
            canvas.repaint() ;
            }
      else
            {
            celsiusField.setText("") ;
            }
      }
else ...
```

- We use the getText method to extract the string in the Celsius temperature field and store it in the String variable c1.

- Now we want to convert the string to a double value, which we do using the statement starting"c2 = . . . "—we explain how this mechanism works in Section 19.4.2. If the characters typed into the field are not a valid double literal, this conversion will fail. We therefore arrange to catch any NumberFormatException. The Boolean variable isValid records whether or not the conversion succeeded. If it did, the result is in the double variable c2.

- If the input was valid, we convert it to Fahrenheit using the Temperature class, round it to two decimal places, convert it back to a String, and insert the result in the Fahrenheit text field with the setText method. Finally, we need to use the repaint method to request that the thermometer be redrawn with the new mercury level.

- If the input was invalid, we simply reset the Celsius text field to all blanks. We do not change the Fahrenheit text field nor redraw the thermometer.

16.7.3   Drawing the Thermometer

We now consider the Canvas2 class. It has a single instance variable to hold a reference to the parent Chapter16n2 instance, just as in the previous program, and we set this from the argument passed to the Canvas2 constructor method:

```
class Canvas2 extends Canvas
    {
    Chapter16n2 parent ;

    public Canvas2(Chapter16n2 f)
        {
        super() ;
        parent = f ;
        } // end of constructor method
    ...
```

We are not going to discuss in detail the code of the paint method, which draws the thermometer. It uses the methods that we discussed in Section 16.4, such as setColor, drawLine, drawArc, and fillOval. For example, we draw the mercury to the correct height in the tube with the code:

```
double tempC = parent.temp1.getCelsius() ;
int mercuryLength ;
if (tempC < - 11)
   mercuryLength = 0 ;
else if (tempC < 120)
   mercuryLength = (int) (30 + (2.6 * tempC)) ;
else
   mercuryLength = tubeLength ;
g.setColor(Color.red) ;
g.fillRect(cx - innerTubeRadius + 1,
           cy - bulbInnerRadius - mercuryLength,
           2 * innerTubeRadius,
           mercuryLength) ;
```

We extract the current temperature with the getCelsius method of the temp1 instance (of the Temperature class) of the parent instance (of the Chapter16n2 class). We then calculate how long the mercury should be and store it in mercuryLength. Finally, we draw a filled rectangle of an appropriate color and size at a suitable position.

We mark the thermometer with some standard temperatures (0 and 100 degrees Celsius, 32 and 212 degrees Fahrenheit), and we want to position the labels correctly. We set up a Font and a FontMetrics object as before, calculate a width w0 using the stringWidth method on the longest string, and calculate half the height of this font h0 using the getAscent method. This method gives the distance (in pixels) between the baseline (upon which all the characters rest, except those with descenders, e.g., lowercase *g* and *y*), and the top of the uppercase characters.

```
Font f1 = new Font("Helvetica", Font.BOLD, 14) ;
FontMetrics fm1 = g.getFontMetrics(f1) ;
int w0 = fm1.stringWidth("212F"),
    h0 = (fm1.getAscent() / 2) ;

g.drawString("100C",
             cx - 50 - w0,
             cy - bulbOuterRadius - tubeLength + 20 + h0) ;
```

There are a selection of other methods in the FontMetrics class for finding other details of the font dimensions; for example, getDescent gives the distance from the baseline to the bottom of characters with descenders such as *g* and *y*.

16.8   Menus, Files, and Images (Optional)

In the programs presented so far in this chapter, all the pictures or diagrams we wanted to display have been drawn using the draw and fill methods supplied by the Abstract Windowing Toolkit. But there is another source of visual data to a Java program: pictures scanned into the computer and held in one of the standard formats for representing them, such as GIF or JPEG. Java provides as part of the AWT a number of methods for displaying such pictures, usually referred to as *images*. Most of the facilities for manipulating images, (e.g., scaling and clipping) are beyond the scope of this book. But our final pair of programs in this chapter show you how to display images with the facilities provided by Java. We take the opportunity in these programs to introduce you to a few slightly more complex parts of the AWT, which you may find useful in writing your programs. We are going to introduce menus, file dialogs, and the handling of mouse events in these two programs.

In the first program, `Chapter16n4.java` (Figure 16.13), we allow the user to select a file that contains an image, and the program then attempts to display it in the center of the window. Rather than having all the buttons on permanent display, we put them on a menu attached to a menu bar at the top of the window.

Figure 16.13: Displaying an image

16.8.1 Setting Up Menus

We begin by setting up the menu system. We are going to set up a single menu containing two buttons: Load to select an image file to display and our old friend the Quit button. It seems to have become a tradition in GUI design that a menu of rather miscellaneous functions is called the File menu, and that is what we have done here. We need to declare instance variables (of type `MenuItem`) for the two menu buttons so that we can find out which one has been selected:

```
public class Chapter16n4 extends Frame
                              implements WindowListener, ActionListener
   {
   Canvas4 canvas ;
   MenuItem load, quit ;
   ...
```

Here is the code in the constructor method for the Chapter16n4 class to set up the menu:

```
Menu menu = new Menu("File") ;
load = new MenuItem("Load") ;
menu.add(load) ;
load.addActionListener(this) ;
quit = new MenuItem("Quit") ;
menu.add(quit) ;
quit.addActionListener(this) ;
MenuBar menuBar = new MenuBar() ;
menuBar.add(menu) ;
setMenuBar(menuBar) ;
```

We create an object of type Menu; this will be labeled "File" in the menu bar. We then add the two menu buttons to it with suitable labels and register that we want to find out when either of them is selected. We then create a menu bar (an object of type MenuBar), add the menu to it, and use the setMenuBar method to add it to the Chapter16n4 instance that we are constructing. We can add a menu bar only to a class derived from Frame, so we cannot have menus attached to arbitrary panels.

We now need to be able to take action when one of the menu items is selected. We handle this in very much the same way we handled buttons in the earlier programs. We have an actionPerformed method in the Chapter16n4 class, and we check for which item was selected in the usual way:

```
public void actionPerformed(ActionEvent event)
   {
   if (event.getSource() == quit)
      {
      dispose();
      System.exit(0);
      }
   else if (event.getSource() == load)
      loadFile() ;
   } // end of method actionPerformed
```

There are a number of other useful features of menus. Suppose we declare the following instance variables:

```
public class Chapter16n4a extends Frame
                              implements WindowListener, ActionListener
```

```
        {
    MenuItem buttonA1, buttonA2, buttonA3,
         buttonA4, buttonA5, buttonA6, buttonA7,
         quit,
         buttonB1p1, buttonB1p2, buttonB1p3,
         buttonB2p1, buttonB2p2, buttonB2p3, buttonB2p4 ;
    int noOfOptions = 7 ;
    CheckboxMenuItem[] options = new
                            CheckboxMenuItem[noOfOptions] ;

    . . .
```

Then we have the following piece of code in the constructor for `Chapter16n4a`:

```
Menu menuA = new Menu("MenuA") ;
buttonA1 = new MenuItem("Button A1") ;
menuA.add(buttonA1) ;
buttonA1.addActionListener(this) ;
buttonA2 = new MenuItem("Button A2") ;
menuA.add(buttonA2) ;
buttonA2.addActionListener(this) ;
buttonA3 = new MenuItem("Button A3") ;
menuA.add(buttonA3) ;
buttonA3.addActionListener(this) ;
menuA.addSeparator() ;
buttonA4 = new MenuItem("Button A4") ;
menuA.add(buttonA4) ;
buttonA4.addActionListener(this) ;
buttonA5 = new MenuItem("Button A5") ;
menuA.add(buttonA5) ;
buttonA5.addActionListener(this) ;
buttonA6 = new MenuItem("Button A6") ;
menuA.add(buttonA6) ;
buttonA6.addActionListener(this) ;
buttonA7 = new MenuItem("Button A7") ;
menuA.add(buttonA7) ;
buttonA7.addActionListener(this) ;
menuA.addSeparator() ;
menuA.add(new MenuItem("Quit")) ;
```

In `MenuA`, we have a large number of buttons, so we use the `addSeparator` method to put the buttons into three groups:

```
Menu menuB = new Menu("MenuB") ;
Menu menuB1 = new Menu("MenuB1") ;
buttonB1p1 = new MenuItem("Button B1.1") ;
menuB1.add(buttonB1p1) ;
buttonB1p1.addActionListener(this) ;
```

```
buttonB1p2 = new MenuItem("Button B1.2") ;
menuB1.add(buttonB1p2) ;
buttonB1p2.addActionListener(this) ;
buttonB1p3 = new MenuItem("Button B1.3") ;
menuB1.add(buttonB1p3) ;
buttonB1p3.addActionListener(this) ;
menuB.add(menuB1) ;
Menu menuB2 = new Menu("MenuB2") ;
buttonB2p1 = new MenuItem("Button B2.1") ;
menuB2.add(buttonB2p1) ;
buttonB2p1.addActionListener(this) ;
buttonB2p2 = new MenuItem("Button B2.2") ;
menuB2.add(buttonB2p2) ;
buttonB2p2.addActionListener(this) ;
buttonB2p3 = new MenuItem("Button B2.3") ;
menuB2.add(buttonB2p3) ;
buttonB2p3.addActionListener(this) ;
buttonB2p4 = new MenuItem("Button B2.4") ;
menuB2.add(buttonB2p4) ;
buttonB2p4.addActionListener(this) ;
menuB.add(menuB2) ;
```

In MenuB, we have two submenus, MenuB1 and MenuB2, each with its own set of buttons. If you click MenuB1, it brings up that submenu with its three buttons.

```
Menu menuC = new Menu("MenuC") ;
options[0] = new CheckboxMenuItem("Monday") ;
options[1] = new CheckboxMenuItem("Tuesday") ;
options[2] = new CheckboxMenuItem("Wednesday") ;
options[3] = new CheckboxMenuItem("Thursday") ;
options[4] = new CheckboxMenuItem("Friday") ;
options[5] = new CheckboxMenuItem("Saturday") ;
options[6] = new CheckboxMenuItem("Sunday") ;
for (int i = 0 ; i < noOfOptions ; i++)
    {
    options[i].addItemListener(this) ;
    menuC.add(options[i]) ;
    }

MenuBar menuBar = new MenuBar() ;
menuBar.add(menuA) ;
menuBar.add(menuB) ;
menuBar.add(menuC) ;
setMenuBar(menuBar) ;
```

In MenuC, we have a number of check boxes, each of which (independently) records an option as "checked" (on) or "unchecked" (off). Since we have a number of check boxes, we have declared an array of them, called a constructor method for each one, and then registered a listener for each and added them to a menu. Each time we click one of these check boxes, it changes state (toggling between true and false), and the current state is indicated on the menu. The `itemStateChanged` method (of the `ItemListener` interface) is called every time the user clicks one of the check boxes and it changes state:

```
public void itemStateChanged(ItemEvent event)
    {
    if (event.getSource() == options[0])
        System.out.println("the 'Monday' option was clicked") ;
    ...
```

The state of a check box starts out as false. We can set it to a particular state with the `setState` method, and we can find out its state with the `getState` method.

16.8.2 Selecting a File

Returning to our `Chapter16n4` program, the Load menu item called the method `loadFile` to allow the user to select a file containing an image and then have this displayed. Here it is:

```
private void loadFile()
    {
    FileDialog d = new FileDialog(this, "Load File", FileDialog.LOAD) ;
    d.setDirectory("... path name at which to start selection ...") ;
    d.setVisible(true) ;
    filename = d.getFile() ;
    directory = d.getDirectory() ;
    canvas.repaint() ;
    } // end of method loadFile
```

We set up an instance of the class `FileDialog`. This requires three arguments:

- The owner of the dialog. This is the instance of the class `Chapter16n4` with which this dialog is to be associated, so we can use the keyword `this`.

- A string to appear as the title for the window that is going to be popped up for the dialog; we have chosen `"Load File"`.

- One of two constants: `FileDialog.LOAD` if we are planning to read from the file, which is what we are doing here, or `FileDialog.SAVE` if we are planning to write to the file.

We then set an initial file directory from which the user can select the file and call the method `setVisible` to display the file dialog box. The system waits until the user selects a file and then clicks a button to indicate that the dialog is complete.

At this point, we extract the name of the selected file with the `getFile` method. If no file has been selected, a `String` of length zero is returned. Since the user can change the directory in the file dialog, you should extract this as well with the `getDirectory` method.

16.8.3 Displaying an Image

Having obtained the name of a file and a directory, we request that the canvas be repainted, attempting to display an image obtained from this file. Here is the paint method in the Canvas4 class:

```
public void paint(Graphics g)
    {
    Dimension d = getSize() ;
    int cx = d.width / 2,
        cy = d.height /2 ;
    // draw a line around the edge of the canvas
    g.setColor(Color.black) ;
    g.drawRoundRect(2, 2, d.width - 5, d.height - 5, 20, 20) ;
    if (parent.filename != null)
        {
        String fullname = parent.directory + parent.name ;
        Image image =
                Toolkit.getDefaultToolkit().getImage(fullname) ;
        g.drawImage(image,
                    cx - (image.getWidth(this) / 2),
                    cy - (image.getHeight(this) / 2),
                    this) ;

        // write the name of the file under the image
        Font f1 = new Font("TimesRoman", Font.PLAIN, 14) ;
        FontMetrics fm1 = g.getFontMetrics(f1) ;
        int w1 = fm1.stringWidth(parent.filename) ;
        g.setColor(Color.black) ;
        g.setFont(f1) ;
        int ctx = cx - (w1 / 2) ;
        int cty = cy + (image.getHeight(this) / 2) + 30 ;
        g.drawString(parent.filename, ctx, cty) ;
        }
    else
        {
        // write the message "No File" in the center of the canvas
        Font f1 = new Font("TimesRoman", Font.PLAIN, 14) ;
        ...
        }
    } // end of method paint
```

We set up the full name of the file fullName from the information saved by the loadFile method in the Chapter16n4 class. Then we read the file and construct an instance of the Image class with the statement:

```
Image image = Toolkit.getDefaultToolkit().getImage(fullname) ;
```

Finally, we draw it with:

```
g.drawImage(image,
            cx - (image.getWidth(this) / 2),
            cy - (image.getHeight(this) / 2),
            this) ;
```

The first argument (of type Image) is the image we want to draw. The second and third arguments are the position at which it is to be drawn (the top left corner, as usual), and we have arranged that it will be displayed in the center of the canvas because we have calculated the coordinates of the center of the canvas (cx, cy) The methods getWidth and getHeight enable us to find out the dimensions of the image. The fourth argument (of type ImageObserver) enables us to keep track of the progress of creating and drawing the image, checking that it is successful, and so on. This is beyond the scope of this book; we simply set the fourth argument to this.

16.8.4   Tracking the Mouse

Finally, we are going to modify the program so that the image is positioned at the point where we last clicked the mouse. There are a number of methods to allow us to take action depending on various things that the user can do with the mouse. We select the mouseClicked method (of the MouseListener interface). We are interested only in mouse clicks within our canvas, so we specify that our class Canvas5 implements the MouseListener interface:

```
class Canvas5 extends Canvas implements MouseListener
    {
    ...
```

We need to register that this class is responsible for dealing with mouse clicks, so we add a statement to the constructor method:

```
public Canvas5(Chapter16n5 f)
    {
    super() ;
    parent = f ;
    addMouseListener(this) ;
    } // end of constructor method
```

Here is the method mouseClicked (in the Canvas5 class):

```
public void mouseClicked(MouseEvent event)
    {
    mx = event.getX() ;
    my = event.getY() ;
    repaint() ;
    } // end of method mouseClicked
```

The argument event contains the coordinates of the mouse click, and we extract these with the getX and getY methods. We store the information in the instance variables (mx, my) in the `Canvas5` class and call for the canvas to be redrawn (with `repaint`). In the `paint` method, we position the image at (`mx`, `my`) instead of at (`cx`, `cy`) as we did before.

The `MouseListener` interface requires us to implement four other methods, which are dummies:

```
public void mousePressed(MouseEvent event) {}
public void mouseReleased(MouseEvent event) {}
public void mouseEntered(MouseEvent event) {}
public void mouseExited(MouseEvent event) {}
```

16.9   Key Points in Chapter 16

- A *graphical user interface,* or *GUI,* is an increasingly popular way of interacting with a program. It presents a number of interaction elements to the end user, including windows (for text or graphics of various types), menus, buttons, text areas, and so on. The user interacts with these elements via mouse and keyboard.

- Java provides the platform-independent *Abstract Windowing Toolkit,* or *AWT*, a standard set of facilities for building GUIs across all platforms. To write GUI programs in Java, we derive new classes from those provided in the AWT.

- A central feature of a GUI program is the *event loop.* The program waits for an event to occur and, depending on the event, carries out the appropriate action. Events that may occur include button clicks or window exposure/resizing. The event loop is within the AWT and does not appear in our program. We must provide the code for setting up the GUI elements and then for responding to events as they occur.

- A GUI application program has a class derived from `Frame`. The constructor for this class sets up the basic features of the display, with the methods `setTitle`, `setBackground`, and `setSize`, and then it puts the picture elements in the window with the `add` method.

- The position of the elements inside a larger picture component is arranged by a *layout manager*, such as `FlowLayout`, `BorderLayout` (the default for a `Frame`), and `GridLayout`.

- The `main` method in the class calls this constructor to set up an instance of the class and then calls the `setVisible` method to display the window and start the program.

- There must be a `windowClosing` method in the class to allow the program to be terminated if necessary. It can be in the standard form given in Section 16.3.5.

- Possible pictures elements include buttons that can be pressed (the `Button` class), pieces of text to label parts of the window (the `Label` class), and areas where text can be typed in by the user (the `TextField`). There is also a `Panel`, which is a container for other picture elements and which can be positioned inside another `Panel` or the `Frame`.

- A `Canvas` is a picture element on which we can draw lines, fill areas of color, write text, and so forth. The drawing is done with a variety of methods, including `drawLine`, `drawRect`, `drawOval`, `fillRect`, `fillOval`, and so on. We can set the color for these using the `setColor` method and the `Color` class.

- The coordinate system on the canvas is in units of pixels, starts at (0, 0) in the top left corner, and extends downward and to the right.

- The drawing methods are specified in a `paint` method. Each of the methods is associated with a `Graphics` instance passed as the formal argument for the `paint` method. If the canvas needs redrawing, we call the `repaint` method.

- Text is written on a canvas with the `drawString` method. We can set up an instance of the `Font` class and then specify the font for a particular string with `setFont`. If we want to position a string carefully, we need to set up an instance of the `FontMetrics` class and then use the methods `stringWidth`, `getAscent`, and so on.

- An `actionPerformed` method (of the `ActionListener` interface) is called if a button is pressed. We have to register each button with a call of the `addActionListener` method. A reference to the button that has been pressed can be obtained by calling the `get-Source` method applied to the `ActionEvent` argument of the `actionPerformed` method.

- We can extract the text typed into a `TextField` with the `getText` method and set it to a new value with `setText`.

16.10 Exercises

1. Write a GUI version of Exercise 3.1. As shown in Figure 16.14, this should have four text fields and a Complete button.

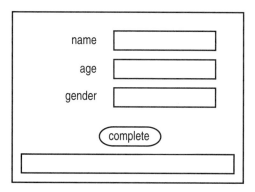

Figure 16.14: Window layout for Exercise 16.1

The user types in a name (forename and surname) in the first field, an age in the second, and a gender in the third. When the Complete button is pressed, the program should set the attributes of a Person instance with the data typed in (checking for missing or invalid values) and then display a message in the fourth field in the form:

```
this person is John Smith (21, male)
```

2. Write a new version of Exercise 4.4, which draws on the screen the two `Card` instances selected. For example, if the four of clubs and the queen of diamonds had been selected, the program should display something like Figure 16.15. If you wish, you can try to draw and display symbols for the four suits.

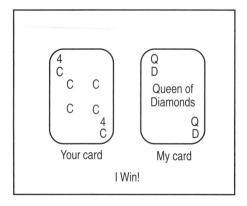

Figure 16.15: Window layout for Exercise 16.2

3. Write a graphical program to display histograms of the characters in a text.

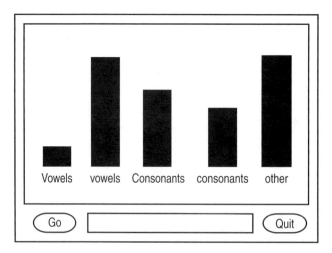

Figure 16.16: Window layout for Exercise 16.3

a. Your program should have an area for displaying a histogram, two buttons (Go and Quit), and a text area (Figure 16.16). If a string of characters is typed in the text area and the Go button is pressed, your program should display a histogram showing:

- The number of uppercase vowels
- The number of lowercase vowels
- The number of uppercase consonants
- The number of lowercase consonants
- The number of other characters

As usual, the Quit button should allow the program to be abandoned.

b. Modify your program to display a scale up the left side of the histogram to give an indication of the number of characters represented by each bar.

4. Read the Java API about the `CheckboxGroup` class. This provides a set of check boxes, only one of which can be "on" at a time. This is sometimes called a group of `radio buttons` because it is like a car radio with buttons for preset stations, only one of which can be depressed at a time.

Change your solution to Exercise 16.1 so that the user specifies the gender attribute with a `CheckboxGroup`.

5. Write a program to draw a map of one floor of a building that you are familiar with. Label each room with a name.

Add a text field to your program. If a valid room name is typed into the field, draw a stick figure in the room specified.

Modify your program so that you can have several stick figures, each with its own name, in the same or different rooms. If the figures are in the same room, can you organize the program to arrange them without overlapping?

6. Write a class `RegionMap` (derived from `Canvas`) that draws and colors a map of a region (e.g., a county) and marks and labels selected locations in the region. It should have the following methods:

- `public RegionMap(String filename)`. This constructor method reads a list of information for the map and locations from a file whose name is supplied as an argument.
- `public void paint(Graphics g)`. This method displays the map and location(s) in the usual way.
- `public void addLocation(String location)`. This method adds the location `location` to those to be displayed.
- `public void clearLocations()`. This method empties the list of locations to be displayed.

The file read by the constructor method contains, on separate lines:

- A count of points on the region boundary
- The *x*-coordinate (in pixels) of the first point on the region boundary
- The *y*-coordinate (in pixels) of the first point on the region boundary
- The *x*-coordinate (in pixels) of the second point on the region boundary
- The *y*-coordinate (in pixels) of the second point on the region boundary and so on
- A count of the locations in the region
- The name of the first location

- The *x*-coordinate (in pixels) of the first location
- The *y*-coordinate (in pixels) of the first location
- The name of the second location
- The *x*-coordinate (in pixels) of the second location
- The *y*-coordinate (in pixels) of the second location and so on

It will look like this:

```
37
253
25
238
25
. . .
22
Bodmin
193
115
Bude
238
45
. . .
```

Write a driver program to test this class.

Modify your program so that it reads in the coordinates in miles, kilometers, or some other more display-independent unit and then converts them to pixels for a suitably sized picture.

7. Provide the task organizer program of Chapter 11 with a graphical interface.

PART 4

Advanced Java

17 Linked Data Structures

18 Recursion and Binary Trees

19 Input and Output in Java

20 Creating and Using Applets

21 Other Features of Java

CHAPTER 17

Linked Data Structures

17.1   Linear and Linked Data Structures

In Chapter 11, we introduced the idea of a priority queue. A priority queue is a *data structure* for holding and releasing information in priority order. Other typical data structures are:

■ A *stack,* such as a stack of plates in a cafeteria (Figure 17.1). On a stack, or last-in, first-out (LIFO) queue, items are removed in reverse order of insertion so that it is always the most recently added item that is the next one to be removed.

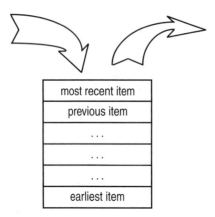

| most recent item |
| previous item |
| . . . |
| . . . |
| . . . |
| earliest item |

Figure 17.1: A stack

■ A *tree,* for example, to represent the relationships within a family (in Figure 17.2, we show only the descent through a single parent, not the marriages).

In Chapter 11, we implemented the priority queue using an array (Figure 17.3). An array is a *linear* data structure in which a sequence of elements is held in a contiguous array of store. We can calculate the position of any particular element by knowing the location of the store area and the index of the element we want to look at.

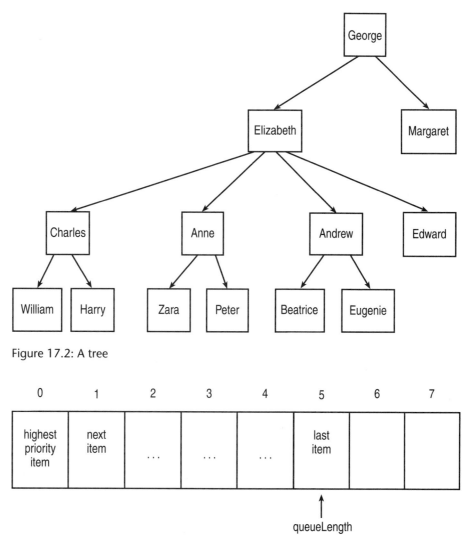

Figure 17.2: A tree

Figure 17.3: Using an array to implement a priority queue

There are a number of problems with holding data structures in an array:

- There are problems, or at least inefficiencies, in inserting or deleting elements in the middle of the array because adjacent elements need to be shuffled along to make room or to close a gap. In Java, we would normally be shuffling pointers to the elements rather than the elements themselves, but for a large structure, this could still be quite time-consuming.

- We have to decide some maximum expected size for the array when we declare it. If we choose too high a value, we are wasting space, which might have been available for some other part of the program. If we choose too low a value, our program will run out of space, or we have to declare a new larger array and move all the elements to this new array.

- It is difficult to implement some of the more complex types of data structures, if we require that the elements are held contiguously in an array. For example, if we had a collection of elements that could be on two lists at the same time, it is not obvious how to arrange them in an array structure.

In fact, the Java system provides a number of data structures, such as the Vector and the Stack, that get around these difficulties. We will look at these structures in Chapter 21, but in this chapter, we look at an alternative way of constructing data structures—by using *linked* elements. In a linked data structure, each element of the structure may be located anywhere in the available computer store, and an element can hold an extra field holding a *reference* to the logically "next" element in the sequence. That is, the extra field contains the *address* of the next element, a *pointer* to the next element. Thus, the priority queue of Figure 17.3 might resemble Figure 17.4 as a linked data structure.

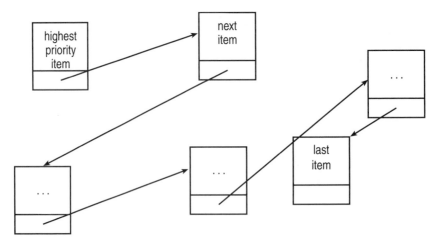

Figure 17.4: Using a linked list to implement a priority queue

Generally, the ability for a program to manipulate storage addresses directly can be dangerous. But Java restricts what manipulation it allows with references to objects in an attempt to ensure that these dangers are avoided.

You will recall that when we declare a variable of an object type, we are in fact setting up a location in the store of the computer capable of referring to an object of the specified type (Figure 17.5).

We can therefore create objects that have one (or more) attributes that act as a reference to another object of the same type. This will enable the first instance in the list to refer to the second as the "next" element in the data structure.

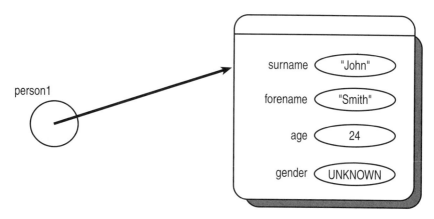

Figure 17.5: A reference to an object

17.2 Implementing a Priority Queue Using a Linked Data Structure

We illustrate the use of linked data structures by reimplementing the priority queue structure introduced in Chapter 11 (as a reminder, see Figure 17.6).

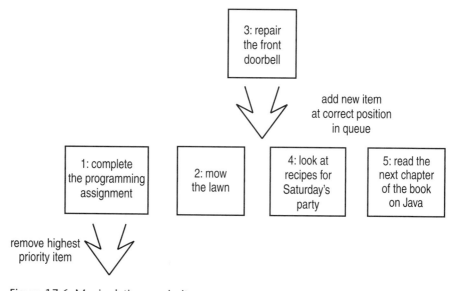

Figure 17.6: Manipulating a priority queue

Each element in the queue is going to contain a priority (an int as before), the data to be held (a String as before), and a next attribute that refers to the next element in the queue (in priority order). The final element in the queue (the one with the lowest priority) has its next attribute set to the value `null` to show that there are no further elements in the queue. The definition for the `QueueNode` class to implement such elements could look like this:

```
class QueueNode
    {
    int priority ;
    String data ;
    QueueNode next ;

    public QueueNode(int p, String d)
        {
        priority = p ;
        data = d ;
        next = null ;
        } // end of constructor method

    . . .
    } // end of class QueueElement
```

Notice that the definition of the class `QueueNode` refers to instances of the very class `QueueNode` that we are defining. Some programming languages have difficulties with this and require us to flag in some way that the class `QueueNode` contains a reference to the class `QueueNode`. This is not a problem in Java.

We have provided a constructor method with which we can set the priority and data attributes to specified values and which initializes the `next` variable to the default value of `null`. It is very important that we never have such a reference variable containing rubbish that might look like the address of a valid element. In fact, Java initializes such instance variables to `null` if they are not explicitly set to a value, but it is good practice to get into the habit of initializing reference values appropriately because other languages may not be so forgiving.

One common source of problems in using linked structures is that a program might use a reference to one type of element as if it were a reference to a different type. Notice here that the attribute `next` can contain a reference only to an instance of the `QueueNode` class (or by polymorphism, to an instance of a subclass of `QueueNode`). Any attempt to store a reference to another type of object in `next`, or to manipulate `next` as if it contained a reference to another type of object, will not be acceptable to the Java system.

Using the `next` attribute, we can insert a link from one queue element to the next (with a lower priority), and the `next` attribute of the last element (with the lowest priority) will contain a value of `null`. But we need to have a way of knowing which is the front element in the queue, which is the one with the highest priority. Thus, we declare a variable `firstPointer`

```
QueueNode firstPointer ;
```

and arrange that it contains a reference to the first element (Figure 17.7). Note that the variable `firstPointer` contains a *reference* to the first element, and not the first element itself.

We need to have some way of creating new objects, putting appropriate values in the instance variables, and storing a reference to the instance in an appropriate place. If, for

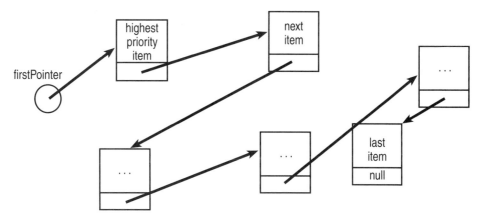

Figure 17.7: Identifying the head of the queue

example, we want the first and only element in the queue to have the priority 5 and data "Lancaster", we could write:

```
firstPointer = new QueueNode(5, "Lancaster") ;
```

The constructor method for the QueueNode class:

- Generates an instance of the QueueNode class.
- In this instance, sets the priority variable to 5 and the data variable to "Lancaster".
- Sets the next variable to the value null to indicate that this is the final element in the queue.
- Passes back a reference to this instance, which we store in the variable firstPointer.

The result of this statement appears in Figure 17.8.

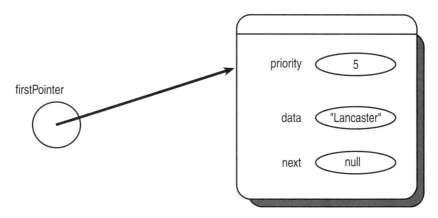

Figure 17.8: After creating the first element of a list

We can access the variables of an instance for which we have a reference (and which have "default" accessibility) by the notation "instance name–dot–variable name." For example, we refer to the `priority` variable of this instance (with the value 5) with `firstPointer.priority` and to the `next` variable (with the value `null`) with `firstPointer.next`.

If we wanted to insert a second element in the queue, with priority 7 and data `"Preston"`, we could write

```
firstPointer.next = new QueueNode(7, "Preston") ;
```

with the result shown in Figure 17.9.

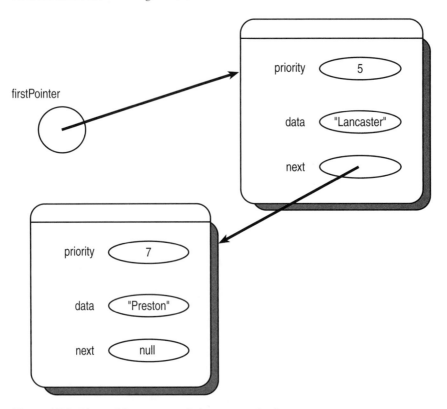

Figure 17.9: After adding a second element to the list

Let us now look at the code for the `PriorityQueue` class with the linked data implementation. We have only one instance variable, a reference to the first element:

```
public class PriorityQueue
    {
    private QueueNode firstPointer = null ;
    ...
```

It would probably be usual to have a second instance variable `queueLength`, which allowed us quickly to find the current length of the queue and which must be updated each time we insert or remove an element. Instead, just to illustrate how it is done, we are going to recalculate the length each time it is required.

17.3   Methods for the `PriorityQueue` Class

We are going to have the same set of methods as before: a constructor method `Priority Queue`, `initialize`, `insert`, `first`, `remove`, `length`, `isFull`, and `isEmpty`:

- The constructor and `initialize` methods simply set `firstPointer` to the value `null`. There are no queue elements to point to, so `firstPointer` must indicate this.

```
public PriorityQueue()
    {
    firstPointer = null ;
    } // end of constructor method
```

```
public void initialize()
    {
    firstPointer = null ;
    } // end of method initialize
```

- The `isEmpty` method is also easy. If `firstPointer` contains the value `null`, the queue is empty. Otherwise, the queue contains at least one element:

```
public boolean isEmpty()
    {
    return (firstPointer == null) ;
    } // end of method isEmpty
```

- One of the advantages of linked data allocation is that we do not have to decide on an upper limit to the size of the data structure we can implement. Thus, the queue can never be full (unless the program has completely run out of store space), so we have:

```
public boolean isFull()
    {
    return false ;
    } // end of method isFull
```

17.3.1   The `length` Method

Next let us look at the `length` method. We are writing this method rather than keeping track of the length of the queue as we go along to illustrate traversal of the linked data structure. Suppose that the queue appears as in Figure 17.10.

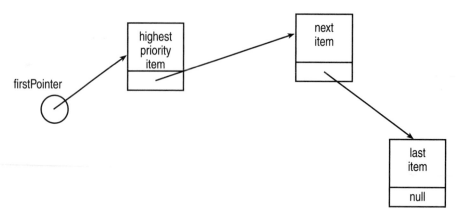

Figure 17.10: An example priority queue

In these circumstances, we want this method to return the value 3. Here is the code:

```
public int length()
    {
    int count = 0 ;
    for (QueueNode pointer = firstPointer ;
        pointer != null ;
        pointer = pointer.next)
        count++ ;
    return count ;
    } // end of method length
```

We initialize an integer count to 0, increment it by 1 for each element in the queue, and return its value as the result of the method.

We are going to traverse the whole linked data structure representing the queue, so we use the for loop. The INITIALIZATION section declares a variable of type QueueNode called pointer and initializes it to the contents of firstPointer. Thus, this variable starts by containing a reference to the first element of the queue (or the value null if the queue is empty) (Figure 17.11).

The MODIFICATION section moves pointer on to the next element with the statement pointer = pointer.next (Figure 17.12).

The TESTING section checks that the variable pointer does not contain a value null, marking the end of the queue.

In Chapter 5, we introduced rules of thumb for choosing between using the for and while statements. The more general statement there noted that we should use a for loop because we are expecting to scan through the complete data structure, even though (as here) we do not know before we start the number of iterations (which is the number of elements in the queue). The INITIALIZATION, TESTING, and MODIFICATION sections implement a pointer control variable rather than the integer control variable we used in Chapter 5.

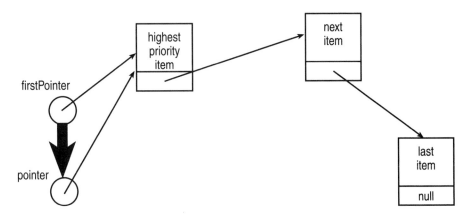

Figure 17.11: The situation after INITIALIZATION

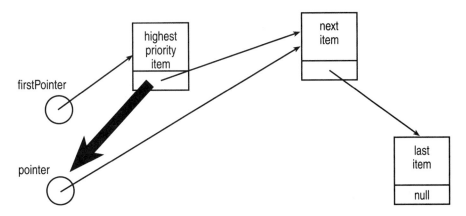

Figure 17.12: The situation after MODIFICATION

17.3.2   *The* first *Method*

The first method needs to return a priority (an int) and the data (a String). We can return an instance of the QueueElement class introduced in Chapter 11 because it encapsulates the priority and data attributes we need. Note the distinction between the QueueElement class from Chapter 11, containing a priority and a data string, and the QueueNode class introduced in Section 17.2, which additionally contains a reference to another instance of the same type.

We need to return a copy of the priority and data values in the first element in the queue—that is, the element pointed to by firstPointer. Thus, we have:

```
public QueueElement first() throws QueueEmptyException
    {
    if (isEmpty())
        throw new QueueEmptyException() ;
```

```
    return new QueueElement(firstPointer.priority, firstPointer.data) ;
    } // end of method first
```

We must check that there is an element in the queue and, if not, throw the exception QueueEmptyException (we defined this exception class in Chapter 15). Remember that the compiler needs to be warned of the possibility that this exception will be thrown with the addition of the throws QueueEmptyException clause to the method header line.

We generate a new QueueElement instance and set its attributes from the first element in the queue (we are effectively doing a *deep* copy, so the returned instance can be modified without affecting the values in the queue), and we return a reference to this instance.

17.3.3   The remove *Method*

Let us now consider the remove method. Here is the code:

```
public QueueElement remove( ) throws QueueEmptyException
    {
    if (isEmpty())
        throw new QueueEmptyException() ;

    QueueElement temp = new QueueElement(firstPointer.priority,
                            firstPointer.data) ;
    firstPointer = firstPointer.next ;
    return temp ;
    } // end of method remove
```

As usual, we check to ensure that the queue is not empty and that there is a first element to remove. We generate a new QueueElement object and set its attributes from the first element in the queue, and we store a reference to this object in the new local variable temp.

We must now remove the current first element from the queue so that the new first element will be what was previously the second element (let us for the moment assume that there is such a second element). The expression firstPointer.next is a reference to (i.e., the address of) the element following that referred to by firstPointer, and so is a reference to the second element. This is the reference that we now want to store in firstPointer. Hence, we write:

```
firstPointer = firstPointer.next ;
```

Before this statement was executed, the situation appeared as in Figure 17.13. Afterward, the situation is as shown in Figure 17.14.

What happens to the area of storage that contains the original first element? Because no reference is made any longer to the instance by the program, a part of the Java system called the *garbage collector* will eventually recover the store area and make it available for further use in some other capacity by the program. The essential point is that we don't have to worry about it; it will be dealt with automatically.

Suppose now that there had been only one element in the queue. Then the next variable in the first (and only) element would have had the value null. The result of executing the statement

```
firstPointer = firstPointer.next ;
```

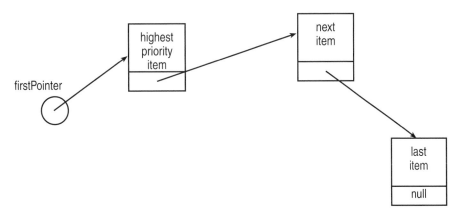

Figure 17.13: Before deleting the first element

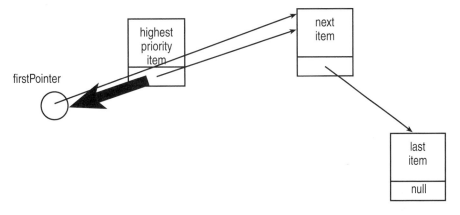

Figure 17.14: After deleting the first element

would therefore have been to put the value null into firstPointer, indicating an empty queue, and this is the correct result.

17.4 The insert Method

The insert method is a bit more complicated. It must work when we insert an element into an empty queue or when the element (according to its priority) should go at the beginning, somewhere in the middle, or at the end of the queue. Here is the code:

```
public void insert(QueueElement d)
    {
```

```
        boolean qStart = true ;
        QueueNode pointer = firstPointer,
                  pointer1 = null ;

        while ((pointer != null) &&
               (pointer.priority <= d.getPriority()))
            {
            pointer1 = pointer ;
            qStart = false ;
            pointer = pointer.next ;
            }

        QueueNode newPointer = new QueueNode(d.getPriority(), d.getData()) ;
        newPointer.next = pointer ;
        if (qStart)
            firstPointer = newPointer ;
        else
            pointer1.next = newPointer ;
        } // end of method insert
```

Notice that we do not conduct any test to see if the queue is full, as this is no longer a possibility.

We first need to find the right place to insert the new element in the queue according to the priority of the element to be added. We are going to use a variable `pointer` of type `QueueNode` to work our way along the queue looking for the right place. Since we do not know whether we are going to look through the whole queue or stop at some intermediate point, we use a `while` loop. The variable `pointer` starts off at the beginning of the queue, so its initial value is the reference to the first element, in `firstPointer`. We scan along the queue until either of two possibilities occurs:

1. We have dropped off the end of the queue, signaled by the fact that `pointer` has the value `null`. If the queue is empty, this causes us to break out of the loop immediately without performing any iterations.

2. The priority of the element to be inserted, which is `d.getPriority()`, is greater (numerically less) than the priority of the element pointed to by `pointer`, which is `pointer.priority`, so the new element should go in front of the element pointed to by `pointer`.

In each iteration, we need to move the variable pointer so it refers to the next element in the list. This is the effect of the statement:

```
pointer = pointer.next ;
```

This takes the reference to the next element (or `null` at the end of the list) held in the `next` attribute of the element referred to by `pointer`, and stores it as the new value of `pointer`.

Unfortunately, when we come out of the loop, the value of `pointer` doesn't quite give us the information we want. What we actually need is, in case 1, a reference to the last element in the queue and, in case 2, a reference to the element just before the one with a lower priority. In either case, we need the element whose `next` attribute is to be modified to refer to the new element we are about to insert, and `pointer` is always one element too far along the queue.

We therefore keep a second variable, pointer1, which we set to hold a reference to the element just before the one referred to by pointer. Before we start, pointer1 is initialized to null. In the loop body, we copy the current value of pointer into the variable pointer1 just before we update pointer to refer to the next element for the next iteration. The effect is that (except at the beginning of the queue) pointer1 always refers to the element just before the element referred to by pointer (Figure 17.15).

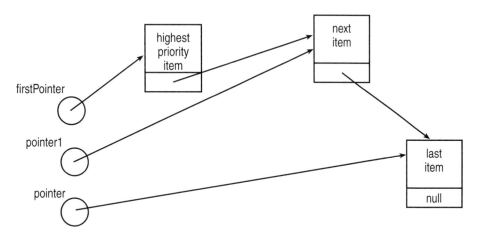

Figure 17.15: pointer1 trailing pointer

If the scanning reaches the end of the queue (because all the elements have a higher priority than the one to be inserted), then pointer will have the value null and pointer1 will refer to the last element in the queue (Figure 17.16).

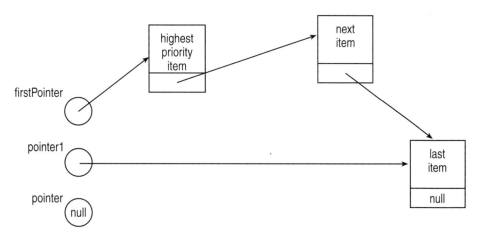

Figure 17.16: Reaching the end of the queue

After we come out of the loop, we have `pointer1` referring to the element just before the one to be inserted. As shown in Figure 17.17, we generate a new `QueueNode` instance, set its attributes to the priority and data passed in the input argument, and put a reference to it (temporarily) into a variable `newPointer` (of type `QueueNode`):

```
QueueNode newPointer = new QueueNode(d.getPriority(), d.getData()) ;
```

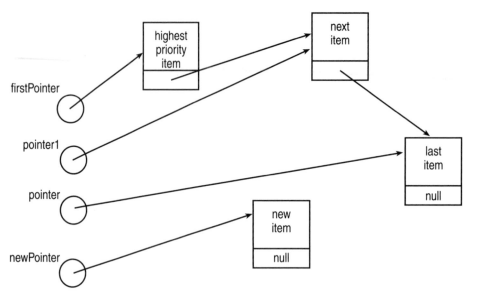

Figure 17.17: Generating the new element

We want the `next` attribute of this new instance to refer to the next element in the queue, and as a result of traversing the loop, a reference to this next element is in the variable `pointer`. Figure 17.18 shows the result of executing the statement:

```
newPointer.next = pointer ;
```

If we were inserting a new final element, `pointer` would contain the value `null`. This is the correct value to insert as the value of the `next` attribute of the new element, currently pointed to by `newPointer`. So this statement still works correctly at the end of the queue.

Finally, we want to link the new element into the queue at the right place. Our first attempt at this might be the following statement (which will in fact require modification)

```
pointer1.next = newPointer ;
```

to insert a reference to the new element as the `next` attribute of the preceding element, the one referred to by `pointer1`. The result is shown in Figure 17.19.

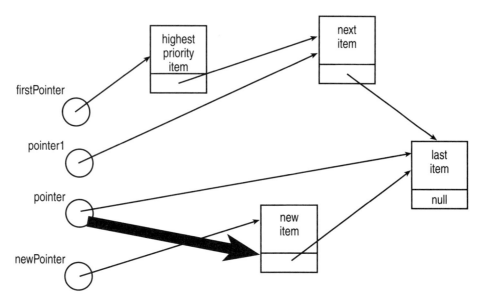

Figure 17.18: Making the new element point to the one that follows it

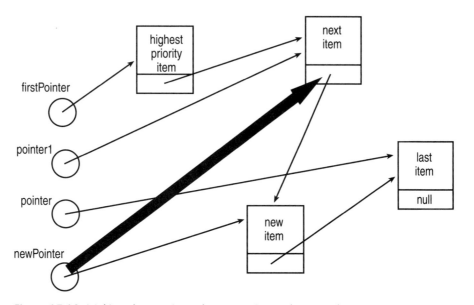

Figure 17.19: Making the previous element point to the new element

There is a slight problem with this. If the new element is to be inserted as the first element in the queue (e.g., because its priority is higher than all elements currently in the queue), there is no "preceding" element, and we need to put the reference to the new element directly in the firstPointer variable. The Boolean variable qStart keeps track of this; it is initialized to true and changed to false on the first iteration (and on all subsequent iterations) when `pointer1` is given a usable value. If qStart has the value true, no iterations of the loop took place, and the variable `firstPointer` is to be updated. Otherwise, `pointer1` has been given a value, which is a reference to the element whose next attribute is to be modified. Hence, the correct version of this step is:

```
if (qStart)
    firstPointer = newPointer ;
else
    pointer1.next = newPointer ;
```

In fact, we could have done without the Boolean variable qStart. We could instead have written the preceding test:

```
if (pointer1 == null)
    firstPointer = newPointer ;
else
    pointer1.next = newPointer ;
```

Figure 17.20 shows the situation when we return from the `insert` method.

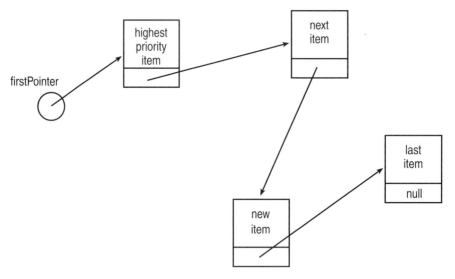

Figure 17.20: The queue after insertion

We have argued that this code for insertion works correctly for the general case of insertion into the middle of a queue and also for the special cases of the beginning and the end of a queue. What about the special case of insertion into an empty queue?

In this case, the variable `firstPointer` has the value `null`, so the initial value of `pointer` will also be `null`. We will exit from the loop without executing any iterations, and qStart will therefore have the value true. We generate a new element in the usual way, its next attribute receives the value null, and its reference goes into firstPointer. We arrive at the situation shown in Figure 17.21, which is the correct setup. Thus, this special case also works.

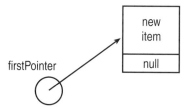

Figure 17.21: Insertion into an empty queue

Finally, what happens if we insert several items with the same priority? The loop that scans for the location in the queue for the new item uses the test <= on the priorities. Thus, a new item is put at the end of the elements in the queue with the same priority.

17.5   Deletion from a Linked Data Structure (Optional)

You will have noticed that, although for the priority queue we must be prepared to insert a new element at any point in the queue, we delete only from the front of the queue, which is particularly simple. If for some reason we wanted to delete an element from an arbitrary place in the queue, we would have the same problem we had with insertion. That is, we have to know where the preceding element is so that we can modify the value held as its next attribute.

Suppose, for example, that we have the variable pointer referring to the element to be deleted and pointer1 referring to the preceding element. We would have to write

```
pointer1.next = pointer.next ;
```

to copy the reference to the element following the one to be deleted into the next attribute of the element preceding the one to be deleted. Before the deletion, we would have a situation resembling that shown in Figure 17.22; afterward, it would resemble Figure 17.23.

Figure 17.24 shows the situation after we return from the delete method and the local variables pointer and pointer1 have disappeared.

Because there are now no references to the area of store associated with the element we have deleted from the queue, it will eventually be recovered by the garbage collector for reuse elsewhere in the program.

The foregoing code for deletion still works if the element being deleted is the last in the queue, in which case pointer.next contains the value null, which gets copied into the next attribute of the element preceding the one we are deleting. It does not work, however, if the element being deleted is the first element in the queue. We would again need some indication of this, either using a Boolean variable qStart as before or perhaps ensuring that pointer1 is set to contain the value null in this case:

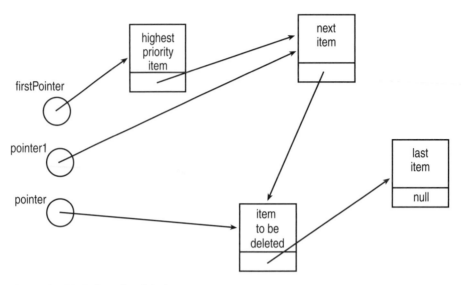

Figure 17.22: Before the deletion

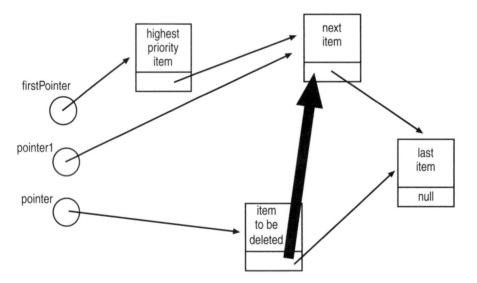

Figure 17.23: After the deletion

```
if (pointer1 == null)
    firstPointer = pointer.next ;
else
    pointer1.next = pointer.next ;
```

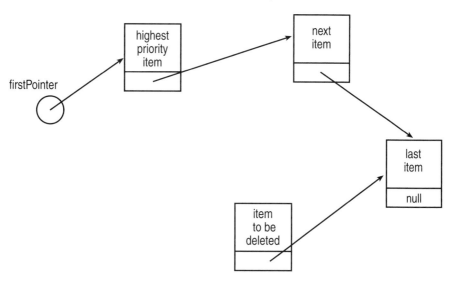

Figure 17.24: The final result of the deletion

We do not need to consider the case of an empty queue here because we are assuming the pointer refers to an element in the queue to be deleted. Depending on how this reference has been obtained, it may be possible for pointer to contain the value null if there is no appropriate element to be deleted. We would then have to test for this special case.

17.6   Doubly Linked Lists (Optional)

In the case of insertion into a priority queue, there is no particular problem in making sure that we establish a reference to the element preceding the insertion point, as we can do this while we are scanning through the queue looking for the appropriate place. But in some situations, we may be in the position of knowing the insertion point without knowing the identity of the preceding element, so we would have to find it by scanning from the beginning.

An alternative would be for each element to contain a reference to the preceding element as well as the following element. The declaration of a QueueNode for such a *doubly linked* list would look like this:

```
class QueueNode
   {
   int priority ;
   String data ;
   QueueNode previous,
            next ;
```

```
public QueueNode(int p, String d)
    {
    priority = p ;
    data = d ;
    previous = null ;
    next = null ;
    } // end of constructor method
} // end of class QueueNode
```

An example of such a list is shown in Figure 17.25.

firstPointer

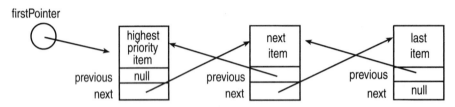

Figure 17.25: A doubly linked list

Suppose we want to insert a new element in a doubly linked list. Let us suppose that `pointer` refers to the element before which we want to insert a new element, and `newPointer` refers to the new element we are about to insert (Figure 17.26). There is no `pointer1` variable, as we can do without it.

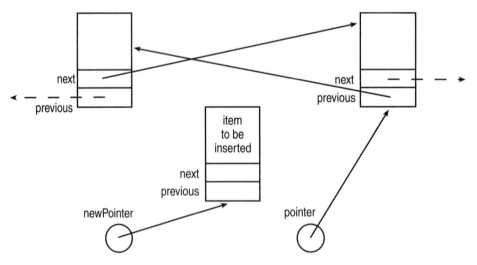

Figure 17.26: Creating a new node for insertion

We need to update four pointers: the `previous` and `next` attributes of this new element, the `next` attribute of the preceding element, and the `previous` attribute of the following element. Here is a first attempt:

```
pointer.previous.next = newPointer ;      // step 1
newPointer.previous = pointer.previous ;  // step 2
newPointer.next = pointer ;               // step 3
pointer.previous = newPointer ;           // step 4
```

Figure 17.27 shows the effect of each statement.

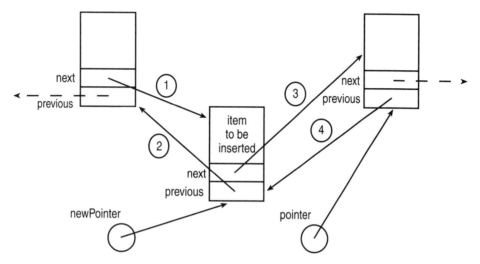

Figure 17.27: After the insertion

This code does not, of course, work properly at the beginning or end of the list. In the first case, at the beginning of the list, `pointer.previous` contains the value `null`, so we could rewrite the code:

```
if (pointer.previous == null)
    {
    firstPointer = newPointer ;
    newPointer.previous = null ;
    }
else
    {
    pointer.previous.next = newPointer ;
    newPointer.previous = pointer.previous ;
    }
newPointer.next = pointer ;
pointer.previous = newPointer ;
```

In the case of insertion at the end of the list, we have said that `pointer` refers to the element after the place we want to insert the new element and so presumably contains the value `null`; thus, we need some other way to locate the insertion position. In the spirit of this example, perhaps we should have a variable `lastPointer` to point to the last element in the list, just as `firstPointer` points to the first element. We leave the details to the reader.

17.7   Using Linked Data Structures

As you will have gathered from the preceding discussion, we have to keep a clear head when writing code to manipulate linked data structures. There are a few well-known situations where it is easy to write erroneous code:

- Sometimes it is possible to have a reference to some type of object, which the program manipulates as if it is a reference to a different type of object. Because Java is a *strongly typed* language, a variable that can hold a reference to one type of object cannot hold a reference to a different type of object; hence, the Java compiler is able to eliminate errors of this sort.

- It is easy to attempt to access an object through a variable that has not been initialized to a suitable value. The Java compiler makes an attempt to catch situations where this has happened, but it is important to get into the habit of initializing reference variables to the value `null` if there is no appropriate value to which to set it. It remains important not to attempt to access an object through a variable initialized to `null`, either by checking carefully to ensure that such situations cannot arise or by explicitly testing for this value before using the reference.

- There are some situations where it is particularly easy to manipulate pointers in the wrong way. One situation is when accessing the "edges" of the linked data structure. For example, in the priority queue code, we needed to be particularly careful when inserting at the beginning and end of the queue. Similarly, if we had a method to provide general deletion from the queue, we would have to be careful to make sure it worked at the beginning and end of the queue.

- We must also be particularly careful when dealing with an empty linked data structure. For example, with the priority queue, we need to ensure that inserting an element into an empty queue works correctly. Similarly, deleting the last element from a queue needs to be checked to ensure that it leaves an empty queue in the correct format for the next insertion.

Let us briefly consider the layout of the `PriorityQueue` code. We have four classes:

- `QueueElement`, containing the priority and data attributes
- `QueueEmptyException`
- `QueueNode`, essentially a `QueueElement` with an extra `next` attribute
- `PriorityQueue`

The first two are exactly the same as for the array implementation of the `PriorityQueue`, which we discussed in Chapter 11. We do not need the `QueueFullException` class, which we needed for the array implementation. These two classes are public, and the source code needs to be in two suitably named files, `QueueElement.java` and `QueueEmptyException.java`, as before.

However, the classes `QueueNode` and `PriorityQueue` are closely connected. We have chosen to put the source code for both these classes into the single file `PriorityQueue.java`. The class `PriorityQueue` is `public` as usual, but the code for the other class starts:

```
class QueueNode
    {
    ...
```

This class therefore has the default protection, which means that it is accessible from all classes in the package, which includes the code of the class `PriorityQueue`. The three instance variables `priority`, `data`, and `next` in this class all have the default protection; thus, in the methods of `PriorityQueue`, we can refer to the variables directly (e.g., as in `firstPointer.priority` and `pointer.next`) without needing to work through `set` and `get` methods. Indeed, the only method we have supplied for the `QueueNode` class is a constructor to set up appropriate initial values.

An alternative strategy could have been to make `QueueNode` inherit its priority and data attributes from `QueueElement` and add another `next` attribute:

```
class QueueNode extends QueueElement
    {
    QueueNode next ;

    public QueueNode(int p, String d)
        {
        super(p, d) ;
        next = null ;
        } // end of constructor method
    } // end of class QueueNode
```

The constructor method for `QueueNode` calls the constructor method for `QueueElement` (using the keyword `super`) and then initializes the `next` attribute. We have to modify the code for the `PriorityQueue` class because we no longer have direct access to the `priority` and `data` attributes, as they are private to the `QueueElement` class. The only way we can access them is via the `getPriority` and `getData` methods. An alternative would have been to give the attributes `protected` or default accessibility in the `QueueElement` class, in which case we would still have direct access from the `PriorityQueue` class.

We are going to look at another example of a linked data structure, a tree, in the next chapter.

17.8   Key Points in Chapter 17

- There are a number of well-known, very useful "high-level" data structures, such as queues, stacks, and trees. These high-level abstractions can be specified and used independently of their implementation; for example, we can define a `Stack` class with a set of operations and hide all details of implementation within the class. This is a further example of an *abstract data type*, as discussed in Chapter 11.

- It is possible to implement these abstract data types using linear, static storage structures such as an array. However, this approach can raise a number of problems, such as fixed maximum capacities and difficulties in rearranging the elements (e.g., to make room for an extra element).

- It is also possible to use dynamic storage structures such as a linked list. An element of such a list (an instance of a particular class) will contain such data as are necessary but also at least one reference attribute (e.g., called next) to refer to another instance of the same class.

- A linked list needs a variable (e.g., called firstPointer) that points to the first element of the list. That first member's reference attribute will point to the next element of this list and so on. The final element will have its reference attribute set to the value null.

- We can traverse a list by using a loop and following the value of the next attribute. A typical loop might look like this:

```
for (NodeClass pointer = firstPointer ;
    pointer != null ;
    pointer = pointer.next)
  . . .
```

This algorithm can be used as the basis for printing, searching, or any general processing of the contents of the list.

- We can insert a new element anywhere in a list. We first use the constructor method to set up a new element, and then we insert the element by manipulating the pointers appropriately, having first scanned through the list looking for the correct position, if necessary.

- If we delete an element from a linked data structure, Java's garbage collector will return it to the available free store once there are no longer references to it.

- We must take care with linked structures (a) to ensure all pointer variables are suitably initialized (perhaps to null), (b) to ensure our algorithms work correctly at the "edges" of the structure," and (c) to ensure that they still work when the structure is empty.

17. 9   Exercises

1. In Exercise 15.2, you used an array to implement a stack of characters as an abstract data type in the class CharacterStack.

   Reimplement the CharacterStack class, this time using a linked list of elements. The only difference from the earlier abstract data type specification is that StackOverflowException will never be thrown by the push method.

   Test your package with the driver and parenthesis checker from Exercises 15.2 and 15.3. These should not need any changes.

2. Add a method `delete` to the `PriorityQueue` class:

`public void delete(int p)`

a. This method should delete the first element in the queue with a priority equal to the value p.

b. Rewrite the method so that it deletes all the elements in the queue with a priority equal to the value p. Check that it still works if all the elements in the queue have this priority.

3. Add a method `merge` to the `PriorityQueue` class:

`public void merge(PriorityQueue q)`

This method takes all the elements in the queue q and inserts them in their correct positions in the queue to which the method is applied. Check what happens to the instance references in the queue q. Should you be using a deep or a shallow copy?

4. Implement a normal (first-in, first-out) queue of `Strings` as an abstract data type `Queue`. Use the same list of methods as for the `PriorityQueue` class and a linked implementation.
Write a method `append` (not part of the `Queue` class)

`public static Queue append(Queue q1, Queue q2)`

which returns a `Queue` that consists of all the elements of q1 (in order) followed by all the elements of q2 (in order). The queues q1 and q2 should be left unchanged, so the `Queue` you return should be a copy.

5. Using the ideas discussed in Section 17.6, reimplement the `PriorityQueue` class as a doubly linked list with instance variables `firstPointer` and `lastPointer` referring to the first and last elements of the queue.
Add a version of the `delete` method discussed in Exercise 17.2.
When you are scanning through the queue in `insert` and `delete` for the appropriate element, do not use a trailing pointer `pointer1`. Instead, have the program work out the neighboring elements from the link variables provided.

6. Write a program that reads from the user the usual information (forename, surname, age, gender) for a sequence of instances of the `Person` class and organize them into two linked lists ordered alphabetically by increasing surname and by increasing age. Then print the two lists in order.

7. A hotel receptionist needs to keep track of who is occupying which hotel room and whether they are in the room at present. Design a system that holds for each occupied room:

- The room number

- A `Person` instance with details of the person occupying the room

- When the occupier checked in

- Whether or not the occupier is currently in the room

The receptionist needs to be able to ask who is occupying a room or which room a person is occupying, since when, and whether they are currently in the room.
Design a `Register` class that holds this information as linked lists of room information, organized by room number and by occupier's name, so that the receptionist can search it by either attribute. The receptionist should be able to check a person into or out of a room and mark that the occupier is currently in the room or not.

8. Figure 17.28 represents a grammar for a simple subset of English. It can be used as a grammar checker as follows:

Start in the state marked with the arrow (here state 1) and with the sentence to be checked. If there is no arc out of this state labeled with the next word of the sentence, the sentence is invalid (at least according to this simple grammar). If there is an arc labeled with the next word of the sentence, follow the arc to the new state. Repeat. When you reach the end of the sentence, interpret "next word" to be the word "STOP." The sentence is valid according to this grammar if you arrive at the final state (marked with a double circle, here 10) at the end of the sentence.

Thus, the sentence *the cat sat on the mat* would cause the program to visit states 1, 2, 3, 6, 7, 8, 9, 10; hence, it is a valid sentence.

Implement a grammar checker using this grammar. It should read in a sentence word by word from a file and match it to the grammar. If the sentence is valid, it should display the sentence and the phrase *is VALID*. If the sentence is not valid, it should display the valid words of the sentence and then the word *ERROR* and the erroneous word.

Thus,

```
the cat sat on the mat
is VALID
```

and

```
the big brown ERROR dog
```

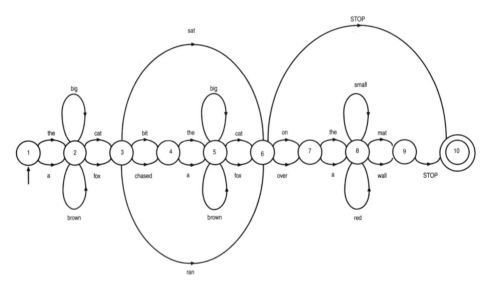

Figure 17.28: A simple English grammar

The class WordFile (derived from BasicFileIo and provided in the javalancs package) provides a method readWord to read successive words from a file:

```
public String readWord()
```

This method reads the next word from the input file and returns it, returning null if
there are no more words.

This diagram is a *finite-state machine*, which is a set of states, including a start state
and one or more finish state, and a set of labeled arcs from one state to another. It is *de-
terministic* because there is never a choice of which arc is the appropriate one to take.
This type of grammar is called a *regular* grammar; it is too simple for English (or Java)
but can be used to define things like time expressions (*ten to six, eleven forty-five*) or the
format of Java identifiers or numbers.

Optional supplementary exercises:

a. Replace the arcs for individual words by arcs for parts of speech (determiner, adjec-
   tive, noun, transitive verb, etc.) and a "dictionary":

```
determiner :- the, a
adjective :- big, brown
noun :- cat, fox
transitive verb :- bit, chased
...
```

b. Provide a way to read the grammar in rather than building it into the program. If
   necessary, assume that there are never more than six arcs coming out of any state.

CHAPTER 18

Recursion and Binary Trees

18.1   Recursion

Suppose we have some task to carry out. We have already discussed the idea of "divide and conquer," where we split up a large task into a number of related subtasks that are easier to implement. Perhaps some subtasks can be further subdivided until we reach a "base task" that cannot be reduced in this way but is directly solvable instead.

There are certain tasks that can be solved by using *recursive* algorithms. With recursion, when we try to subdivide the task, we find that:

- The subtask is exactly the same as the original task, but it works with a reduced amount or value of data. The original task is related to the subtask in some way. A typical recursive expression would involve:

  ```
  task(data) = expression relating to data + task(reduced data)
  ```

- There is a *base task* that works with the smallest or simplest amount of data such as one item of data or the simplest value of that data. If we are processing a collection, the simplest value is a single item; if we are processing a numeric value, then it is 0 or 1:

  ```
  task (simplest data) = fixed answer
  ```

  Notice that the solution to the base task is trivial.

We basically apply the same task algorithm over and over again, reducing the data until we arrive at the base task. Recursion can be a complicated concept to grasp, but you will find that it often offers the simplest solution.

Thus, the strategy we have outlined defines a solution to a task in terms of the same task applied to reduced data, which "bottoms out" at a simple base task. This type of strategy is called *recursion*, and you are going to study its use in programming in this chapter. There is a well-known joke entry in a computer science glossary:

Recursion: *See* Recursion.

This would be *infinite* recursion, as we never make any progress with the task in hand (to define the concept recursion). We must always have an alternative, nonrecursive path so that the recursion eventually stops.

Before we discuss recursion, we need to revisit how ordinary, nonrecursive methods call each other. An application program starts with a main method; let us suppose it calls method1, which then calls method2. When the Java system is executing the statements in the body of method2, it needs to remember where in method1 in came from (so it can return there when method2 has finished) and where in the main method it called method1 (so it can return there when method1 has finished). In principle, this chain of calls could be a long one. Not only must the Java system record where in the preceding method it should return to, but there are other pieces of information about the method that must be remembered so that they can be reinstated when we return—for example, the values of the formal arguments and the local variables. Whenever we leave a method, we return to the method we were previously executing, which means that the information is required in last-in, first-out (LIFO) order. The Java system stores the information about the current methods on a stack called the *run-time stack* (Figure 18.1).

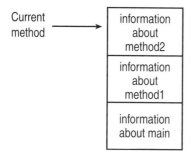

Figure 18.1: The run-time stack

When we use recursion in programming, we have a method whose body contains one or more calls of the same method. A simple example is a program to calculate the factorial of a supplied argument *n*. The *factorial* of a number is the product of all the values from 1 up to and including the number itself (it is defined only for nonnegative values of the argument). Thus, the factorial of 6 is $6 \times 5 \times 4 \times 3 \times 2 \times 1$, or 720. We can give a recursive definition of the factorial function:

```
factorial(n) = 1                         if n = 0
               n x factorial(n - 1)      if n > 0
```

We can program this directly in Java. We have a main method to obtain a value for n from the user and to display the result, and we have a method factorial, which implements the definition directly. It tests for the nonrecursive *base case* (n having a value of 0) and deals with that. Otherwise it makes a recursive call to the factorial method, and uses the result to calculate the answer to the original problem. Note that the recursive call deals with a smaller subtask because it is solving the problem for a value of the argument one less than the original value. To be safe, the factorial method should probably check for a negative value of the argument and stop if it encounters one; otherwise, we could have a case of infinite recursion. Here is the code:

```
import javalancs.* ;

public class Chapter18n1
    {
```

```
public static void main(String[] args) throws Exception
    {
    BasicIo.prompt("number? ") ;
    int n = BasicIo.readInteger() ;
    System.out.println("The factorial of " + n + " is "
                        + factorial(n)) ;
    } // end of method main

private static int factorial(int n)
    {
    if (n == 0)
        return 1 ;
    else
        return n * factorial(n - 1) ;
    } // end of method factorial
} // end of class Chapter18n1
```

How does this work? Suppose the user typed 3 in response to the prompt. Then the main method makes a call factorial(3). Each call of the factorial method effectively causes a new copy of the method to be created, with its own copy of each argument (here n) and local variable (here there are none). These local copies are held in the run-time stack, together with sufficient information for the program to "unwind" each recursive call back to where it came from. In fact, the information held is exactly the same as what Java holds for a nonrecursive method; it does not need to treat a recursive method as a special case. Figure 18.2 shows what happens for a call of factorial(3).

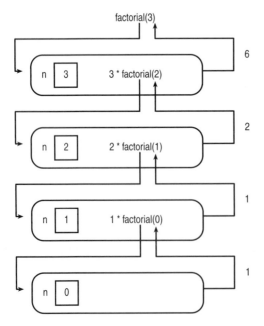

Figure 18.2: A recursive call of factorial

The arrows down the left side of Figure 18.2 represent successive recursive calls of the factorial method, with smaller and smaller values of the argument n. Eventually, the base case (when the value of the argument is 0) is reached, at which time the method returns a value of 1. Then the recursion unwinds, following the arrows at the right side of Figure 18.2, in each case returning a suitable value, until the topmost (original) call of factorial returns a value of 6, which is output by the main method.

There is a cost to the use of recursion. As we have pointed out, for each recursive call, the Java environment needs to keep a separate copy of all the arguments and local variables (in this case, it is only the argument n), together with sufficient information to enable the "unwinding" of the recursion to take place successfully.

It so happens that with the factorial function there is also an iterative solution available, which is just as clear as the recursive solution:

```
private static int factorial(int n)
   {
   int result = 1 ;
   for (int i = 1 ; i <= n ; i++)
       result *= i ;
   return result ;
   } // end of method factorial
```

Before we enter the loop, we set the result to the base case when n is 0. Then in the loop, we simply multiply by successive values from 1 up to the value of the supplied argument; (remember that a *= b means the same as a = a * b).

It is always possible to rewrite a recursive solution as an iterative solution. In some cases, this may be quite difficult because we essentially have to simulate the operation of the run-time stack (i.e., implement the recursion winding and unwinding illustrated in Figure 18.2). As we have pointed out, there is an overhead in using recursion because the environment has to save and restore a certain amount of local information as we move from one copy to the next of the recursive method. But in some cases, it is so much easier to think of a solution to a programming problem in recursive terms that this is the most effective strategy for doing it.

18.2   Solving the Towers of Hanoi Problem

We now look at a different problem and contrast the recursive and iterative solutions to it. This is the *Towers of Hanoi* problem (Figure 18.3), which was invented as a puzzle in 1883. You will find it on pages 57–58 in *Mathematical Puzzles and Diversions* by Martin Gardner (Penguin, 1965).

We have three pegs called A, B, and C. On one peg, we have a number of disks; in this example, there are three, although there were eight in the original puzzle. We start off with all the disks on peg A, with each disk smaller than the one it rests on. The problem is to move all the disks from peg A to peg B, making use of peg C if we wish, but there are two rules for moving the disks:

- We can move only one disk at a time.

- When we move a disk, it must start and finish resting on a larger disk (or of course, on the stand).

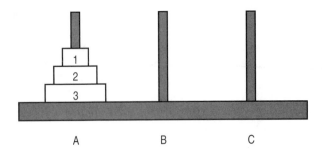

Figure 18.3: The Towers of Hanoi

Thus, we could start by moving disk 1 from peg A to peg B. We could then move disk 2 from peg A to peg C. This is in fact the only reasonable move, as we could not move it to peg B (this is occupied by a smaller disk), and it doesn't make sense to move disk 1 from peg B back to peg A or on to peg C, as we would be wasting moves. We could then move disk 1 from peg B to peg C (on top of a larger disk). We have now successfully moved the top two disks from peg A to peg C, making use of peg B, and taking three moves (Figure 18.4).

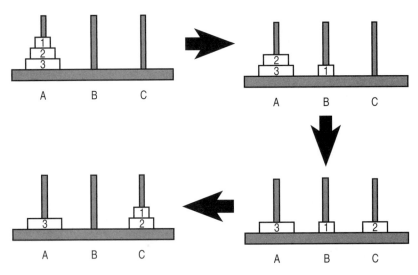

Figure 18.4: Moving disks 1 and 2 to start the process

We can now move disk 3 from peg A to peg B, so it is in the correct final position (Figure 18.5).

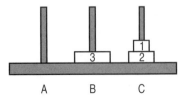

Figure 18.5: Moving disk 3 to the final position

Now all we need to do is move disks 1 and 2 back from peg C to peg B, and we are done. But in principle, we know how to move a stack of two disks from one peg to another because we have already done it in Figure 18.4 (except that it was from peg A to peg C, instead of peg C to B). This final set of moves is shown in Figure 18.6.

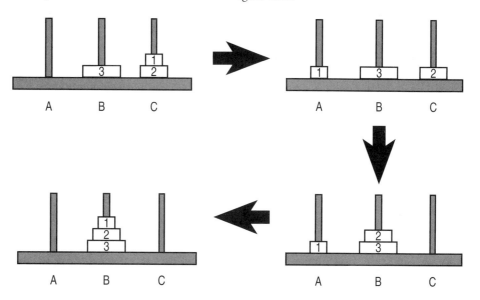

Figure 18.6: Moving disks 1 and 2 to complete the process

Thus, we can solve the problem for three disks using 3 + 1 + 3, or 7, moves.

18.2.1 A Recursive Solution to the Towers of Hanoi Problem

The previous section suggests a recursive solution to the general problem with n disks:

```
public static void hanoi(int n, Peg fromPeg, Peg toPeg, Peg
                         helpPeg)
    {
    if (n == 1)
        moveDisk(fromPeg, toPeg) ;
    else
        {
        hanoi(n - 1, fromPeg, helpPeg, toPeg) ;
        moveDisk(fromPeg, toPeg) ;
        hanoi(n - 1, helpPeg, toPeg, fromPeg) ;
        }
    } // end of method hanoi
```

If there is a stack of one disk to move (the base case), we can do that directly. If we need to move a stack of more than one disk from a peg fromPeg to a peg toPeg:

- We first have to move all but the bottom disk of the stack from `fromPeg` to the third peg `helpPeg`; this is a smaller problem, so we presumably know how to do this (recursively).

- Then we are free to move the bottom disk of the stack from `fromPeg` to `toPeg`.

- Finally, we move the remaining disks of the stack back from the `helpPeg` to `toPeg`, making use of our knowledge of the recursive procedure for moving a smaller number of pegs.

Whenever we are moving a stack of disks from one peg to another, we can make use of the third peg. It may have disks on it, but they will always be bigger than the ones we are moving, so they will not affect our strategy.

We would start the process going by writing something like

```
hanoi(n, pegA, pegB, pegC) ;
```

and the result for three disks would be a sequence of seven moves:

```
move disk from A to B
move disk from A to C
move disk from B to C
move disk from A to B
move disk from C to A
move disk from C to B
move disk from A to B
```

We have implemented the `Peg` objects as consisting simply of their names (A, B, and C), and our `moveDisk` method is:

```
public static void moveDisk(Peg fromPeg, Peg toPeg)
    {
    System.out.println("Move disk from " + fromPeg + " to " +
                    toPeg) ;
    } // end of method moveDisk
```

If we want the program to print the number of each disk as we move it, we would have to keep track of where each disk was as the solution progresses, but we have not bothered to do this. Someone following the computer's instructions would be able to use the specification of the pegs involved to make the right move at each stage.

If we are going to get the computer to make the moves in the Towers of Hanoi problem, then this recursive solution is a good one. It is clear how it works (and that it works), and it is obvious how many moves are required. It is $2^n - 1$ moves for n disks (you can prove this using recursion). Thus, one disk requires one move, two disks require three moves, three disks require seven moves, and so on. When the puzzle was invented in 1883, it was claimed that it was based on a real set of three pegs with 64 disks in the Great Temple of Benares, and the world would end when all the disks had been moved. The number of moves for 64 disks is about 18 followed by 18 zeros, which gives us several thousand million years at one move per second.

But if you try and carry out this strategy "by hand," you will find a major problem. You will have difficulty keeping track of where you are in the strategy—that is, which move you are implementing for a particular stack of disks, inside the strategy for a bigger stack, inside the strategy for a bigger stack still, and so on. The recursive solution keeps (on the run-time stack in the computer) all this information about where it has reached inside a sequence of nested strategies. Consequently, as we have seen in implementing the recursive solution, it doesn't really ever need to look at the pegs to see what disk is where because it knows this from its internal information. For a human being, it would be better not to keep all the information on our personal run-time stack (as it is pretty shallow) and instead make use of information about which disk is physically on which peg at any particular time.

18.2.2 *An Iterative Solution to the Towers of Hanoi Problem*

Thus, we are led to consider an iterative solution to the Towers of Hanoi problem. Here it is:

```
public static void hanoi(int n, Peg fromPeg, Peg toPeg, Peg
                          helpPeg)
    {
    if n is odd
        "cyclically" means fromPeg => toPeg => helpPeg =>
                                    fromPeg ;
    else
        "cyclically" means fromPeg => helpPeg => toPeg =>
                                    fromPeg ;

    while (true)
        {
        move the smallest disk one peg cyclically ;
        if (all the disks are on the toPeg)
            break ;
        make the only possible move not involving the smallest peg ;
        }
    } // end of method hanoi
```

This would be a sufficient algorithm for a human. It would be obvious from looking at the current situation of the pegs and disks which is the smallest disk, where it is, and what "the only possible move not involving the smallest peg" is. But we have to work a bit harder for an iterative computer solution.

We now have to reimplement the Peg objects to simulate the stack of disks that they contain at any time. We provide a method noOfDisks to tell us how many disks are on a peg at any time and top to tell us the number of the uppermost disk on a peg (with a large number if the peg is empty). We have also added a public instance variable called successor to the Peg class so we can record what *cyclically* means. The iterative hanoi method in detail would now look something like this:

```
public static void hanoi(int n, Peg fromPeg, Peg toPeg, Peg
                          helpPeg)
    {
    if (n % 2 == 1)
        {
```

```
          fromPeg.successor = toPeg ;
          toPeg.successor = helpPeg ;
          helpPeg.successor = fromPeg ;
          }
      else
          {
          fromPeg.successor = helpPeg ;
          helpPeg.successor = toPeg ;
          toPeg.successor = fromPeg ;
          }

      while (true)
          {
          Peg smallest = fromPeg ;
          if (toPeg.top() < smallest.top())
              smallest = toPeg ;
          if (helpPeg.top() < smallest.top())
              smallest = helpPeg ;
          Peg newSmallest = smallest.successor ;
          Peg otherPeg = newSmallest.successor ;

          moveDisk(smallest, newSmallest) ;
          if (toPeg.noOfDisks() == n)
              break ;
          if (smallest.top() < otherPeg.top())
              moveDisk(smallest, otherPeg) ;
          else
              moveDisk(otherPeg, smallest) ;
          }
    } // end of method hanoi
```

If you run this version, you will see that it generates exactly the same sequence of moves as the recursive solution, but it is not obvious that it will do so. Although the iterative solution is probably the best for a human, it has a number of general disadvantages. It is certainly not obvious that carrying out this procedure will in fact move the stack of disks in the desired way. And it is not obvious how many moves are required.

Thus, we see that there will be recursive and iterative solutions to a problem, and there may be particular advantages for each.

18.3   Binary Trees

In the previous chapter, we looked at some simple abstract data types and considered how to implement them using linked data structures, where one element contains a reference to one or more other elements. In this chapter, we consider how to implement *trees* using such linked data structures. As you will see, it is often useful to think in terms of recursive algorithms when we implement strategies for manipulating or traversing a tree.

To motivate our discussion, we consider the following problem. Suppose we have a very large text (let's say, hundreds of thousands of words) and we want to make a list of all the words that occur in the text along with a count for how many times each word occurs. In principle, the program to do this is very simple:

```
set the list of words to empty
while there is another word in the text
    look the word up in the list
    if it is in the list
        add one to its count
    else
        make an entry in the list for this word and set its count to one
display the list of words and their associated counts
```

The problem is: What is the most efficient way to store our list of words? Here are some possibilities:

- We could keep the words and counts in an array. When we read the next text word, we need to see if it has occurred before. Thus, we scan the array from the beginning. If we find the word in the array, we add 1 to the count and we are done with this text word. If we reach the end of the array, the word has not occurred before, so we simply add it in the first free space at the end of the array.

   If the word is in the array, we search on average halfway through the array before finding it. If the word is not in the array, then we search all the way through the array to find that out. In either case, we have an $O(n)$ process; with twice as many words in the lexicon, we could expect to take twice as long to search.

- You have seen that we can sometimes improve the situation by keeping the array in sorted order. If we did this, the searching could be done by binary search, which is an $O(\log n)$ process and clearly an improvement. But when we have to add in a new word, we have to shuffle around the array of words to make room for it, and this is still an $O(n)$ process.

- A third possibility is to use a *binary tree*.

A tree in computer science consists of a number of nodes or elements arranged like a family tree (one that shows descent from a common ancestor but not marriage)—see, for example, the inheritance hierarchy in Section 13.3. Each element is joined by a line or *arc* to its parent element, except that there is one element, the *root* element, that has no parent. The root is always drawn at the top of the page with the tree growing downward, like a family tree but unlike a botanical tree. The elements at the bottom of the tree, with no children, are called *leaves*.

In a general tree, an element may have any number of children, but in a *binary* tree, it must have no more than two children. Figure 18.7 shows an example of a binary tree made of the distinct words in the text *now is the time for all good people to come to the aid of the party*.

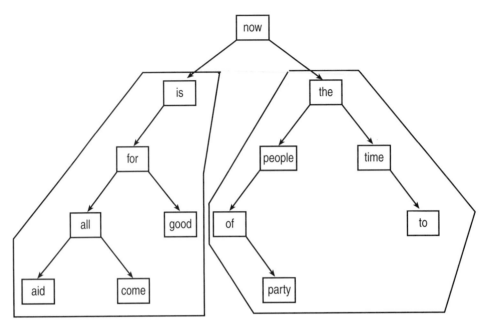

Figure 18.7: A binary tree

A *subtree* is a connected portion of a tree that is itself a tree. Thus, each of the sections enclosed in a line in Figure 18.7 is a subtree of the original tree. In fact, the two subtrees are called the *left* and *right subtrees* of the root node.

We can give a recursive definition of a binary tree:

- A binary tree is either empty
- Or it consists of a root element, a left binary tree, and a right binary tree.

Consider the tree (Figure 18.8) consisting only of the word *aid*. It could be considered as a root element, with empty left and right binary trees. So, considered by itself, it is a binary tree.

Figure 18.8: A binary tree with a single element

Now consider the tree in Figure 18.9. This is also a tree by the same argument.

Figure 18.9: Another binary tree with a single element

Now look at the tree in Figure 18.10. The element *all* could be considered a root element, and we have already proved that the *aid* and *come* elements, each considered by itself, are binary trees. Hence, these are respectively the left and right binary trees of the element *all*, and the whole thing is also a binary tree.

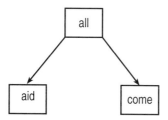

Figure 18.10: A tree with three elements

By following through this type of argument, we could show that the whole of Figure 18.7 is a binary tree rooted at the *now* element.

We have left out one important property of a binary tree. It is so arranged that all the elements in the left binary tree are ordered before (in this case, alphabetically earlier than) the element in the root, which is ordered before all the elements in the right binary tree.

18.3.1   Searching and Updating a Binary Tree

Here is how we use the binary tree to search for an element, for instance, the word *search*. We start at the root, and we compare the item we are searching for with the item in that element:

- If we have a match, we have found the element we are looking for (in the problem under discussion, we would add 1 to the count of occurrences at this element).

- If the item we are searching for is ordered before the item in this element (i.e., it is alphabetically earlier), then we look at the root of the left binary subtree.

- If the item we are searching for is ordered after the item in this element (i.e., it is alphabetically later), then we look at the root of the right binary subtree.

- If the procedure requires us to look at a particular element that does not exist (that binary subtree is empty), then the item we are searching for is not in the tree. Furthermore, the correct place for this item in the tree is the point we have just reached.

To apply this procedure to the word *search,* we proceed as follows:

- We first compare *search* with *now*. It is alphabetically later, so we visit the right subtree (with root *the*).

- We next compare *search* with *the*. It is alphabetically earlier, so we visit the left subtree (with root *people*).

- We next compare *search* with *people*. It is alphabetically later, so we visit the right subtree (which is empty).

Thus, the word *search* is not in the binary tree. If we wish to insert it in the tree, we must create an element as the root of a new right binary subtree for the element containing *people* (Figure 18.11).

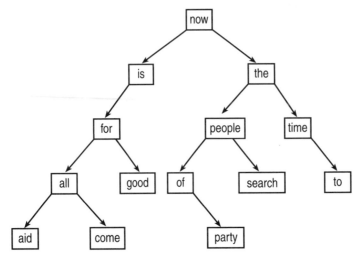

Figure 18.11: A tree with *search* added

Now if we search for the word *search*, we would have the following:

- We first compare *search* with *now*. It is alphabetically later, so we visit the right subtree (with root *the*).

- We next compare *search* with *the*. It is alphabetically earlier, so we visit the left subtree (with root *people*).

- We next compare *search* with *people*. It is alphabetically later, so we visit the right subtree (with root *search*)

- We next compare *search* with *search*, and we have found the matching element

A well-organized binary tree can be searched in time O(log *n*), as with binary search. But we can also insert a new element at the appropriate position in the tree in time O(log *n*). We specified that the binary tree should be "well-organized," which means that the elements should be well spread out, as in the preceding example. Whether this is true depends on the order in which we introduce new elements in the tree. Suppose someone had perversely sorted the words in our text into reverse order before we read them in so that the text reads *to time the people party of now is good for come all aid*. Now if we construct a binary tree in the same way as before, we arrive at the situation shown in Figure 18.12. If we try and search, or insert into, such a binary tree, we are essentially doing linear search. So we are back at an O(*n*) algorithm.

There are mechanisms for taking an unbalanced binary tree (e.g., the one in Figure 18.12) and making it more balanced or for reorganizing the tree as we go along so that it remains relatively balanced as we add new elements. More information is given on binary search trees in

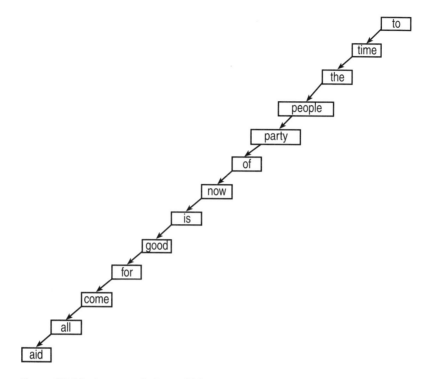

Figure 18.12: A very unbalanced binary tree

textbooks on the study of computer algorithms, such as Chapter 4 of Alfred V. Aho, John E. Hopcroft, and Jeffrey D. Ulmann's *The Design and Analysis of Computer Algorithms* (Addison-Wesley, 1974) or Chapters 3 and 11 *of Data Structures and Algorithms: A First Course* by Iain T. Adamson (Springer, 1996). In the problem we are considering, we ignore this issue because we assume that the words occurring in our text file are not in any particular order and that our list of words is therefore likely to end up reasonably balanced.

18.3.2 Writing the Code for the Binary Tree

We start by creating a class LexiconNode for an element of the lexicon; this needs to contain the word, the count of occurrences, and a pointer to each of the two subtrees, the left and the right. We are going to need a constructor for objects of this type. If we give the constructor a String argument that is the word to be inserted, we can set the count to 1 and the pointers for the left and right subtrees initially to null:

```
class LexiconNode
    {
    String word ;
    int occurrenceCount ;
    LexiconNode left, right ;
```

```
public LexiconNode(String s)
    {
    word = s ;
    occurrenceCount = 1 ;
    left = null ;
    right = null ;
    } // end of constructor method
} // end of class LexiconNode
```

We next create a class `Lexicon` to represent our list of words. This is to have two instance variables: a pointer `first` to the root element of the tree and a count `elementCount` of how many elements are in the tree (i.e., how many distinct words are in the tree). Thus, we can extract this information without having to recalculate it when required. The constructor and `getElementCount` methods are trivial. They are shown in the following portion of the `Lexicon` class definition:

```
class Lexicon
    {
    LexiconNode first ;
    int elementCount ;

    public Lexicon()
        {
        first = null ;
        elementCount = 0 ;
        } // end of constructor method

    public int getElementCount()
        {
        return elementCount ;
        } // end of method getElementCount

    ...
```

18.3.3   Adding a Word Occurrence to the Lexicon

We now write the add method to search for a specified word in the lexicon and take appropriate action—increment the count if the word is already in the lexicon or insert it with a count of 1 if not. We could write a recursive or an iterative version of this, and we start with an iterative version:

```
public void add(String search)
    {
    if (first == null)
        {
        first = new LexiconNode(search) ;
        elementCount++ ;
        return ;
        }
```

```
LexiconNode pointer = first ;
while (true)
    {
    int result = search.compareTo(pointer.word) ;
    if (result == 0)
        {
        pointer.occurrenceCount++ ;
        return ;
        }
    else if (result < 0)
        {
        if (pointer.left == null)
            {
            pointer.left = new LexiconNode(search) ;
            elementCount++ ;
            return ;
            }
        else
            pointer = pointer.left ;
        }
    else // result > 0
        {
        if (pointer.right == null)
            {
            pointer.right = new LexiconNode(search) ;
            elementCount++ ;
            return ;
            }
        else
            pointer = pointer.right ;
        }
    }
} // end of method add
```

We first check for the special case of the tree being completely empty. In this case, we create an instance of the LexiconNode class containing the word we have read, and we insert it as the root element of the tree, pointed to by first.

Otherwise, we start scanning through the tree (iteratively) looking for the correct position for this word search. We have a LexiconNode variable called pointer, which points to the tree element that we are currently considering. We initialize it to point to the root element of the tree at first. Then we go around a loop until we have found or inserted the appropriate element.

We compare the word search for which we are searching against the word in the current element of the tree pointer.word. We use the compareTo method to compare them because we want a three-way comparison: equal, search earlier in the alphabetical ordering, search later in the alphabetical ordering. Make sure you check which way around you want this to work; the first version of this code had the test the wrong way around, and the lexicon was displayed in reverse alphabetical order.

If the element referred to by `pointer` is the same as the word `search`, we are almost done. We increment the count associated with this element, and then we have finished.

If the word `search` is alphabetically earlier than the element at position `pointer`, we need to explore its left subtree. If the left subtree is not empty, we can move our `pointer` to the root element of that subtree:

```
pointer = pointer.left ;
```

If the left subtree is empty, then we have nearly finished. We know that this word `search` is not in the tree, but it should be inserted as the root element of the left subtree of the element pointed to by `pointer`. So:

```
pointer.left = new LexiconNode(search) ;
```

We treat the third case, when the word `search` is alphabetically later than the element at position `pointer`, in a very similar way. Again the element referred to by `pointer` may or may not have a right subtree.

There are several ways to write a recursive version of the `add` method. One looks almost exactly the same as the iterative version. Here is another way to write it:

```
public void add(String search)
    {
    first = addToTree(first, search) ;
    } // end of method add

public LexiconNode addToTree(LexiconNode pointer, String search)
    {
    if (pointer == null)
        {
        elementCount++ ;
        return new LexiconNode(search) ;
        }
    else
        {
        int result = search.compareTo(pointer.word) ;
        if (result == 0)
            pointer.occurrenceCount++ ;
        else if (result < 0)
            pointer.left = addToTree(pointer.left, search) ;
        else // result > 0
            pointer.right = addToTree(pointer.right, search) ;
        return pointer ;
        }
    } // end of method addToTree
```

The add method calls the `addToTree` method at the root level with the word to be added.

Suppose we pass as the first argument of the addToTree method the address of the tree or subtree into which the word is added. The problem is that, if this (sub)tree is null, we have to set up a new LexiconNode containing the word and then put the reference to it somewhere. We cannot pass it back as an argument because it is the value of the reference to the LexiconNode that is passed to the method, and changing the formal argument would not change the actual argument. So we pass back the reference to the new LexiconNode as a return value to be stored in the appropriate place. If the first argument was not null, we pass back as a return value the LexiconNode reference we were given.

18.3.4 Outputting the Lexicon Information

Finally, we need a display method for the Lexicon class to list in alphabetical order all the words and associated counts we have stored. This time, we are going to do a recursive version because there is a natural recursive way of defining how to do this:

```
for any binary tree:
    display the left subtree
    display the root element
    display the right subtree
```

Incidentally, in the theory of binary trees, this is called an *inorder* traversal because we visit the root element in between the visits to the left and right subtrees. There are also a *preorder* traversal, when we visit the root element before the left and right subtrees, and a *postorder* traversal, when we visit the root element after the left and right subtrees. They can both be defined recursively in a way similar to the inorder traversal.

We write a private method displayLexiconElement to implement this recursive procedure

```
private void displayLexiconElement(LexiconNode current)
    {
    if (current != null)
        {
        displayLexiconElement(current.left) ;
        System.out.println(current.word + " " + current.occurrenceCount) ;
        displayLexiconElement(current.right) ;
        }
    } // end of method displayLexiconElement
```

and we call this from a public method display:

```
public void display()
    {
    displayLexiconElement(first) ;
    } // end of method display
```

How would you write this as an iterative method? It is likely that you would have to use a stack to hold the various subtrees waiting to be dealt with, so to some extent you will be implementing a version of the run-time stack of the recursive version.

In the recursive methods we have been examining, we have examples of *direct* recursion where there is at least one explicit call of a method X in the body of the method X. It is also possible to have *indirect* or *mutual* recursion where, for example, method A might call method B and method B might call method A. As before, there must be some alternative course of action; otherwise, we would have infinite recursion. In some programming languages, we have to warn the compiler of mutual recursion because it expects each method to be declared before it is called (and how can we have this, since one of A and B must precede the other in the file?). But in Java, the compiler is clever enough to deal with this situation without any requirement for an explicit warning from the programmer.

18.4   Key Points in Chapter 18

- *Recursion* involves describing the solution to a problem in terms of a simpler, smaller problem that is in some way related to the original problem.

- A recursive method thus typically contains one or more calls to itself with a "smaller" argument. When this argument is numeric, it may simply be the value of the argument minus 1. When it is a string or array or linked list, it may be the same structure with one less element.

- The recursive mechanism involves use of the run-time stack, which results in an overhead. However, the recursive solution to a problem may be more intuitive than an iterative one.

- A *binary tree* consists of a number of elements, each of which consists of some data and references to left and right subtrees (either or both of which may be null). There is a *root* element at the base of the tree. We can implement an element as an instance of a class that contains two instance variables of the same type as the class being defined.

- We can use a recursive method to traverse a binary tree to visit and process each of the elements in turn.

18.5   Exercises

1. The following are *Fibonacci* numbers. The first two numbers are both 1, and each subsequent number is the sum of the preceding two numbers:

   1, 1, 2, 3, 5, 8, 13, 21, . . .

   Write a recursive method to find the *n*th Fibonacci number for *n* specified in the argument. Write a program to test your method.
   Write an iterative method to perform the same calculation.

2. There is a function of two variables called Ackermann's function, which has a recursive definition:

```
ackermann(m, n) = 1                      if m = 0
                  2                      if m = 1 and n = 0
                  m + 2                  if m > 1 and n = 0
                  ackermann(ackermann
                  (m - 1, n), n-1)       otherwise
```

Write a program to prompt the user for values of m and n and calculate the result. What is the value of ackermann(2, 1)? What about ackermann(4, 3)?

3. You want to print the contents of a string in reverse. Write a recursive method that:

   ▪ Outputs the last character of the string.

   ▪ Removes the last character.

   ▪ Calls itself again with the shorter string.

4. Write a program to use the Lexicon class to print a list of all the distinct words in a large file of text. Make sure that your program is case insensitive; for example, you should treat *the* and *The* as the same word.

   The class WordFile (derived from BasicFileIo in the javalancs package) provides a method to read the next word from an input file and return it, returning null if there are no more words.

   In a sentence, the punctuation marks are usually written right next to the words, as in *the (red) cat sat on the mat.* Arrange your program so that, as far as possible, it eliminates these punctuation marks from the list of words.

5 Create a class SortedIntegerList to hold a set of integers in sorted order. This class should provide the following services:

   ▪ add to add a new integer to the list; this should check that the value is not already in the list.

   ▪ toString to return the list of integers in sorted order.

   The SortedIntegerList should be implemented as a binary tree, but all details of the implementation should be hidden from the user.

   Write a suitable driver application program to test the class.

6. Add a delete method to the SortedIntegerList class to delete an element with a specified value.

   Tip: It is easy to delete an element from a binary tree if it has no dependent elements (just delete it) or only one dependent element (replace the element to be deleted by its dependent element). If it has two dependent elements, it is slightly more difficult. You have to look for the "next" element (or the "previous" element) in the inorder sequence, delete it from its current location, and insert it instead of the element to be deleted. This new element you have deleted must have no or one dependent element, so we know how to deal with this situation (see pages 68–71 of *Data Structures and Algorithms: A First Course* by Iain T. Adamson, Springer, 1996).

7. Here is a way to write a program to make a computer play a game of tick-tack-toe (noughts-and-crosses):

   ▪ Starting from the current position, generate all possible moves the computer can make from this position; this leads to a number of new positions. For each of these positions, generate all possible moves by the opponent, leading to another set of new positions. For each of these, generate all possible moves by the computer.

   Carry on like this until each position is a win for either the computer or the opponent or there are no more possible moves and the game is a draw.

   This can be represented (Figure 18.13) by a tree of possible positions, with the current position as the root element. This is sometimes called the *game* tree.

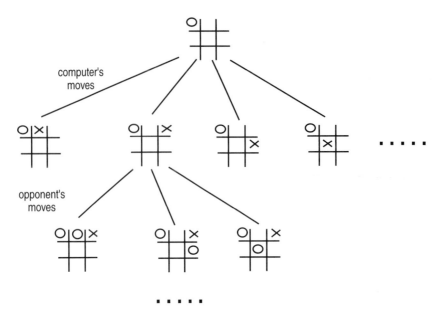

Figure 18.13: A game tree

- Mark each final position with 1 if it is a win for the computer, −1 if it is a win for the opponent, and 0 if it is a draw.

- Suppose you have a position X where it is the computer's move, and all the positions you can reach by one move from X are marked with either 1, 0, or −1. If any of these resulting positions is marked 1, select one at random and write against X the number 1 and the selected move. If none of the resulting positions is marked 1, but some are marked 0, select one at random and write against X the number 0 and the selected move. Otherwise, if all the resulting positions are marked −1, select one at random and write against X the number −1 and the selected move.

  This implements the idea that the computer always chooses a winning move if there is one or plays to draw otherwise.

- Suppose you have a position X where it is the opponent's move, and all the positions you can reach by one move from X are marked with either 1, 0, or −1. If any of these resulting positions is marked −1, select one at random and write against X the number −1 and the selected move. If none of the resulting positions is marked −1, but some are marked 0, select one at random and write against X the number 0 and the selected move. Otherwise, if all the resulting positions are marked 1, select one at random and write against X the number 1 and the selected move.

  This implements the idea that the opponent similarly always chooses a winning move if there is one or plays to draw otherwise.

- Work back up the tree, applying this procedure (called *minimaxing*—can you see why?). Eventually, you arrive at the root node. Make the move you have written against this element. This is the best move you can make (actually, it may be one of the best moves).

Write a method that, given a position, returns the numerical value and the move assigned to the position by the foregoing procedure.

Write a program, based on this method, that plays the game against a human opponent. The human and the computer should alternate for the first move.

Note ∎

The numerical value returned for a position indicates the result if both players play as well as possible: 1 is a certain win for the computer, –1 is a certain win for the opponent, 0 is a draw. Apply the method to the empty opening position of a game. What does the resulting value tell you about the game?

8. In Exercise 18.7, we suggested that you generate the tree and then traverse it, assigning values to the various elements. If you do this, you must visit all an element's dependent elements before you can calculate the value for the element. Thus, the traversal looks like this:

```
for the game tree:
    visit the first subtree
    visit the next subtree
    . . .
    visit the last subtree
    visit the root element to assign a value
```

This is a *postorder* traversal.

Actually, you do not need to keep the entire tree. You need to keep only the path from the root to the element you are currently examining. The traversal for the current element looks like this:

- Visit the first subtree and remember the value and associated move.
- Visit the next subtree and remember the value and associated move if it is an improvement.
- And so on.
- Visit the last subtree and remember the value and associated move if it is an improvement.
- Pass back the value and the move that arrived at this element.

Although you generate and visit the whole tree, you do not actually need to set the tree up as a data structure. You need to keep only a stack representing the path from root to element. Rewrite your method to work this way.

9. Write a program to place eight chess queens on an 8 by 8 chessboard so that none of them can capture each other; that is, no two of them must be on the same row, column, or diagonal line (Figure 18.14).

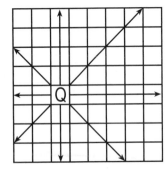

Figure 18.14: A queen on a chessboard

Note ▪

Tip 1: There must be exactly one queen on each row. You could write a recursive method that tries to place a queen on each square of row i; if this is an acceptable position, given the queens already placed in rows $1 \ldots i-1$, call the same method again to consider positioning the queen everywhere in row $i + 1$.

Tip 2: The obvious data structure for holding the proposed queen structure is a two-dimensional array representing the board and whether each square is occupied or not. A better data structure may be a one-dimensional array that specifies for each row which column the queen is in.

Optional Supplementary Problem: Extend the program to make it display all possible positions for the eight queens, not only the first one encountered. Can you make it display only the distinct positions (i.e., eliminating all mirror image positions etc.)?

CHAPTER 19

Input and Output in Java

19.1 Input and Output Systems

Any useful program must have some connection with the outside world. There are a very few, mostly trivial programs that do not need any input to enable them to do their job (our first Java program, Hello.java, was one). But usually, a program needs some input from the outside world upon which to base its calculations. And any program must output its calculated results somehow; otherwise, what is the point of running it?

In the preceding chapters, you have met a number of ways by which a Java program can communicate with the outside world:

- In Chapter 1, we introduced the System.out object and its associated print and println methods to display at the user's terminal the results of the program's calculations. In this chapter, we explain exactly what sort of object this is and discuss a number of related aspects.

- In Chapter 3, we provided a class called BasicIo that contains a number of methods (e.g., readInteger) to enable a program to read various different types of data (integers, strings, floating-point numbers, etc.) when they are typed in by the user at the keyboard. In this chapter, we reveal the mechanism that underlies the methods of the BasicIo class so that you can write code to enable your program to interact directly with the keyboard.

- In Exercise 5.6, we introduced the BasicFileIo class, which enabled us to write programs that read data from, or write data to, files in the computer's filing system. Again, in this chapter, you will be looking at the mechanisms used by this class to allow us to interact more directly with data in files.

- In Chapter 16, we met the completely different type of input/output system provided by Java's Abstract Windowing Toolkit (AWT), which allows a program to draw various pictures, buttons, and text areas on the computer screen and receive input via the mouse and keyboard. Although we only scratched the surface in that chapter of the facilities provided by the AWT, we will not be pursuing that mechanism further here. You will need to read a more advanced book on the AWT for more information.

- For completeness, we need to mention one other method for the input of small quantities of data to a program: the command-line parameter mechanism introduced in Chapter 3. This is a rather simple mechanism, and we have said all there is to say about it.

In this chapter, we look at the facilities that Java provides for simple input and output to the computer terminal or to the computer's file system. It turns out that this general mechanism can also be used in a number of other areas:

- If we have two or more programs running on a computer at the same time, we may wish to pass data from one to the other. The Java language allows us to specify a program as two or more independent subprograms, or *threads,* which can run on the computer conceptually at the same time. Java allows the communication between these threads to be provided by a form of input/output with the data output by one thread being the input to another thread. This type of mechanism is sometimes called a *pipe;* one program or thread feeds data into one end of the pipe, and another program or thread takes it out of the other end.

- Today, the two communicating programs could be on two different computers connected by some form of communications link. Again, Java organizes the communication of data between our program and a program on another computer by the same overall input/output system. In particular, we can use Java's input/output system to obtain pages and other data from the World Wide Web. We give a brief example of such a program at the end of this chapter.

Many computer programming languages make a distinction between two types of input/output facility, which they see as quite distinct:

- One type of facility is for handling data in the form of (printable) characters, which are arranged in lines of text with the lines of text possibly arranged in pages.

- A completely separate facility is then provided for handling data in the form of binary numbers.

As an example, let us consider how we might output the numeric value 1997:

- The first of the two types of input/output facilities would treat this number as a series of characters representing the decimal digits of the number (Figure 19.1). Exactly how much room this takes will depend on the representation of characters the system is using. Stored in the popular ASCII character representation, each character would take up one (8-bit) byte. Stored using the Unicode character representation used in Java, each character may take up two 8-bit bytes because a much larger range of characters is represented. The number of these units of storage taken up would, in this format, depend on the size of the number; the number 23 would require only two units, 19975 would require five units, and −23 would require three units (one for the character representing the sign and two for the digits).

character 1	character 9	character 9	character 7

Figure 19.1: The number 1997 as a series of characters

- An alternative way of holding the value 1997 is to use the way an integer is held inside the computer. It could be converted into a binary number, which is then held as a series of 4 bytes (Figure 19.2). If we held a smaller number, a negative number, or a larger number (as long as it is less than about 2 billion and fits into a Java int), it would still take 4 bytes to hold the value. Furthermore, this type of format considerably reduces the amount of reformatting required, as compared with holding the number as a series of characters, because the format in which the number is held externally (say, on a file) is almost exactly the same as the format in which it will be held internally (in the store and registers of the computer).

00000000	00000000	00000011	11001101

Figure 19.2: The number 1997 as a (4-byte) binary number

As we have said, most programming languages provide two sets of facilities. One is a set of *character* file or *text* file facilities for handling files of lines consisting of characters. By extension, the computer keyboard and screen are treated as being of this type, as are streams of characters received over a communication line. Then there is a separate set of facilities, a set of *binary* file facilities, to handle data held in the underlying binary format.

Early versions of Java did not make the distinction in this way. The basic input/output facilities provided access to input or output data as a sequence of bytes of binary data, and some of the facilities were specialized to treat such a sequence of bytes as an encoding of a sequence of characters making up a series of lines. In later versions of Java, another set of classes was provided, and these are now the preferred method for handling the input and output of characters. In this chapter, we concentrate on the facilities that Java provides for handling data in the form of lines of (printable) characters, although we will mention briefly the facilities for handling data in binary form.

If we consider input and output between a program and a file, there is another distinction to be made between *sequential* access and *random* access to the file. With sequential access, we start at the beginning of the file and work our way, character by character or byte by byte, toward the end of the file. We could be reading data in from a file that previously exists, or we could be constructing a file from data calculated by the program. With random access, we can jump around the file, accessing one part and then another, without visiting all the parts in between. It is feasible with random access to read part of the file and then change that part of the file without changing (or even reading) the other parts. Thus, if we have a file containing a set of bank accounts, it is feasible with random access to go to the part of the file corresponding to a particular bank account and read it into the computer, to change the data in some way (e.g., to reflect a deposit or withdrawal), and then to write back the revised data without affecting the information held on anyone else's bank account.

With most other types of input/output (e.g., piped to another program or read from the Web) the data have to be treated as sequential. Most of Java's input/output facilities therefore concentrate on providing sequential or *stream* access to data, but there are also facilities for handling random access to file data. In this chapter, we concentrate on sequential access and briefly mention random access in the appropriate place.

19.2 The Java Classes for Input and Output

We first outline the input/output facilities provided by Java for binary data and then discuss the classes provided for character data. All these classes are in the package `java.io`. The basic classes for input/output of binary data (Figure 19.3) are:

- `InputStream` for input of binary data
- `OutputStream` for output of binary data

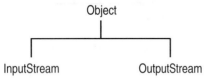

Figure 19.3: The basic classes for input/output of binary data

These are in fact *abstract* classes, and they specify the basic facilities provided by Java for input and output of binary data. The type of input/output provided is, as you can see from the names, *stream* input/output or what we referred to as *sequential* input/output in the previous section. Thus, the `InputStream` class considers input to be a stream or sequence of bytes of information, perhaps structured into binary numbers. Similarly, the `OutputStream` class considers output to be a stream of bytes, again perhaps derived from binary numbers inside the program creating the stream.

All the various different forms of binary input/output are provided by classes derived from these two basic classes (Figure 19.4). The derived classes are arranged in such a way that they can be fitted together smoothly to provide the exact facilities we need. The most important classes are `DataInputStream` for input, derived ultimately from `InputStream`, and `PrintStream` for output, derived ultimately from `OutputStream`.

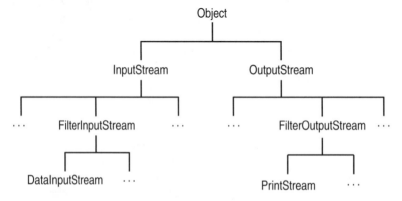

Figure 19.4: Classes for input/output of binary data

You will have noticed that this provides only sequential input/output and does not provide the random access facilities mentioned earlier. For this, there is a separate class `RandomAccess-File` (Figure 19.5). This class is not derived from `InputStream` or `OutputStream`. However, to ensure commonality of facilities where possible, the class `RandomAccessFile` implements two interfaces called `DataInput` and `DataOutput`. The `DataInput` interface is also implemented by the class `DataInputStream`, and the `DataOutput` interface is implemented by a class called `DataOutputStream`, derived, like `PrintStream`, from `OutputStream`.

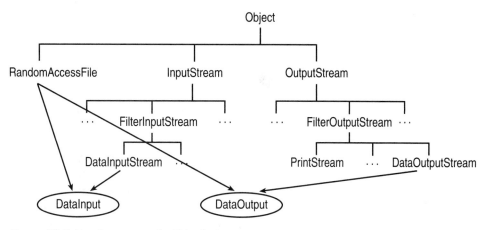

Figure 19.5: Random access facilities in Java

We now turn to the input and output of character data. In early versions of Java, this was done by classes derived from `InputStream` and `OutputStream`. However, from Version 1.1 of Java onward, two new abstract classes, `Reader` and `Writer`, provide (respectively) input and output of streams of characters (Figure 19.6).

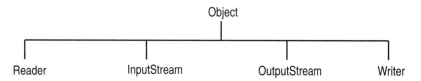

Figure 19.6: The basic classes for input/output

As shown in Figure 19.7, the classes that we discuss in this chapter, such as `BufferedReader` and `PrintWriter`, are derived from these classes (as are a number of other classes, which we will not need to refer to here).

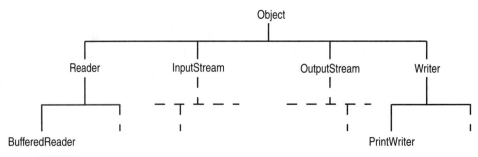

Figure 19.7: Classes for input and output of character data

19.3   The `PrintStream` **Class and** `System.out`

You have already met `System.out`; indeed, we have been using it since Chapter 1 for display-ing strings of characters and numbers. In the package `java.lang` (which is always available in our program and does not have to appear in an `import` statement), there is a class called `System`. This class contains various useful facilities (you have met the method `exit`, which allows us to abandon a program). In particular, it contains three variables:

```
public static final PrintStream err ;
public static final InputStream in ;
public static final PrintStream out ;
```

Thus, `System.out` is an instance of the `PrintStream` class, and it is usually connected to the user's display screen. Sending data to this stream makes it appear sequentially at the user's terminal.

The `PrintStream` class is derived ultimately from `OutputStream` (actually, it is derived from a class called `FilterOutputStream`, which is derived from `OutputStream`). The `PrintStream` class provides a set of methods that outputs values of various types in a suitable form; for example:

```
public void print(boolean b)
public void print(char c)
public void print(double d)
public void print(float f)
public void print(int i)
public void print(long l)
public void print(String s)
```

Each of these methods leaves the current output position immediately after the characters just displayed so that a further call of one of these methods would output a series of characters adjacent to the first call (Figure 19.8).

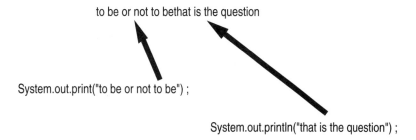

Figure 19.8: Output: `print` followed by `print(ln)`

If we want to start a new line immediately after the characters we have output, we have an equivalent set of methods:

```
public void println(boolean b)
public void println(char c)
public void println(double d)
public void println(float f)
public void println(int i)
public void println(long l)
public void println(String s)
```

This is illustrated in Figure 19.9.

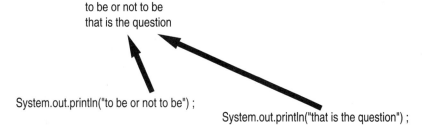

Figure 19.9: Output: `println` followed by `print(ln)`

There is also a method `println` with no argument to start a new line without outputting any preceding value (Figure 19.10).

Normally, a line of characters is held in an internal buffer and not output until a new line is specified. However, the `flush` method outputs any characters currently in the buffer without waiting for a new line. Thus, if we want to prompt the user to input a value, which is to appear on the same line as the prompt, we can write:

```
System.out.print("type the next value required ") ;
System.out.flush() ;
// read in the value
```

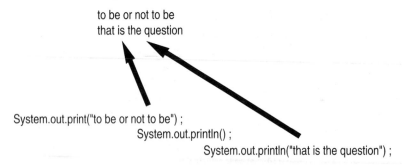

Figure 19.10: Output: Use of print1n with no argument

This is illustrated in Figure 19.11.

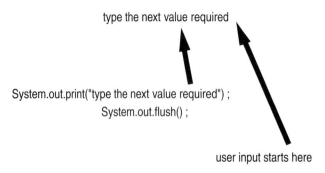

Figure 19.11: Output: Use of the flush method

We can use the concatenate operator + to put together a sequence of values to be printed (Figure 19.12). Here we are attempting to concatenate the String "Today's date is " with the Date object now. In this type of situation, Java attempts to find a toString method for the required class, which should generate some form of String representation of the object. For the Date class, it finds one. If the class does not have a toString method, and neither do any of its ancestor classes, it will ultimately use the toString method of the Object class, and this returns a String that includes the class name.

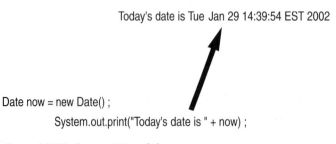

Figure 19.12: Output: Use of the + operator

Those `print` and `println` methods that output numeric values always output exactly as many characters as are required to represent the value specified. If we are trying to output a table of values, this is not quite what we want because we need all the numeric values to appear in fields of the same width (with the positions of the decimal point, notional or otherwise, appearing in a vertical line one above the other). The `writeInteger` method in the `BasicIo` class (in the `javalancs` package) has a second argument to specify the width in characters of the field in which the value of the first argument is output. Similarly, `writeDouble` allows control over the number of decimal places output.

A number of facilities are provided in the `java.text` package for various types of output formatting. These are organized so that the format is appropriate for the locality where the program is currently running (e.g., using the appropriate character to represent the decimal point). As an example, you can use the `NumberFormat` class in this package to specify that a number is to be output with exactly two decimal places as follows:

```
Double num = 123456.789 ;
NumberFormat nf = NumberFormat.getNumberInstance() ;
nf.setMinimumFractionDigits(2) ;
nf.setMaximumFractionDigits(2) ;
System.out.println("the formatted number is " +
                   nf.format(num)) ;
```

There are specialized number formats for outputting percentages and currency amounts and also the `DateFormat` class (again in the `java.text` package) for outputting dates in a suitable local format.

19.3.1   *Output Redirection*

The `System.out` stream is usually connected to the user's screen. In some environments, it is possible to *redirect* the output elsewhere. For example, if we have a Java program `Chapter19n1`, we can run it under the Windows and UNIX operating system with output going to the screen

```
java Chapter19n1
```

or we can run it with the output going to a file `xyz`

```
java Chapter19n1 >xyz
```

No change is required to the program; everything output via the `System.out` stream is redirected to the file `xyz`. Sometimes this redirection causes problems because there are really two different types of data being output:

- The results of the program's calculations, which we presumably do want to be sent to the file (for subsequent printing or further processing).

- Messages to the user to do something, such as to input a value or take note of an error condition, which we would still like to come to the user's screen.

For this reason, the Java environment actually provides two `PrintStream` objects: `System.out` and `System.err`. We should send any result data to `System.out` as before, and these can be redirected to a file if appropriate. However, prompts and error messages should be sent to `System.err`:

```
System.err.print("type in the next value ") ;
System.err.flush() ;
// read a value into x
System.out.println("the value of " + x + " squared is " + x * x) ;
```

If we run this with redirection, the prompt still comes to the user's screen, and the final line is redirected to the file.

19.4 The BufferedReader Class and System.in

We have noted that the System class contains a declaration of the variable in:

```
public static final InputStream in ;
```

Thus, System.in is an instance of the InputStream class, and it is usually connected to the user's keyboard. Actually, InputStream is an abstract class, so System.in must in fact be an instance of a concrete class derived from InputStream. It is usually a BufferedInputStream, which is a class derived from InputStream with additional functionality.

To use this InputStream in a convenient way, we need to add more functionality. In particular, it is a stream of characters, so we are going to use the class BufferedReader, which is derived from the abstract Reader class. We construct an instance of a BufferedReader from the System.in stream with which we are provided as follows:

```
BufferedReader din = new BufferedReader(new
                           InputStreamReader(System.in)) ;
```

This takes the System.in stream, "wraps" an InputStreamReader around it (to turn the bytes from the stream into characters), and then wraps a BufferedReader (which we have called din) around that to provide a useful collection of facilities.

The most useful method we have available as a result of this is one called readLine, which reads the next line of input from the keyboard (up to, but excluding, the keystroke that indicates the end of the line, Return or Enter) and returns this line as a String. Here is a piece of code that reads successive lines from the keyboard and displays them (with println) until the user types in a line consisting of no characters:

```
BufferedReader din = new BufferedReader(new
                           InputStreamReader(System.in)) ;
System.err.println("type in some lines, please") ;
while (true)
    {
    String line = din.readLine() ;
    if (line.length() == 0)
        break ;
    System.out.println("the line was **" + line + "**") ;
    }
System.out.println("**end of input**") ;
```

One small improvement might be that we would like to treat a line consisting only of spaces as if it was a line consisting of no characters and therefore terminating the loop. To do this, we could use the `trim` method from the `String` class (which deletes all leading and trailing spaces and tab characters):

```
BufferedReader din = new BufferedReader(new
                                InputStreamReader(System.in)) ;
System.err.println("type in some lines, please") ;
while (true)
    {
    String line = din.readLine().trim() ;
    if (line.length() == 0)
        break ;
    System.out.println("the line was **" + line + "**") ;
    }
System.out.println("**end of input**") ;
```

19.4.1 Tokenizing an Input Line

Once we have read in a line of characters, we can process it. Usually, a line can be expected to contain a succession of values or *tokens* (numbers, strings, etc.) separated by what is sometimes called *whitespace* (spaces or tab characters) (Figure 19.13).

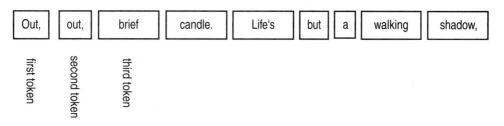

Figure 19.13: A line of characters divided into tokens

We could write some code to separate a line into tokens, but Java provides a `StringTokenizer` class (in the `java.util` package) that does it for us. We first construct an instance of the `StringTokenizer` class from the line we have read in, and then we have available two methods:

- `nextToken` to return a `String` that is the next token or sequence of characters between whitespace.

- `hasMoreTokens`, which tells us if there are any more tokens to process on this input line.

Here is some code to read a sequence of lines from the keyboard and display the successive tokens (using `println`):

```
BufferedReader din = new BufferedReader(new
                                InputStreamReader(System.in)) ;
```

```
System.err.println("type in some more lines, please") ;
while (true)
    {
    String line = din.readLine().trim() ;
    if (line.length() == 0)
        break ;
    StringTokenizer st = new StringTokenizer(line) ;
    while (st.hasMoreTokens())
        System.out.println("the token was **" +
                            st.nextToken() + "**") ;
    }
System.out.println("**end of input**") ;
```

Each line is read in, checked for an empty (or whitespace-only) line, and then tokenized. As long as there are some more tokens on this line (indicated by the hasMoreTokens method), we display the next token (provided by the nextToken method).

This version of the StringTokenizer assumes that the characters separating the tokens are one or more spaces or tab characters (or a newline character if we had constructed a String containing such characters). Another constructor for the StringTokenizer class allows us, as a second argument, to specify a String of characters, any of which is to be treated as a separator. Suppose we wanted to tokenize a line where the individual tokens are separated by the vertical line character|; we could write:

```
StringTokenizer st = new StringTokenizer(line, "|") ;
```

If we wanted to split the tokens at space, comma, or full stop, we could write:

```
StringTokenizer st = new StringTokenizer(line, " ,.") ;
```

19.4.2   Converting Strings to Numeric Values

There is one other thing we will want to do, at least with some of the tokens. If the String we have read in represents a numeric value, we want that value rather than the character string.

Java provides us with the static methods parseInt (in the Integer class) and parseDouble (in the Double class). These take a String as argument and return an int or a double, respectively (there are similar methods for long and float). Here is an example:

```
System.err.println("type an integer followed by a double") ;
String line = din.readLine().trim() ;
StringTokenizer st = new StringTokenizer(line) ;
int firstValue = Integer.parseInt(st.nextToken()) ;
System.out.println("the first value is " + firstValue) ;
double secondValue = Double.parseDouble(st.nextToken()) ;
System.out.println("the second value is " + secondValue) ;
```

For simplicity, we have omitted the calling of the hasMoreTokens method, which would ensure that there is a value to convert. You can see now why we hid this inside the BasicIo class when you were starting to program in Java!

What happens if we type in a string that cannot be converted to an appropriate number? We get a NumberFormatException. It would be better if we caught this exception and told the user to try again. Here is a revision of the code to try to ensure that the user types in a sensible pair of values:

```
BufferedReader din = new BufferedReader(new
                              InputStreamReader(System.in)) ;
System.err.println("type an integer followed by a double") ;
boolean invalidInput = false ;
int firstValue = 0 ;
double secondValue = 0.0 ;
do
    {
    String line = din.readLine() ;
    StringTokenizer st = new StringTokenizer(line) ;
    try {
        firstValue = Integer.parseInt(st.nextToken()) ;
        secondValue = Double.parseDouble(st.nextToken()) ;
        invalidInput = !isInputOK(firstValue, secondValue) ;
        }
    catch (NumberFormatException e)
        {
        invalidInput = true ;
        }
    if (invalidInput)
        System.err.println("ERROR: retype both values") ;
    }
while (invalidInput) ;
System.out.println("the first value is " + firstValue) ;
System.out.println("the second value is " + secondValue) ;
```

As before, we read in a line, tokenize it, and try to extract the integer and double values from the characters read. If we succeed, we call a method we have provided called isInputOK to tell us whether or not the two values are acceptable—for example, that each lies in a suitable range and that the combination of the two values is also acceptable. On the basis of the (Boolean) value returned, we set the value of the Boolean variable invalidInput. If this has the value true, we print an error message. In this example, the error message is particularly unhelpful; we should really have made the isInputOK method return much more information about what it doesn't like about the input values, and then we could construct a more helpful error message. We put all this code inside a loop (in this case, a do ... while loop, where the test is at the end), and the code is repeated until the invalidInput variable is set to false, indicating that the values are now acceptable. We can then proceed to make use of the values read in.

We now want to trap the exceptions. We put the conversion of the strings to numeric values inside a try block, and we catch the exception NumberFormatException. If this exception occurs, we want to set the Boolean variable invalidInput to true so that we print the error message and repeat the loop at least one more time.

Since the isInputOK method does not give us any information about which value is erroneous, we have required the user to type both values in again. It might be better:

- To read in the first value, convert that to a number (catching any exceptions), and test that it has a sensible value.

- And then to read in the second value on a new line, convert that to a number (catching any exceptions), and test that it has a sensible value (both considered by itself and considered in combination with the first value).

In this way, we would be able to print more precise error messages and require the user to retype only the minimum of information.

19.4.3 *Redirecting Input*

In Section 19.3.1, we discussed redirection of the System.out stream to a file. On some systems, we can do the same for System.in. Under the Windows and UNIX operating systems, if we run our Java program with

```
java Chapter19n1 <text.data
```

then System.in is connected to the file text.data rather than to the user's keyboard. If we make a BufferedReader from System.in, as we did earlier, we can use the readLine method to read successive lines of characters from this file, using exactly the same mechanism as if the lines came from the user's keyboard. What happens if the program reads past the last line in the file? In this case, the readLine method returns the value null rather than a String. We can test for this if we want:

```
BufferedReader din = new BufferedReader(new
                            InputStreamReader(System.in)) ;
System.err.println("type in some more lines, please") ;
while (true)
    {
    String line = din.readLine() ;
    if (line == null)
        {
        System.err.println("fell off the end of the file") ;
        break ;
        }
    line = line.trim() ;
    if (line.length() == 0)
        break ;
    StringTokenizer st = new StringTokenizer(line) ;
    while (st.hasMoreTokens())
        System.out.println("the token was **" +
                        st.nextToken() + "**") ;
    }
System.out.println("**end of input**") ;
```

We have to check that the value returned is a `String` (rather than `null`) before we can apply the `trim` method to it. The prompt message will still be sent to the user's screen, even though we are reading in from a file. Input redirection is a useful mechanism if we want to read in from either the keyboard or a file. If we know we want to read from a file, it is better to use the `FileReader` facilities discussed in Section 19.6.2.

19.5   Files and File Handling

We now look at the facilities provided by Java to allow us to manipulate, and in particular read data from and write data to, files in the filing system on our computer. We could use the redirection features mentioned in the Sections 19.3.1 and 19.4.3 if they are available on our platform. Or we could use the facilities we have provided as the `BasicFileIo` class to allow simple access to file data. But to do serious work with the file system, we need to understand the facilities that Java provides.

We start with a brief reminder about the structure of the filing system on a computer; for more details, refer to Section 1.6. Useful information is held in *files* in the filing system, and files may be grouped together into *directories* (sometimes called *folders*). When we start to use the system, we will be placed at some position within this tree, the *current directory*, and there will be facilities for making some other directory the current directory. If we want to refer to a file in the current directory, we specify its name. Files in other directories are specified by a *path name* from the current directory or from the filing system's *root directory*.

Java provides a `File` class that allows us to manipulate files as a whole from within a Java program. We start by declaring a variable of this type, specifying the name of the file as an argument to the constructor:

```
File file1 = new File("text1.data") ;
```

This allows us to manipulate a file called `text1.data` in the current directory. There does not actually have to be a file with this name in the current directory; we can find out if there is one with the `exists` method:

```
BufferedReader din = new BufferedReader(new
                                  InputStreamReader(System.in)) ;
System.err.print("type a file name: ") ;
System.err.flush() ;
String fileName = din.readLine().trim() ;
File file1 = new File(fileName) ;
System.err.print("the file '" + fileName) ;
if (file1.exists())
    System.err.println("' exists") ;
else
    System.err.println("' does not exist") ;
```

Similarly, we can find out if we are allowed to read the file (with the `canRead` method) or write to it (with the `canWrite` method) and how long it is (in bytes) with the `length` method. We can find out whether the file is a directory with the `isDirectory` method; if it is, we can get back a list of all the files in it with the `list` method, which returns an array of `Strings` that are the file names in the directory. You will see an example of `isDirectory` and `list` in Section 19.6.2.

When we constructed the `File` instance, we specified the name of a file in the current directory. We could have specified a path name:

```
File file1 = new File("misc/letters/toBeth") ;
```

This assumes that the separator between directory names in the path is /, which is correct for a UNIX system but not a Windows system, where we would write `misc\letters\toBeth`. The Java `File` class provides several constants specifying system-dependent values like this. In particular, it provides a `String` constant `separator`, which specifies the separator between directories in a path on the current platform; thus, we could write:

```
File file1 = new File("misc" + File.separator + "letters" +
                      File.separator + "toBeth") ;
```

There are also `File` constructors with two arguments: the first specifying the directory (either a `File` that we have already constructed or a `String` that is the path name) and the second a `String` representing the name of the file.

Once we have constructed a `File` instance, we can manipulate the file in the filing system with which it is connected. We can

- Delete the file with the `delete` method.

- Rename the file with the `renameTo` method.

- Create a directory with the `mkdir` method (and then presumably go on to create some files in this directory).

19.6   Reading and Writing Files

Of course, what we really want to do is read information from, or write information to, a file. For this, Java provides streams called `FileReader` and `FileWriter`, derived from `Reader` and `Writer`, respectively (Figure 19.14). To make the data easy to manipulate, we usually want to add an extra layer of functionality on top of these types of streams.

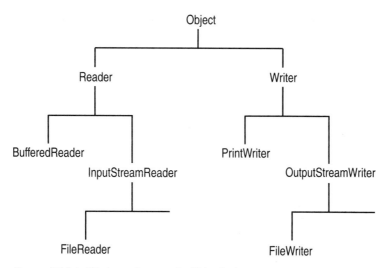

Figure 19.14: File input/output facilities in Java

19.6.1 Writing to a File

We first consider output. We would like to write to a file using the print and println methods described in Section 19.3, but to do this, we have to use the PrintWriter class that provides the same menu of methods rather than the PrintStream class. We provide a PrintWriter via the FileWriter class. Here is an example:

```
BufferedReader din = new BufferedReader(new
                                InputStreamReader(System.in)) ;
System.err.print("type a file name: ") ;
System.err.flush() ;
String fileName = din.readLine().trim() ;
PrintWriter pout = new PrintWriter(new FileWriter(fileName)) ;

int noLines = 0 ;
while (true)
    {
    System.err.print("next line? ") ;
    System.err.flush() ;
    String line = din.readLine().trim() ;
    if (line.length() == 0)
        break ;
    noLines++ ;
    pout.println(noLines + ":" + line) ;
    }
```

```
pout.close() ;
System.err.println(noLines + " lines output to file '" +
                    fileName + "'") ;
```

We obtain a file name (the variable fileName) from the user, and we create a PrintWriter instance pout. We do this by first constructing a FileWriter with the specified file name and then wrapping the functionality of a PrintWriter around it. This will create the file if it doesn't exist or set it to empty and ready to write into if it does exist. If we did not have permission to write to the file, we would get a FileNotFoundException.

We have used a FileWriter constructor that requires a String specifying the file name (or more generally, the path name); another version of the constructor takes a File instance as an argument. Since we have wrapped the PrintWriter functionality around the FileWriter, we can use all the usual print and println methods. Here each line consists of a line number, a colon, and then whatever was typed in by the user. When we have finished, we should use the close method to close the file, breaking the link between the program and the file.

19.6.2   Reading from a File

We now consider input, and we are going to look at the program Chapter19n4.java to display the contents of any specified file. To make it a bit more interesting, we have written a graphical user interface to this program, making use of the menu facilities introduced in the program Chapter16n4.java in Chapter 16. When the user selects the Load button on the menu, the method loadFile is called as before. The full program is available on the Web site (see Appendix A), but loadFile looks like this:

```
private void loadFile()
    {
    FileDialog d = new FileDialog(this, "Load File",
                               FileDialog.LOAD) ;
    d.setVisible(true) ;
    fileName = d.getFile() ;
    directory = d.getDirectory() ;
    try {
        File file = new File(directory, fileName) ;
        if (file.isDirectory())
            {
            String[] list = file.list() ;
            String text = "" ;
            for (int i = 0 ; i < list.length ; i++)
                text += list[i] + "\n" ;
            area.setText(text) ;
            }
        else // file is not a directory
            {
            FileReader file0 = new FileReader(file) ;
            BufferedReader file1 = new
                            BufferedReader(file0) ;
```

```
                String text = "" ;
                while (true)
                    {
                    String line = file1.readLine() ;
                    if (line == null)
                        break ;
                    text += line + "\n" ;
                    }
                file1.close() ;
                area.setText(text) ;
                }
        }
    catch(IOException ex)
        {
        System.err.println("ERROR: " + ex) ;
        }
    } // end of method loadFile
```

As before, the facilities provided by the FileDialog class allow the user to select the name of a file to read (and a directory). We then create an instance of the File class, given the directory and file names supplied by the user (using a version of the File constructor that takes these as two separate String arguments) and find out if it is a directory or a normal file.

If it is a directory, we obtain a list of the names of the files contained in it with the list method. We are going to display this information with an instance of a class TextArea, which allows multiple lines of text to be displayed, scrolling through the text if it is large enough. We have declared area as an instance variable of type TextArea in the class Chapter19n4 (which extends Frame, as usual for graphical interfaces). In the constructor for the Chapter19n4class, we specify that the text area is to have 10 rows and 50 columns:

```
public class Chapter19n4 extends Frame
                                implements ActionListener
    {
    TextArea area ;
    ...

    public Chapter19n4()
        {
        ...
        area = new TextArea(10, 50) ;
        add("Center", area) ;
        } // end of constructor method

    other methods ...
```

When we want something displayed, we call the method setText, passing it the String that we want to display (with \n characters where we want the new lines to start).

If the file is not a directory, we want to read its contents. This time, as an illustration, we first create a FileReader called file0, passing as the argument to the constructor method the

File instance `file` that we have already set up. Then we wrap a `BufferedReader` called `file1` around it to give us the functionality we need.

We read the data from the file using the `readLine` method provided as part of the `BufferedReader` facilities, and we create a suitable string to pass to the `setText` method of the `TextArea` instance. When there are no more lines to read, the `readLine` method returns the value `null` instead of a `String`. If the number of lines warrants it, the `TextArea` instance will allow us to scroll through the file.

If the file did not exist, or it was not readable, the exception `FileNotFoundException` would be thrown. We catch any `IOExceptions` that are thrown (`FileNotFoundException` is derived from `IOException`) and output an error message.

Since we have wrapped a `BufferedReader` around the `FileReader`, all the usual BufferedReader facilities are available. Similarly, all the discussion of `StringTokenizers` in Section 19.4.1 still applies; we could have tokenized each line after reading it in if that had been what we wanted. When we have finished reading the file, we remember to close it with the `close` method.

19.7   Binary Files (Optional)

So far, we have assumed that all the files that we read and write consist of lines of characters. When we read, say, an integer from such a file, we read it as a series of printable characters. We then have to turn them somehow into the binary format in which such numbers are held in the store of the computer (we don't have to do this ourselves; Java supplies methods to allow us to do it). But as discussed in Section 19.1, we could store an `int` value in a file as 4 bytes in a format much closer to how it is held internally.

The streams `DataInputStream` and `DataOutputStream` provide methods for reading and writing data in this binary format. We could write a binary integer:

```
BufferedReader din = new BufferedReader(new
                              InputStreamReader(System.in)) ;
System.err.print("type file to write to ") ;
System.err.flush() ;
String fileName = din.readLine().trim() ;
DataOutputStream dout = new DataOutputStream(new
                              FileOutputStream(fileName)) ;

System.err.print("type integer to write ") ;
System.err.flush() ;
String number = din.readLine().trim() ;
int number1 = Integer.parseInt(number) ;

dout.writeInt(number1) ;
dout.close() ;
```

We construct a suitable `FileOutputStream` and wrap a `DataOutputStream` around it (just as we wrapped a `PrintWriter` around a `FileWriter`). Then we can write an `int` in binary format with the `writeInt` method. There are methods for writing all the other primitive data types; consult the documentation for the `DataOutputStream` class. If we look at this file with a suitable program (not a normal editor because that expects printable characters; on UNIX, we can use the `od` program), we will see that 4 bytes have been written containing the binary value of the integer we specified.

We can read data back from the file in binary format in a similar way, using the `readInt` method of the `DataInputStream` class:

```
BufferedReader din = new BufferedReader(new
                                InputStreamReader(System.in)) ;
System.err.print("type file to read from ") ;
System.err.flush() ;
String fileName = din.readLine().trim() ;
DataInputStream din1 = new DataInputStream(new
                                FileInputStream(fileName)) ;

int number = din1.readInt() ;
System.err.println("the number was " + number) ;
din1.close() ;
```

19.8   Random Access Files (Optional)

We have treated files in the filing system as streams of data; we can start at the beginning of an empty file and write data items one after another to the file. Or we can start at the beginning of the file and read our way through it from beginning to the end (or as far as we want to read). When we open a file, we decide whether we are going to be reading from it or writing to it opening a `FileReader` or a `FileWriter` as appropriate.

But we might need to move around from one part of a file to another to modify the file selectively without visiting all the parts in between. For example, if we imagine a file containing information about a lot of bank accounts and we have to record a deposit or a withdrawal, we would want to go to the part of the file containing that account, read in the information about the account, change the balance, and write the information back to the appropriate part of the file without reading or affecting the other bank accounts in any way.

Java has a class called `RandomAccessFile` that provides this type of access to the data. When we construct an instance of this class, we specify the file (as a `String` or a `File`) and a "mode" that is either `r` (meaning that we can only read the file this time) or `rw` (meaning that we can read and write to the file this time).

We can go to a particular position in the file with a method called `seek`. The position is specified as a number of bytes from the beginning of the file. If we specified the position as the length of the file, we could add new information at the end of the file.

When we have placed ourselves at the appropriate position in the file, we can then read or write information. As we have mentioned, the `RandomAccessFile` class actually implements two interfaces, `DataInput` and `DataOutput`, which are also implemented by the classes `DataInputStream` and `DataOutputStream`. So in fact, we have methods similar to those we have already seen: `readInt`, `writeInt`, and so on. Random access files are discussed in more detail in Chapter 23.

19.9   Accessing Other Computers (Optional)

An important feature of Java is its use over networks of computers, and the language provides a comprehensive range of facilities for communication between one computer and another. This topic is beyond the scope of this book, but we mention the basic features to whet your appetite.

The most basic facility provided by Java is a class `Socket` (in the package `java.net`). We can open a communication link by setting up a `Socket` specifying the name of the computer and the port number we wish to connect to:

```
Socket socket = new Socket(hostName, portNumber) ;
```

We can then construct a character reader or writer around this link (assuming it can be expected to transmit characters) and use the usual methods:

```
BufferedReader stream = new BufferedReader(new
                              InputStreamReader(socket.getInputStream())) ;
String line = stream.readLine() ;
```

Java provides facilities for access to the World Wide Web, and we conclude this chapter with a simple example of this:

```
BufferedReader din = new BufferedReader(new
                              InputStreamReader(System.in)) ;
System.err.print("URL? ") ;
System.err.flush() ;
String urlString = din.readLine().trim() ;

try {
    URL url = new URL(urlString) ;
    BufferedReader stream = new BufferedReader(new
                              InputStreamReader(url.openStream())) ;

    while (true)
        {
        String line = stream.readLine() ;
        if (line == null)
            break ;
        System.out.println(line) ;
        }
    }
catch(IOException ex)
    {
    System.err.println("ERROR: " + ex) ;
    }
```

We request a Uniform Resource Locator (URL) from the user—that is, an address on the Web, such as www.lancs.ac.uk. We then

- Create an instance of the class URL (in the package java.net) using this String.

- Create an input stream to read from this location on the network with the openStream method.

- Wrap a BufferedReader around this input stream to allow us to use the usual facilities.

As before, we now have the usual range of BufferedReader methods. Here we use the readLine method to obtain successive text lines. We are assuming it is a text file, such as a normal Web page of information with interspersed HTML markers.

We need to catch any exceptions thrown by the process of making the connection. For example, if we type in rubbish at the user prompt, we are likely to get a MalformedURLException (derived from IOException).

19.10   Key Points in Chapter 19

- Java provides a host of classes in the package java.io to support input to and output from an application. The main (abstract) classes are InputStream, OutputStream, Reader, and Writer, and a number of useful classes are derived from these fundamental classes.

- System.out is an instance of the PrintStream class, which provides convenient output facilities to the screen. This means that print, println, and flush (all of which we have used with System.out) are actually methods that belong to the PrintStream class.

- In some systems (e.g., UNIX and Windows), we can redirect System.out from the screen to a file using the > symbol. For example,

```
java TestProgram >results
```

places the output from the TestProgram application (everything that is written to System.out) in the file results.

- System.err is another PrintStream instance available to us. Like System.out, this outputs to the screen, but when System.out is redirected, System.err still outputs to the screen. This is useful if the application needs to prompt the user—for example, for an item of input data.

- System.in is an instance of a concrete subclass of InputStream. To use System.in in a convenient way, we need to add functionality by wrapping it in an instance of the BufferedReader class:

```
BufferedReader din = new BufferedReader(new
                         InputStreamReader(System.in)) ;
```

BufferedReader provides a number of useful methods, such as readLine, to read the entire next line as a String.

- It is often useful to split up a line into recognizable tokens (and also to throw away any unwanted whitespace). Java provides the class `StringTokenizer` (in the package `java.util`) to support this:

```
StringTokenizer st = new StringTokenizer(line) ;
if (st.hasMoreTokens())
    {
    String word = st.nextToken() ;
    ...
```

Another version of the StringTokenizer constructor method allows us to choose the characters that separate the tokens.

- To handle the management of files, Java provides the `File` class with the following methods:

- `exists`	finds out if the file exists
- `canRead, canWrite`	finds out if we can read from and write to the file
- `length`	finds out how many bytes long it is
- `isDirectory`	finds out if it is a directory
- `list`	finds out what files a directory holds
- `delete`	deletes a file
- `renameTo`	renames a file
- `mkdir`	creates a new directory

- To read and write files, Java provides the classes `FileReader` and `FileWriter`, respectively. As with `System.in`, it is often useful to wrap instances of these classes as instances of another class that provides additional functionality.

- For example, if we wrap up a `FileWriter` instance within a `PrintWriter` instance, we can use the `print` and `println` methods we are used to:

```
PrintWriter pout = new PrintWriter(new FileWriter(fileName)) ;
...
pout.println("I am writing to the file") ;
...
pout.close()
```

- Similarly, we can wrap a `FileReader` instance within a `BufferedReader` and provide the `readLine` method:

```
BufferedReader fin = new BufferedReader(new
                          FileReader(fileName)) ;
...
String line = fin.readLine() ;
...
fin.close()
```

At the end of the file, readLine returns null.

- The DataInputStream and DataOutputStream classes (derived from InputStream and OutputStream, respectively) provide methods that allow us to read and write the basic Java types in binary—for example, readInt and writeInt for int values.

- In addition to reading and writing data sequentially (i.e., starting at the beginning of the file and working through it, reading or writing data), we sometimes need to have *random* or *direct* access to a file. Java has a RandomAccessFile class that provides this kind of access. In addition to the methods that DataInputStream and DataOutput-Stream provide, there is also a seek method that allows us to change our position within the file as required.

19.11 Exercises

1. Write a program that reads a sentence typed in as a single line at the keyboard and outputs each word on a separate line. This program should not use any of the facilities of the BasicIo class and should use the StringTokenizer class to split the line into words. Words can be assumed to be sequences of nonwhitespace characters separated by whitespace.

2. Write a program that prompts the user to type in the path name of a file and then prints the components of the path one per line. Thus, if the path name is "roger/Java/done/prog1", it should output:

```
roger
Java
done
prog1
```

Modify the program so that it indicates whether the path is *absolute* (it starts with the file separator symbol) or not.

3. Rewrite your solution to Exercise 16.6 (the RegionMap class) so that:

- The argument to the constructor is a BufferedReader rather than a file name (so the driver program will open the appropriate file and wrap it up in a BufferedReader as the actual argument for the constructor method).

- The x- and y-coordinates of each point on the boundary and the name, x- and y-coordinates of each location, should now be held one per line in the file as follows:

```
37
253, 25
238, 25
...
22
Bodmin, 193, 115
Bude, 238, 45
...
```

You should decide what ranges of x- and y-coordinate values are appropriate, and your program should validate the input values accordingly.

4. Write a program that prompts the user for a file name and then outputs whether a file of that name exists in the current directory. If it does, it should also output:

- Whether the file can be read from or written to.

- How long the file is.

- Whether it is a directory.

5. A file contains information about students in a computer programming course. Students have supplied a number of lines of information about themselves, and these have been collected together into a single file. Each student's information should commence with a line consisting only of the word DATA, followed by five lines containing the surname, one or more forenames, the practical class number (in the range 10 to 20), the college (one of Bowland, Lonsdale, Cartmel, County, Furness, Fylde, Pendle, and Grizedale), and the name of the major course. Unfortunately, at the time the students typed in this information, they had not yet learned about the importance of accuracy in data input. You can therefore expect a number of errors in the data supplied, and your program should do as much checking as possible, outputting information about any problems encountered.

Your program should input a file of student information as described and output a list of all students in alphabetical order of surname, a list of students in each practical class, and a list of students in each college.

You should write a short report indicating what types of error your program would be unable to check for.

6. Write a program that reads a file of sales details and prints invoices for the sales. The first version of the program should expect the file to consist of several sets of sales details, one per customer, in the form:

```
SALE sales number
sales date (in the form 4/5/2002)
customer name and address in the form "name / first line of address /
second line of address ..."
number sold, item description, cost per item for the first item
(separated by / characters)
number sold, item description, cost per item for the second item
(separated by / characters)
number sold, item description, cost per item for the third item
(separated by / characters)
...
END
```

Each sales invoice should resemble Figure 19.15.

SALE by Java Industries Ltd

INVOICE NUMBER: 12345

TO: customer,
           address1,
           address2

TODAY'S DATE: 5/6/2002   DATE OF SALE: 4/5/2002

NUMBER	DESCRIPTION	ITEM COST	TOTAL COST	SALES TAX
number of 1st item	description of 1st item	item cost of 1st item	total cost of 1st item	tax on 1st item
number of 2nd item	description 2nd item	item cost of 2nd item	total cost of 2nd item	tax on 2nd item
number of 3rd item	description of 3rd item	item cost of 3rd item	total cost of 3rd item	tax on 3rd item
. . .				
TOTAL		total of this column	total of this column	total of this column

PLEASE PAY: sum of total cost + total sales tax

TERMS: 30 DAYS

Figure 19.15: Sales invoice for Exercise 19.6

Today's date should be obtained from the Java system using the Date class. The user should be prompted for the sales tax rate; it should fall in the range 5% to 10%.

Modify the program so that the sales information gives a code number for each customer and item sold. Details of customers (name and address) and items (description and cost) should be looked up in separate files using these code numbers.

CHAPTER 20

Creating and Using Applets

20.1   Creating Applets

So far, the Java programs we have written have been *applications*. An application runs in a completely *stand-alone* fashion, and the user directly requests the system to start it by typing a command or clicking an icon. Most programs in other languages are applications. Now we are going to look at how to write what the Java system calls *applets*. An applet is a program that can be downloaded across the World Wide Web and run as part of a page displayed by a browser such as Netscape Navigator or Microsoft Internet Explorer.

An applet program is derived from the class `Applet` in the package `java.applet`. The `Applet` class is derived from the `Panel` class, which is part of the Abstract Windowing Toolkit we explored in Chapter 16. An applet is displayed as a panel on the browser page on which it puts appropriate data and through which it reacts to user input.

In Chapter 16, you had an example of drawing a happy face. The program had a Change button with which we could change it to a sad face (and then back again). For our first example of an applet, we will take this AWT example and change it from an application program to an applet. Here is the code for the main part of the applet, the class `Chapter20n1`:

```
import java.awt.* ;
import java.awt.event.* ;
import java.applet.* ;

public class Chapter20n1 extends Applet
                            implements ActionListener
    {
    Canvas1 canvas ;
    Button change ;
    String welcomeName ;
    boolean isSmiling ;

    public void init()
        {
        setLayout(new BorderLayout()) ;
        welcomeName = "World" ;
        isSmiling = true ;
        setBackground(Color.green) ;
```

```
        canvas = new Canvas1(this) ;
        add("Center", canvas) ;

        Panel p = new Panel() ;
        p.setLayout(new FlowLayout()) ;
        change = new Button("Change") ;
        p.add(change) ;
        change.addActionListener(this) ;
        add("South", p) ;
        } // end of method init

    public void actionPerformed(ActionEvent event)
        {
        isSmiling = !isSmiling ;
        canvas.repaint() ;
        } // end of method actionPerformed
    } // end of class Chapter20n1

    ...Canvas1...
```

We start off with a class `Chapter20n1` derived from `Applet` (we have to import the package `java.applet` to make this work). As before, this has four instance variables:

- `canvas`, a reference to an object of the class `Canvas1`, which we will create as part of this program. It will be almost exactly the same as the `Canvas1` class you studied as part of the `Chapter16n1.java` program in Chapter 16. We need to refer to this object because, as before, we have to request that it be redrawn when the Change button is pressed.

- `change`, a reference to the Change button.

- `welcomeName`, a `String` variable to form part of the welcoming message that we are going to write on the screen.

- `isSmiling`, a Boolean variable to remember the current state of happiness of the face.

In the program `Chapter16n1.java`, we had a constructor method for the class `Chapter16n1`, in which we laid out the components we wanted to display, and a `main` method, which called the constructor and set things going. In an applet, we instead write a single method called `init`, and this is called by the browser when the applet is being started. It contains all the initial instructions to lay out the panel to be displayed as follows:

- The class `Chapter16n1` was derived from the `Frame` class, which has a default layout manager `BorderLayout`. We now have to set this explicitly because `Applet` is derived from the `Panel` class, which does not have a default layout manager:

    ```
    setLayout(new BorderLayout()) ;
    ```

- In the earlier program, we obtained a name for the welcoming message from a command-line parameter and passed it as an argument to the constructor. This route is not available for an applet, so for the present, we set `welcomeName` to a default string. Later, we will see how an applet can be passed parameters.

- We initialize the value of isSmiling to true as before.

- We set the background color.

- In the earlier program, we set the title to appear at the top of the window and we specified the initial size of the window. Both of these are set up in a different way for an applet from outside the program.

- We then set up the canvas and the button exactly as before and register that an action is to be performed when the button is clicked. Notice that we have provided only the Change button. We have a different mechanism for stopping an applet when we leave the page on which it is displayed.

- The actionPerformed method needs to deal with only the Change button now. It reverses the value of the isSmiling Boolean variable and requests that the canvas be repainted.

- We no longer need the windowClosing method or the other methods associated with the WindowListener interface.

- Our Canvas1 class is very much as before. It contains a constructor method to store the reference to the Chapter20n1 instance for later use and a paint method. The latter draws the face on the canvas with a mouth shape indicated by the Boolean variable parent.isSmiling and writes a message including the string parent.welcomeName.

20.2 Using Applets

We compile our Java applet in the usual way

```
javac Chapter20n1.java
```

to generate the code file Chapter20n1.class. How are we going to run it? Ultimately, we are going to run it from a browser. For the moment, while we are still debugging the code of our applet, there is a simpler and rather more straightforward mechanism—using a program provided as part of the Software Development Kit (SDK) called the *appletviewer*.

An applet is always invoked (even by the appletviewer) through an HTML page. We write a very simple HTML page, put it in a file, and call it Chapter20n1.html:

```
<html>
<title>
This is my first Applet
</title>
<body bgcolor="ffffff">
<p>
Here is my first example of an applet,
written in the Java programming language,
to display a happy face.
<center><p>
<applet code="Chapter20n1.class" width=500 height=400>
```

```
</applet></center>
<p>
If you click on the "Change" button,
it will change to a sad face;
if you click on it again,
it will change back to a happy face.
That's all it does.
<center><p>
<a href="http://www.lancs.ac.uk/">Click here when you've finished</a>
</center>
</body>
</html>
```

In a page of HTML, portions of text are enclosed in HTML tags. Thus, the text "This is my first Applet" is enclosed between a *begin title* tag `<title>` and an *end title* tag `</title>`, indicating that the text is to be displayed in the browser's title area when this page is being viewed. HTML tags start with the character <, followed by the name of the tag, followed by the character >; end tags have the character / before the tag name. A tag may have one or more *attributes* in the format "attribute name = attribute value". For example, the bgcolor (i.e., background color) attribute of the body tag (indicating what is to be displayed in the main browser window) is set to "ffffff" (i.e., white), and the width attribute of the applet tag is set to 500. For more details on HTML see *Using HTML: The Definitive Guide* by Bill Kennedy and Chuck Musciano (Sebastopol, CA: O'Reilly & Associates, 2000).

Text enclosed in "`<a>` ... `</a>`" tags indicates a link to another page. If we click text enclosed in this way (indicated by an underline when the text is displayed), the browser fetches the page indicated by the href attribute and displays it. Thus, if we click the text "Click here when you've finished", the browser fetches a page from the Web site "www.lancs.ac.uk" (actually Lancaster University's home page) and displays it. The value of the href attribute, the address of a place on the Web, is called a *Uniform Resource Locator (URL)*. It has a standard format. The characters "http:" mean *Hypertext Transfer Protocol*, indicating that the normal Web protocol is to be used for obtaining and displaying this new page. The next part indicates the name of a Web server computer, and there may be a third part that indicates a particular file on the Web server.

The only part of this file that is really required at present is the two lines

```
<applet code="Chapter20n1.class" width=500 height=400>
</applet>
```

because the appletviewer ignores all the rest (the browser won't be so cavalier). This HTML page says that

- An applet is to be run.

- Its code is to be found in the file Chapter20n1.class in the same directory as the HTML page.

- It is to be displayed in an area 500 pixels wide by 400 pixels high (this replaces the call of the `resize` method we used in Chapter 16).

If we now give the command

`appletviewer Chapter20n1.html`

it will display the applet in a window (Figure 20.1) so that we can test whether all its features work.

Figure 20.1: Viewing our first applet with the appletviewer

When we are reasonably satisfied that the applet is free of bugs, we can try running it in earnest. We start a browser and point it at the file `Chapter20n1.html`. Alternatively, we could insert a reference to this file on another HTML page and reach it that way. Whichever way we do this, the browser will display our applet (Figure 20.2), and we can try out the button and see that it works. Unlike the situation with the appletviewer, the browser deals properly with the other information that we put in the file `Chapter20n1.html`. For instance, the `<title>` tag causes the string `"This is my first Applet"` to be displayed in the browser's title area.

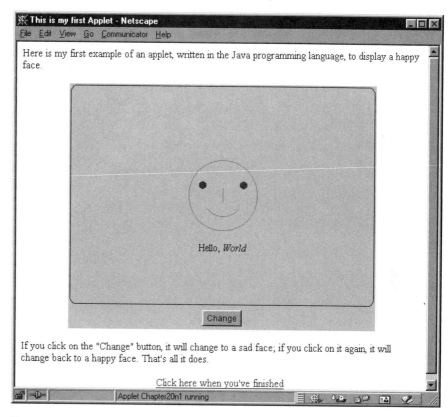

Figure 20.2: Viewing our first applet with a browser

20.3 More about Applets

In the original happy face program in Chapter 16, we were able to pass a string to the program through a command-line parameter. We can do something similar with applets, in that we can put parameters in the HTML page and have the applet read them when it starts. Suppose we rewrite the HTML page with a <param> tag between the <applet> and the </applet> tags:

```
<applet code="Chapter20n1.class" width=500 height=400>
<param name="who" value="Roger">
</applet>
```

Now in the init method, we set up the welcomeName instance variable using the getParameter method as follows:

```
welcomeName = getParameter("who") ;
if (welcomeName == null)
    welcomeName = "World" ;
```

The getParameter method searches for a parameter whose name field is who (it is sensitive to case) and returns the corresponding value field (as a String). In this case, it will return Roger. If it cannot find an appropriately named parameter, it returns the value null. We can have as many parameters as we want as long as they all have different name fields.

We have so far used only the init method for the Applet class. In fact, the Applet class provides four methods that we can override: init, start, stop, and destroy. Let us modify our applet again:

- We add as the first line of our init method the line:

```
System.err.println("call of 'init' method") ;
```

- We add three more methods:

```
public void start()
    {
    System.err.println("call of 'start' method") ;
    } // end of method start

public void stop()
    {
    System.err.println("call of 'stop' method") ;
    } // end of method stop

public void destroy()
    {
    System.err.println("call of 'destroy' method") ;
    } // end of method destroy
```

We now rerun our applet under the browser but with the Java Console window open, so we can see any messages sent to System.err by our applet. We will see that when the applet starts, it calls init and then start. If the browser is not displaying the applet (the browser is iconified or we have moved to a different page), then the stop method is called. When the applet is displayed again, the start method (but not the init method) is called. Finally, the destroy method is called when the browser stops.

Often, we need to write only the init method. But if we are doing some extensive calculation (perhaps we are animating a display), we should stop when the page is not being displayed and start when the page is being displayed again; the stop and start methods allow us to do this.

20.4 A Useful Applet

We are now going to look at a simple but useful applet that displays a copy of any of the source code files for the programs described in this book, as specified by the user of the applet. On the host computer, in the directory that holds the original copy of the HTML page Chapter20n2.html and this applet Chapter20n2.class, we also store:

- A copy of the source text file for each of the programs (e.g., the files `Chapter15n0.java` and `Chapter19n2.java`).

- A list (the file `programList`) of all these text files, with an indication for each one of which chapter it belongs to (sorted into an appropriate order) in this format:

```
chap15/Chapter15n3.java
chap15/Chapter15n4.java
chap15/Chapter15n4a.java
chap15/Chapter15n5.java
chap15/Temperature.java
chap16/PriorityQueue.java
chap16/QueueElement.java
chap16/QueueEmptyException.java
chap17/Chapter17n1.java
chap17/Chapter17n2.java
chap17/Chapter17n3.java
chap17/Chapter17n4.java
```

When the HTML page and the associated applet are downloaded to the user's computer (the *client* computer) and the applet begins to run, it downloads the `programList` file and extracts the appropriate information for the user. When the user has selected a program to look at, the applet downloads that file and displays it. The mechanism is shown in Figure 20.3, and the user's view of the applet is shown in Figure 20.4.

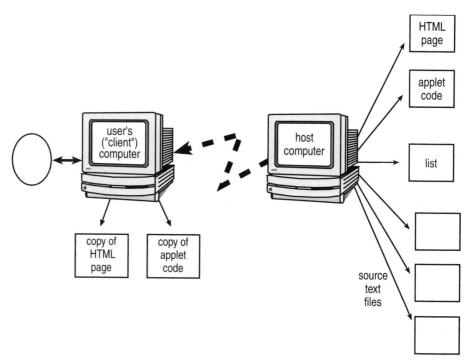

Figure 20.3: The mechanism of the `Chapter20n2` applet

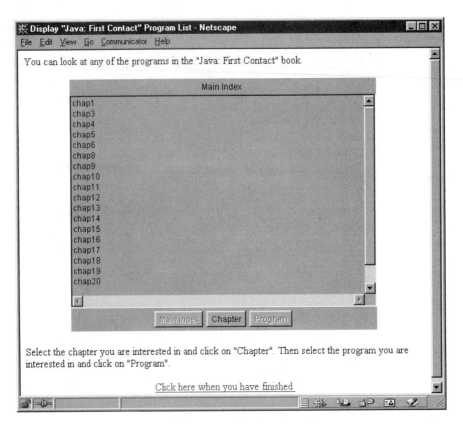

Figure 20.4: The user's view of the `Chapter20n2` applet

There is a central area to display either a list of items that could be displayed or the text of the selected file (this is an instance of the `TextArea` class that you met in the previous chapter), a label at the top to indicate what we are looking at, and three buttons to allow the user to navigate through the information provided. We start with a list of chapters. When the user selects a chapter and clicks the Chapter button, the applet lists all the programs in that chapter. When the user selects a particular program and clicks the Program button, the applet displays the source text of that program.

In some of the examples of using the Abstract Windowing Toolkit in Chapter 16, we would have put these buttons on a menu, allowing them to appear only when needed, but we cannot do that here. A `Menu` instance can be attached only to an instance of a class derived from `Frame`, and applets are derived from the `Panel` class rather than the `Frame` class. Hence, we display the buttons along the bottom of the applet.

We do not give a full listing of the code for the program here because it is given in Appendix D.2. Notice the following points, however:

- This applet uses a lot of facilities provided by six different Java packages, so we need to import all these packages.

- In the class Chapter20n2 (derived from Applet), we have instance variables for all the AWT components that we are going to need to manipulate during the course of the program: the label label at the top of the panel, the text area area in the middle, and the three buttons main, chap, and prog at the bottom.

- In the init method, we first read the file programList from the host computer and set up data structures containing the information; this is done in the private method readIndex, which you will look at shortly. We then specify details of the main panel and add the label, text area, and three buttons in the usual way.

  We want the text to appear in the center of the label field, so we use a version of the Label constructor that allows us to specify this.

- In this applet, we want to ensure that the user can click only the appropriate button or buttons at any particular time. For example, when the applet starts, the user could click the Chapter button but not the Main Index or Program buttons. We therefore disable the first and third buttons with the setEnabled method with the argument set to false; for completeness, we ensure that the Chapter button is enabled with the setEnabled method with the argument set to true. When the applet is displayed, the disabled buttons will appear dimmed and do not react to the user.

20.4.1 *The* readIndex *Method*

In the readIndex method, we first want to read the programList file from the host computer. The standard way to refer to the location of a piece of information on the Web is with a Uniform Resource Locator, or URL. Java therefore provides the URL class (in the package java.net) to model this important feature of Web structure. The method getDocumentBase returns an instance of the URL class that refers to the *document base*—that is, the location on the host computer where the HTML page and other documents can be found. In particular, this is the location of the programList file. There is also a getCodeBase method for returning a URL for the location of the applet code on the host computer if it is different from the document base.

One form of the URL constructor method allows us to specify a URL as context and a String to represent a file within that context. The line

```
URL index = new URL(getDocumentBase(), "programList") ;
```

uses this constructor to create a URL for the file programList within the context returned by the getDocumentBase method. That is, we construct a URL for the file programList in the same directory on the host computer as the original version of the HTML page that caused the applet to be started.

We can then create an instance of the BufferedReader class to read this file

```
BufferedReader stream = new BufferedReader(new
                        InputStreamReader(index.openStream())) ;
```

and then we can read the lines of the file with

```
String line = stream.readLine() ;
```

until we reach a null line.

All sorts of things can go wrong with this process, and this would cause various exceptions to be thrown. For example, the URL that we are trying to set up may not make sense, in which case the MalformedURLException (derived from IOException) would be thrown. Thus, we have to include this code in a try block. If an exception is caught, the program outputs an error message.

From the lines read in, we create two data structures: an array called progs (which contains details of the individual entries in the list) and a String called indexString. The latter is a list of chapter names extracted from the first components of the lines (the part up to the / character). We have made use of the StringTokenizer class to divide each line into the chapter name before the / character and the program name after. We also keep only one version of each chapter name, relying on the fact that the list is in alphabetical order. We use this indexString to set up the text area in the init method.

In this version of the program, we use arrays to hold the information about chapters and programs, and we have to decide an upper limit to the array sizes; we have used the constant MAX_NO_OF_PROGRAMS, which we have set to 200. In Chapter 21, we rewrite the applet using a Java class called Vector, which allows us to ignore the issue of how many programs there are to list.

20.4.2   The actionPerformed Method

We now look at the code of the actionPerformed method. This consists of three sections corresponding to the three buttons. We are going to look in detail at the code corresponding to the Chapter button, which is the only one that is enabled when the applet starts.

The program expects the user to have double-clicked on a particular line of the main index before pressing the Chapter button. The TextArea class provides two methods to enable the program to find out exactly which sequence of characters in the text the user selected. The getSelectionStart method tells us the position of the first character selected within the text string, and the getSelectionEnd method tells us the position of the last character selected within the text string.

The program uses these methods to obtain the position of the selected string of characters within indexString. It then uses information that was stored by the readIndex method in the array progs when indexString was set up to establish which line of the array was indicated and hence the name of the chapter selected. We leave it to you to follow through the code.

We chose to use a TextArea instance to display the list of chapter names and the getSelectionStart and getSelectionEnd methods to establish which one the user is interested in. In fact, Java provides a List class in the AWT to simplify this type of operation, and you could try looking at the API documentation and then modifying the program to use a List.

The program then goes through the original array progs looking for all program source text names belonging to this chapter. It makes a list of these names in an array progs1 and sets up a new text string indexString1 of the names to insert in the text area with the setText method. The contents of the label field at the top of the applet are changed to the chapter name using a setText method belonging to the Label class. Finally, the appropriate buttons are enabled or disabled.

If the Program button is clicked, a sequence of actions takes place that is similar to the actions for the Chapter button. We obtain the start and finish position of the selected text, establish which entry in the `progs1` array corresponds to it, and hence which program file has been specified (in the variable `thisProg`).

We take the file name `thisProg` and construct a URL for this file in the context of the directory given by the `getDocumentBase` method.

```
URL t = new URL(getDocumentBase(), thisProg) ;
```

We open this as a stream and wrap a `BufferedReader` around it:

```
BufferedReader stream = new BufferedReader(new
                            InputStreamReader(t.openStream())) ;
```

Then we read in the lines of the file and display them:

```
while (true)
   {
   String line = stream.readLine() ;
   if (line == null)
       break ;
   ...
```

20.5   Security Aspects of the Use of Applets

A feature that we might like to add to the applet is a Save button so that we could save to a file on our local filing system the source code of any program we find interesting, but we cannot do this. While an applet is running in a browser, a *Security Manager* keeps track of anything the applet might try to do and disallows what has been decided is too dangerous (you can watch the error messages on the Java console in your browser). You should note that the applet viewer is not so careful; it will let your applet do things locally, which the Security Manager on your browser thinks are too dangerous to be done by an applet brought from another site and run on your computer.

An applet running in a browser cannot do either of the following:

1. It cannot read or write to a local file or in fact have any interaction with the local filing system. After all, it might corrupt some of our files, or it might take copies of interesting files and pass them back to the originating site.

2. It cannot in general communicate with any other computer. This is a bit too restrictive. An applet is allowed to communicate with the site where it originated; in fact, we did that in the applet you just looked at. But it cannot access any other computer. If it needs to access other parts of the Net, it will have to communicate with a program on the originating computer, which can then access the Net and pass back information as required.

There are a number of other restrictions, such as not being able to call the `System.exit` method, but these are the main ones.

20.6   Key Points in Chapter 20

- An *applet* is a Java program that can be downloaded across the World Wide Web and is executed as part of a Web page by a Java-aware browser.

- Applets are derived from the Applet class (in the java.applet package), and this class in turn is derived from the Panel class of the Abstract Windowing Toolkit. Applets are thus graphical in nature.

- When an applet starts, the init method is called. This is similar to the constructor method for the class derived from Frame in an AWT program. The main differences are that we do not set the title or size of the window, the default layout manager is FlowLayout, and we cannot use menus.

- Applets are compiled like ordinary Java applications but cannot be executed by the Java interpreter. They are always invoked via an HTML page using the <applet> tag.

- To execute an applet, we can use a Java-aware browser, or during development and testing, we can use the *appletviewer* provided as part of the Software Development Kit (SDK).

- We can pass information from the HTML page to a running applet with the HTML <param> tag.

- We can obtain a URL for the directory containing the HTML page on the originating computer with the getDocumentBase method, and then we can read a file from that location as follows:

```
URL url = new URL(getDocumentBase(), fileName) ;
BufferedReader stream = new BufferedReader(new
                                InputStreamReader(url.openStream())) ;
while (true)
    {
    String line = stream.readLine() ;
    if (line == null)
        break ;
        . . .
```

- Because applets are executed locally on our machine, there are a number of security restrictions on what applets can do. These restrictions include no interaction with our local file system and no communication with Web sites other than the applet's originating site.

20.7   Exercises

1. Take the program Chapter16n2.java (discussed in Chapter 16) to perform temperature conversion between Celsius and Fahrenheit and to display a thermometer and convert it to run as an applet.

2. Revise the task organizer, discussed in Chapter 11, to run as an applet.

3. Write a simple version of a Java applet that would allow a vacationer to access information about accommodations over the World Wide Web. You will be supplied with a file `propertiesList` that contains details of the accommodations for one state in America (in fact, the data supplied are for Kansas), and there will be one line per property. It will contain the location, the price, possibly an indication that the food is vegetarian (indicated by the characters `vegetarian`), the name of the property, and the contact telephone number (all separated by / characters). For example, the file might begin:

```
Topeka / 145 / vegetarian / Shawnee Hotel / 555-1838
Wichita / 72 / Maize Motel / 555-6784
...
```

When the applet is running, it displays a map of the state in question. The user should be able to specify a location (e.g., `Topeka` or `Wichita`) or the word `any` (which matches any location), a range of prices (e.g., $100 to $150), and whether or not they require vegetarian food. The applet should then search the list and display all the matching properties, indicating the location of the property or properties on the map. Figure 20.5 shows a simple version of such an applet.

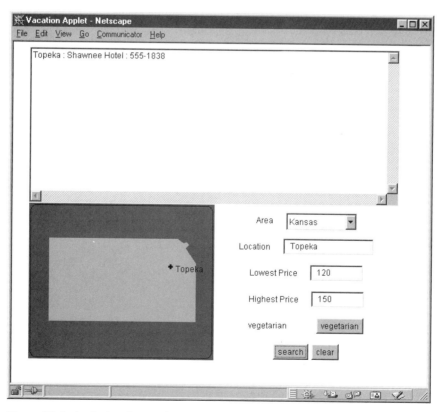

Figure 20.5: A window layout for Exercise 20.3

The task of writing this applet can be broken down into three main parts:

a. A class `PropertiesList` to handle the searching of the list of properties.

b. A class `RegionMap` to handle the drawing and displaying of the map.

c. A class `VacationApplet` derived from the `Applet` class, which handles the overall graphical user interface and calls the methods of the other two classes. In particular, it calls the constructor methods of the other two classes, passing them instances of the `BufferedReader` class representing files of information on the host computer required by these classes. These `BufferedReader` classes should be set up using the `getDocumentBase` method.

Accessing of the `propertiesList` file should be done by the class `PropertiesList` with the following methods:

- `public PropertiesList(BufferedReader din)`. This constructor method reads the properties list from the `BufferedReader` supplied as the argument.

- `public void searchProperties(String location, int lowerPrice, int upperPrice, boolean vegetarian)`. This method sets the arguments for searching the list for properties that match the user's specified location, price range, and vegetarian food requirements.

- `public boolean hasMoreProperties()`. This method indicates whether there are any more properties matching the current search requirements.

- `public PropertyDetails nextProperty()`. This returns the next property matching the current search requirements. It returns an instance of a class `Property-Details`, which should have the methods:

```
public String getLocation()
public String getName()
public String getTelephone()
```

The drawing of the map should be done by the class `RegionMap` (see Exercise 19.3).

CHAPTER 21

Other Features of Java

21.1 Vectors and Other Java Data Structures

In the `Chapter20n2` applet you studied in the last chapter, we needed to store various collections of information such as details of the lines read in over the Web and how they are positioned in the text area. In that example, we used arrays of instances of a class called `ProgramDetails` for this.

But as you know, there is a problem with arrays; we have to decide ahead of time how big the array should be, and we have to make sure we never attempt to exceed this limit. We did not bother to do this in the example program because we knew that we had declared an array size that was going to be big enough (at least for the present), but this is extremely poor programming practice. Before adding an element to the array, we should have first checked that the current number of elements was less than the value `MAX_NO_OF_PROGRAMS`.

Furthermore, if the information had not been sorted into alphabetical order in the original file, we would have wanted to rearrange the elements in the array as we read them in, shuffling the elements around to get them into the correct order. We could alternatively have used a linked data structure, which does not have capacity restrictions and allows insertion into the middle of a list without rearranging the elements on either side.

21.1.1 The Vector Class

In Java, there is another possibility. In the `java.util` package, there is a class called `Vector`, and this provides us with what is essentially an array, but we do not have to worry about capacity restrictions; it reorganizes itself to accommodate new elements. Furthermore, it provides methods for conveniently inserting elements in the middle of the `Vector` without the user having to worry about shuffling other elements to make room. Why have we not revealed the existence of the `Vector` data structure to you before so that you could avoid learning about arrays and linked lists? There are a couple of reasons:

- Many languages do not provide an equivalent of the `Vector` data structure, although they do have equivalents of arrays and (usually) the means to construct linked data structures. Thus, to ensure that you have programming skills that transfer to other languages, you need to have studied these other features.

- There are some issues in the use of `Vectors` (and some of the other data structures provided by Java) that require you to know about the Java class hierarchy and how to cast objects from one type to another.

We start the new version of the `Chapter20n2` code by creating an instance `mainIndex` of the `Vector` class:

```
Vector mainIndex = new Vector() ;
```

We do not have to say anything about the expected maximum size of the `Vector`. If we wish, we could specify an initial size or an initial size and a size of *increment*—that is, how many new positions to allocate to the `Vector` each time the system makes it bigger. But if we do not specify these, the `Vector` will organize them behind the scenes.

We can now add elements (instances of the class `ProgramDetails`) to the `Vector` with the `addElement` method; this adds the element to the end of the `Vector` (Figure 21.1):

```
ProgramDetails newPD = new ProgramDetails(firstString,
                        secondString, firstMarker, secondMarker) ;
mainIndex.addElement(newPD) ;
```

or

```
mainIndex.addElement(new ProgramDetails(firstString,
                        secondString, firstMarker, secondMarker)) ;
```

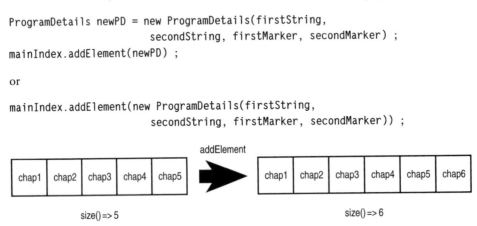

Figure 21.1: Using `addElement` on a `Vector`

At any time, we can find out how many elements are in a `Vector` with the method `size`. The elements stored in the `Vector` are numbered from 0 to 1 less than the value returned by `size`. Some things we can do with a `Vector` are:

- We can add an element into the `Vector` at position i (Figure 21.2) with the `insertElementAt` method (shuffling up the elements currently at i ... `size()-1`):

  ```
  mainIndex.insertElementAt(newPD, i) ;
  ```

  The second argument must be in the range 0 to `size`. If it is equal to `size`, this is equivalent to a call of `addElement`.

insertElementAt(... , 2)

| chap1 | chap2 | chap3 | chap4 | chap5 |

| chap1 | chap2 | chap2a | chap3 | chap4 | chap5 |

Figure 21.2: Using `insertElementAt` on a `Vector`

- We can change the element at a particular position (Figure 21.3) with the setElementAt method, discarding the element that was previously there:

```
mainIndex.setElementAt(newPD, i) ;
```

The second argument must be in the range 0 to 1 less than size.

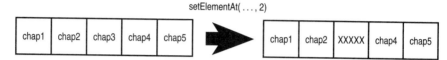

Figure 21.3: Using setElementAt on a Vector

- We can delete an element from the Vector (Figure 21.4) with the removeElementAt method:

```
mainIndex.removeElementAt(i) ;
```

The argument must be in the range 0 to 1 less than size. All elements with a higher index value are shifted down.

Figure 21.4: Using removeElementAt on a Vector

At some point, we want to look at an element in the Vector, say, at position i, with the elementAt method:

```
ProgramDetails tempPD = mainIndex.elementAt(i) ;
```

Unfortunately, this does not work. You will have noticed that when we set up the Vector in the first place, we did not specify that it was a Vector of ProgramDetails instances, as we would if we had been declaring an array. In fact, a Vector is a Vector of Objects, and (using polymorphism) we can insert Objects of any type into a Vector. But when we want to extract an element, as we do in the preceding statement, we are trying to copy an instance of the Object class to a variable that holds references to instances of the class ProgramDetails, and the Java compiler will not let us do this. We have to *cast* the object that we get back from the Vector to the correct type:

```
ProgramDetails tempPD = (ProgramDetails) mainIndex.elementAt(i) ;
```

This means that when this statement is executed, a check will be made that the object returned from the Vector is from the class ProgramDetails. If it is, it can be assigned to the variable tempPD. But if it is not, a ClassCastException will be thrown.

You can see that this is not entirely satisfactory. If we have two `Vectors` for different types of objects, and by mistake we add an instance of one type to the `Vector` that is to hold instances of the other type, then we will not discover it until we try to extract the element and get a `ClassCastException`. The compiler has nothing to say about it, because all it knows about a `Vector` is that it is a `Vector` of `Objects` so that the extraction of an instance of any class is perfectly legitimate. Similarly, adding the offending element to the `Vector` is acceptable because it is clearly an `Object`. What can we do about this?

- In some languages (e.g., Ada and C++), there is an extra feature to deal with this problem. In these languages, it is possible to specify, for example, what it means for a `Vector` to hold elements of type SOMETHING, even though we have not defined exactly what that SOMETHING is. We can then write all the methods for the class `Vector` assuming that the elements are of this type; for example, the `addElement` method takes an argument of type SOMETHING, and `elementAt` returns an element of type SOMETHING. Then, at some later stage, we can say that we require a `Vector`, and at that point, we have to specify what type the SOMETHING is (we might specify it earlier, but we certainly don't have to specify it when we first define what a `Vector` is). Then the compiler can check that any element being inserted into or extracted from the `Vector` is of the specified type. This feature (which is sometimes called *genericity*) is not available in Java.

- We could ensure that the `ClassCastException` does not occur by inserting program checks that an object taken from a `Vector` is the appropriate type and taking suitable action. This would make use of some of the features to be discussed briefly in Section 21.3. But there are problems with this: (a) the checking is still being done while the program is running rather than (much more safely and cheaply) while the program is being compiled; (b) the programmer has to insert the tests explicitly; and (c) it is not clear what the "suitable action" would be, except to stop the program with an error message.

- We could build a new derived class `VectorOfProgramDetails` and write versions of all the relevant methods that would have the `Vector` element as type `ProgramDetails`. But this is a lot of work, and it is work that is in principle redundant (except for security) because the code of the original `Vector` class contains all the relevant coding details.

- The final possibility is that we ensure as programmers that we are aware of this problem and are just very careful. But this is not entirely satisfactory. In fact, this is an area where the Java language does not really provide a fully satisfactory way of dealing with the problem of genericity.

In our new version of the `Chapter20n2` applet, we have searched through a `Vector` looking for entries for a particular chapter using a `for` loop:

```
for (int i = 0 ; i <mainIndex.size() ; i++)
    {
    ProgramDetails current = (ProgramDetails) mainIndex.elementAt(i) ;
    ...
```

In fact, the `Vector` class (like many of the data structures provided by Java) has a method called `elements` that returns an object which implements an interface called `Enumeration` (in the package `java.util`). This interface specifies that there will be two methods, `hasMoreElements` and `nextElement`, that enable us to look at each element in turn of the underlying data structure. We could rewrite the preceding loop:

```
Enumeration enum = mainIndex.elements() ;
while (enum.hasMoreElements())
    {
    ProgramDetails current = (ProgramDetails) enum.nextElement() ;
    ...
```

The enumeration returns an `Object`, so we have to cast it to the correct type, as before. This is rather like the `hasMoreTokens`/`nextToken` methods of the `StringTokenizer` class, but with those methods, an object of a particular type (a `String`) was returned.

The `Vector` class also provides a selection of methods for searching a `Vector` for an element that matches an `Object` supplied as an argument.

We have discussed and implemented versions of a *stack,* or last-in, first-out store, where the elements are held like a stack of plates in a cafeteria with access only to the top plate. Java provides a `Stack` data structure, derived from `Vector`, which implements the usual "push" and "pop" methods. Note that it is a `Stack` of `Objects`.

The `Vector` and `Stack` classes (and the `Hashtable` class discussed in the next section) have been available since the earliest versions of Java. More recent versions (from Version 1.2 onward) have generalized these into an interface called `Collection` (in the `java.util` package) for a general collection of objects and its subinterfaces `List` (where there is order among the objects) and `Set` (where there are no duplicates). The `java.util` package then provides various classes that implement these interfaces; for example, an `ArrayList` implements the `List` interface and is rather like a `Vector`.

21.1.2 *The* Hashtable *Class*

Another useful data structure is a `Hashtable`. Here we can store an element together with an associated key value and then recover the element by quoting its key value:

```
Hashtable ht = new Hashtable() ;
ht.put("shakespeare", new PersonDates(1564, 1616)) ;
ht.put("austen", new PersonDates(1775, 1817)) ;
ht.put("dickens", new PersonDates(1812, 1870)) ;
ht.put("trollope", new PersonDates(1815, 1882)) ;
ht.put("bronte", new PersonDates(1818, 1848)) ;
ht.put("eliot", new PersonDates(1819, 1880)) ;
...
```

We declare a `Hashtable`. If we wished, we could have specified an initial capacity and a *load factor* (a number in the range 0.0 to 1.0, which specifies the point at which the system should make the `Hashtable` larger).

We use the `put` method to add an element (here an object of type `PersonDates`) and its key value (here a `String`) to the `Hashtable`. We cannot use anything as a key for a `Hashtable`; it has to be an object instance (e.g., a `String`). This is because the `Hashtable` applies two methods (`equals` and `hashcode`) to the key; since both of these methods are provided in the `Object` class, and every class inherits from `Object`, the code of the `Hashtable` class can safely invoke these methods.

We have been a bit cavalier in that the `Hashtable` stores only one element with any particular key value. If we try and store a second element with this key value, it will indeed store it but will return the element previously stored with this key value (rather than `null`). We should therefore check the return value:

```
PersonDates result = (PersonDates) ht.put("bronte",
                              new PersonDates(1816, 1855)) ;
if (result != null)
    System.err.println("duplicate information") ;
```

We can extract information with the `get` method quoting a key. We have to cast the object returned to the appropriate type, and the previous discussion about genericity applies here. A value `null` is returned if there is no entry for this key value.

```
BasicIo.prompt("type author's name ") ;
BufferedReader din = new BufferedReader (new InputStreamReader (System.in)) ;
String name = din.readLine().trim() ;
PersonDates p = (PersonDates) ht.get(name) ;
if (p == null)
    System.err.println("I have no information about " + name) ;
else
    System.err.println(name + " was born in " +
                    p.getBirthDate() + " and died in "
                    + p.getDeathDate()) ;
```

We can remove an element with a particular key from the hash table (with `remove`), and we can remove all the elements (with `clear`). If we want to scan all the elements in a `Hashtable`, we can use the `Enumeration` interface, as with the `Vector`:

```
Enumeration hashElements = ht.elements() ;
Enumeration hashKeys = ht.keys() ;
while (hashKeys.hasMoreElements())
    {
    System.out.print(hashKeys.nextElement()) ;
    PersonDates p1 = (PersonDates) hashElements.nextElement() ;
    System.out.println(" was born in " + p1.getBirthDate() +
                    " and died in " + p1.getDeathDate()) ;
    }
```

There is also a class called `Properties`, derived from `Hashtable`, where both the key and element are of type `String`. It has additional methods to load a property list from a file (or more generally, an `InputStream`) and output them to an `OutputStream`.

21.2 Strings **and** StringBuffers

So far, when we have wanted to handle strings of characters, we have used the String class, which is the standard way of manipulating strings in Java. As long as we want to treat strings as single complete entities, or perhaps just inspect the individual characters (with the charAt method), the String class is adequate.

However, if we want to change individual characters of a String, we have a problem because the instances of the String class are *immutable*—that is, we cannot change them in any way. If, for example, we want to change the i th character of the String s0 to the character 'X', we have to do something like:

```
s0 = s0.substring(0, i) + 'X' + s0.substring(i + 1) ;
```

We use the substring method and the concatenate operator to create a completely new String, and then the reference to this String is assigned to the variable s0. At some later stage, Java's garbage collector will realize that there is no reference to the original String, so its storage area will then be recovered. This is obviously an inconvenient mechanism for the programmer to use. It is also an inefficient way for Java to manipulate strings of characters because it has to create a completely new String and recover the old one even if only one character is changed.

Thus, Java provides the StringBuffer class (in the java.lang package) for use if we are planning to do extensive modification to a string of characters:

- We start by using a StringBuffer constructor method to construct a StringBuffer instance out of a String. Hence, if line is a String (perhaps read in from a file), we generate a StringBuffer instance containing the same characters:

```
StringBuffer line1 = new StringBuffer(line) ;
```

- We can find out the number of characters in the StringBuffer with the length method:

```
System.out.println("there are " + line1.length() + "
                    characters") ;
```

- We can inspect individual characters in the StringBuffer with the charAt method, just as with a String (character numbering starts at 0):

```
if (line1.charAt(5) == '0')
    ...
```

- Unlike the String class, we can change the character at a particular position with the setCharAt method:

```
line1.setCharAt(i, 'X') ;
```

- We can insert a character at a particular position (shuffling the rest of the characters up) or append a character at the end with the insert and append methods:

```
line1.insert(j, 'Y') ;
line1.append('Z') ;
```

- Finally, we can convert the StringBuffer instance back to a String with the toString method:

```
line = line1.toString() ;
```

21.3 Run-Time Type Information (Optional)

While a Java program is running, it keeps track of the type of all the objects that exist at any particular time. It is sometimes useful to find out the class of an object so that the appropriate action can be taken. Suppose we have a method, one of whose arguments could be an instance of any of a number of different classes (so we declare it as of type Object). We can use the operator instanceof (which returns a Boolean value) to test at run time to see what type the argument is:

```
public static void funnyMethod(Object x)
    {
    if (x instanceof String)
        {
        System.err.println("It was a String **" + x + "**") ;
        }
    else if (x instanceof Integer)
        {
        System.err.println("It was an Integer **" + x + "**") ;
        }
    else
        {
        System.err.println("It was something else **" + x + "**") ;
        }
    } // end of method funnyMethod
```

We are relying here on the fact that any object has or inherits a method toString, which the println method can call to obtain printable information from the object. Here is a main method to call funnyMethod:

```
public static void main(String[] args)
    {
    funnyMethod("Hello, World") ;
    funnyMethod(new Integer(42)) ;
    funnyMethod(new Date()) ;
    } // end of method main
```

We could not have written funnyMethod(42) because this would be an actual argument of type int, which (unlike Integer) is not derived from Object.

The class `Object` has a useful method `getClass`, which can tell us the class of an instance. It actually returns an instance of the class `Class`, which has a method `getName` that returns the name of the class. Thus, we could write in our `funnyMethod`:

```
. . .
else
    {
    System.err.println("It was a " +
                    x.getClass().getName() + " **" + x + "**") ;
    }
} // end of method funnyMethod
```

These features of Java are quite useful to find out what type an instance might be when debugging a program. But it is extremely poor practice to make extensive use of them in programming because it is against the spirit of polymorphism, and we are evading many of the type checks that the Java compiler helpfully provides.

21.4 Threads (Optional)

If you watch carefully when your browser is loading in a new page, you may see that when there is an image to be loaded, the rest of the page is displayed and the image appears a bit later, chunk by chunk. It looks as if what is happening is that the browser continues to look after its principal task, displaying the main features of the page, and delegates a separate task to another program, which obtains the image data from the host site and displays it as it arrives. Similarly, if we request that something is printed, the browser will delegate this task to another program and in the meantime carry on as before, dealing with user input and so on.

This is a general and common feature of a modern computer system. We can have several separate "things" going on effectively at the same time. There are a number of different terms for these things that can be executing simultaneously. The terms *process* and *task* are often used, but the Java term is *thread*. When the browser needs to display an image, it starts a separate thread to do this, and then the main thread of the browser carries on as before to display the rest of the page (and if another image appears, another thread could be started).

How the computer deals with having several threads around at the same time depends on exactly how the system is set up. The most likely scenario is that the computer will in fact execute only one of the threads at a time but will share its attention to each thread in turn so that they all make reasonable progress with the tasks that have been delegated to them. In some systems, the computer executes a thread until it voluntarily decides it has done enough for the present (perhaps it has requested a remote computer for the next piece of data and is awaiting the result), at which point the computer chooses another thread to run for a bit. In this case, the threads have to be cooperative and voluntarily relinquish control from time to time. Other systems use *preemptive scheduling*, where each thread gets a share of the time available, and it then loses control to another thread whether or not it has reached a "natural break." Finally, some systems contain several processing units so that more than one thread can actually be executed at the same time.

Many modern programming languages provide some sort of mechanism to allow the programmer to specify that two or more tasks can be carried on at the same time and to specify how the several tasks can pass information back and forth between them. The fact that Java supports *multithreading* is one of the important features of the usefulness of the language. However, writing programs where the different parts can operate in parallel is a complex problem because we have to ensure that the interactions between the several parts take place in a disciplined manner. The Java features for multithreading are therefore beyond the scope of this book.

In this section, we demonstrate a simple program that executes multiple threads, and we indicate one of the common pitfalls and how Java deals with it. For more information on multithreading in Java, see *Core Java* by Gary Cornell and Cay S. Horstmann (SunSoft Press, 1996) or *Exploring Java* by Patrick Niemeyer and Joshua Peck (Sebastopol, CA: O'Reilly & Associates, 2000).

We start with a program that does not have multiple threads. We have a class `ProcessString` with a single instance variable `originalString`. This variable is set to a suitable value from an argument passed to its constructor method when we declare an instance of the class:

```
class ProcessString
    {
    private String originalString ;

    public ProcessString(String string)
        {
        originalString = string ;
        } // end of constructor method

    OTHER METHODS

    } // end of class ProcessString
```

The class has a method `run` that consists mainly of a loop that goes on forever. In this loop, we convert the "next" character of `originalString` to uppercase, display it on the screen, wait for a second, and repeat.

The waiting is done by calling a method `sleep` (in the `Thread` class) with one argument, the length of time in milliseconds to sleep. The `Thread` class is in the `java.lang` package, so we do not need any `import` statement for this. When the program has slept that period of time, it is woken up by an `InterruptedException`; thus, we put the call of the `sleep` method into a `try` block and catch the result. The corresponding `catch` does nothing but allows us to proceed around the loop.

```
public void run()
    {
    int offset = 0 ;
    while (true)
        {
        String s = originalString.substring(0, offset) +
```

```
                            Character.toUpperCase(originalString.charAt(offset)) +
                            originalString.substring(offset + 1) ;
              System.out.println("**" + s + "**") ;
              offset++ ;
              if (offset == originalString.length())
                  offset = 0 ;
              try {
                  Thread.sleep(1000) ;
                  }
              catch (InterruptedException e)
                  {
                  }
              }
      } // end of method run
```

The main method (in a class Chapter21n4) sets up an instance of the ProcessString class with a suitable string and gets it going by calling its run method:

```
public class Chapter21n4
    {
    public static void main(String[] args)
        {
        ProcessString p1 = new ProcessString("lancaster") ;
        p1.run() ;
        } // end of method main
    } // end of class Chapter21n4
```

If we run this program, it will keep writing to the screen

```
**Lancaster**
**lAncaster**
**laNcaster**
**lanCaster**
**lancAster**
**lancaSter**
**lancasTer**
**lancastEr**
**lancasteR**
**Lancaster**
**lAncaster**
...
```

until we stop it (with Ctrl + C or something similar). Figure 21.5 is a sketch of what is happening.

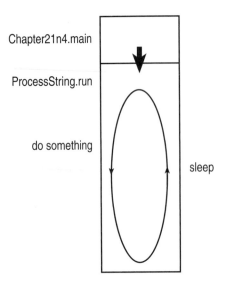

Figure 21.5: Executing `Chapter21n4`: A single thread

Now we are going to make the `ProcessString` class run as a thread separate from the `main` method (which we will modify to do something, so we can see that multithreading is indeed taking place). If we want to treat a class as a thread, it must implement an interface called `Runnable`, which requires that we have a method (with no arguments and no return value) called `run`. We have already done this, so we can rewrite the beginning of this class:

```
class ProcessString implements Runnable
    {
    private String originalString ;
    ...
```

Then we have to turn the class into a thread, which we do in its constructor method:

```
public ProcessString(String string)
    {
    originalString = string ;

    Thread thisThread = new Thread(this) ;
    thisThread.start() ;
    } // end of constructor method
```

This uses the `Thread` constructor to make a thread out of this instance of the class `ProcessString` and stores a reference to it in the variable `thisThread`. Then we get it going with a call of the method `start` belonging to the `Thread` class.

Back in the `main` method of the `Chapter21n4` class, we set up an instance of the `ProcessString` class as before. However, we no longer need to call its `run` method. When we call the constructor for ProcessString, it calls the start method, and this eventually calls the run method (it knows that there will be one because that is guaranteed by the fact that ProcessString implements the Runnable interface). All the main method has to do is carry on, doing something "useful." We wait in an infinite loop, displaying the message "Hello again" every 5 seconds:

```
public class Chapter21n4
    {
    public static void main(String[] args)
        {
        ProcessString p1 = new ProcessString("lancaster") ;

        while (true)
            {
            System.out.println("Hello again") ;
            try {
                Thread.sleep(5000) ;
                }
            catch (InterruptedException e)
                {
                }
            }
        } // end of method main
    } // end of class Chapter21n4
```

If we run this, we get something like the following

```
Hello again
**Lancaster**
**lAncaster**
**laNcaster**
**lanCaster**
**lancAster**
Hello again
**lancaSter**
**lancasTer**
**lancastEr**
**lancasteR**
**Lancaster**
Hello again
**lAncaster**

...
```

until we stop it. Figure 21.6 is a sketch of what is happening now.

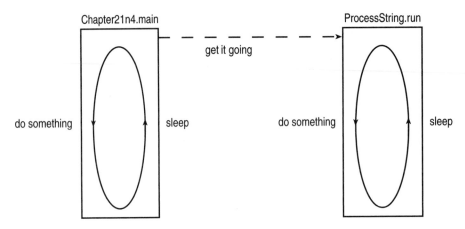

Figure 21.6: Executing `Chapter21n4`: Two threads

Now try changing the beginning of the `Chapter21n4` code to set up several separate `ProcessString` instances:

```
public class Chapter21n4
    {
    public static void main(String[] args)
        {
        ProcessString p1 = new ProcessString("lancaster") ;
        ProcessString p2 = new ProcessString("preston") ;
        ProcessString p3 = new ProcessString("kendal") ;

        while (true)
            {
            ...
```

If we compile and run this, we get

```
Hello again
**Lancaster**
**Preston**
**Kendal**
**lAncaster**
**pReston**
**kEndal**
**laNcaster**
**prEston**
**keNdal**
**lanCaster**
**preSton**
**kenDal**
```

```
**lancAster**
**presTon**
**kendAl**
Hello again
**lancaSter**

...
```

and so on. The execution of the three `ProcessString` threads and the `main` thread are all interleaved (Figure 21.7).

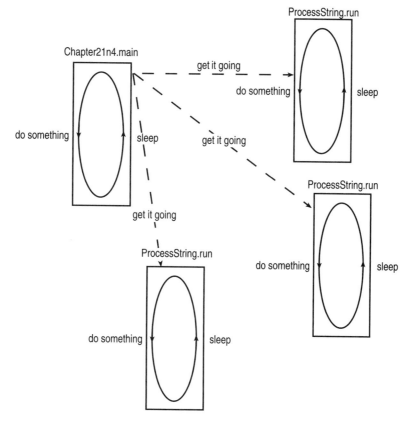

Figure 21.7: Executing `Chapter21n4`: Four threads

21.4.1 Synchronizing Threads

There is a problem with running several threads at the same time. In this simple program, each thread was totally independent and did not need to interact with any other thread or with any shared information. But a more serious use of threads might have a `run` method looking like this:

```
public void run()
    {
    while (true)
        {
        chooseTaskFromCommonTable() ;
        doTheTask() ;
        go to sleep for a bit ;
        }
    } // end of method run
```

We imagine a common task table where all the threads look from time to time to choose the next task, remove the task from the table, and then do it. But suppose two threads both try to look at the task table at the same time. They might both choose the same task and both try to do it.

We need to make sure that, while one thread is in the chooseTaskFromCommonTable method, no other thread can get into it until the first one has finished choosing a task, removed it from the table, and left the method. To ensure orderly entry to such a method, Java provides the keyword synchronized:

```
synchronized void chooseTaskFromCommonTable()
    {
    ...
    } // end of method chooseTaskFromCommonTable
```

This tells the Java system that only one thread is allowed to be in the method at a time. Any other threads wanting to enter must form an orderly queue and enter one at a time, when the preceding thread has finished.

21.5 Key Points in Chapter 21

- A Vector is a dynamic data structure supplied by Java. It allows us to maintain a heterogeneous collection of objects. We can think of it as an array that can grow and shrink as required; it also allows insertion of elements at specified locations without the need to shuffle elements.

- When we extract an element from a Vector, it is a reference to an Object, and we must cast it to the appropriate class if we are to use that element correctly.

- If we wish to process the elements of a Vector sequentially, we can use the elements method to return an Enumeration instance. Subsequently, we can use the hasMoreElements and nextElement methods to process the elements (which again have to be cast to the correct class).

- A Stack class is available, derived from Vector, with additional "pop" and "push" methods.

- A Hashtable class is also available. We can store data elements with an associated key using put and can retrieve elements later using get by supplying the appropriate key. If we put two elements with the same key value, the first is replaced by the second.

- If we wish to manipulate a string of characters, we can convert it from a String to a StringBuffer. The methods charAt and setCharAt allow us to inspect and modify individual characters, and the toString method allows us to convert the StringBuffer back to a String.

- At run time, we can find out the class that an instance belongs to by using the instanceof operator.

- It is often the case that computer systems run separate "things" at apparently the same time. These things are commonly known as *processes* or *tasks*; in Java, the term is *threads*.

- It is possible to write a class and make it into a thread so that we can arrange to have several parts of our program all running at the same time.

21.6   Exercises

1. We implemented our PriorityQueue class in Chapters 11 and 17 as a single queue ordered by the priority (and within the priority, in a first-in, first-out manner). Assume there are only four priority levels (1 = Urgent, 2 = High, 3 = Medium, 4 = Low).

   Reimplement the PriorityQueue as four Vectors, one for each level of priority. Make sure the details of your implementation are completely hidden from the class user.

   Implement methods deleteElement and changePriority for this class. You specify a queue element to be deleted, or whose priority is to be changed, by giving a version of the String held in the element. Your program should not require an exact match between the two Strings; "matching" Strings should be allowed to differ at least in the number of spaces and the capitalization.

2. In Exercise 15.2, you used an array to implement a stack of characters as a class CharacterStack. In Exercise 17.1, you reimplemented it as a linked list.

   This time implement it using the Java Stack class, still presenting the same CharacterStack methods to the outside world. Test it with your driver program.

3. A British postcode is a string of characters that generally corresponds to a particular range of houses in a particular street in a particular town. Many service firms today, when receiving a telephone call, first ask the caller for their postcode. They look this up, confirm the street and town name with the caller, and then ask the caller for their house number, which can be checked against the range given by the postcode.

   Write an applet that, when started, reads a file of information from the host computer where each line is in the form:

   postcode / first house number / last house number / street / town

   The applet should set up a Hashtable with this information and then display the appropriate piece of information for the user when they type in a postcode.

4. Write a Java program that *justifies* the text in a file so that it has smooth left and right margins. That is, the program should rearrange the text in the file so that all the lines (except possibly the last in each paragraph) are the same length.

The program should prompt the user for (a) the name of the file containing the text to be arranged, (b) the name of the file to contain the justified text, and (c) the required number of characters per line of text.

Paragraphs in the input file are marked by an empty line or one containing only spaces. No word in the input file should be longer than 20 characters, and the number of characters per line specified by the user should be in the range 40 to 100 characters, but your program should check both of these constraints.

No line in the output file should contain more than the specified number of characters. Normally, there should be a single space between one word and the next on the line, but extra spaces should be added so that the line has the correct number of characters (unless it is the final line of a paragraph).

As an example, if the user specified 50 characters, and the input file began

```
Introduction: Objects   and   Classes

Object-orientation         (or OO)
is a technique which      has pervaded
all aspects of computer science over the past decade or so.

Object-oriented ways of thinking have been applied to software
system design,       operating systems, programming languages
and database    systems, to name but a few areas       impacted
by this recent    technology. In this chapter, we will
introduce some of the basic concepts of object-orientation.
```

the output file should begin like this

```
Introduction: Objects and Classes

Object-orientation (or OO) is a technique which
has pervaded all aspects of computer science over
the past decade or so.

Object-oriented ways of thinking have been applied
to  software  system  design,  operating  systems,
programming  languages  and  database  systems,  to
name  but  a  few  areas  impacted  by  this  recent
technology.  In  this  chapter,  we  will  introduce
some of the basic concepts of object-orientation.
```

PART 5

Object-Oriented Design

22 Object-Oriented Design

23 Case Study: Implementing the
Personal Organizer 1

24 Case Study: Implementing the
Personal Organizer 2

25 Criteria for a Good Object-Oriented
Design

CHAPTER 22

Object-Oriented Design

22.1 Software Engineering

In this part of the book, we address issues of object-oriented design. Before concentrating on this particular aspect of programming, we need to examine design in the wider context of software engineering and the software life cycle.

Ever since the identification of a software "crisis" in the late 1960s, it was realized that a new engineering approach to the building of large-scale software systems was required. The increase of hardware power (both in speed and size) made it possible to envision large and powerful software systems. However, it was as if someone capable of creating an artifact that allowed people to cross a small body of water (a wooden plank across a stream) was now being asked to build a bridge across a large body of water (the railway bridge over the Mississippi River or the Firth of Forth) using the same techniques.

The problem is one of scale. Just as we would never expect a structural engineer to approach these two problems in the same way, it was clear that programmers couldn't expect the same techniques that allow us to build programs with hundreds of lines of code to scale up to hundreds of thousands of lines. Thus, the discipline of *software engineering* was born.

To give a simple example of why such practices came into being, consider a large software system. These systems have upwards of a quarter of a million lines of code. Typical examples include:

- Stock exchange trading systems
- Production line control systems
- Emergency command and control systems
- Insurance proposal systems
- Telephone switching systems (4 million lines of code)
- Spreadsheets (half a million lines of code)

In terms of person years of effort needed to create one of these systems, it is clear that no one person (or even a small team of people) could hope to build it. It is also clear that no one person would be able to understand the detailed working of the system. The age-old problem-solving technique of "divide and conquer" comes into play. There will be an overall architectural design in place, which in turn will be divided into subsystems. Subsystems in turn may be fragmented into a logical set of smaller subsystems. We continue this process until we arrive at a level of subsystem that a few people (a small group) will be able fully to design, implement, and test.

Each subsystem should present a "simple" and clearly defined interface to the other subsystems. This enables us to construct the overall system from these building blocks.

22.2   The Software Life Cycle

Most introductory books on programming focus on the coding of rather small programs; we have been in the position of the person placing a plank across a stream. The problems we have faced have not been overwhelmingly large; they have been well within the capability of one person to solve. In large-scale systems, it is easier to see that there are a number of phases that the creation of a software artifact passes through. In our small problems, we have gone through all of these phases, but you may have done this so quickly that you scarcely noted their existence.

The collection of phases is known as the *software life cycle*. For the purposes of this book, we present one of the earliest and simplest versions: the *waterfall* model (Figure 22.1). The software process is generally more complicated than this model depicts; however, it does describe the broad phases that software development follows and is sufficient for our present needs.

The model consists of the following steps:

- Requirements
- Design
- Coding
- Testing
- Maintenance

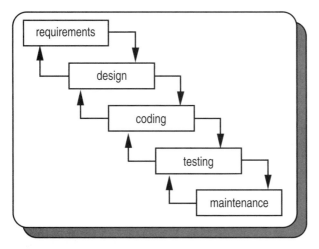

Figure 22.1: The waterfall life cycle

We now examine each of these steps in more detail.

22.2.1   Requirements

This phase is aimed at answering the "what" question: What problem is the system intended to address? This involves requirements *analysis* and *definition*. The services, constraints, and goals of the system are elicited from the potential system users. They are then defined in a form understandable by both users and developers. This software specification is passed on to the designers.

22.2.2   Design

Armed with a set of requirements for the system they have to build, the designers now face the "how" question: How will we build the system so that it behaves as specified by the requirements? It is this phase that we will concentrate on in this part of the book. The end result of this process is a detailed design document.

22.2.3   Coding

Next the design is passed on to a team of programmers and implementers whose job is to realize the design in a working system. The act of programming has been the focus of much of this book, but it is important to realize that this part of the life cycle (in conjunction with design) accounts for only about 30 percent of the total costs.

22.2.4   Testing

Testing, although placed at this point in the life cycle, is something that we would expect to take place during the coding phase. The aim of modern software engineering is to approach the production of large software systems through the use (and reuse) of existing "black box" modules. We have already discussed how objects meet the requirements for such black boxes and shown how it is possible to write "driver" programs whose job is to exercise (and test) objects. This can be thought of as *unit* testing.

At this point, we would expect testing to refer to *system* testing. When we put together all the black boxes, does the complete system perform as expected? Did we get the design right? Does it meet all the requirements? Can the users understand and use it? Problems that arise at this point might be addressed by returning to coding: A fairly minor bug has been uncovered. It could be worse and reveal a problem with the system design, in which case the design would have to be reconsidered. Even worse, it could indicate an error in the specification of the requirements.

22.2.5   Maintenance

Strictly speaking, maintenance isn't really part of the life cycle in the same way as the earlier phases. This occurs after the system has been completed and delivered and typically requires twice the effort that development required. Maintenance is intended to address any problems that arise in the everyday use of the system. Unfortunately, it may raise issues that can be addressed only by returning to the earlier parts of the life cycle.

We may uncover bugs that even exhaustive testing failed to find; they may be fixable by programmers or may reveal deeper design flaws. Users may find the system does not perform as they expected, or it makes a simple task much more difficult than it should be. This means there is a flaw in the requirements; either they were incomplete or just plain wrong. The requirements themselves may change due to external forces. If the application mirrors some real-world constraints, like the legal or financial system, and they undergo some changes (e.g., a change in the tax laws, such as eligibility, tax rates, etc.), then the application must reflect those changes. The introduction of the application itself may cause changes in the way people work outside the application; these changes may in turn have an impact on the application.

This concludes our "whistle-stop tour" of the life cycle; of necessity, it is (by its very nature) brief, and we refer you to texts such as *Software Engineering* (Sommerville, 2000) for further details.

The difference between planks and bridges has been captured in the phrases *programming in the large* and *programming in the small*. To a great extent, we have been concentrating on the latter. Although we cannot hope to cover programming in the large in a book of this nature, we intend to give you an appreciation of what it means and to provide some examples of what we might call programming in the medium.

22.3   Design

A full example of the design of a large-scale software system is beyond the scope of this book (or indeed of just about any book). What then do we hope to achieve in this final part of the book? First, we will present a small example and develop it from an informal description through to a fully coded Java implementation. By applying some design techniques in the small, as it were, we hope to provide some appreciation of the techniques in general. Second, we believe you will find the techniques useful as your implementation experiences move from small programming problems to the medium-scale programming projects that you may encounter in the rest of your training.

When facing these larger problems, it may even be required that you first prepare a specification (which is beyond the scope of this book) and a fully documented design. In this case, you should find the techniques and notations presented here of some use.

22.3.1   The Design Process

Broadly speaking, the design process is an iterative sequence of refinements, moving from an informal design outline toward a finished design. We can start with a broad outline of how we think the system can be realized and move through a number of refinements, including an informal design, a more formal design, and finally, the completed design. At each step, we add more details and refine our design, making it more and more formal.

Like the waterfall life cycle, this is an iterative process. As we start to think more deeply about our informal design and try to flesh it out by decomposing it into more detailed subdesigns, we may find our original intentions are too difficult to realize. We must therefore reconsider the earlier steps in our design and amend them accordingly.

22.3.2   *Functional Design*

Object-oriented design is a fairly recent development, achieving widespread adoption only in the late 1980s. Prior to its arrival, the most commonly used software design strategy was *functional* design. This strategy involves decomposing the design into functional components with system state information held in a shared data area. By comparison, in object-oriented design, system state is decentralized, and each object manages its own state information.

Consider this crude comparison of the two approaches. In functional design, the data that are worked on by the components are passed between them; each component applies some transformation and passes the (transformed) data onto the next component for further processing. In object-oriented design, it is not data that are transmitted among the components, but commands (messages that are requests for services from the other components).

These design approaches are not in opposition; they are complementary. They will be applied when deemed most appropriate by the software engineer(s). Perhaps for some systems, each approach will be applied to different subsystems when deemed suitable.

22.4   Object-Oriented Design (OOD)

As you have seen, objects possess a number of very desirable features for software engineers. They are an implementation of the module concept, identified early as an important "black box building block" for complex software systems. They can be easily understood as individual stand-alone entities. They are appropriate reusable components. For some systems, there may be obvious real-world entities that can be mapped onto system objects. In Chapter 2, we discussed the concept that everyday entities can be considered, and modeled, as objects (remember the CD player?).

Something worth considering is the relationship between OOD and OOP (object-oriented programming). They are related but distinct. As Java programmers, we can exploit the fact that our design will consist of a set of class definitions and clearly defined relationships between the classes (be it inheritance or clientship), which we can readily map onto a language that is itself object-oriented. However, there is absolutely nothing to prevent us from using OOD to produce a design that we can, although probably with more effort, realize in a non-OO programming language.

We can carry this argument a step earlier in the life cycle; there are now object-oriented requirement analysis techniques. The objects we identify in the requirements phase can naturally be carried forward into the design phase.

22.4.1   *Capturing Our Design: A Design Notation*

We will use and adapt a notation suggested in *The Object-Oriented Systems Life Cycle* (Henderson-Sellers and Edwards, 1990), which we will refer to as H-S&E.

H-S&E realize the importance of representing both single objects and class definitions and suggest we can do both using the same notation. They refer to such generic capabilities as *O/C* (object/class). Figure 22.2 presents a representation of a single object/class. At the top of the rounded rectangle, we give the O/C name. On the borders of the rectangle, we have the publicly available attribute(s) and method(s). Within the rectangle, we have the private attribute(s) and method(s). Attributes are contained in ovals, and methods are within rectangles.

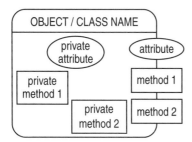

Figure 22.2: A single object/class

We are interested in two types of relationships between O/Cs: These are *inheritance* and *clientship*. We capture them in the notation as follows:

- Inheritance is represented by a thick arrow pointing from superclass to subclass, starting and ending at the borders of the rounded rectangle.

- Clientship is denoted by a circle within the body of an O/C, containing the start of a thin arrow pointing to the boundary of the server O/C.

In Figure 22.3, you see that obj1 is the superclass of obj3, and obj2 is a server for obj1. An example you have seen earlier in the book is given in Figure 22.4, where you see that Person is the superclass of Student, and OurDate is a server for later versions of Person.

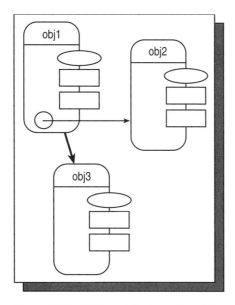

Figure 22.3: O/Cs and their relationships

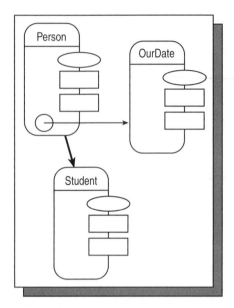

Figure 22.4: `Person`, `Student`, and `OurDate` represented as an H-S&E diagram

22.4.2   Object Identification

Unfortunately, one of the hardest parts of OOD is also the very first step we must take: *object identification*. A number of approaches have been suggested, but there is really no single automatic process we can follow. Designers must use their skill and experience to help. This poses something of a Catch-22 scenario for any text purporting to "teach" object-oriented design.

Identification of objects includes the objects themselves, their attributes, their associated operations, and their interrelationships. One technique for generating a "first cut" is a grammatical approach (Robinson 1992, Booch 1986). We highlight nouns and verbs in the natural language description of what the system is to do. The nouns identify objects, and the verbs (actions) identify operations or object services. Other approaches to object identification can be found in Coad and Yourdon's OOA/OOD method (Coad and Yourdon 1991a, 1991b).

Great care must be taken with the grammatical approach. We cannot assume nouns are always objects or verbs services. In addition, the writer of the system description may assume that knowledge is shared by the designer; if this is not the case, then important objects and services may be omitted.

As a simple worked example, let us consider the following text that describes part of the functionality of a personal organizer. Nouns are italicized, and verbs are in bold.

> The *telephone directory organizer* **provides** *surnames*. The *user* **searches** for existing *phone numbers* by *surname*. The *organizer* **displays** the *information* regarding an *entry*, and the *user* **adds** new *entries*. Once an *entry* has been **displayed**, the *user* can **browse** forward or backward through the *entries*.

From this simple analysis, we can identify the nouns and verbs shown in Table 22-1.

Nouns	Verbs
telephone directory organizer	search
user	provide
phone numbers	display
surname(s)	add
(information regarding an) entry	browse
(new) entries	

Table 22.1: Nouns and Verbs from the Description

This is only the start of the process; it is a deceptively easy way of generating a first cut. We must now weed out "false" objects, decide what is to be modeled as an object or as an attribute, and decide what is and what is not a method. Often, we must fall back on our experience to help us make these decisions.

Trying to move from our initial identification of nouns and verbs, we can see that some nouns refer to attributes. For example, if we accept an *entry* as an object, then surely *surname* and *phone number* should be attributes of that object (see Table 22.2).

Candidate	Objects	Attributes	Methods
	entry	phone number surname	
	telephone directory organizer		search display add browse
	user		
	entries		

Table 22.2: Candidate Objects, Attributes, and Methods

The *user* appears in the description because users are the source of system commands. We do not need to model the user formally in our design.

We are by no means finished. For example, we have not defined all the methods required. We may also need to add more attributes; for example, for a directory entry, we will at least wish to add a forename. A proposed set of initial classes is shown in Figure 22.5.

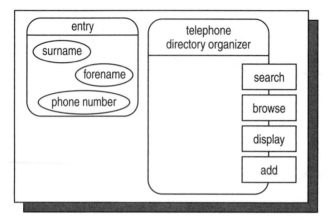

Figure 22.5: Proposed initial classes

There are other objects to define as well. We have begun to define a single entry; however, we will need to represent a collection of entries (as seen from our table of candidate objects). From our earlier experience of designing and using systems, we can visualize this collection as a database of directory entries. Just like a database management system, we will expect our collection to manage the addition, retrieval, and organization of entries.

We will expect this database to provide most of the functionality of the directory organizer. When a user asks to search for an entry, we would expect this request to be passed on almost unchanged to the database; similarly, a request to add a new entry would be passed on unchanged. Thus, the add and search methods of the directory organizer should be handled by the database. However, the browse and display methods are more closely related to the user interface than to the database.

What is actually required is some means for the user interface to retrieve a "named" entry, which it then displays. Browsing will be achieved in the user interface by retrieving the next or previous entry (thus satisfying the "browse forward or backward" requirement). The actual service provided by the database (Figure 22.6) will be getEntry.

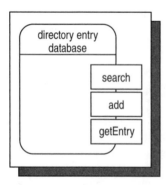

Figure 22.6: The directory entry database

Returning to our example, the telephone directory system (Figure 22.7) is essentially intended to be an interactive one driven by user commands. Note that we have added a new command, stop. Even though this was not mentioned in the original English specification, we clearly need some mechanism for terminating a session.

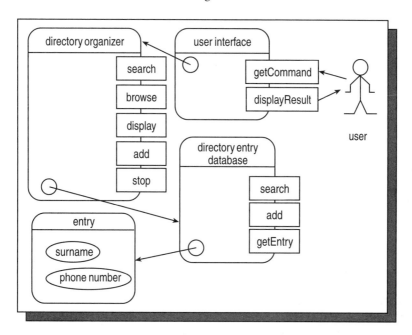

Figure 22.7: The complete system

In the next chapter, we shall move toward implementation through the process of detailed design. Following this, we will discuss a possible implementation of the design. Finally, we will present guidelines for a good object-oriented design.

22.5   Key Points in Chapter 22

- Software engineering came into being in response to the software crisis caused by the scaling up of computing power, which enabled the development of more ambitious software systems.

- The software crisis can be summarized as the difference between *programming in the small* and *programming in the large*. Techniques for placing a plank over a stream (in the small) do not scale up to those for building a bridge over a river (in the large). Software engineering is intended to support developments in the large.

- The *software life cycle* describes the phases through which a software artifact passes during its creation. The *waterfall* model names these phases as requirements, design, coding, testing, and maintenance.

- The design process is an iterative sequence of refinements starting from an informal design and adding more detail as we move toward a complete design.

- Prior to object-oriented design (OOD), the most common technique was *functional* design. In this approach, the design is decomposed into functional components that apply some transformation to data and pass on the (transformed) data to the next component for further processing.

- *Object-oriented design* is said to model the real world more closely. For example, there are everyday artifacts that can be considered, and modeled, as objects. Moreover, we can apply object orientation to the life cycle activities on either side of design—namely, requirements and coding. This means that an object identified during the requirements phase can be tracked through design and coding.

- Identifying objects is the first step in OOD. One approach is to apply a simple grammatical analysis and identify nouns and verbs, where nouns are taken to be objects and verbs are methods. This is only a first cut, and the results should be treated with care. For example, some nouns may refer to attributes rather than objects.

- Our design can be captured and documented using a suitable notation.

22.6   Exercises

1. For the application that you wrote for Exercise 17.7 (the hotel reception system), produce an H-S&E diagram to document the final structure of your program.

2. The description of the telephone directory organizer has been extended as follows:
   "When it is no longer necessary to keep someone's contact details, you can delete their entry from the directory. You can also update entries in the following two ways:
   a. Someone's phone number changes
   b. Someone's surname changes"
   Carry out the noun and verb approach to identify candidate objects, attributes, and methods in this description. Extend Figure 22.7 to show how your design can accommodate these additional requirements.

3. Here is an informal description of an information system based on a person's birthday:
   "The user provides the system with their date of birth. The system calculates the day that the person was born on, how long they have lived in months, weeks, and days, and presents them with a line from the poem about days of birth ('Monday's child is fair of face, . . .')."
   Apply the noun and verb approach to identify candidate objects, attributes, and methods in this description. Produce an initial H-S&E diagram to document your design.

4. Here is an informal description of a theater booking system:

"The theater booking system allows the booking office clerk to select information about a particular performance (specified by day and time—matinee or evening). The clerk can examine the status of a given seat (booked or unbooked) and change its status if required.

Customers may request single seats (row and seat number) or a range of seats (row, start and end seat numbers). They may also ask the clerk to check by specification; that is, "Have you a row of four adjacent seats?" or "Have you a block of seats 3 by 6?" For each seat booked, the name of the customer should be recorded as contact information. Seats are identified by a row (character) and a number.

The system should maintain persistent information regarding the status of seats for each performance. The system should be configurable for different seat layouts (assume there is a single floor of seats)."

Apply the noun and verb approach to identify candidate objects, attributes, and methods in this description. Produce an initial H-S&E diagram to document your design.

22.7 References

Booch, G. 1986. Object-Oriented Development. *IEEE Transactions on Software Engineering*, SE-12, No. 2 (February): 211–221.

Coad, P., and E. Yourdon. 1991a. *Object-Oriented Analysis* (2nd ed.). Englewood Cliffs, NJ: Yourdon Press, Prentice Hall.

———. 1991b *Object-Oriented Design.* Englewood Cliffs, NJ: Yourdon Press, Prentice Hall.

Henderson-Sellers, B., and J. M. Edwards. 1990. The Object-Oriented Systems Life Cycle. *Communications of the ACM*, 33, No. 9 (September): 142–159.

Robinson, P. J. 1992. *Hierarchic Object-Oriented Design.* Englewood Cliffs, NJ: Prentice Hall.

Sommerville, I. 2000. *Software Engineering* (6th ed.). New York: Addison-Wesley.

CHAPTER 23

Case Study: Implementing the Personal Organizer 1

23.1 First Steps in the Design

In this chapter, we move forward from the design stage into detailed implementation. Our problem is to implement the Java personal organizer (JPO), part of which is the telephone directory service we designed in the previous chapter. We intend to build a prototype application. A *prototype* is a system that exhibits most, if not all, of the functionality of the final application and allows implementers and users to experiment with the application. We will also provide a graphical user interface (GUI) for the prototype.

Initially, we could be said to be involved in detailed design; that is, we are exploring options as to how the prototype can actually be implemented. We are still addressing the "how" question, although at a much lower level. We still face a number of decisions based on how we will implement our design.

We begin by discussing the actual implementation of the telephone directory. We already know what the contents of a directory entry will look like; what we have to decide is how we will organize the directory, both on the filing system and in the program.

23.2 File Organization

Before continuing work on refining the design of our classes, we turn our attention to some lower level details of how we will organize our data on the filing system. Our telephone directory (and the elements that it consists of) must be *persistent*. That is, the information it contains must survive across executions of our application—no one would want to spend time inputting lots of telephone information, close down the application, and then start it up again at some later time only to find that all the data have disappeared.

We will use a number of files to save our data. The next point to consider is how best to organize the structure of those files to support our application.

23.2.1 Index Sequential Access

If you examine a physical telephone directory, you will detect a standard organization. Each page consists of an alphabetized list of subscribers; at the top of each page is the name of the first subscriber on the page. The list of names from the tops of the pages is known as an *index*. This type of organization has been used in database management systems and is known as an *index sequential storage structure*. For further details on index structures, see Chapter 5 of *Fundamentals of Database Systems* (Elmasri and Navathe 1994).

Here is a brief description of such a structure. We maintain two files: one for the index and one for the main file. The main file contains the actual data (in our case, the person's contact details), and the index file contains the index. We can consider the index and main files to consist of a sequence of *blocks*. The size of a block in bytes is normally a power of 2 (let's say 512).

The most common organization is one in which both the main file and the index file are kept in sorted order. In our case, we will want to retrieve by surname, so we will keep our data in alphabetical order according to surname. An index entry will consist of a surname (where the surname is the first name in a main file block) and a pointer to a main file block (in our case, the number of the block). In Figure 23.1, we assume that an index block contains three index entries (in practice, we would expect it to hold a lot more) and a main file block can contain only two directory entries.

In database terminology, the main file consists of a sequence of *records*. A record is a collection of *fields* (or attributes) of interest. In this example, we can say that our directory entries are the records we are interested in, and they have three fields: surname, forename, and phone number.

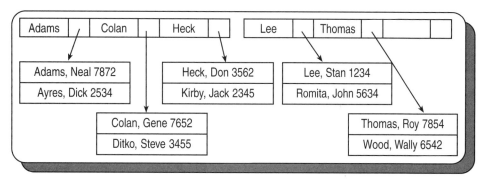

Figure 23.1: An example of an index sequential file

Figure 23.1 is an example of a *sparse* index because not every surname in the main file has a corresponding index entry. This situation is analogous to a real telephone directory; at the top of each page, we have the first surname to appear on that page. The name at the top of the page is the same as an index entry.

Given a surname, how do we find the matching details? The simplest algorithm would use a linear sequential search of the index entries. Suppose that the search surname is equal to the current index surname or greater than the current index surname and less than the next index surname (Figure 23.2). Then the matching entry, if it exists, should be present in the main file block pointed to by the current index pointer.

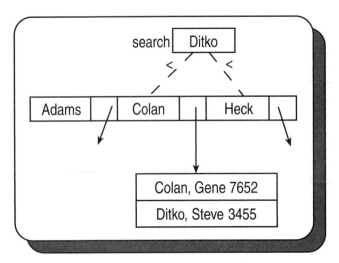

Figure 23.2: A sample search, where `Colan` < `Ditko` < `Heck`

Linear sequential searches are not so efficient when there is a large search space; we can take advantage of the sorted nature of the index and apply the binary search technique (see Section 9.4).

For our prototypical personal organizer, we have decided on a different organization. It is a simpler technique; we do not need to consider the file as consisting of blocks, nor do we have to worry about keeping the main file in sorted order. This approach will be sufficient to get our prototype application up and running. Because of the black box nature of our design, this does not prohibit a move to a more complex organization at a later date should the demands on our application require it.

Our main file is going to act as a *heap*; this means that new records are going to be added at the end of the file as they arrive. Our main file is thus not going to be in sorted order. We will maintain the sorted order in our index and will have an index entry for every record in the main file. This is an example of a *dense* index (Figure 23.3).

23.2.2   The Main File

The general way we will retrieve information is as follows: Given a surname, we will look up the corresponding entry in the sorted index. The index entry will contain the number of the record that contains the required information. We will then fetch the corresponding record from the main file and display it to the user.

If the record doesn't exist, we will return a marker to indicate this condition (it may be in the form of a null record). If we have more than one record with the same surname, we will return the first occurrence.

Given a record number, how can we locate the corresponding record? The record number is the number of the record within the heap. We will number the record "slots" in the heap from 0 upward. We want to transform this record number into a position within the main file and to read the requisite number of bytes directly from that position.

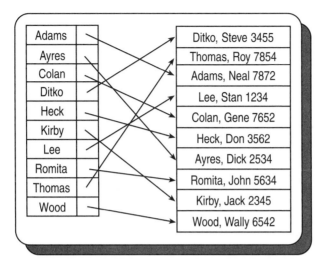

Figure 23.3: A dense index operating on a heap main file

Java files have no inherent structure of their own. They are viewed, like files in the UNIX operating system, as unbounded byte streams. They consist of a sequence of bytes addressed from zero. Any structure must be imposed by the application that uses the file. The first thing to do is to consider our detail records as having a fixed size; that is, all records in the file have exactly the same size. The size of our record must now be calculated; our `Entry` class has three fields: two `String`s and an `int`. We know that an `int` occupies 4 bytes on every Java platform. `String`s are, in a sense, unbounded, so we have to decide how big we are going to make them as far as the stored record is concerned. We have decided to make our surname and forename each 15 bytes long. This means a stored record will have $(15 \times 2) + 4$ bytes, or 34 bytes.

To store the contents of a Java `String` in a file, we can first convert the `String` into an array of bytes. We do this using the `String` method `getBytes`. We can then write the bytes directly to the file. We are using a `RandomAccessFile` in our example; we shall discuss this class shortly.

However, as we discussed earlier, we are imposing a fixed-size record structure on our file. We must ensure that we write 15 bytes into the file and not just the number of characters contained in the string. We need to:

- Convert the `String` into an intermediate array of bytes.
- Copy these bytes into an array of 15 bytes.
- Pad out the remaining unused bytes (we will use the null byte as padding).

We implement this algorithm as a method as follows:

```
private byte[] process(String str)
    {
    byte[] res = new byte[RECORD_STRING_SIZE] ;
    byte[] temp = str.getBytes() ;
```

```
        for (int i = 0 ; i < str.length() ; i++)
            res[i] = temp[i] ;
        for (int i = str.length() ; i < RECORD_STRING_SIZE ; i++)
            res[i] = '\0' ;
        return res ;
        } // end of method process
```

We can use this as follows when writing to a file:

```
String inString, outString ;
RandomAccessFile file = new RandomAccessFile("file.dat", "rw") ;
static final int RECORD_STRING_SIZE = 15 ;
```

...

```
// declare and create a new byte array
byte[] b1 = process(outString) ;
file.write(b1) ;
```

When we read bytes back from the file, we must first place them in a byte array. We can then use a `String` constructor that takes a byte array and converts it into a `String`.

```
// declare and create a new byte array
byte[] b1 = new byte [RECORD_STRING_SIZE] ;
file.readFully(b1) ;
inString = new String(b1) ;
```

Unfortunately, our job is not quite finished. Consider how we will be using the filed data in our application. If we write the byte array that contains the 5 characters that make up the name `Smith`, we also write 10 null characters (making up the 15 bytes of RECORD_STRING_SIZE). When we read back 15 bytes from the file and convert them back into `inString`, we will find we have the `Smith` characters but also 10 null characters.

In our experience, when printing `inString`, Java will output only as far as the first null character. Thus, `inString` appears to be correct. However, when comparing the value of `inString` with another `String` (as we will do when looking for a match with a search key), the string `Smith` will not match with the contents of `inString` because it has only 5 characters whereas `inString` has 15.

To overcome this problem, we used the following steps. We convert `inString` into an array of characters. We then use our method `sizeOf` to count the number of nonnull characters. Finally, we construct a new `String` from the array of characters using the size we have obtained. This will successfully convert `Smith` followed by 10 null characters into just `Smith`, as we require.

```
char[] temp = inString.toCharArray() ;
size = sizeOf(temp, inString.length()) ;
inString = new String(temp, 0, size) ;
```

```
private int sizeOf(char[] chArray, int length)
   {
   int i = 0 ;
   while ((chArray[i] != 0) && (i < length))
       i++ ;
   return i ;
   } // end of method sizeOf
```

Our main file will contain a number of record slots, each 34 bytes long. Because we are using fixed-sized records, this gives us a very simple way of calculating the start (byte) address of any record contained in the file:

```
bytePos = recordNumber * RECORD_SIZE ;
```

Finally, we require direct access to any record. That is, if we need record number 5, we do not want to start at the beginning of the file and sequentially read (and throw away!) the first five records (numbers 0 to 4) to get to the record we want. We want to move directly to the start (byte) address of the record and read in RECORD_SIZE bytes from that position.

As far as our internal representation is concerned, we will adopt a "one-record-at-a-time" approach. Whenever we need an entry from the file, we will read it into an `Entry` object.

23.2.3 The RandomAccessFile Class

Java provides a `RandomAccessFile` class that supplies exactly the functionality we require. This class has the same capabilities as `DataInputStream` and `DataOutputStream` plus the `seek` method, which allows us to change our current position in the file dynamically.

It is worth noting that `RandomAccessFile`, `DataInputStream`, and `DataOutputStream` share two interfaces (`DataInput` and `DataOutput`). Thus, although they are at different points on the inheritance hierarchy, the use of interfaces guarantees that all three of the classes provide the same functionality (which is specified in the two interfaces).

To open a `RandomAccessFile`, we use a constructor as follows:

```
RandomAccessFile myInput = new RandomAccessFile("in.dat", "r") ;
```

The first argument is the name of a file, and the second is an access mode specifier. We can open a `RandomAccessFile` for reading (as just shown, using "r") or for writing and reading (using "rw" as in our earlier example).

We can read and write arrays of `bytes` (among other things like `chars`, `doubles`, `floats`, etc.). In our example, we have used `readFully` instead of `read`. These methods are specified in the `DataInput` interface. The difference between these two methods is:

- `read( )` reads data into an array of bytes, blocking until at least some data are available.

- `readFully( )` reads data into an array of bytes, blocking until all the data are available.

Finally, the main reason we want to use `RandomAccessFiles` is the ability to change our current position in the file randomly. For this, we use the `seek( )` method. To use this, we provide a `long` argument specifying the new location in the file we wish to read from or write to as follows:

```
myInput.seek((long) 100) ;
```

This would change our current position in the file to byte 100.

23.2.4   The Index

We now turn our attention to how we are going to represent and handle the index. We make the following assumptions:

- We do not know in advance how big the index is going to become.

- However, we do know it will never be so big that we cannot store all of it in main memory.

An index element will be modeled by the IndexElem class, which contains two attributes: a key (in this case, the surname) and an integer (the number of the entry within the main file that contains full details on the person). For the moment, we assume distinct surnames. The index will thus be a collection of IndexElem objects.

Now we have to decide on the internal representation of the index. An initial candidate might be a simple array of IndexElems; arrays have to be fixed in size in Java, so we would have to decide how big the array was going to be. However, in our earlier assumptions, we do not know how big the array might become. We could make an arbitrary decision and guess how big it would ever be and proceed from there. Alternatively, we could model the index as a linked list.

However, we know that Java provides a number of classes for dynamically growing (and shrinking) collections, so we might consider these instead. First, we turn to the Vector class.

23.2.5   Suitability of the Vector *Class for Internal Representation of the Index*

At first sight, the Vector class might seem ideal. It can store any objects and grows and contracts as required. Moreover, remember that the index must be maintained in sorted order. A new entry as it arrives cannot be appended to the end of the index in "heap" fashion. We must find out where it belongs in the index and insert it there. If we modeled the index as an array, we would have to shift along every subsequent entry in the array to make room for it. Using a linked list removes this problem. So, too, does the Vector class; it will take care of all these details on our behalf.

However, we do not use the index only for storing information; we must also be able to retrieve those data on request. In our application, we would provide a surname and expect to get a suitable index element in reply. How can we search the Vector for a surname? The Vector class provides a contains method:

```
v.contains(searchKey)
```

This returns true if the searchKey can be found and false otherwise. A Vector is capable of handling heterogeneous collections; in our case, however, all the contents will be IndexElem instances. The searchKey must therefore be an IndexElem instance.

However, this means we can only find out if the Vector contains exactly the same object as the one we are now searching for. In most cases, the IndexElem we used to insert the information will not now be the same one we are using as the searchKey.

For example, consider the following fragment of Java code:

```
IndexElem ieOne = new IndexElem ("Jones", 2) ;
Vector index = new Vector() ;
index.addElement(ieOne) ;
IndexElem ieTwo = new IndexElem("Jones", 2) ;
boolean res = index.contains(ieTwo) ; // result will be false
```

The reason the result is false is because, although the Vector contains a reference to ieOne (which has state identical to that of ieTwo), it does not contain a reference to the actual instance ieTwo. In other words, we do not want to base the result of contains on object references but rather on the contents (or state) of the objects. This *content-based retrieval* is one of the prime functions of database systems.

Even here, we do not want to use all the state of the searchKey; we know only the surname, not the record number (which is the information we are after). The Vector class calls the equals method to decide if the searchKey is equal to an element it contains.

This inability to retrieve by key prohibits the direct use of the Vector class.

23.2.6 *Suitability of the* Hashtable *Class for Internal Representation of the Index*

Hashtables are an attempt to provide direct access to internal data structures. Based on the value of a key, the position of the data within the structure is calculated and the data are stored there. Retrieval is by the same mechanism:

```
table.put(key, data) ;
```

We can use the put method to add our (surname, record number) pairs to the Hashtable. We can get rid of our IndexElem class, as the hashtable has replaced it. Because our key is a String, an object class that is treated specially as part of the Java language, the correct equals method is called, and we can indeed retrieve data from this structure. However, if our key was, say, IndexElem, we would have exactly the same problems as we faced with the Vector class and its use of equals.

However, what happens if our directory stored more than one person with the same name?

```
table.put ("Smith", 3) ;
table.put ("Smith", 54) ;
```

The second put call overrides the original data (3). The put method returns an Object result, which we can check for this situation arising. However, the question remains: What to do about the situation?

Probably the largest objection to the use of the Hashtable class in our situation is the requirement for sorted order. We want the user to be able to browse backward and forward through the sorted data. We have already decided to realize the main file as a heap, so we look to the index mechanism to provide that sorted order. By its very nature, a hashtable does not keep data in sorted order. It "scatters" the data across its storage structure.

23.2.7   *Using the* Vector *Class Indirectly*

We return to the Vector class. As you recall, this class was pretty good as far as inserting data was concerned; it was retrieval that let us down. We can use clientship instead of direct use or inheritance. We can define an Index class that contains a Vector instance as one of its attributes. Requests to add data to the index can eventually be passed on to the Vector. Retrieval (or contains) can be implemented by the Index class as follows:

- Convert the Vector into an Enumeration.

- Scan the Enumeration for the appropriate searchKey; return true if found and false otherwise.

23.3   The Classes in Detail

In this section, in conjunction with our discussion on how we will organize the file structures, we will decide what further classes and services are required to support our DirBase (directory entry database) class.

DirBase is the main object for the telephone directory application. It hides from its clients all details of how the directory is actually implemented. The abstraction it presents is an alphabetically ordered sequence of directory entries.

DirBase	Attributes	Methods
		contains
		getEntry
		add
		open
		close

Table 23.1: DirBase Attributes and Methods

As shown in Table 23.1, we can define five major services:

- contains. Given a surname, this returns the number (position) of the first directory entry that contains that surname if it exists. Otherwise, it returns –1. This implements the "search" functionality seen in Figure 22.7.

- getEntry. Given the position of a directory entry, this returns that entry.

- add. This adds a directory entry to the ordered sequence.

- open and close. These open and close a directory entry database.

In this and subsequent tables, we have omitted the constructor method(s); they are implicit for each class we design.

DirEntry is the class that represents an entry (or a record) in the main file; it consists of the attributes and methods shown in Table 23.2.

DirEntry	(Private) Attributes	Methods
	surname	getSurname
	forename	getForename
	phoneNumber	getPhoneNumber

Table 23.2: DirEntry Attributes and Methods

According to our specification, there is no need to alter or individually change attributes of a directory entry. We have therefore not provided any mutator methods. It is only at construction time that attribute values can be provided. However, we will need selector methods (the user interface will want to choose the individual attributes to present them to the user); these are getSurname, getForename, and getPhoneNumber, all of which return the corresponding attribute value.

IndexElem contains the attributes and methods shown in Table 23.3. Like our DirEntry class, we assume there is no need for mutator methods. However, we will need to select the individual attributes; the methods getKey and getNumber return the corresponding attribute value.

IndexElem	(Private) Attributes	Methods
	recordNumber	getNumber
	key	getKey
		equals

Table 23.3: IndexElem Attributes and Methods

When searching the contents of the index, we will need to find out if an index element contains the surname we are looking for. We have chosen to override the equals method to do this. The new equals method returns true if this index element contains the surname we are looking for and false otherwise.

The Index class supports the ordered sequence abstraction; the methods are listed in Table 23.4.

Index	Attributes	Methods
		contains
		indexOf
		elementAt
		addElement

Table 23.4 Index Attributes and Methods

The details of these methods are as follows:

- `contains`. Given a surname, this returns true if the surname is in the index and false otherwise.
- `indexOf`. Given a surname, this returns the position of the first such surname if present and −1 otherwise.
- `elementAt`. Given a position, this returns the index element at that position.
- `addElement`. Given an index element, this adds it to the index at the correct position (maintaining the sorted order).

You can see how the first three methods can be used together to ensure we access the index safely—that is, retrieve only valid index elements:

```
if (index.contains("Smith"))
    element = index.elementAt(index.indexOf("Smith")) ;
```

or

```
int pos = index.indexOf("Smith") ;
if (pos != -1)
    element = index.elementAt(pos) ;
```

This concludes our high-level design of the four classes that make up the functionality of the `DirBase`.

23.3.1 *Filing System Considerations*

We discussed earlier how we would organize the filing system for our index sequential structure. We have reached a point in our design where we consider the main file. We will identify the need for additional methods that we have not featured in our design thus far.

To reiterate, the main file will contain an unordered sequence of directory entries. The index contains a *record number* that relates to a position within the main file. Given a record number, we want to retrieve the corresponding directory entry from the main file:

```
DirEntry dirEnt = new DirEntry() ;
dirEnt.read(recordNumber) ;
```

We will also need to write a directory entry to the main file:

```
dirEnt.write(recordNumber) ;
```

It seems natural to associate these input/output methods with a `DirEntry` object. However, we will also require methods that open and close the underlying file. If you recall that we can think of a class as both a definition and a collection of all instances of a class, then we can associate the `open` and `close` methods with the `DirEntry` class. We make them `static` so that they belong to the class rather than to individual instances. They will be called by the `open` and `close` methods of `DirBase`.

We can now sketch our possible implementation of the `DirBase.getEntry` method:

```
indElem = index.elementAt(pos) ;
entryNum = indElem.getNum() ;
dirEnt.read(entryNum) ;
```

We can also outline the `DirBase.contains` method with argument, say, `"Smith"`:

```
int pos = index.indexOf("Smith") ;
if (pos != -1)
    {
    IndexElem element = index.elementAt(pos) ;
    dirEnt.read(element.getNumber()) ;
    }
```

The last method of `DirBase` to consider is `add` with arguments, say, `"Smith"` and 1948:

```
dirEnt = new DirEntry("Smith", 1948) ;
dirEnt.write(pos) ;
indElem = new IndexElem("Smith", pos) ;
index.addElement(indElem) ;
```

In Table 23.5, we list the revised attributes and methods of the `DirEntry` class.

DirEntry	(Private) Attributes	Methods
	surname	getSurname
	forename	getForename
	phoneNumber	getPhoneNumber
		read
		write
		(static) open
		(static) close

Table 23.5: Revised `DirEntry` Attributes and Methods

In a similar fashion, we must make the index elements persistent. They, too, will require a `read` and a `write` method. However, responsibility for opening and closing the file containing the index elements rests with the `Index` class. Table 23.6 lists the revised attributes and methods of the `IndexElem` class.

IndexElem	(Private) Attributes	Methods
	recordNumber	getNumber
	key	getKey
		equals
		read
		write

Table 23.6: Revised IndexElem Attributes and Methods

For the prototype, we assume we can hold all of the index in memory at run time. Unlike our directory entries, which we read/write individually as required, we need only read the whole index in when we begin and write it all out when we finish. We call these methods load and save. These methods will process the contents of the index and, for each index element, will call the appropriate read or write method belonging to the IndexElem class. The Index class will open and close the file as required. Table 23.7 lists the revised methods of the Index class.

Index	Attributes	Methods
		contains
		indexOf
		elementAt
		addElement
		load
		save
		open
		close

Table 23.7: Revised Index Attributes and Methods

You may wonder why we have decided to have load as well as open and save as well as close. This is because the operations of opening and closing the index file are fundamental operations; we may at a later date decide that the index is too large to be loaded in all at once and move to an approach similar to that taken with the directory entries. Or we may offer the facility to save the contents of the index periodically even though we are not finished using it. We do not wish to tie up two distinct operations under one single method, although there would seem little harm in doing so in our prototype. We are, however, thinking about the flexibility of our design and subsequent implementation for future development and maintenance.

23.3.2 Clientship

Finally, in this section, we describe the clientship relationships between our four new classes and also the RandomAccessFile class that we shall be using. We have summarized this information in Table 23.8, and we capture our complete design in Figure 23.4.

	DirBase	Index	IndexElem	DirEntry	RandomAccessFile
DirBase	•	yes	yes	yes	no
Index	no	•	yes	no	yes
IndexElem	no	no	•	no	yes
DirEntry	no	no	no	•	yes
RandomAccess File	no	no	no	no	•

Table 23.8: Clientship Relationships in Our Design

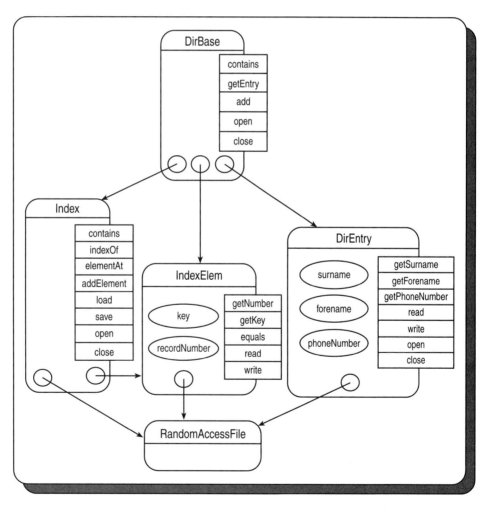

Figure 23.4: Our complete design

23.4   Moving toward Implementation

In the following sections, we look at the classes we have identified as parts of the system, and we provide headers and descriptions of the services that instances of the classes will have to offer.

23.4.1   The DirBase Class

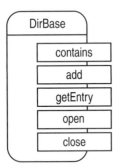

Figure 23.5: The DirBase class

This class is shown in Figure 23.5 and contains the following methods:

- public int contains(String surname). The abstraction presented to the DirBase client is an ordered sequence of entries. Given a surname, this method returns the position of the first entry in the ordered sequence that contains that surname. It returns −1 if the surname is not present in the system.

- public DirEntry getEntry(int posNumber). This method gets an entry from the main file. The posNumber here refers to the entry's position in the sorted sequence of entries. Sequential calls of getEntry with an incrementing posNumber will thus see a stream of entries in sorted order.

- public void add(String surname, String forename, int telNumber). This method adds a new directory entry to the system.

- public void open(String dbName). This method opens the named directory database.

- public void close(). This closes the current directory database.

23.4.2   The DirEntry class

The DirEntry class (Figure 23.6) is intended to represent a directory entry. It possesses three private attributes: forename and surname to represent the person's names and phoneNumber to represent that person's phone number. Some of the methods of the class are intended to manipulate and manage these three attributes. They are as follows:

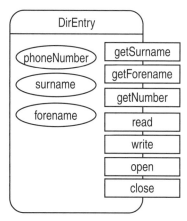

Figure 23.6: The DirEntry class

- `public String getSurname( )`
- `public String getForename( )`
- `public int getNumber( )`

These are the traditional `get` methods for the private attributes of the class.

The next two methods do not actually manipulate individual entries but are instead involved with the file in which entries will be stored:

- `static public boolean open (String filename)`. This method opens a (random access) file. Part of the internal state of a `DirEntry` object is a random access file, which is set via this method. The method returns true if the file was successfully opened and false otherwise.

- `static public void close( )`. This method closes the (random access) file associated with the `DirEntry` object.

The last two methods are for reading and writing `DirEntry` information to and from the main file:

- `public void read(int recNum) throws IOException`
- `public void write(int recNum) throws IOException`

These interface routines calculate the start byte address of the entry in the file according to the argument `recNum` and use the `RandomAccessFile.seek` method to make that our current position in the main file. They then handle the conversion of the internal attributes of `DirEntry` into a byte stream suitable for storage and loading from the file and read or write from the calculated position.

Remember, here we take *record number* to refer to the entry's position within the main file. The *position number* in `DirBase` refers to the position of the index entry for the record within the sorted index.

23.4.3   *The* IndexElem *Class*

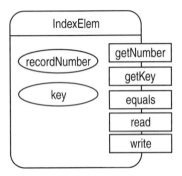

Figure 23.7: The IndexElem Class

This class is shown in Figure 23.7 and has the following methods:

- `public String getKey()`
- `public int getNum()`

These are selector methods for the two private attributes.

- `public boolean equals(String key)`. This method returns true if the key associated with the calling object is equal to the key of the argument and false otherwise.

The next two methods use the `elemNum` argument to seek a position in the (random access) file before reading or writing an `IndexElem`:

- `public void read(RandomAccessFile file, int elemNum)`
                                         `throws IOException`
- `public void write(RandomAccessFile file, int elemNum)`
                                         `throws IOException`

23.4.4   *The* Index *class*

This class is shown in Figure 23.8 and has the following methods:

- `public boolean contains(String searchKey)`. If the `String searchKey` is contained within the `Index`, this method returns true and false otherwise.
- `public int indexOf(String searchKey)`. If the `String searchKey` is contained within the index, this method returns its position within the index and −1 otherwise.
- `public IndexElem elementAt(int pos)`. This returns the index element residing at the given position.
- `public void addElement(IndexElem pie)`. This method adds the index element `pie` to the index maintaining its sorted order.

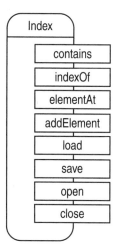

Figure 23.8: The Index class

The next four methods relate to the persistent nature of the index:

- `public boolean open(String filename)`. This method attempts to open the named file; it returns true if successful and false otherwise. The `RandomAccessFile` object is maintained as part of the internal state of the `Index`.

- `public void close()`. This method closes the file.

As discussed earlier, in our initial prototype, we have decided to treat the index as a complete entity rather than as individual blocks. Thus, when our application starts, we need to read all of the index file into the `Index` object. Similarly, when we shut down the application, we need to save the contents of the `Index` object in the index file. These next two methods are intended to take care of this problem:

- `public void load() throws IOException`

- `public void save() throws IOException`

23.5 Key Points in Chapter 23

- When designing a system that requires persistent data, these will normally be stored in a file. The use the application will make of these data influences how we choose to organize the layout of the file(s) involved.

- Our telephone directory application suggested the use of the *index sequential access* structure. This involves two files: an index and a main file. Normally, the main file contains a sequence of records sorted by the field we will most commonly use for retrieval (here the surname). The index file contains a sequence of entries, again in sorted order.

Each entry contains one search field (the surname) and a pointer to the main file block that contains that surname in its first record.

- Care must be taken when converting Strings to byte arrays for storage in files, and vice versa, because it is possible to end up with a String with trailing null bytes, which are invisible on printing. This particularly causes problems when comparing Strings.

- The java.io package provides a RandomAccessFile class that supports random access to a file through the seek method that allows us to change our location in the file randomly.

- For our telephone directory application, we identified four classes: DirBase, DirEntry, IndexElem, and Index. The Index class uses a Vector instance as an attribute to support its operation.

- Filing system considerations caused us to make further design decisions and resulted in extensions to the design of our four classes to accommodate the need for persistence.

- Finally, we provided detailed method headers for each class.

23.6   Exercise

1. Continuing your work on the theater booking system (see Exercise 22.4), you should extend your design to take into account the persistent nature of the booking information. You may wish to consider using inheritance to add persistence to the classes you have already designed. This is discussed in Section 24.5.

23.7   Reference

Elmasri, R., and S.B. Navathe. 1994. *Fundamentals of Database Systems* (2nd ed.). Redwood City, CA: Benjamin/Cummings.

CHAPTER 24

Case Study: Implementing the Personal Organizer 2

24.1 Completing the Implementation

In this chapter, we continue the implementation process for the Java personal organizer (JPO). We present the source text for the four classes we have designed. We also discuss the process of testing the behavior of the classes through the provision of an application to set up an initial personal organizer from a text file and a text-based version of the final application. We can think of the latter as a kind of extended test harness for the classes involved.

We discuss and present the final graphical version of the application. We then discuss the extensibility of our design and implementation.

24.2 Implementations of DirBase, Index, IndexElem, and DirEntry

In the next four sections, we present and discuss the Java source code produced for each class following the design given in Section 23.4.

24.2.1 DirEntry *Class Source and Commentary*

This class has the three attributes from the design and the associated get methods:

```
int phoneNumber ;
String forename, surname ;

// selector methods ...
public String getSurname()
    {
    return surname ;
    } //end of method getSurname
```

```
public String getForename()
    {
    return forename ;
    } // end of method getForename

public int getNumber()
    {
    return phoneNumber ;
    } // end of method getNumber
```

Next we have the constructor method:

```
public DirEntry (String fName, String sName, int number)
    {
    forename = fName ;
    surname = sName ;
    phoneNumber = number ;
    } // end of constructor method
```

Then we consider the main file methods. They are static because they are associated with the class rather than individual objects:

```
static RandomAccessFile file ;
public static boolean open(String fileName)
// tries to open the named file; returns "true" if
// successful, "false" otherwise
    {
    boolean res = true ;
    try {
        file = new RandomAccessFile(fileName, "rw") ;
        }
    catch (IOException e)
        {
        res = false ;
        }
    return res ;
    } // end of method open

public static void close()
// closes the currently opened file
    {
    try {
        file.close() ;
        }
    catch (IOException e)
        {
        }
    } // end of method close
```

Next we provide the ability to read and write individual `DirEntry` objects. We begin by declaring some constants to represent the size (in bytes) of a `dirEntry` in the file. We have decided that the largest string we will handle will have 15 characters (bytes). As a `dirEntry` is made up of two such strings (one for forename and one for surname) plus an integer (representing a phone number), we can calculate the total size of an entry:

```
// details of the number of bytes a "dirEntry" occupies
// on the filing system
private static final int RECORD_STRING_SIZE = 15 ;
private static final int RECORD_SIZE =
                            (RECORD_STRING_SIZE * 2) + 4 ;
```

Here are the `read` and `write` methods:

```
public void read(int recNum) throws IOException
// read a record from the specified RandomAccessFile
    {
    file.seek((long) recNum * RECORD_SIZE) ;
    phoneNumber = file.readInt() ;
    byte[] b1 = new byte [RECORD_STRING_SIZE] ;
    file.readFully(b1) ;
    forename = new String (b1, 0) ;
    byte[] b2 = new byte[RECORD_STRING_SIZE] ;
    file.readFully(b2) ;
    surname = new String (b2, 0) ;
    } // end of method read

private byte[] process(String str)
    {
    byte[] res = new byte[RECORD_STRING_SIZE] ;
    byte[] temp = str.getBytes() ;
    for (int i = 0; i < str.length(); i++)
        res[i] = temp[i] ;
    for (int i = str.length(); i < RECORD_STRING_SIZE; i++)
        res[i] = '\0';
    return res;
    } // end of method process

public void write(int recNum) throws IOException
    {
    file.seek((long) recNum * RECORD_SIZE) ;
    file.writeInt(phoneNumber) ;
    if (forename == null) throw new
        IOException("trying to output unset forename") ;
    byte[] b1 = process(forename) ;
    file.write(b1) ;
    if (surname == null) throw new
```

```
        IOException("trying to output unset surname") ;
    byte[] b2 = process(surname) ;
    file.write(b2) ;
    } // end of method write
```

We do not include the additional code discussed in Section 23.2.2, which handles the additional null bytes that occur when we convert a byte array to a `String`. This is because we don't really need to as far as entries in our main file are concerned. All we ever do with these entries is display them, and `System.out.println` appears to stop printing characters in a `String` as soon as it reaches a null character. It is of concern only when we want to compare two `Strings`, as we do when searching the `Index` for a match, so we will see the code again in Section 24.2.2.

Finally, we present a couple of additional methods. First, we override `toString`, which is often useful:

```
public String toString()
    {
    return surname + ", " + forename + " " +
        phoneNumber + " " ;
    } // end of method toString
```

Second, we provide a method that "clears" a `dirEntry` to a "null" entry. This operation is useful when we wish to return a `dirEntry` if we were unable to fetch one from the main file:

```
public void clear ()
// clear a "dirEntry" to appropriate "empty" values
    {
    forename = surname = null ;
    phoneNumber = 0 ;
    } // end of method clear
```

The first line of this method sets both the `String` attribute references `forename` and `surname` to `null`.

24.2.2 IndexElem *Class Source and Commentary*

This class has the two attributes identified in the design plus associated constructors and selector methods:

```
String key ;
int recordNumber ;

// constructor methods ...
public IndexElem(String k, int rNum)
    {
    key = new String(k) ; // make a deep copy of the String
    recordNumber = rNum ;
    } // end of constructor method
```

```
// selector methods ...
public String getKey()
    {
    return key ;
    } // end of method getKey

public int getNum()
    {
    return recordNumber ;
    } // end of method getNum
```

Now we turn our attention to input and output of IndexElems. As with DirEntry, we begin by declaring some constants to represent the size of a String in a file and the size of a complete IndexElem.

```
// input/output methods and constants

static final int RECORD_STRING_SIZE = 15 ;
static final int IE_SIZE = RECORD_STRING_SIZE + 4 ;
```

As we discussed previously, we have to take care about reading back Strings from a file because they are padded out with null characters when written. We present here again our sizeOf method and how it is used in our read method.

```
private int sizeOf(char[] chArray, int length)
    {
    int i = 0 ;
    while ((chArray[i] != 0) && (i < length))
        i++ ;
    return i ;
    } //end of method sizeOf

public void read(RandomAccessFile file, int recNum)
                            throws IOException
    {
    int size ;
    file.seek((long)recNum * IE_SIZE) ;
    recordNumber = file.readInt() ;
    byte[] b1 = new byte [RECORD_STRING_SIZE] ;
    file.readFully(b1) ;
    key = new String (b1, 0) ;

    char[] temp = key.toCharArray() ;
    size = sizeOf(temp, key.length()) ;
    key = new String(temp, 0, size) ;
    } // end of method read
```

```
private byte[] process(String str)
    {
    // as seen earlier
    } // end of method process

public void write(RandomAccessFile file, int recNum)
                              throws IOException
    {
    file.seek((long)recNum * IE_SIZE) ;
    file.writeInt(recordNumber) ;
    byte[] b1 ;
    if (key == null)
        throw new IOException("trying to output an unset key") ;
    b1 = process(key) ;
    file.write(b1) ;
    } // end of method write
```

Finally, an extra method is the ever-useful `toString` override:

```
public String toString()
    {
    return key + " " + recordNumber ;
    } // end of method toString
```

24.2.3   Index *Class Source and Commentary*

We begin with the attributes of this class:

```
Vector v ;                  // the index's home in main memory
RandomAccessFile file ;     // the index's home on the filing system
```

Our constructor initializes our `Vector` attribute:

```
public Index()
    {
    v = new Vector(10) ;
    } // end of constructor method
```

While moving from our detailed design to implementation, we realized that we would need a method that returns how many elements our `Index` contains; thus, we provided a `size` method as described next. When a request is made to find out the size (the number of current elements in our index), we delegate this to our `Vector` attribute and return the results directly:

```
public int size()
// return the number of index elements in the index
    {
    return v.size() ;
    } // end of method size
```

Similarly, when we need to return an element at a specific position, we delegate this to our Vector attribute. However, although Vectors are capable of storing any Object reference, we know that only IndexElems will be maintained in the Vector attribute of the Index class. This means we can safely cast the result of the Vector method to IndexElem:

```
public IndexElem elementAt(int pos)
// return the index element at the requested position
    {
    return (IndexElem) v.elementAt(pos) ;
    } // end of method elementAt
```

We move on to our two "search" methods: contains and indexOf. Both take a String searchKey argument that will contain the surname that corresponds to the phone number we are after. They treat the contents of the Vector attribute as an Enumeration instance. We then loop through the contents of the Vector and test each one for equality with the search key. As soon as we find a match, we terminate the loop.

The contains method returns a Boolean result true if the searchKey is in the index and false otherwise:

```
public boolean contains(String searchKey)
// given a search key, this method looks at each
// index element.
// if it finds the required key, it returns "true";
// "false" otherwise.
    {
    boolean res = false ;
    Enumeration e = v.elements() ;
    IndexElem ie ;
    while (e.hasMoreElements() && !res)
        {
        ie = (IndexElem)e.nextElement() ;
        res = searchKey.equals(ie.getKey()) ;
        }
    return res ;
    } // end of method contains
```

The indexOf method returns the actual position of the search key within the index and −1 if not found:

```
public int indexOf(String searchKey)
// given a search key, this method examines each
// index element.
// when it finds a match, it returns the position of
// the element within the index; −1 otherwise.
    {
    boolean flag = false ;
    int res = -1, count = 0 ;
    Enumeration e = v.elements() ;
```

```
    IndexElem ie ;
    while (e.hasMoreElements() && !flag)
        {
        ie = (IndexElem)e.nextElement() ;
        flag = searchKey.equals(ie.getKey()) ;
        if (flag) res = count ;
        count++ ;
        }
    return res ;
    } // end of method indexOf
```

Next we come to the addElement method. This is probably the largest method in the Index class. This is because it is concerned with maintaining the sorted order of the Index; we can't just add the element directly to the Vector attribute:

```
public void addElement(IndexElem pie)
// this method adds an index element to the index,
// maintaining the sorted order
    {
    // find out where the element belongs
    boolean flag = false ;
    int cres = 0, res = 0, count = 0 ;
    Enumeration e = v.elements() ;
    String add, current ;
    IndexElem ie ;

    // special case -- empty vector
    int vSize = v.size() ;
    if (vSize == 0)
        {
        v.addElement(pie) ;
        return ;
        }

    add = pie.getKey() ;

    while (e.hasMoreElements() && !flag)
        {
        ie = (IndexElem)e.nextElement() ;
        current = ie.getKey() ;
        cres = add.compareTo(current) ;
        if (cres <= 0)
            {
            flag = true ;
            res = count ;
            }
        count++ ;
        }
```

```
// if the new string is larger than the last
// element
if (!flag) res = count ;

// at last we know where the new index element
// belongs ...
v.insertElementAt(pie, res) ;
} // end of method addElement
```

We have two special cases to consider. First, is this the first element in the Vector? Second, is this larger than the last element in the Vector? In between, we must find out where the new element should be placed within the current index.

We start with the simplest case: Is the Vector currently empty? We can find out by using the Vector.size() method. If it is empty, we add the element and leave.

If it isn't, we must find out where it belongs. We extract the surname from the index element we are trying to add. As in our "search" methods, we treat the contents of the Vector attribute as an Enumeration instance and loop through. We compare the String from the element we are trying to add with the surname String from the current index element. As soon as we find a stored surname that is less than or equal to the new surname, we terminate the loop because we have found out where to store the new index element.

As part of the scanning loop, we keep a count of which element we are looking at. When the loop terminates because we have found a stored surname less than or equal to the surname to be added, res is set to the position where we should add the new element.

Having left the loop, we need to take into account why the loop terminated. We terminate the loop because either:

- We have found a stored surname less than or equal to the surname being added, as we have described.

- We have run out of index elements to look at without finding a suitable stored surname.

If it is the latter, the surname to be added is greater than any of the stored surnames and should be added at the end of the Vector attribute. We can check this by examining the value of the Boolean variable flag; if it is false, then we did not find a suitable surname, and we set the value of res to the value of count.

At this point in the method, res contains the position where the new element is to be added to the Vector attribute regardless of whether it belongs somewhere within the Vector or at the end. We can finally add the element to the Vector.

We move onto the input/output methods by which we achieve the persistence of the Index. We start with the basic open and close methods that open and close the underlying file used to store the Index:

```
// input/output methods ; for the
// persistence of the index
```

```
public boolean open(String fileName)
    {
    boolean res = true ;
    try {
        file = new RandomAccessFile(fileName, "rw") ;
        }
    catch (IOException e)
        {
        System.out.println("problem in Index.open") ;
        System.exit(0) ;
        res = false ;
        }
    return res ;
    } // end of method open

public void close()
    {
    try {
        file.close() ;
        }
    catch (IOException e)
        {
        // not doing anything intelligent
        }
    } // end of method close
```

Now we come to the load and save methods. As we have discussed, unlike the directory entries themselves (which are individually read and written as necessary), all of the elements contained in the index are loaded up when our application starts running. Similarly, when the application terminates, all of the elements are stored back in the file:

```
public void save() throws IOException
// saves the index elements in the file
    {
    Enumeration e = v.elements() ;
    IndexElem ie ;
    int count = 0 ;

    file.seek((long) 0) ;

    while (e.hasMoreElements())
        {
        ie = (IndexElem)e.nextElement() ;
        ie.write(file, count) ;
        count++ ;
        }
    } // end of method save
```

In the save method, we begin by using the seek method associated with the RandomAc-cessFile class. We must make sure that we are at the start of the file before doing any writes. If we didn't, chances are we would be appending the index at the end of the file. If this is not the first time we've used the file, this would probably have the effect of placing the current version of the index after the old version.

Again, we treat the contents of the Vector attribute as an Enumeration instance and loop through those contents, writing each IndexElem individually.

```
public void load( ) throws IOException
// loads the index elements from the file
// into main memory
    {
    IndexElem ie = new IndexElem( ) ;
    boolean goOn = true ;
    int count = 0 ;

    file.seek((long) 0) ;

    while (goOn)
        {
        try {
            ie.read(file, count) ;
            count++ ;
            }
        catch (IOException e)
            }
            goOn = false ;
            }
        if (goOn)
            {
            v.addElement(ie) ;
            ie = new IndexElem( ) ;
            }
        }
    } // end of method load
```

In the load method, we again ensure that we are at the start of the file by using seek. We read in a new IndexElement from the file and add it directly to the Vector element. We don't need to make sure the index is in sorted order because we know it will always be saved in this order. We can use Vector.addElement instead of Index.addElement.

We control the loop that processes the file through the detection of an *end-of-file* excep-tion. As long as this exception has not been thrown, we add the IndexElement to the Vector attribute.

Finally, we again have an additional method to assist with debugging the Index class; this prints the index elements in the index. We can therefore see at a glance if entries are being added in alphabetical order:

```
public void print()
// debugging method ... prints out all the
// index elements in the index
    {
    Enumeration e = v.elements() ;
    IndexElem ie ;
    System.out.println("index contains ...") ;
    while (e.hasMoreElements())
        {
        ie = (IndexElem)e.nextElement() ;
        System.out.println(ie) ;
        }
    } // end of method print
```

24.2.4   DirBase *Class Source and Commentary*

The DirBase class contains a single attribute

```
static Index index ;
```

which represents the Index client.

Its constructor method takes a single String argument that acts as the name of the directory entry database. Using the String concatenation operator, it adds a ".ind" extension to denote the index file and ".dat" to denote the main file. It passes requests on to the Index object and the DirEntry class to open these files. It loads the Index object from the index file:

```
public DirBase(String dbName)
    {
    index = new Index() ;
    index.open(dbName + ".ind") ;
    try {
        index.load() ;
        }
    catch (IOException e)
        {
        // if we can't load the index, not much
        // point in continuing ...
        System.exit(0) ;
        }
    index.print() ;
    DirEntry.open(dbName + ".dat") ;
    } // end of constructor method
```

The constructor therefore implicitly opens up the "database" (actually, the index and main files). We must have a matching close method:

```
public void close()
// close the database down ...
// delegates to the Index and DirEntry classes ...
    {
    try {
        index.save() ;
        index.close() ;
        DirEntry.close() ;
        }
    catch (IOException e)
        {
        System.exit(0) ;
        }
    } // end of method close
```

We now present the add service. It does a fair bit of delegation. First it creates a new DirEntry instance using its arguments. It finds out where the end of the main file is by asking the index what size it currently is. This gives it the "next record slot," and it calls DirEntry.write accordingly. Having added the DirEntry to the end of the main file heap, it now creates a new IndexElem instance and adds that to the index (using Index.addElement to ensure sorted order is maintained):

```
public void add(String sname, String fname, int number)
// adds a directory entry triple to the system ...
    {
    // create a new "DirEntry"
    DirEntry rec = new DirEntry(fname, sname, number) ;

    // find out where the end of the main file is
    int nextRecSlot = index.size() ;

    try {
        // write the new entry into the main file
        rec.write(nextRecSlot) ;
        }
    catch (IOException e)
        {
        System.err.println("DirBase.add " + e) ;
        System.exit(-1) ;
        }

    // create a new index element for the entry
    IndexElem ie = new IndexElem(sname, nextRecSlot) ;

    // add it to the index
    index.addElement(ie) ;

    } // end of method add
```

Now we come onto the search (`contains`) and retrieve (`getEntry`) methods. The `contains` method takes a search key and, by delegation, uses `Index.contains` to find out if the search key is present in the index. If so, it uses `Index.indexOf` to get its position in the index; otherwise, it returns −1:

```
public int contains (String surname)
// given a key surname, return its position in
// the index. If it is not present, return -1
    {
    int recNum = -1 ;
    if (index.contains(surname))
        {
        recNum = index.indexOf(surname) ;
        }
    return recNum ;
    } // end of method contains
```

Once we have a position within the index, we can obtain the `DirEntry` indicated by the index entry. The `getEntry` method obtains the index element at that position, extracts the associated record number (the position of the directory entry in the main file), and uses `DirEntry.read` to retrieve the entry from the file, which it returns as its result:

```
public DirEntry getEntry(int recNum)
// given a position in the index, return the record
// indicated by that index element
    {
    int mainRecNum, position ;
    DirEntry rec = new DirEntry() ;

    // get the relevant index element
    IndexElem ie = index.elementAt(recNum) ;

    // extract the main record number from the
    // index element
    mainRecNum = ie.getNum() ;

    try {
        // read the directory entry
        rec.read(mainRecNum) ;
        }
    catch (IOException e)
        {
        // make it into a "null" entry
        rec.clear() ;
        }
    return rec ;
    } // end of method getEntry
```

Strictly speaking, this next find method could be implemented by the client because it really combines contains and getEntry. However, it was provided for client convenience:

```
public DirEntry find (String surname)
// this method combines "contains" and "getEntry"
// for the convenience of the client.
// given a key "surname", this returns the matching
// directory entry.
// If not found, returns a "null" entry.
    {
    int recNum = contains(surname) ;
    if (recNum == -1)
        {
        DirEntry empty = new DirEntry() ;
        empty.clear() ;
        return empty ;
        }
    return (getEntry(recNum)) ;
    } // end of method find
```

Next we come to two debugging methods. One prints out the current state of the index by delegation, passing a "print" request on to the index. The second involves more implementation work because it reads through the main file, printing each directory entry individually. Arguably, this method should be part of the DirEntry class:

```
public void indexPrint()
// debugging method ...
    {
    index.print() ;
    } // end of method indexPrint

public void mainPrint()
// debugging method ...
// sequentially read and display the contents of the
// main file, one record at a time.
    {
    int i = 0 ;
    DirEntry rec = new DirEntry() ;
    boolean goOn = true ;

    while (goOn)
        {
        try {
            rec.read(i) ;
            }
        catch (IOException e)
            {
```

```
                        // we expect "end-of-file" to occur,
                        // so stop the loop when it does.
                        goOn = false ;
                        }
                if (goOn) System.out.println(i + " ' + rec) ;
                i++ ;
                }
        } // end of method mainPrint
```

Finally, we provide a `size` method so that clients can find out how many records are in the directory entry database. Again, this is implemented by delegation to the `Index` instance:

```
public int size()
// return how many records are currently in the system
    {
    return index.size() ;
    } // end of method size
```

24.3 Testing What We Have Done So Far

At this point, we want to test the various classes we have designed and implemented. We propose two programs to do this. First, because it can be tedious to enter lots of test data interactively, we want to have an initialization (`Init`) program. It will read text from a file (through standard input) and then store the corresponding records in a `DirBase`. This will allow us to test the methods for:

- Opening and closing the index and main files.
- Generally accessing the stored data.
- Adding entries to the index (are they being kept in alphabetical order?).

The format of the data is:

```
surname forename phoneNumber
```

24.3.1 Using a StreamTokenizer

We can use a `StreamTokenizer` to help us process the data in the file. You met `String-Tokenizer` in Section 19.4.1; `StreamTokenizer` is similar except that it operates on streams. It acts like a lexical analyzer on our input stream reader and breaks the input into tokens. To use a `StreamTokenizer` (in the package `java.io`), we wrap an input stream inside an instance. Thereafter, we can use the method `nextToken` to return the next token in the stream. The result of `nextToken` is an `int` that represents the kind of token we have just processed; these are coded as class constants:

- TT_EOF—end of file
- TT_EOL—end of line
- TT_NUMBER—numeric value
- TT_WORD—text

The StreamTokenizer instance provides two public attributes: nval and sval. The nval attribute is a double and stores the numeric value if the result of nextToken was TT_NUMBER. The sval attribute is a String that contains the text if the result of nextToken was TT_WORD. Notice that these are public, so we can access them directly without using selector methods.

A general structure that we could apply to process a stream of input might be as follows:

```
StreamTokenizer stin = new
        StreamTokenizer(mySomeInputStream) ;
boolean goOn = true ;
int myNumber ;
StringmyText ;

while (goOn)
    {
    result = stin.nextToken() ;
    switch (result)
        {
        case TT_EOF : // finished processing!
            goOn = false ;
            break ;
        case TT_EOL : // do something or just ignore it
            break ;
        case TT_NUMBER :
            myNumber = (int) stin.nval ;
            // process the value
            break ;
        case TT_WORD :
            myText = new String(stin.sval) ; // deep copy
            // process the value
            break ;
        default :
            System.err.println("StreamTokenizer.nextToken produced strange
    result") ;
            break ;
        }
    }
```

Anywhere we have a "simple fixed structured format" for input, a StreamTokenizer can prove very useful indeed.

We now turn to the design of the Init program (Figure 24.1).

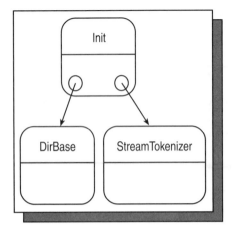

Figure 24.1: High-level design of Init

```
import java.io.* ;
import java.util.* ;

public class Init
    {

    public static void main(String[] args)
                                throws IOException
        {
        StreamTokenizer din = new StreamTokenizer(System.in) ;
        int tok ;
        String sName = new String() ;
        String fName = new String() ;
        int pNum = 0 ;
        boolean goOn = true ;
        DirBase db = new DirBase("telinfo") ;
```

We begin with a number of declarations. The ones of most interest are those involving the StreamTokenizer and the DirBase classes. The StreamTokenizer constructor associates the stream with standard input (from the keyboard or redirected from a file). The DirBase constructor, which operates as an "open" method, takes the name of a directory entry database, which we assume is currently empty.

```
        while (goOn)
            {
            tok = din.nextToken() ;
            if (tok != din.TT_EOF)
                {
                if (tok == din.TT_WORD)
```

```
                    sName = din.sval;
            else
                {
                System.out.println("expected a surname") ;
                System.exit(1) ;
                }

            tok = din.nextToken() ;
            if (tok == din.TT_WORD)
                fName = din.sval ;
            else
                {
                System.out.println("expected a forename") ;
                System.exit(1) ;
                }

            tok = din.nextToken() ;
            if (tok == din.TT_NUMBER)
                pNum = (int) din.nval ;
            else
                {
                System.out.println("expected a phone number") ;
                System.exit(1) ;
                }

            if (tok != din.TT_EOF)
                db.add(sName, fName, pNum) ;
            }
        else
            goOn = false ;
        }
```

The `while` loop in the preceding code is the workhorse of the initialization application. As long as there are tokens left in the stream, we will keep going. In the body of the loop, we try to extract three tokens: one for the surname, one for the forename, and one for the telephone number. We attempt some error checking because we expect a word, followed by a word, followed by a number. If this order is broken, we print an error message and terminate the application.

If we arrive safely at the end of the loop body, we should have the components of a directory entry. We use `DirBase.add` to add this entry to the directory entry database.

```
        System.out.println("index is ") ;
        db.indexPrint() ;
        db.close() ;
        } // end of main method
    } // end of class Init
```

Finally, we print out the state of the index contained within the `DirBase` class and close down the directory entry database.

Now that we have successfully implemented and tested our `DirBase` class (and by extension and delegation, the classes that support it) using our `Init` application, it would be possible to incorporate the `Init` functionality as a method within `DirBase`. Note also that our design completely hides details of the `DirBase`-supporting classes (`Index`, `IndexElem`, and `DirEntry`) from clients of `DirBase`. We shall see in the next chapter that this is a desirable property of design.

24.3.2   Text-Based Interface: Intermediate Application and Testing

Our second test program is a complete implementation of the final functionality of the system. However, the interface is text-based rather than graphical. The commands we want to support include some we have already identified plus a couple for testing and for user assistance:

- `stop`. This command closes down the application and asks the `DirBase` to ensure persistent data are saved and all associated files are closed.
- `find <surname>`. Provided with a surname, this uses the `DirBase` to find out if an entry with that surname exists. If it does, the entry is displayed on the screen.
- `add <surname, forename, number`. This adds this entry to the `DirBase`.
- `help`. This prints a list of commands supported by the application.

The next two commands are useful only for testing with small amounts of data. Imagine using them with a telephone directory with thousands of entries:

- `indexPrint` This prints the current state of the index.
- `mainPrint` This prints the current contents of the main file.

```
import java.io.* ;
import java.util.* ;
import javalancs.* ;

public class Main
    {
    static DirBase dirBase ;
```

We begin with two "interactive" methods. To make classes as reusable as possible, we have to be careful as to how much interaction they have with the user. For example, if we were providing a class that may be used as part of an embedded system, there is little use in having extensive dialog with the user because:

1. There may not be a direct user.

2. The system may not be connected to a keyboard.

In our case, we have tried to limit direct interaction with `DirBase` and its supporting classes. This is partly because we knew we would have to provide a graphical interface, and here again, we expect most interaction to take place via graphical components such as windows, menus, buttons, and text fields rather than directly through the keyboard.

For the keyboard user to access the `find` and `add` methods of `DirBase`, then, we provide a couple of "enveloping" interactive methods:

```
private static void findInteractive() throws IOException
    {
    String sname ;
    BasicIo.prompt("type surname: ") ;
    sname = BasicIo.readString() ;
    DirEntry rec = dirBase.find(sname) ;
    System.out.println(rec) ;
    } // end of method findInteractive

private static void addInteractive() throws IOException
    {
    String sname, fname ;
    int number ;
    BasicIo.prompt("Surname: ") ;
    sname = BasicIo.readString() ;
    BasicIo.prompt("Forename: ") ;
    fname = BasicIo.readString() ;
    BasicIo.prompt("Number: ") ;
    number = BasicIo.readInteger() ;
    dirBase.add(sname, fname, number) ;
    } // end of method addInteractive
```

The next method is the workhorse of the text-based application. It reads in single-character commands from the user and uses a `switch` statement to decide which action to take; often, as you would expect, this involves calling a `DirBase` method:

```
private static void interpCommands() throws IOException
    {
    String com ;
    boolean goOn = true ;

    while (goOn)
        {
        BasicIo.prompt("> >") ;
        com = BasicIo.readString() ;

        switch (com.charAt(0))
            {
            case 's' : goOn = false ; break ;
            case 'f' : findInteractive() ; break ;
            case 'a' : addInteractive() ; break ;
            case 'i' : dirBase.indexPrint() ; break ;
            case 'p' : dirBase.mainPrint() ; break ;
            case 'h' : listCommands() ; break ;
```

```
                    default :
                        System.out.println("Unknown command") ;
                        break ;
                    }
            } // end of command loop

    } // end of method interpCommands
```

Notice, as an alternative to providing the two interactive methods, we could have included the code we needed as part of the appropriate `case` statement. However, as you can see, it is very simple to read and understand the `case` statement as it stands. Including the code of the interactive methods here might have complicated the overall `switch` statement.

Finally, we present the `main` method itself and a simple method that will list the commands available to the user:

```
private static void listCommands()
    {
    System.out.println("s : stop \n f : find \n a : add") ;
    System.out.println("i : index print \n p : records print") ;
    System.out.println("h : help") ;
    } // end of method listCommands

public static void main(String[] args)
                            throws IOException
    {
    dirBase = new DirBase("telinfo") ;
    interpCommands() ;
    dirBase.close() ;
    } // end of main method

} // end of class Main
```

24.3.3   What Are We Testing?

We have written these two "intermediate" applications for the purpose of testing the classes we have designed and implemented. We want to ensure that they operate as expected. What are we looking for?

- When we open a `DirBase`, are the index and main files opened as expected?
- When we close a `DirBase`, are the index and main files closed correctly, with the expected information within?
- When we add a new directory entry to a `DirBase`, is the index updated correctly? Is the entry appended to the end of the main file as we expect?

When we are concerned with files, it is often helpful to have some way other than the application itself to examine the contents and layout of the files we are using. UNIX has a very useful od facility that allows us to view the contents of the file in various ways.

Issues of adding new entries focus on the sorted order of the index. Is it maintained? What we need to test are the boundary conditions: What happens when we add an entry:

- To an empty `DirBase`?
- That belongs at the end of the `DirBase`?
- That belongs at the start of the `DirBase`?
- That belongs in the middle of the `DirBase`?

We should test the system with a list of entries that are:

- In random order
- In order
- In reverse order

Finally, we must consider being able to find entries in the `DirBase`. Again, the emphasis is on boundaries. We should search for entries that we know:

- Are at the start of the ordered list
- Are at the end of the ordered list
- Are in the middle of the ordered list
- Do not exist

24.4   Graphical User Interface: The Final Prototype Application

Now that we are confident that the classes and files we have designed work as expected, we can turn our attention to providing a graphical user interface (GUI) for our personal organizer. Most users now expect fairly sophisticated graphical interfaces and would reject an application that provided the kind of user interface our test harness has. Java's AWT and Swing classes at least ease the implementation problem of generating such a graphical interface. However, this does not help us handle the graphical design problems of such interfaces. Clearly, it will be simpler to come up with a slap-dash interface that is very graphical, but such an interface may not be very useful.[1]

The graphical user interface we designed can be described as follows. The main window displays a title for the general application and a number of buttons, one for each function of the JPO and a general Done button to terminate the session. As we have implemented only one aspect of the personal organizer, we have only one button for the directory function.

---

[1]The issues of graphical interface design are beyond the scope of this book; interested readers should refer to Ben Schneiderman, *Designing the User Interface* (2nd ed.). (Reading, MA: Addison-Wesley, 1992).

The DirGui (directory interface) displays two buttons: one for New (interactively introduce new records to the system) and one for Done. For finding entries, we have a Find label and a blank text field. To initiate a search, the user types a surname value to be found and terminates it with the Return key. An earlier design and implementation consisted of a Find button and a blank text field. However, using the system in practice showed that a user needed to undertake two separate actions to initiate a search: typing in the search key and then pressing a button. The original design felt unsatisfactory, and thus, we switched to the current design and implementation.

The BrowseRecGui (browsing found records interface) has label and text-field pairs, one for each record attribute. It also has three buttons: the perennial Done button plus Forward (>>) and Backward (<<) buttons to support that mode of browsing.

The NewRecGui (new record interface) similarly has label and text-field pairs plus two buttons: Done and Enter. The latter causes the record, if fully specified, to be stored in the DirBase.

A sketch of the proposed interface is shown in Figure 24.2.

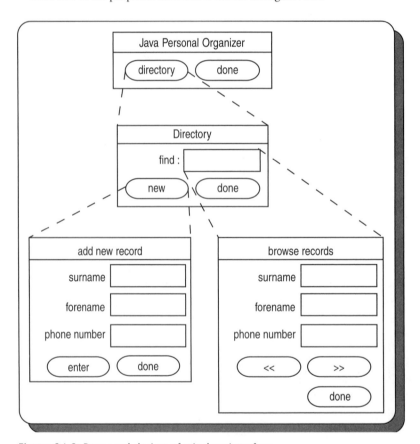

Figure 24.2: Proposed design of window interface

Each window has a corresponding class of its own. This means that we can map the design quite readily onto the partial H-S&E diagram shown in Figure 24.3.

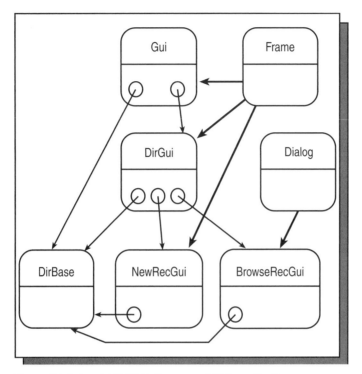

Figure 24.3: Partial H-S&E diagram of GUI application

All of our GUI classes will have to communicate with the `DirBase` to search and retrieve records from it. They will also contain references to several AWT classes, including `Buttons`, `Labels`, and `TextFields`. As you can imagine, showing this in a diagram would lead to quite a clutter. When you examine the source code for the application, you will also find a reference to the `AlertDialog` class that inherits from the AWT `Dialog` class.

Screen shots of the GUIs for the organizer and the directory, and the actions of browsing and adding new records, are shown in Figures 24.4 to 24.7. The code for these GUI classes is given in Appendix D.3.

Figure 24.4: The organizer

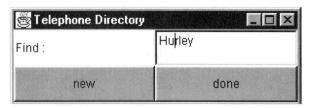

Figure 24.5: The directory

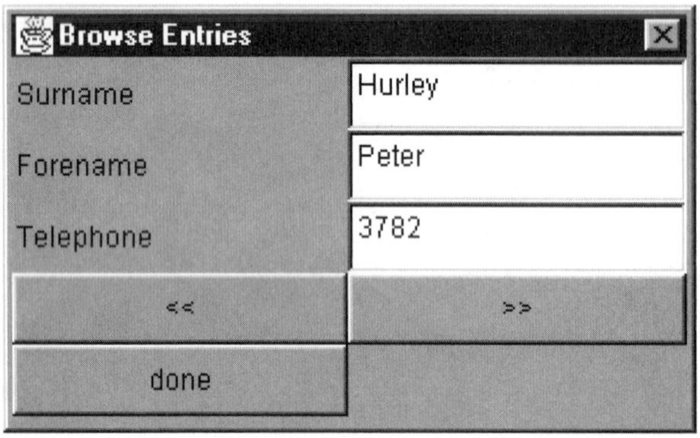

Figure 24.6: Browsing records

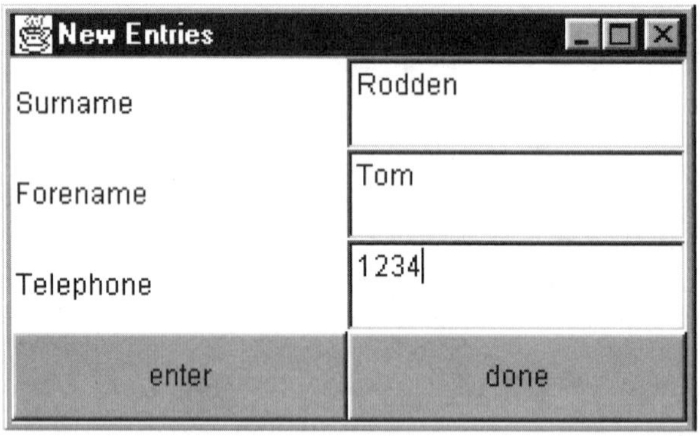

Figure 24.7: Adding a new record

24.4.1   *Testing the Graphical Interface*

We should repeat the set of tests that we carried out on the text-based version of our application. As you will recall, those tests involved adding and locating entries at the boundaries and in the middle of our ordered list. The graphical interface gives us the additional ability to browse through the ordered list; we should ensure that this browsing presents the entries in the correct order.

24.5   Using Inheritance

In this example, we have used inheritance only in our GUI classes. We did not exploit the feature in our JPO classes. This is because (obviously!) either our design did not call for it or because we were unable to use it. Once we had uncovered the unsuitability of using the `Vector` class directly, we could not introduce a new class `Index` that inherited directly from `Vector`. Instead, we had to use clientship to exploit those features of `Vectors` that were suitable.

Clearly, there will be cases where inheritance is more suitable; we have presented scenarios of inheritance in action earlier in this book. Let's stay with our JPO design for a moment and consider possible uses for inheritance if we were to evolve our design.

We quite deliberately named the `DirEntry` class to reflect the fact that we were treating the information contained within it as a classic example of a record in data processing. We were not modeling a person (as we have done so many times throughout this book), but a directory entry.

Consider, however, a computer dating agency. Its employees will also maintain a database of records about people, but when processing these data, they will often have to compare two people to gauge their suitability for each other. It will be more natural for the designers and programmers to think of people at this point rather than records. We can use inheritance to support this. We can design the class `Person`, which contains information regarding individuals. We can have a subclass `PersistPerson`, which contains the support for making `Person` information persistent (i.e., saving it between applications).

We have a clear division of concepts; on the one hand, we have the pure `Person` class, which can contain methods only about people. For example,

```
int compatible(Person p)
```

This method could return a measure between 0 and 100 to show how compatible the calling `Person` object is with the argument `Person` object.

On the other hand, we have the `PersistPerson` class (Figure 24.8), which contains methods and management information about opening and closing the `Person` database and for reading, writing, and retrieving information from that database. Because of polymorphism, everywhere we expect a `Person` instance, we can use a `PersistPerson` instance instead. Designers and developers of the `Person` class can think exclusively in terms of `Person`. Users and clients of the `Person` class, who are developing software in terms of `PersistPerson`, can quite happily use their `PersistPerson` instances with the `Person` class.

This separation of interests might be useful even for the JPO application. Now that the system is up and operational, it may occur to the users that they need to delete entries. This does not appear in the requirements and so will probably send us back to the design phase. We hope we can "massage" our existing design so that it has minimal impact on the current implementation.

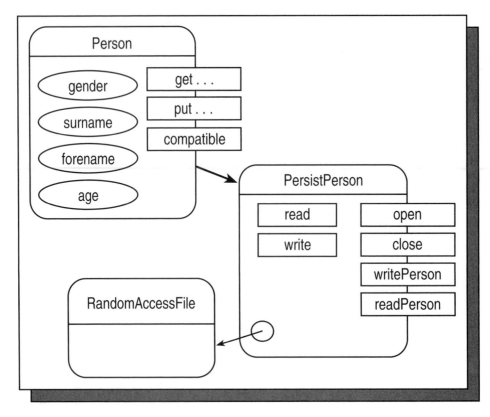

Figure 24.8: Extending the Person class through inheritance

One possible approach is to add management information to a DirEntry; we can have a Boolean flag that tells us if the record is "in use" or has been "deleted." We can see there is a difference between this attribute and the existing three attributes; what we have at the moment can all be presented to the user and is truly part of the information we would expect to find in a telephone directory. The new attribute has to do with the management of the information on the filing system. Even here, it might be useful to think of a directory entry and of a persistent directory entry.

24.6   Key Points in Chapter 24

- The StreamTokenizer class (in the package java.io) is very useful as a lexical analyzer for simple fixed structure files.
- We propose the use of a text-based interface to act as a test application for the classes developed as the result of the design process.

- Where our application is "data intensive," it is often useful to prepopulate our database for test purposes. The populating application is also a useful test of our classes.

- It is useful to identify tests that exercise the boundary conditions of our application.

- When producing a GUI, the appearance and behavior of the GUI should also be designed and prototyped.

- Although not graphically illustrated by the Java personal organizer example, inheritance is an important consideration during the design process.

24.7 Exercises

1. Show how the `contains` method of the `Index` class could be realized by using the `indexOf` method. Why could this be considered a better implementation option?

2. You should now implement the birthday system, which you started designing in Exercise 22.3. Note that there may be existing classes you have written or have been given in this book that you could use instead of writing brand-new ones.

   For the birthday system, you should provide a GUI interface that allows the user to input a date of birth and that presents the various items of information. It should also allow users easily to provide different dates of birth as often as they wish.

   You may want to produce a text-based interface to test your classes.

3. a. Write down a requirements statement for the diary component of the JPO. This should be only a short paragraph.
   b. Using the noun-and-verb approach, begin the design process by identifying possible objects, services, and attributes.
   c. Design a number of classes to support the diary component; produce H&S-E diagrams to illustrate your design and the interrelationships among the classes.
   d. Implement an `Init`-style application to test your diary classes.
   e. Design a suitable GUI that will extend the existing JPO interface to include the diary component.
   f. Finally, integrate your diary component software with the JPO.

4. Consider our suggested computer dating application.
   a. Implement a version of the `Person` class, ensuring it contains the following attributes:
      - Age
      - Gender (male, female)
      - Marital status (single, married, divorced, widowed)

      Include the following methods:
      - `eligible` Returns true if the person can be legally married and false otherwise.
      - `canMarry` Returns true if the person can be legally married to the person provided as the argument to the method and false otherwise.

      Write a small test application.
   b. Implement a subclass `PersistPerson`, which implements a "next free slot" file.
   c. Write an `Init`-style application that creates a `PersistPerson` file.
   d. Write an application that examines the contents of a `PersistPerson` file and generates:
      - A list of all those who are not eligible to marry (forename and surname).
      - A list of all pairs of people who could marry each other (forename and surname).

5. For the theater booking system, you should provide a GUI interface for the clerk; this should include a two-dimensional display of the theater's seats and their status. You should have a set of panels that allow the clerk to:
   - Book individual seats.
   - Book a row of specified seats.
   - Book a block of specified seats.
   - Search for and display a row of required seats.
   - Search for and display a block of required seats.

   You may assume that the representation of the theater (a collection of seats) can be held in main memory. You may assume there will not be a theater with more than 10 rows and 10 seats in each row.

   When the clerk asks for information about a new performance (i.e., one for which nobody has previously requested seats), the system should:
   - Initialize the theater appropriately.
   - Create the file that maintains the persistent representation of that performance.

   The layout of a theater should be stored as characters in a file. This could be:

```
XXXXXXXXXX
XXXXXXXXXX
-XXXXXXXX-
-XXXXXXXX-
--XXXXXX--
--XXXXXX--
---XXXX---
---XXXX---
----XX----
----XX----
```

   You should assume that seats are indicated by a row (letter) and a position within the row (number).

   You may want to:
   - Produce a text-based interface to test your classes.
   - Provide an application that initializes the state of a performance from a text file.

CHAPTER 25

Criteria for a Good Object-Oriented Design

25.1   Introduction

In this chapter, we present a number of criteria that are drawn from several sources in the literature (Coad and Yourdon, 1991a, 1991b; Korson and McGregor, 1990) and are thought to be aspects of good design for a program. Some of these criteria have origins in preobject work on the modular concept for software, but as you might expect, they are equally valid for objects.

25.2   Cohesion

Designs are made up of collections of pieces. For example, an object is a collection of attributes and methods. Cohesion addresses the degree to which the pieces actually belong together. In a good design, we are looking for strong cohesion. Issues of cohesion can be considered for classes, methods, and the inheritance structure.

When we define a class, we want the attributes and methods to be cohesive. We might expect classes to be naturally cohesive because they ideally model some real-world entity. There should be no redundant attributes or methods; they should all contribute to the responsibilities of an instance of the class.

In the example in Figure 25.1, every attribute and method is contributing to the responsibility of the class: to represent and maintain index elements. There are no redundant attributes; there are only the two required components of an index element. Two of the methods are selectors and one is a mutator (clear), all operating on the two attributes of the class. One method is the standard toString, and two more relate to the persistent nature of the index elements within a file.

The public methods of a class should all be *operators* of the class. That is, they all operate on the (hidden) attributes of the class. There should be no redundant methods.

Similarly, methods should carry out one, and only one, function. We should avoid methods that do only part of a function or indeed methods that do more than one thing. When methods do more than one thing, clients may not fully appreciate this or misunderstand the general purpose of the method. We can say that the "unknown" other purpose is a "side effect" and may cause system behavior that the user will find confusing, to say the least.

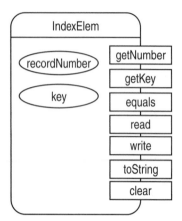

Figure 25.1: The IndexElem class

Again, with reference to the IndexElem class, if we were to provide conventional mutators, we would intentionally provide a single set mutator. In other examples, we have had a set method for each attribute, and this is often acceptable. However, the way in which we will use index elements means that whenever we set up such an element, we will always set values for both the search key and the record number:

```
indElem.set("Sommerville", 3) ; // instruction set 1
```

```
indElem.setKey("Sommerville") ; // instruction set 2
indElem.setRecordNumber(3) ;
```

The two sets of instructions in the preceding code are functionally equivalent, but the second set means we accomplish our aim in two steps; setKey and setRecordNumber are two distinct methods that contribute to our single aim.

Methods that accomplish more than one aim can be confusing. To start with a ludicrous example, consider our Person class. Imagine if the act of setting the value of a person's surname also incremented the person's age. If users aren't aware of this, they could get a surprise when they access the person's age:

```
fred.setAge(5) ;
fred.setSurname("Jones") ;
System.out.println(fred.getAge()) ; // surprise for user
```

If we give the method a sensible name, this exposes the ludicrous nature of what we have done:

```
fred.setSurnameAndIncrementAge("Jones") ; // something
                                          // wrong with our design
```

A more sensible example might be to consider that whenever a user sets a person's surname, we should clear the forename because we assume the user is in the process of changing the person's entire name.

```
myPerson.setSurname("Jones") ;
myPerson.setForename("Bill") ;        // OK

myPerson.setSurname("Smith") ;
myPerson.setForename("Jane") ;        // OK
```

There are a number of problems with this. What if Jane marries Bill? We just want to change her surname and leave her forename alone:

```
jane.setSurname("Smith") ;
jane.setForename("Jane") ;
// Jane marries Bill
jane.setSurname("Jones") ;       // we've set the surname
                                 // but lost Jane's forename
```

Even simpler, the action of setSurname assumes an ordering to the operations. We must set the surname before we set the forename:

```
bill.setForename("Bill") ;
bill.setSurname("Jones") ;       // we've set the surname
                                 // but lost Bill's forename
```

It seems pointless to insist on such an ordering.

We return to an earlier example, the Temperature class (see Section 8.5), which maintains two private attributes, celsius and fahr, and a link between them. When we set the Celsius attribute, we make sure the Fahrenheit attribute has the correct equivalent (and vice versa). Unless users have a clear idea of what is going on—the class is intended to model a single temperature but maintain a dual representation of that temperature using two different scales—they might not understand what appears to be happening:

```
myTemperature.setFahr(34.2) ;
System.out.println(myTemperature.getFahr()) ;
myTemperature.setCelsius(12.4) ;
System.out.println(myTemperature.getCelsius()) ;
System.out.println(myTemperature.getFahr()) ;
```

If they assume there are actually two distinct temperatures, they will be surprised to see that the second printing of the Fahrenheit information is different from the first. They might consider the alteration of the Fahrenheit value to be an unwanted (or at least, not understood) side effect of setting the Celsius value.

Perhaps a better design that should lead to less confusion would be to replace the two set-Fahr and setCelsius methods with a single set method:

```
myTemperature.set(34.2, Temperature.FAHRENHEIT) ;
myTemperature.set(12.4, Temperature.CELSIUS) ;
```

The class could contain two public constants, FAHRENHEIT and CELSIUS, which would allow users to specify the scale they are using. Similarly, we could have one get method:

```
myTemperature.get(Temperature.FAHRENHEIT) ;
myTemperature.get(Temperature.CELSIUS) ;
```

We use the constants to specify the scale in which we want the temperature to be returned.

A good guideline for ensuring cohesion of methods is to say that designers should be able to describe a method with a single imperative English sentence containing a single verb and a single direct object.

```
setCelsius: set the value of the Celsius attribute to the value of the
actual argument and set the Fahrenheit attribute to the equivalent value.
```

This detailed description has already broken the guideline.

```
setSurnameAndIncrementAge: set the value of the surname attribute to the
value of the argument, and increment the value of the age attribute.
```

Here we see two verbs and two direct objects.

When we link two classes via inheritance, we should also be asking whether these two classes should really be linked together or, more generally, how strong we consider that link to be. As you know, the inheritance mechanism captures the semantic concepts of generalization and specialization. When we make one class a subclass of another, we need to consider whether that subclass really is a specialization of its superclass. Have we accurately captured real-world semantics, or are we using inheritance as some kind of "useful trick"?

When we model an employee as a subclass of person, it appears to model the real-world situation if we consider the situation in terms of sets and subsets. The set of employees is a subset of all people. Similarly, if we consider the attributes and methods, everything a person has (surname, age, etc.) an employee does, too. And an employee has some additional attributes such as salary and tax code.

It is a bit harder to defend our suggested use of `Person` and `PersistPerson` in Section 24.5 as superclass and subclass. This certainly has very little to do with the real world and much more to do with aspects of software. `PersistPerson` has additional methods, but those methods relate to how we can load and save individual `Person` objects in a file; there is no equivalent real-world concept of a `PersistPerson`. The specialization here refers to how the object will be used in the computer system.

25.3   Coupling

An object-oriented program consists of an *object space*. Objects (clients) can call upon the methods of other objects (servers) to get their work done. Objects are naturally dependent on each other and can be said to be interconnected. Coupling refers to the degree of interconnection.

If parts of a system are tightly coupled (strongly connected), then changes to one part of the system will have a "knock-on" effect on other parts. Ideally, when we change one part of the system, we want to limit the impact of that change on other parts of the system. We want to have weak coupling. Another benefit of weak coupling is that if we want to understand what a particular object does (if we are trying to maintain the software), we shouldn't have to understand many other classes as well.

We can envision the way objects interact as a process of message passing. To reduce object coupling, then, we need to reduce the number of messages sent and received by individual objects. Moreover, the amount of data sent as part of a message (the arguments to a method call) should also be kept to a minimum.

The inheritance structure is one place where high coupling is desirable, but only when used properly. If it is used improperly, there are ways to avoid high-inheritance coupling:

- Use a mechanism whereby a subclass can explicitly reject attributes from its superclass. This is not possible in Java.

- Use a subclass that is not using attributes of its superclass.

25.3.1   *The Law of Demeter*

As reported in Wilfs-Brock and Johnson's, "Surveying Current Research in Object-Oriented Design" in *Communications of the ACM* (1990), the Demeter project (lead by Karl Lieberherr at Northeastern University) is developing CASE tools and their theoretical foundations to improve the productivity of object-oriented designers and programmers. They have produced a rule, the Law of Demeter, which minimizes coupling between classes.

The law states that one should not retrieve part of an object and then perform an operation on that part, but should instead perform the operation on the original object, which can perform the operation by delegating it to the part.

In our JPO design, the `DirBase` contains a reference to an `Index` object. When we add a new telephone directory entry, the `DirBase.add` method delegates the process of adding a new index element to the `Index object`. Our design obeys the Law of Demeter (Figure 25.2).

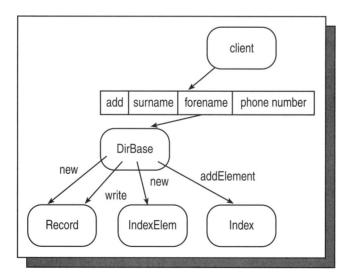

Figure 25.2: Obeying the Law of Demeter

Here's how we might break the law (Figure 25.3):

- Add a new method `getIndex` to `DirBase`.
- Use `getIndex` to obtain a reference to the `DirBase` `Index` object:

  `myIndex = dirBase.getIndex() ;`

- Now the client program has to create an appropriate index element (so we need previously hidden details on how to use the `IndexElem` class).
- Then we add the element (again, needing previously hidden details of the `Index` class).

The law enforces information hiding. If we do not follow the law, users can retrieve a subpart of an object and work on it directly. If the structure of the subpart changes, it affects all clients (direct or, in this case, indirect) of the subpart. In a sense, the encapsulation we find so desirable in the object model has broken down. If we obey the law, the change to the subpart affects only direct clients. It shouldn't affect us.

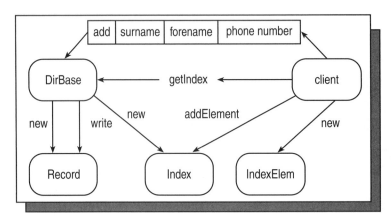

Figure 25.3: Breaking the Law of Demeter

When we obey the law, clients of `DirBase` do not need to know anything about `Index` and `IndexElem`. Changes to `Index` and `IndexElem` should have an impact only on `DirBase`. When we break the law, such changes will almost certainly require changes to the clients of `DirBase` as well.

Our discussion in Section 10.7 regarding the use of an `OurDate` instance to represent a `Person`'s date of birth can now be interpreted in terms of the Law of Demeter.

25.4   Clarity

Clarity is obviously a good characteristic of any artifact we expect other people to use and understand. This can, of course, include our Java source code. What we say here briefly about design can equally be applied to our programming. We should use sensible names for our classes, attributes, and methods. They should be common names (nothing fancy) that users can be expected to understand. We should have consistency of naming; you have seen this with our mutator and selector methods throughout this book (with names starting with `get` and `set`).

We have also used capitalization in a careful and consistent way throughout the book. We have used it within names to indicate "visible spaces"; for example, *get surname* is written as `getSurname`. An alternative approach is to use an underscore as a visible space, as in `get_surname`. It is important to pick a convention and stick with it.

Capitalization has been used to indicate the name of a class; the *person* class is written `Person`. This allows easy distinction between class names and instance, attribute, and method names. Finally, we have used all capital letters for constants, and it is here that we have also used underscores, as in `MAX_STRING_LENGTH`.

The names of classes should reflect their responsibilities. If we can't think of a good, simple name for the class we have designed, we should take a closer look at the design! The responsibility of a class should be derivable from its name (e.g., `DirBase`, `Index`, and `IndexElem` seem pretty self-descriptive class names, although some might say they are too much of an abbreviation).

25.5 Extensibility of Our Design

A fairly good measure of the quality of our design is to consider how resilient it is to change. In this section, we consider extending our Java personal organizer in two ways to see how flexible our current design is and how well it will cope with the proposed alterations.

As far as personal organizers go, our JPO is simple; it provides only a telephone directory. There is plenty of room for extending the capabilities of the system. What we want to consider here is the robustness of our design process. How easy is it to extend the system, and how much disruption does it cause to the software we have already written?

25.5.1 *Adding an Email Attribute to a Directory Entry*

Consider first a minor change; we want our telephone directory also to handle a person's email address. This may be a minor change, but it has repercussions to quite a few classes.

We have to extend our `DirEntry` class to have an additional attribute (`eMail`) and alter a number of associated methods (`toString`, `read`, and `write` to name but three). We need to extend our constructor method(s) to cope and add a new `getEmail` method. These extensions can be realized using inheritance.

We have to extend our stored record to have an additional 15 (or more) bytes to deal with the email address. Notice that this presents problems that cannot be easily handled by inheritance. Our `read` and `write` methods, as they are currently implemented, need to know the overall size of an entry (be it index or directory) in the file to calculate the starting byte position of an entry from an entry number. We would require a fairly major reorganization of how this is achieved to cope with inheritance. This is because we require information to go from a subclass to a superclass (and this is opposite to the usual flow of information in inheritance techniques).

It would have to be the subclass's responsibility to work out the starting byte position and then call a version of the superclass's read method to read in the attributes that it knows about from that start byte.

Our BrowseRecGui class will have to take account of the new attribute that it must now display.

25.5.2   Adding a Diary Feature to the Personal Organizer

A more major change is to add completely new functionality. Consider the addition of a diary feature, as proposed in Exercise 24.3. We can reuse some of our experience of designing and implementing the telephone directory.

We must decide what a diary entry looks like. It may be a String of some length, or we may require something a bit more structured—that is, "indexed" by time of day. Whatever we decide, we can treat a diary entry as a class (DiaryEntry) and as a fixed-sized record for the file.

As far as the diary is concerned, we may decide that there are a maximum of 366 days in any year and that we will maintain a file, one for each year, consisting of 366 DiaryEntry slots on the filing system. Given a date (day, month, and year), we can calculate which day of the year this is (dayYear), and this will be the number of the slot the corresponding DiaryEntry occupies within the file for that year. We can, as before, calculate the start (byte) address of the diary entry and read it into a DiaryEntry object.

However, if you are like us and do not have a very dense diary, you may feel this is very wasteful of filing system space. We can try to do something very similar to the telephone directory and use an index sequential storage structure. The diary file could again be a heap, and our index would be sorted according to day, month, and year.

However we choose to organize the diary, we could deliver a DiaryBase object for the system. This has minimal impact on the existing system; we need to provide a set of GUI interface classes and add a Diary button to the main menu, but otherwise, little else has to change. In other words, we can apply our design experience in providing the directory entry database to the task of building the diary entry database.

25.6   Key Points in Chapter 25

- *Cohesion* is a measure of how well pieces of a design or implementation belong together. In a good design, we are looking for strong cohesion.

- *Coupling* is the degree of interconnection among pieces. We are aiming at weak coupling; the more an object can stand alone, the less likely that changes to that object will have a "knock-on" effect.

- The Law of Demeter provides a rule that, if adhered to, minimizes coupling.

- *Clarity* is a measure of how easily users can understand and use an artifact. Naming, textual, and layout conventions can greatly assist clarity.

- *Extensibility* is how easily we can extend an existing design or application. Ease of extension is a sign of good design.

25.7 Exercises

1. In Exercise 20.3, we presented a problem regarding vacation accommodations. In essence, we had predesigned the application you were to build. We would like you to examine the structure and design of this application and assess it for quality.

2. In the telephone directory work, we placed the ability to browse in the user interface. This is not necessarily the right decision. If we had decided to test the browsing ability in the text-based interface, we would have duplicated the code. It may have been better to place support for browsing in the `DirBase` class. Decide on the service interfaces and additional state within the `DirBase` class to support the browsing activity and rewrite the `BrowseRecGui` method accordingly.

3. The need to delete and update directory entries has become pressing. Continue the design work from Exercise 22.2 to produce an amended set of classes for the `DirBase` application. Implement and test these classes. Develop the `Init` and text-based test applications to handle the new functionality. Extend the Java personal organizer GUI classes to cope with the additional capabilities.

   A possible approach to handle deletion would be to add a new Boolean attribute, `inUse`. You may wish to use inheritance to distinguish between those attributes that truly belong to a directory entry and those that manage the entries within the system. The `Init` application will have to ensure that `inUse` is set to true for each directory entry it sets up.

   The question now arises of what to do with the `DirEntry` slots in the file that are not in use. We can change our view of the `DirEntry` file from a heap to a "next free space" model. In other words, we want to reuse the "empty" slots. Note that if there are no empty slots, we return to using the file as a heap.

   You should make appropriate changes to the `add` functionality so that it searches for the next empty slot before falling back on the heap technique.

4. Select an applet you are familiar with from your exploration of the Web. Critique the software and, as far as possible, the design of the applet.

25.8 References

Coad, P., and E. Yourdon. 1991a. *Object-Oriented Analysis* (2nd ed.). Englewood Cliffs, NJ: Yourdon Press, Prentice Hall.

———. 1991b. *Object-Oriented Design*. Englewood Cliffs, NJ: Yourdon Press, Prentice Hall.

Korson, T., and J. D. McGregor. 1990. Understanding Object-Oriented Design: A Unifying Paradigm. *Communications of the ACM,* 33, No. 9 (September): 40–60.

Wilfs-Brock, R. J., and R. E. Johnson. 1990. Surveying Current Research in Object-Oriented Design. *Communications of the ACM,* 33, No. 9 (September): 104–124.

APPENDIX A

Getting Started with Java

The precise details of how to get started with Java depend on your computer and the source of your Java environment. Here we list the main steps you have to go through to be able to study the Java programming language; further up-to-date information is available at the Web sites that follow:

- First you need an environment in which you can compile and execute Java programs. The standard one, the environment described in this book, is the Software Development Kit (SDK) from Sun Microsystems. This can be downloaded over the Web from the Sun Web site (java.sun.com). The site gives details of the downloading process. This book describes the version of Java current in December 2001 called JAVA 2 Platform: Standard Edition: Version 1.3; it is available for Microsoft Windows, Linux, and Solaris systems.

  The SDK supplies a command-line compiler (javac) and bytecode interpreter (java), together with a number of other utility programs (e.g., appletviewer and javadoc).

  To run the compiler and other programs from any directory, you need to set the PATH variable for your system. This is described in the installation instructions supplied with all the SDK distributions. These instructions also describe how to set the CLASSPATH variable if you need to do this.

  There are also other more integrated environments for Java development, such as Symantec Café or Borland JBuilder.

- While you are programming, you need to refer to the extensive Java API—that is, the documentation for the standard Java classes. You can browse the API on the Sun Web site, or for convenience, you can download a copy of the API during the installation process.

- You will need a suitable editor so that you can write and revise the source text of your Java programs.

- This book makes use of a number of specially written classes such as the Person class in Chapter 3 and the BasicIo class for providing simple keyboard input to a Java program. These are connected together as a package javalancs, which can be downloaded from this book's Web site:

  www.comp.lancs.ac.uk/computing/users/rgg/jfcBook/

  In the folder on your computer containing the Java SDK (usually called something like jdk1.3.1_01), there will be a folder called jre (for *Java Runtime Environment*). In this folder, create a folder called classes and inside this a folder called javalancs. Copy the class files from the book's Web site into this folder. If you wish, you can store the class files elsewhere, but if you do, you will have to set the CLASSPATH variable accordingly.

- This book's Web site also contains the API for the classes in the javalancs package, the code for all the examples discussed in the text, and other useful information.

- Extensive information is available on the Sun Web site, including an online Java tutorial. Other useful sources of information and example Java programs are at www.jars.com and www.javaboutique.com.

APPENDIX B

Keywords in Java

This appendix lists all the keywords in Java, together with the numbers of the chapters where the main uses of the keyword are explained. These keywords are *reserved;* that is, you cannot use them as names of variables, methods, and so on.

abstract (14)

boolean (4, 6)

break (4, 5)

byte (6)

case (4)

catch (15)

char (6)

class (3, 7)

const[a]

continue (5)

default (4)

do (5)

double (6)

else (4)

extends (12)

false (4)

final (8)

finally (15)

float (6)

for (5)

goto[a]

if (4)

implements (14)

import (3, 8)

instanceof (21)

int (6)

interface (14)

long (6)

native[b]

new (3)

null (3, 17)

package (3, 8)

private (8)

protected (8)

public (3, 8)

return (7)

short (6)

static (8)

strictfp[b]

super (13)

switch (4)

synchronized (21)

this (8)

throw (15)

throws (15)

transient[b]

true (4)

try (15)

void (3, 7)

volatile[b]

while (5)

[a] Reserved for possible use.
[b] Not discussed in this book.

ASCII and Unicode Characters

Here we list the basic printable ASCII characters, the corresponding Unicode encoding (which is in hexadecimal, as explained in Section 6.6), and the decimal equivalent.

ASCII Character	Unicode Encoding	Decimal Equivalent
space	\u0020	32
!	\u0021	33
"	\u0022	34
#	\u0023	35
$	\u0024	36
%	\u0025	37
&	\u0026	38
'	\u0027	39
(	\u0028	40
)	\u0029	41
*	\u002a	42
+	\u002b	43
,	\u002c	44
-	\u002d	45
.	\u002e	46
/	\u002f	47
0	\u0030	48
1	\u0031	49
2	\u0032	50
3	\u0033	51
4	\u0034	52
5	\u0035	53
6	\u0036	54
7	\u0037	55
8	\u0038	56
9	\u0039	57
:	\u003a	58
;	\u003b	59
<	\u003c	60
=	\u003d	61
>	\u003e	62
?	\u003f	63
@	\u0040	64
A	\u0041	65

ASCII Character	Unicode Encoding	Decimal Equivalent
B	\u0042	66
C	\u0043	67
D	\u0044	68
E	\u0045	69
F	\u0046	70
G	\u0047	71
H	\u0048	72
I	\u0049	73
J	\u004a	74
K	\u004b	75
L	\u004c	76
M	\u004d	77
N	\u004e	78
O	\u004f	79
P	\u0050	80
Q	\u0051	81
R	\u0052	82
S	\u0053	83
T	\u0054	84
U	\u0055	85
V	\u0056	86
W	\u0057	87
X	\u0058	88
Y	\u0059	89
Z	\u005a	90
[	\u005b	91
\	\u005c[a]	92
]	\u005d	93
^	\u005e	94
_	\u005f	95
`	\u0060	96
a	\u0061	97
b	\u0062	98
c	\u0063	99
d	\u0064	100
e	\u0065	101
f	\u0066	102

---

[a] Note this character has to be written '\u005c\u005c'.

ASCII Character	Unicode Encoding	Decimal Equivalent
g	\u0067	103
h	\u0068	104
i	\u0069	105
j	\u006a	106
k	\u006b	107
l	\u006c	108
m	\u006d	109
n	\u006e	110
o	\u006f	111
p	\u0070	112
q	\u0071	113
r	\u0072	114
s	\u0073	115
t	\u0074	116
u	\u0075	117
v	\u0076	118
w	\u0077	119
x	\u0078	120
y	\u0079	121
z	\u007a	122
{	\u007b	123
l	\u007c	124
}	\u007d	125
~	\u007e	126

Program Listings

D.1 Person.java

This is the code of the Person class (see Chapters 7 and 8). You will notice the comments in this code look slightly different from the other listings in the book. This is because the comments are in a format that enables them to be extracted automatically by a program called javadoc to create the documentation for the Person class that you have been accessing with a browser. Thus, for example, the javadoc program knows that a line containing @param contains a description of one of the arguments of a method.

```java
package javalancs ;

/*...*
 * Represents simple facts about a person
 * @author Roger Garside
 * First Written: January 15, 1997
 * @version Last Rewritten: November 28, 2001
 */

public class Person
    {
    // Person Class Constants

    /*
     * Constant - the upper limit for the age
     */
    private static final int UPPER_AGE = 150 ;

    /**
     * Constant - unknown gender
     */
    public static final int UNKNOWN = 99 ;

    /**
     * Constant - male gender
     */
    public static final int MALE = 1 ;

    /**
     * Constant - female gender
     */
    public static final int FEMALE = 2 ;

    // Person Instance Variables
```

```
/*
 * the person's (single) forename
 */
private String forename ;

/*
 * the person's surname
 */
private String surname ;

/*
 * the person's age
 */
private int age ;

/*
 * the person's gender
 */
private int gender ;

// Person Constructor Methods

/**
 * Creates an instance of the Person class with default values
 * (forename = "NONE", surname = "NONE", age = 0, gender = UNKNOWN)
 */
public Person()
    {
    forename = "NONE" ;
    surname = "NONE" ;
    age = 0 ;
    gender = UNKNOWN ;
    } // end of constructor method

/**
 * Creates an instance of the Person class with specified attribute
 * values
 * @param f forename of the person
 * @param s surname of the person
 * @param a age of the person
 * @param g gender of the person
 */
public Person(String f, String s, int a, int g)
    {
    if (f.length() < 1)
        {
        System.err.println("invalid forename argument in constructor") ;
        System.exit(1) ;
        }
    forename = f ;
    if (s.length() < 1)
```

```
                {
                System.err.println("invalid surname argument in constructor") ;
                System.exit(1) ;
                }
        surname = s ;
        if ((a < 0) || (a > UPPER_AGE))
                {
                System.err.println("invalid age argument in constructor") ;
                System.exit(1) ;
                }
        age = a ;
        if ((g != MALE) && (g != FEMALE) && (g != UNKNOWN))
                {
                System.err.println("invalid gender argument in constructor") ;
                System.exit(1) ;
                }
        gender = g ;
        } // end of constructor method

// Person Class Methods

/**
 * returns the upper limit for a valid age
 * @return the upper limit for a valid age
 */
public static int getUpperAgeLimit()
        {
        return UPPER_AGE ;
        } // end of method getUpperAgeLimit

// Person Instance Methods - Selectors

/**
 * returns the forename attribute of the person
 * @return the forename attribute of the person
 */
public String getForename()
        {
        return forename ;
        } // end of method getForename

/**
 * returns the surname attribute of the person
 * @return the surname attribute of the person
 */
public String getSurname()
        {
        return surname ;
        } // end of method getSurname
```

```java
/**
 * returns the age attribute of the person
 * @return the age attribute of the person
 */
public int getAge()
    {
    return age ;
    } // end of method getAge

/**
 * returns the gender attribute of the person
 * @return the gender attribute of the person
 */
public int getGender()
    {
    return gender ;
    } // end of method getGender

/**
 * returns the gender attribute of the person as a String
 * @return the gender attribute of the person as a String
 */
public String getGenderString()
    {
    String x = "unknown" ;
    switch (gender)
        {
        case MALE :
            x = "male" ;
            break ;
        case FEMALE :
            x = "female" ;
            break ;
        case UNKNOWN :
            x = "unknown" ;
            break ;
        }
    return x ;
    } // end of method getGenderString

// Instance Methods - Mutators

/**
 * set the forename attribute of the person
 * @param f the forename of the person
 */
public void setForename(String f)
    {
    if (f.length() < 1)
        {
        System.err.println("invalid forename argument in 'setForename'") ;
```

```
            System.exit(1) ;
            }
        forename = f ;
        } // end of method setForename

/**
 * set the surname attribute of the person
 * @param s the surname of the person
 */
public void setSurname(String s)
    {
    if (s.length() < 1)
        {
        System.err.println("invalid surname argument in 'setSurname'") ;
        System.exit(1) ;
        }
    surname = s ;
    } // end of method setSurname

/**
 * set the age attribute of the person
 * @param a the age of the person
 */
public void setAge(int a)
    {
    if ((a < 0) || (a > UPPER_AGE))
        {
        System.err.println("invalid age argument in 'setAge'") ;
        System.exit(1) ;
        }
    age = a ;
    } // end of method setAge

/**
 * set the gender attribute of the person
 * @param g the gender of the person
 */
public void setGender(int g)
    {
    if ((g != MALE) && (g != FEMALE) && (g != UNKNOWN))
        {
        System.err.println("invalid gender argument in 'setGender'") ;
        System.exit(1) ;
        }
    gender = g ;
    } // end of method setGender

// Other Person Methods

/**
 * increase the age of the person by the specified amount
```

```
         * @param n the number of years by which the age attribute should
         * be increased
         */
        public void increaseAge(int n)
            {
            if ((n < 1) || (age + n > UPPER_AGE))
                {
                System.err.println("invalid age in 'increaseAge'") ;
                System.exit(1) ;
                }
            age += n ;
            } // end of method increaseAge

    /**
     * set the full name of the person in one operation
     * @param f the forename of the person
     * @param s the surname of the person
     */
    public void setFullName(String f, String s)
        {
        if ((f.length() < 1) || (s.length() < 1))
            {
            System.err.println("invalid name arguments(s) in 'setFullName'") ;
            System.exit(1) ;
            }
        forename = f ;
        surname = s ;
        } // end of method setFullName

    /**
     * return the formal title of the person
     * @return the formal name of the person ('Mr' or 'Ms', initial, surname)
     */
    public String formalTitle()
        {
        String s;

        if (gender == MALE)
            s = "Mr " ;
        else if (gender == FEMALE)
            s = "Ms " ;
        else
            s = "" ;
        return s + forename.charAt(0) + ". " + surname ;
        } // end of method formalTitle

    /**
     * return a string representing the person
     * @return details of the person ('forename surname (age: gender)')
     */
    public String toString()
```

```
        {
        return forename + ' ' + surname + " (" + age + ": " +
                getGenderString() + ')' ;
        } // end of method toString

    /**
     * return a copy of the person
     * @return a copy of the Person instance
     */
    public Person copy()
        {
        Person result = new Person() ;
        result.forename = new String(forename) ;
        result.surname = new String(surname) ;
        result.age = age ;
        result.gender = gender ;
        return result ;
        } // end of method copy

    } // end of class Person
```

D.2 Chapter20n2.java

This is the applet to access copies of the programs used in this book (see Section 20.4).

```
/*
 *
 * applet to display demonstration Java program source code
 *
 * Written by: Roger Garside
 *
 * First Written: February 2, 1997
 * Last Rewritten: December 18, 2001
 *
 */

import java.applet.* ;
import java.awt.* ;
import java.awt.event.* ;
import java.io.* ;
import java.net.* ;
import java.util.* ;

public class Chapter20n2 extends Applet
                                    implements ActionListener
    {
    // picture elements
    private Label label ;
    private TextArea area ;
```

```
private Button main, chap, prog ;

private static final int MAX_NO_OF_PROGRAMS = 200 ;

// list of all programs available
private int noOfPrograms ;
private ProgramDetails[] progs = new
                        ProgramDetails[MAX_NO_OF_PROGRAMS] ;
private String indexString ;
// list of programs for current chapter
private int noOfPrograms1 ;
private ProgramDetails[] progs1 = new
                        ProgramDetails[MAX_NO_OF_PROGRAMS] ;
private String indexString1 ;

/*
 *
 * init
 *
 */

public void init()
    {
    readIndex() ;

    setLayout(new BorderLayout()) ;
    setBackground(Color.green) ;
    label = new Label("Main Index", Label.CENTER) ;
    add("North", label) ;

    // set up the text area
    area = new TextArea(20, 80) ;
    area.setText(indexString) ;
    add("Center", area) ;

    // set up the buttons
    Panel p = new Panel() ;
    p.setLayout(new FlowLayout()) ;
    main = new Button("Main Index") ;
    p.add(main) ;
    main.addActionListener(this) ;
    main.setEnabled(false) ;
    chap = new Button("Chapter") ;
    p.add(chap) ;
    chap.addActionListener(this) ;
    chap.setEnabled(true) ;
    prog = new Button("Program") ;
    p.add(prog) ;
    prog.addActionListener(this) ;
    prog.setEnabled(false) ;
    add("South", p) ;
    } // end of method init
```

```
/*
 *
 * readIndex
 *
 */

private void readIndex()
    {
    try {
        // access the file "programList"
        URL index = new URL(getDocumentBase(), "programList") ;
        BufferedReader stream = new BufferedReader(new
                        InputStreamReader(index.openStream())) ;

        // read the program list into the array "prog"
        // and the chapter names into the string "indexString"
        noOfPrograms = 0 ;
        indexString = "" ;
        String previousFirst = "" ;
        while (true)
            {
            String line = stream.readLine() ;
            if (line == null)
                break ;
            StringTokenizer st = new StringTokenizer(line, "/") ;
            String first = st.nextToken() ;
            String second = st.nextToken() ;
            if (noOfPrograms >= MAX_NO_OF_PROGRAMS)
                {
                System.err.println("too many programs") ;
                System.exit(1) ;
                }
            progs[noOfPrograms] = new
                        ProgramDetails(first, second) ;
            if (!first.equals(previousFirst))
                {
                if (indexString.length() != 0)
                    indexString += '\n' ;
                progs[noOfPrograms].start =
                        indexString.length() ;
                indexString += first ;
                progs[noOfPrograms].finish =
                        indexString.length() ;
                }
            previousFirst = first ;
            noOfPrograms++ ;
            }
        }
    catch (IOException ex)
```

```
                    {
                    System.err.println("ERROR: " + ex) ;
                    }
            } // end of method readIndex

    /*
     *
     * actionPerformed
     *
     */

    public void actionPerformed(ActionEvent event)
            {
        // deal with "Main Index" button
        if (event.getSource() == main)
            {
            label.setText("Main Index") ;
            area.setText(indexString) ;
            main.setEnabled(false) ;
            chap.setEnabled(true) ;
            prog.setEnabled(false) ;
            }
        // deal with "Chapter" button
        else if (event.getSource() == chap)
            {
            // get the line selected
            int start = area.getSelectionStart() ;
            int finish = area.getSelectionEnd() ;
            // look for the entry in the "prog" array
            int i = 0 ;
            while ((i < noOfPrograms) && (start > progs[i].finish))
                i++ ;
            if (i == noOfPrograms)
                System.err.println("no chapter selected") ;
            else
                {
                // extract a list of programs in this chapter into the
                // array "prog1" and the string "indexString1"
                String thisChap = progs[i].first ;
                noOfPrograms1 = 0 ;
                indexString1 = "" ;
                for (int j = 0 ; j < noOfPrograms ; j++)
                    if (progs[j].first.equals(thisChap))
                        {
                        progs1[noOfPrograms1] = new
                                ProgramDetails(thisChap, progs[j].second) ;
                        if (indexString1.length() != 0)
                            indexString1 += '\n' ;
                        progs1[noOfPrograms1].start =
                                indexString1.length() ;
                        indexString1 += progs[j].second ;
```

```
                            progs1[noOfPrograms1].finish =
                                      indexString1.length() ;
                            noOfPrograms1++ ;
                            }
                label.setText(thisChap) ;
                area.setText(indexString1) ;
                main.setEnabled(true) ;
                chap.setEnabled(false) ;
                prog.setEnabled(true) ;
                }
            }
// deal with "Program" button
else if (event.getSource() == prog)
        {
        // get the line selected
        int start = area.getSelectionStart() ;
        int finish = area.getSelectionEnd() ;
        // look for the entry in the "prog1" array
        int i = 0 ;
        while ((i < noOfPrograms1) && (start > progs1[i].finish))
            i++ ;
        if (i == noOfPrograms1)
            System.err.println("no program selected") ;
        else
            {
            // access the appropriate file of source text
            String thisProg = progs1[i].second ;
            try {
                URL t = new URL(getDocumentBase(), thisProg) ;
                BufferedReader stream = new
                            BufferedReader(new InputStreamReader(t.openStream())) ;
                String textString = "" ;
                while (true)
                    {
                    String line = stream.readLine() ;
                    if (line = = null)
                        break ;
                  if (textString.length() != 0)
                        textString += '\n' ;
                    textString += line ;
                    }
                label.setText(thisProg) ;
                area.setText(textString) ;
                main.setEnabled(true) ;
                chap.setEnabled(false) ;
                prog.setEnabled(false) ;
                }
            catch (IOException e1)
                {
                System.err.println("ERROR: " + e1) ;
                }
```

```
                    }
                  }
               } // end of method actionPerformed
            } // end of class Chapter20n2

class ProgramDetails
    {
    String first, second ;
    int start, finish ;

    /**
     * constructor
     */
    public ProgramDetails(String f, String s)
        {
        first = f ;
        second = s ;
        start = -1 ;
        finish = -1 ;
        } // end of constructor method
    } // end of class ProgramDetails
```

D.3   The GUI Source Code for the Java Personal Organizer

D.3.1   The Gui Class

```
// Gui class (main program)
// =========

import java.awt.* ;
import java.awt.event.* ;
import java.io.* ;
import java.util.* ;

public class Gui extends Frame implements WindowListener, ActionListener
    {
    // link to directory component
    static DirBase dirBase ;

    // application window components

    Button dirButton, doneButton ;
    DirGui myDirGui ;

    public Gui()
        {
        super("Java Personal Organizer") ;
```

```
        setup() ;
        }// end of constructor method

// setup the window for the application
public void setup()
    {
    setSize(300,60) ;
    setLayout(new GridLayout(1,2)) ;

    dirButton = new Button("directory") ;
    doneButton = new Button("done") ;

    add(dirButton) ;
    add(doneButton) ;

    dirButton.addActionListener(this) ;
    doneButton.addActionListener(this) ;

    show() ;

    myDirGui = new DirGui(dirBase) ;
    } // end of method setup

// Process actions

public void actionPerformed (ActionEvent event)
    {
    if (event.getSource() == doneButton)
        {
        dirBase.close() ;
        // shutdown the program
        System.exit(0) ;
        }
    else if (event.getSource() == dirButton)
        {
        myDirGui.show() ;
        }
    } // end of method actionPerformed

public static void main(String[] args) throws IOException
    {
    dirBase = new DirBase("telinfo") ;
    Gui myGui = new Gui() ;
    } // end of main method

public void windowOpened(WindowEvent event) {}
public void windowIconified(WindowEvent event) {}
public void windowDeiconified(WindowEvent event) {}
public void windowClosed(WindowEvent event) {}
public void windowActivated(WindowEvent event) {}
public void windowDeactivated(WindowEvent event) {}
```

```
public void windowClosing(WindowEvent event)
    {
    dispose() ;
    System.exit(0) ;
    } // end of method windowClosing

} // end of class Gui
```

D.3.2   *The* DirGui *Class*

```
// DirGui class
// ============

import java.awt.* ;
import java.awt.event.* ;
import java.io.* ;
import java.util.* ;

public class DirGui extends Frame implements WindowListener, ActionListener
    {

    // link to directory component
    DirBase dirBase ;

    // application window components

    Button newButton, doneButton ;
    Label findLabel = new Label("Find: ") ;
    TextField sNameField ;
    String sName ;

    BrowseRecGui myBrowseRecGui ;
    NewRecGui myNewRecGui ;

    public DirGui(DirBase db)
        {
        super("Telephone Directory") ;
        dirBase = db ;
        setup() ;
        }// end of constructor method

    public void setup()
    // setup the window for the application
        {
        setSize(300,100) ;
        setLayout(new GridLayout(2, 2)) ;

        sNameField = new TextField(10) ;
        newButton = new Button("new") ;
        doneButton = new Button("done") ;
```

```
        add(findLabel) ;
        add(sNameField) ;
        add(newButton) ;
        add(doneButton) ;

        sNameField.addActionListener(this) ;
        newButton.addActionListener(this) ;
        doneButton.addActionListener(this) ;

        myBrowseRecGui = new BrowseRecGui(this, dirBase) ;
        myNewRecGui = new NewRecGui(dirBase) ;
        } // end of method setup

public void actionPerformed (ActionEvent event)
    {
    DirEntry rec ;
    int recNum ;

    if (event.getSource() == doneButton)
        {
        setVisible(false);
        }
    else if (event.getSource() == newButton)
        {
        myNewRecGui.show() ;
        }
    else if (event.getSource() == sNameField)
        {
        sName = new String(sNameField.getText()) ;
        System.out.println("request to find "+sName) ;
        recNum = dirBase.contains(sName) ;
        if (recNum != -1)
            {
            rec = dirBase.find(sName) ;
            System.out.println(rec) ;
            myBrowseRecGui.load(rec,recNum) ;
            myBrowseRecGui.show() ;
            }
        else
            {
            rec = new DirEntry  () ;
            rec.clear() ;
            myBrowseRecGui.load(rec,-1) ;
            myBrowseRecGui.show() ;
            }
        }
    } // end of method actionPerformed

public void windowOpened(WindowEvent event) {}
public void windowIconified(WindowEvent event) {}
public void windowDeiconified(WindowEvent event) {}
```

```
        public void windowClosed(WindowEvent event) {}
        public void windowActivated(WindowEvent event) {}
        public void windowDeactivated(WindowEvent event) {}

        public void windowClosing(WindowEvent event)
            {
            dispose() ;
            } // end of method windowClosing

        } // end of class DirGui
```

D.3.3   *The* BrowseRecGui *Class*

```
// BrowseRecGui class
// ==================

import java.awt.* ;
import java.awt.event.* ;
import java.io.* ;
import java.util.* ;

class BrowseRecGui extends Dialog implements WindowListener, ActionListener
    {

    int recNum = 0 ;
    DirBase dirBase ;

    // application window components

    Button fwdButton, revButton, doneButton ;
    TextField fName, sName, telNo ;
    Label fNameLabel, sNameLabel, telNoLabel ;

    public BrowseRecGui(Frame parent, DirBase db)
        {
        super(parent, "Browse Entries", true) ;

        setSize(300,180) ;
        setLayout(new GridLayout(5, 2)) ;

        fName = new TextField(10) ;
        sName = new TextField(10) ;
        telNo = new TextField(10) ;

        fNameLabel = new Label ("Forename") ;
        sNameLabel = new Label ("Surname") ;
        telNoLabel = new Label ("Telephone") ;

        add(sNameLabel) ;
        add(sName) ;
        add(fNameLabel) ;
```

```
        add(fName) ;
        add(telNoLabel) ;
        add(telNo) ;

        revButton = new Button("<<") ;
        fwdButton = new Button(">>") ;
        doneButton = new Button("done") ;
        add(revButton) ;
        add(fwdButton) ;
        add(doneButton) ;

        revButton.addActionListener(this) ;
        fwdButton.addActionListener(this) ;
        doneButton.addActionListener(this) ;
        dirBase = db ;
        } // end of constructor method

public void actionPerformed (ActionEvent event)
        {
        DirEntry rec = new DirEntry() ;
        if (event.getSource() == doneButton)
            {
            setVisible(false) ;
            }
        else if (event.getSource() == revButton)
            {
            if (recNum != -1)
                {
                recNum-- ;
                // implement wrapround
                if (recNum < 0)
                    recNum = dirBase.size() - 1 ;
                rec = dirBase.getEntry(recNum) ;
                load(rec,recNum) ;
                }
            }
        else if (event.getSource() == fwdButton)
            {
            if (recNum != -1)
                {
                recNum++ ;
                // implement wrapround
                if (recNum > dirBase.size()-1)
                    recNum = 0 ;
                rec = dirBase.getEntry(recNum) ;
                load(rec,recNum) ;
                }
            }
        } // end of method actionPerformed
```

```
        public void load(DirEntry rec, int rNum)
        // given a "dirEntry", this loads up the graphic display accordingly
            {
            fName.setText(rec.getForename()) ;
            sName.setText(rec.getSurname()) ;
            telNo.setText(Integer.toString(rec.getNumber())) ;
            recNum = rNum ;
            }

    public void windowOpened(WindowEvent event) {}
    public void windowIconified(WindowEvent event) {}
    public void windowDeiconified(WindowEvent event) {}
    public void windowClosed(WindowEvent event) {}
    public void windowActivated(WindowEvent event) {}
    public void windowDeactivated(WindowEvent event) {}

    public void windowClosing(WindowEvent event)
        {
        dispose() ;
        } // end of method windowClosing

    } // end of class BrowseRecGui
```

D.3.4   The NewRecGui Class

```
// NewRecGui class
// ===============

import java.awt.* ;
import java.awt.event.* ;
import java.io.* ;
import java.util.* ;

class NewRecGui extends Frame implements WindowListener, ActionListener
    {

    int recNum ;
    DirBase dirBase ;
    String fName, sName, telNoStr ;

    // application window components

    Button enterButton, doneButton ;
    TextField fNameTf, sNameTf, telNoTf ;
    Label fNameLabel, sNameLabel, telNoLabel ;

    public NewRecGui(DirBase db)
        {
        super("New Entries") ;
```

```
        setSize(300,180) ;
        setLayout(new GridLayout(4, 2)) ;

        fNameTf = new TextField(10) ;
        sNameTf = new TextField(10) ;
        telNoTf = new TextField(10) ;

        fNameLabel = new Label ("Forename") ;
        sNameLabel = new Label ("Surname") ;
        telNoLabel = new Label ("Telephone") ;

        add(sNameLabel) ;
        add(sNameTf) ;
        add(fNameLabel) ;
        add(fNameTf) ;
        add(telNoLabel) ;
        add(telNoTf) ;

        enterButton = new Button("enter") ;
        doneButton = new Button("done") ;
        add(enterButton) ;
        add(doneButton) ;

        enterButton.addActionListener(this) ;
        doneButton.addActionListener(this) ;

        sNameTf.addActionListener(this) ;
        fNameTf.addActionListener(this) ;
        telNoTf.addActionListener(this) ;
        dirBase = db ;
        } // end of constructor method
public void actionPerformed (ActionEvent event)
    {

    if (event.getSource() == doneButton)
        {
        setVisible(false) ;
        }
    else if (event.getSource() == enterButton)
        {
        if ((sName == null) || (fName == null) ||
            (telNoStr == null))
            {
            AlertDialog id = new AlertDialog(this,
                        "Incomplete record specified") ;
            }
        else
            {
            int telNo;
            telNo = Integer.parseInt(telNoStr) ;
            dirBase.add(sName,fName,telNo) ;
```

```
                        sName = null ;
                        fName = null ;
                        telNoStr = null ;
                        sNameTf.setText(null) ;
                        fNameTf.setText(null) ;
                        telNoTf.setText(null) ;
                        }

                }
            else if (event.getSource() == sNameTf)
                {
                sName = new String(sNameTf.getText()) ;
                }
            else if (event.getSource() == fNameTf)
                {
                fName = new String(fNameTf.getText()) ;
                }
            else if (event.getSource() == telNoTf)
                {
                telNoStr = new String(telNoTf.getText()) ;
                }
            } // end of method actionPerformed

        public void windowOpened(WindowEvent event) {}
        public void windowIconified(WindowEvent event) {}
        public void windowDeiconified(WindowEvent event) {}
        public void windowClosed(WindowEvent event) {}
        public void windowActivated(WindowEvent event) {}
        public void windowDeactivated(WindowEvent event) {}

        public void windowClosing(WindowEvent event)
            {
            dispose() ;
            } // end of method windowClosing

        } // end of class NewRecGui
```

D.3.5   *The* AlertDialog *Class*

```
// AlertDialog class
// ================

import java.awt.* ;
import java.awt.event.* ;

public class AlertDialog extends Dialog
                                implements WindowListener, ActionListener
        {
        protected Button button ;
        protected Label label ;
```

```java
public AlertDialog(Frame parent, String message)
    {
    super(parent,"ALERT",false) ;

    this.setLayout(new BorderLayout(15, 15)) ;

    label = new Label(message) ;
    this.add("Center",label) ;

    button = new Button("Okay") ;
    Panel p = new Panel() ;
    p.setLayout(new FlowLayout(FlowLayout.CENTER,15,15)) ;
    p.add(button) ;

    button.addActionListener(this) ;
    this.add("South",p) ;

    this.pack() ;
    this.show() ;
    }// end of constructor method

public void actionPerformed (ActionEvent event)
    {
    if (event.getSource() == button)
        {
        this.setVisible(false) ;
        this.dispose() ;
        }
    } // end of method actionPerformed

public void windowOpened(WindowEvent event) {}
public void windowIconified(WindowEvent event) {}
public void windowDeiconified(WindowEvent event) {}
public void windowClosed(WindowEvent event) {}
public void windowActivated(WindowEvent event) {}
public void windowDeactivated(WindowEvent event) {}

public void windowClosing(WindowEvent event)
    {
    dispose() ;
    } // end of method windowClosing

} // end of class AlertDialog
```

Index

{} (braces) in compound (selection) statements, 90
{} (braces) in Java programs, 22
; (semicolon), in Java statements, 23
&& (ampersands), short circuit operator, 100, 133
\ (backslash) as escape character, 156
\ (backslash) in path names, 15
= (equal sign), assignment operator, 55
== (equal signs), relational operator, 92
% (percent sign), as modulus operator, 148
+ (plus sign), concatenation operator, 62–63
// (slashes), comment indicator, 57
/ (slash), in path names, 15
<applet> tag, 487
<param> tag, 489

A
absolute path names, 15
abstract classes, 333–338
abstract classes, polymorphism, 338–340
abstract data type, 290
abstract methods, 334
Abstract Windowing Toolkit (AWT), 366
access modifiers, 22
access rights and subclasses, 304–305
accessing other computers, 478–479
accumulator, 10
ActionEvent class, 385
actionPerformed() method, 376–377, 385, 494
actual arguments, 67, 177–182
actual arguments, changing contents of, 263–266
actual arguments, passing, 182–185
addElement() method of Vector, 500
address, 9, 408
airplane reservations, example of programming with inheritance, 305–310
AlertDialog class, source code, 612–613
algorithms, 3–5
ampersands (&&), short circuit operator, 100, 133
animation, 383–386
API (Application Program Interface), 20
Applet class, 484
Applet, using, 486–489
applet. See also applications; programs
    actionPerformed() method, 494–495
    appletviewer, 486
    compiling, 486
    creating, 484–486
    definition, 16, 484
    document base, 493
    example, 490–495
    getDocumentBase() method, 493
    HTML code, example, 486–490
    invoking, 486
    parameters, 489–490

readIndex() method, 493–494
    security, 495
    tag <applet>, 487
    URLs, getting, 493–494
appletviewer, 486
application, 20, 484
Application Program Interface (API), 20
application programs, 2
applications. See also applets; programs
    program structure, example, 48–49
arc, of a tree, 443
arguments
    actual, 67, 177–182
    changing the contents of an object, 263–266
    definition, 23 See also parameters
    formal, 67, 177, 178–182
    modes of passing, 182–185
    ordering of actual and formal, 179
    to methods, 147
arithmetic operations, data requirements, 10
arrays
    and data structures, 406–409
    as arguments, 234–237
    as collections of elements, 218–221
    assigning values to, 219–220
    columns, 237
    definition, 6, 406
    indexes, 219
    length attribute, 219
    literal array expressions, 219–220
    looping through, 218–221
    multi-dimensional, 237–240
    nonrectangular, 241–242
    of objects, 221–223
    rows, 237
    searching
        binary search, 226–227
        serial searches, 223–226
    sorting, 227–233
    two-dimensional, 237
ASCII character set, 156
ASCII characters, list of, 590–592
ASCII data types, 156–157
assignment statement, 56, 145
assignment statement, on Strings, 159
attributes
    default initialization values, 191
    definition, 32, 174
    extracting by method, 60–63
    protected, 304–305
    setting by method, 57–60
AWT (Abstract Windowing Toolkit), 366

B
background colors, 373
backslash (\), as escape character, 156

backslash(\), in path names, 15
base case, in recursion, 435
base class, in an inheritance relationship, 298
base task, in recursion, 434
basic data types, 142–147
binary file facilities, 459
binary files, 476–477
binary search, of an array, 226–227
binary trees
    code for, 447–452
    description, 442–452
    inserting elements, 448–451
    listing contents of, 451–452
    root elements, 444–445
    searching, 445–447
    subtrees, 444
    updating, 448–451
bit, 9
black box mechanisms, 30
blocks, in a file, 531
body, of a loop, 113
body, of a method, 23, 175
boolean algebra, 97
boolean expressions
    description, 86, 92–95
    loops, 121, 132–134
    precedence of operators, 98
    selection statements, 86–89
boolean type, 96–101, 155
Boolean wrapper class, 162–165
border layout manager, 374
braces ({})
    in compound statements, 90
    in Java programs, 22
break statement
    as part of a switch statement, 102
    break out of a loop, 124–126
    the labeled break, 137
BrowseRecGui class, source code, 608–610
browsers, 16
    Java-aware, 16, 19
BufferedReader class, 466–471
buffers, flushing, 24–25
Button class, 375
buttons, 367, 375
byte type, 151–153
Byte wrapper class, 162–165
bytecodes, 19
bytes, 9

C
C language and Java history, 17–20
C++ language and Java history, 17–20
call by reference, 260–266
call by value, 184
call by value returned, 184

calling methods, 39, 54
calling overridden methods, 325–327
calling process, 179
canRead() method of File, 472
Canvas class, 372
canvas
    definition, 372
    drawing on, 378–382
    writing text on, 382–383
Canvas0 class
    drawArc() method, 380–382
    drawLine() method, 379
    drawOval() method, 380
    drawPolygon() method, 382
    drawRect() method, 379
    drawRoundRect() method, 380
    drawString() method, 382–383
    fillOval() method, 382
    fillPolygon() method, 382
    fillRect() method, 382
    fillRoundRect() method, 382
canWrite() method of File, 472
case sensitivity, 54
case statement, 102
casting, of types, 152, 501
catch clause, exceptions, 356
catching exceptions, 353, 355–363
Chapter16n0 class
    actionPerformed() method, 376–377
    constructor method, 372–375
    main() method, 376
    windowClosing() method, 377–378
char type, 156–157
Character class, 162–165
character file facilities, 459
character string data types, 156–157
charAt() method of String, 161, 505
child class, in an inheritance relationship, 298
circular buffer, data structure, 281
clarity, 584–585
class, 29–32, 43–46
class constants, 195–196
class keyword, 173
class Math, 201
class methods, 66
class providers, 170
class template, 45
class users, 170
class variables, 196–197
class, definition, 30
class, introduction, 22
classes
    abstract, 333–338
    ActionEvent, 385
    Applet, 484
    Boolean, 162–165

BufferedReader, 466–471
Button, 375
Byte, 162–165
Canvas, 372
Canvas0. See entry "Canvas0 class"
Chapter16n0. See entry "Chapter16n0 class"
Character, 162–165
concrete, 333
constructor methods, 171–172
constructor methods, creating an instance,
    189–192
DataInputStream, 476–477
DataOutputStream, 476–477
defining, 172–175
DirBase, 538, 544, 560–564
DirEntry, 539, 541, 544–545, 549–552
Double, 162–165
duplicate names, 193–194
encapsulation, 169–170
end users, 170
extending, 297–299
File. See entry "File class"
FileDialog, 397
FileReader, 474–476
FileWriter, 473–474
finding for objects, 506–507
Float, 162–165
Font, 383
Frame, 372
grouping, 206–210
grouping, description, 52–53
Hashtable, 503–504
holes in the scope, 212
import statement, 52–53, 209–210
Index, 539–540, 542, 546–547, 554–560
IndexElem, 539, 542, 546, 552–554
InputStream, 460–462
Integer, 162–165
lexical conventions, 185–186
Long, 162–165
main, 202–206
Math, 201
naming conventions, 185–186
Object, 317–319
OurDate, 250–253
OutputStream, 460–462
overloading, 193–194
package statement, 207
packages, 52, 206–210
Panel, 484
permission levels, 214
Person, definition, 49–51
Person, methods, 171, 175–178
PrintStream, 462–466
PriorityQueue class. See entry "PriorityQueue class"
private methods, 198–200

QueueElement, 272
QueueElement, 272
QueueNode, 410
RandomAccessFile, 459, 477–478
RandomAccessFile class, 535
scope, 210–214
Short, 162–165
signature, 193
Socket, 478
Stack, 408, 503
static methods, 66, 201
StreamTokenizer, 564–568
String. See entry "String class"
StringBuffer, 160, 505–506
System.err, 465–466
System.in, 466–471
System.out, 462–466
testing, 107–110
TextField, 387
this keyword, use of, 214
uninitialized variables, 190
URL, 493
Vector. See entry "Vector class"
visibility
    interclass, 214
    intraclass, 210–214
wrapper, 162–164
classpath, 52, 208
client, computer, 491
clientship, 523
clientship relationships, in JPO, 542–543
coding phase, in software life cycle, 520
cohesion, 279–582
command-line parameters, 72
comments, definition, 22
comment, inclusion in source text, 57
communicating programs, 458
communications link, 458
comparing values, 92–95
compile time, 12, 53
compilers, 7
compiling applets, 486
compiling Java programs, 23
compound selection statements, 90–92
computer, hardware components, 8–9
concatenating strings, 62
concatenation operator, on Strings, 62, 158
constants, definition, 6
constants, description, 63–65
constructor, 68–71
constructor chaining, 315
constructor methods
    and inheritance, 314–315
    creating an instance, 189–192
    definition, 54
    description, 68–71

Person class, 171–172
  with arguments, 192
content-based retrieval, of data, 537
continue statement, in a loop, 136
control structures. See also exceptions; looping; selection
  definition, 59, 113
control variables, 115
controlling expression, 102
coordinate system, 379–381
coupling, 582–584
current directory, 14, 471

D
data modeling, 293–298
data structures, 406 See also linked data structures
  and arrays, 406–409
  hashtables, 503–504
  linear, 406–409
  stack, 169
  Stack, 503
  strings, 505–506
  vectors, 499–503
data types
  ASCII, 156–157
  boolean, 96–101, 155
  byte, 151–153
  char, 156–157 see also String class
  character string, 156–157
  definition, 290
  description, 40–42
  escape sequences, 156–157
  float, 153–155
  floating-point, 153–155
  int, 147–151
  integer values, 147
  long, 151–153
  short, 151–153
  special characters, 156
  Unicode, 156–157
  whole numbers, 147–153
DataInputStream class, 476–477
DataOutputStream class, 476–477
decision making
  boolean expressions
    description, 86, 92–95
    precedence of operators, 98
    selection statements, 86–89
  break statement, 102
    the labeled break, 137
  else keyword, 89
  selection
    (braces), in compound statements, 90
    boolean expressions, 86–89
    comparing values, 92–95
    definition, 89
    else keyword, 89

relational operators, 92–95
  switch statements, 101–107
  syntax, 90–92
  truth tables, 97
decision statements, 85–89
declaring objects, 53–57
declaring, a String variable, 157
declaring, a variable of a basic type, 143
declaring, an object, 142
deep copy, definition, 257
deep copy, examples, 278, 280, 416
default case statement, 103
delete() method of File, 472
deletion, from a linked data structure, 423–425
dense index, 532
derived class, in an inheritance relationship, 298
design notation, 522–523
design phase, in software life cycle, 520
design process, 521–524
difference, between base and derived class, 299
DirBase class, 538, 544, 560–564
direct recursion, 451
directories, 206–210, 471 See also folders
  current, 14, 471
  definition, 14
  root, 14–15, 471
directory handling, 471–472
DirEntry class, 539, 541, 544–545, 549–552
DirGui class, source code, 606–608
displaying a graphical object, 376
displaying an image, 398
divide and conquer, 434, 518
do loops, 134–136
document base, 493
Double class, 162–165
double data types, 153–155
doubly linked lists, 425–428
drawArc() method of Canvas0, 380–382
drawing area, 367
drawing geometric shapes, 379–382
drawLine() method of Canvas0, 379
drawOval() method of Canvas0, 380
drawPolygon() method of Canvas0, 382
drawRect() method of Canvas0, 379
drawRoundRect() method of Canvas0, 380
drawString() method of Canvas0, 382–383
driver programs, see also test harness, 107
dynamic method binding, 325

E
elementAt() method of Vector, 501–502
elements() method of Vector, 503
else keyword, 89
encapsulation, 169–170
end users, of a class, 170
endsWith() method of String, 161

enumerated types, 63
Enumeration interface, 502–503
equal sign (=), assignment operator, 55
equal signs(==), relational operator, 92
equals() method, 110, 161
equalsIgnoreCase() method, 161
error handling. See exceptions
escape character, 156
escape sequences, 156
event driven programs, 367
event loops, in graphical program, 367
events, detecting, 376–377
exception handler, 351
exceptions
    catch clause, 356
    catching, 353, 355–363
    defining, 353–354
    definition, 351
    description, 351–353
    finally clauses, 361–363
    throw statement, 354–355
    throwing, 354–356
    throws clause, 352
    try blocks, 355–361
    try clause, 355
exists() method of File, 471
exponential methods, 154
expressions, as arguments in methods, 147
extending a class, 297–299
extends keyword, 297
extensibility, of design, 585–586

F
fields, in a record, 531
FIFO (first in, first out), 271
file access, sequential, random, 459
File class
    canRead() method, 472
    canWrite() method, 472
    delete() method, 472
    exists() method, 471
    isDirectory() method, 472
    list() method, 472
    mkdir() method, 472
    renameTo() method, 472
file handling, 471–472
    binary files, 476–477
    checking existence, 471
    DataInputStream class, 476–477
    DataOutputStream class, 476–477
    deleting, 472
    File class. See entry "File class"
    FileReader class, 472, 474–476
    FileWriter class, 472–474
    listing, 472
    network files, 478–479
    RandomAccessFile class, 535

    reading, 474–476
    readLine() method, 476
    renaming, 472
    seek() method, 477
    Socket class, 478
    writing, 473–474
file organization
    index sequential access, 530–532
    main file, 532–535
    RandomAccessFile class, 535–536
file, selection in graphics, 397
FileDialog class, 397
FileReader class, 474–476
Files, and filing systems, 14–15
FileWriter class, 473–474
filing systems, 14–15
fillOval() method of Canvas0, 382
fillPolygon() method of Canvas0, 382
fillRect() method of Canvas0, 382
fillRoundRect() method of Canvas0, 382
final keyword, 317
finally clauses, 361–363
first() method of PriorityQueue, 415–416
flags, 204
Float class, 162–165
float type, 153–155
floating point data types, 153–155
floating point operators, 154
floating reference, 259
flow layout manager, 374
flow of control See also decision making; looping defini-
    tion, 59
flowcharting, 86
flush() method, 24–25, 463
flushing a buffer, 463
flushing buffers, 24–25
folders, 471 see also directories
folders, definition, 14
Font class, 383
font style, 383
for and while loops, when to use either, 126–127
for loops, 115–120
for statement, 115–120
formal and actual arguments, objects as, 263–266
formal arguments, 67, 177–182
formal arguments, changing contents of, 263–266
formal arguments, passing, 182–185
Frame class, 372
functional design, 522

G
garbage collection, 160
garbage collector, 416
generalization, 293, 294, 333
genericity, 290, 502
getDocumentBase() method, 493
getText() method, 391

graphical interface, simple program with, 368–372
Graphical User Interface (GUI). See GUI (Graphical User Interface)
graphical user interface, for JPO, 571–574
graphical user interfaces, 366–368
grid bag layout manager, 376
grid layout manager, 375
Gui class, source code, 604–606
GUI (Graphical User Interface)
  animation, 383–386
  background colors, 373
  border layout manager, 374
  Button class, 375
  buttons, 367, 375
  canvas
    definition, 372
    drawing on, 378–382
    writing text on, 382–383
  Canvas0 class. See "Canvas0 class" entry
  Chapter16n0 class. See entry "Chapter16n0 class"
  closing windows, 377–378
  coordinate system, 379–381
  definition, 366
  detecting events, 376–377
  displaying a (graphical) object, 376
  drawing geometric shapes, 379–382
  event driven programs, 367
  event loops, 367
  files, selecting via graphics, 397
  flow layout manager, 374
  Frame class, 372
  images
    displaying, 398–399
    positioning, 399–400
  in Java Personal Organizer (JPO), 571–574
  keyboard input, 77–80
  layout managers, 374–376
  menus, 393–397
  platform independence, 366
  sample program, 368–372
  TextField, getting text from, 389–391
  thermometer picture, 386–392
  titles, 372–373
  tracking the mouse, 399–400
  window size, 373

H
Hardware, definition, 8
Hashtable class, 503–504
Hashtable class, use within JPO, 537
hashtable data structures, 503–504
hasMoreTokens() method, 467–468
heap, 532
heterogeneous collections, 322–325
hiding references, to other objects, 266–267
high-level programming languages, 5–8
hole, in scope, 212

home pages, on the Web, 16
HTML (Hypertext Markup Language)
  applet example, 490–495
  definition, 16
HTML page, 486
HTML tag attributes, 487
HTML tags, 487
http (hypertext transfer protocol), 487
Hypertext Markup Language (HTML)
  applet example, 490–495
  definition, 16
Hypertext Transfer Protocol ("http:"), 487

I
identifier, 54
if keyword, 89
if statements, 89–95 See also switch statements
images, displaying, 398–399
images, positioning, 399–400
immutable, 160
imperative language, 5
implicit root, of inheritance hierarchy, 317–319
import statement, 52–53, 209–210
indentation, 89
indeterminate looping, while, 121–123
Index class, 539–540, 542, 546–547, 554–560
index sequential access, to a file, 530–532
index sequential storage structure, 531
index, dense, 532
index, of an array, 219
index, sparse, 531
IndexElem class, 539, 542, 546, 552–554
indexOf() method of String, 162
indirect recursion, 452
infinite loops, 115
infinite recursion, 434
information hiding, 36, 169, 267, 290
inheritance hierarchy, 306, 316–317
inheritance lattice, 341
inheritance
  and information hiding, 327
  data modeling, 293–298
  definition, 44
  extending a class, 297–299
  generalization, 293, 294, 333
  implicit root, 317–319
  multiple, 341
  overriding inherited methods, 300–303
  polymorphism, 319–322
  preventing, 317
  set membership, 293
  single, 341
  specialization, 293, 294
  the class Object, 317–319
  within the JPO, 575–576
initialize() method of PriorityQueue, 275, 413
inorder traversal, of a tree, 451

input and output, Java classes for, 460–462
input systems, 457–459
input
    BufferedReader class, 466–471
    character strings in a graphical interface, 386–398
    converting strings to numeric values, 468–470
    from keyboard, 77–80
    hasMoreTokens() method, 467–468
    InputStream class, 460–462
    redirecting, 470–471
    System.in, 466–471
    tokenizing, 467–468
    white space, 467
InputStream class, 460–462
insert() method of PriorityQueue, 278–281, 417–423
insertion sort, 227
instance methods, 66
instance variables, 174. See also attributes
instances, definition, 31
instances, description, 43–46
instruction cycle, 11
instructions, 9
int type, 147–151
Integer class, 162–165
integer division, 148
integer expressions, 82
integer operations, 148
integer values data types, 147–153
integer variables, 80–84
interclass visibility, 214
interface, 340–346
interfaces, 36
Internet, 15
interpreters, 19
intraclass visibility, 210–214
isDigit() method of Character, 164
isDirectory() method of File, 472
isEmpty() method of PriorityQueue, 276, 413
isFull() method of PriorityQueue, 276, 413
isLetter() method of Character, 164
isLowerCase() method of Character, 164
isUpperCase() method of Character, 164
isWhitespace() method of Character, 164

J
Java applets. See applets
Java applications, 20
Java Development Kit (JDK), 20
Java language, and history with C/C++, 17–20
Java Personal Organizer. See JPO
Java programs
    access modifiers, 22
    arguments, 23
    basic format, 21–24
    body of a method, 23
    braces, 22

    classes, 22
    comments, 22
    compiling, 23
    getting started, 588
    method headers, 22
    methods, 22
    parameters, 23
    running, 23
    statements, 23
java, interpreter command, 23
javac command, 23
JPO
    classes. See entries "DirBase class", "DirEntry class",
        "Index class", "IndexElem class"
    clientship relationships, 542–543
    diary feature, 586
    file organization
        index sequential access, 530–532
        main file, 532–535
        RandomAccessFile class, 535–536
    filing system, 540–541
    index
        definition, 536
        suitability of Hashtable class, 537
        suitability of Vector class, 536–537, 538
    inheritance, 575–576
    persistent data, 530
    source code
        AlertDialog class, 612–613
        BrowseRecGui class, 608–610
        DirBase class, 560–564
        DirEntry class, 549–552
        DirGui class, 606–608
        Gui class, 604–606
        Index class, 554–560
        IndexElem, 552–554
        NewRecGui class, 610–612
    StreamTokenizer, 564–568
    testing, 564–571, graphical interface, 574–575
    user interface
        graphical user interface (GUI), 571–574
        text-based, 568–570

K
keyboard input
    for variables, 77–80
    GUI (Graphical User Interface), 386–391
    programs, 72, 77–80
    prompting for, 77–80
    System.in, 466–471
keywords, list of, 589

L
labeled breaks, 137
late binding, 325
Law of Demeter, 583–584

layout managers, 374–376
leaves, of a tree, 443
left subtree, 444
length() method of PriorityQueue, 276, 413–415
length() method of String, 159
length, attribute of an array, 219
lexical conventions, 185–186
LIFO (Last In First Out), 169
linear data structures, 406–409
    definition, 406–409
    edge precautions, 428
    empty structures, 428
    priority queues
        definition, 408–409
        deleting elements, 416–417, 423–424
        description, 409–413
        doubly linked lists, 425–428
        empty structures, 413
        first element values, 415–416
        inserting elements, 417–423
        length, 413–415
    PriorityQueue class. See entry "PriorityQueue class"
    uninitialized variables, 428
    use of, 428–429
list() method of File, 472
literal array expression, initializing an array, 219–220
literals
    definition, 6
    double, 153
    float, 153
    in arguments, 62
    String, 157
load factor, for a stack, 503
local variable, 53, 180
logical operators, 96
Long class, 162–165
long type, 151–153
looping
    control variables, 115
        initialization, 116–117
        integer, 414
        modification, 116–117
        pointer, 414
        testing, 116–117
    indeterminate iterations121–123
    predetermined iterations, 115–120
    through arrays, 218–221
loops
    Boolean expressions, 121, 132–134
    breaking out of, 124–126
    continue statement, 136
    description113–115
    do loops, 134–136
    for loops, 115–120
    infinite, 115
    labeled breaks, 137

nested loops, 127–132
    tested at beginning
        for statement, 115–120
        while statement, 121–123
    testing at end, 134–136
    testing in middle, 124–126
    while loops, 121–123

M
machine code, 9–13
Main class, 202–206
maintenance phase, of software life cycle, 520
Math class, 201
menus, set-up, 393–397
message passing, 40
method call, format, 58
method headers, 22
method signature, 193
method, introduction, 22, 30
methods()
    actionPerformed(), 376–377, 385, 494
    addElement() of Vector, 500
    canRead() of File, 472
    canWrite() of File, 472
    charAt() of String, 161
    delete() of File, 472
    drawArc() of Canvas0, 380–382
    drawLine() of Canvas0, 379
    drawOval() of Canvas0, 380
    drawPolygon() of Canvas0, 382
    drawRect() of Canvas0, 379
    drawRoundRect() of Canvas0, 380
    drawString() of Canvas0, 382–383
    elementAt() of Vector, 501–502
    elements() of Vector, 503
    endsWith() of String, 161
    equals(), 110
    equals() of String, 161
    equalsIgnoreCase() of String, 161
    exists() of File, 471
    fillOval() of Canvas0, 382
    fillOval() of Canvas0, 382
    fillPolygon() of Canvas0, 382
    fillPolygon() of Canvas0, 382
    fillRect() of Canvas0, 382
    fillRect() of Canvas0, 382
    fillRoundRect() of Canvas0, 382
    fillRoundRect() of Canvas0, 382
    first() of PriorityQueue, 415–416
    flush(), 24–25, 463
    getDocumentBase(), 493
    getText(), 391
    hasMoreTokens(), 467–468
    indexOf() of String, 162
    initialize() of PriorityQueue, 275, 413
    insert() of PriorityQueue, 278–281, 417–423

isDigit() of Character, 164
isDirectory() of File, 472
isEmpty() of PriorityQueue, 276, 413
isFull()of PriorityQueue, 276, 413
isLetter() of Character, 164
isLowerCase() of Character, 164
isUpperCase() of Character, 164
isWhitespace() of Character, 164
length() of PriorityQueue, 276, 413–415
length() of String, 159
list() of File, 472
mkdir() of File, 472
nextToken() of StringTokenizer, 467
paint(), 368, 378
parseDouble() of Double, 164
parseInt() of Integer, 164
pow() of Math, 154
print(), 24
println(), 24
prompt() of BasicIo
readIndex() of Chapter20n2, 493–494
readLine() of BufferedReader, 479
remove() of PriorityQueue, 277–278, 416–417
removeElementAt() of Vector, 501
renameTo() of File, 472
repaint(), 368
replace() of String, 162
round() of Math, 155
seek(), 477
setBackground(), 373
setCharAt() of StringBuffer, 505
setElementAt() of Vector, 501
setLayout(), 374
setSize(), 373
setText(), 391
setTitle(), 372
size() of Vector, 500
startsWith() of String, 161
substring() of String, 161
toLowerCase() of Character, 163
toLowerCase() of String, 162
toString() of Double, 164
toUpperCase() of Character, 163
toUpperCase() of String, 162
trim() of String, 162
methods
  arguments to, 147
  body of, 23
  calling, 39, 54
  class, 66
  class or static, 201
  constructor, definition, 54
  constructor, description, 68–71
  definition, 22, 30
  exponential, 154
  flushing buffers, 24–25

  for String class, 157–160
  in derived classes, 327–329
  mutator, 57, 144
  overloading, 193–194
  overridden, calling, 327
  overriding, 300–303
  Person class, 171, 175–178
  printing strings, 24
  private198–200
  prompting for keyboard input, 77–80
  recursion, 435–437
  replacing, 300–303
  selector, 146
    definition, 60
  static, 66, 201
  using, 65–66
  values returned from, 185
  void, 67
mkdir() method of File, 472
module, 36
module provider, 170
modulus operation, 148
mouse tracking, 399–400
multi-dimensional arrays, 237–240
multiple references, to the same object, 255–259
multithreading, 508
mutator methods, 57, 144
mutual recursion, 452

N
naming, 41
naming conventions, class names, 185–186
nested loops, 127–132
network files, 478–479
NewRecGui class, source code, 610–612
nextToken() method of StringTokenizer, 468–469
nonrectangular arrays, 241–242
null value, 70, 410

O
O(log n) algorithm, 227, 443, 446
O(n log n) algorithm, 233
O(n) algorithm, 225, 443, 446
O(n²) algorithm, 233
object, 29–32
Object class, 317–319
object declaration, 53–57, 142
object identification, in design, 524–527
object orientation, 29
object space, 582
object, as arguments, 253–255, 260–266
object, single, 36–39
object, software, 32–39
object-oriented design
  clarity, 584–585
  cohesion, 279–582

coupling, 582–584
definition, 522–527
design notation, 522–523
design process, 521–524
extensibility, 585–586
functional design, 522
Law of Demeter, 583–584
object identification, 524–527
object space, 582
software engineering, 518–519
software life cycle, 519–521
strong cohesion, 579
system testing, 520
unit testing, 520
object-oriented programming, 8
object-oriented programs, 39–40
objects
arrays of, 221–223
as arguments, 253–255, 260–266
call by reference, 260–266
declaring, 53–57
deep copy, 257
definition, 29
displaying a graphical object in a GUI, 376
extracting attributes, 60–63
finding class of, 506–507
floating reference, 259
hiding reference to, 259
multiple references to, 255–259
return values, 261
setting attributes, 57–60
shallow copy, 257, 278–279
single, 36–39
software, 32–35
using, 65–66
within objects, 249–253
operating systems, definition, 2
ordinal type, 102
OurDate class, 250–253
output systems, 457–459
output
OutputStream class, 460–462
PrintStream class, 462–466
redirection, 465–466
System.err class, 465–466
System.out, 462–466
OutputStream class, 460–462
overloading, classes, 193–194
overloading, methods, 69
overriding, inherited methods, 300–303

P
package statement, 207
packages, 52, 206–210
pages, on the Web, 16
paint() method, 368, 378

Panel class, 484
param: tag <param>, 489
parameter definition, 23. See also argument
parent class, 298
parseDouble() method of Double, 164, 468
parseInt() method of Integer, 164, 468
parts-explosion situation, 249
Pascal's triangle, 241–242
passing messages, 40
passing values into an object, 180
pathname, or path name, 14, 471
percent sign (%) as modulus operator, 148
permissions, classes, 214
permissions, subclasses, 304–305
persistent data, 530
Person class
definition, 49–51
methods, 171, 175–178
source code for, 593–599
person.java, source code, 593–599
pipes, communication between programs or threads, 458
platform independence
GUI (Graphical User Interface), 366
Java applets, 18
WWW (World Wide Web), 17
plus sign (+), concatenation operator, 62–63
pointer, 408
polymorphism
and abstract classes, 338–340
and heterogeneous collections, 322–325
constructor chaining, 315
constructor methods, 314–315
description, 319–322
dynamic method binding, 325
inheritance, 318–319
late binding, 325
popping a stack, 169
postorder traversal, of a tree, 451
pow() method of Math, 154
precedence of operators, arithmetic operations and
    Boolean comparisons, 150
precedence of operators, Boolean comparisons, 98–100
predetermined looping, for, 115–120
preemptive scheduling, 507
preorder traversal, of a tree, 451
print() method, 24
printing strings, 24
println() method, 24
PrintStream class, 462–466
priority queues
definition, 271, 408–409
deleting elements, 416–417, 423–424
description, 409–413
doubly linked lists, 425–428
empty structures, 413
first element values, 415–416

implementation using linked data structure, 409–413
implementation with an array, 275–280
implementation with an array, 275–280
inserting elements, 417–423
length, 413–415
PriorityQueue class
    description, 271–275
    first() method, 415–416
    initialize() method, 275, 413
    insert() method, 278–281, 417–423
    isEmpty() method, 276, 413
    isFull() method, 276, 413
    length() method, 276, 413–415
    remove() method, 277–278, 416–417
    testing, 282–287
    using, 287–289
    with a circular buffer, 281–282
    with an array, 275–280
private keyword, 174, 304
private methods, 198–200
procedural language, 6
procedure, 6
process, see thread, 507
processor, as computer component, 9
processor, definition, 2
program counter, 11
programming in the large, 521
programming in the small, 521
programming with inheritance, introduction, 298–299
programming, definition, 2–8
programs. See also applets; applications
    case studies. See Java Personal Organizer (JPO); task
        organizer program
    command line arguments, 72
    definition, 2, 9
    keyboard input, 72, 77–80
    structure, example, 48–49
prompt() method of BasicIo, 77
prompting for keyboard input, 77–80
protected keyword, 214, 304
prototype, 530
public keyword, 173, 304
pushing a stack, 169

Q
queue, data structure, 271
QueueElement class, 272
QueueNode class, 410

R
random file access, 459, 477–478
RandomAccessFile class, 535
readIndex() method of Chapter20n2, 493–494
reading, from a file, 474–476
reading, values from keyboard, 77–80
readLine() method, 479
records, in a database or file, 531

recursion, 331
    description, 435–437
    direct, 451
    indirect, 452
    infinite, 434
    mutual, 452
    run-time stack, 435
    Towers of Hanoi problem
        description, 437–442
        iterative solution, 441–442
        recursive solution, 439–441
recursive algorithm, 434
redirecting input, 470–471
redirection output, 465–466
reference, 55, 235, 249, 408, 410
    anonymous, 259
    floating, 259
relational operators, 92–95
relative path names, definition15
remove() method of PriorityQueue, 277–278, 416–417
removeElementAt() method of Vector, 501
renameTo() method of File, 472
repaint() method, 368
repetition, 113–115
repetition statements, see also looping; loops, 113
replace() method of String, 162
requesting services, 40
requirements phase in software life cycle, 520
reserved words, 54
reserved words, list of, 589
return keyword, 176
return references, objects as return values, 261
return values, 60, 185, 260–266
right subtree, 444
robust programs, 351–353
root directories, 14–15, 471
root elements, binary trees, 444–445
root, of a tree, 443
round() method of Math, 155
rows, 237
run time, 12, 53
run-time stack, the calling process, 435
run-time type information, 506–507

S
scheduling, preemptive, 507
scientific notation, 153
scope, 53, 210–214
searching, an array, 223–226
Security Manager, of applets in browsers, 495
security
    applets, 495
    WWW (World Wide Web), 17
seek() method, 477
selection
    (braces), in compound statements, 90
    boolean expressions, 86–89

comparing values, 92–95
definition, 89
else keyword, 89
if statements, 89–95
relational operators, 92–95
switch statements, 101–107
syntax, 90–92
selector methods, 60, 146
semicolon(;), in Java statements, 23
sequencing, 59
sequential file access, 459
service provider, 36
set membership, 293
setBackground() method, 373
setCharAt() method of StringBuffer, 505
setElementAt() method of Vector, 501
setLayout() method, 374
setSize() method, 373
setText() method, 391
setTitle() method, 372
shallow copy, definition, 257
shallow copy, example, 278–279
short type, 151–153
Short wrapper class, 162–165
short-circuit operator of AND and OR, 100, 133
signature, 193
single inheritance, 341
single objects, 36–39
size() method of Vector, 500
slash(/), in path names, 15
slashes(//), comment indicator, 57
Socket class, 478
software crisis, 518
Software Development Kit (SDK), 20
software engineering, 36, 518–519
software life cycle, 519–521
software life cycle, waterfall model, 519–521
software objects, 32–35
Software, definition, 8
sort, insertion, 227
sorting arrays, 227–233
sparse index, 531
special characters data types, 156
specialization, 293, 294
specialization, 293, 294
Stack class, 408, 503
stack data structures, 169
Stack data structures, 503
stack, data structure, 169, 406
stack, run-time, 435
stand-alone, applications, 484
startsWith() method of String, 161
state, of an object, 29–30
statements, 23, 90–92
    compound, 90, 120
    single or simple, 90, 120
static methods, 66, 201

store, 9
store location, 9
stream access, to data, 459
StreamTokenizer class, using, 564–568
String class, 505–506
    charAt() method, 161
    description, 157–160
    endsWith() method, 161
    equals() method, 161
    equalsIgnoreCase(), 161
    indexOf() method, 162
    length() method, 159
    replace() method, 162
    startsWith() method, 161
    substring(), 161
    toLowerCase() method, 162
    toUpperCase() method, 162
    trim() method, 162
StringBuffer class, 160, 505–506
strings, converting to numeric values, 468–470
strong cohesion, 579
strongly typed language, 84, 428
subclass, 298
subclasses, permissions, 304–305
substring() method of String, 161
subtrees, 444
super keyword, 314, 327
super keyword, and use within constructor methods,
    314–315
super keyword, and use within overriding methods, 327
super keyword, rules of use, 314
super() method, 314–315
superclass, 298
Superclass constructor, 314–315
Superclasses, single versus multiple, 340–341
Swing graphical classes, 367
switch keyword, 101
switch statements, 101–107. See also if statement
synchronizing threads, 513–514
system testing, 520
System.err class, 465–466
System.in class, 466–471
System.out class, 462–466

T
Task Organizer Program
    abstract data types, 290
    data types, 290
    description, 270–271
    genericity, 290
    information hiding, 290
    PriorityQueue class
        description, 271–275
        testing, 282–287
        using, 287–289
        with a circular buffer, 281–282
        with an array, 275–280

task, see thread, 507
test harness, 107 See also driver program
testing phase, in software life cycle, 520
testing, a new class, 107–110
testing, boolean expression at end of loop, 134–136
testing, the JPO, 564–571
text area, 367
text file facilities, 459
text-based interface, for JPO, 568–570
TextField class, 387
TextField, getting text from, 389–391
thermometer picture, 386–392
this keyword, use of, 214
threads, description, 458, 507–514
threads, synchronizing, 513–514
throw statement, 354–355
throwing exceptions, 354–356
throws clause, exceptions, 352
titles, GUI, 372–373
tokenizing input, 467–468
tokens, 467
toLowerCase() method
    Character class, 163
    String class, 162
toUpperCase() method
    Character class, 163
    String class, 162
Towers of Hanoi problem
    description, 437–442
    iterative solution, 441–442
    recursive solution, 439–441
tree, data structure, 406, 442
trees, 406
trim() method of String, 162
true/false comparisons, 86
truncation, 155
truth tables, 97
try blocks, 355–361
try clause, exceptions, 355
two-dimensional arrays, 237
type casting, 152, 501
type checking, 12, 84–85
type information, at run-time, 506–507
types, 40–43. See data types
typing rules for whole number types, 152

U
Unicode character set, 156
Unicode characters, list, 590–592
Unicode data types, 156–157
Uniform Resource Locator (URL), 478
unit testing, 520

unwinding recursive calls, 436
URL (Uniform Resource Locator), 478
URL class, 493

V
variables
    accessing the value of, 146
    boolean type, 96–101
    declaring, 142–144
    definition, 5
    extracting values, 146
    in a class, 196–197
    in an instance, 174
    initializing, 80
    integer, 80–84
    keyboard input for, 77–80
    ordinal types, 102
    setting values, 144–146
    type checking, 84–85
    uninitialized, 190
Vector class
    addElement() method, 500
    description, 408, 499–503
    elements() method, 503
    removeElementAt() method, 501
    setElementAt() method, 501
    size() method, 500
    use within JPO, 536–537, 538
visibility, interclass, 214
visibility, intraclass, 210–214
void keyword, 176
void methods, 67

W
waterfall model, of the software life cycle, 519–521
Web browsers. See browsers
while loops, 121–123
while statement, 121–123
white space, 467
whole number data types, 151–153
windowClosing() method, 377
windowListening interface, 377
windows, closing, 377
words, 9
World Wide Web (WWW), 484
    description, 15–17
    platform independence, 17
    security, 17
wrapper classes, 162–164
wrapper object, creating an instance of, 163
writing, to a file, 473–474